EDUCATION AND SOCIETY
A Reader

EDUCATION AND SOCIETY
A READER

Kevin J. Dougherty
Manhattan College

Floyd M. Hammack
New York University

HARCOURT BRACE JOVANOVICH, PUBLISHERS

San Diego   New York   Chicago   Austin   Washington, D.C.
London   Sydney   Tokyo   Toronto

To Beth, Josephine, Maren and John and their
spouses and children, and to the memory of my
father.

K.J.D.

To my mother, Nancy, Andrew, and Philip.

F.M.H.

Requests for permission to make copies of any part of the
work should be mailed to: Copyrights and Permissions
Department, Harcourt Brace Jovanovich, Publishers,
Orlando, Florida 32887.

ISBN: 0-15-520735-0
Library of Congress Catalog Card Number: 89-84235
Printed in the United States of America

PREFACE

This book is the product of a close collaboration. The spark for the collaboration came when Floyd Hammack suggested to Kevin Dougherty that they work together on a book for students in social foundations of education and sociology of education. A central aim of this collaboration has been to utilize our different locations and experiences—one of us teaches in a department of sociology and the other in a school of education—to illuminate the shared concerns of these often-distant endeavors. At the same time, we have tried to combine the analysis of the social context of education with the study of the day-to-day operation of schools. By this union, we hope to do two things: (1) to put social science to work, illuminating the problems encountered by professional educators, and (2) to enrich social science theory, by reinforcing the movement away from seeing education just as a variable to also viewing it as an institution whose structure and processes must be understood.

Our study of education has been guided by two key precepts. The first is that to study comprehensively a complex institution such as education we must explore its connections with other important social institutions, such as the economic and political systems. These connections establish the context within which education takes place and strongly influence what goes on in its name. The second is that to analyze education itself structurally, we need to trace the interconnections among its different levels—national, state, and local. In studying these links between levels, social scientists emphasize how phenomena at one level constrain events at lower levels. Thus, to understand why students differ in what and how much they learn, we need to study not just individual students' and teachers' traits, but also how classroom behavior is molded by the way the American educational system is structured. This interest in the nested nature of educational phenomena is reflected in the organization of the book. We move from the national level down to the local district and school levels and, ultimately, to individual teachers and students. And at the individual level, we trace students' careers into, through, and out of school.

Although we began with the idea of compiling a reader, the book evolved into something more. As our discussions progressed, we decided that the introductions to the readings should be more informative than such introductions usually are. Hence, *Education and Society* is now as much a textbook as a reader. It has extensive introductions that frame and supplement the readings, which in turn are intended to extend and give flavor to the themes raised in the introductions.

The production of this book has been a joint venture. Together we drew up a list of topics the book should address and a list of readings it should include. Three main rules governed our selection of readings. First, we wished to have articles that addressed a wide range of empirical research, policy issues, and theories about the social role of education. Second, because our main audience is students, the selections should be both readable and solidly founded in educational scholarship. Finally, because educational research, policy, and theory have been changing rapidly, most of the readings should be of recent vintage. The task of securing permission for reprinting these readings was undertaken by Floyd Hammack. Kevin Dougherty took responsibility for editing readings down to manageable size.

The introductions were the product of both collaborative and independent effort. We discussed what points the introductions should address and then divided the task of writing them. Kevin Dougherty wrote the introductions to Chapters 2, 3, 5–7, and 9. Floyd Hammack wrote the introductions to Chapters 4, 8, and 10. The general introduction, Chapter 1, was primarily written by Floyd Hammack, with Kevin Dougherty preparing the final draft. We both commented extensively on all the introductions, and the final versions thoroughly reflect our collaboration.

The book benefited from insightful comments from several sources. The reviewers commissioned by the publisher—David Labaree, Michigan State University; Philip Altbach, State University of New York at Buffalo; and William Boyd, The Pennsylvania State University—played an important role in alerting us to certain topics and readings and suggesting ways the introductions could be improved. We also benefited greatly from the comments of several friends and colleagues—Mark Alter and Charles B. Hayes, New York University's School of Education, Health, Nursing, and Arts Professions; Jerome Karabel, University of California at Berkeley; Katherine McClelland, Franklin and Marshall College; David Riesman, Harvard University; and David Swartz, Wesleyan University. Katherine McClelland gave a particularly close and thoughtful reading of all the introductions. In addition, anyone familiar with Jerome Karabel and A. H. Halsey's *Power and Ideology in Education* (1977) will realize our debt to its delineation of theory and research in education.

Julia G. Berrisford, our acquisitions editor at Harcourt Brace Jovanovich, deserves our great thanks for helping us bring this book to fruition. She suggested important topics and readings and commissioned excellent reviews. Her comments made the introductions more topical and readable, and her sense of humor enlivened our discussions. Ruth Cottrell, our production editor, very efficiently and pleasantly managed the conversion of our manuscript into a book. Our manuscript editor, Elizabeth Judd, was helpful in catching errors, both grammatical and conceptual.

Finally, we wish to thank our wives, Beth Stevens and Nancy Walker, for providing intellectual and emotional sustenance for this project. In the midst of their own busy professional careers, they gave us ideas and tolerated the time this book took away. Andrew C. Hammack made Floyd's life especially rich during the work on this book, and the School of Education, Health, Nursing, and Arts Professions provided him a sabbatical leave that allowed book and family to coexist.

Contents

Chapter 4
Teachers, Teaching, and the Organizational Dynamics of Education in the United States   168

Chapter 5
Access and Opportunity in Education   247

Chapter 6
Factors Influencing Academic Learning

Chapter 7
Factors Influencing Nonacademic Learning

Chapter 8
Students with Special Needs

EDUCATION AND SOCIETY
A Reader

1

General Introduction

Education is again a topic of central concern in American society. Since the "Year of the Reports" (1983), public focus has remained on education. Many people today speak of a "crisis" in education, and politicians have made the condition of education a campaign issue at all levels of government. This crisis is described in quite varied and even opposed terms. Some speak of a sharp drop in the quality of education, leading us to fail in economic competition with the Japanese and Europeans. Others decry a lack of equality, as evidenced by the very high dropout rates of working-class and minority youth. Still others talk about a lack of morality in the schools or the imposition of alien values.

This variety of concerns, all expressed in impassioned terms, leaves one puzzled. Which of these criticisms is correct? Even if we determine which criticism is correct, how do we solve the problem it points to? After all, education has been said to be in crisis many times before. In fact, many of the charges being made today have been made many times before. The concern about poor quality was made in the 1950s and even earlier. The concern about lack of educational opportunity was raised before, in the 1960s and earlier. So why do we have yet another educational "crisis"? Even if real, does this new crisis have any easy solution? Is it simply a matter of raising standards or spending more money? But one would think that if any obvious changes in schools would dramatically improve education, we would have discovered and implemented them by now.

This book aims to help you address these issues by thoroughly reviewing how social science conceptualizes and studies contemporary educational issues. Our belief is that social science can powerfully cut through the tangle of conflicting claims about the cause of education's perennial problems and illuminate new paths of action.

SOCIAL SCIENCE'S CONTRIBUTIONS TO EDUCATION

Social science's contributions to understanding and shaping education are quite numerous and varied. But we will explore how it can aid understanding

1

and action by examining three important and representative issues: the sources of the recurrent sense of crisis in American education, the causes of why so many students are not learning well, and the bases of the strong relationship between family background and educational achievement.

With regard to the current crisis in education, social science shows that this sense of crisis is not new and that like previous crises it stems from the fact that the debaters usually have very high, and often conflicting, expectations of schooling. The United States expects far more from education than virtually any other society. Americans believe that education is the key to national well-being. As a result, we expect schools to prepare students for adult occupational roles, provide equal opportunity to pursue education as far as possible, inculcate knowledge of a common heritage and culture, breed respect for the cultural differences among groups, be uniformly excellent across the country, and be responsive to their local communities. Any of these goals is hard to reach, especially given the complexity of the social world and the limits of our knowledge. Hence, because our expectations about education are so high and we take schooling so seriously, there is a built-in predisposition to be unhappy with the schools, with this unhappiness breaking out every so often.

But this recurrence of a sense of crisis is also due to the fact that our goals for education are often contradictory. For example, our concern to prepare students for their adult occupational roles leads us to emphasize excellence and getting students to come to a realistic appreciation of their abilities. But this leads to practices like curriculum tracking and special programs for the gifted that inhibit the pursuit of another goal: equality. Similarly, in our pursuit of excellence and equality we have been moving to a more centralized school system, with a greater role for the state and federal governments, but this conflicts with the goal that schools should be locally controlled and responsive to their local communities. Finally, we want to instill a common cultural experience, so we provide public schools. But at the same time we want to preserve religious, language, and ethnic differences among families, so we support private schooling.[1]

Because of this conflict of goals many end up disappointed with how the schools perform. If the schools try to meet two different and partially contradictory goals they may meet neither particularly well. Even if they do concentrate on one goal, they end up ignoring another, leaving the partisans of that goal unhappy. What one observer will take as evidence of the school's failure another will take as evidence of its success. As a result, schools lurch from one emphasis to another, and the recurrent crises in education have a cyclical nature, with concern about one goal (such as higher standards in the 1950s) being replaced with worry about another goal (such as equality in the 1960s), only to have the first concern return (higher standards in the 1970s and early 1980s) (Kirst and Meister, 1985).

Social science research can be helpful to educational scholars and practitioners in a second way, explaining why so many students are not learning

---

[1]Chapter 2 discusses these various views of what are and what should be the goals of schooling.

well. This question has been a major concern of those who now see education as in crisis. The explanations often given by laypeople and many educational policymakers center either on pupils' deficiencies (lack of ability or motivation, often due to a poor home life) or teachers' deficiencies (lack of ability, poor training, or inadequate standards). But social science research suggests that this focus is off target: It is too individualistic and misses the importance of social structure. The effectiveness of instruction does not depend mostly on the qualities of individual students or teachers but to a very large degree on the way schools are organized. Our national school system is a very complex structure broken up into public and private systems, districts, individual schools, curriculum tracks within schools, and smaller learning groups within classrooms. Each level has been found to have a major effect on other levels and a profound impact on how well students learn in the classroom (Barr and Dreeben, 1983; Slavin, 1987). The sometimes distant and strained relationships between parents, students, teachers, and administrators are often the product of such structural features as school size and organization. American schools are typically larger than schools in other countries and more bureaucratized. Hence, American teachers are less able to engage in the close collaboration with parents and students that is typical of Japanese schools (Shimahara, 1978). Furthermore, the fact that our educational system is fairly decentralized, in comparison to many other countries, has a major effect on the resources students have available. Our lack of a centralized system makes the quality of our schools highly variable across states and districts within states, with the result that students in some areas get far more resources devoted to their education than do students in other areas.[2]

Third and finally, social science research illuminates a question that has come up repeatedly in recent years and has long perplexed educators, policymakers, and researchers: Why is there such a strong relationship between students' social background and their level of educational achievement? This question has become key as education has come to be so important in influencing economic success. Social science research helps to untangle the myriad and often subtle ways students' social class, race, and gender affect how students and schools interact with each other. For example, social scientists have found that working-class students are more likely to end up in the slower groups and lower tracks and receive less encouragement from teachers than their middle-class or upper-class counterparts, even without teachers intending or being aware that this happens.[3] This difference in treatment contributes in turn to producing social class differences in levels of academic performance. But this research has not simply cataloged obstacles to equal education, it has also suggested policy. Social scientists have been identifying and studying schools that are unusually effective in educating working-class and nonwhite pupils.

The structural and organizational emphasis of the social sciences, particularly sociology, can greatly deepen our understanding of education and

---

[2]Chapter 3 and 4 both examine how our schools are organized in ways that are different from other countries and what impact these structural differences have on how our schools operate.

[3]Chapter 6 reviews the literature on curriculum tracking thoroughly.

improve educational practice. But it is only recently that this promise has begun to bear fruit. To understand this, we have to examine the history of the social scientific study of education.

THE HISTORY OF THE SOCIAL SCIENCE OF EDUCATION

The French sociologist Emile Durkheim (1858–1917) was among the first social scientists to explore the relationship between education and society. His lectures to teachers in training at French universities around the turn of the century helped launch the social science study of education (Durkheim, 1956, 1961, 1977). He asked what are the consequences for society of different forms of education, and he traced the form and content of schools back to the structure of the societies in which they were rooted. He was particularly interested in how education helps a society cohere in the midst of rapid change induced by industrialization.

But Durkheim's pioneering studies of education did not strongly influence early research on education in the United States. The social scientific study of education was very weak until recent years.

To be sure, schools of education have long paid attention to social science. In the development of teacher education, the social sciences—especially psychology and sociology—along with the fields of history and philosophy were identified as important sources of ideas and knowledge for educators. These four disciplines came to be called the "foundations" in schools of education. But of these foundation disciplines only educational psychology really prospered. It is the largest of the foundation disciplines, with its own journals, texts, and professional associations. Meanwhile, while having some success, educational history and philosophy have been much smaller in size than educational psychology and are frequently combined into a single department. And educational sociology, finally, has virtually disappeared after considerable growth during the early years of this century. The name is seldom used today, and separate departments or programs within schools of education are rare. At the same time, educational sociology also faded from departments of sociology. Despite the vote of confidence from Durkheim, one of sociology's founding fathers, sociologists paid little attention to education until the last 20 years.

As sociology of education drifted from the immediate concerns of educators and sociologists, educational psychology moved to fill the gap. Educational psychology was able to devise instruments that provided educators with apparently scientific procedures for educating the vast diversity of students brought into schools by the expansion of elementary and especially secondary education in the early 20th century. Educational psychologists developed the IQ test and theories of cognitive growth and development that gave educators seemingly rational ways of classifying students and providing instruction appropriate to their needs and abilities. As the historian David Tyack relates,

[E]ducators were increasingly serving as the gatekeepers to opportunity. In this task schoolmen turned more and more to "scientific" measures of ability and achievement. What they sought was a technology which would enable them to differentiate children, for selection was a prerequisite to specialized treatment. Through such a technology the needs of the students, the needs of the educational system, and the needs of the larger society could be more precisely calibrated and the connecting parts more smoothly meshed. (1974: 199)

But while it is clear that educators have been aided by the rise of educational psychology, with its focus on how teaching techniques can be tailored to student characteristics (Brophy and Good, 1986), it is equally clear that many of the central problems of schooling remain unsolved. We are still disappointed and frustrated by the many students who do not finish high school. Too many of those who do finish high school are unable to find gainful employment and take their places as adults in our society. The technologies furnished by educational psychology have not eliminated the dilemmas of American education. And, if we take testing as an example, we would have to say that educational psychology's contribution has been a mixed blessing. Test results, however informative, have not enabled educators to create effective schools. Nor have they helped schools to overcome the difficulties posed by race and class differences. In fact, many argue that educational testing has exacerbated the problem of educational inequality (Persell, 1977).

As the limits of educational psychology have become more evident, sociological interest in schools has revived. In the late 1960s, education again became a major interest to sociologists (Brookover and Erickson, 1975; Coleman and others, 1966; Jencks and others, 1972; and Sewell and Hauser, 1975).[4] Especially as education has become so important to occupational success, sociologists came to realize they could not understand fundamental social processes in this country without closely studying education and educational processes.[5]

Sociology's rediscovery of education has not been without its problems, however. It has shifted the center of gravity of sociology of education from schools of education to departments of sociology in colleges of arts and sciences,[6] with the result that sociologists tend to study education more for the

---

[4]Although less heralded than the others, Wilbur Brookover has exerted a great influence on education. In recent years, he and his colleagues have developed much of the empirical basis for the "effective schools" movement (Brookover and others, 1979). See Chapter 6 for further discussion.

[5]Sociologists' rediscovery of education was accompanied by a similar growth of interest in education on the part of anthropologists and economists, an interest symbolized by the founding of the journals *Anthropology and Education Quarterly* in the late 1960s and *Economics of Education Review* in the 1980s.

[6]A good illustration of the shifting base of sociology of education is provided by the history of the *Journal of Educational Sociology*. After its birth at New York University's School of Education in 1928, it became *Sociology of Education* in the early 1960s, when it was adopted by the American Sociological Association.

sake of sociology than of education (Hansen, 1967). Sociology is a discipline that largely embraces the canons of science, esteeming objectivity and the ability to abstract and generalize. It tries to be value-free and theoretical.[7] Education, on the other hand, is by everyone's agreement a value-laden and pragmatic activity. Educational choices can and should be informed by research, but educational problems and decisions remain normative, linked to goals and aspirations. Education is also pragmatic in that teachers and administrators have to run and maintain schools and achieve increasingly specific educational goals. Necessarily educators are inclined to value concrete knowledge that spells out how to diagnose and address the problems they face.

But this difference of emphasis has greatly attenuated in recent years. Many of the most prominent sociologists of education in recent years are located in schools of education and are conducting research that is closely attuned to the problems of practicing educators (Barr and Dreeben, 1983; Brookover and others, 1979; Hawley and others, 1982; and Metz, 1978). And sociologists in academic departments of sociology have also become more receptive to the needs of practitioners in that they have become much more concerned not only with pointing out how educational phenomena are related to larger social structures but also with working out the precise connections between the two (Karabel and Halsey, 1977).

This book in fact represents both strands within the sociology of education. One of us is located in a department of sociology and the other in a school of education. Uniting us is a shared concern with making the connections between education and the larger society in a way that not only deepens our general knowledge of society but also sheds light on educational processes in a manner useful to educational practitioners and researchers. By closely studying the interaction between education and the social, political and economic structures that surround it, we can better understand how society works, for education plays a key role in preparing workers for the economy and citizens for the state. At the same time, this contextualizing of education deepens our understanding of education itself because it illuminates how education works and where we must look if we wish to change it. Many aspects of schooling that seem to be purely educational are closely tied to social and political problems in the larger society (Bowles and Gintis, 1976; Hurn, 1985; and Jencks and others, 1972). Thus, the solutions to educational problems are not always educational. And if the solutions are educational, they lie as often in modifying the structure of schools as in changing students or teachers. Sociological research has made clear that student performance depends as much on how instruction is organized as on student or teacher characteristics.[8]

[7]There is a limit, of course, to any discipline's objectivity. See Curtis and Petras (1970), Kuhn (1962), Friedrichs (1970), and Young (1971) for analyses of objectivity in sociology and in science.

[8]See Chapter 6 for more on what affects student achievement.

LOOKING AHEAD

The remainder of this book is divided into nine chapters, each with an introduction followed by readings.

The sequence and content of these chapters reflects our orientation to education. Because we attach great importance to matters of theory and method, Chapter 2 is devoted to examining the main theories of the nature and social origins of schooling and the main methodological prescriptions for studying it. In addition, all the subsequent chapters will make explicit how they draw on these general theories and methods to illuminate specific questions. Because we believe that schools' structural characteristics greatly condition the teacher-student relationship, we begin our empirical analysis of education by examining in Chapters 3 and 4 the American school system's main structural features, how these contrast with those of other advanced industrial societies, and how they shape the way schools work. With this background, in Chapters 5 through 9, we trace students' careers into, through, and out of the schools. Finally, in Chapter 10, we examine the current debate over the future of education, noting the various positions advanced and critiquing their claims.

Each chapter begins with an extensive introduction that sets out the main issues that have been raised concerning the aspect of education in question. Each introduction is then followed by readings that amplify and concretize the points raised in the introduction. We have sought selections that address both the questions most interesting to social scientists and the technical and substantive issues critical to educational practice.

In what follows in this introduction, we provide a more detailed description of the contents of each chapter. Chapter 2 examines how social scientists approach two main questions in the study of education: What are the social origins and purposes of education, and how should we go about studying it? Several readings address the first question, explicating the functionalist, Marxist, and Weberian perspectives and the work of Pierre Bourdieu and John Meyer. As part of the analysis of the Marxist position, we note the considerable differences between the class reproduction position of Bowles and Gintis and the "resistance" or class conflict position of Michael Apple, Henry Giroux, and Paul Willis. The question of research methodology, of how one studies education, is addressed by the introduction and a selection by Ray Rist. These discuss the various views as to the appropriate level of analysis (societal, organizational, or interactional) and the best means of gathering and analyzing data (the qualitative-quantitative debate). We conclude this discussion of research methodology by arguing for studies that examine more than one level and combine different means of gathering and analyzing data. As an exemplar of such analyses, we describe the work of Basil Bernstein.

Chapter 3 and Chapter 4 are concerned with the structure of education and how it sets boundaries for the interaction between students and teachers. In Chapter 3, we assay the different ways contemporary societies provide educational services to their citizens. Because societies vary so greatly, we have selected readings dealing with vastly different societies: from Ponape in the South Seas to Japan, the Soviet Union, and the United States. This variety of educational systems brings home the fact that the American educational system is unusual in its size, degree of decentralization, and range of expected functions. Besides detailing these features, the chapter draws out their implications for how American schools operate.

The fourth chapter draws on some of the most practical research offered by the social sciences. Each selection highlights a different aspect of the organization of American education: teacher preparation, the relationships between teachers and students, the interaction between superintendents and local school boards, and the relations between schools and their immediate communities. The central idea is that the organization of American schools takes certain distinctive forms that shape what occurs in the classroom. American schools are unusual to the degree that they operate under three different structures of authority: bureaucracy, professionalism, and democracy. These three structures are by no means entirely compatible and create tensions that are recurrent and typically American: for example, the conflict between schools' claim to authority over what to teach and parents' claim that the schools are teaching values inimical to those of the home or the local community.

With the structure of education in mind, we move toward the classroom. In Chapters 5 through 9, we trace students' careers in the schools: observing who goes to school and for how long, tracking students' experiences while in school, and picking students up as they emerge from school and go into the labor force. Chapter 5 sets the stage for Chapters 6 through 9 by posing the key sociological question of the role education plays as a gateway between children's family origins and their adult destinations. It describes how family background (especially class and race) affects students' likelihood of remaining in high school, entering college, and graduating from college.

Chapters 6 and 7 move us from describing schools' impact on learning to explaining it. We have separated these effects into academic and nonacademic outcomes, with each receiving a chapter. Academic learning prepares students to be technically able to meet their adult roles by transmitting such skills as reading, writing, and arithmetic. It is produced primarily by the formal curriculum—the texts and exercises teachers and students experience. Nonacademic learning is concerned not with skills but motivation (values, attitudes, and behaviors), with preparing students to perform their adult roles willingly and not just competently. It is the product of both the formal curriculum and the informal curriculum of school rules and the nature of the teacher-student relationship.

The question of what determines student academic learning is quite controversial and has prompted quite varied responses, as can be seen in the number and range of selections in Chapter 6. To make sense of this confusion, the chapter identifies two main types of explanation: a "student-centered" explanation that attributes class, race, and sex differences in learning to family upbringing or, in some cases, genetic differences; and a "school-centered" explanation that stresses the impact of school characteristics such as curriculum tracking, the climate of expectations for student performance, or amount of time students are kept on task. In examining the school-centered explanation, the chapters gives considerable attention to the "effective schools" literature. The chapter stresses that, despite their differences, the school-centered and student-centered explanations are not entirely opposed. They represent different poles of the interaction between students and schools. How much students learn is a product not only of their backgrounds, not only of the types of schools they encounter, but of a combination of the two. Hence, both student-centered and school-centered explanations need to be joined in any powerful theory of why students differ in how much they learn.

Chapter 7 addresses the nonacademic (or noncognitive) values and attitudes that schools teach. The selections illuminate different ways in which schools contribute to the formation of students' personalities. Taking a functionalist position, Robert Dreeben examines how schools transmit the values of achievement, universalism, specificity, and affective neutrality. Jean Anyon, influenced by the Marxism of Bowles and Gintis, examines how schools inculcate in children differing in class background and class destination contrasting personality traits: initiative for executives, obedience for workers, and constrained creativity for middle managers. In a Weberian vein, Alan Peshkin examines the role of Christian fundamentalist schools in preserving a particular subgroup (status group) culture. Finally, Dougherty and Hammack review the literature on the noncognitive effects of college, raising fundamental questions about the meaning of these purported effects.

Schools are ideologically committed to treating all students equally, but must cope with students who have special learning needs to which educators must respond. The four selections in Chapter 8 address the special needs of blacks, non–English speakers, females, and the handicapped in examining the issues of desegregation, bilingual/bicultural education, the education of females, and schooling for the learning disabled. The chapter examines the basis of "specialness" (asking how groups come to be identified as in need of special services), how those special services are defined and delivered, and the consequences of special education for schools and children.

Chapter 9 examines what is for many observers the key function of schooling: providing access to jobs. Drawn from sociology and economics, the readings in Chapter 9 raise the question of whether the strong relationship between educational attainment and occupational success exists because school imparts job skills or because it simply provides a convenient credential that employers and professionalizing occupations can use to determine who should get the best jobs. In addition, the chapter examines employment trends and their implications for education. It questions the conventional wisdom that American schools have to produce many more scientists and engineers, noting the evidence that the biggest growth will be in much more modest occupations.

Finally, Chapter 10 surveys the continuing debate over education sparked by the 1983 report of the National Commission on Excellence in Education, *A Nation at Risk*. It begins with this report and then moves to a variety of other contributions to the debate by the conservative Heritage Foundation, liberal educator Theodore Sizer, the Holmes Group of deans of schools of education, and radical commentators Ann Bastian and colleagues. These reports are followed by articles evaluating their findings and value assumptions. In addition, Chapter 10 analyzes why the reform movement arose this decade and why it has proved so politically popular and resilient.

We think education is particularly exciting today. After more than a decade in which national attention and priorities were directed elsewhere, education is once again seen as of central importance to our society. Resources once channeled to other concerns are now being redirected to education, and the lives of students and teachers are more open to change today than they have been for a long time. We believe that as the transformation of American education continues, the voices represented in this book hold great promise for improving educational research and practice.

REFERENCES

Barr, Rebecca, and Robert Dreeben. 1983. *How Schools Work*. Chicago: University of Chicago Press.

Bowles, Samuel, and Herbert Gintis. 1976. *Schooling in Capitalist America*. New York: Basic Books.

Brim, Orville G., Jr. 1958. *Sociology and the Field of Education*. New York: Russell Sage.

Brookover, Wilbur B. 1949. "Sociology of Education: A Definition." *American Sociological Review* 14 (June): 407–415. Reprinted in Ronald M. Pavalko (ed.), *Sociology of Education: A Book of Readings*. Itasca, IL.: Peacock, 1968.

_____, and Edsel Erickson. 1975. *Sociology of Education*. Homewood, IL: Dorsey Press.

_____, Charles Beady, Patricia Flood, John Schweitzer, and Joe Wisenbaker. 1979. *School Social Systems and Student Achievement: Schools Can Make a Difference*. New York: Praeger.

Brophy, J. E., and T. L. Good. 1986. "Teacher Behavior and Student Achievement." In Merlin C. Whittrock (ed.), *Handbook of Research on Teaching*, pp. 328–375. New York: Macmillan.

Coleman, James S., Ernest Q. Campbell, Carol J. Hobson, James McPartland, Alexander M. Mood, Frederick Weinfeld, and Robert L. York. 1966. *Equality of Educational Opportunity*. Washington, D.C.: Government Printing Office.

Curtis, James E., and James W. Petras (eds.). 1970. *The Sociology of Knowledge: A Reader*. New York: Praeger.

Durkheim, Emile. 1956. *Education and Sociology*, trans. Sherwood D. Fox. Glencoe, IL: Free Press.

_____. 1961. *Moral Education*, trans. Everett K. Wilson and Herman Schaurer. New York: Free Press.

_____. 1977. *The Evolution of Educational Thought*, trans. Peter Collins. London: Routledge and Kegan Paul.

Friedrichs, Robert W. 1970. *A Sociology of Sociology*. New York: Free Press.

Gross, Neal. 1959. "Some Contributions of Sociology to the Field of Education." *Harvard Educational Review* 29 (fall): 275–287.

Hansen, Donald A. 1967. "The Uncomfortable Relation of Sociology and Education." In Donald A. Hansen and Joel E. Gerstl (eds.), *On Education—Sociological Perspectives*, pp. 3–35. New York: Wiley.

Hawley, Willis, and others. 1982. *Strategies for Effective School Desegregation: Lessons from Research*. Lexington, MA: Lexington Books. (See the Hawley selection in Chapter 8.)

Hurn, Christopher J. 1985. *The Limits and Possibilities of Schooling: An Introduction to the Sociology of Education*. 2nd ed. Boston: Allyn and Bacon.

Jencks, Christopher, Marshall Smith, Henry Acland, Mary Jo Bane, David Cohen, Herbert Gintis, Barbara Heyns, Stephan Michelson. 1972. *Inequality*. New York: Basic Books.

Karabel, Jerome, and A. H. Halsey (eds.). 1977. *Power and Ideology in Education*. New York: Oxford University Press.

Kirst, Michael W., and Gail Meister. 1985. "Turbulence in American Secondary Schools: What Reforms Last?" *Curriculum Inquiry* 15: 169–186.

Kuhn, Thomas S. 1962. *The Structure of Scientific Revolutions*. Chicago: University of Chicago Press.

Metz, Mary Haywood. 1978. *Classrooms and Corridors*. Berkeley: University of California Press. (See the excerpt in Chapter 4 of this book.)

National Commission on Excellence in Education. 1983. *A Nation at Risk*. Washington, D.C.: Government Printing Office. (Excerpted in Chapter 10 of this book.)

Persell, Caroline Hodges. 1977. *Education and Inequality*. New York: Free Press.

Sewell, William, and Robert Hauser. 1975. *Education, Occupation, and Earnings*. New York: Academic Press.

Shimahara, Nobuo. 1978. "Socialization for College Entrance Examinations in Japan." (Reprinted in Chapter 3 of this book.)

Slavin, Robert E. 1987. "Cooperative Learning and the Cooperative School." *Educational Leadership* 45 (November): 7–13.

Strike, Kenneth A. 1985. "Is There a Conflict Between Equity and Excellence?" *Educational Evaluation and Policy Analysis* 7 (winter): 409–416.

Trent, William T., Jomills Henry Braddock, II, and Ronald M. Henderson. 1986. "Sociology of Education: A Focus on Education as an Institution." In *Review of Research in Education* 12: 295–336. Washington, D.C.: American Educational Research Association.

Tyack, David B. 1974. *The One Best System: A History of American Urban Education*. Cambridge, MA: Harvard University Press.

Waller, Willard. 1961. *The Scoiology of Teaching*. New York: Wiley.

Young, Michael F. D. (ed.). 1971. *Knowledge and Control: New Directions for the Sociology of Education*. London: Collier-Macmillan.

2

Theory and Method: Perspectives on the Nature of Education and How to Study It

Schooling in the United States is a very complex enterprise. As Chapter 1 notes, it is a multilevel institution oriented to many different, often contradictory goals. This complexity poses two central problems for social scientists studying education: How should they view the nature of education, and how should they go about studying it? Faced with the complex nature of education, we need to find a way to focus on its fundamental features, free of unimportant details. This is where social science theory enters. Like a map, theory is essentially a simplification of reality designed to let us focus on the forest rather than the trees. But if we are to study education, we need not only a theory of education to focus our attention on the object of study, but also guidance on how to cut into it in order to explore its features. Here is where research methodology becomes key, for it suggests how we can gather information about education and analyze it.

The task of this chapter is to explore the variety of general theories and methods that social scientists have developed to study education. These general theories and methods lay the basis for the studies of specific educational topics that are reviewed in Chapters 3 through 10. Hence, as we go through those chapters, we will note when a study draws on one or the other of the theories and methods covered in this chapter.

THEORIES ON THE NATURE OF EDUCATION

One would hope that social science theory could give us one map of education. But instead it has produced many theories of the nature of education—its social role and origins. As in the parable of the blind men and the elephant, education can be described from many different perspectives, each of which is true but is also incomplete. This variety of perspectives seems to be an inescapable feature of being human, because social life may be too complicated to be brought within one theory.

The first four readings in this chapter cover the main theories that social scientists have developed to describe the social role of education: functionalism, various forms of Marxism (especially class reproduction theory and resistance or class conflict theory), Weberianism, the work of Pierre Bourdieu, and the work of John Meyer. In each case, we will briefly describe the theory's analysis of the social role and origins of education and review the major criticisms that have been made of the theory.

Functionalism

Until the 1960s, the functionalist perspective dominated research not only on education but on society generally.[1] Functionalists view society as an interrelated set of institutions—such as education, the family, and the economy—each of which performs specialized "functions" that allow the society to survive and that benefit members of society. Functionalists sometimes envision society as an organism and a social institution as an organ—such as the heart—that performs a function that the organism needs to survive. In the functionalist view, society is characterized by harmony and consensus because its institutions are governed by a shared culture (values and norms) and because they perform different but complementary functions.[2] The task of social science research in the functionalist view is to determine the precise functions of a social institution and how those functions interrelate with the functions of other social institutions.[3]

In keeping with the general functionalist perspective, David Goslin in "The Functions of the School in Modern Society" lists the major social needs that schools meet for American society as a whole. These social functions are transmitting the fundamental culture on which American institutions rest and selecting and preparing students for adult occupations. Functionalists argue that schools have a unique role in transmitting the fundamental values and norms of society, because they serve as "halfway houses" that ease children's transition between the personalized world of the family and the impersonal

---

[1]The leading contributors to the functionalist theory of education have been Durkheim (1956, 1961, 1977), Parsons (1959), Clark (1962), Dreeben (1968), and Trow (1961). These works are cited under the heading of "functionalism" in the reference section at the end of this introduction.

[2]The statements above are particularly true of functionalist theory stemming from the work of Talcott Parsons and less true of that growing out of the work of Robert Merton (1968). Mertonian functionalism more openly acknowledges, through the concept of "dysfunction," that society is subject to a considerable degree of disharmony and incoherence. However, unlike Parsons, Merton has had very little influence on the study of education. See Goslin (1965) and Dreeben (1968).

[3]An institution's functions are not necessarily the same as its stated intentions, for these "manifest functions" are usually coupled with "latent functions," which often are unintended, go unnoticed, and undercut its public goals. For example, although college catalogs rarely state it, college has a latent function of providing young adults a place to meet socially appropriate friends or spouses.

world of adult occupational and civic life. Schools also play a unique role in occupational selection and preparation because they give children access to occupational knowledge that parents do not have and they permit job selection to be freed from favoritism, thus allowing children to rise above their parents' economic station. While these functions are central, Goslin also notes that schools meet other functions as well: providing parents with child care during the day, allowing prospective mates to meet, and effecting social reforms such as racial integration.[4]

A close cousin of functionalism is human capital theory in economics. This theory focuses on the role of education in preparing students for occupations. It argues that education does this by giving students "human capital" in the form of skills and other traits that make them productive workers whom employers want to hire (Becker, 1964; Schultz, 1961).

Functionalism has been closely tied to the ideal of "meritocracy," that is, of a society in which all members have an equal chance for educational and economic success regardless of their family background (Bell, 1973; Young, 1958).[5] Politically, the meritocratic ideal has given rise to liberal social policies that rely on the schools to achieve greater social equality. Functionalists, like Goslin, argue that education promotes greater equality because it provides the skills and attitudes necessary to perform higher skilled and better paying jobs. Because privileged groups are not alone in being able to learn these skills and attitudes through school, Goslin argues that schooling contributes to equality of opportunity and therefore to social mobility: that is, to children being able to make more money and work in more prestigious occupations than their parents.

The functionalist account of education's origins is much sketchier than its analysis of education's social functions. Essentially functionalists argue that educational expansion has been the product of economic change, with popular demand acting as the connecting link. According to Trow (1961) educational expansion has been driven by the desire of parents to ensure greater economic opportunity for their children by securing more education for them. Fueling this popular demand has been the evolution of the U.S. economy, as it has moved from an agrarian society with simple skill requirements and little need for formal schooling to an industrial society requiring complex skills and advanced educational training.

Functionalism has proved a very popular view of the social role of education. It seems to provide a "hardheaded" rationale for educational expansion and reform. It allows advocates of greater access to education to argue that it benefits not only disadvantaged individuals and groups but also society as a whole through greater economic growth (Karabel and Halsey,

---

[4]Goslin also argues that schools maintain the distinctive culture of different ethnic and religious groups. This point is not typically functionalist, but rather is made usually by followers of the sociologist Max Weber. We will come to this when we discuss the selection by Randall Collins.

[5]Put in somewhat different terms, meritocracy is about equality of opportunity but not equality of result. In a meritocratic society, inequality would be tolerated if it is based on individual capacity and achievement rather than inherited advantage.

1977: 10, 13). Moreover, functionalism has been around for a long time. For example, in his celebrated 1848 report when he was Secretary of the Massachusetts State Board of Education, Horace Mann anticipated several of Goslin's points, arguing that education creates social mobility and prevents class warfare, encourages economic growth, protects popular government by creating informed citizens, stops crime and disorder by inculcating moral values, and promotes health through physical education (Mann, 1891: 215).

Functionalism has enormously enriched scholarship in education by urging us to look past its surface details to the fundamental ways it serves society. In so doing, we come to appreciate why education is so important to our society and how it differs from other social institutions. But while appreciated for its contributions, functionalist theory has also been severely criticized. In particular, critics of functionalism have denounced it for ignoring that society is divided into various groups (races, sexes, and social classes) that often differ fundamentally in their interests and goals. Far from being characterized by consensus and equilibrium, societies are often dominated by conflict and disequilibrium. Moreover, far from preparing skilled workers for the economy and allowing children to rise economically above their parents, education provides relatively few job-relevant skills and has not created any greater economic equality (Bowles and Gintis, 1976: chap. 4; Collins, 1979: chaps. 1–2).[6]

The other theories covered in this chapter reject the functionalist perspective to a greater or lesser extent. But they also disagree among themselves as to what are the social role and origins of education.

Marxism

Marxism has long been one of the foremost alternatives to functionalism. It stems from the work of the German social theorists and revolutionaries, Karl Marx (1818–1883) and Friedrich Engels (1820–1895). As with other great social movements, ranging from Islam to Christianity, Marxism has many internal differences of opinions, with different factions arguing sometimes quite opposed positions but claiming to be true to the words of the founder. What Marxists of whatever stripe share is a view of society as fundamentally organized around an economy divided between the capitalist class, which owns the means of production (income-producing property), and the working class, which does not own the means of production and therefore must work for the capitalist class. This fundamental class division produces a class struggle that reverberates throughout society. As with all other major social institutions in a capitalist society, education becomes enmeshed in the struggle between the capitalist class and the working class.[7]

The selection by Martin Carnoy, "Marxism and Education," reviews the main approaches Marxists have taken toward understanding education.

---

[6]For criticisms of functionalism generally, see Dahrendorf (1968: chap. 4) and Gouldner (1970). For more on education and social mobility, see Chapter 5.

[7]For useful introductions to Marxism, see Giddens (1971) and Tucker (1978).

He distinguishes two main camps, which are tied to two different key Marxian concepts: correspondence and contradiction.

Class Reproduction or Correspondence Position[8] What has been called the class reproduction approach picks up on the concept of correspondence: that is, Marx's argument that the various parts of capitalist society fit together in such a fashion that they reflect and perpetuate the fundamental nature of capitalist society as a system in which the capitalist class economically exploits the working class. The class reproduction camp, whose best-known representatives are Samuel Bowles and Herbert Gintis (1976), argues that education in capitalist society reflects the hierarchical structure of the capitalist firm—for example, the capitalist firm's division between managers and workers and use of money as an incentive reappear in education as the division between teachers and students and the use of grades as incentives. Because of this resemblance, schools "reproduce" (perpetuate) capitalist society in three ways: channeling students into different levels in the capitalist work hierarchy in a way that corresponds to their family background, so that workers' children become workers and capitalists' children become capitalists; socializing students to have the skills and attitudes appropriate to those different levels (obedience for workers, but self-initiative for managers); and legitimating or justifying these processes of allocation and socialization as in the interests of all.[9]

The class reproduction school explains the expansion of education largely in terms of the self-conscious efforts of members of the capitalist class desirous of preserving their interests. They note that the major turning points in educational development have coincided with periods of major transformation of the economy, especially shifts in skills requirements (with the rise of white collar jobs and the role of science and technology in industry) and class structure (as farmers and self-employed people are driven into the working class). These economic changes lead members of the capitalist class to seek changes in the educational system: new programs to provide the skills now needed by their firms, and increasing enrollment of working-class children who might otherwise be a source of social turmoil. Capitalists can secure these changes because of their general political power and because they directly influence education through their command of resources for educational research, innovation, and training.[10]

---

[8]Representatives of the class reproduction school are Althusser (1971), Bowles and Gintis (1976), Carnoy (1974, 1975), and Carnoy and Levin (1976). Look under "Marxism: Correspondence or Class Reproduction Position" in the list of references.

[9]Bowles and Gintis have changed their views since 1976, putting greater emphasis on how education on occasion contradicts the interests of the capitalist class. This shift moves them into a position not far from that of the resistance or class conflict position discussed below. See Bowles and Gintis (1981).

[10]Bowles and Gintis also discuss, but do not employ in their analysis, another channel of capitalist influence, which they call "pluralist accommodation." It operates through the fact that parents and government officials tailor their actions to the requirements of a changing economy not because of capitalist command but because they perceive this accommodation to be in their own interest (Bowles and Gintis, 1976: 236–237).

The class reproduction version of Marxism has had great influence on the study of education. At the same time, it has been greatly criticized—both by the class conflict school of Marxism (which we will cover next) and by non-Marxists—for overemphasizing the degree to which education benefits the capitalist class and has been shaped by it.

Resistance or Class Conflict Position[11]   This group agrees with the class reproduction camp that schools reproduce the position of the capitalist class and therefore capitalist society itself. But the resistance camp stresses the reproduction of capitalist ideology more than the reproduction of the skills a capitalist economy needs. Moreover, the resistance position criticizes the class reproduction camp for stressing correspondence to such a degree that it forgets contradiction: the Marxian idea that capitalist society is deeply divided by the struggle between classes and therefore is self-destructive. Schools, they argue, do not reproduce capitalist social relations smoothly or perfectly. Schools are committed not just to preparing workers for a capitalist economy but also to advancing the ideal of equality of opportunity. Hence, they are also the sites of struggle by subordinate groups to resist capitalist values and domination and to instead defend alternative values and interests. Working-class, minority, and female students and parents try to gain greater access to education (Carnoy and Levin, 1985). Moreover, within school, they try to resist teachers' authority. Paul Willis has been particularly hailed for his exploration of this phenomenon in his study of a small group of delinquent high school students in England. He shows how their delinquency was really resistance, one originating out of a keen awareness of and hostility to the way the school's values and purposes differed from and repudiated their working-class background (Willis, 1981).

Because of the demands and resistance of oppressed groups, schools do not just defend, but also disrupt, capitalist economic processes. They turn out highly educated students in greater numbers than the capitalist labor market can absorb. They produce workers who care more for democracy than for submitting to the authoritarianism of the capitalist work hierarchy (Apple, 1982: 14–15; Carnoy and Levin, 1985: chap. 6).

Reflecting its emphasis on contradiction as well as correspondence, the class conflict or resistance position views school expansion as the product not just of capitalist commands but also of democratic demands on the part of the working class, nonwhites, and women. In fact, some argue that capitalist and popular forces have alternated in their control over the schools, with capitalists in ascendancy in the 1900s, in the 1950s, and in the 1980s, but democratic forces in the 19th century, the 1930s, and the 1960s (Carnoy and Levin, 1985: 1–15; Katznelson and Weir, 1985: 10–27).

---

[11]This group includes Apple (1982, 1987), Aronowitz and Giroux (1985), Carnoy and Levin (1985), Katznelson and Weir (1985), Wexler (1976), Willis (1981), and Wrigley (1982). We place Carnoy and Levin's later work in the class conflict camp because of their explicit repudiation of their earlier perspective (1985: 2–3). See the readings listed under "Marxism: Resistance or Class Conflict Approach" in the list of references.

If the class reproduction camp overly emphasizes the school's submission to capitalist imperatives, resistance theory tends to fall into the opposite mistake: overly stressing the influence of workers and students. For example, resistance theorists tend to identify any adolescent rebellion with anticapitalist resistance (Aronowitz and Giroux, 1985: 105–106).[12] Furthermore, resistance theory does not say enough about when, why, and how schools act independently of capitalist interests and direction. Resistance scholars talk of education's "relative autonomy" from capitalism but often never specify the origins and limits of this autonomy.[13] Finally, when discussing capitalist influence, the resistance or class conflict camp tends to view it in overly narrow terms, largely agreeing with the class reproduction camp that it is based on the capitalist class's direct intervention in policymaking. This misses less overt forms of power such as ideological dominance (in which policymakers benefit a certain group because they share its beliefs and values) and the "power of constraint" (policymakers take actions in a group's interest because they want access to resources that group controls).[14]

A failing common to the Marxist position, particularly the class reproduction camp, is an almost exclusive focus on social class, to the point that the role of government (as an independent actor) and of ethnic, racial, and gender groups is downplayed.[15] This is where the Weberian perspective makes a major contribution.

Weberianism

The Weberian perspective—whose origins lie with the work of the German sociologist Max Weber (1864–1920)—is illustrated by the selection by Randall Collins, "Some Comparative Principles of Educational Stratification."[16] Like the Marxists, Weberians argue that schools have been shaped by the desires of special interest groups. But while agreeing with Marxists on the important influence of social classes, Weberians also stress the role of other groups: in

[12]Resistance theory's romantic view of adolescent rebellion may stem from the Left's need in the 1970s and 1980s to find a new revolutionary actor in the face of the waning radicalism of the labor movement and the 1960s social movements (nonwhites, students, and women).

[13]This lack of detail is particularly evident in the work of Aronowitz and Giroux (1985) and Apple (1982, 1987). Other class conflict Marxists do better insofar as they argue that schools enjoy some autonomy because other actors—especially workers—fight the capitalist class for voice over school (Carnoy and Levin, 1985; Katznelson and Weir, 1985; and Wrigley, 1982). But even here more needs to be said about when noncapitalist forces are best able to exert an influence over the schools. For more criticism of the resistance school, see Wexler (1987).

[14]Some members of the resistance school do give importance to the capitalist class's ideological power (Apple, 1982; Aronowitz and Giroux, 1985), but only Apple has developed this idea at length. The "power of constraint," which has affinities with Bowles and Gintis's (1976: 236–237) notion of "pluralist accommodation," has been developed and applied in Dougherty (1988), Kingston (1986), and Murphy (1982).

[15]Apple (1982, 1987), however, does note the importance of the state and of gender and racial divisions.

[16]This analysis is amplified in Collins (1979). Other representatives of the Weberian perspective include Archer (1979, 1982) and Ringer (1979). For more on the Weberian perspective, see Giddens (1971) and Weber (1978). For these references, look under "Weberianism" in the reference section.

particular, government heads and "status groups" (such as occupational, ethnic, and religious groups).[17]

As Collins notes, heads of government have an independent interest in controlling their subjects and have long used schooling for this purpose. Schools ideologically indoctrinate the mass population. And they serve as recruiting grounds for government officials, ensuring that they have been properly trained and indoctrinated.

Status groups, meanwhile, have used education for two different purposes: maintaining the cohesion of the group; and helping the group compete with other groups for wealth, prestige, and power. Schooling can be used to maintain group cohesion by transmitting and reinforcing a status group's distinctive culture, as in the case of religious denominations that set up religious schools to keep their children within the flock.[18] Status groups also use schooling as a way to compete for prestige, wealth, and power. Status groups can raise their prestige by schooling their members in whatever is considered high culture in a society, whether it be knowledge of classical music and modern art as in our society or knowledge of poetry and calligraphy as in ancient China. Furthermore, status groups can use education to get access to wealth and income by restricting access to powerful and well-paying jobs to those holding the educational credentials that happen to be common among the status group in question. Finally, a status group can use education to dominate other status groups by schooling those groups in its own culture (Collins, 1979: chap. 2, 5–6).

In *The Credential Society* (1979), Collins applies this general Weberian perspective to explaining the development of education in the United States. He finds little evidence of government initiative, unlike Europe. But he does find that status groups, especially religious denominations and ethnic groups, have greatly spurred the development of education by, for example, founding denominational schools and colleges.

Weberianism provides a valuable correction to Marxism in bringing attention to the importance of actors other than social classes, particularly the capitalist class. But the cost of this greater openness is that Weberians— especially American Weberians—tend to downplay the importance of social class. Nonetheless, the Weberian and Marxist positions are similar in many regards: both reject functionalism's assumption of social consensus and argue that a fundamental feature of society is the conflict between different groups for resources. And where the two positions are different, they can be combined so as to offset their respective weaknesses. An illustration of how these positions can be fruitfully combined can be found in the work of the French sociologist Pierre Bourdieu and his followers.

---

[17]Status groups are defined by a common culture and style of life: job, education, religion, family customs, language, and even food. Hence, ethnic groups such as Jews or Irish-Americans provide examples of status groups.

[18]For an excellent example of a status group using schooling to reinforce its solidarity, see the selection by Peshkin, "God's Choice," in Chapter 7 of this book, which describes the "Christian academies" founded in recent years by fundamentalist Protestant denominations.

Bourdieu

The selection by David Swartz, "Pierre Bourdieu: Culture, Education, and Social Inequality," covers Bourdieu's powerful but complex work on education.[19] Bourdieu's main concern is how the dominant class is able to pass on its privileged position to its children in such a manner that this inheritance of privilege seems legitimate. Bourdieu's focus on the dominant class recalls Marxism. But Bourdieu also draws on Weber because his dominant class includes not only the owners of large firms but also those who are highly educated, whether or not they are wealthy. He includes, in other words, not only those high in economic capital but also those high in "cultural capital" (cultural knowledge and educational credentials).[20]

Bourdieu argues that for both "fractions" of the dominant class the transmission of privilege occurs through schooling. Dominant class children tend to secure upper-class positions because they tend to do well in school. Schools expect students to possess cultural knowledge and styles (such as knowledge of the arts and classical music and ease in using formal language) that are most often found among members of the dominant class.[21] Hence, dominant-class students are much more likely to do well on tests, graduate from high school, and go on to the university than their less advantaged peers. Moreover, working-class children take themselves out of the competition because their expectations are lowered by the fact that they rarely see people of their background succeed in school.

Bourdieu's analysis of the development of education combines elements of both the Marxian and Weberian arguments. Like the Marxists, he sees education as changing as capitalism has shifted from the nineteenth economy of small, family-owned firms to the 20th-century economy of large corporations. But unlike the Marxists, he does not focus on capitalists' need for more highly skilled workers or for a way to control potential dissidents. Rather, he draws on the Weberian argument that educational change is tied to status groups' competition for prestige, wealth, and power. For Bourdieu, as capitalism has changed, families—particularly upper-class and middle-class families—have shifted from trying to ensure their children's future by passing on economic capital (property) to passing on cultural capital, by getting them as much education as possible.

Bourdieu's theory provides a powerful and suggestive way to think of the social role of schooling. It combines the class emphasis of Marxism with the interest in status groups of Weberianism.[22] However, his perspective has flaws. Bourdieu leaves little room for conflict and contradiction; like the class

---

[19]For a sampling of Bourdieu's writings and critical views of his work, look under "Pierre Bourdieu" in the list of references.

[20]Marxists largely restrict the dominant class to those who are the owners and very top executives of business firms and exclude those who are highly educated if they are not wealthy.

[21]This is particularly true in France, where Bourdieu lives, but is also true of the United States. See DiMaggio and Mohr (1985).

[22]Bourdieu has been strongly influenced as well by the work of Emile Durkheim, who had a great impact on the functionalists. However, his Durkheim is the one of the *Evolution of Educational Thought* rather than *Moral Education* or *Education and Sociology*.

reproduction Marxists, his school functions too smoothly in reproducing the privileged position of the dominant class. Bourdieu's argument is also flawed by the often vague and inconsistent way he uses concepts and his sometimes quite casual use of empirical data (DiMaggio, 1979: 1467–1469; Swartz, this book).

John Meyer

John Meyer and his colleagues also break with the assumptions underlying functionalism, but in a way quite different from the Marxists or Weberians.[23] Rather than viewing the school as a dependent institution simply serving the needs of society or of a dominant group, Meyer views it as an institution that shapes society. Moreover, to the extent it serves a social purpose, it is not by providing job-relevant skills but by providing a means of organizing society. Education creates categories of knowledge (such as academic disciplines and professional expertise) that people defer to, divides people into different occupations according to these categories of knowledge (expert or possessor of knowledge as versus layperson or nonpossessor of knowledge), and allocates people into these occupations. In the process of creating these categories of knowledge and people, schools socialize not just their students but the whole of society. This socialization does not take part through any direct inculcation but through people's acceptance of the categories of knowledge and people that education defines. For example, students become "educated" people not by direct instruction but by accepting this category and choosing to develop the behavior considered appropriate to it (Meyer, 1977: 61, 65–70). To capture education's role, Meyer describes it as a "religion" or "myth": "As religions do, it provides a legitimating account of the competency of citizens, the authority of elites, and the sources of the adequacy of the social system to maintain itself in the face of uncertainty" (Meyer, 1977: 72).

Meyer and his colleagues attribute the development of education not to competing classes or status groups but rather to nation builders. They have argued that the main proponents of school expansion in 19th-century America were Protestant, Republican farmers wishing to create a common national culture based on the values of individualism, free enterprise, and republican government (Meyer, Tyack, Nagel, and Gordon, 1979). Furthermore, Meyer and his colleagues state that Third World countries have spurred the development of their schools because this creates national unity and because an educated population has come to be seen as an indicator of a modern, progressive state (Meyer and Hannan, 1979).

Meyer's emphasis on how education shapes society and his doubt that it provides technical skills offers an important corrective to other theories' view that education is a passive instrument for realizing the interests of particular groups or even of society as a whole and to the economistic emphasis of

[23]Meyer's view of education has very strong affinities to Durkheim's (1965) work on primitive classification and religion and Ivan Illich's (1970) view of education as a secular religion. For writings by Meyer and his colleagues, look under "John Meyer" in the references.

technological functionalism and the Marxist class reproduction school. But Meyer's corrective is too effective. His illuminating analysis of how education shapes society is not coupled with equal attention to how society shapes education. And in stressing how education does not provide technical skills, he ignores the instances where it does.

RESEARCH METHODOLOGY

Just as social scientists studying education are powerfully divided by their theories of the social role and origins of education, so too are they divided by their views as to what are the best methods for studying education. These methodological divisions run along two lines: the proper level of analysis, and the proper way of gathering and analyzing data.

Levels of Analysis

Chapter 1 notes that school systems are structures composed of multiple levels, ranging from the societal (the entire educational system) to the organizational (the district or school) to the interactional (the individual classroom or even the teacher-student dyad). As a result, different positions have emerged on which level is the most important to study. Scholars taking a "structural" perspective believe that one should focus on the societal or organizational levels, because these set limits on, or even determine, what goes on at lower levels. Structural scholars take a macroscopic view of education, focusing on such questions as the interaction between education and other major institutions; how and why educational systems develop; and which groups have the most influence in shaping education. Meanwhile, scholars taking an "interactional" perspective have a microscopic view of society. They believe that larger-scale social structures, whether schools or even entire societies, are real only to the extent they are built up from individual or small-group behavior. For example, interactionists argue that in order to understand how class differences in education are produced we need to study the interaction between individual teachers and students, observing how unequal results come out of the interplay of teachers' images of students and students' images of themselves and of teachers.[24]

As Chapter 1 indicates, we believe that both the structural and interactional perspectives are valid and need to be combined.[25] The societal and organizational levels do set limits on what occurs at lower levels of education. We cannot understand what occurs within U.S. classrooms unless we understand that they operate within organizations that are simultaneously bureaucratic, professional, and democratic and that those organizations operate in turn within a society that is organized around a capitalist economy

---

[24]For more description and critique of the interactionist approach in education, see Karabel and Halsey (1977: 44–61); Jacob (1988); Atkinson, Delamont, and Hammersley (1988); and Wexler (1987).

[25]Karabel and Halsey (1977) and Apple (1982) have made a powerful case for this combination.

and a democratic government and puts great emphasis on both vocational preparation and equality, bureaucracy and local control. Hence, in Chapters 3 and 4 of this book, we examine the societal and organizational levels of education. At the same time, the analysis of education is not complete unless it shows how those macroscopic factors work themselves out at the interactional level. Once we have used a structural analysis to determine the social functions of education—for example, the production of workers for the economy—we must draw on the interactional perspective to analyze how the transactions between teachers and students produce those social functions. Hence, Chapters 6 and 7 of this book draw heavily on the interactional perspective to illuminate how educational effects are produced.

Our advocacy of a fusion of structural and interactional perspectives is shared by others. A number of excellent examples of such a fusion are available. One can think of the notable studies by Bernstein (1973a, 1973b, 1975, 1982, 1986), Durkheim (1977), Apple (1982), Barr and Dreeben (1983), and Willis (1981). Basil Bernstein has been particularly noteworthy for his insistence on studies that connect different levels of education and society and the richness of the interconnections he has noted. He is most famous for his argument that class differences in educational outcomes arise from differences in language style, which in turn arise from class differences in family structure (Bernstein, 1973a, 1973b). But he has also done pathbreaking work on the connection between social structure and classroom pedagogy, as in his argument that the unstructured "open classroom" frequently found in the lower grades reflects the lifestyle of the "new middle class" of professionals and managers, while the traditional classroom fits the lifestyle of the working class and the old middle class of small shopkeepers. This second strand of research has flowed from Bernstein's interest in how the class structure impresses itself on, and is transmitted by, three main "message systems" in schools: curriculum, pedagogy, and evaluation (testing) (Bernstein, 1975, 1982, 1986).[26]

Data Gathering and Analysis

The second methodological question social scientists face is how to gather and analyze data. For many, this question has pitted two different general methods: "quantitative" and "qualitative." Quantitative scholars use statistical methods to analyze numerical data gathered through experiments and questionnaire surveys. Qualitative scholars, on the other hand, tend to favor nonstatistical methods to analyze data gathered through participant observation, informal interviews, and analysis of documents.

The selection by Ray Rist, "On the Relations Among Educational Research Paradigms: From Disdain to Detente," contrasts the quantitative and qualitative approaches along several dimensions. The quantitative approach tends to

---

[26]In many ways, his project both draws on and deepens Bourdieu's notions of cultural capital and habitus. For an excellent critical commentary on Bernstein as a synthesizer of the structural and interactional perspectives, see Karabel and Halsey (1977: 62–71). For Bernstein's work, see the section in the references entitled "Basil Bernstein."

be positivist, adhering to the view that the social sciences can and should emulate the natural sciences. Hence, quantitative research emphasizes the following: studying observable behavior; discovering laws of behavior that hold across different societies and time periods; breaking phenomena down into their component parts; and stressing the reliability (consistency) of findings more than their validity (correctness).[27] The qualitative approach, on the other hand, tends to be antipositivist, viewing the social sciences as being quite different from the natural sciences. Hence, it is characterized by the following: studying the meanings people attach to their behavior; discovering regularities of behavior, but acknowledging that they cannot be general laws because human beings are capable of reflecting on and thus changing their behavior; refusing to break phenomena down into isolated parts but instead observing the total complex in which behavior occurs; and stressing the validity more than the reliability of findings.[28]

Until recently, the quantitative approach dominated educational research, reflecting the strength of educational psychology. But in the last few years, qualitative methods have been coming to the fore. This shift reflects in part the fact that few educators have mastered the mathematics necessary for quantitative research. But more importantly, there is growing impatience with the fact that quantitative research often does not provide a clear guide for practice because it abstracts too much from the day-to-day life of schools.

The debate between qualitative and quantitative methods should not lead us, however, to simply favor one over the other. Just as we have argued for the usefulness of combining structural and interactional analyses, we also argue for joining quantitative and qualitative methods, a stand that Ray Rist endorses as well. Each method captures an important, but limited, part of social reality. Quantitative methods are particularly good in spotting and describing general educational patterns—such as the higher dropout rate for working-class or nonwhite youth—but they cannot answer by themselves the question of how those patterns come into being: for example, the precise conditions that lead minority students to leave high school. Qualitative methods, though, are highly useful in helping us understand how people interact with each other to produce educational patterns. However, because qualitative studies are usually small scale, they cannot tell us how general certain patterns are. Hence, any complete analysis of an educational phenomenon will need to draw on both methods.[29]

---

[27]While quantitative scholars tend to be positivist, this is not always the case. Many scholars who are explicitly antipositivist use quantitative methods not to discover "general laws" but empirical regularities of behavior that can well be historically and culturally specific.

[28]For excellent reviews of the various qualitative research approaches, see Jacob (1988) and Atkinson, Delamont, and Hammersley (1988). For an analysis of the philosophical roots of the quantitative and qualitative positions, emphasizing their ties to the philosophical schools of realism and idealism, see Smith (1983).

[29]We are indebted to Katherine McClelland for this point and for the point that quantitative research is not always allied to a positivist perspective.

CONCLUSIONS

Our review of the dominant perspectives on education's social role and origins and on how best to study education suggests the need to creatively synthesize the theories already available, in the belief that each has a piece of the truth, even if distorted. Like a map, a theory enhances our awareness of certain parts of our environment but at the cost of hindering our awareness of other parts. Each has strengths that are different from, and complement, the strengths of the other.

Several theories of the social role and origins of education (Marxism, Weberianism, and the work of Pierre Bourdieu) alert us to how education can be used as a weapon in group conflict for wealth, prestige, and power, with each approach variously highlighting the interests of social classes, racial or ethnic groups, and government officials. Functionalism, meanwhile, alerts us to the ways in which education might serve the interests of the entire society, whether for technical skills or for cultural cohesion, rather than just a subset. And John Meyer's work, finally, suggests that education is not simply an agent of other institutions of society, but also is active in its own right, creating new forms of knowledge and behavior and new kinds of people.

Similarly, the debates over how best to conduct research suggests the usefulness of combining the strengths of structural and interactional analyses and qualitative and quantitative data-gathering and analysis methods. For example, structural analyses illuminate the role that education plays in the transmission of social privilege, but we need interactional studies to tie down precisely how this occurs.

While urging this theoretical synthesis, we would also raise two cautions. The first is that theories should be combined carefully. Theories cannot simply be assembled as just so many spare parts. Each theory embodies a comprehensive worldview that informs its specific statements and often puts them at odds with those of other theories. This problem has particularly plagued attempts to combine functionalist theory with Marxist and Weberian theories. The second caution is that we should not view our theoretical work as only taking the form of assembling various existing theories. Even assembled together, the existing theories still provide us an incomplete understanding of education's social role. Hence, we need to be engaging in new theorizing as well.

REFERENCES

General References

Atkinson, Paul, Sara Delamont, and Martin Hammersley. 1988. "Qualitative Research Traditions: A British Response to Jacob." *Review of Educational Research* 58 (summer): 231–250.

Barr, Rebecca, and Robert Dreeben. 1983. *How Schools Work.* Chicago: University of Chicago Press.

Bell, Daniel. 1973. *The Coming of Post-Industrial Society.* New York: Basic Books.

Dahrendorf, Ralf. 1968. *Essays in the Theory of Society.* Stanford: Stanford University Press.

Dougherty, Kevin. 1988. "Educational Policymaking and the Relative Autonomy of the State." *Sociological Forum* 3 (summer): 400–432.

Giddens, Anthony. 1971. *Capitalism and Modern Social Theory.* Cambridge, England: Cambridge University Press.

Gouldner, Alvin. 1970. *The Coming Crisis of Western Sociology.* New York: Basic Books.

Illich, Ivan. 1970. *Deschooling Society.* New York: Harper & Row.

Jacob, Evelyn. 1988. "Clarifying Qualitative Research: A Focus on Traditions." *Educational Researcher* 17 (January-February): 16–24.

Karabel, Jerome, and A. H. Halsey (eds.). 1977. *Power and Ideology in Education.* New York: Oxford University Press.

Kingston, Paul W. 1986. "Theory at Risk: Accounting for the Excellence Movement." *Sociological Forum* 1 (fall): 632–656.

Murphy, Raymond. 1982. "Power and Authority in the Sociology of Education." *Theory and Society* 11: 179–203.

Smith, John K. 1983. "Qualitative versus Quantitative Research." *Educational Researcher* 12 (March): 6–13.

Tucker, Robert C. 1978. *The Marx-Engels Reader,* 2nd ed. New York: Norton.

Wexler, Philip. 1987. *Social Analysis of Education.* London: Routledge and Kegan Paul.

Young, Michael. 1958. *The Rise of the Meritocracy.* London: Thames and Hudson.

Functionalist Approaches

Becker, Gary. 1964. *Human Capital.* New York: National Bureau of Economic Research.

Clark, Burton. 1962. *Educating the Expert Society.* San Francisco: Chandler.

Dreeben, Robert. 1968. *On What Is Learned in School.* Boston: Addison-Wesley. (See the excerpt in Chapter 7 of this book)

Durkheim, Emile. 1956. *Education and Sociology,* trans. Sherwood D. Fox. Glencoe, IL: Free Press.

_____. 1961. *Moral Education,* trans. Everett K. Wilson and Herman Schaurer. Glencoe, IL: Free Press.

_____. 1965. *The Elementary Forms of the Religious Life.* New York: Free Press.

_____. 1977. *The Evolution of Educational Thought,* trans. Peter Collins. London: Routledge and Kegan Paul.

Goslin, David. 1965. *The School in Contemporary Society.* Atlanta: Scott, Foresman. (See the excerpt in this chapter.)

Mann, Horace. 1891. *Life and Works of Horace Mann.* Vol. 4: Annual Reports. Boston: Lee and Shepard.

Merton, Robert K. 1968. *Social Theory and Social Structure.* Rev. ed. New York: Free Press.

Parsons, Talcott. 1959. "The School Class as a Social System." *Harvard Educational Review* 39: 297–318.

Schultz, Theodore W. 1961. "Investment in Human Capital." *American Economic Review* 51: 1–17. Reprinted in Jerome Karabel and A. H. Halsey (eds.), *Power and Ideology in Education,* pp. 313–324. New York: Oxford University Press, 1977.

Trow, Martin. 1961. "The Second Transformation of American Secondary Education." *International Journal of Comparative Sociology* 2: 144–166. Reprinted in Jerome Karabel and A. H. Halsey (eds.), *Power and Ideology in Education,* pp. 105–118. New York: Oxford University Press, 1977.

Marxism: Correspondence or Class Reproduction Position

Althusser, Louis. 1971. "Ideology and Ideological State Apparatuses." In *Lenin and Philosophy and Other Essays*. New York: Monthly Review Press.

Anyon, Jean. "Social Class and the Hidden Curriculum of Work." *Journal of Education* 162 (1980): 67–92. (See the excerpt in Chapter 7.)

Bowles, Samuel, and Herbert Gintis. 1976. *Schooling in Capitalist America*. New York: Basic Books.

Carnoy, Martin. 1974. *Education as Cultural Imperialism*. New York: McKay.

_____(ed.). 1975. *Schooling in a Corporate Society*. New York: McKay.

_____, and Henry Levin (eds.). 1976. *The Limits of Educational Reform*. New York: Longman.

Marxism: Resistance or Class Conflict Approach

Apple, Michael. 1982. *Education and Power*. Boston: Routledge and Kegan Paul.

_____. 1987. *Teachers and Texts*. Boston: Routledge and Kegan Paul.

Aronowitz, Stanley, and Henry Giroux. 1985. *Education Under Siege*. South Hadley, MA: Bergin and Garvey.

Bowles, Samuel, and Herbert Gintis. 1981. "Education as a Site of Contradictions in the Reproduction of the Capital-Labor Relationship: Second Thoughts on the 'Correspondence Principle.' " *Economic and Industrial Democracy* 2: 223–242.

Carnoy, Martin, and Henry Levin. 1985. *Schooling and Work in the Democratic State*. Stanford: Stanford University Press.

Katznelson, Ira, and Margaret Weir. 1985. *Schooling for All*. New York: Basic Books.

Wexler, Philip. 1976. *The Sociology of Education: Beyond Equality*. Indianapolis, IN: Bobbs-Merrill.

Willis, Paul. 1981. *Learning to Labour*. New York: Columbia University Press.

Wrigley, Julia. 1982. *Class Politics and Public Schools: Chicago, 1900–1950*. New Brunswick, NJ: Rutgers University Press.

Weberianism

Archer, Margaret S. 1979. *Social Origins of Educational Systems*. London and Beverly Hills: Sage.

Archer, Margaret. 1982. "Introduction: Theorizing About the Expansion of Educational Systems." In Margaret Archer (ed.), *The Sociology of Educational Expansion*, pp. 3–64. Beverly Hills, CA: Sage.

Collins, Randall. 1979. *The Credential Society*. New York: Academic Press.

Giddens, Anthony. 1971. *Capitalism and Modern Social Theory*. Cambridge, England: Cambridge University Press.

Ringer, Fritz. 1979. *Education and Society in Modern Europe*. Bloomington, IN: Indiana University Press.

Weber, Max. 1978. In Guenther Roth and Claus Wittich, eds., *Economy and Society*. 2 vols. Berkeley, CA: University of California Press.

Pierre Bourdieu

Bourdieu, Pierre. 1984. *Distinction: A Social Critique of the Judgment of Taste*. Cambridge, MA: Harvard University Press.

_____, and Jean-Claude Passeron. 1977. *Reproduction in Society, Culture and Education.* Beverly Hills, CA: Sage.

_____, and Luc Boltanski. 1978. "Changes in Social Structure and Changes in the Demand for Education." In Salvador Giner and Margaret Scotford Archer (eds.), *Contemporary Europe: Social Structure and Cultural Patterns,* pp. 197–227. London: Routledge and Kegan Paul.

DiMaggio, Paul. 1979. "Review Essay: On Pierre Bourdieu." *American Journal of Sociology* 84 (6): 1460–1474.

_____, and John Mohr. 1985. "Cultural Capital, Educational Attainment, and Marital Selection." *American Journal of Sociology* 90 (May): 1231–1261.

Lamont, Michele and Annette Lareau. 1988. "Cultural Capital: Allusions, Gaps, and Glissandos in Recent Theoretical Developments." *Sociological Theory* 6 (fall): 153–168.

Swartz, David. Forthcoming. *Cultural Domination: Pierre Bourdieu and Contemporary Social Theory.* Chicago: University of Chicago Press.

John Meyer

Meyer, John W. 1977. "The Effects of Education as an Institution." *American Journal of Sociology* 83 (July): 55–77.

_____, and Brian Rowan. 1978. "The Structure of Educational Organizations." In Marshall W. Meyer and associates, *Environments and Organizations,* pp. 78–109. San Francisco: Jossey-Bass.

_____, and Michael Hannan (eds.). 1979. *National Development and the Modern World System.* Chicago: University of Chicago Press.

_____, David Tyack, Joane Nagel, and Audri Gordon. 1979. "Public Education as Nation-Building in America." *American Journal of Sociology* 85: 591–613.

Basil Bernstein

Bernstein, Basil. 1973a. *Class, Codes, and Control.* vol. 1. London: Paladin.

_____. 1973b. *Class, Codes, and Control.* vol. 2. London: Routledge and Kegan Paul.

_____. 1975. *Class, Codes, and Control.* vol. 3. London: Routledge and Kegan Paul.

_____. 1982. "Codes, Modalities, and the Process of Cultural Reproduction: A Model." In Michael Apple (ed.), *Cultural and Economic Reproduction in Education,* pp. 304–355. London: Routledge and Kegan Paul.

_____. 1986. "On Pedagogic Discourse." In John G. Richardson (ed.), *Handbook of Theory and Research for the Sociology of Education,* pp. 205–240. New York: Green-wood Press

The Functions of the School in Modern Society

DAVID A. GOSLIN
American Institutes of Research

Before an attempt can be made to assess the impact of changes that are taking place in our society on the school, some attention must be given to the question of what role the school plays vis-à-vis the society and its members. All societies, whether a modern industrialized society like our own or an isolated and primitive tribal society of past or present, are composed of a number of interrelated parts, each of which contributes in some manner to the ongoing character of the society. Every society, for example, must make some provision for collective decision-making if it is to survive for any significant period of time. Similarly, all societies must develop ways of allocating scarce resources, material and nonmaterial, and every society must make some provision for regulating the sexual behavior of its members in order to insure both the continuation of the society over time and the adequate socialization of new members.

The purpose of this chapter is to examine the relationship of that part of the modern society concerned with the maintenance and transmission of culture—the institution of education—to the other parts of the society as a whole. In particular we shall be concerned with what members of the society expect from their schools and how these expectations influence the educational process in the United States.

Each of the different institutions within the society, including the educational system, have important functions[1] in relation to the system as a whole and to its other parts. Thus many of the decisions made by government will have important consequences not only for the society as a whole but also for the functioning of other parts of the system, such as the family or the school. And, conversely, child rearing practices in the family are likely to affect what goes on in the school and, at least in the long run, governmental processes.

The conception of society as a system of interrelated parts is neither novel nor particularly sophisticated, yet it is frequently overlooked in efforts to understand the workings of a particular part of the system. For example, if one wishes to make any real headway in the analysis of the teaching process in American elementary schools, the particular student-teacher relationship must be set in a context that includes some consideration of the various functions performed by education as well as the ways in which other aspects of the social system influence the school. To consider only one of many possible consequences of this interdependence, if certain groups within the society view the elementary school primarily as a place to send children to get them out of the house, then this view of the school's function will almost certainly have an effect on what goes on in the school.

THE TRANSMISSION OF CULTURE

From the standpoint of the society as a whole, and often of groups within the society, the primary function of education is the maintenance of culture. "Man's capacity to learn, to organize learning in symbolic forms, to communicate this learning as knowledge to other members of the species, and to act on the basis of learning or knowledge is the source of all cultural phenomena. . . . Any culture and the civilization based upon that culture must depend upon the ability of the civilization to articulate and transmit its learning as semiautonomous, cognitive systems. These represent the accumulated knowledge in every field of inquiry and comprise the subject matter in all education. This is what we mean when we speak of the school's responsibility in transmitting a cultural heritage."[2]

Culture, of course, includes more than just the "accumulated knowledge in every field of inquiry." It includes the values, beliefs, and norms which have been passed down from generation to generation, albeit with frequent modifications, throughout the history of the society. "Education transmits a common cultural fund to the next generation and in the process helps to bring hordes of young barbarians to adult ways that are continuous with the past."[3]

The transmission and accumulation of culture from generation to generation has been the distinguishing characteristic of man since the earliest beginnings of human society. The role of formal education in this process has thus been significant throughout only a fraction of man's history. As Burton Clark points out, "the earliest 'educational systems' were no more than a woman instructing a daughter or a man and a boy walking, talking, and working together. In the Stone Age, we may bet, there were no elementary classes in flint chipping; a boy learned to chip flints by watching adults."[4] As the store of man's knowledge has grown and the groups in which he lives have become more complex, the development of specialized facilities to take over where the family leaves off in this process of cultural transmission has become necessary. During most of recent history and extending as far back as the days of the Greek and Roman civilizations, formal education was restricted to a tiny minority of the society's members, usually the ruling elite or members of religious orders. The Industrial Revolution, however, in addition to producing a flood of innovations that caused the reservoir of man's knowledge and technical skills to burst its heretofore relatively narrow confines, radically altered the social structure of the society. No longer was the family the primary unit of production, as was the case in a predominantly agrarian economy. Instead a large number of men (not to mention women and children) found themselves leaving the home every day to work in manufacturing plants or offices. This shift in the basic social structure of the society (which tended to split up the family unit), together with a growing variety of available occupational positions (each requiring somewhat different skills and knowledge), made it impossible for new members of the society to continue to learn by observation of their parents alone. Not only did the young have more choices as to what skills they might acquire, than their parents, but no longer did the breadwinner of the family work where his children could watch him and learn from him.

"In brief, formal schooling became a necessity as the home and the community became ineffectual, even incompetent, in training the young for adulthood through informal contact. A new class of cultural agents—the teachers of the commoners—grew up. The changing nature of knowledge and work brought the children of the common man into the schoolhouse and gave to the schools a greatly broadened and deepened role in cultural transmission and continuity."[5]

To the extent that current trends in our society continue to accentuate this separation of occupational and family roles, we may predict that the function of the school as a primary agent of cultural transmission will be enhanced. We may not conclude, however, that the family is no longer important as a socializing agent, or that the school has taken over all of what used to be the family's functions in regard to the socialization of the young and the transmission of culture. Although there appears to be a trend toward admission of children to schools in this country at earlier ages, the family still serves as virtually the sole agent of socialization during the critical first four or five years of the child's life. It is during this period that the child learns to talk and forms the initial significant social relationships that will greatly influence his adaptation and accommodation in subsequent interpersonal situations. The child also begins to internalize the social values and normative prescriptions and proscriptions that will make it possible for him to function as a member of an orderly society during the remainder of his life.

Nor does the family lose its interest in the child when he reaches school age. In most cases parents, brothers and sisters, and members of the extended family (aunts, uncles, cousins, et cetera) will continue to exert strong socializing influences throughout the period of the child's formal education and, to a lesser extent, thereafter. As we shall see in subsequent discussions, it is likely that many of the special problems with which the school must contend stem from this division of responsibility for socialization of the young. Not only must the school begin with children who have already acquired a set of values (some of which may conflict with values that the school is committed to inculcating), but it must continue to deal with parallel and sometimes competing influences from the family (not to mention the child's peer group) during the time that the child is in its care.

These problems are further complicated by the fact that in this country the school traditionally has been viewed in a service relationship to the family, rather than as a legitimate independent socializing influence. This relationship between the family and the school is perhaps understandable in light of the fact that it is the family that is usually held responsible for faulty socialization and not the school. But this does not make the school's task any easier. Our society has come to expect the school to transmit to the child an enormously complex culture which includes not only a great deal of accumulated knowledge and many complex skills, both intellectual and physical, but an even more sophisticated and complicated set of values and norms which comprise the ideological basis of our cultural heritage.

It is a frequently acknowledged fact that the stability and continuity of our society as presently constituted depends not only on the ability of its citizens to read, write, and complete their income tax forms, but on their belief in and adherence to the political, religious, and social principles on which the institutions of the society are based. Thus the school is expected to teach the child something about such diverse ideals as democracy, the rule of law, free enterprise, and even the desirability of monogamous marriage.[6] And it is also expected to persuade future citizens of the society of the necessity of behaving in accordance with these principles and practices.

Socialization, even within the context of a formal educational system such as the school, involves much more than the learning of skills and the acquisition of information about how the society works or how it should work. Learning that results from more or less formal pedagogical procedures constitutes only a part of the preparation of the child for behaving in accordance with the roles of a participating adult member of the society. Perhaps the most important part of the socialization process involves the unconscious assimilation and internalization of beliefs, values, and patterns of behavior of significant others with whom the individual comes in contact. The preschool child soon begins to emulate aspects of the behavior of his parents, his brothers and sisters, and certain of his peers. As new figures are added to the circle of significant others surrounding the child—his teacher, his classmates, perhaps certain television personalities—the resulting influences on his behavior become increasingly diverse and complex. The possibility of conflict in the emulated behaviors is also increased, and the child must face the task of ranking the people with whom he deals, consciously or unconsciously, in terms of the influence he will permit them to have on his behavior.

Since most children spend a considerable part of their waking hours in school or in school-related activities, it is not surprising that those whom the child encounters in school can have an important influence on his behavior, including the formation of his value system, his attitudes about various social norms, and his behavior in general. It is only through widening his circle of significant others that the individual has an opportunity to prepare himself adequately for the diverse roles which the adult in our society must assume. To function adequately as an adult, the child must learn not only the roles of father or mother but also those of student, teacher, group leader, and, eventually, wife or husband. Boys must learn something about the role of family provider, be he businessman or factory worker; while girls frequently must be able to assume the role of secretary or career woman along with their roles as wife and mother. Although it is obvious that children do not for the most part learn a great deal about some of these roles until they have reached the status of an adult, many of the decisions that a child must make (and in which, although he may receive assistance from his family, his teacher or guidance counselor, or other adults, he is often left on his own) require him to know something about what is expected of individuals occupying various positions in the adult society. In addition, a child begins to acquire more generalized capacities for assuming adult roles at an early age. The school plays a major role, for example, in helping children learn to control their emotions, to deal with as well as assume positions of authority, and to recognize the existence of status hierarchies in social groups.

It is also clear that even if it were deemed desirable to keep children from learning about adult roles, such a course would be impossible without isolating young people from all contact with the adult world. With the rapid development of the mass media, especially television, children are exposed to this world earlier, with greater frequency, and in greater detail than ever before. The influence of the mass media is clearly a fact of modern life that must be considered in any discussion of the processes of socialization and cultural transmission.

A frequently overlooked aspect of the socialization process that has great relevance to any discussion of the functions of the school in modern society concerns the nature of the intellectual process itself. Among other things, socialization involves learning how to solve problems of all sorts. The acquisition of problem-solving techniques is an integral part of the educational process, although this is not always made explicit, perhaps in part because of the current state of our understanding of intellectual processes. It is not completely clear, for example, which of the various ways of going about solving different kinds of problems is of greatest overall usefulness and whether certain techniques are more useful in some situations than in others. Many scholars have advocated an essentially inductive approach to certain kinds of problems, whereas others have maintained that a deductive approach is of greatest usefulness. Learning theorists have not yet fully explored the relative roles of reward and punishment in the learning process, and although during recent years most educators have clung steadfastly to the assumption that optimum learning takes place under conditions of reward, it is not entirely clear that this is the case in all learning situations. Even assuming that some kind of positive reinforcement is most felicitous to learning, it might turn out that rewards intrinsic to the learning situation itself—for example, enjoyment in the activities involved—are all that are needed in certain kinds of learning. The intrusion into the situation of potentially conflicting external rewards from a teacher or parent may serve only to impede the process.

Although new insights into learning and thinking processes are forth-coming all the time, relatively little attention has been given to the problem of how these discoveries relate to what is going on in the school and, more importantly, to what should go on in the school. If one of the most important functions of the school is to teach children how to learn and to solve problems, then it would appear to be reasonable to inquire about what young people are being taught along these lines and whether the techniques they are learning will be of greatest usefulness to them as they assume responsibilities as adult members of the society. Obviously it is important for those individuals who are in positions where they must make decisions affecting the society to be able to adapt effectively to the continually changing demands upon them and to learn how to handle their responsibilities in the most efficacious way. The responsibility of the school in preparing society's members for such positions involves more than the inculcation of technical knowledge along with a smattering of tradition. Of even greater importance is the school's responsibility for teaching the child how to use whatever skills and knowledge he may possess. The educator's responsibility does not permit him to ignore the question of how children are being taught to solve problems and absorb new knowledge. The technique for approaching new information that is acquired by the child in the course of his experiences in school may turn out to be the most important part of the educational process.

SUPPORTING THE DISCOVERY OF NEW KNOWLEDGE

Although the primary function of the school may be the transmission of existing knowledge and tradition, educational institutions have paradoxically also been expected to play an important role in the encouragement and implementation of change. The university has always been a focal point of the search for new knowledge, and a great part of the flood of new ideas and innovations that have produced such rapid change in our society has originated in institutions of higher learning. During the past half century, as the rate of discovery has accelerated, the emphasis on research as a major function of colleges and universities has become of even greater significance. The result has been that the highest academic standing and prestige are increasingly being awarded to those members of the faculty who contribute the most to knowledge and the discovery of new ways of dealing with the physical, psychological, and social world. Much to the distress of many educators and despite frequent claims to the contrary, the teacher in higher education is not accorded prestige and financial rewards commensurate with those received by the researcher. That this trend is having and will continue to have an effect on the quality of the educational process, at all levels, is hard to deny (perhaps, for example, it will improve secondary school teaching by driving dedicated teachers out of the college ranks).

The role of educational institutions in fostering change and innovation is particularly notable at the college and university level, but elementary and secondary schools are expected to play their part in this process as well. Both through the encouragement of creative activities on the part of students and through the inculcation of social values having to do with the desirability of progress based on achievements in the sciences and in other fields of knowledge, the school plays a major role in influencing the rate of change in the society.

Not only does it have a responsibility to prepare children for dealing with the rapidly changing society they will encounter as adults, but if the society is to continue to progress at its current pace, the educational system must continue to produce individuals who will take over the task of developing new knowledge and techniques. As the cultural heritage on which our technology is based expands, the amount of preparation necessary before an individual can make a contribution to our basic store of knowledge grows along with it. The increasing technological complexity of the society has therefore had a profound effect on elementary and secondary education. Even in the primary grades, for example, efforts are being made to revise traditional curriculum content, particularly in mathematics and the sciences, at least in part in order to meet the demands of a society that has accepted change as an ideal to be strived for with all of the resources at its disposal.

ALLOCATING INDIVIDUALS TO POSITIONS IN SOCIETY

Every society must make some provision for deciding which of its members shall occupy the various positions in the society and perform the roles necessary for its continuation and development. Although the number and variety of positions to be filled varies from society to society, it has thus far been true in every society that the available positions have carried with them unequal responsibilities for and demands upon their occupants. Some jobs are more difficult than others, some are more dangerous, and some are more distasteful; some require special training or skills. For this reason and because it is fairly clear that the skills required for some positions are rarer than for others (e.g., the doctor, the judge), the world has not yet seen a society in which the occupants of all positions were accorded equal rewards or status. As a result there is competition among the members of the society (at least within those groups in which competition is permitted) for those positions receiving the greatest rewards and carrying with them the greatest responsibility and prestige. In his utopian *Walden Two*, B. F. Skinner solved this problem by mandating that the occupants of the most distasteful or boring positions would work significantly *fewer* hours but would receive equal rewards from the community—thus making garbage collection a particularly attractive occupation, especially for the artist or musician who values free time more than having an interesting job.[7] Thus far, however, although we have perhaps been moving in these directions, the desirability as well as the possibility of attaining such an ideal is open to question.

Traditionally, most societies have made use of a variety of ascribed or inherited characteristics in allocating individuals to positions or at least in deciding which groups of individuals will have an opportunity to compete for certain classes of positions. Family background, race, religion, order of birth, and sex are examples of ascribed characteristics which have been and frequently still are used as major determiners of the positions an individual may hold in society. However, the rapidly expanding technology of modern society has created a situation in which it has become increasingly important that individuals occupy positions for which they are well suited. As Ralph Linton pointed out in his analysis of status and role in human societies, the better adjusted the members of any society are to their statuses and roles, the more smoothly the society is likely to function.[8] As the requirements for fulfilling various positions become more complex and require not only longer training but greater ability, ascribed characteristics of individuals turn out to be less useful as criteria for allocating positions efficiently than measures of the individual's achievement and ability.

As the school has taken over from the family a greater share of the responsibility for socializing the young, it has also become the focus of many of the child's activities. The performance of the child in school serves therefore as one of the most important early measures of his abilities and energy. With the rise of mass education the school functions as an integral part of the process of status allocation in four ways: (1) by providing a context in which the individual can demonstrate his abilities, (2) by channeling individuals into paths that lead in the direction of different occupations or classes of occupations, (3) by providing the particular skills needed to fulfill the requirements of various positions, and finally (4) by transferring to the individual the differential prestige of the school itself.

In theory, development of public educational facilities in the United States has made it possible for any child to acquire the skills necessary to fulfill virtually any position in the society within the limitations of the individual's own abilities. Although the theory does not always work in practice (we shall examine some of the reasons for this in a subsequent chapter), it is nevertheless true that the school offers most children a unique opportunity to show what they can do. Although we have not as yet reached the point where access to all the different positions in the society is determined by an individual's abilities or even his educational background—ascribed characteristics still play an important part in influencing selection for many positions[9]—the evidence is overwhelming that educational achievement makes a great deal of difference in the kinds of opportunities open to a given individual, regardless of what other attributes he may have.

From the beginning the school operates as the arbiter of the individual's achievement. As the child progresses through the educational system, the decisions that must be made about the kinds of training he may select and the opportunities for advancement open to him are, for the most part, left to the school. The child and his parents may influence these decisions, but in the majority of cases the school plays the major role. It is in this process that the school probably exerts its greatest influence on the allocation of status. The decision as to whether the student will be allowed to take the courses required for college admission, for example, looms as one of the critical choice points in determining the individual's subsequent occupational status.

The skills and knowledge the individual acquires during the course of his education are, of course, important factors in the process of job allocation. But schools are not all equal in the quality of the education they provide or even in the kinds of specific training they offer. Consequently, the individual's long-range occupational opportunities may be determined by the kinds and quality of the educational experiences open to him. We have not yet reached the point where all members of the society have equal access, limited only by their abilities, to the various kinds of training possible. Regional and local differences in resources available for educational facilities, and discrimination in the allocation of what resources there are, severely restrict the opportunities of many members of the society. The situation has been improved in recent years, and the prospect of increased Federal government involvement in education has brightened the picture considerably, both with respect to increasing the total supply of resources available and to ensuring their equitable distribution. As our society becomes technologically more complex, continued progress in providing access to educational facilities will be an important factor in the maintenance of our present rate of growth. Two significant developments in this area, the widespread use of standardized tests in evaluating individuals and the appearance of the junior college, will be discussed in Chapter VI.

Finally, because some schools are better than others, the reputation and prestige of the school is likely to become a factor in subsequent evaluations of the individual, regardless of his actual training or capabilities. Thus the young man who graduates from an Ivy League college may find that there are more job opportunities available to him than to the graduate of a less prestigious college, even though the latter student might be equally qualified. Similarly, the private preparatory school graduate has less trouble getting into many colleges than his public school counterpart (excluding students who attend a few highly prestigious public schools), not only because he may have received better training but in part because of the reputation and prestige of his school. Although there is little data available on this point, the prestige of one's secondary school or college probably makes less difference at present due to the growing demand for well-trained personnel and to the increasing use of objective measures of ability and achievement (e.g., standardized tests) in both college admissions and job allocation. Indeed, one series of studies has indicated[10] that where social class background is taken into account in evaluating the influence of the reputation of one's school or college on subsequent opportunities, the hypothesized relationship disappears. We shall return to a further examination of this problem when we take up the larger question of maximum utilization of manpower in a later chapter.

OTHER FUNCTIONS OF THE SCHOOL

We have briefly considered each of the primary functions of the school in modern society, but like most social institutions, the school has a number of other functions which appear to be tangential to its main role in the society and sometimes tend to conflict with its primary functions. These secondary functions include: (1) the role of the school in providing mothers with relief from the task of taking care of their children during a significant part of the day, which in turn makes possible the addition of large numbers of married women to the labor force, (2) the part played by the school in the courtship process and its consequent influence on mate selection, (3) the use of the school to maintain the cultural identity and therefore the stability of subgroups within the society, and (4) the use of educational institutions to effect social reforms. . . .

NOTES

1. See Wilbert E. Moore, *Social Change* (Englewood Cliffs, N.J.: Prentice-Hall, Inc., 1963), pp. 6–11, for a brief discussion of this problem. Moore uses the term "function" to refer to "the intended or unintended consequences of action" (p. 28).

2. Vincent Ostrom, "Education and Politics," in *Social Forces Influencing American Education,* ed. Nelson B. Henry (Chicago: The National Society for the Study of Education, 1961), pp. 10–12. Distributed by the University of Chicago Press.

3. Burton R. Clark, *Educating the Expert Society* (San Francisco: Chandler Publishing Company, 1962), p. 11.

4. *Ibid.,* p. 12.

5. *Ibid.,* p. 15.

6. *Ibid.,* p. 15.

7. B. F. Skinner, *Walden Two* (New York: Macmillan Company, 1962).

8. Ralph Linton, *The Study of Man* (New York: D. Appleton-Century Co., 1936).

9. Although most people think immediately of racial discrimination in this context, it should be noted that race is only one of several ascribed characteristics that influence the allocation of positions. Sex is a more important basis for discrimination in many situations, for example.

10. Alexander W. Astin, " 'Productivity' of Undergraduate Institutions," *Science,* CXXXVI (April 13, 1962).

Some Comparative Principles of Educational Stratification

RANDALL COLLINS
University of California, Riverside

What determines the structures and contents of educational systems? A great deal of research in the sociology of education has taken an existing structure and its content for granted and concentrated on describing the social processes that occur within it. We are left with the question of why a given educational system exists—what conditions or forces produce it, sustain it, change it, or even abolish it. This theoretical question has often been answered from a functionalist or social-order perspective, which explains education by citing its contributions to the integration or productivity of society. Alternatively, education may be explained as a weapon in the struggles for domination that make up the phenomenon of stratification, whether considered from the viewpoint of Marxist theory, Weberian theory, or some mixture of the two.

The social-order approach, long accepted rather uncritically by many American social theorists, has a number of crucial weaknesses. In its most general formulation—that education socializes young people into the existing social order[1]—the theory is causally underdetermined. Its apparent truth is tautological. The proposition justifies *any* educational structure after the fact; it does not explain why one particular structure exists rather than some other, and therefore it is not subject to empirical validation. Some functionalist theorists have attempted to evade this difficulty by formulating more specific kinds of social demands that education fulfills: they assert either that education provides specific technical skills or that educational history follows an empirically demonstrable series of stages which evolve from primitive to advanced forms. The evidence usually cited for the first model is the rise over the last century in a given Western country's educational attendance; for the second model, the standard evidence is a set of educational-attendance figures for societies differing on a measure of economic productivity such as per-capita gross national product.[2] The two specifications of functionalist theory often overlap, since many evolutionary models posit that schooling expands to meet the increasing need for technically skilled workers in industrial and especially in advanced or "post-industrial" societies.

These efforts to salvage functionalist theory are not very successful, in my opinion. A close look at the evidence indicates that schooling does not supply specific technical skills, as functionalists contend.[3] Furthermore, as we shall see, historical patterns of educational development have been caused by factors other than increasing sophistication of industrial techniques.

These problems with the functionalist viewpoint lead me to believe that the most fruitful new developments in the attempt to explain the evolution and change of educational systems involve the stratification or domination approach. Like the functionalist approaches, the approaches to education which focus on domination have also varied. The Marxist approach has several versions. In the *Communist Manifesto*, Marx and Engels demanded free and universal access to education, a theme that has persisted in liberal as well as radical critiques of class differences in educational access and attainment. More sophisticated Marxist positions have emerged in recent years. Louis Althusser theorizes that education is a mechanism of domination that reproduces the unequal relationship of capitalist production.[4] Samuel Bowles and Herbert Gintis, arguing from a detailed empirical basis, stress education's role in producing a compliant labor force.[5] Standing at least one tenet of Marxism on its head, Alain Touraine interprets the class struggle of each historical period as a conflict between the ruling class, which controls productive skills, and the subordinate classes, which possess only labor power.[6] In this view, education is the basis of modern class domination, and struggles over educational access become the new focus of class struggle.

These Marxist approaches thus include a simple view of education as an unequally distributed good, a sophisticated view of education as a mechanism of domination, and a technocratic, evolutionary view of educationally derived skills as the prime basis of modern stratification. In my view, exponents of the domination approach are on the right track. Althusser's theory, however, shares functionalism's weakness of treating education as part of a given structure without showing, by empirical detail or historical comparison, the conditions for one sort of education rather than another. Bowles and Gintis provide the most specified and empirically bolstered theory, but their single causal dynamic, I shall argue, needs to be incorporated into a larger set of stratifying processes.

Although the Weberian approach rejects the Marxian emphasis on the causal preponderance of the economic structure and its historical evolution, the Weberian approach is, to a degree, a sophisticated version of the Marxian tradition. That is, Weberians do see economic interests based on property divisions as key bases of group organization, of intergroup conflict, and of historical change.[7] But, in contrast to Marx, Weber also pointed out that organizational resources, especially those of state and private bureaucracies, and cultural resources, above all religious traditions (but also secular ones such as education), can create and channel additional interest groups and conflicts.[8] Three lines of societal division—economic, organizational-political, and cultural (or in Weber's terms, "class," "party," and "status")—mesh, so that economic classes or organizational politicians are stronger if they also possess the unity that comes from common cultural resources. But the three types of resources may be differentially distributed; strong ethnic, national, religious, or other cultural divisions can shape struggles for economic or political domination into patterns very different from those emerging along class lines. There are many kinds of stratification systems, and with the proper conceptual tools one may show the conditions for each.

My approach may be broadly characterized as Weberian. I see education as part of a multisided struggle among status communities for domination, for economic advantage, and for prestige. This approach allows the incorporation of a multiplicity of particular causes into an overall explanation, since it regards social structure as the result of the mobilization of a variety of resources and interest groups within a common arena. It even permits us to salvage the main intellectual contribution of the social-order tradition as it applies to education—Durkheim's theory of education as an agent of moral socialization and hence as the secular equivalent of religion in modern society.[9] Durkheim shows that participation in rituals—whether religious, political, or educational—promotes group identification, and that myths or symbols that are the focus of rituals become marks of membership in distinctive social groups and the referents of moral legitimacy. Put in this fashion, the Durkheimian theory points the way out of its own major weakness, its obliviousness to the stratifying effects of education and to the social struggles that surround it. For procedures inculcating social membership can be used by particular groups in a stratified society both to cement their own boundaries and to morally legitimate themselves in the eyes of others.[10] In its overgeneralized form, the Durkheimian theory simply asserts that education integrates entire, undifferentiated societies; in a more limited form, it is useful in showing education's contribution to integrating particular groups in situations of conflict and domination. This version of Durkheim fits naturally with the Weberian concept of stratification through status groups.

In what follows, I will attempt to show how the positive insights of the Durkheimian, Marxian, and even practical-skills approaches to education may contribute to a multidimensional Weberian model of stratification. I will also try to specify the types of educational systems to which each approach applies. My overall concern will be with the interaction of the economic, organizational, and cultural aspects of stratification; I shall attempt to show that in the long run the interaction of these spheres generates a market-like structure. Since this pattern is difficult to see except at a macroscopic level, a word about comparative historical evidence and method is in order. . . .

PRACTICAL SKILLS

The most common modern interpretation of the role of education is that it meets the demand for technical skills. Most contemporary evidence, however, contradicts this interpretation.[11] The content of most modern education is not very practical: educational attainment and grades are not much related to work performance, and most technical skills are learned on the job. Although work skills are more complex in *some* modern jobs than in most preindustrial jobs, in many modern jobs they are not. Similar patterns appear in an overview of societies throughout history.

In tribal societies, children are trained for adult work primarily through informal apprenticeship in which they watch and later help their parents or other relatives.[12] The more complex and advanced crafts, such as metal working or the art of the shaman or medicine man, may be learned by secret apprenticeship outside the family. The same pattern characterizes the training of craftsmen in literate civilizations. Greco-Roman artisans, for example, learned their skills solely through apprenticeship, usually within the family; this approach was used for medicine (at that time, as in all areas until the late nineteenth century, a craft with little real effectiveness), for such advanced crafts as architecture and construction engineering, and for the various arts.[13] After the conquest of Greece by the Romans (circa 190 B.C.), many skilled craftsmen were slaves, who were excluded from any formal schooling. This exclusion did not detract from the quality of their practical work, although it did keep the power and prestige of their occupations low.

The pattern of learning the most useful and complex practical skills by apprenticeship is common to the civilizations of China, Japan, India, Islam, and medieval and early modern Europe. Although probably illiterate and certainly not formally educated, the craftsmen of these civilizations were not sharply different in skill or innovativeness from those of the industrial world. After all, it was the craftsmen of medieval Europe and China who produced the beginnings of the machine revolution over a long period starting at least as far back as A.D. 900.[14] Even during England's full-scale takeoff into industrialism in the early nineteenth century, the level of education was generally low, and what education did exist was by and large nontechnical in content.[15]

The one practical skill often taught in specialized schools has been literacy. The origins of literate education are in the priestly administrations of ancient Mesopotamia and Egypt, where children were trained in schools for the career of scribe.[16] Some of those schools were attached to temples; others were probably run by private schoolmasters. The scribe might be a government administrator, especially in the rather totalitarian Egyptian dynasties, or an independent practitioner who engaged in letter writing for the populace. Some merchants also were literate. Apparently, however, literacy training usually approximated an apprenticeship, since the assistant (in Mesopotamia often an adopted son) of an independent scribe accompanied his trainer, practiced the fundamentals of the trade, and gradually came to copy and then share in his trainer's work.

Such practical education almost always has been highly unritualized. Even in the more formal schools, we know of no attendance requirements, examinations, grades, or degrees; proficiency was sufficiently tested in practice. In highly commercial periods, the middle classes have attempted to acquire skills in literacy and arithmetic. Thus we find education for these ends among the commercial classes of Japan's Tokugawa period and of the prosperous periods in European history since the High Middle Ages.[17] But practical education of this sort has generally been quite different from the ritualized and status-ostentatious education of elites of those societies. Arithmetic and the reading and writing of the vulgar languages have usually been taught in family or apprenticeship settings or in low-status private schools without the formalized public credentials of official, high-status institutions.

At times, though, practical education has involved a ritualized superstructure. This generally has occurred where an occupational group has been politically powerful and has possessed strong collective organization, as in the case of a guild or self-regulating profession. Under these conditions, the occupation group can monopolize skills and require a lengthy period of servitude for trainees through formal requirements for length of apprenticeship, examinations (such as producing a master-work), and ceremonial procedures of promotion. In Italy and Germany in the late Middle Ages, training was sometimes lengthened so artificially that journeymen revolted, producing some of the earliest instances of overt class warfare.[18] In contrast, the politically powerless Greco-Roman craftsmen were apprenticed informally and promoted to full active status solely on the basis of adequate performance.

Perhaps ritualized training first appeared in tribal societies where cohorts of young people underwent ritual segregation, ordeals, and formal initiation into the society of adults.[19] Specialists in magic and witch doctoring, whose skills were heavily dependent on the psychological effects of their ceremonies, often underwent very ritualized secret apprenticeships. The same was true of iron workers in many West African tribes and in medieval Japan, who derived a great deal of prestige from their ability to make weapons.[20]

In summary, most practical education has involved students working as assistants to experienced workers.[21] Schools have sometimes been established in cases where the fundamental components of practical skill could be learned by repetitious drill, such as in the acquisition of literacy and arithmetic skills. Usually such schooling has been unritualized and aimed at developing proficiency in the most efficient manner. This has been particularly true where dominant social classes have had a ritualized form of education and practical work has been relegated to unprivileged middle or lower classes. At times, though, powerful groups have incorporated practical education into a ritualized educational system. In the United States, for example, a formal structure surrounds elementary education, which alone among all levels of modern education bears a clear relationship to economic productivity.[22] The more elaborate organizational form, though, must be explained by factors other than the demand for practical skills, and to these social factors we now turn.

STATUS-GROUP MEMBERSHIP

Weber defined a status group as a community based on a common culture that provides a consciousness of membership (and hence of the boundaries with nonmembers) and, usually, some claim to prestige and legitimacy in the social order.[23] The key resource for the creation and maintenance of such communities, then, is a common culture. It should be borne in mind that Weber acknowledged the importance of both status-group and class stratification. Cultural resources frequently are stratified by economic class and are one of the weapons that classes can use to become powerfully organized. Cultural resources may also produce status-group divisions within classes or even across them, most notably in the forms of nationalism and ethnicity. In every case, we should remember that cultural resources are *means* and that groups organized on their basis may have a variety of *ends:* groups are not confined to struggling for prestige but may also try to use their culturally based organization to monopolize economic and power positions.

In historical perspective, education has been used more often for organizing status groups than for other purposes. Since the defining locus of status-group activity is leisure and consumption, status-group education has been sharply distinguished from practical education by the exclusion of materially productive skills. Because status groups have used a common culture as a mark of group membership, status-group education has taken the form of a club and has included much ceremony to demonstrate group solidarity and to publicly distinguish members from nonmembers. This club aspect characterized the activities of Chinese gentlemen who met for genteel conversation and poetry writing, as well as the periodic festivals put on for the Greek public by students, an elite sector of the population.[24]

Status-group education, then, has been ceremonial, aesthetic, and detached from practical activities. Its rituals rarely have dramatized rankings within the group; formal grades, competitive examinations, and degrees usually have been absent. Where competitions have occurred, as in the games and contests of the Greeks, they have shown the group as a whole and have emphasized the leisure of group members and spectators. The main distinctions have been between insiders and outsiders, not among members of the group. Frequently, there have been no formal attendance requirements, and the absence of formal degrees has reflected the fact that acquisition of the status group's culture is the object of education. In contrast with bureaucratic forms of education, the test has come in one's participation in the leisure activities of the status group, and the organization of the schools has been only incidental to that end.

Status-group education has predominated in societies controlled by aristocracies and other wealthy, leisured classes. In Greece and Rome, it arose out of the age-group initiations of the quasi-tribal period.[25] With the development of highly stratified city-states, warrior training evolved into a set of games (what we now call the basic track and field events), singing, and eventually reading and writing traditional poetry, especially the warrior epics of Homer. Participation in this culture, particularly in the games and festivals of the schools, became the mark of upper-class status, especially as a middle class of merchants and soldiers developed due to changes in the economy and in warfare. The exclusiveness of education was threatened during the fifth century B.C., when, in the midst of political revolutions and expanding commerce, wandering teachers known as sophists offered instruction in the art of argument, or rhetoric, to all who could pay the price. This threat to the cultural domination of the upper classes was headed off, however, as education in rhetoric and grammar was added to the standard sequence of schooling involving sports and festivals. This form of education lasted for eight hundred years, through the Roman conquest of Greece, and was eventually adopted with only minor changes by the Romans. The Greek upper classes in cities throughout the eastern Mediterranean used possession of this culture to distinguish themselves from the surrounding "barbarians," even if the latter might be cultivated Syrians, Egyptians, or Romans.

In China, the first educated men were diviners or sages, who read oracles for the court and probably passed their skills along through apprenticeship.[26] Since these skills eventually developed into a full-fledged writing system, this early education may be seen as a form of "practical" training. The period of Confucius, Lao Tzu, and other teachers (circa 500–200 B.C.) was also one of predominantly practical training in that education was usually directed to training advisors for the competing courts. With the unification of China under the Han dynasty (circa 200 B.C.–A.D. 200), the Confucian form of education developed into a bureaucratic selection device. Selection, though, was based largely on aesthetic skills, and, as social status outside as well as within government service came to depend on education, the aesthetic elements in education developed still further. In later dynasties formal examinations were judged exclusively on the bases of literary skill and beauty of calligraphy. The leisure pursuits of Chinese gentlemen of this era centered on poetry writing and painting; the prestigious form of sociability was the "literary gathering" where literature was read and discussed. This emphasis on aesthetics was even more pronounced during periods of weak dynasties or of political decentralization. An example was the period of A.D. 200–600, when Confucianism was displaced by a highly poetic and artistic form of Taoist mysticism, whose practitioners cultivated an individualism which entailed a total disregard for formal educational requirements or doctrines.

There are many other examples of aesthetic education for the gentry. In India, from the beginnings of literacy, education was closely associated with status-group prestige. Brahmin priests monopolized knowledge of the Vedic traditions and thereby helped not only to close off entry to their caste but also to legitimate the caste system.[27] For the original Brahmins, education was a "practical" training in religious and magic skills. As a complex commercial society developed, however, the Brahmin caste became less an occupational group of priests and more an educated caste of landholders and administrators for the various princes. Among the lower castes, religious movements developed which emulated the old Brahmin religious purity and mystical doctrine, because this was a route toward improving one's social prestige. Within the upper levels, both the Brahmin and the warrior and the merchant castes developed a more secular culture, including poetry, drama, dance, a science of love-making, and art, which displayed their membership in the privileged leisure classes. The height of this culture, in which private teachers apparently taught the rich, occurred during the wealthy Gupta period from A.D. 300 to 700.

Similarly, in the Heian court of early Japanese civilization (A.D. 1000), men and women courtiers developed an elaborate culture of poetry writing and art appreciation and even produced the first great Japanese works of prose fiction, largely through informal family education.[28] In the Islamic world, education developed from religious training in the holy scriptures and laws to a form of culture that, in the cosmopolitan cities of prosperous periods, provided entertainment and status for the wealthy.[29] Especially in the court circles of centers such as Baghdad and Cordova, this culture included not only a pious acquaintance with religious tradition, but also a knowledge of semi-religious and even secular traditions of poetry, philosophy, and science.

In Europe, informal education as the basis of status emulation was most prominent during the Renaissance, especially in the wealthy commercial cities of Italy, but also in Germany, the Netherlands, France, and England.[30] Poetry writing and allusions to the classics were marks of prestige in everyday social life. Status groups were further organized around the patronage of artists, scientists, and scholars, and around "academies" that held formal meetings for members to discuss and be entertained by their own culture. The schooling involved in acquiring this culture was largely individual and private and was carried out in rivalry with the formal organization of the universities. Eventually, however, the status culture based on aesthetic activities began to be inculcated more formally as schools were established, and for several centuries (from 1500 to 1800) the schools succeeded in attracting the children of the elite. These schools included the "colleges" organized by the Jesuits, which in France became the *lycées;* the English boarding schools that came to be known as public schools; and similar schools in Germany that originally were called academies and, later, gymnasia. They became secondary schools only when the combination of bureaucratization and incorporation of humanistic culture into the universities made university education a more important foundation of elite status. For the German universities, this occurred around 1800; for the French, English, and American universities, after 1870. In modern university systems, high social prestige has usually been attached to schools that have concentrated, in their curricula, on the classics or on a literary and relatively impractical form of modern culture—schools such as Oxford and Cambridge in England and the Ivy League schools in the United States.

Well-organized status groups have not been confined to the upper classes, however. Under conditions of an expanding commercial economy and a political system with some dispersion of authority, less dominant classes have been able to claim greater prestige and to organize their communities more strongly by developing their own cultures. Such middle-class education (as among the "merchant princes" of the Renaissance) sometimes has emulated the aesthetic culture of the upper class, but more usually it has taken a religious form. Examples of the latter were the academies of dissenting Protestant sects in England and Germany during the early Industrial Revolution.[31] We can even see this religious form in the educational movements of the English working class during the nineteenth century—the Sunday schools and Workingmen's Improvement Associations.[32] The workingmen's movement was oriented towards enhancing its discipline and used rituals to increase its social respectability. Education in the movement was used not to enhance work skills, but to make a claim for higher social status and even to assist in political organizing. Similarly, in Islam, the upper-class education provided by the *ulema*—the teacher-judges who interpreted the holy law and were patronized by the wealthy—was challenged by the mystical Sufi cults among metal workers, rug makers, and other urban artisans.[33] These Sufi secret societies, which combined craft apprenticeship with religious learning, were often vehicles for political opposition to the dominant classes, and in Baghdad in the eleventh century they discredited and destroyed the secular, aesthetic culture of the courts.

There have been times when a rebellious class, sensing a shift in the resources that underlie the organization of power, has gone to the extreme of developing a culture which is the opposite of the existing dominant culture. Thus the *philosophes* of eighteenth-century France mocked the traditional religious culture and the classical culture and promoted in their stead the ideal of a modern culture based on science and technology.[34] This cultural ideal appealed to a new status group, which included the emerging administrators of the state, especially members of the new technical branches of the military. This group provided the organizational basis for the revolution of 1789–1800. In England, the utilitarians espoused a similar ideal, although less successfully; their technocratic ideology, although embodied in a number of schools, failed to overthrow the traditional culture of the elite. Still, technocratic ideology has remained a unifying theme in middle-class and, to some extent, labor politics since the early 1800s.[35] This ideology has influenced Communist doctrine, as shown in the Soviet educational system's emphasis on technical education as the sole legitimate qualification for dominant positions.[36]

The contents of status-group education, then, vary predictably with the class situations of the groups that espouse them. We find aesthetic education, often combined with games and a reverence for tradition, in the status cultures of privileged upper classes. Moral respectability, usually in the form of religious doctrine, has been the cultural ideal of moderately aspiring middle classes or upper working classes. Rising classes in revolutionary periods have often taken practical and scientific education as their cultural ideal. Perhaps, though, we are generalizing about rebellious groups from a set of cases that is too historically limited; the more universal principle might be that revolutionary groups draw on whatever cultural form can be claimed to be both progressive and sharply distinct from traditional status claims.

BUREAUCRACY

Bureaucracy is a style of organization based on rules and regulations, written reports, and files of records. The use of such written materials tends to make control appear abstract and generalized; bureaucracy makes possible the separation of the individual officeholder from the powers of the position. Bureaucracy helps to solve the crucial problem of rulers and other leaders of organizations: the tendency to lose control of subordinates because they appropriate their positions as their own and thus become independent of their chiefs. Other characteristics of bureaucracy also serve the purpose of control. The specialization of tasks limits the individual's powers and makes him or her more dependent on the cooperation of other specialists. The multiplication of ranks and the setting of regular career sequences with limited periods in each office keep officials concerned with their organizational futures and motivated toward higher offices. Formal examinations maximize the impersonality and competitiveness of the system when they are the basis for entrance into the bureaucracy or promotion within it. Not all bureaucratic organizations have used all these control devices, however. There have been many quasi-bureaucracies which have mixed bureaucratic controls with mechanisms of hereditary aristocracy, purchase of position, or various informal arrangements; research tends to confirm that no organization is without some informal structure.[37] . . .

Medieval Europe and the Bureaucratic Church

In medieval Europe, the greatest centralizing power was the papacy. Between 1050 and 1300, it made a bid for theocratic control, based on possession of the only large-scale literate organization in Europe. The church began to bureaucratize internally through the growth of the papal chancery, which became steadily more important in settling property matters among the many wealthy monasteries and cathedrals; the chancery then moved to regain control of church appointments from the feudal lords.[38] The universities, which proliferated from the early twelfth century onwards, arose in response to employment opportunities in the church bureaucracy. Though there were no formal examinations for church offices, the tendency arose for the pope to appoint bishops from the ranks of those holding doctorates in theology and canon law. Clerics seeking appointment to lower-ranking parish positions had their names submitted on lists prepared by their university officials; it appears that it was not necessary for candidates to have a degree but only to have been in attendance.

These schools were the first in world history to be bureaucratized internally. While schooling preparatory to the university consisted of informal literacy training by monks or local parish priests, the universities developed an elaborate internal structure. They had a series of courses, examinations, and degrees. Specialized courses (canon law, secular law, medicine, theology) branched off from the study of the lower arts. Specific periods of attendance were required for various degrees: two years for the Bachelor of Arts, four more for the Master of Arts, and up to eight more for higher degrees in theology.

Although grades do not seem to have been assigned and students varied in age from the early teens through the thirties, in other respects the schools involved considerable standardization, hierarchy, and specialization—especially in comparison to the schools of the Orient or the schools of Mediterranean antiquity. This internal bureaucratization seems to have evolved in response partly to the increasing bureaucratization of the papacy, partly to increasing competition for recommendations for church appointments, and partly to the increasing competition of teachers for students. The teachers took the unprecedented step of organizing themselves into a guild—*universitas* meant "guild" in medieval Latin. The guild seems to have designed the university structure of internal specialization and required hierarchies of courses as a means of sharing students and extending the period of paid instruction. (Students paid their professors individually for their instruction.) Thus, during the twelfth and thirteenth centuries, the number of years required to attain the valuable doctorate in theology gradually extended to sixteen, as the competition for high church positions increased.[39]

As various principalities, kingdoms, and cities consolidated their power, however, the papacy's bid for domination of Europe failed, and the church again became the captive of contending states. From the fourteenth century onwards, student enrollment dropped sharply, and the structure of the university began to change. In England, where this process went furthest, the higher faculties disappeared, and the universities became collections of colleges or private residential halls in which students were instructed by tutors rather than university professors. Thus, the failure of the bureaucratic church-state led to the decline of bureaucratic education.

The development of modern school systems resulted from the consolidation of strong European bureaucratic states that were independent of the Catholic church. These secular school systems taught in the national language rather than the pan-European language of church Latin.[40] The militarily expansive and rigidly bureaucratized Prussian state led the way in the seventeenth and eighteenth centuries in building a public school system at the elementary and university levels and in drawing state officials from among holders of university degrees. During this same period, the French state created military and engineering schools so as to draw its administrators from a source independent of the aristocracy and the powerful church-controlled schools. The Russian state, in its efforts to centralize control, went to the extreme of making aristocratic status dependent on government service, which in turn was tied to state-defined school qualifications. England, virtually up until the end of the nineteenth century, maintained a relatively patrimonial form of government administration—including the purchase of military commands, widespread patronage politics, and local administration by amateur gentry—and placed the least emphasis on publicly supported education. Only with the civil-service reforms beginning in 1870 did the English government begin to build a public school system, to revive the ancient but long moribund universities, and to create new universities.[41]

In general, any strong, centralized state or church tends to be bureaucratically organized; the bureaucratic control devices themselves are the prime basis of its centralized authority. Such a state or church provides a demand for education, but the relationship between the state or church and the educational system may take several forms. In the weakest form, the state or church simply provides a market for schools that spring up independently, as in many Islamic states, the medieval papacy, and the Chinese Empire. The Ottoman and late Roman empires represent an intermediate form, in which the state oversees and offers some financial support for existing educational institutions. State influence on education is fairly strong where examinations are required for entrance to government office, as in Imperial China, Germany after 1800, and Britain after 1870. The state is most deeply involved in education where it requires school attendance. Attendance was compulsory for aristocrats in Tokugawa Japan and in Russia, but only in the last few centuries has it been required of the general population, beginning with Germany in the eighteenth century, followed by the United States, France, Japan, Italy, and Russia in the nineteenth and by England and other countries in the twentieth.

It is here that the recent Marxist argument—that schooling is used as a device for ensuring labor discipline and, hence, is developed by the dominant class in its own interest—takes on great relevance.[42] Clearly, this argument applies only to modern mass education, not to the elite education that characterized most pre-modern educational systems and that continues to comprise the elite stratum of modern educational systems. With this specification, the labor-discipline argument does find empirical support. Consider, for example, the conservative and conformist values expressed in school texts throughout the period of mass education, and the efficacy of primary schools in inculcating unreflective political loyalty.[43] Yet although modern education does discipline the lower social classes, the demand for labor discipline per se does not explain why some industrial societies have large mass-education systems and why some have small ones. For example, the educational system is huge in the United States, relatively large in Russia and Japan, and tiny in Britain, France, and Germany, even though the need for labor discipline is presumably the same in all industrial societies. (Compare the figures from the early 1960s shown in table 1.) Nor does the demand for labor discipline explain the existence of segregated class systems in some societies but not in others.

Historical evidence indicates that mass, compulsory education was first created not for industrial, but for military and political, discipline. The first compulsory, state-supported elementary schools were established in the early eighteenth century by Denmark and Prussia, and later by Japan, to accompany the creation of mass conscript armies.[44] In England, where a highly traditional military organization and the aristocracy's near deadlock on political power survived until the late nineteenth century, it was only with military and political reforms and the concomitant organization of a powerful working-class party that a compulsory school system was envisioned.

Capitalists' interest in using education to ensure labor discipline may have been a force behind the development of mass, compulsory education in some

TABLE 1

	Percent completing secondary school	Percent attending university	Percent graduating from university
USA	75	39	18
USSR	47	19	9
Japan	57	11	11
France	30	11	–
England	12	6	5
West Germany	11	6	–

Sources: Torsten Husen, "Social Structure and the Utilization of Talent," in *Essays on World Education,* ed. George Z. F. Bereday (New York: Oxford Univ. Press, 1969), p. 80; Philip J. Idenberg, "Europe: In Search of New Forms of Education," in *Essays,* ed. Bereday, p. 281; Nicholas De Witt, "Basic Comparative Data on Soviet and American Education," *Comparative Perspectives on Education,* ed. Robert J. Havinghurst (Boston: Little, Brown, 1968), pp. 55–56; John E. Blewett, trans. and ed., *Higher Education in Postwar Japan: The Ministry of Education's 1964 White Paper* (Tokyo: Sophia Univ. Press, 1965), pp. 113, 118, 122, 158–9.

of these countries, but it was not the central motive: Prussia and Japan established compulsory schooling well before extensive industrialization, and England long after. The safer generalization is that bureaucratic states impose compulsory education on populations which are seen as potential threats to state control, and that those economic classes which are influential in the state will help define the nature of the "threat."

Finally, it seems clear that the initial impetus behind the development of bureaucratized schooling did not come from the bureaucratization of business enterprises. Bureaucracy within private business organizations developed quite late. There are few examples of it before the late nineteenth century in the United States.[45] The industrial organizations of England, France, and Germany in the early and middle nineteenth century did make considerable use of record keeping, and some of these organizations were large enough to have a degree of specialization and of administrative career hierarchy, but educational requirements and examinations were not part of this structure. Most nineteenth-century British or German clerks were trained through work "apprenticeship" after elementary schooling in literacy. Even in the twentieth century, managers in Britain and Germany have tended to have had little formal education, because the higher schools have been connected with careers in government and the elite professions.[46] The civil-service exams for which students prepare have reflected the culture of the elite status group, exemplified in England by knowledge of the Greek and Latin classics and in Germany by knowledge of philosophy and law. Where industrial and commercial bureaucracies have emphasized educational requirements for employees—above all in the United States, Japan, and Russia and to a lesser degree in France—the educational system has taken the lead and business has responded.[47] This has resulted in a tendency for formal requirements to increase in both spheres.

CONCLUSION: TOWARDS A THEORY OF CULTURAL MARKETS

We have seen that there are different types of education, each with its own determining conditions. Several of these conditions may operate simultaneously, resulting in a variety of types of education that coexist or even combine into a single, complex system. This is especially the case in the modern industrial world, where a great many interests in education have been mobilized. Sometimes these interests have conflicted, but they have nevertheless collectively resulted in a larger system of educational stratification. This system, I would suggest, is a market for cultural goods in which various sources of demand mesh with sources of supply. The effects of this market are usually not foreseen by the individual parties involved. Among these effects are changes in the rates of growth of educational systems, in the price and purchasing power of educational credentials, and in the structure of educational systems. Finally, crises may arise as the parties react to the unforeseen outcomes of the cultural market.

We have examined three types of education. Training in practical skills exists in any economy but is usually built informally into the work process. The practical skills of literacy and numeracy have been especially demanded, and sometimes provided by special teachers, wherever there has been literate administration or the development of commerce. Education in the leisure culture of a status group has prospered in relatively peaceful periods during which there is decentralized competition within a wealthy aristocracy, within a prosperous bourgeoisie, or within a rising working class; the nature of the status culture has varied with the groups involved. Highly formal educational systems with specified time sequences, examinations, and elements of compulsion have developed as bureaucratic devices are used, especially by centralized states, to control officials, feudal aristocracies, or, in modern periods of mass political mobilization, the general population.

Historically, these types of education have sometimes combined. To be sure, some of them are theoretically incompatible; for example, aristocratic status education has emphasized aesthetic and leisure themes that are explicitly intended to oppose both practical training and the narrower specializations of thoroughly bureaucratic education. But in practice, these seemingly incompatible types of education have appeared in combination. For example, familiarity with the status culture of the aristocracy has often been used as a criterion for selection of government officials in bureaucratic systems. The Chinese examination system tested the genteel skills of poetic composition and use of literary allusions, just as the British civil-service examinations tested knowledge of the literary classics. In modern times, bureaucratic and compulsory mass education has incorporated elements of practical education by training students in literacy and arithmetic. Similarly, secondary schooling, which developed in post-Renaissance Europe as a support for the status cultures of the prosperous classes, has been incorporated into a standard sequence of educational levels leading up to the university.

Bureaucratization has been the principal means for combining different types of education. The essence of bureaucratic controls is a stress on the keeping of formal regulations and records; any content, whether it be originally aesthetic, religious, legal, scientific, or practical, may be fitted into this system. Thus we find strong bureaucratic states and churches emphasizing various kinds of educational contents: the Chinese classics and the martial arts of Tokugawa Japan, the rhetoric of the late Roman Empire, the dialectics of the medieval university, the inflexible legal canons of Islamic culture, the Greek and Latin classics of British and German elite education, and the sciences of the elite schools in France and the Soviet Union. What all these educational programs have in common is structural formality; grades, examinations, required sequences, and set time periods for instruction that are absent from the pure forms of practical and status-group education. In bureaucratic structures, however, students know that the content of education is arbitrary: even if education is ostensibly aimed at cultivating practical skills, relatively few of these skills, at least in the modern world, seem to stay with students once they have passed through the system and received their credentials.

The various kinds of demand for education—practical, status-group, and bureaucratic—may be viewed more broadly as part of a *cultural market* in which social actors simultaneously attempt to attain certain goals. The interest of government in bureaucratic control over particular classes may mesh with the interest of these very classes in improving their cultural attainments for the sake of status. Thus, we find a symbiosis between the control interest of the Chinese emperors and the status interest of the gentry and, more ironically, between government concern for compulsory educational indoctrination of the modern masses and some interest in status mobility on the part of those masses. The interest of capitalists in ensuring labor discipline adds yet another demand to this market,[48] as does the interest of a particular ethnic group in maintaining its opportunities vis-à-vis other ethnic groups.

The extent to which education develops in different societies and historical periods varies according to the nature of their cultural markets. Abstractly, we may see that cultural markets require a common currency and independent sources of supply and demand for cultural goods.

A *common cultural currency* derives from an elite culture, which has undisputed dominance because it legitimates a wealthy and powerful group.

The *supply of cultural goods* (or cultural capital, in Pierre Bourdieu's term[49]) is determined by the availability of teachers, of material resources for schools, of sufficient economic productivity or stratification to permit leisure for cultural activities, and of methods for producing (and especially mass-producing) books and writing materials.

The *demand for cultural goods* is determined by the number of individuals or groups who feel there is a potential payoff from education and by the economic and political resources they have to make their demands effective. The interests motivating these demands can be of all three types discussed above—practical training, status-group training, and bureaucratic control.

Since, in principle, the demand for training in practical skills can be satisfied on the job, such training has been demanded in the form of schooling only where occupations and professions have been monopolistically organized through a formal credential system. The desire for training in the culture of a status group has been a stronger source of demand for formal education. Competition over status-group membership or group prestige has been strong during periods of political decentralization or political instability under a unified market economy. It has been even stronger when many culturally distinct ethnic groups live within a common system of economic or political stratification. Situations of ethnic competition have tended to increase the salience of the cultural sphere, first, because the basis of ethnic differences has been cultural and, second, because particular ethnic groups have attempted to use devices for cultural inclusion and prestige as crucial weapons for controlling top economic and political positions. Thus we find in India that the market for status-group education was largest during prosperous, politically decentralized periods when the extraordinary range of ethnic groups was channeled into the occupational monopolies of the caste system. Similarly, status-group education was particularly important in the Hellenistic empires built by Greek conquest of the culturally distinct Middle Eastern and Mediterranean states; in the ethnically diverse Islamic empire; in medieval Europe when an ethnically heterogeneous people were united by the papacy; and in the United States since the immigrations of the mid-nineteenth century.

The demand for cultural goods has also depended on the extent of political opposition to the dominant classes. Where governments have faced only a small politically mobilized class in the population, their demand for education as a bureaucratic control has been quite limited. Where a large population has been mobilized, however, the control interest of bureaucratic elites has been correspondingly large.

The development of a complex school system may itself create an additional demand for employees socialized by its own procedures. Furthermore, due to internal struggles for control, a school system may bureaucratize the careers of its own teachers.

Finally, a source of increases in demand has been population growth, if it has been connected with an existing interest in education. For example, as the Chinese population grew from the sixteenth century onward and as economic changes mobilized an increasing proportion of that population, the number of aspirants for government positions increased steadily. Similarly, population growth played into a mobilized interest in education to create the college-attendance boom of the United States in the 1960s.

What may this market model explain? The ramifications, I believe, are numerous; here it is possible to mention only a few. The varying rates of growth of educational systems (including negative rates) are, in principle, calculable from such a model. And the rate of growth relative to the availability of payoffs in the surrounding society will determine the purchasing power of education for those who acquire it. For example, the demand for education in China increased from the sixteenth through the nineteenth centuries, but the number of government positions was kept virtually constant. Thus, the cultural price of education increased: the examination system was gradually elaborated, resulting in a series of examinations that might take a scholar thirty years to complete.[50] In all educational systems there have been similar processes in which the demand for educational credentials has increased without a commensurate increase in payoffs. Oversupply of graduates may result in upper-level unemployment where job requirements remain constant, as occurred in Germany in the 1920s and in many Third World nations in the 1960s.[51] Where credential seekers are mobilized and able to put pressure on the government to expand the educational system, as in modern democracies, the cultural market adjusts by increasing the formal-training requirements for any given position and, sometimes, by increasing the number of positions for which such formal credentials are required.[52] The situation is analogous to inflation of a monetary currency, which results in a decrease in purchasing power.

The parties that enter the cultural marketplace usually are involved in social conflicts of some sort—whether struggles by economic classes for domination, revolution, or self-improvement, or the more complex conflicts that result when class struggle meshes with the prestige struggle of ethnic or other status groups. The differences among the main types of educational structures in the modern world can be explained by differences among lineups of contending interests.

The most prominent difference is between "sponsored-mobility" systems, such as those of Britain and most other Western European countries, and "contest-mobility" systems, such as those of the United States and the Soviet Union.[53] In the former type, children's careers are determined early, usually at the end of primary school. Some children proceed into elite university-preparatory schools stressing traditional high culture; others enter terminal vocational schools; and still others end their education at the elementary level. The group that enters the elite track is virtually guaranteed admission into and graduation from each succeeding level. For this group, mobility is said to be sponsored. In a contest-mobility system, there is no single decision point. Nearly all students are channeled into comprehensive secondary schools, and there is continuous attrition and competition for admission to each higher level.

Class-segregated, sponsored-mobility systems have emerged where there has been a radical mobilization of the middle or working class that has resulted in cultural polarization around distinctively commercial and technical educational ideals, but the upper class has nevertheless managed to maintain power. When such a social division occurs, educational systems have split, too: the middle and working classes are given distinctive educational enclaves while careers in the dominant occupations and political institutions remain monopolized by those who have moved through an elite educational system that maintains the traditional high culture. Contest-mobility systems, on the other hand, have emerged in industrial societies where class conflict has been submerged within a single market for cultural respectability. This may occur, as in the United States, where class differences are subordinate to divisions among many competing ethnic groups, or, as in the Soviet Union (which is also a multi-ethnic society dominated by a particular ethnic elite), where organized class conflict was eliminated, leaving only a single cultural standard for competition.

Conflict over economic interests is not eliminated in multi-ethnic situations, but it is fragmented among a much larger number of contending groups. This leads to greater competition for cultural credentials. Economic outcomes are not necessarily affected by whether class conflict is fragmented in this way; rates of mobility seem to be quite similar in societies with both sponsored and contest structures of education and seem to be quite stable over time when either type of system expands. The differences lie, rather, in the political and cultural spheres: the sponsored-mobility structure keeps class cultures quite distinct and fosters class-based ideological parties, while the contest-mobility structure seems to blur class identification in politics. In sponsored-mobility systems, a sharp split is maintained between elite culture and low culture, while mass, popular cultural movements seem more prevalent in contest-mobility systems.

Inflation of educational credentials is especially likely in contest-mobility systems. For example, the United States has experienced this kind of educational inflation since at least the middle of the nineteenth century. From 1870 to 1970, school-attendance rates rose dramatically at every level, and higher levels were created and expanded as the lower ones filled up. At the same time, educational requirements for employment at all levels increased correspondingly, adjusting to the inflated supply of cultural currency. Such an inflationary process does not necessarily go on indefinitely; the downturn in educational attendance since approximately 1970 and the cultural revolution of student-protest movements and dropout culture of the 1960s are instances of reactions that may occur when a culture-producing system has been expanding in an inflationary way for some time.

An inflationary system, even if it merely expands the supply of currency while leaving the rest of the stratification system in a state of dynamic equilibrium, nevertheless affects cultural consciousness by mobilizing increasing proportions of the population in struggles for control of the stratification system. Such mobilization can become politically dangerous to an authoritarian government, which may react by cutting down the educational system. There are a number of instances of this in Chinese history (most recently in the 1960s) and in nineteenth-century Russian history. Or disillusionment may set in among the purchasers of cultural credentials. This was behind the precipitous drop in European university enrollments in the period after the Reformation, and something similar seems to be developing in America today. Finally, the currency itself can break down. The prestige of a particular elite culture and that culture's accompanying political and organizational domination may give way to independent currencies, as when the separate national cultures of early modern Europe replaced the old international culture of the medieval church. Although it would be hazardous to predict a future change of this magnitude for the United States, we certainly see a trend in this direction in the recent attacks on Anglo-Protestant cultural domination and the efforts towards a new cultural pluralism.

Our understanding of such possibilities depends on the construction of a workable theory of cultural markets. As yet, we are only beginning to see what such a theory would include and what it might explain. Its prospects are extensive. If we have come to see education as basic to our current system of stratification, an exploration of this phenomenon which moves beyond a naive, functionalist view suggests a major reformulation of all stratification analyses. For the interaction of cultural organization with the material economy is the key to all structures of domination, and the concept of the cultural market may provide a means of encompassing multifaceted interests and conflicts within a single explanatory structure.

NOTES

1. Robert Dreeben's *On What Is Learned in School* (Reading, MA: Addison-Wesley, 1968) is a recent formulation of this position.
2. Use of the second type of evidence involves the fallacy of assuming that static cross sections present a historical sequence actually followed by all societies; the historical approach shows that this assumption is not justified. See Daniel Bell, *The Coming of Post-Industrial Society* (New York: Basic Books, 1973); and Frederick Harbison and Charles A. Myers, *Education, Manpower, and Economic Growth* (New York: McGraw-Hill, 1964).
3. Randall Collins, "Functional and Conflict Theories of Educational Stratification," *American Sociological Review*, 36 (1971), 1002–19.
4. Louis Althusser, "Ideology and Ideological State Apparatuses," *Lenin and Philosophy and Other Essays* (London: New Left Books, 1971), pp. 123–73.
5. Samuel Bowles and Herbert Gintis, *Schooling in Capitalist America: Educational Reform and the Contradictions of Economic Life* (New York: Basic Books, 1976).
6. Alain Touraine, *Production de la Société* (Paris: Éditions du Seuil, 1973).
7. See Max Weber, *Economy and Society* (New York: Bedminster Press, 1968), especially pp. 932–37 and 998–1002.
8. Pierre Bourdieu develops this tradition in a highly original manner. He views the realm of symbolic status as a market for cultural capital in which social struggle is shaped not only by the various competing classes, but also by the autonomous structure of the cultural marketplace itself. *Esquisse d'une Théorie de la Pratique* (Geneva: Droz, 1972), pp. 227–43.
9. Emile Durkheim, *Moral Education* (New York: Free Press, 1961).
10. This process is explained in Randall Collins, *Conflict Sociology* (New York: Academic Press, 1975), chs. 2–4.
11. Collins, "Functional and Conflict Theories."
12. Robert J. Havighurst, "Education in Hopi Society," in *Comparative Perspectives on Education*, ed. Robert J. Havighurst (Boston: Little, Brown, 1968), pp. 3–10; and Mircea Eliade, *The Forge and the Crucible* (New York: Harper & Row, 1957), pp. 53–108.
13. Henri Irenée Marrou, *A History of Education in Antiquity* (New York: New American Library, 1964), pp. 262–66.
14. Lynn White, Jr., *Medieval Technology and Social Change* (New York: Oxford Univ. Press, 1962); and Joseph Needham, *Science and Civilization in China* (Cambridge, Eng.: Cambridge Univ. Press, 1954–1956), I–IV.
15. In 1837, for example, only 20 to 25 percent of the children in the larger English industrial towns were attending schools for any length of time, and the proportions were doubtless lower in the countryside. English science in this period was overwhelmingly developed and carried out by amateurs, and there was little formal teaching in science in the schools and

universities. Brian Simon, *Studies in the History of Education, 1780–1870* (London: Lawrence & Wishart, 1959), p. 170; and John Theodore Merz, *A History of European Thought in the Nineteenth Century* (New York: Dover, 1965), I, 250–67.

16. Marrou, pp. xv–xix; Henri Frankfort, John A. Wilson, and Thorkild Jacobsen, *Before Philosophy* (Baltimore: Penguin Books, 1949), pp. 71–102; and Edward Chiera, *They Wrote on Clay* (Chicago: Univ. of Chicago Press, 1938).

17. Ronald P. Dore, *Education in Tokugawa Japan* (Berkeley: Univ. of California Press, 1964), pp. 214–90; D. E. Smith, *History of Mathematics* (New York: Dover, 1958), I, 194–268; Bernard Bailyn, *Education in the Forming of American Society: Needs and Opportunities for Study* (Chapel Hill: Univ. of North Carolina Press, 1960).

18. Max Weber, *General Economic History* (New York: Free Press, 1961), pp. 107–27.

19. Shmuel N. Eisenstadt, *From Generation to Generation* (Glencoe, Ill.: Free Press, 1956).

20. Eliade, *The Forge and the Crucible*.

21. This has been the case not only for heavy manual pursuits, but also for the skilled crafts and administrative and ritual skills. The training of priests in both Eastern and Western religions has historically been primarily by apprenticeship, even in the case of the literate churches. See Marrou, pp. 419–51; and Melford E. Spiro, *Buddhism and Society* (New York: Harper & Row, 1970).

22. Collins, "Functional and Conflict Theories," p. 1006.

23. Weber, *Economy and Society*, pp. 926–39.

24. Max Weber, *The Religion of China* (New York: Free Press, 1951), pp. 119–33; Marrou, *History of Education*, pp. 147–64.

25. Marrou, *History of Education*; and Ramsey MacMullen, *Roman Social Relations* (New Haven, Conn.: Yale Univ. Press, 1974), pp. 81, 107–15.

26. Fung Yu-lan, *A Short History of Chinese Philosophy* (New York: Free Press, 1966).

27. Romila Thapar, *A History of India* (Baltimore: Penguin Books, 1966), pp. 136–66; Max Weber, *The Religion of India* (New York: Free Press, 1958), pp. 123–33; and Mysore N. Srinivas, "Sanskritization," in *Social Change in Modern India* (Berkeley: Univ. of California Press, 1955), pp. 1–45.

28. Ivar Morris, *The World of the Shining Prince: Court Life in Ancient Japan* (Oxford: Oxford Univ. Press, 1964).

29. William H. McNeill, *The Rise of the West* (Chicago: Univ. of Chicago Press, 1963), pp. 476–80.

30. Joseph Ben-David, *The Scientist's Role in Society* (Englewood Cliffs, N.J.: Prentice-Hall, 1971), pp. 59–65, 80–82; and Collins, *Conflict Sociology*, pp. 485–87.

31. Nicholas Hans, *New Trends in Education in the 18th Century* (London: Routledge & Kegan Paul, 1951). The disciplined, upward-striving tone of the German dissenting academics is noted by Max Weber in *The Protestant Ethic and the Spirit of Capitalism* (New York: Scribners, 1930).

32. Edward P. Thompson, *The Making of the English Working Class* (Harmondsworth, Eng.: Penguin Books, 1963).

33. A. J. Arberry, *Sufism: An Account of the Mystics of Islam* (London: Allen & Unwyn, 1940); and Bernard Lewis, "The Islamic Guilds," *Economic History Review*, 8 (1937), 20–37.

34. Ben-David, *The Scientist's Role in Society*, pp. 88–97; and James K. Finch, *The Story of Engineering* (New York: Doubleday, 1960), pp. 137–38, 159–60.

35. Elie Halévie, *The Growth of Philosophical Radicalism* (Boston: Beacon Press, 1955); and William H. G. Armytage, *The Rise of the Technocrats* (London: Routledge & Kegan Paul, 1965).

36. Nigel Grant, *Soviet Education* (Baltimore: Penguin Books, 1968); David Granick, *The Red Executive* (New York: Doubleday, 1960), pp. 46–73; and Zbigniew Brzezinski and Samuel P. Huntington, *Political Power: USA/USSR* (New York: Viking Press, 1965), pp. 129–90.

37. Weber, *Economy and Society*, pp. 956–1110; and Collins, *Conflict Sociology*, ch. 6.

38. Richard W. Southern, *Western Society and the Church in the Middle Ages* (Baltimore: Penguin Books, 1970); Nathan Schachner, *Medieval Universities* (New York: A. S. Barnes, 1962); Hastings Rashdall, *The Universities of Europe in the Middle Ages*, rev. ed. (London: Oxford Univ. Press, 1936); and Philippe Ariès, *Centuries of Childhood: A Social History of Family Life* (New York: Knopf, 1962), pp. 137–75.

39. Schachner, p. 135.

40. Ariès, p. 167; Lawrence Stone, *The Crisis of the Aristocracy* (New York: Oxford Univ. Press, 1967), pp. 303–31; Reinhard Bendix, *Nation-Building and Citizenship* (New York: Wiley, 1964),

pp. 89–92; and Walter H. Bruford, *Germany in the Eighteenth Century* (Cambridge, Eng.: Cambridge Univ. Press, 1935), pp. 122–24.

41. Joseph R. Gusfield, "Equalitarianism and Bureaucratic Recruitment," *Administrative Science Quarterly*, 2 (1958), 521–41. A detailed Weberian account is given in Hans-Eberhard Mueller. "Bureaucracy and Education: Civil Service Reforms in Prussia and England as Strategies of Monopolization," unpublished paper, Swarthmore College, Swarthmore, Pa., 1974.

42. Bowles and Gintis, *Schooling in Capitalist America*.

43. Richard de Charms and George H. Moeller, "Values Expressed in American Children's Readers," *Journal of Abnormal and Social Psychology*, 64 (1962), 36–142; and Robert D. Hess and Judith V. Torney, *The Development of Political Attitudes in Children* (Chicago: Aldine, 1967).

44. Bendix, *Nation Building and Citizenship*, pp. 88–93. Japan created a universal, compulsory elementary-school system as part of its program of military reform, as it moved from relying on exclusively samurai armies to mass-conscript ones, according to Dore, *Education in Tokugawa Japan*, pp. 222, 250–51, 297–98.

45. Alfred D. Chandler, "The Coming of Big Business," in *The Comparative Approach to American History*, ed. C. Vann Woodward (New York: Basic Books, 1968), pp. 220–37; and Reinhard Bendix, *Work and Authority in Industry* (New York: Wiley, 1956), pp. 198–253.

46. David Granick, *The European Executive* (New York: Doubleday, 1960), pp. 240–300; and Roy Lewis and Rosemary Stewart, *The Managers: A New Examination of the English, German, and American Executive* (New York: New American Library, 1961), pp. 58–75.

47. Collins, "Functional and Conflict Theories," pp. 1003–4, 1014–16; Koza Azumi, *Higher Education and Business Recruitment in Japan* (New York: Teachers College Press, 1969); and Pierre Bourdieu, Luc Boltanski, and Monique de Saint Martin, "Les Stratégies de Reconversion: Les Classes Sociales et le Système d'Enseignement," *Social Science Information*, 12 (1974), 61–113.

48. Bowles and Gintis, in *Schooling in Capitalist America*, similarly suggest that an impersonal market mechanism can bring about the creation of a school system in response to the predominant demands in the class structure.

49. Pierre Bourdieu and Jean-Claude Passeron, *La Réproduction* (Paris: Les Éditions de Minuit, 1970).

50. Chang, *The Chinese Gentry*; Franke, *Reform and Abolition*.

51. Walter M. Kotschnig, *Unemployment in the Learned Professions* (London: Oxford Univ. Press, 1937); and Bert F. Hoselitz, "Investment in Education and Its Political Impact," in *Education and Political Development*, ed. James S. Coleman (Princeton, N.J.: Princeton Univ. Press, 1965), pp. 541–65.

52. Weber noted this inflationary tendency in bureaucratic employment requirements in Europe in his day. Weber, *Economy and Society*. Another period of credential inflation occurred in Germany around 1800, when a mass of applicants for government positions crowded the universities, producing a reform which consisted of an extension of educational requirements to more positions. See Bruford, *Germany in the Eighteenth Century*, pp. 248–68; Henri Brunschwig, *La Crise de l'Etat Prussien* (Paris: Presses Universitaires de France, 1947); Hans Rosenberg, *Bureaucracy, Aristocracy, and Autocracy* (Cambridge, Mass.: Harvard Univ. Press, 1958); Franz Schnabel, *Deutsche Geschichte im Neunzehnten Jahrhundert* (Freiburg, Germany: Verlag Herder, 1959), I, 408–57. Inflationary phenomena have been especially noticeable in the expansion of American education since the late nineteenth century, as well as in France since World War II. See fn. 47. William G. Spady shows that the relative gaps in education among American social classes have remained constant throughout the twentieth century despite mass increases in the *absolute* level of schooling. "Educational Mobility and Access: Growth and Paradoxes," *American Journal of Sociology*, 72 (1967), 273–86. Similar results for France are reported by Pierre Bourdieu and Jean-Claude Passeron in *Les Héritiers* (Paris: Les Éditions de Minuit, 1964) and in *La Réproduction*.

53. The distinction is originated by Ralph H. Turner in "Sponsored and Contest Mobility and the School System," *American Sociological Review*, 25 (1960), 855–67. Turner bases his distinction on the supposed primacy of the value of ascription or achievement. In my view, however, such values (if in fact they exist outside the mind of the analyst) result from social structure rather than vice versa.

Marxism and Education

MARTIN CARNOY

Stanford University

. . . For Marxists, education is crucial to the issue of reproduction and its counterpart, social change. Because they consider capitalist society to be organized in the interest of capitalists and managers, how are the relations of production, the division of labor, and social classes reproduced from generation to generation? In the present version of the traditional American view (pluralism), reproduction and change take place through representative democracy that reflects changing consensual values. In the Marxian approach, this "consensus" about what society should be and where it should be heading is absent; yet, capitalism continues to be the prevailing mode of production. Orthodox Marxist theories argue that reproduction is carried out largely by capitalists in the production sector itself—by a series of tactics that keep labor fearful of any attempts to organize against employers and that maintain a division of labor along class lines—and through the repressive (juridical and army/police) apparatuses of the capitalist state.

More recent Marxian analyses, however, give greater weight in the reproduction process to superstructure. This is where schooling comes in. For it is in schooling that reproduction takes its most organized form: Children go to school at an early age and are systematically inculcated with skills, values, and ideology suited to their class and that fit into the type of economic development consistent with continued capitalist control. Marxists argue that through the schools and other superstructural institutions the capitalist class reproduces the forces of production (labor, the division of labor, and the division of knowledge) and the relations of production—the latter predominantly by the maintenance and development of a "legitimate" ideology and set of behavior patterns (culture).

Reproduction in the interest of a particular social class implies the existence of class antagonism and the potential for class struggle. It is this notion of class struggle inherent in all aspects of capitalist development and capitalist institutions, structure, and superstructure that forms the basis of a Marxian theory of social change. Capitalists' organization of institutions for reproduction means that there is resistance to capitalists' concept of economic and personal development and to their necessary control of that development. Again, a Marxian analysis of schooling in the context of social change is couched in this all-pervasive class struggle. . . .

In the early 1970s, some sociologists and economists challenged traditional views of education's relation to mobility and work. Although Bourdieu and Passeron in France had already published a non-Marxian alternative to traditional sociological theory—*Reproduction* (1970; Eng. trans. 1977)—and Baudelot and Establet a Marxian one—*L'école capitaliste* (1971)—a group of radical political economists in the United States began writing empirical analyses that attacked the assumptions of mainline human capital theory. Samuel Bowles's "Unequal Education and the Reproduction of the Social Division of Labor" (1971; in Carnoy, 1975) and Herbert Gintis's "The New Working Class and Revolutionary Youth" (1971) and his critique of Illich's *Deschooling Society* in the *Harvard Educational Review* (Gintis, 1972) were the beginning of a Marxian analysis of U.S. education. These contained many of the ideas that would appear in their later work. Bowles argued that the educational system in the United States was developed to fill the needs of capitalists in a growing economy, and that, contrary to the American dream, the school system helps preserve the status structure from generation to generation rather than helping to generate interclass mobility. To confront the reality of American education, Gintis went on, meant understanding that it reproduced the structure, relations, and patterns of the workplace. It was the structure of values and relationships in capitalist production that was capitalist education; to suggest changing schooling or abolishing it without taking into account changes in the structure of production put the shoe on the wrong foot. Education had to be analyzed through the structure of capitalist development as a whole.

Althusser's influence on this theory of "correspondence" (as it was called) is obvious. Carnoy's work at that time was similarly structuralist. Carnoy tried to show in *Education as Cultural Imperialism* (1974) that Third World education had conformed to imperialist purposes in different stages of capitalist development. In India, West Africa, Latin America, and even within the United States, schools were shaped by the needs of capitalist development. Third World peoples were educated in terms of their role in the international division of labor dominated by the emerging industrial country bourgeoisies. So, far from becoming a liberating force running counter to exploitative colonial economic, social, and political institutions, colonial education necessarily supported and expanded those exploitative relations from the very nature of the imperialist, capitalist project. Colonial education not only was, but had to be, oppressive and produce a passive, colonized, subjugated worker.

Bowles and Gintis's *Schooling in Capitalist America* (1976) appeared two years later and represented the zenith of a structuralist theory of American education. Using a combination of historical and statistical analysis, they presented a model that makes educational reform a function of changes in production. Such changes in production—themselves a result of class conflict—determine the subsequent changes in the way that schooling is called upon to reproduce relations in production.

There are three important implications of the Bowles and Gintis analysis: First, the dominant group in the ruling class turns to superstructure to mediate the inherent class conflict in production (Althusser's view), but that class conflict in the superstructure is *not* particularly successful in influencing the shape and functions of the educational system—neither its organization nor content:

> The evolution of U.S. education over the last century and a half was the result of a compromise—granted an unequal one—between the capitalist class and the very social classes it had unintentionally but nonetheless inexorably created. Though the business interests often struck their compromise under severe duress and . . . did not always prevail, they were highly successful in maintaining ultimate control over the administration of educational reform (Bowles and Gintis, 1976:240).

Second, Bowles and Gintis put primary emphasis on the *reproductive function* of the schools in all the different stages of U.S. capitalist development. Reproduction is defined in the Althusserian sense: The reproduction of labor power—the allocation of skilled labor to different parts of the hierarchy based on the pupil/worker's social class background—and the reproduction of the social relations of production. Thus, the reproduction of economic inequality and the legitimation of the inequality (as well as the legitimation of the capitalist relations of production) get top billing in the Bowles and Gintis analysis. The actual production of skills and their contribution to capital accumulation is discussed in their analysis of university education but not emphasized relative to the ideological-repressive functions of schooling.

Third, Bowles and Gintis emphasize the correspondence of the structure (production) and the education system (superstructure) and play down contradictions in the superstructure and their implications for production. Indeed, the main purpose of the study is to show the causal connection between changes in capitalist relations of production and educational reform. They show, for example, that attempts at alternative education in the aftermath of the 1960s achieved little more than marginal educational improvement in the face of an unchanged economic system. Although they made the schooling experience better for many young people in school, none of the attempts was capable of addressing the major problems facing U.S. society in the 1970s. "The notion that the U.S. school system does—or ever can, under capitalism—effectively serve the interests of equality or human growth is going by the boards" (Bowles and Gintis, 1976:263).

Bowles and Gintis made a significant contribution to understanding the reproductive role of schooling. Their analysis spawned a virtual deluge of Marxian analyses, many of them critical of "correspondence" theory and *Schooling in Capitalist America's* emphasis on schooling's "economic" function. But, to the study's credit, its main point—that capitalist education reproduces capitalist relations of production and its division of labor—has generally withstood this criticism.

Recent analyses have focused on two issues: First, there has been a return to the works of Bourdieu and Passeron in France and Bernstein in England on the practices of education itself, and how these do or do not reproduce dominant (bourgeois) behavior and values. Writers like Michael Apple (1979) and Jean Anyon (1981) concentrate on social practices in schools and how these, in and of themselves, transmit dominant class ideologies. Thus, the emphasis here is on schools as cultural—not just economic—institutions, and on hegemony and counterhegemony rather than correspondence between base and superstructure.

The second issue is the relative absence of contradiction in correspondence theory. It is deterministic rather than dialectic. The best single analysis to date of dialectics in education is by Henry Giroux (1981), but the work of Carnoy and Levin (see Levin, 1980) looks at the problem in a somewhat different way. Comparing these approaches can help us understand what the current debates are in Marxian writings on education.

Apple—identifying his own analysis closely with the Gramscian view of a relatively autonomous superstructure—argues not only that economic structure does not insure a simple correspondence between it and schooling, but that schools help recreate the conditions necessary for ideological hegemony to be maintained (1982a: 17). Hegemony does not just come about; it must be "worked for in particular sites like the family, the workplace, the political sphere, and the school" (Apple, 1982a: 18). Apple concentrates on the manner in which this hegemony is partly produced through day-to-day curricular, pedagogical, and evaluative interactions in the school. And although he acknowledges the economic function of schooling, he is much more interested in schools as cultural institutions. Schools not only contribute to the reproduction of the social division of labor, but to the creation of ideological hegemony and the reproduction of power—this is where the form and content of the curriculum become especially important.

CORRESPONDENCE AND CONTRADICTION

The second piece of Apple's analysis that responds to Bowles and Gintis's characterization of schooling as a place of reproduction is his insistence that there is working-class resistance to school practices. Based in part on Paul Willis's study of English working-class youth (1981), Apple argues that schools themselves are producers of culture and ideology and, like the workplace, they are produced in ways that are filled with contradiction and by a process that is itself based on contestation and struggle (Apple, 1982a, p. 27). So he focuses on the contradictions that take place in the formation of culture and ideology; that is, in the creation of hegemony.[1] This Gramscian notion of contradiction in superstructure, then, makes hegemony and contradictions in hegemony central to the reproduction of social relations. Interferences with the "hidden curriculum" and school practices are a primary contradiction in the reproductive process.

Giroux (1981) argues in this same vein:

> Schooling must be studied, on the one hand, as part of a critical theory of society which is logically prior to and inclusive of a radical theory of education. On the other hand, schooling must be seen not only as part of a "global" dimension of oppression, but must also be studied in its own right . . . proponents of a genuinely radical educational theory will have to spend more time in understanding how the many variables at work in the classroom encounter, reproduce and contradict the prevailing ideologies and social relationships in the larger society (Giroux, 1981:78–9).

Giroux also makes a much more specific attack on Althusser's (and Bowles and Gintis's) notion of "economic" class relations as dominant in the analysis of ideology. In such a notion, Giroux argues, consciousness loses its capacity as an active force. And the sociocultural forces that mediate between the forces of production and consciousness are also lost. Like Apple, he turns to schooling as an "active cultural sphere" that functions both "to sustain and resist" the values and beliefs of the dominant society. Again, in reacting to correspondence theory, he emphasizes contradictions in ideological reproduction, specifically in the form and content of school curricula, teaching practices, and school administration, which has its own ideological content (Giroux, 1981:99).

In their own recent work (1982), Carnoy and Levin also argue that contradiction is a key variable in understanding the reproductive role of schooling but take a rather different tack from Apple and Giroux. For them, not only are ideology and production part and parcel of the same structure of social class relations (as Bowles and Gintis's work contends), but so are production and reproduction. Schools *are* ideological apparatuses but they are ideological in the sense that they attempt to reproduce the social relations of production and the class division of labor. Political power and belief systems are subject to struggle, as Giroux contends, and formal schooling, as part of the state's apparatuses, is relatively autonomous from production. But the primary contradictions in education are contradictions in reproducing social relations of production. The struggle in schools is not over the idea or concept of capitalism but over capitalist development itself, and in that sense it is intimately connected to social conflict outside the school—conflict rooted in material relations. It *is* true that domination can, has, and does exist without capitalism, but to understand schooling in capitalist countries requires analysing schools as reproducers of *capitalist* social relations.

Contradictions in reproduction for us are therefore closely related to the contradictory nature of production. The social division of labor and capitalist social relations are unjust and undemocratic. They are based on an economic system that survives by exploiting labor and passing on production's social costs to workers and consumers. First and foremost, schooling is accepted to the degree that it is and even demanded because it prepares young people for the work force. Willis's (1981) description of resistance among English working-class youth to schools' dominant ideology—their rejection of individualism, conformity, and academic credentials—or Anyon's (1982) analysis of "accommodation and resistance" among schoolgirls—particularly their desire to attain skills for work—takes place in part because the designated workplace (for women, the home) has no room for the kinds of mobility and economic gain expectations generated by schooling *as a reproductive institution*. Once youth understands the world outside the school and the ideology promulgated inside do not correspond, the school's practices become dysfunctional for those who attend. Resistance in schools to school curriculum and practices is indeed resistance to ideological reproduction. But that contradiction must be subsumed within the primary contradiction in the reproductive function of schooling itself: The losers in an unjust system of production get less schooling and less employment-relevant schooling than the winners, and that is evident to both winners and losers.

This is not to deny that schools attempt to reproduce ideology through curriculum content and form and that this generates resistance. However, this interpretation of Gramsci that emphasizes the struggle over ideology and consciousness underplays the notion that the basis of struggle resides in social classes and in groups like women and blacks (whose roles in society are related to social class roles). That struggle often succeeds in making significant economic and social gains for the working class (and women and blacks), gains that change the nature of capitalist production and influence the reproductive role of schooling. The struggle also takes place over schooling, but largely concerns expanding schooling and attempting to alter it to *better* incorporate working class youth, women, and minorities into the more rewarding work in capitalist production. This is not the result of false consciousness, but the expression of subordinate groups struggling for greater benefits in a conflictual social and political context. The *primary* manifestation of class struggle in the schools is therefore one over getting more education, not less. Resistance to schooling by working-class youth is important, but secondary. The main contradictions still take place in production, even while the struggle has shifted to a struggle over resources commanded by the state rather than the private sector. But in private production, the contradictions of an ever-expanding educational system are also felt—in highly schooled workers who are dissatisfied with menial jobs, and in a highly educated, articulate, unemployed labor force.

WHERE IS THE DEBATE NOW?

Educators themselves—especially in U.S. schools of education—have not been significantly touched by the Marxian debate on education. But social scientists have and perhaps more than even in France, the discussion in the United States has been particularly sophisticated and extensive, both in theoretical and empirical terms.

The differences in theoretical approaches are the result of disagreements over the way a social system reproduces itself. This boils down to disagreement over whether social reproduction relies primarily on the production and reproduction of ideology (consciousness and dominant culture), or whether it relies on reproducing the division of labor in and the social relations of *production*. Of course, all the writers we have discussed agree that ideology and production are difficult to separate, but the question is whether primary contradictions occur in production and direct production-related reproduction or in hegemony, where hegemony is interpreted as the dominant ideological forms and content.

Nevertheless, the Gramscian and the class struggle approaches to reproduction and education are not mutually exclusive, as Apple (1982a) and Giroux (1981), among others, have noted. Ideology and consciousness play an important role in capitalist development, particularly in the United States, characterized by a relatively weak state and powerful ideology. It is no accident that American Marxists have turned so avidly to analyzing education as a site of ideological struggle and to the promotion of counterhegemony in schools as a principal strategy for social change. The heritage of Paul Goodman and other 1960s radical educators is still felt.

The point here is that the debate does not have to be resolved; more important is to extend the currently narrow influence of Marxian writings in education to the actors themselves—to parents, workers, communities seeking ways out of the current fiscal crunch, and even to the embattled, conservative teacher training colleges and teachers' unions. The struggle over education exists already, but if intellectuals can use Marxian analyses to increase consciousness of the hegemonic forms and content—the hidden curriculum—in schooling, contradictions can be accentuated and an alternative pedagogy developed as part of that struggle.

NOTE

1. This is precisely what Baudelot and Establet (1971) argued some ten years earlier in France in reaction to the work of Bourdieu and Passeron, but with an Althusserian twist: The formation of culture and ideology is in fact rooted in (and inseparable from) the reproduction of the capitalist division of labor and the relations of production. However, Apple sees power and the reproduction of dominance as separate from capitalist production—that is, ideology can form the basis of power and power relations can be reproduced by controlling the production of ideology. Thus, contradictions in the production of ideology are paramount in breaking down existing (unequal) power relations.

BIBLIOGRAPHY

Altbach, Philip; Arnove, Robert; and Kelly, Gail (eds.). *Comparative Education.* New York: Macmillan, 1982.

Altbach, Philip, and Kelly, Gail (eds.). *Education and Colonialism*. New York: Longman, 1978.

Althusser, Louis. "Ideology and Ideological State Apparatuses." In Althusser, Louis. *Lenin and Philosophy and Other Essays*. New York: Monthly Review Press, 1971.

Althusser, Louis, and Balibar, E. *Reading Capital*. London: New Left Books, 1970.

Anyon, Jean. "Schools as Agencies of Social Legitimization." *International Journal of Political Education* 4 (1981).

_____. "Interaction of Gender and Class: Accommodation and Resistance by Working-class and Affluent Females to Contradictory Sex-role Ideologies." In Walker, S., and Barton, L. eds. *Gender, Class, and Education*. London: The Falmer Press, 1982.

_____. *Social Class and Gender in U.S. Education*. London: Routledge & Kegan Paul, 1983.

Apple, Michael. "The New Sociology of Education: Analyzing Cultural and Economic Reproduction." *Harvard Educational Review* 22 (November, 1978).

_____. *Ideology and Curriculum*. Boston: Routledge & Kegan Paul, 1979.

_____. *Education and Power*. Boston: Routledge & Kegan Paul, 1982a.

_____. (ed.). *Cultural and Economic Reproduction in Education*. Boston: Routledge & Kegan Paul, 1982b.

Baudelot, Christian, and Establet, Roger. *L'école capitaliste en France*. Paris: Maspero, 1971.

Bernstein, Basil. *Class, Codes and Control*. V.3. London: Routledge & Kegan Paul, 1977.

Bourdieu, Pierre and Passeron, Jean-Claude. *Reproduction*. Beverly Hills: Sage, 1977.

Bowles, Samuel. "Unequal Education and the Reproduction of the Social Division of Labor." In Carnoy, Martin (ed.). *Schooling in a Corporate Society*. 2nd edition. New York: McKay, 1975.

Bowles, Samuel, and Gintis, Herbert. *Schooling in Capitalist America*. New York: Harper & Row, 1976.

_____. "Reply to Sherry Gorelick." *Monthly Review* 30 (November, 1978).

Broady, D. *Critique of the Political Economy of Education: The Prokla Approach*. Stockholm: Stockholm Institute of Education, 1980.

Broccoli, Angelo. *Antonio Gramsci y la Educacion como Hegemonia*. Mexico: Editorial Nueva Imagen, 1977.

Buci-Glucksmann, Christine. *Gramsci and the State*. London: Lawrence and Wishart, 1980.

Carnoy, Martin. "Class Analysis and Investment in Human Resources: A Dynamic Model." *Review of Radical Economics* 3 (Fall/Winter, 1971).

_____. *Education as Cultural Imperialism*. New York: David McKay, 1974.

_____. (ed.). *Schooling in a Corporate Society*. 2nd edition. New York: McKay, 1975.

_____. "Education, Economy, and the State." In Apple, M. (ed.). *Cultural and Economic Reproduction in Education*. Boston: Routledge & Kegan Paul, 1982.

Carnoy, Martin, and Levin, Henry (eds.). *The Limits of Educational Reform*. New York: Longmans, 1976.

_____. *The Dialectics of Education and Work*. Stanford University, 1982 (mimeograph).

Collins, Randall. *The Credential Society*. New York: Academic Press, 1979.

Dale, Roger; Esland, G.; and MacDonald, M. (eds.). *Schooling and Capitalism*. London: The Open University Press, 1976.

Deem, Rosemary (ed.). *Schooling for Women's Work.* London: Routledge & Kegan Paul, 1980.

Eisenstein, Zillah (ed.). *Capitalist Patriarchy and the Case for Socialist Feminism.* New York: Monthly Review Press, 1979.

Entwistle, H. *Antonio Gramsci: Conservative Schooling for Radical Politics.* Boston: Routledge & Kegan Paul, 1979.

Foucault, Michel. *Discipline and Punish.* New York: Random House, 1977.

Freire, Paolo. *Pedagogy of the Oppressed.* New York: Seabury Press, 1973a.

_____. *Education for Critical Consciousness.* New York: Seabury Press, 1973b.

Friedenberg, Edgar Z. *Coming of Age in America.* New York: Random House, 1965.

Gintis, Herbert. "The New Working Class and Revolutionary Youth." *Socialist Revolution* (1971).

_____. "Towards a Political Economy of Education: A Radical Critique of Ivan Illich's Deschooling Society." *Harvard Educational Review* 42 (1972).

Giroux, Henry A. *Ideology, Culture, and the Process of Schooling.* Philadelphia: Temple University Press, 1981.

Gitlin, Todd. "Television's Screens: Hegemony in Transition." In Apple, M. (ed.). *Cultural and Economic Reproduction in Education.* Boston: Routledge & Kegan Paul, 1982.

Goodman, Paul. *Growing Up Absurd.* New York: Random House, 1956.

_____. *Compulsory Mis-Education.* New York: Horizon Press, 1964.

Gorelick, Sherry. "Undermining Hierarchy: Problems of Schooling in Capitalist America." *Monthly Review* 29 (October, 1977).

Gramsci, Antonio. *Selections from Prison Notebooks.* New York: International Publishers, 1972.

Greer, Colin. *The Great School Legend: A Revisionist Interpretation of American Public Education.* New York: Basic Books, 1972.

Holt, John. *How Children Fail.* New York: Pitman Publishing, 1964.

Illich, Ivan. *Deschooling Society.* New York: Harper & Row, 1971.

Jencks, Christopher, et al. *Inequality.* New York: Basic Books, 1972.

_____. *Who Gets Ahead?* New York: Basic Books, 1979.

Kaestle, Carl, and Vinovskis, Maris. *Education and Social Change in Nineteenth Century Massachusetts.* New York: Cambridge University Press, 1980.

Karabel, Jerome, and Halsey, A. H. (eds.). *Power and Ideology in Education.* New York: Oxford University Press, 1977.

Karier, Clarence; Violas, Paul; and Spring, Joel. *Roots of Crisis: American Education in the Twentieth Century.* Chicago: Rand McNally, 1973.

Katz, Michael. *The Irony of Early School Reform.* Cambridge, Mass.: Harvard University Press, 1968.

Kozol, Jonathan. *Death at an Early Age.* Boston: Houghton Mifflin, 1967.

_____. *Free Schools.* Boston: Houghton Mifflin, 1972.

Lazerson, Marvin. *Origins of the Urban School.* Cambridge, Mass.: Harvard University Press, 1971.

Lenhardt, Gero. "Educational Politics and Capitalist Society: Marxist Perspectives on Educational Reform in the Federal Republic of Germany." Berlin: Max Planck Institute, 1979 (mimeograph).

Levin, Henry. "The Dilemma of Comprehensive Secondary School Reforms in Western Europe." *Comparative Education Review* 22 (October, 1978).

_____. "Workplace Democracy and Educational Planning." In Carnoy, M.; Levin, H.; and King, K. *Education, Work, and Employment—II.* Paris: International Institute of Educational Planning, 1980.

Marx, Karl, and Engels, Friedrich. *The German Ideology.* New York: International Publishers, 1972.

Mouffe, Chantal (ed.). *Gramsci and Marxist Theory.* London: Routledge & Kegan Paul, 1979.

Neill, A. S. *Summerhill.* New York: Hart, 1960.

Norton, T. M., and Ollman, Bertell (eds.). *Studies in Socialist Pedagogy.* New York: Monthly Review Press, 1978.

Offe, Claus. "Advanced Capitalism and the Welfare State." *Politics and Society* (Summer 1972).

_____. "The Theory of the State and the Problem of Policy Formation." In Lindberg, Leon et al. (eds.). *Stress and Contradiction in Modern Capitalism.* Lexington, Mass.: Lexington Books, 1975.

_____. "Laws of Motion of Reformist State Policies." Mimeograph, 1976.

Poulantzas, Nicos. "The Problem of the Capitalist State." *New Left Review* 58 (1969).

_____. *Political Power and Social Classes.* London: New Left Books, 1973.

_____. *State, Power, Socialism.* London: New Left Books, 1978.

Reich, Michael. *Racial Inequality: A Political-Economic Analysis.* Princeton: Princeton University Press, 1981.

Sarup, M. *Marxism and Education.* London: Routledge & Kegan Paul, 1978.

Sennett, Richard, and Cobb, Jonathan. *Hidden Injuries of Class.* New York: Vintage Books, 1973.

Sharp, Rachel. *Knowledge, Ideology, and the Politics of Schooling.* London: Routledge & Kegan Paul, 1980.

Shor, Ira. *Critical Teaching and Everyday Life.* Boston: South End Press, 1980.

Spring, Joel. *Education and the Rise of the Corporate State.* Boston: Beacon Press, 1972.

_____. *The Sorting Machine.* New York: David McKay, 1976.

Willis, Paul. *Learning to Labor.* New York: Columbia University Press, 1981.

Young, Michael F. D. (ed.). *Knowledge and Control.* London: Collier-Macmillan, 1971.

Young, Michael, and Whitty, Geoff (eds.). *Society, State, and Schooling.* Rimger, England: The Falmer Press, 1977.

Pierre Bourdieu: Culture, Education, and Social Inequality

DAVID SWARTZ
Wesleyan University

The expansion of higher education and the growth in the number of graduates since World War II have undoubtedly contributed to a major change in social class relations in the advanced industrial societies. But observers differ on the nature of the change. For some, expanded educational opportunity has generated considerable social mobility and thereby helped to erode the traditional links between career achievement and inherited social status. For others, however, educational expansion has created new forms of social stratification that impede progress toward greater equality. This is the position taken by Pierre Bourdieu, who is one of France's leading social theorists and critics of higher education.[1]

Bourdieu is one of the first sociologists to take a critical look at the popular public policies of expanding educational opportunity in order to reduce social inequality. Though educational levels in all Western democracies have seen tremendous improvement during the last 30 years, glaring inequities in wealth, income, and status persist. Bourdieu's theory helps us understand how it is possible for educational expansion to actually perpetuate rather than attenuate social inequality.

A key question running throughout Bourdieu's work is how do inequalities of privilege and power persist intergenerationally without conscious recognition and public resistance. The answer, he contends, can be found by exploring how cultural resources—especially educational credentials—can be used by individuals and groups to perpetuate their positions of privilege and power.[2] Bourdieu maintains that the educational system—more than the

This article appears here for the first time.

family, church, or business firm—has become the key institution for the transmission of social inequality.

The system of higher education, according to Bourdieu, functions to transmit privilege, allocate status, and instill respect for the existing social order. Although their manifest function is to teach knowledge and skills, educational institutions, in fact, perform a latent function of contributing to the "reproduction" of the social class structure by reinforcing cultural and status cleavages among classes.[3] To illustrate, Bourdieu observes that contemporary Western democracies rely more on indirect, symbolic forms of power and control than upon direct, physical violence to maintain social hierarchies. The widespread belief in formal equality, for example, makes it difficult for dominant groups to overtly monopolize privileged positions and exclude subordinate group members. Dominant groups have nonetheless found in higher education a more discreet means of preserving their privileged access to desirable occupational positions. Higher education transmits social inequalities without apparently violating democratic ideology "by transmuting them into academic hierarchies" (Bourdieu and Passeron, 1977: 153).

SOCIAL CLASS AND SCHOOLING

Four themes recur in Bourdieu's work on education. First, Bourdieu finds that students' academic performance is strongly related to parents' cultural background. Bourdieu claims that education contributes to the maintenance of an unequal social system by allowing inherited cultural differences to shape academic achievement and occupational attainment. Second, Bourdieu systematically relates the selective process of education to social class structure without reducing this relationship to one of simple class determinism. Social class background is filtered through a complex set of factors that interact in different ways at different levels of schooling. This process is particularly visible for academically successful working-class students who rely more heavily on the school than on their family environment for acquiring cultural resources. Bourdieu argues that working-class students can succeed academically, but he goes on to note that they pick up a stilted, formal academic style that is very different from the easy, eloquent style of successful upper class students. Third, higher educational institutions are *socially* as well as academically segmented into a system of interinstitutional tracks. Bourdieu argues that degree of success in the labor market depends not only on the *amount* of education received but also upon the *kind*—especially the social status of the institution attended. Much of his work focuses on the differences between the *Grandes Écoles* (elite professional schools in France) and the universities.[4] Fourth, Bourdieu argues that educational institutions are not simply an adjunct of more decisive institutions in society. Rather, they develop their own organizational and professional interests, which may deviate significantly from the interests of the dominant class.

Parental Cultural Background and Academic Success:
Habitus and Cultural Capital

To show how parental background affects students' academic performance, Bourdieu uses the concepts of "habitus" and "cultural capital." Akin to the idea of class subculture, habitus refers to a set of relatively permanent and largely unconscious ideas about one's chances of success and how society works that are common to members of a social class or status group.[5] These ideas or, more precisely, *dispositions* lead individuals to act in such a way as to reproduce the prevailing structure of life chances and status distinctions. Habitus, then, represents a cultural matrix, varying by people's background, that generates self-fulfilling prophecies.[6]

Bourdieu maintains that whether or not youths stay in school depends on their perceptions of the likelihood that people of their social class will succeed academically. His concept of habitus posits that "there is a close correlation between *subjective hopes* and *objective chances*, the latter tending to effectively modify attitudes and behavior by working through the former" (Bourdieu, 1974: 44). A child's ambitions and expectations with regard to education and career are the structurally determined products of parental and peer or reference-group educational experience and cultural life. Working-class youth in France do not aspire to high levels of educational attainment because, according to Bourdieu, they have internalized and resigned themselves to the limited opportunities for school success that exist for those without much cultural capital.[7] Bourdieu's emphasis, then, is on selection through self-selection.

In addition to class habitus, class differences in *cultural capital* also affect educational attainment. Cultural knowledge and style operate as carriers of social inequality. Bourdieu finds it useful to think of culture—especially in the form of educational credentials (scholastic capital)—as a kind of asset that can be inherited or purchased with time, energy, and money and then exchanged for occupations with high status and incomes. His concept of cultural capital covers a wide variety of resources including verbal facility, general cultural awareness, information about the school system, and educational credentials. Bourdieu points to an *unequal distribution of cultural capital*. Social classes differ greatly in levels of educational attainment and patterns of cultural consumption. Most higher education degrees in France, for example, are held by children of professionals; very few are held by children of farmers and factory workers.

Bourdieu focuses on how the higher educational system reproduces, rather than redistributes, the unequal distribution of cultural capital. Even prolonged exposure to university instruction does not fully compensate working- and middle-class youth for their initial handicap in cultural capital. French schools, he finds, tend to emphasize the forms of knowledge and cultural ideals and styles that are cherished above all by dominant social groups. He suggests that the traditional program of humanist studies, which characterizes the preparatory track for entrance to the university and elite professional schools in France, does not provide the technical skills needed in the job market. The humanities can be appreciated only by students whose economic background virtually assures them of economic security. Moreover, this program of study acts as a selection device: Academic success in the humanities requires general cultural awareness and a refined and elegant style of language. Curriculum content and style, then, offer advantages to those who possess the "educationally profitable linguistic capital" of "bourgeois language": its tendency "to abstraction, formalism, intellectualism, and euphemistic moderation" reflects a literary and cultured disposition that is found most often among the dominant classes.

Because of the emphasis placed on the spoken as well as written word, the traditional preference in French schools for the eloquent lecture helps secure the privileges of those rich in cultural capital. Bourdieu makes the interesting observation that even the physical organization of the French university—lecture halls and amphitheaters rather than small seminar rooms or even libraries—testifies to the preeminence of the spoken word. By failing to provide compensatory coursework adapted to meet the language deficiencies of those without cultural capital, traditional pedagogy fulfills the function of serving dominant class interests by demanding "uniformly of all its students that they should have what it does not give": namely, a practical and informal mastery of language and culture that can be acquired only in the dominant class family. Style as much as content becomes the mechanism whereby cultural privilege is reinforced and cultural disadvantage is left unattended.

The classic oral and essay examinations, like the traditional form of instruction, present advantages to those richest in cultural capital. Such examinations tend to measure ability in linguistic expression as much as mastery of subject matter. For example, in his analysis of the *aggrégation*, the national competitive examination leading to teaching posts at the secondary and university level, Bourdieu finds that candidates who distinguished themselves by eloquence in writing and speech tend to be given preference (Bourdieu and de Saint Martin, 1974). The novelty of Bourdieu's analysis of the national competitive examinations is the demonstration that class bias enters into this supposedly neutral and objective system for channeling successful candidates into top leadership positions in business, education, and state administration. These national examinations represent the highest level of achievement within the French educational system and symbolize the triumph of democratic, secular, and state-controlled education over the interests of church, region, and social class. While these examinations, in theory, promulgate the ideals of democratic equality and meritocratic achievement, Bourdieu forcefully argues that, in practice, they favor those who are culturally privileged.

Cultural Capital and Selection

Bourdieu's (Bourdieu and Passeron, 1977) analysis of results from a language test administered to university students illustrates how the educational system translates the student's initial degree of educational opportunity and amount of cultural capital into characteristically academic traits. Cultural capital and "degree of selection" are the fulcrum concepts used to interpret the test results. Students of dominant class origin obtain high test scores on all types of vocabulary questions, from the definition of scholastic concepts to those that presuppose a more general cultural background. By inheriting the most socially valued forms of cultural activity from parents who usually have some university education, these cultural heirs are able to cash in cultural capital on good academic performance.

Working-class students can score just as well as upper-class students on questions involving academic concepts, since these working-class students themselves represent a highly select academic group. These few working-class survivors have compensated for their initial lack of general cultural capital by acquiring a scholastically based cultural capital through exceptional intellectual ability, individual effort, and unusual home or social circumstances. However, these working-class students do not score as well on questions requiring broad cultural knowledge, because they lack the cultural background of their upper-class schoolmates. Meanwhile, large numbers of middle-class students receive the lowest scores because they represent a less highly select academic group than the few working-class survivors and because they have less cultural capital than their dominant-class counterparts.

A Socially Stratified Higher Education System

Bourdieu observes that *type* and *prestige* of educational institution attended are as influential on later careers as number of years spent in schooling. The third theme of his work, then, is that educational institutions are socially stratified. This is certainly the case in France where a highly stratified educational system sorts and channels individuals into different career tracks. Of particular significance is the elite sector of postsecondary professional schools (*Grandes Écoles*) that parallel the French universities.[8] A rough equivalent in the United States would be the difference between the Ivy League and state universities. The *Grandes Écoles* are at the pinnacle of French higher education: They are academically more selective than the universities; they prepare graduates for leadership roles in higher education, government and the economy; and they provide their graduates with valued alumni networks that help advance students' careers. Whereas entrance to the university requires no more than the successful completion of the *baccalauréat*, entrance to the academically prestigious *Grandes Écoles* requires intensive and specialized postsecondary preparation (usually two years) for passing the highly competitive entrance examinations. Thus, the *Grandes Écoles* represent the institutional embodiment of the meritocracy. Bourdieu's work, however, demonstrates that the sharp status distinction between the universities and the *Grandes Écoles* is a *social* as well as academic one, for the latter recruit in large measure from the dominant class.

Relative Autonomy

Bourdieu's approach establishes linkages between the social class structure and educational processes and institutions. But—and this is the fourth recurring theme in Bourdieu's work—he does not reduce the relationship between social class structure and the selective function of education to one of simple class determinism. Bourdieu writes (Bourdieu and Passeron, 1977) of the "relative autonomous" status of the educational system to indicate that educational institutions are not just an adjunct of more decisive institutions in society. While the educational system functions to reproduce the social structure, there can be a significant lack of synchronization between an educational system and the demands of the labor market. Bourdieu points out that the educational system obtains a certain autonomy from outside institutions through its self-reproductive capacity and its vested interest in protecting the value of scholastic capital. Referring to Durkheim, Bourdieu cites the educational system's capacity to recruit its leadership from within its own ranks as the reason for its unusual historical continuity and stability, analogous more to the church than to business or the state (Bourdieu and Passeron, 1977: 195–198)[9] Education's virtual monopoly over recruitment, training, and promotion of teachers allows the educational system to adapt its programs and activities to its own specific needs for self-perpetuation. For example, the intergenerational transmission of a humanist cultural tradition in the traditional French university has stood at cross-purposes with the more contemporary concern for utilitarian knowledge encouraged by industrialization. This has undoubtedly been one important source of anticapitalist sentiment among many well-educated French people. It also helps explain why the French academic profession has strongly resisted repeated efforts by state planners to more closely align the curriculum with the practical needs of business.[10]

CLASS-BASED EDUCATIONAL INVESTMENT STRATEGIES

Bourdieu analyzes the post–World War II expansion of the French educational system in terms of social class "strategies of reproduction" through which middle- and dominant-class groups have tried "consciously or unconsciously, to maintain or improve their position in the structure of class relations by safeguarding or increasing their capital" (Bourdieu and Boltanski, 1977: 198). Groups protect or advance their positions within the social hierarchy by preserving, reinforcing, or transforming their stock of capital. Building on the work of Max Weber,[11] Bourdieu views social class as a composite of capitals: social capital (for example, family prestige and connections), economic capital (such as wealth and income), and cultural capital (for example, academic credentials, language style, and general knowledge). The different kinds of capital may be accumulated, monopolized, or exchanged in order to maintain or improve one's position in markets. Classes are marked off from each other by differences in the *volume* of total capital, whereas differences in *types* of capital holdings delimit groups within the same class. The substantial possession of almost every kind of capital sets apart the dominant class (for example, professionals, managers, and capitalists) from all other groups in the stratification order. Within this dominant class, however, wealthy cultural capitalists, such as lawyers and professors, differ from industrial owners in basing their claims to power on cultural capital rather than on economic capital.

In order to maintain or improve their positions in the stratification order, different classes pursue different kinds of educational investment strategies. The intellectual elite traditionally invests in education and thus accumulates considerable cultural capital. This fraction of the dominant class has assured the reproduction from generation to generation of professors, writers, and artists in France. As the main carriers of the humanist tradition in French culture, this cultural elite works to protect its cultural capital from devaluation—that is, from bending academic requirements to the changing skill needs of the labor market. These wealthy cultural capitalists tend to defend the merits of liberal arts instruction, to oppose reform measures that would give a vocational orientation to university instruction, and to argue for the complete autonomy of the university. They also tend to orient their youth toward the *Grandes Écoles*, particularly the highly prestigious and selective *École Normale Supérieure*, which prepares teachers for secondary schools and universities.

Other dominant-class fractions have pursued different strategies to maintain their positions of power and privilege. In the face of democratic ideals of equality and new administrative and legal restrictions, it has become increasingly difficult simply to inherit economic wealth and power. Big business leaders, who are wealthy in economic capital but only moderately wealthy in cultural capital, have responded to the decline of the family firm by "converting" their economic capital into cultural capital in the form of academic degrees. These degrees allow them easy, but also legitimate, access to top managerial positions in the larger French firms. On the other hand, those quite wealthy in both cultural and economic capital, such as doctors and lawyers, have intensified their accumulation of cultural capital in order to compete successfully for the same top business positions and to protect their professional positions against newly successful middle-class *arrivistes*. Both of these privileged class fractions dominate the prestigious professional schools, such as *L'École Polytechnique* and *L'École Nationale d'Administration*, whose graduates are channeled directly into top leadership posts in the government administration and large corporations.

Meanwhile, middle-class groups (for example, shopkeepers) have started investing in higher education since World War II in order to obtain economic security in a job market that increasingly requires formal qualifications. Traditionally low in cultural capital, these groups have invested in the expanding universities. Not surprisingly, therefore, these middle-class groups have demanded that curriculum and instruction be oriented toward the acquisition of usable knowledge and skills for the job market. They have been frustrated by the continuation of the traditional emphasis on the humanities and on forms of instruction that do not assist students who enter education with little inherited cultural capital.

Bourdieu's analysis of the varying and often conflicting educational investment strategies of different class groups demonstrates that the stakes in education are not the same for everyone. He perceptively suggests that the increased demand for academic credentials represents more than a response to increased skill demands in the labor market. Rather, Bourdieu ties higher educational expansion since World War II to changes in the cultural and economic capital of social classes and to conflicts over access to positions of power and privilege.

EDUCATIONAL EXPANSION AND CRISIS

Bourdieu argues that prior to the 1960s—the period of rapid educational expansion—the traditional higher educational system in France was characterized by a high degree of harmony among teachers and students, because both held considerable cultural capital and represented very select social groups. Rapid and extensive educational expansion, however, has fundamentally altered this traditional harmony. It has created a fundamental gap between expectations and rewards for both teachers and students. The growing disenchantment, confusion, and tension within French universities since the 1960s is explained not simply by increases in numbers but also by increased heterogeneity of the university population. University expansion was limited largely to junior level faculty. Senior positions remained fixed and so, too, the promotion possibilities of the many new junior faculty.

In addition, teachers have found themselves facing increased numbers of less highly selected, middle-class students who do not possess the cultural background that has traditionally been taken for granted. Middle-class students have found that the humanist orientation of the universities offers little assurance of obtaining the practical skills needed to compete in a tight job market. These changes, Bourdieu suggests, have created frustrated expectations among both faculty and students that led to the May 1968 student revolt and underlie the contemporary crisis in French higher education (Bourdieu, 1988).

SOME CRITICISMS

A theoretical framework that highlights certain issues or problems often does so by excluding others from proper analysis. Bourdieu's focus on the cultural dimensions of social inequality permits him to illuminate very subtle mechanisms in schooling that contribute to the persistence of social stratification. But this focus also excludes from analysis the relationship of schooling to the state and organized interest groups. Bourdieu argues convincingly that education reproduces social class relations by not redistributing cultural capital. But he ignores the fact that social class inequality is also perpetuated through government educational policies and the power of organized interest groups.[12] Educational planning and policymaking, for instance, are carried out more by government officials than by relatively autonomous teachers and professors. Moreover, one should not overlook the important lobby of labor and teaching unions. And business interests, even in France, are not entirely absent from universities, as the increasing switch in curriculum to scientific and business-oriented studies suggests (Isamberg-Jamati and Segré, 1971).

Bourdieu's conception of social classes as deploying various types of capital in their pursuit of advantage may work better for some groups than for others. This conceptualization adequately explains the behavior of middle- and dominant-class groups that have capital to invest; it is doubtful, however, whether the same model applies as well to working-class groups that do not hold much capital.

The idea of social reproduction stands as a healthy reminder that expanded educational opportunity may well be compatible with enduring social inequality. Nevertheless, one must wonder whether Bourdieu's theory works too smoothly. He may, in fact, be overestimating the capacity of a class-divided social system to endlessly protect and regenerate itself. This may be seen in his use of the concept of habitus.

Bourdieu's analysis of student self-selection through a habitus involving a very strong correlation between objective possibilities and subjective aspirations is insightful but not entirely convincing. First, if Bourdieu's concept of habitus helps describe situations where expectations are adjusted to objective opportunities so that the dominated actually participate in their own domination, it also misses the miscalculations of objective probabilities that are a common feature of individual and group perceptions (O'Gorman, 1986). The high aspirations among American blacks after World War II for a college education, despite overwhelming evidence of limited career opportunities in the professions, represents just one striking example of a disjunction between hopes and real chances.[13] Second, Bourdieu's concept of habitus does not adequately account for sudden shifts in expectations. And third, the concept of habitus—with its idea of action as governed by largely unconscious ideas—does not fit well the actions of those groups that pursue highly self-conscious educational investment strategies. The educational behavior of the French middle class exemplifies the second and third problems in Bourdieu's concept of habitus. After World War II, middle-class families suddenly began to invest in the credentials market, despite a history of poor results. Moreover, this middle-class behavior was governed not so much by taken-for-granted past experience but by a highly conscious future-oriented perspective.

CONCLUSION

The merit of Bourdieu's work is to have examined important components of latent conflict between dominant and subordinate groups over access to valued educational resources. With almost 50 percent of American youth now obtaining some form of postsecondary education, inequality in occupations and incomes may result, as Bourdieu suggests, from differences in *type* and *prestige* of institution attended as well as *amount* of education received. Bourdieu's central claim is that cultural-capital transmission through education plays a key role in the perpetuation of social inequality. His theory of education does much to illuminate the more subtle aspects of social differentiation and contains important insights that need further discussion and research in the sociology of education.

NOTES

1. Pierre Bourdieu holds the chair of sociology at the prestigious College de France. He directs the Center for European Sociology and his own sociological journal, *Actes de la Recherche en Sciences Sociales*. Much of his published work on education has been in collaboration with Monique de Saint Martin and Jean-Claude Passeron.

2. Bourdieu's exploration of the relationship between culture and domination is not limited to the study of education but spans a broad spectrum of substantive areas of investigation, ranging from the study of peasants, kinship, fertility, unemployment, art, literature and social classes to sports, religion, law, politics, and intellectuals (Brubaker, 1985).

3. Bourdieu uses the term *reproduction* sociologically to designate the transmission of social class privilege from parents to children.

4. The *Grandes Écoles* are academically selective postsecondary institutions that parallel the French university and provide professional and technical training for top positions in government, education, and business. Particularly important are the École Polytechnique, which trains engineers, the École Nationale d'Administration, which trains senior civil servants, and the École Normale Supérieure, which trains teachers for the French secondary schools and universities. A rough equivalent in the United States would be the most prestigious business, law, and graduate schools.

5. This presentation of Bourdieu's ideas on education is directed toward an undergraduate audience. For more detailed and nuanced discussions of Bourdieu's conceptual language, see Brubaker, (1985) Dimaggio (1979) and Swartz (1977, 1981, and forthcoming).

6. Bourdieu defines this key concept as "a system of lasting, transposable dispositions which, integrating past experiences, functions at every moment as a *matrix of perceptions, appreciations, and actions* and makes possible the achievement of infinitely diversified tasks, thanks to analogical transfers of schemes permitting the solution of similarly shaped problems" (Bourdieu, 1977b: 82–83).

7. See Ogbu in Chapter 6 of this book for a similar discussion of the sources of the lower college aspirations of American blacks.

8. In addition to the universities and *Grandes Écoles,* French higher education includes a broad range of vocational and technical schools that for the most part do not require the *baccalauréat* (roughly equivalent to the high school diploma) and recruit most of their students from the lower middle class or working class.

9. The reference to Durkheim concerns his little-known, but most fundamental work in the sociology of education (Durkheim, 1977).

10. In the United States, the political leadership has made a similar attempt to subordinate the curriculum to the demands of business, but with somewhat greater success than in France. See Chapter 10 of this book.

11. The Weberian perspective is also represented in this book by the Collins selection "Some Comparative Principles of Educational Stratification" (see Chapter 2).

12. In the United States, the high cost of college tuition as well as cultural differences helps distinguish the college population from those who do not seek any college education. In France, tuition costs are minimal.

13. See Rosenbaum (1976) for evidence of a similar disjunction in which students misperceive the consequences of being placed in one or another secondary school track.

REFERENCES

Bourdieu, Pierre. 1971. "Intellectual Field and Creative Project." In M. F. D. Young (ed.), *Knowledge and Control: New Directions for the Sociology of Education*, pp. 161–88. London: Collier Macmillan.

_____. 1974. "The School as a Conservative Force: Scholastic and Cultural Inequalities." In John Eggleston (ed.), *Contemporary Research in the Sociology of Education*, pp. 32–46. London: Methuen.

_____. 1977a. "Cultural Reproduction and Social Reproduction." In Jerome Karabel and A. H. Halsey (eds.), *Power and Ideology in Education*, pp. 487–511. New York: Oxford University Press.

_____. 1977b. *Outline of a Theory of Practice*. London: Cambridge University Press.

_____. 1988. *Homo Academicus*. Stanford, CA.: Stanford University Press.

_____, and Luc Boltanski. 1977. "Changes in Social Structure and Changes in the Demand for Education." In Salvador Giner and Margaret Scotford Archer (eds.), *Contemporary Europe: Social Structures and Cultural Patterns*, pp. 197–227. London: Routledge and Kegan Paul.

_____, and Jean-Claude Passeron. 1977. *Reproduction in Society, Culture, and Education*. Beverly Hills, CA.: Sage.

_____, and Jean-Claude Passeron. 1979. *The Inheritors: French Students and Their Relation to Culture*. Chicago: University of Chicago Press.

_____, and Monique de Saint Martin. 1974. "Scholastic Excellence and the Values of the Educational System." In John Eggleston (ed.), *Contemporary Research in the Sociology of Education*, pp. 338–71. London: Methuen.

Brubaker, Rogers. 1985. "Rethinking Classical Theory: The Sociological Vision of Pierre Bourdieu." *Theory and Society* 14(6): 745–775.

DiMaggio, Paul. 1979. "Review Essay: On Pierre Bourdieu." *American Journal of Sociology* 84(6): 1460–1474.

Durkheim, Emile. 1977. *The Evolution of Educational Thought*. London: Routledge and Kegan Paul.

Isamberg-Jamati, Viviane, and Monique Segré. 1971. "Systèmes Scolaires et Systèmes Socio-Economiques." *L'Année Sociologique* 22: 527–541.

Ogbu, John U. 1979. "Social Stratification and the Socialization of Competence." (Reprinted in Chapter 6 of this book.)

O'Gorman, Hubert. 1986. "The Discovery of Pluralistic Ignorance: An Ironic Lesson." *Journal of the History of the Behavioral Sciences*. 22 (October): 333–347.

Rosenbaum, James E. 1976. *Making Inequality: The Hidden Curriculum of High School Tracking*. New York: Wiley.

Swartz, David. 1977. "Pierre Bourdieu: The Cultural Transmission of Social Inequality." *Harvard Educational Review* 47 (November): 545–555.

_____. 1981. "Classes, Educational Systems and Labor Markets: A Critical Evaluation of the Contributions by Raymond Boudon and Pierre Bourdieu to the Sociology of Education." *European Journal of Sociology* 22: 325–353.

_____. Forthcoming. *Culture and Domination: Pierre Bourdieu and Contemporary Social Theory*. Chicago: University of Chicago Press.

On the Relations Among Educational Research Paradigms: From Disdain to Detentes[1]

RAY C. RIST

U.S. General Accounting Office

To the extent, as significant as it is incomplete, that two scientific schools disagree about what is a problem and what a solution, they will inevitably talk through each other when debating the relative merits of their respective paradigms. In the partially circular arguments that regularly result, each paradigm will be shown to satisfy more or less the criteria that it dictates for itself and to fall short of a few of those dictated by its opponent. . . . Since no paradigm ever solves all the problems it defines and since no two paradigms leave all the same problems unsolved, paradigm debates always involve the question: Which problems is it more significant to have solved?

> —Thomas S. Kuhn, The Structure
> of Scientific Revolutions

"Hard vs. soft." "Quantifiers vs. describers." "Scientists vs. critics." "Rigor vs. intuition." It is merely restating the obvious to suggest that the dichotomies represented by such trite cliches have too long dominated comparative discussions of varying research strategies in education. The complexities and nuances of research approaches are reduced to simple and rigid polarities. Thus the emergence of methodological provincialism reflected in the reification of the terms "qualitative methodology" and "quantitative methodology." The dialectic and interaction among all efforts to

From *Anthropology and Education Quarterly* 8:2 (1977). Reproduced by permission of the American Anthropological Association and the author. Not for further reproduction.

"know" or to "understand" are obscured. Further, we only hinder and cripple ourselves by a continued fixation upon what is "good" about one approach or "bad" about another. As once suggested by Homans (1949), issues of methodology are issues of strategy, not of morals.

In the quest to transform the appropriate into the orthodox, there is an inevitable distortion and skewing of the research effort. Nearly twenty years ago, C.W. Mills warned against this tendency with his castigation of those researchers who become so enamored of one method to the exclusion of all others that they take the method as an end in itself. These researchers he terms "abstract empiricists" (Mills, 1959).

The refusal to recognize that there are different ways of "knowing" does not mean they do not exist. They do. The very fact of educational research being multiparadigmatic generates a symposium such as this. I take it to be our task here to analyze the convergent and divergent orientations inherent in our varying methodological approaches. In this way, we also may arrive at a better understanding of the possible interrelations among these differing means of approaching the social reality we all seek to comprehend.

Before moving to an analysis of these various methodologies, a short aside with regard to the title of this paper is necessary. It is my view that a situation of detente is rapidly evolving with respect to the broad categories of quantitative and qualitative research. There are at least two reasons. First, there is a general recognition among some researchers and even more practitioners that no one methodology can answer all questions and provide insights on all issues. In short, no one approach has a hegemony in educational research. Second, the internal order and logic of each approach is sufficiently articulated that it is difficult, if not impossible, to foresee the time they would merge under some broader, more eclectic research orientation.

I am not one normally to go to foreign affairs for my imagery, but I do believe that a set of accommodations is emerging whereby the various approaches, while maintaining profound tensions and different epistemological orientations, are recognizing the right of "peaceful coexistence." This coexistence both constrains and stimulates intellectual growth and development of the research efforts guided by one or another of the basic orientations. It constrains in the sense that the parameters of what is viewed as "acceptable" research are rather formal; it stimulates in that the energies of each methodology are turned inward and thus pushed towards greater refinement and sophistication (cf. Rist, 1975).

But as with all imagery, there is some slippage between the ideal and the actual. First, there is surely the question of dominance. We are not dealing with a situation of parity among the various research methodologies. Quantitative research is *the* dominant methodology in educational research. It is more widely published, taught, accepted, and rewarded in educational research circles than any other approach. In the extreme, quantitative research is characterized as equivalent to "The Scientific Method." For example, in their widely used methodological primer, Campbell and Stanley (1963:3) term this methodological orientation "the only available route to cumulative progress." Having taken this view of quantitative research methods, it becomes understandable why those who posit an alternative set of assumptions and principles for educational research are frequently disparaged as employing an effort less than that exalted by the canons of scientific inquiry, i.e., the scientific method.

Second, there is the possibility that neither approach does, in fact, see it to be in its own best interest to pursue a policy of detente. This would be for the simple reason that neither orientation believes it particularly relevant whether any other exists or not. That is, we may have a situation in which the internal structure and principles are so self-contained and so nonreliant on external influences that the presence of other orientations is superfluous. I do not believe this to be the case, but it does remain a distinct possibility.

RESEARCH PARADIGMS IN EDUCATION

Given that current research efforts in education are paradigmatic, it is well to spell them out in more detail prior to any comparative analysis. Building upon the work of Kuhn, Patton (1975:9) defines a paradigm in these terms:

> A paradigm is a world view, a general perspective, a way of breaking down the complexity of the real world. As such, paradigms are deeply embedded in the socialization of adherents and practitioners, telling them what is important, what is legitimate, what is reasonable. Paradigms are normative; they tell the practitioner what to do without the necessity of long existential or epistemological consideration. But it is this aspect of a paradigm that constitutes both its strength *and* its weakness—its strength in that it makes action possible, its weakness in that the very reason for action is hidden in the unquestioned assumptions of the paradigm.

It is important to ferret out these "unquestioned assumptions" and subject them to examination before one attempts to assess the relative contributions of various research strategies. This is so because ultimately, the issue is not research strategies, *per se*. Rather, the adherence to one paradigm as opposed to another predisposes one to view the world and the events within it in profoundly differing ways (cf. Becker, 1967; Gouldner, 1970). The power and pull of a paradigm is more than simply a methodological orientation. It is a means by which to grasp reality and give it meaning and predictability. As Kuhn (1970:46) has suggested:

> That scientists do not usually ask or debate what makes a particular problem or solution legitimate tempts us to suppose that, at least intuitively, they know the answer. But it may only indicate that neither the question nor the answers are felt to be relevant to their research. Paradigms may be prior to, more binding, and more complete than any set of rules for research that could be unequivocally abstracted from them.

If paradigms do, in fact, constitute more than a "set of rules for research," then it is necessary to elaborate upon the ways that they do. In this way, the research orientations are themselves grounded in a perspective beyond simple questions of methodological procedure.

When we speak of "quantitative" or "qualitative" methodologies, we are, in the final analysis, speaking of an interrelated set of assumptions about the social world which are philosophical, ideological, and epistemological. They encompass more than simply data gathering techniques.

To assume otherwise about the nature of methodology is to imply that it is "atheoretical," suitable for valid scientific use by any knowledgeable user. On the contrary, the selection of a particular methodology is profoundly theoretical, regardless of its relative availability. Research methods represent different means of acting upon the environment. To choose one line of action over and against another is to have foregone others available from a different perspective and orientation. Each method reveals peculiar elements of symbolic reality. And to accentuate one aspect of that reality vs. another is to influence both observations and conclusions (Denzin, 1970:298). All knowledge is social. The methods one employs to articulate knowledge of reality necessarily flow from beliefs and values one holds about the very nature of that reality.[2] In personalistic terms, I believe this same point can be made, for example, by comparing the methods of classroom observation represented by Ned Flanders and Jules Henry, or Jane Stallings and Philip Jackson.

Recognizing full well that I may be guilty of the same reification of orientations that I criticized earlier, I would nevertheless like to pursue an assessment of the quantitative and qualitative approaches by placing them in juxtaposition. Creating this dichotomy is done with the aim of capturing the underlying and fundamental elements in each paradigm. The strategy here will be twofold: first, a very brief set of comments about the epistemological nature of each methodology and, second, a comparison of several dominant motifs and patterns that serve to clarify the alternative emphases inherent in each approach.

QUANTITATIVE ORIENTATIONS

Quantitative methodologies assume the possibility, desirability, and even necessity of applying some underlying empirical standard to social phenomena. Based on these premises, there has arisen a concerted and widespread effort to formally test nomothetic propositions. Such research is assumed to contribute towards creating enduring theoretical structures. In fact, Suppes (1974) suggests that theorizing on the basis of such data collection procedures becomes the principal duty of researchers and that in due course, those who follow in the footsteps will erect "theoretical palaces" on the foundations now being laid.

Quantitative research holds to a view that the progression of knowledge moves on a continuum from observation to experimentation to theoretical development. I believe it is safe to say that the emphasis has been the latter linkage, between experimentation and theoretical development, as opposed to the former, between observation and experimentation.[3] This may be the result, at least in part, of the fact that for the quantitative researcher, working at the level of inductive statistics is intrinsically more interesting than working with descriptive statistics (cf. Blalock, 1960:4). From this orientation, it is less challenging and less creative to describe than to infer and induce properties of a population on the basis of known sample results. As Blalock notes (1960:5):

> Statistical inference, as the process is called, involves much more complex reasoning than does descriptive statistics, but when properly used and understood becomes a very important tool in the development of a scientific discipline. Inductive statistics is based directly on probability theory, a branch of mathematics.

But aside from whether one statistical approach is more challenging and creative than another, there remains for the quantitative researchers the belief that knowledge is cumulative and that the verification of what is known through experimentation is central to the scientific endeavor. As Campbell and Stanley (1963:2) have suggested regarding experimentation, it is "the only means for settling disputes regarding educational practice, the only way of verifying educational improvements, and the only way of establishing a cumulative tradition in which improvements can be introduced without the danger of a faddish discard of old wisdom in favor of inferior novelties."

Stated in this way, the paradigm governing quantitative methodologies is one derived from the natural sciences. Human events are assumed to be lawful; man and his creations are part of the natural world. The development, elaboration, and verification of generalizations about that natural world become the first task of the researcher. From that one aspires to amass empirical generalizations; then to refine and restructure them into more general laws; and finally to weave these scattered and disparate laws into coherent nomothetic theory. In short, efforts are predicated upon a belief in the correctness of the scientific method as it is practiced in the natural sciences.[4, 5]

QUALITATIVE ORIENTATIONS

The epistemological questions raised by qualitative methodology challenge the presuppositions of the natural science approach to scientific investigation. Whereas the latter may assume that the study of observable deeds and expressed words is adequate to produce knowledge about man and his natural world, qualitative methodologies assume there is value to an analysis of both the inner and outer perspective of human behavior. In the German, the term is *verstehen*. This inner perspective or "understanding" assumes that a complete and ultimately truthful analysis can only be achieved by actively participating in the life of the observed and gaining insights by means of introspection.

Emphasis is placed upon the ability of the researcher to "take the role of the other," to grasp the basic underlying assumptions of behavior through understanding the "definition of the situation" from the view of the participants, and upon the need to understand the perceptions and values given to symbols as they are manipulated by man. Qualitative research is predicated upon the assumption that this method of "inner understanding" enables a comprehension of human behavior in greater depth than is possible from the study of surface behavior, the focus of quantitative methodologies. As Filstead (1970:6) has noted:

> Qualitative methodology refers to those research strategies, such as participant observation, in-depth interviewing, total participation in the activity being investigated, field work, etc., which allow the researcher to obtain first-hand knowledge about the empirical social world in question. Qualitative methodology allows the researcher to "get close to the data," thereby developing the analytical, conceptual, and categorical components of explanation from the data itself.

This view of the means by which knowledge and understanding are developed is essentially one of inductive analysis. Theory begins with an extrapolation from "grounded events." One begins not with models, hypotheses, or theorems, but rather with the understandings of frequently minute episodes or interactions that are examined for broader patterns and processes (cf. Glaser and Strauss, 1967). It is from an interpretation of the world through the perspective of the subjects that reality, meaning, and behavior are analyzed. The canons and precepts of the scientific method are seen to be insufficient; what are needed are intersubjective understandings.[6]

Having sketched in broad strokes what Gouldner (1970) would term the "domain assumptions" behind these two methodological orientations, what follows is an effort to examine several issues in more detail. Specifically, qualitative and quantitative methodologies will be assessed in terms of the polarities of reliability vs. validity, objectivity vs. subjectivity, and holistic vs. component analysis. While any number of such dyads could be constructed, these three should provide a sufficient map upon which to chart the convergences and divergences of the two research paradigms in question.

RELIABILITY VS. VALIDITY

Implicit in much that has been said thus far is that paradigms provide the framework or boundaries within which researchers structure their inquiry. They suggest what is appropriate to study, what questions to ask, what aspects of the phenomenon to emphasize, what standards for analysis, and what forms of interpretation to apply. Thus in any comparison of qualitative and quantitative research paradigms, there is the immediate question of emphasis (cf. Myrdal, 1972:161). Succinctly, it is my view that the emphasis within quantitative methodologies on an emulation of the scientific method has led it to emphasize reliability while qualitative methodologies have emphasized validity.[7]

The very nature of quantitative research in accentuating the cumulative properties of hypothesis testing and theory building necessitates a high degree of consensus among scientists (cf. Merton, 1957:448). Or, in the terms of Thomas Kuhn, quantification is at the very heart of the paradigm of "normal science." Such "science" is not possible if there is not a high degree of replicability and consistency among findings.

But all is not harmonious or parsimonious among the quantitatively oriented researchers. An emphasis upon reliability has its limits. As Cronbach has noted in this regard (1975:124):

> The time has come to exorcise the null hypotheses. We cannot afford to pour costly data down the drain whenever effects present in the sample "fail to reach significance." . . . Let the author file descriptive information, at least in an archive, instead of reporting only those selected differences and correlations that are nominally "greater than chance." Descriptions encourage us to think constructively about results from quasi-replications, whereas the dichotomy significant/non-significant implies only a hopeless inconsistency. The canon of parsimony, misinterpreted, has led us into the habit of accepting Type II errors at every turn, for the sake of holding Type I errors in check. There are more things in heaven and earth than are dreamt of in our hypotheses, and our observations should be open to them.

Or consider this quote from Deutscher (1970:33):

> We have been absorbed in measuring the amount of error which results from inconsistency among interviewers or inconsistency among items on our instruments. We concentrate on consistency without much concern with what it is we are being consistent about or whether we are consistently right or wrong. As a consequence, we may have been learning a great deal about how to pursue an incorrect course with a maximum of precision . . . Certainly zero reliability must result in zero validity. But the relation is not linear, since infinite perfection of reliability (zero error) may also be associated with zero validity.

When one turns to qualitative methodologies, the emphasis is quite different. Here the concern with validity is central. The researcher is encouraged to get close to the data, to develop an empathetic understanding of the observed, to be able to interpret and describe the constructions of reality as seen by the subjects, and to be able to articulate an inter-subjectivity with regard to the phenomenon being studied. As Patton (1975:19) has noted: "The overriding issue in the *verstehen* approach to science is the meaning of the scientist's observations and data, particularly its meaning for participants themselves. The constant focus is on a valid representation of what is happening. . . ."

Ideally, both paradigms would want high reliability and high validity. But the reality of the different emphases suggests that along this continuum, one orientation is the mirror opposite of the other. And this should immediately make apparent how, in the debates over the relative merits of the two paradigms, each finds fault in the other for the absence of its own strength. Quantitative researchers castigate qualitative researchers on their lack of reliability and their lack of work towards a cumulative body of "scientific knowledge." In an effort to meet this criticism, qualitative researchers at times make an almost pathetic attempt to argue for the "inter-rater reliability" among their field observers—a defensiveness suggesting that the manner in which quantitative researchers have defined "the scientific method" does hold a powerful appeal.

Alternatively, qualitative methodologies fault the quantitative researchers for not understanding the "meanings" behind their statistical formulations. Thus the dictum, "Statistical realities do not necessarily coincide with cultural realities." A correlation on paper may, in reality, be no correlation at all. This I take to be the caution voiced by Deutscher whom I just quoted. Parenthetically, I do not find much sense of alarm or concern among quantitative researchers about this question of validity. It may well be that the pursuit of the natural science model of research is so well established and so ingrained that questions of validity take an obvious backseat to issues of reliability.

SUBJECTIVITY VS. OBJECTIVITY

In the debate among those of the two paradigmatic persuasions, perhaps nowhere are nerves rubbed more raw than in the assessment of subjectivity vs. objectivity. While objectivity is considered the *sine qua non* of quantitative methodologies, qualitative approaches emphasize the need for *verstehen* or a subjective interpretation of the social phenomena in question. Having stated the dichotomy in this manner, it is necessary immediately to say that the meanings attached to these terms have been constantly confused, and the perspective that extols the one is used to condemn the other.

But following the lead of Scriven (1972:94–95), I agree that quantitative methods are no more synonymous with what we assume when we use the term "objectivity" than are qualitative methods synonymous with what we assume coincides with the term "subjectivity." As Scriven suggests: "Errors like this are too simple to be explicit. They are inferred confusions in the ideological foundations of research, its interpretations, its applications."

Attempting to ferret out the confusions in understanding, Scriven (p. 95) provides the following definitions:

> The terms "objective" and "subjective" are always held to be contrasting, but they are widely used to refer to two quite different contrasts, which I shall refer to as the *quantitative* and *qualitative* senses. In the first of these contrasts, "subjective" refers to what concerns or occurs to the individual subject and his experiences, qualities, and disposition,

while "objective" refers to what a number of subjects or judges experience—in short, to phenomena in the public domain. The difference is simply the *number* of people to whom reference is made, hence the term "quantitative." In the second of the two uses, there is a reference to the *quality* of the testimony or to the report or the (putative) evidence, and so I call this the "qualitative" sense. Here "subjective" means unreliable, biased, or probably biased, a matter of opinion, and "objective" means reliable, factual, confirmable, or confirmed, and so forth.

It is in the second sense, in the "quality" of the report, that the tension between qualitative and quantitative methodologies becomes heated. It is precisely to avoid the fate of unreliable, biased, or opinionated data that reliability is stressed in quantitative approaches. But for the same goal, qualitative researchers will seek validity through personalized, intimate understandings of the social phenomena, stressing "close in" observations to achieve "factual, reliable, and confirmable" data. Having said this, we come full circle to the first part of Scriven's set of definitions. For at this point, the quantitative methodologist would pursue confirmation through the use of a number of subjects, while the qualitative methodologist might undertake an intensive case study of a small group or even some particular individuals. We are back to a reconfirmation of the view that the very basis by which to confirm or dispute, to accept or reject, to "know," are paradigm dependent.

Scriven's 1972 article is entitled "Objectivity and Subjectivity in Educational Research." I find it an important contribution to the effort to detach the traditional connotation of "subjectivity" from qualitative research and "objectivity" from quantitative research. Scriven has argued that instead there are two basic components to any scientific endeavor—prediction and understanding. Prediction, of course, has long been accepted as a goal of the scientific effort, though in its reified form, it has been reduced to simply an assessment of reliability. When he turns to the role of understanding in science, Scriven notes (1972:127):

> . . . Understanding, properly conceived, is in fact an "objective" state of the mind or brain and can be tested quite objectively; and it is a functional and crucial state of the mind, betokening the presence of skills and states that are necessary for survival in the sea of information. There is nothing wrong with saying, in this case, that we have simply developed an enlightened form of inter-subjectivism. But one might also equally well say that we have developed an enlightened form of subjectivism—put flesh on the bones of empathy.

I agree here with Patton (1975:22) that the strength of Scriven's analysis lies in his suggesting that the notion of dual perspectives goes to the very heart of the tension between the quantitative and qualitative paradigms. For in the final analysis, such a perspective suggests that two researchers, working from different theoretical assumptions and different methodological orientations, may literally not see the same phenomenon, though involved in simultaneous observation. Or as Kuhn has suggested (1970:113), "something like a paradigm is necessary to perception itself." In only a slightly different context, the same issue is spoken to by Smith and Geoffrey (1968:255) in their comments on what they termed the "two realities problem."

It is one thing to recognize these differences in the basis of analysis and interpretation; it is another to set them in concrete and declare a cold war. The continued disdain implied by the selective and pejorative use of the terms "objective" and "subjective" when speaking of alternative methodological approaches does damage far beyond any reasonable intellectual clarity they might provide. And the rubble generated by such acrimony only gets in the way of our work on the question posed by Kuhn at the beginning of this paper, "Which problem is it more significant to have solved?"

COMPONENT VS. HOLISTIC ANALYSIS

Understandings of causality are at the heart of the scientific endeavor. Whether this pursuit of knowledge is for its own sake or to establish a basis from which to intervene to modify current conditions, the articulation of cause and effect relations is of the utmost priority. And once again, in a comparison of quantitative and qualitative methodologies, there are basic differences in how the analysis of causality is undertaken. The manner in which the topic of investigation is defined, the modes of data collection, the means of analysis, and the presentation of findings all diverge between these two paradigmatic approaches for the study of causal relations (cf. Rist, 1978). Neither, of course, represents an omnibus strategy for all assessments of causality, but it is apparent that within each framework rather elaborate strategies do exist.

Within the quantitative orientation, the emphasis upon the ability to manipulate variables is critical for the reason that such manipulation is central to experimentation. And as noted earlier in the quote from Campbell and Stanley, experimentation is the final arbiter of educational practice, educational improvements, and the cumulation of educational knowledge. Thus the rationale for the large number of experimental studies with a defined set of variables, one of which is the treatment variable, and the effort to separate out cause and effect. In fact, the very names of the statistical methodologies used in the assessment of these cause-effect relations gives evidence of the emphasis upon component analysis—multiple regression analysis, partial correlation analysis, linear regression analysis, nonlinear regressional analysis, correlation matrix analysis, etc.

Patton (1975:29) has nicely commented upon this relation of experimentation and educational research:

> Treatments in educational research are usually some type of new hardware, a specific curriculum innovation, variations in class size, or some specific type of teaching style. One of the major problems in experimental educational research is clear specification of what the

treatment actually is, which infers controlling all other possible causal variables and the corresponding problem of multiple treatment interference and interaction effects. It is the constraints posed by controlling the specific treatment under study that necessitates simplifying and breaking down the totality of reality into small component parts. A great deal of the scientific enterprise revolves around this process of simplifying the complexity of reality.

The rationale used by quantitative methodologists for employing component analysis is stood on its head, so far as qualitative methodologists are concerned. From their perspective, it is precisely because reality cannot be broken down into component parts without the severe risk of distortion that a holistic analysis is necessary. Focusing on a narrow set of variables necessarily sets up a filtering screen between the researcher and the phenomena he is attempting to comprehend. Such barriers, from the vantage point of those employing a holistic analysis, inhibit and thwart the observer from a necessary closeness to the data, from an understanding of what is unique as well as what is generalizable from the data, and from perceiving the processes involved in contrast to simply the outcomes.

The reactions among some qualitative researchers to the extreme emphasis upon component analysis to the virtual exclusion of holistic analysis in our studies of American education have been strident. Consider this comment by Deutscher (1970:33) on the use of component analysis in the evaluation of educational programs:

> We knew that human behavior was rarely if ever directed, influenced or explained by an isolated variable; we knew that it was impossible to assume that any set of such variables was additive (with or without weighting); we knew that the complex mathematics of the interaction among any set of variables, much less their interaction with internal variables, was incomprehensible to us. In effect, though we knew they did not exist, we defined them into being.

To reiterate, there is no omnibus strategy for our study of causality. Rather, what appears more realistic is to assume that different methodological approaches are appropriate for different levels of analysis and for different levels of abstraction. The methodology should follow the answering of the questions of for whom and for what ends the analysis is being undertaken (cf. Broadhead and Rist, 1976). Regardless of the methods employed, the assessment of any causal relation should be for reasons of its being important, not simply because it can be done. The very parsimony of saying that the method should match the problem, however, may hide as much as it elucidates. For if the analysis of this paper is correct, then stating the problem, giving it definition and form, as well as selecting the appropriate methodological techniques for its analysis are all the result of the paradigmatic spectacles one sees fit to wear.

I do not want to carry this imagery much further, but if we are serious about our quest for an understanding of the social reality about us and the causal relations within it, then what may be most needed are researchers capable of wearing bi-focal or even tri-focal lenses. In this regard, I am particularly impressed with the sensitivity demonstrated by Shapiro in her evaluations of innovative Follow Through classrooms. She seems well to have sensed the nuances of classroom life that necessitated a combination of qualitative and quantitative methodologies to achieve an accurate portrayal of the impact of Follow Through. Consider, for example, these comments (Shapiro, 1973:541):

> The relevance and appropriateness of the classroom and the test situation as locations for studying the impact of schooling on children requires reevaluation. Each can supply useful information, but in both situations the evidence is situation-bound. Neither yields pure measures, and it is necessary to consider the type of school situation the children are in and the developmental status, as well as the social and sociological factors that determine or have determined the children's expectations, perceptions, and styles of thinking and communication with other children and adults. What may be an appropriate situation for assessing some groups may lead to misevaluation of others. . . . It is an old chestnut that psychological dimensions cannot be defined in terms of their physical equivalence: psychologists who are trying to study the impact of different kinds of experience on different kinds of children must be able to shift their expectations and tools depending upon the contexts in which they are working.

CONCLUSIONS

There are several rather straightforward conclusions to be drawn from the preceding analysis.

First, if in fact we do find ourselves in a situation of multiple paradigmatic perspectives on educational research, then it is not appropriate to think in the near future of there being a "grand synthesis" of quantitative and qualitative methodologies. If the two major paradigms do exist as outlined here, each with its own internal order and logic, and neither finds its present framework for analysis unsuitable, they will continue to prosper. It would only be when one or another of the approaches no longer believed in the utility and appropriateness of its paradigm that new syntheses might become possible. This may already be happening on the fringes of each paradigm, but surely not at the center. In this light, the spirit of detente may be the most we should anticipate.

Second, the fact that these two paradigms are in tension over the very most basic assumptions upon which they base their research efforts opens up the potential for a dialectic where the resolution is not an "either/or" but each answering a part of the question at hand. If each approach does provide a perspective which tends to be the mirror opposite of the other, the creative effort becomes one of finding ways to take these partial images of reality and piece them into a new orientation or perspective.[8] It may well be that some of the most intellectually stimulating and exciting developments in educational research over the next decade will be in working out the implications of the dialectic. If breakthroughs are to come, they will happen, as Kuhn (1970:110) suggests, when "scientists see new and different things when looking with familiar instruments in places they have looked before." It may well be that when the "familiar instruments" of quantitative and qualitative methodologies are juxtaposed, we will "see new and different things."

Third, and a paradox in light of the second point, is that with these two paradigms moving in their own spheres and with their own rules of evidence and acceptability in their respective communities, we confront one more example of the phenomenon of contemporary research leading to divergences rather than convergences. As each methodology is now more sophisticated than ever, as basic concepts are overhauled and refined, as new distinctions formulated, and as the sheer amount of research evidence continues to grow, we find new arguments and complications rather than new answers and resolutions. Speaking on this issue as it relates specifically to social policy research, Cohen and Weiss (1976) have noted:

> The improvement of research on social policy does not lead to greater clarity about what to think or what to do. Instead, it usually tends to produce a greater sense of complexity. This result is endemic to the research process. For what researchers understand by improvement in their craft leads not to greater consensus about research problems, methods and interpretations of results, but to more variety in the ways problems are seen, more divergence in the ways studies are carried out, and more controversy in the ways results are interpreted. It leads also to a more complicated view of problems and solutions, for the progress of research tends to reveal the inadequacy of accepted ideas about solving problems. The ensuing complexity and confusion are naturally a terrific frustration both to researchers who think they should matter and to officials who think they need help.

If Cohen and Weiss are accurate in their assessment, their comments suggest that a situation of multiple visions and understandings of reality is unescapable. And the task still remains of how then to piece our collage of realities together. Which leads to my fourth and final point.

We suffer for the lack of appropriate language and conceptual frameworks for locating both paradigms in a relation to one another. I am not sure we would recognize the collage even if we saw it. And one consequence among many of this lack of coherent organizing principles is that we probably will have to reconcile ourselves to a number of ultimately fruitless endeavors and wasted deadends. As we set out to explore these tangled and complex multiple realities with tangled and complex methodologies, the odds appear stacked against us.

But I suspect for many of us there remains the vision of developing a means to comprehend the diversities and nuances of the educational experience. And if we can come to comprehend it, then perhaps we will find the will to transform it. To learn of the ways in which to make learning and schooling both stimulating and exciting experiences for children would be no mean feat. And there are few other tasks more worthy of our efforts.

NOTES

1. I wish to acknowledge the fruitful comments from Harold L. Hodgkinson on this topic. Our discussion sharpened for me several key issues raised in this paper.

2. There is yet a further philosophical issue here as well. Not only does the use of one methodological approach as opposed to another change the means by which one perceives the reality under study, but also the very reality to which a researcher has applied a method is itself continually in a state of change. As all knowledge is social, so also all reality is social. To wait for absolutes is to wait for Godot. Social systems are ongoing, regardless of how stable they may appear. Put differently, no methodology allows us to step twice in the same stream in the same place.

3. Cf. this quote from Cronbach (1975:124): "Originally, the psychologist saw his role as the scientific observation of human behavior. When hypothesis testing became paramount, observation was neglected, and even actively discouraged by editorial policies of journals. Some authors now report nothing save F ratios."

4. I raise this only as an aside, but I find it of interest that, to my knowledge, there has been no systematic tracing out of the manner in which natural science methods have been brought over into the social and behavioral sciences. Are there adaptations and mutations in the transfer process? What aspects of natural science methodology are relevant? Which are not? Are those branches of the natural sciences which are not experimental in nature (astronomy and geology, for example) able to contribute to our methodological sophistication? The analysis necessary for the answers is in the domain of the sociology of knowledge. And in the absence of such answers, I wonder if we are not at times a bit hasty to accept the "natural science" model as, in fact, the one from which current quantitative approaches have come.

5. For a more elaborate and more complete analysis of the epistemological underpinnings between the scientific method and the natural sciences, I suggest the following sources which I found extremely beneficial: Thomas Kuhn, *The Structure of Scientific Revolutions;* Ernest Nagel, *The Structure of Science;* and Abraham Kaplan, *The Conduct of Inquiry.*

6. To suggest several citations which provide the epistemological underpinnings for the use of qualitative methodologies, I would offer the following: Alfred Schutz, *The Phenomenology of the Social World;* Herbert Blumer, *Symbolic Interactionism;* and George H. Mead, *Mind, Self, and Society.*

7. I find Patton's summary (1975) of these two concepts quite sufficient. "Reliability concerns the replicability and consistency of scientific findings." One is particularly concerned here with inter-rate, inter-item, interviewer, observer, and instrument reliability. Validity, on the other hand, concerns the meaning and meaningfulness of the data collected and instrumentation employed. Does the instrument measure what it purports to measure? Does the data mean what we think it means?

8. We may have one promising example at hand of the potential for a creative breakthrough once two paradigms are placed in a dialectic with one another. I am referring to the strides we have made in the heredity-environment debate over individual intelligence. So long as each existed without having to account for the other, little progress was made. But after a period of attempting to grasp the contributions of each in relation to its alternative, new insights are flourishing and promising research avenues opening up.

REFERENCES

Becker, H.S. "Whose Side Are We On?" *Social Problems* 14:239–47, 1967.

Blalock, H.M. *Social Statistics.* New York: McGraw-Hill, 1960.

Broadhead, R.A., and R.C. Rist. "Gatekeepers and the Social Control of Social Research." *Social Problems* 23:325–26, 1976.

Campbell, D.T., and J.C. Stanley. *Experimental and Quasi-Experimental Designs for Research*. Chicago: Rand McNally, 1963.

Cohen, D., and J. Weiss, "Social Science and Social Policy: Schools and Race." Paper presented to the International Symposium on "Education, Social Science and the Judicial Process," National Institute of Education, Washington, D.C., February, 1976.

Cronbach, L.J. "Beyond the Two Disciplines of Scientific Psychology." *American Psychologist* 30:116–127, 1975.

Denzin, N.K. *The Research Act: Introduction to Sociological Methods*. Chicago: Aldine, 1970.

Deutscher, I. "Words and Deeds: Social Science and Social Policy." In W.J. Filstead (ed.). *Qualitative Methodology*. Chicago: Markham, 1970.

Filstead, W.J. *Qualitative Methodology*. Chicago: Markham, 1970.

Glaser, B., and A. Strauss. *The Discovery of Grounded Theory*. Chicago: Aldine, 1967.

Gouldner, A. *The Coming Crisis in Western Sociology*. New York: Basic Books, 1970.

Homans, G. "The Strategy of Industrial Sociology." *American Journal of Sociology* 54:330–337, 1949.

Kuhn, T.S. *The Origins of Scientific Revolutions*. Chicago: University of Chicago Press, 1970.

Merton, R.S. *Social Theory and Social Structure*. Glencoe (Ill.): Free Press, 1957.

Mills, C.W. *The Sociological Imagination*. New York: Oxford, 1959.

Myrdal, G. "How Scientific Are the Social Sciences?" *Journal of Social Issues* 28:151–70, 1972.

Patton, M.Q. *Alternative Evaluation Research Paradigm*. Grand Forks: University of North Dakota Press, 1975.

Rist, R.C. "Race, Policy, and Schooling." In I.L. Horowitz (ed.). *The Use and Abuse of Social Science*. New Brunswick (N.J.): Trans-Action Books, 1975.

_____ *The Invisible Children: School Integration in American Society*. Cambridge: Harvard University Press, 1978.

Scriven, M. "Objectivity and Subjectivity in Educational Research." In H.B. Dunkel, et al. (eds.). *Philosophical Redirection of Educational Research*. Chicago: National Society for the Study of Education, 1972.

Shapiro, E. "Educational Evaluation: Rethinking the Criteria of Competence." *School Review* 81:523–49, 1973.

Smith, L., and W. Geoffrey. *The Complexities of an Urban Classroom*. New York: Holt, Rinehart, and Winston, 1968.

Suppes, P. "The Place of Theory in Educational Research." *Educational Researcher* 3(6):3–10, 1974.

3

The Structure of
Educational Systems

This chapter and the next set the stage for the interactional analysis in Chapters 6 and 7. As stated in Chapters 1 and 2, a fundamental theme of this book is that many of the most typical features of U.S. schools stem from the way those schools are organized. If we want to know the causes of differences in student performance or teacher morale, we first need to examine the structure within which teachers and students work. Our examination of the structure of U.S. schooling is divided into two chapters. This chapter operates at the societal level, describing the overall structure of the United States educational system and comparing it to the educational systems of other societies, particularly Japan and the Soviet Union. Chapter 4, meanwhile, will move to the organizational level—that of the school district or individual school—to examine the roles of teachers, administrators, students, and parents.

THE TYPES OF EDUCATION

Before describing the structure of the U.S. educational system and putting it in context, we need to clarify what we mean by education. A very basic point is that education and schooling are not synonymous. Education is the more encompassing concept, referring to the general process by which a social group—whether an entire society or a just a family—transmits attitudes, beliefs, behaviors, and skills to its members.[1] Within these broad boundaries, education greatly varies, with educational scholars typically distinguishing three general types: formal, nonformal, and informal education (LaBelle, 1976: 21–24). These different kinds of education can be distinguished accord-

---

[1]Synonyms for education are socialization and enculturation.

ing to where they take place, the characteristics of teachers, the methods of instruction, and what is learned.

Informal education takes such forms as family child rearing, peer group socialization, and learning skills such as auto repair and guitar playing largely on one's own. It takes place in the context of everyday, intimate relationships, with teachers being family members or friends and learning occurring through observation and imitation ("hands on"). Formal education or schooling, meanwhile, takes place outside the family in institutions (which we call schools) that specialize in education, are led by teachers who are not students' intimates and whose principal occupation is education, and stress learning more through verbal and written description and guided inquiry rather than observation and imitation. Nonformal education, finally, includes on-the-job training, agricultural extension programs, and family planning outreach programs. It differs from informal education in taking place outside the family, but it also differs from formal education in that it does not take place in schools and its aims are more specific and short-term.

Virtually all societies utilize all three forms of education, but they differ in the relative predominance of these forms. In highly industrialized societies such as the United States, formal education rivals, if not exceeds, nonformal and informal education in importance and use of society's resources. But in nonindustrialized societies, informal education dominates, with formal and nonformal education only marginally present.

The opening piece in this chapter, N. J. Colletta's "Education Without Schools: Learning Among the Ponapeans," illuminates the nature of education in nonindustrialized societies (and the central characteristics of informal education in our own society) by examining education in a society largely devoid of formal and nonformal education. Colletta explores education in Ponape, a Pacific Island tribal society whose educational system is almost exclusively built around informal education. Colletta explores how the Ponapeans raise their children to assume their adult family, work, and religious roles. He emphasizes how this education largely occurs in the course of everyday life as a parent who is cooking or making a canoe lets a child take a hand.

Modern industrialized societies share a common emphasis on formal education. Yet within this similarity of policy, there are also enormous differences. The U.S. school system is quite different in many regards from those of other advanced industrial societies. Before we analyze those differences, and the implications they hold for U.S. education, let us paint the main characteristics of the U.S. school system.

THE U.S. SCHOOL SYSTEM DESCRIBED

The selections by Hammack and Dougherty sum up the main characteristics of the U.S. school system. In "The Structure of American Elementary and Secondary Education," Floyd Hammack focuses on two features of the school system: governance and the organization of instruction. With regard to governance, he describes the relative roles of national, state, and local government, noting that the United States is unusual in that national control is far weaker than in most other countries and, conversely, state and local control is far stronger. With regard to the organization of instruction, he notes the considerable similarity among U.S. schools due to the U.S. commitment to common and comprehensive schooling. For example, most U.S. secondary school students attend schools that offer both academic and vocational programs. This contrasts with the typical European formula—although one that is waning—of providing separate academic and vocational high schools. Hammack notes, however, that U.S. schooling does differentiate among students both within schools (in the form of curriculum grouping or tracking) and between schools (in the form of the public/private division and differences among schools in student body composition).

The selection by Kevin Dougherty, "The American Higher Education System," examines the wide variety of U.S. colleges, how the U.S. higher education system arose, and how that system differs from those in other advanced industrial societies. Dougherty classifies U.S. colleges along four axes: the degrees and programs they offer, who controls them, the characteristics of their student bodies, and their prestige. These different kinds of colleges arose at different times, so he also traces the history of the U.S. higher education system from colonial times on. Finally, he shows how the U.S. higher education system is very different from those of other advanced industrial societies: It is much larger, less nationally directed, and more varied in types of institutions.

Both Hammack and Dougherty call attention to the fact that when we discuss U.S. education, we should not focus on public education alone. Like many other societies, the U.S. educational system has a strong private school sector. Private schools enroll 13 percent of all secondary students and 23 percent of all college students in the United States (U.S. Department of Education, 1987; 38, 52, 122). Many private schools are little different from public schools: enrolling a wide variety of students; offering a broad curriculum; and if they provide religious education, largely restricting it to chapel and courses specifically on religion.[2] But a good number of private schools are quite distinctive: In particular, the elite private schools and colleges and the rapidly multiplying Christian academies and colleges.[3]

U.S. EXCEPTIONALISM

As described above, the U.S. school system may seem commonplace and even commonsensical. Is there really any other way to reasonably organize a

---

[2]One major difference between private schools and public schools is that private schools enroll more students who are white and from more economically privileged families. For example, the median family income of private school students is 40 percent higher than that of public school students. Similarly, only 7 percent of private school students, but 16 percent of public school students, are black (Bianchi, 1982: 240, 245).

[3]For more on elite private schools, see Hammack and Cookson (1980) and Cookson and Persell (1985).

school system? In fact, there are quite varied ways. Even nations similar to ours diverge considerably from us in how they organize their school systems, and these structural differences result in quite substantial differences in how their systems operate and how they affect students. Six divergences stand out between the U.S. school system and those of other advanced industrial societies.

First, the U.S. school system is much larger. This is a product not just of our large population but also of the fact that our schools enroll a far larger *proportion* of students, particularly among those above the age of compulsory school attendance. For example, in 1982, college students represented 5.4 percent of the entire U.S. population, while the comparable percentage was 2.3 in West Germany, 2.2 in France, 2.0 in Japan and the Soviet Union, and 1.6 in the United Kingdom (United Nations Economic, Scientific, and Cultural Organization, 1985, III:241–245).

Second, the U.S. school system is far less centralized than the school systems of most advanced industrial societies (Hopper, 1977). Most other industrial societies largely vest control of their school systems in a national ministry of education that finances the schools and sets basic rules for curriculum, admission and graduation, and teacher education, hiring, and promotion. Such a pattern of strong national centralization, with minimal local voice, can be seen in Japan, France, Italy, and the Soviet Union (Ignas and Corsini, 1981; King, 1979).[4] In the United States, meanwhile, the states have constitutional sovereignty over education and, furthermore, allow local districts great power over the day-to-day functioning of the schools (Campbell and others, 1980; Wirt and Kirst, 1982: 192–193).[5] This decentralization of authority is enhanced by the fact that U.S. schools receive most of their funds not from the national government but from state and local sources.

Because of its greater decentralization, the U.S. school system is less homogeneous across different regions of the country than are the school systems in other advanced industrial societies. In comparison to French students living in different regions of their country, U.S. students living in different states encounter greater differences in how much is spent on their education, how educated their teachers are, and what education they are provided.

The United States is not devoid of centralizing tendencies in its educational system, however. U.S. schools in different states are more similar, after all, than schools in different countries. One of the most important centralizing tendencies is the great mobility of our population, so that people moving from one state to another have demanded in the new state what they had been

---

[4]Two major exceptions are West Germany and Britain. West Germany vests its *Länder* (states) with educational governance in a manner similar to the United States. Britain gives its local educational authorities considerable autonomy. However, it is less than that enjoyed by U.S. school districts and it was significantly curtailed by the Educational Reform Act of 1988, which installed the beginnings of a national curriculum (Ignas and Corsini, 1981: 412—413; King, 1979: 190–196; "Educational Reform Act," 1988).

[5]The United States does not mention education in its national constitution, unlike many other countries which make education a fundamental responsibility of the national government.

used to in their home state. In addition, the federal government, state governments, and a host of private organizations (ranging from accrediting associations to test manufacturers) foster a considerable degree of homogeneity in educational policy across the country (Campbell, Cunningham, Nystrand, and Usdan, 1980: 325–340; Iannaccone, 1967: 374–377; Wirt and Kirst, 1982: 81–88, 194–201).[6]

The selection by Brian Holmes, "Education in the Soviet Union," illuminates the main characteristics of the nationally centralized school systems typical to Continental Europe and Japan by examining the school system in the Soviet Union. Aside from providing an excellent synopsis of Soviet education, Holmes illuminates the Continental European pattern of utilizing nationally centralized control as a means of providing equal and homogeneous education nationwide.[7]

A third distinctive feature of the U.S. school system is that it is much less driven by examination requirements than are many other school systems. In good part because the U.S. system is much less centralized, it does not have the system of nationwide exams that are present in most other advanced societies and that powerfully mold students' educational careers. In most other countries, exams taken before high school determine the kind of high school one can attend and exams taken at the end of high school determine whether one can go on to higher education and what kind of college one can attend. As a result, exam taking assumes a critical and hellish importance in such countries as Japan, France, Germany, the Soviet Union, and England. In the United States, though, one can still get into college without doing well on the Scholastic Aptitude Test (SAT) or American College Test (ACT) or even taking them at all. However, the U.S. exemption from the "examination hell" may be disappearing as states and local school districts increasingly require students to pass a minimum competency test to receive a high school or college diploma (Airasian, 1987).[8]

The selection by Nobuo Shimahara, "Socialization for College Entrance Examinations in Japan," explores the key role of these examinations in Japanese education. Entrance into prestigious occupations in Japan is tightly connected to the prestige of the university one enters. In turn, entrance to prestigious universities is entirely dependent on how one does on the once-a-year national college entrance examination. As a result, secondary schools and even elementary schools in Japan focus their energy on preparing their students for the college entrance exam. Moreover, a huge network of private academies (*jukus*) has sprung up to provide after school coaching for the exam, beginning as early as elementary school. In the process of exploring

---

[6]For more on this point, see the essays by Hammack and Dougherty in this chapter.

[7]The strong centralization of the Continental European and Japanese education systems may be breaking down, however. Increasingly, Soviet and Japanese educators are calling for more local autonomy and less emphasis on strong direction by the national ministry of education (Barringer, 1988).

[8]This increased emphasis on examinations has been strongly encouraged by the recent spate of educational commissions, such as the National Commission on Excellence in Education. See Chapter 10 for more.

the Japanese examination system, Shimahara provides a powerful synopsis of the Japanese school system and a careful assessment of the functions and dysfunctions of the Japanese college examination system for Japanese society.[9]

While the U.S. school system is less centralized and therefore less homogeneous across regions than the systems in most other industrial societies, our system is also *more* homogeneous *within the same district.* This is the fourth major difference among industrial societies. The United States has long enrolled its students in "comprehensive" schools: that is, institutions that offer both academic and vocational subjects. Most other advanced industrial societies—with the exception of the Soviet Union and Japan— traditionally have had strongly differentiated secondary and postsecondary educational systems. Until recently, many students have enrolled in special- ized high schools: whether vocational schools or elite academic high schools (the English grammar school, the French lycée, and the German gymnasium). In turn, higher education in most advanced societies has been strongly divided between academically oriented universities and less prestigious, vocationally oriented technical and teacher training institutions.[10] This cur- ricular division has tended to coincide with class divisions. The elite academic secondary schools and the universities have long drawn disproportionately from the upper class and upper middle class. Meanwhile lower middle-class and working-class students have gone to vocational schools and low-prestige comprehensive schools and, if they reached higher education, technical and teacher training colleges. In the United States, meanwhile, students of all classes largely attend comprehensive schools and colleges, because of the relatively small number of exclusively vocational or academic schools and colleges.[11]

But if U.S. schools evidence greater homogeneity within the same district, this is purchased in good part through greater heterogeneity *within* the school. This is the fifth difference between American schools and those of other countries. Unlike Japan, France, and the Soviet Union, U.S. schools extensively group students within schools according to apparent ability and interests and, as a result, social class and ethnicity (Ignas and Corsini, 1981; King, 1979).[12] For example, many U.S. high schools maintain a college

[9]For other analyses of the Japanese education system, see King (1979), Ignas and Corsini (1981), Rohlen (1983), and White (1987). For cautions about the dangers of uncritically copying Japanese educational practices, see Ohanian (1987).

[10]In the last 20 years, European school systems have been moving in the direction of greater curricular homogeneity. "Comprehensive" secondary schools have been multiplying and grow- ing in enrollments and prestige (Ignas and Corsini, 1981; King, 1979; Levin, 1978). Similarly, there has been a growing amalgamation between the universities and technical institutes. However, European education still remains more differentiated by curriculum than is the case in the United States.

[11]There is greater differentiation between schools at the higher education level than at the precollege level. Schools that are largely vocational make up a larger proportion of U.S. colleges than they do of U.S. high schools.

[12]See the introduction to Chapter 6 for more on the association between students' track placement and their social class and ethnicity.

preparatory track for students presumed to be college material, a vocational track for those expected to enter blue collar jobs, and a general or commercial track for those expected to enter lower-level white collar jobs or, perhaps, college. The U.S. combination of comprehensive schools with internal tracking is by no means necessary. Other school systems, such as the Japanese and the Soviet, seem to have been able to provide comprehensive schools without resorting to a great deal of internal tracking.[13]

The sixth and final divergence is that U.S. schools typically take on far more tasks than is typical in other societies. We expect our schools to address such problems as poor driving, drug abuse, sexual ignorance, and poor nutrition at home. As a result, American schools are full of courses and programs that rarely show up in the curricula of comparable societies: drivers' education, drug education, health and sex education, and school lunch programs.

CONCLUSIONS

When seen in comparative perspective, the U.S. school system has many clearly distinctive characteristics. It is very large, a product not only of our country's large size but also its unusual commitment to having everybody graduate from high school and large numbers attend college. The U.S. school system is also quite decentralized and therefore variable across regions of the country. And within schools, students are often grouped into different tracks or curriculum groups. But at the same time, the American school system is committed to enrolling the bulk of its students in comprehensive schools, rather than in separate academic and vocational schools.

These structural features of the U.S. system carry at least five major implications for how U.S. schools operate, implications that we will explore in subsequent chapters. First, the huge size of the American educational system means that it absorbs a large proportion of government revenues. In 1984, education took up 14 percent of all government revenues and 35 percent of state and local governments' direct general expenditures (U.S. Bureau of the Census, 1986: 257, 280, 293). As a result, education plays a very central role in U.S. politics, perhaps more so than in any other industrial society. This is demonstrated by the great attention garnered by the current educational reform movement, discussed in Chapter 10, which was catalyzed by the National Commission on Excellence in Education in its 1983 report, *A Nation at Risk*.

Second, the decentralization of U.S. education—a product of our commitment to local control—generates again and again certain conflicts that are absent or much more muted in other countries. Three examples come to mind. Because of decentralization, schools have been recurrently embroiled

---

[13]Several educational commentators have argued that we should move in this direction as well, dispensing largely or entirely with tracking or curriculum grouping (Adler, 1982; Sizer, 1983). See Chapter 10 for more on this.

in controversies pitting parents and educators in a fight for influence over school policy. Acting in the name of local control, groups of conservative parents have frequently attacked educators for pushing values that are antithetical to theirs. For example, in recent years, fundamentalist Christian parents have accused educators of subverting family values by pushing "secular humanism" through courses in evolution, sex education, and values clarification (Hillocks, 1978; Page and Clelland, 1978). And this call has been taken up at the national level by various New Right organizations. (See the discussion of the Heritage Foundation in Chapter 10.) On the other hand, other parents, often from minority groups, have criticized educators for making fateful decisions about their children's education—such as closing schools or assigning their children to lower tracks—that are unfair or done without proper consultation. Consequently, as Chapter 4 demonstrates, U.S. schools are less completely and securely bureaucratized and professionalized, as evidenced by teachers' lower status, than is common in most other industrial societies.

Also because of decentralization, Americans often see a conflict between democracy and educational equality, whereas in most countries these are seen as intimately tied together. Because Americans define democracy as requiring locally controlled schools, many have categorized egalitarian policies such as school desegregation and court-ordered busing as undemocratic insofar as they infringe on local control. The most obvious example has been the controversy, discussed by the Hawley reading in Chapter 8, between those favoring busing and those favoring "neighborhood schools." This controversy comes up much less often in societies where democracy is seen as lodged in the national government rather than local government and where schools are not seen as a property of local citizens but an arm of the national government and thus proper instruments of national policies, such as racial desegregation.

Finally, because of decentralization, our schools are heavily dependent on local tax revenues. Consequently, they differ widely in how much tax revenues they can raise and thus how much they can spend on pupils. As a result, efforts to equalize funding across districts have preoccupied educational policymakers—and to some degree citizens—over the last 20 years. Yet, such controversies are rare abroad, since in most countries school funding is a responsibility of national government, so that regional variations in school spending are much smaller than here.

A third implication of the unusual character of the U.S. school system flows from its commitment to "common schooling" and therefore avoiding separate academic and vocational schools. The commitment to common schooling arises from the American goals of equality of opportunity and democratic citizenship and belief that the school plays a unique role in advancing both. (See Chapters 2 and 10 for more.) Hence, issues of equality and citizenship are more quickly turned into educational issues in this country than most. As Chapter 5 discusses, social movements to uplift oppressed groups—ranging from blacks and women to the physically handicapped—have typically put as big a stress on securing equal access and treatment in the schools as in the economy and other realms of life. As a result, the category of "students with special needs," discussed in Chapter 8, is very important educationally and politically in the United States.

Fourth, the U.S. system's commitment to common schooling has created great pressure for curriculum tracking within schools. While other educational systems tend to differentiate their educational programs *between* schools, the United States tends to differentiate *within* schools in the form of different tracks or curriculums. As a result, curriculum tracking is quite important in U.S. schools, as Chapter 6 shows, and it has attracted the same political controversy as has selective schooling in England, France, and Germany.

Finally, the breadth of the U.S. high school curriculum, stemming from the U.S. penchant to give schools major responsibility for such tasks as drivers' education and drug education, helps explain the recurrent concern that U.S. schools try to do too much and that we need to "get back to basics." As Chapter 10 discusses, a common explanation for the relatively poor performance of U.S. students in comparison to students in other nations is that too much of our students' attention is wasted on "frills," rather than basic subjects such as English, science, and mathematics.

REFERENCES

Adler, Mortimer. 1982. *The Paideia Proposal*. New York: Macmillan.

Airasian, Peter W. 1987. "State Mandated Testing and Educational Reform: Context and Consequences." *American Journal of Education* 95 (May): 393–412.

Barringer, Felicity. 1988. "Soviet Students Now Asking 'Why?' " *New York Times*, February 17, 1988, p. B8.

Bianchi, Suzanne. 1982. "Private School Enrollments." In Alan C. Kerckhoff (ed.), *Research in Sociology of Education and Socialization*, vol. 3, pp. 233–258. Greenwich, CT: JAI Press, Inc.

Campbell, Roald F., Luvern L. Cunningham, Raphael O. Nystrand, and Michael D. Usdan. 1980. *Organization and Control of American Schools*. 4th ed. Columbus, OH: Merrill.

Cookson, Peter W., Jr., and Caroline Hodges Persell. 1985. *Preparing for Power*. New York: Basic Books.

"Educational Reform Act." 1988. *Times Educational Supplement* 3761 (July 29): 9–12.

Hammack, Floyd M., and Peter W. Cookson, Jr. 1980. "Colleges Attended by Graduates of Elite Secondary Schools." *Educational Forum* 44 (May): 483–490.

Hillocks, George. 1978. "Books and Bombs: Ideological Conflict in the Schools." *American Journal of Education* 86: 632–654.

Hopper, Earl. 1977. "A Typology for the Classification of Educational Systems." In Jerome Karabel and A. H. Halsey (eds.), *Power and Ideology in Education*, pp. 153–166. New York: Oxford University Press.

Iannaccone, Laurence. 1967. *Politics in Education*. New York: Center for Applied Research in Education.

Ignas, Edward, and Raymond Corsini (eds.). 1981. *Comparative Educational Systems*. Itasca, IL: Peacock.

King, Edmund. 1979. *Other Schools and Ours.* 5th ed. New York: Oxford University Press.

LaBelle, Thomas J. 1976. *Nonformal Education and Social Change in Latin America.* Los Angeles: University of California at Los Angeles.

Levin, Henry. 1978. "The Dilemma of Comprehensive Secondary School Reforms in Western Europe." *Comparative Educational Review* 22 (October): 434–451.

Ohanian, Susan. 1987. "Notes on Japan from an American Schoolteacher." *Phi Delta Kappan* (January): 360–367.

Page, Ann L., and Donald A. Clelland. 1978. "The Kanawha County Textbook Controversy." *Social Forces* 57 (September): 265–281.

Peshkin, Alan. 1986. *God's Choice: The Total World of a Fundamentalist Christian School.* Chicago: University of Chicago Press. (See the excerpt in Chapter 7.)

Rohlen, Thomas. 1983. *Japan's High Schools.* Berkeley: University of California Press.

Sizer, Theodore R. 1983. "High School Reform." *Phi Delta Kappan* 64 (June): 679–683. (Reprinted in Chapter 10.)

United Nations Educational, Scientific, and Cultural Organization. 1985. *Statistical Yearbook, 1985.* Paris: UNESCO.

U.S. Bureau of the Census. 1986. *Statistical Abstract of the United States, 1987.* Washington, D.C.: Government Printing Office.

U.S. Department of Education. 1987. *Digest of Education Statistics, 1987.* Washington, D.C.: Government Printing Office.

White, Merry. 1987. *The Japanese Educational Challenge: A Commitment to Children.* New York: Free Press.

Wirt, Frederick, and Michael Kirst. 1982. *Schools in Conflict.* Berkeley, CA: McCutchan.

Education Without Schools: Learning Among the Ponapeans

N. J. COLLETTA
World Bank

Northeast of New Guinea and about 8° above the equator lies the highly volcanic island of Ponape, the crow's nest of the Eastern Caroline Islands.[1] Ethnographically, Ponape is part of the greater cultural area known as Micronesia or "tiny islands." But as Mason suggests, the concept of Micronesia as a homogeneous cultural area, bordering Melanesia on the south and Polynesia on the east, loses its utility when confronted with the vast heterogeneity of cultures and languages within its bounds.[2]

The Ponapeans are predominantly an agrarian people who tend to live on dispersed agricultural plots rather than in consolidated villages or in the district center enclaves, although government employment and schooling have increased their steady gravitation toward the latter. The physical environment of the island, with its geographic isolation, high rainfall, and fertile coastal plains, has structured the evolution of a subsistence agrarian economy functioning on an extended communal family effort as a means of assuring survival. It is the informal transmission of the knowledge, skills, attitudes, and beliefs commensurate to this mode of subsistence that this article shall focus upon.

EDUCATION—AN INDIGENOUS PERSPECTIVE

The feast was well underway. The men had just completed the uhmw (ground oven) under the watchful eyes of Daro and the others. A multitude of breadfruit lay roasting under the heap of banana leaves and simmering stones. Daro proceeded to lay his single small bread-fruit in the miniature uhmw he and his companions had so skillfully duplicated. Observing this event, his father, in a proud, joking manner acclaimed, "Now you may get married my son, you are a real Ponapean man." . . . the air filled with conjoint laughter. . . . Daro was but six years old.

The above narrative, as related by a Ponapean, connotes an educational process different from Western schooling. Here, and in situations less clearly defined but much more common to the daily life of Ponapeans, knowledge, values, and skills are continually transmitted and renewed incidentally by word and by example.

Education as exhibited in formal schooling is a relatively recent innovation, but the operational phenomenon itself, in terms of learning and pedagogy, is firmly rooted in the history of man's struggle with nature from time immemorial. Anthropologists, centering on the process of encultura-tion, have long alluded to educational practices of mankind in their ethnographies.

In 1943, at a symposium on education and culture, Robert Redfield addressed his comments to the informal day-to-day situations in which tradition was communicated and modified.[3] Later, Melville Herskovits pursued the notion of education in the broader context of a total learning system, distinguishing between the three components of education, encul-turation, and schooling.[4] He claimed that while education encompassed all realms of human teaching and learning, enculturation pertained primarily to nondirected learning, while schooling was that aspect of education per-formed by trained specialists in designated locations at particular time intervals.

Edwin Smith, when addressing himself to the process of indigenous education in Africa, divided it into three distinct areas: the "formal," as when a person is apprenticed to a trade or when the traditional rules of conduct are impressed through initiation rites; the "informal," as when young people learn by direct imitation; and the "unconscious," as when children in their play unknowingly follow impulses which have a social end and which are stimulated by the actions of their older models.[5]

"In short, a well-educated person, from a cultural point of view, is a person who, to paraphrase [Eric] Fromm, wants to do what he ought to do—the 'oughtness' being defined by his culture."[6] The process of transmis-sion itself is referred to in as many ways as there are discrete disciplinary paradigms. Sociologists speak of socialization, psychologists talk of condi-tioning, anthropologists refer to enculturation, and educators beg and borrow from all of these disciplines and label it education. But the actual "process" still pleads understanding and clarification.

With this brief perspective in mind, we shall investigate the process of informal learning among the Ponapeans of Micronesia.

Birth and Infancy

A Ponapean child enters the world with much merriment and happiness. The child is seen not only as a gift from heaven, but also as an addition to the communal labor force and insurance for the parents in old age.

A girl usually wishes to go home to her mother to have the baby. Mothers and sisters are frequently present at the birth, but brothers are strictly excluded. Girls are expected to be stoic during childbirth, and it is very rare to hear any outcries or demonstrations of pain. The umbilical cord is buried immediately after birth to guard against black magic or any other spiritual antagonism.

The status of the young man and woman changes after the birth of their first child when they are considered officially to have entered the adult world with all its responsibilities. It is generally felt that the first girl belongs to the mother's family, the first boy to the father's family, and all others to the couple themselves. Soon after the arrival of the baby, both grandmothers come and stay for a couple of months to help the nursing mother. The girl's mother takes care of her and the household chores, while the boy's mother takes care of the baby.

Indulgence is the rule as the infant is rarely out of the arms of various family members, especially the grandmothers, aunts, and older sisters. Sometimes the mother will let the baby cry, but another family member will caress it, as a crying baby is thought to indicate a lack of love and thus could bring shame on the entire family. Even in later years, a crying child will be granted its wish in order to prove parental love. A grandmother caring for her eighteen-month-old grandson quickly excused herself from an interview when the child began to cry, explaining, "I'm sorry but I can't talk to you now because the boy is crying." She proceeded to fondle and play with the child until he was happy again. She never hit or yelled at the child, saying, "Hitting him is wrong, he is too young, he would not even understand what he has done wrong. Wait until he can understand. Then he may be punished. To spank him now is only to teach him to cry."

The infant's legs and feet are often massaged with coconut oil so that his first steps will be strong. The Ponapeans prefer to bathe the child in the mornings because they believe that the morning water is the cleanest. Since it is also the coldest, they often rub the child down with coconut oil to protect his tender body from the harsh effects of the water. Coconut oil is considered to be highly medicinal and is frequently used to guard the child against fungus and to help heal cuts.

The baby sleeps in the same room as the rest of the family and usually near the mother. The child is free to nurse whenever he is hungry. The nursing mother is given the best food, so that she will produce much milk. It is believed that the mother must eat as much as possible in order to keep her milk flowing strong. She does not work much for the first month as too much action is thought to sour the milk. She must not bathe in cold water for the same period for fear of drying up the milk. The mother is supposed to eat during the night because the Ponapeans believe that this is the best time for the mother to produce milk. The Ponapeans will never wake a sleeping baby because they believe that a baby does most of its growing when asleep.

Weaning begins from six to twelve months when the mother starts to give the baby bananas and papaya to eat. Before the baby has teeth, special foods are prepared, but for convenience, mothers generally prefer to wait until the baby can eat regular food. Weaning is gradual and geared to the child's pace. A widely accepted psychoanalytic belief holds that such unlimited breast feeding (orality) results in a character marked by a great level of interpersonal affection and generosity.[7] These are certainly traits exhibited in later life by the Ponapeans, especially as evidenced at the feast. It should also be noted that prolonged breast feeding is linked to high affectivity and dependence between parent and child which are also dominant Ponapean character traits.

When a child is able to walk, he is expected to relieve himself outside the house, but is forbidden to go near the outhouse for fear that he might fall through the hole. He usually follows the example of the other children as they go about their toilet activities. In this act the child initiates his natural mode of learning by imitation and by being controlled through fear of public (peer group) shame.

The family is careful to see that the firstborn will not be jealous of a new arrival. The firstborn will sleep with the father while the newborn sleeps with the mother. Sometimes the firstborn will be spanked if he hits his new sibling, but usually the mother will say, "This is your baby whom you must love." Although every family seems to treat the sibling jealousy problem differently, there are often enough people around so that the first child does not suffer much loss of attention.

When the infant reaches his first birthday, a feast is given to confirm ritualistically his survival of the difficult first year. In some instances naming the baby is withheld until this occasion for superstitious fear of premature death.

Adoption is a common practice, especially if one family has an abundance of children and another has few. It is not necessary that a very close relative adopt a child, but the person should be in the same clan. Usually a woman will adopt a girl and a man a boy. One cannot reclaim a child unless he is mistreated and runs home. One must pay to take an older child back if he has not run away, since it is considered that repayment must be made for the time and effort put into rearing the child. Sometimes there are arguments between families if the real parents do not like the way that their child is being reared, but for the most part adoption seems to go smoothly for all concerned.

When the child begins to crawl, he typically becomes the ward of the eldest daughter and is carried almost continually. Thus the dual functions of child care and training for motherhood are combined. When the child begins to walk, he takes his place in the extended family "pecking order" of playmates, and childhood officially commences.

Childhood
A child is encouraged to start helping with the family chores as soon as he is able to walk. Beginning with the task of fetching for the mother, the child

will later carry water, sweep, gather firewood, and care for younger siblings. He is rarely forced into more complicated work, but he is encouraged to watch. The Ponapeans closely observe their children's behavior, and if one seems interested in a particular skill, his curiosity is quickly fed. The initial interest, however, comes from the child.

During this period the play group becomes the primary educational institution for the child. Through various forms of play the children mimic adult behavior, strengthen their muscles, stimulate their intellect, and develop their power of observation, imagination, and imitation. It is common to see children constructing and sailing miniature boats, spearing fish, sling-shooting fowl, and imitating dances and songs they have seen their parents perform on festive occasions. It is quite evident that this play is a direct practice of adult roles. The play group is sexually mixed and structured along a hierarchical order determined by age, with all members usually coming from the same extended family or clan. The group is marked by a great deal of freedom from parental involvement as the members of the group guide, reprove, and cultivate each other's behavior. It is here that the foundation for shame as the mechanism for social control and the adult character trait of extreme social sensitivity are firmly inculcated. At this stage also the respect and security of rank and place in the social order are first incurred.

During this period, too, the fundamental rule of all Ponapean education is laid down: All learning and teaching transpires in real life situations. There is no sharp cleavage between the life space of the child, his physical environment, and the adult world. Children are not isolated from parents in separate physical structures or caste-like categories. All take active part in family life, religious rites, and economic processes. One observes and participates when ready. The readiness is intrinsically determined by the individual and encouraged with expectations of success by significant others in the form of adults and peers. Moments of instruction are not segregated from moments of action. Learning occurs through self-initiated activity in which individuals are in total sensory involvement with their environment.[8] Ponapean indigenous education is not just a listening process where the burden rests upon the teacher, but is a full educational experience with the learner actively seeking what he needs to know. Securing and developing keen perceptive powers are firmly grounded in Ponapean cosmology. They approach the world in a balanced sensate manner. They are "wholistic" and "relational" rather than "analytical" in their world view.

All education is in response to social demands. Knowledge is sought where it is thought to be meaningful and a useful guide to one's survival. The basic principles of Ponapean indigenous education are deeply rooted in the experiences of childhood. The identification with and mimicry of adult roles become a lucid learning process sanctioned and guided by the group in the context of daily living.

Youth
At about age ten the child becomes more active in the economic life of the family. The boys take on such responsibilities as gathering and cutting

firewood and feeding the pigs, while the girls wash, cook, and care for the younger children. The earlier indulgence pattern and the unrestrained freedom of childhood now fade into the constraints and responsibilities of family cooperation. All skills are learned by working side-by-side with the elders. The prolonged observation and practice of childhood begin to get their full test as learning proceeds through private trial to public performance. A youth will humbly refuse to attempt a task unless he is sure that he can perform it correctly and thus avoid public embarrassment. Identification, prolonged observation, and confident participation become the fundamentals of learning. The entire extended family interacts as both teachers and learners. Siblings, parents, uncles, and aunts all become crucial educators in the Ponapean lineage network. Community education and apprenticeship work hand and hand as the growing youth who wishes to acquire a particular skill attaches himself to a clan member who possesses the skill he desires.

Knowledge and skills common to daily survival (*tiak en sop*) are free for the observation, but matters dealing with magic, medicine (*winani*), ritual, and legend (*loquia puta put*) are much more difficult to acquire. It is believed that these areas are highly sacred and are to be passed on to select individuals within a specific clan. Different clans control different areas of knowledge which are often testimony to the clan's status. Elders who control a specific area of knowledge within the clan release it gradually over time. It is common practice not to reveal all one knows until death is near. If knowledge is divulged earlier, it is believed that certainly status, and possibly life itself, will begin to fade. Individuals are usually selected to receive certain areas of knowledge with their temperment in mind. For example, magic and medicine are typically taught to the child who exhibits the most even disposition and silent tongue, so that he can be trusted not to divulge or misuse the secrets. These secrets are not entrusted to the individual until he is well past the age of twenty, and even then they are given piecemeal until his teacher's dying moments.

Legend and ritual are frequently taught in the same manner. But one may also obtain this knowledge by close observation at feasts, through song and dance, and around the kava stone. One Ponapean made the analogy between his learning of certain legends and the putting together of a jigsaw puzzle. "First I would spend much time with different elders listening to their tales, but one has to be cautious since it is our custom not to tell all or at least not to tell it truthfully. Then I would have to compare the different versions of the legend given to me and piece them together to arrive at the real version." It is further contended that such sacred knowledge may be transmitted through dreams and spiritual inspiration. Occasionally this knowledge is traded, sold, or given as a marital dowry.

Attitudes, values, and beliefs are often implicitly transmitted through Ponapean sayings and proverbs. Such maxims as "The quietness of a man is like the fierceness of a barracuda" convey moral lessons and social attitudes.

Other advanced technical skills, such as the intricate tying of the feast house poles, the building of a canoe, and the planting of yams, are also highly guarded and diligently transmitted. These skills, like all other knowledge, are kept in the clan for status purposes and are usually imparted within the clan according to individual interest and dexterity. If a child shows interest in canoe construction, he will be singled out to learn that particular skill. Each child will be given at least one skill, although many will acquire several in varying degrees of mastery.

Another matter of considerable importance that is taught both directly and indirectly during this period is "right relations" or interpersonal gestures of respectful behavior. This lesson is usually demonstrated in the home and at the feast house, where parents will point out to the child the behavior which should be accorded certain titles of rank such as the Nahnmwarki. The child is also taught the high language (*maing*) to be employed when addressing nobility and the polite language forms for addressing elders. He learns not to touch those above him, especially the head of an elder, to speak softly, and to stand below people of rank when addressing them.

The feast is the one comprehensive educational experience continually repeated before the eyes of the entire community, for here rituals are performed, songs are sung, dances transpire, legends are told around the kava stone, and special foods are prepared, all in an atmosphere imbued with the acknowledgement of rank, status, and prestige. In this context, the inculcation of skills, moral teachings, and attitudes of respect culminate to reinforce ritualistically the social solidarity of the group. The traditional feast can be somewhat envisioned as the nearest functional analogy to the modern day formal school in its emphasis on instruction, indoctrination, and social selection.

Mechanisms of Social Control

Need dispositions or motivational tendencies within a culture are often both a creation and a creator of the value patterns of the controlling social structure under endemic environmental conditions, with the control being maintained through a system of rewards and punishments.

The dominant forces of behavioral control at work in Ponapean society can be categorized as: intrinsic situational mechanisms; threats and corporal punishment; supernatural sanctions; ridicule and shaming; praise and prestige; and material reward.

Both Spiro[9] and Lee[10] have elaborated on the notion of intrinsic motivation which applies in describing motivational tendencies among the Ponapeans. The unity of social sphere between adults and children, the immediate utilization of acquired knowledge, the reality and meaningfulness of the learning situation (in terms of survival), and the near "total expectation" that the individual is willing and capable of cultural acquisition serve as internalized incentives to self-actualization and the realization of social norms. Ponapean children deeply desire adult status and are constantly reminded of their proximity to that state. One continually hears such phrases as *"Ke sohte cock wia ohl en Ponpei,"* or "Can't you do it like a Ponapean *man*?" One informant told how his father took him to work on a canoe when he was a small boy. When he exhibited the slightest interest, his father quickly placed a small adze in his hand and told him to work on a section. He claims this early granting of responsibility and verbal support gave him a strong feeling of personal worth and intrinsic motivation. He went on to recall that after that occasion he frequently pleaded with his father to allow him to work on the canoe.

Fear of the spiritual world is utilized to control behavior from early childhood onward. Little children are often disciplined with the threat that a spirit will harm them. Later in life these same adults exhibit a tremendous fear of "*riyala*" of spiritual curse.

Although parents are generally permissive during early childhood, they enforce strict discipline (*kakos*) from about age ten. Threats of loss of inheritance and shame are preferred techniques of controlling adolescents, but corporal punishment is not precluded. If the child is small enough, a mother will often project the threat of physical retaliation onto a stranger or an ominous animal. This gesture serves to place the discipline outside the nuclear family and to preserve the affective harmony of the parent-child relationship. This also explains why the avuncular role is frequently one of disciplinarian in the extended family.

Ridicule and shame are probably the most typical forms of control in Ponapean society. Children are especially quick to point out shortcomings or public blunders in the most explicit terms, while elders are more apt to utilize humor and more subtle nonverbal forms of ridicule and shame. In general, as one enters adolescence, public abuse is withheld in favor of the defensive posture of mutual respect behavior. It then becomes a social taboo to shame openly or to be shamed.

The other side of ridicule and shame, praise and prestige, are equally effective in the control of behavior. The bestowal of titles under the "prestige economy" provides the Nahnmwarki an important motivating and control-ling device. Individual praise for acts of bravery, generosity, and skill are common reinforcements. Although it is accepted practice to deny obsequi-ously all public praise, this behavior sometimes makes the praise seem even more outstanding. An American teacher in the community college related an experience that she had with this cultural trait. When she began teaching, she publicly praised one of the students, and he denied the praise. She continued to praise him lavishly as he profusely continued to deprecate his abilities. Finally, she stopped, realizing that she was being led by his self-denial to honor him far beyond initial intent.

As in every known society, some form of material benefit accrues to certain behaviors. In Ponape, a highly titled person will receive a larger portion of food in the distribution at the feast, although traditionally he is also expected to contribute generously. Land inheritance and marital dowry are common entities used as a means of control. And finally, knowledge, which indirectly relates to material gain and social status (payment for practicing magic or medicine or renown for knowing legends or certain skills or rituals like the proper butchering of a dog), is a central avenue of social recognition and control among the Ponapeans.[11]

All mechanisms of social control are related to and supportive of the ongoing social structure of Ponapean society. This society is centered in the institution of the matrilineal clan and actualized through the practice of competitive feasting.

In essence, the indigenous Ponapean educator plays upon the student's curiosity, wonder, fear of the unkown, respect for elders, pride, desire for acceptance, powers of self-restraint, rivalry, and covert competition in the control and molding of the cultural character.

Thought Processes and Methods of Persuasion

The Ponapean tends to make mental associations which are concrete and immediate rather than abstract and defined in terms of multiple causation. He learns by listening, watching, or doing, not by reading. He stores no knowledge in symbols remote from contemporary application. His educational emphasis is placed on a specific act of behavior in a concrete situation. Connections are more of significance and finality than causal in nature. Classification, experimentation, and abstraction may occur for practical knowledge (i.e., totemic classification), not as an end in itself.

In a sense, the Ponapean has internalized nature's values and norms. The structural aspect of his life remains permanent and undisturbed, while the functions or events are merely reconstructed to meet predetermined ends. There is no reflective choice, only spontaneous, uncritical, and immediate action. It is a matter of the sacred over the secular, or, as Piaget labelled it, "egocentric logic" in which an intuitive jump is made from premise to conclusion in a "wholistic" leap of faith supported by personal and visual schemas of analogy and socially determined values.[12] Thus in the forming of their opinions, emotional response takes the place of logical demonstration. Fixed values and limited needs (as governed by the ascriptive social structure) ascertain the meaning and arrangement of perceptions into streams of thought, while the phenomenon of perception itself is one of total sensory involvement in a restricted physical environment.

It is important to note certain related themes in the indigenous educational process. First, select knowledge is hierarchically aligned with age and status and is passed down in an authoritarian manner. There is little personal initiative in the learning process for acquiring highly specialized knowledge, such as magic and medicine, which differs from more general knowledge related to daily survival. The Ponapean mode of transmission, surrounded by a deeply internalized respect for the wisdom of the aged, favors rote memorization and direct imitation over free thought and creative initiative. It must also be remembered that imitation is a unique learning skill that is itself unconsciously learned through constant repetition. In short, when discussing the educational process, one has to consider not only the content to be learned but also the structure of the learning environment and the structure of the learning style itself.

In Ponapean culture the question "why" is rarely directed in pursuit of causal explanation. Not only is causation assumed to be self-evident in the concrete nature of the learning context, but this question would also be viewed as an affront to the Ponapean norms of respect behavior, thus a culturally antisocial response. One story of an American science teacher's efforts to teach multiple causation goes as follows:

> One day I decided to dramatically illustrate to a science class *why* it rained. I proceeded to set up a terrarium and to demonstrate the water cycle as I had so successfully done on numerous occasions in the States. I carried through the experiment explaining and showing the causes of rainfall while the whole class sat in utter boredom. When the class ended I asked the Ponapean teacher what I had done wrong. At first he made excuses such as the 'class is tired, it is the end of the week,' so as not to embarrass me. I persisted and finally he quixotically responded, 'You know that it rains, I know that it rains, don't you think the class knows that it rains?' . . . I departed in silence.[13]

It seems as if they perceive secondary analysis as a useless expenditure of energy. The knowledge that it rains is sufficient, why know more?

It is frequently implied that preindustrial peoples, such as the Ponapeans, do not have the capacity for the scientific method and processes of reflection and abstraction. Paul Radin,[14] Levi-Strauss,[15] and other eminent scholars have presented sufficient evidence to the contrary. They demonstrate the existence of highly scientific modes of inquiry and thought among so-called primitive peoples. But as Dewey has pointed out, "Environmental deprivation as experienced in the limited physical mobility of isolated primitive tribes has not been conducive to innovative utilization of the scientific method in reshaping the environment."[16] This is surely one explanation for the Ponapean disregard for in-depth analysis. Moreover, the fragmental nature of secondary analysis is not in line with the traditional relational, wholistic Ponapean world view alluded to earlier.

It is also possible that the authoritarian nature of the Ponapean social structure which stresses interpersonal dependence and exhibits a lack of opportunities for decision-making in the formative years could contribute greatly to this form of cognitive development. In his study of indigenous education among the Pueblo Indians of the Southwest, F. C. Spencer observed a similar developmental phenomena and referred to the overall education process of the Pueblo as one of "arrested development."[17]

The road to becoming a Ponapean adult is long and arduous, and one's control over one's life remains rather minimal as long as one's parents are living. Freedom of physical movement is great. Freedom of mental diversion is heresy.

The methods of persuasion common to Ponapean social interaction are quite supportive of the above mental processes. There is the deference to age-related position or rank. One's position in the social hierarchy can be employed to command direct obedience, as personal power by age and title is legitimized throughout the entire social structure. To deny a social superior this mental deference is to cast doubt upon the social order itself. Secondly, there is the accepted proverb or "cultural truism," which timely expressed will often win an argument. Again, this is illustrative of the submission of individual logic to historically accepted statement as passed down for generations. To question the idiom is to confront the collective consciousness. Finally, there is the subtle process of indirect logic, whereby one plays upon the pride, shame, or public consciousness of the other to convince him of a certain point. When a favor is requested, for instance the emotive reasons are always given first, until the request, though still unverbalized, becomes evident. This is quite different from the Western style of first presenting the fact or question and then straining for reasons to support it. A good example of this custom was observed one afternoon when one Poлapean male approached another to borrow his canoe. There was no direct request. The borrower initially commented on how he had to go to town to buy milk for his child. Then he mentioned how hard it rained the previous night and how muddy the paths were. Finally, the owner of the canoe submitted (in my presence) that he take his canoe. The first response was clever hesitation, "Your canoe is most worthy, but I really can't . . ." This, of course, brought on insistence by the canoe owner, "You must!" Finally the borrower succumbed, "if you insist." The ritual was complete.

Having examined some of the more prominent aspects of informal education among the Ponapeans, we must now turn our attention to the all-important question of "Education for What?"

Education For Permanence

Ponapean education is essentially social in character. Although it may tend to such activities as skill training and mental discipline, its primary purpose is the enhancement of social solidarity—the preservation and transmission of the culture as it exists. In its aims Ponapean education is distinctly unprogressive, serving to perpetuate existing conditions (continuity) rather than to induce an element of unrest and chance (discontinuity). This is not to denigrate all aspects of Ponapean indigenous education, such as the interrelating of thought, act, and function; the stress of learning through participation in real life experiences; and the employment of intrinsic motivation inherent in the joy and meaningfulness of a learning activity and other such facets described in the preceding pages. It would be difficult to deny that modern progressive educators have more often than not looked to the origins of man for some of their more "progressive" concepts.

The major task of Ponapean indigenous education is the inculcation of the values of the group and the perpetuation of those group values through the linkage of past tradition with present action and future generations. Human and material innovations are more likely to be adapted to the social structure, rather than the social structure being adapted to them.

Ponapean indigenous education is tradition bound, conservative, and authoritarian in nature. It educates to reproduce itself. Lineage becomes not only a biological construct but also an important educational concept inasmuch as the family is the central educational institution. Education is consensus rather than conflict oriented. Social harmony and cultural continuity become the overriding themes.

The Ponapean accepts his needs as fixed and predetermined by a social structure which incorporates both spiritual and natural orders. He maintains an aesthetically balanced sensory perception on reality, virtually unmarred by the filtering mechanisms of a highly technological society. His experiences and meanings are affectively (as opposed to cognitively) biased by a clear perception and unquestioning acceptance of socially defined reality. Complex choice and decision-making are not a conditioned part of his mind. Cognition (discrimination and generalization) does not occur as a matter of free will (independent decision among multiple alternatives), but as an act of social conformity. He sustains a tolerant perception on reality without judgment. There is little individual selective perception of reality, nor is there abstract discrimination and deduction about perceptions. One's life chances are predetermined. There is little risk-taking, control of natural events, or notion of discontinuity. There is no concept of directed change. Immutability is not only a trait, but a goal of Ponapean society and informal education.

Today this highly functional, informal education process is experiencing the greatest challenge to its survival, the American formal school. Inherent in this challenge is a threat to the very existence of Ponapean traditional culture. The future looms large for the disjunction between informal and formal learning on Ponape, but the fact remains—education need not transpire in the sole context of schools!

NOTES

1. This article is derived from data collected in a larger study conducted by the author on the role of education in cultural character change among the Ponapeans. The study was funded by the Ford Foundation and would have been impossible without their generous assistance.

2. L. Mason, "The Ethnology of Micronesia," in Andrew P. Vayda, ed. *People and Cultures of the Pacific: An Anthropological Reader.* Garden City, N.Y.: Natural History Press, 1967.

3. Robert Redfield, "Education in a Western Guatemalan Highland Village," *American Journal of Sociology,* Vol. 48, 1943.

4. Melville Herskovits. *Man and His Works.* New York, N.Y.: Alfred A. Knopf, 1956.

5. Edwin H. Smith, "Indigenous Education in Africa," in E. E. Evans-Pritchard et al., eds. *Essays Presented to C. G. Seligman.* London: K. Paul, French, Trubner, 1934, pp. 319–340.

6. M. E. Spiro, "Education in a Collective Settlement in Israel," *American Journal of Orthopsychiatry,* Vol. 25, 1955, p. 290.

7. Eric Erikson. *Childhood and Society.* New York, N.Y.: W. W. Norton, 1950.

8. For a more detailed epistemological investigation into the notion of sensory relation to one's environment, see any of Marshall McLuhan's major works.

9. M. E. Spiro, "Social Systems, Personality, and Functional Analysis," in Bert Kaplan, ed. *Studying Personality Cross-Culturally.* New York. N.Y.: Harper & Row, 1961, pp. 93–127.

10. Dorothy Lee, "Autonomous Motivation," in Frederick Gruber, ed. *Anthropology and Education.* Philadelphia, Pa.: University of Pennsylvania Press, 1961, pp. 1903–2021.

11. Knowledge is highly regarded in such a communal society where limited material entities are shared by most people thus diminishing the ultimate worth of material goods. But with the greater influx of material goods on Ponape, coupled with new types of knowledge, this phenomenon is gradually changing. Communal practices are falling prey to capitalistic laws of supply and demand, and open competition is replacing atavistic forms of cooperation and covert competition.

12. Jean Piaget. *Language and Thought of the Child.* New York, N.Y.: Harcourt, Brace and Co., 1932.

13. Quoted from an interview, Kolonia, Ponape 1971.

14. Paul Radin, *The Primitive Man as Philosopher.* New York, N.Y.: D. Appleton and Co., 1927.

15. C. Levi-Strauss. *The Savage Mind.* Chicago, Ill.: University of Chicago Press, 1970.

16. John Dewey, *Democracy and Education.* London, England: The Free Press, 1916.

17. F. C. Spencer, "Education Among the Pueblo Indians: A Study in Arrested Development," in Irving King, ed. *Social Aspects of Education.* New York, N.Y.: Macmillan, 1914.

Education in the Soviet Union

BRIAN HOLMES

. . .

HISTORY

Beginnings

It would be a mistake to accept uncritically that the present system of education in the Soviet Union has its origin in the Revolution of 1917. Much of what goes on today in Soviet schools resembles practices in Western European schools. Nicholas Hans[1] notes that on the eve of the Revolution the Russian tradition in education included an emphasis on social rather than child-centered aims. It was secular rather than dominated by the Church. Curricula were scientific-utilitarian in character, and humanism influenced the tone of education. Productive work was regarded as part of general education, and the notion of Russian nationalism found a place. Many of these features of a tradition molded by Peter the Great, Catherine II, and Alexander I show the influence of the French encyclopedists and physiocrats of the eighteenth century.

Hans regards Peter the Great as the founder of the Russian educational tradition. On his return from England in 1700 Peter founded a modern school of mathematics and navigation in Moscow along the lines of the mathematical school of Christ's Hospital in England. In taking this as his model for his reform, Peter consciously introduced scientific-utilitarian characteristics and weakened the classical tradition. Later Catherine II, drawing heavily on French ideas, accepted the Austrian school system as a model for the new system she hoped to introduce in Russia. It, too, was scientific-utilitarian, secular, and coeducational.

There can be little doubt that of the Western European influences in the Soviet system of schooling those derived from France and French encyclopedism are the most obvious. The break with classicism made it relatively easier for Russian and Soviet educationists to establish curricula in which more attention was paid to mathematics and the natural sciences than to literary subjects. And among the latter, modern foreign languages rather than "classical" foreign languages receive the most attention. Doubtless the war against Napoleon influenced Russian opinion, and while the reforms of Alexander I (who ascended the throne in 1801) owed much to French ideas, subsequently the movement to resist foreign innovations and emphasize Russian traditions grew stronger. Insofar as education retained a strong Western orientation, it was limited to that received by the upper and middle classes. . . .

The Revolution is taken as the start of a new era. Its purpose was first to remove the inequalities of a previous regime and thus establish a foundation on which the achievements of culture, science, and art could be made accessible to all men and women whether they were manual workers or professional people. Czarist policies had created great inequalities. The situation inherited by the Soviet government was particularly bad in the hinterlands where national minorities were not allowed to have their children taught in their native language. Among the 100 nationalities the Russians constitute more than half the total population of the Soviet Union. The Ukrainians come next. In czarist days forty-eight nationalities had no written language of their own. Workers of non-Russian origin were almost totally illiterate. Soviet policy[2] was designed to equalize provision by creating written languages (over forty nationalities have done so).

Faced with this situation, the Communists set out after the Revolution to destroy the ideology of bourgeois schools and to build a Communist society with the help of the schools. These were to help mold the character of individuals to create a generation of new Soviet men and women. High levels of general and specialized training were to develop the spiritual potential, the political maturity, the ideological-moral, and general culture of all young people. In addition schools were to train them to work in productive industry. Thus explicit in the aims of Soviet education from the start was the notion of all-round development and all-round training of individuals.[3] . . .

Current Status

. . . Equality and brotherhood rather than liberty dominate the aims of educational provision. Consequently in practice Soviet educationists make every attempt to create a unified system of schooling throughout the whole country. This means for them a unified curriculum, the same syllabus and textbooks for each subject, the same methods of teaching, and the same examinations. It also means that salary schedules and per capita expenditures should be the same throughout the country. Uniformity is an objective; equality the aim. They justify a measure of centralized control that would be unacceptable in countries where liberty is stressed at the expense of equality.

Belief in a unified system of schooling is not simply a matter of political philosophy. In the Soviet Union it receives psychological and epistemological justification. According to Soviet educationists the use of IQ tests is suspect. They are neither objective nor scientific and should be administered only to diagnose brain damage and other defects. The physiological basis of Soviet educational psychology is derived from the work of I. P. Pavlov. Insofar as it is behavioristic, it provides support for the environmentalists. Given the same conditions, the argument might run, individuals will reach the same level of achievement. Serious failure is due to physiological causes. Given this kind of commitment, it is not surprising that Soviet educational psychologists can dismiss the value of Freudian and Piagetian[4] theories while looking with more favor on the theories of B. F. Skinner and R. G. Crowder. It also explains some of the conclusions reached when proposals were made to reduce primary schooling from four to three years. These conclusions were that far more children than had been previously thought possible are capable of learning abstract principles and deducing from them a wide range of detailed information. Uniformity of provision can be justified on psychological grounds.

It is also possible to do so by reference to a theory of knowledge that asserts that using the methods of scientific inquiry, absolute and entirely objective knowledge can be acquired. In this theoretical framework what is taught and how it is taught are not and should not be matters of subjective opinion but the outcome of scientific investigation. Subjectivism has no place in the preparation of syllabuses, textbooks, and manuals about teaching methods. When describing their research, Soviet educationists seem to call more heavily on documentary material than on empirical evidence. . . .

APPLICATIONS

Curriculum, Academic
. . . In general, curricula are the same throughout the country and are encyclopedic at all three levels or stages—primary, secondary, and tertiary. In the first three grades emphasis is placed on the native tongue and mathematics but a range of other subjects is prescribed. They include history, geography, and the natural sciences. For selected pupils, a modern foreign language is introduced in the second grade. The most popular foreign language is English, but French and German can be studied.

At the next stage, from the fourth through the eighth grade, curricula in the schools of the fifteen autonomous republics are by intention the same, although each republic has the power to adapt the content of schooling to meet its own needs. This finds most obvious expression in the medium of instruction. In Latvia, for example, Latvian is the medium of instruction for those children whose parents choose to send them to these rather than to Russian-language schools. A similar choice is open to parents living in other non-Russian-speaking republics.

It should be noted that while a majority of Soviet citizens (about 60 percent) speak Russian as their native tongue, more than 100 languages and dialects are spoken throughout the vast nation of 250 million inhabitants. These languages differ, of course. Some are major languages spoken by many people, are written, and have a considerable literature. Others do not satisfy these criteria. The languages spoken by nomadic tribes in the far north of the Soviet Union are in the process of being written and have no literature. The freedom given to pupils to learn through the medium of their own native tongue introduces considerable variety into the system as a whole.

Nevertheless, in schools throughout the Soviet Union all pupils must study the same subjects. Their own language, if not Russian, a modern foreign language from the fifth grade on, mathematics, physics, chemistry, biology, history, and geography constitute the core of a common nationwide curriculum. Additional subjects vary somewhat in the different grades, but in general the balance is in favor of mathematics and the physical and biological sciences. In the early 1960s major studies were carried out by members of the Academy of Pedagogical Sciences[5] with the intention of improving the curriculum. In scope, however, it remains much as before, but a considerable amount of new knowledge and concepts have been included in the syllabi of the subjects.

Textbooks, whether in Russian or other languages, are the same everywhere, and interpretations of content in the exact sciences are the same. Language teachers within a prescribed framework may introduce illustrative material of their own choice. In history, textbooks and teachers consistently offer a materialistic interpretation. Similar, authorized interpretations of biological phenomena are commonly taught. All such interpretations are regarded as "scientific" and therefore not open to serious reconsideration.

The accumulation of "scientific" knowledge in recent decades has made it difficult to include everything in a curriculum offered to and followed by all pupils. In the seventh grade "options" were recently introduced so that some pupils at least could add to their basic knowledge of some subjects by taking courses based on up-to-date information and new concepts. The number of such optional courses in the seventh and eighth grades is strictly limited, for these two grades complete the period of compulsory schooling.

The ninth and tenth grades (and in non-Russian-speaking republics the eleventh grade as well) constitute what is called "complete secondary education." In these grades options are offered, and pupils can specialize to some extent before going on to tertiary education. These options are designed to provide potential scientists, linguists, or social scientists with up-to-date knowledge relevant to the major courses they propose to study later.

Other pupils at this stage may be offered additional courses in the "basic" subjects, for example Russian and mathematics. These options are intended not so much for potential university and institute students but for pupils who are not expected to do more than complete a secondary school course successfully. This kind of differentiation in terms of the curriculum implies that some pupils are not as capable as others of covering a common range of subjects in the same time and of reaching the same level of achievement. It also suggests that high achievers can benefit from specialized additional knowledge before they go on to a university or institute.

Such differentiation of content is not representative.[6] For the most part, all ninth and tenth grade pupils take the same subjects, and these as before include mathematics, language, the natural sciences, and the social sciences. In addition, pupils are introduced to dialectical materialism as a basic philosophical component, which is also included in the content of courses in institutions of higher education. . . .

Student Evaluation[7]

. . . Of the relatively few universities Moscow and Leningrad enjoy the highest prestige and select from a large number of applicants the few who can be accepted. These universities, like other similar institutions, have their own entrance examinations. In the case of Leningrad University special boarding schools help children from rural areas, where the quality of teaching may be lower than in the cities, to prepare for the university's entrance examinations. During the five-year university course leading to a diploma students tend, within a faculty system, to concentrate attention on a limited number of subjects but some general subjects are compulsory in laid-down curricula. As part of their specialist studies students are instructed in methods of teaching. In lecture seminars, for example, at the University of Moscow, students of English study aspects of the language as well as ways of teaching them. A feature of the system ensures that young people who are not able to gain admission to full-time courses can complete higher education part-time. Institutes of higher education, universities, polytechnics, and pedagogical institutes provide part-time evening courses for working people.[8] Frequently full-time *Komsomol* students help run these courses, which lead to comparable awards to those obtained by full-time students. Correspondence courses also make it possible for working people outside the major cities to return to a sequence of studies that may have been interrupted. Faculty members in city institutes participate in these correspondence courses by visiting centers in provincial capitals and other parts of the country. Correspondence students are encouraged to visit the major institutions in order to follow short courses regularly. . . .

ROLES

Administration

Since 1966 there has been an all-Union Ministry of Education, responsible for preschool, primary, and general secondary schools. The all-Union Ministry of Higher and Specialized Secondary Education has a longer history. It is responsible for universities, polytechnics, pedagogical institutes, and technical schools. The Ministry of Health, however, looks after medical institutions. The Ministry of Agriculture and the Ministry of Communications are responsible for educational facilities in their respective spheres. The Ministry of

Culture has under its general supervision conservatories, art schools, theatrical and cinema institutes, and so on. The State Committee for Vocational Training is in charge of training skilled workers in a network of vocational schools. Responsibility for education and training is thus shared by a number of all-union ministries.

There are fifteen union republics each with its own constitution and a ministry of education, which is subordinate to the Ministry of Education of the Soviet Union. Autonomous republics are constituent parts of the union republics and have their own ministries of education. In addition, regions, territories, areas, cities, and districts complete a complex pattern of administrative control. The principle of democratic centralism, however, ensures that each executive body is responsible to a local Soviet (committee) of Working People's Deputies. These committees and bodies are linked in a hierarchy that ensures that educational problems are tackled on a national level and local needs are met. The authorities take pride in the fact that the Ministry of Education of the Soviet Union is responsible for ensuring equality of provision throughout the country.

Major principles of policy were laid down in the Fundamental Legislation of the Soviet Union and the Union Republics on Public Education adopted in 1973. Apart from the provisions made in the Constitution, the legislation[9] is designed to ensure that there is a unified system of schooling through which all pupils can pass smoothly from the lower to the higher stages. To guarantee this curricula, syllabuses, and textbooks (even in the different languages) are the same. Education is secular and schools are coeducational. The role of the Communist party in the formulation of policy is crucial. . . .

SYSTEM IN ACTION

In general schools serve a particular neighborhood. Preschool institutions are organized by the department of public education, factories and other industrial enterprises, local government bodies, and collective farms. Kindergartens are frequently situated so as to serve families living in adjacent apartment blocks. Great attention is paid to the physical well-being and early socialization of the young children. Many of them learn to read and write, however, and are frequently more advanced socially and educationally when they enter the first grade than children who are starting school for the first time.

Almost 11 million children attend nursery school and kindergartens.[10] Since 1920 when 250,000 children were in crèches or attending kindergartens and playgrounds, numbers have risen enormously, and particularly since 1961 when 3 million children were enrolled. This growth reflects the high proportion—about 50 percent of the work force—of women who work in industry, commerce, and the professions, and the speed with which young couples are being rehoused so that grandmama is no longer with them and able to look after the children while their parents are at work.

Nursery schools and kindergartens are usually fairly small, often taking care of less than 300 children from the immediate neighborhood. They are often surrounded by a square of apartment blocks. This arrangement frequently means that the parents of most of the pupils work at the same local factory which may, in fact, help to support the school by buying extras for it. Parents pay a small amount per month but it is not intended to meet more than a tiny proportion (about one fifth of the total cost of caring for and feeding their children while they are at work).

To meet the needs of parents, nursery schools and kindergartens may open at 7 o'clock in the morning. Staff may be on duty until 8 o'clock at night. In some cases, two groups of teachers work in two six-hour shifts with children split into groups of twenty in the nursery class up to three years of age and into classes of twenty-five for children between the ages of four and seven. Some children may live at a kindergarten for five days of the week, returning home at week-ends. Most are picked up between 5 and 6 o'clock by one of their parents after work.

Daily routines are designed to prepare a child for school. They include short lessons in reading, writing and speech, counting, music, craftwork, poetry, and physical education. The number of lessons per week increases as the children grow older. Each day, however, they are given substantial and well-balanced meals. They walk and play when possible in the open air and sleep in dormitories after their mid-day meal. They are trained to look after themselves and to mix with other children. Medical doctors visit regularly, and trained nurses are in permanent attendance. Children are checked for complaints like tuberculosis. Great attention is given to the health of these young children, and their diet, sequence of injections, and general progress are recorded. Delicate and otherwise handicapped children may be sent to special kindergartens. There special facilities are available, but the aim is to prepare children to take their place eventually in a regular school. . . .

Surveys have shown, and indeed the assessments of first grade teachers confirm, that nursery school children are on average better developed mentally and physically than those who have been kept at home—some justification of the Zankov theory. They are more sociable and more easily able to concentrate on schoolwork. Among nursery school children entering first grade, a higher proportion than among those who have not attended preschool institutions had had defects of speech, hearing, and physical movement corrected. Intellectually they are able to apply their knowledge to new situations more quickly than the others.

All children, unless they are very seriously handicapped, must attend school when they reach the age of seven. The majority go to regular neighborhood schools and remain there for at least eight years of compulsory schooling or for ten years, enabling them to complete secondary education. This period is extended to eleven years in the non-Russian-speaking union republics. Primary schooling now lasts for three years instead of, as before, for four years. During this period children stay with the same teacher who is also responsible for all their lessons. After the third grade pupils are taught by specialist subject teachers and move from one classroom to another.

September 1 is a very special day.[11] It is the day on which the school year begins. Nearly 50 million Soviet children return to school after the holidays.

Among them are the seven-year-olds who are starting regular school. In the Baltic republics they start at the age of six. Everywhere, however, great efforts are made to make them feel that the first day at school is a happy and important occasion. Boys in white shirts and girls in starched white pinafores carry bunches of flowers as they make their way to school. Older pupils and teachers welcome and look after the beginners. It must be said that this early enthusiasm is sustained throughout their school life. To assume that Lenin's admonition to Young Communists to "study, study, study," explains the obvious enthusiasm for learning is too simple. The rewards for doing well at school are evident in Soviet life. Even so, teachers sometimes complain, as elsewhere, that young people do not work as hard as they used to and are less interested in studying. . . .

In the first four grades pupils have twenty-four lessons per week.[12] In the fifth and sixth grades the number is thirty. In addition, two extracurricular lessons with a choice of subjects are taken in the seventh grade. This number rises to four in the eighth grade and to six in the ninth and tenth grades. The total number of lessons in any subject is calculated on a yearly basis. Over the ten years of schooling mathematics tops the list followed closely by Russian grammar, Russian literature, history, physics, and a modern foreign language come next but occupy less than a third of the time devoted to either mathematics or Russian grammar. Two lessons each week are given over both to physical training and to shop. Some selection of subjects is now possible in and after the seventh grade.

Pupils attend school six days a week. They have five or six lessons a day (a maximum of thirty-six per week) depending on their age and up to three-hours homework a night. Many students remain in school after formal lessons are over in what are termed "prolonged day" school.[13] In 1975 almost one sixth of the total number of schoolchildren were in such groups. Most of them were from one of the first three classes. The growth in these schools has helped to meet the needs of children whose parents work. Lunch is served to these and other pupils during one of the twenty-minute recesses. The three-course hot meal costs parents a very small amount of money. After lunch, children may play in the school yard or a neighboring park and do their lessons or attend hobby circles under the guidance of teachers. They return home at five or six o'clock. . . .

The school year lasts until May 20 or June 1. Midwinter and spring breaks are short, but the summer holidays last for three months. Every summer about 15 million school children go off to Young Pioneer, school, health, or tourist camps. The Young Pioneer Camps accept any child. In their early days they were rather simple affairs. Now a Young Pioneer Camp has all the amenities of a small town, including stadiums, buildings for clubs and hobby circles, and so on as well as dormitories and dining rooms which may accommodate up to 600 persons. Factories and trade unions contribute generously to provide good camps for the children of workers. Children who remain in the towns and cities may attend special camps and may participate in excursions, sports, and organized walks.

Life at a university or pedagogical institute in the Soviet Union is similar in many respects to student life anywhere else. The number of lecture-seminars per week is heavy and prescribed. Classes are usually small, and methods of teaching take into account the maturity and motivation of students. A required course is dialectical materialism. Other required courses ensure that in spite of considerable specialization in a faculty or department the content of higher education is fairly broad. In all institutions and departments great attention is paid to a scientific knowledge of the subject. Rigorous criteria of scholarship are laid down, and students are expected to meet these criteria. In language classes textual analysis is frequently combined with oral practice and references to methods of teaching the material. In physics classes, students work in laboratories performing basic experiments from instructions on worksheets. Teaching is reminiscent of what goes on in universities in England. Students take examinations at the end of each academic year and prepare a dissertation for their diploma, which they receive usually after five years of study. Subsequently some may proceed by thesis to a *kandidat* degree—somewhat comparable to a Ph.D. in England and North America. Without a higher doctorate, an academic cannot become a full professor. Promotion within the academic world is consequently dependent upon scholarship as measured by research and publication.

Students training to be schoolteachers devote a great deal of time acquiring mastery of the subject they are going to teach in middle and complete secondary schools. Less time than some teachers would wish is spent on psychological and foundation studies but during their training, students spend some time in schools on supervised teaching practice. Specially appointed members of the faculty are concerned with methods of teaching and teaching practice. A majority are highly qualified in their subject. This is perhaps less so among faculty members in departments of primary education in which students intending to teach in kindergartens or the first three grades of school are trained. More attention is paid in these departments to psychology and child development, and, of course, the class teacher is responsible for all the subjects taught to children between seven and ten and hence is less of a subject specialist than the secondary school teacher.

Universities are run along traditional lines. The rector as administrative head is elected for a limited period of time from among the professors. He is assisted by deputy rectors with specific responsibilities. The universities' relationships with the All-Union Ministry of Higher Education are laid down in regulations and in practice are conducted in the light of tradition and convention. The fact that a great deal of applied research is carried out in special institutes associated with the university and financed by government industrial contracts makes it possible to draw a distinction between university- and government-sponsored research.

Within the university faculties are organized in departments. The concept of the chair persists. Its holder has associated with him teachers and research workers. As in other European universities the chair is specific to a field of enquiry, and it is the responsibility of the chair to develop his subject as he thinks fit. As mentioned, no professor can occupy a chair without a doctorate. Such academics, of course, dominate the work of a university and enjoy considerable freedom to pursue their research in accordance with their own interests. Some areas of enquiry are obviously more sensitive than others as the Lysenko controversy some twenty years ago demonstrated. Evidently developments in the social sciences and in education are more susceptible to ideological political pressures than is work in the pure and applied natural sciences.

PROSPECT[14]

According to Marxist-Leninist theory the future of education in the Soviet Union will depend on the rate and success of moves to create a truly Communist society. From a Soviet point of view it is necessary to place the achievements made since 1917 in the longer perspective of the historical development of societies.

Thus, the author of "The Communist Party of the Soviet Union" in *Soviet Union*[15] states that the October Revolution and the establishment of Soviet power signified that the first program of the Bolshevik party had been fulfilled, and the second program of the party had been fulfilled when, after the Great Patriotic War (World War II) the economy of the country had been rehabilitated and the victory of socialism assured. In educational terms the achievement of nationwide literacy represented the completion of a major program. The next task of the Communist party was to universalize general secondary and polytechnic education.

The history of this endeavor is frequently told in statistics.[16] The period of compulsory schooling was gradually increased—first in towns and cities, then in the rural areas. Universal eight-year schooling was introduced in 1958. Between 1939 and 1959 the number of people with a secondary education increased 3.7 times. By 1975 the ten-year secondary education was available virtually to everyone. In 1976–1977 there were 159,000 schools including 52,000 ten-year schools attended by 46.5 million pupils. Nearly 5.25 million pupils completed eight years of compulsory schooling in 1976, and of these 97 percent went on in general secondary schools or in other establishments providing secondary education. Plans for 1976–1980 included the provision of general education for some 7 million pupils of whom 4.5 million were known to be in rural areas.

In 1977 the system of vocational training enrolled 3.5 million boys and girls in 6,100 schools. More than 1,000 specialist courses were on offer. Increasingly young people attending these technical vocational schools can complete a general education that will give them access to an institution of higher education. Early in 1977 some 40 percent of those enrolled in day vocational schools were in this position. Urban schools train young people for industry, construction work, and transport, trade and municipal services. Rural schools train tractor drivers and machine operators who will work on the farms. Practical training occupies up to 60 or 70 percent of the total time and is given first in factory or farm schools and then in industrial plants or on farms.

Specialized secondary schools admit young people who have completed either eight years of compulsory schooling or ten years in a general education school. One group of specialized secondary schools trains people for industry, commerce, and agriculture. A second group trains paraprofessional workers such as elementary school teachers, medical staff, musicians, art workers, seamen, and so on. For pupils who have only eight years of schooling, the general education and theoretical and practical training as a specialist lasts three or four years. For pupils who have completed the ten-year school, a course in a specialized secondary school lasts two or three years. These years are largely devoted to practical instruction. Altogether in 1976–1977, there were 4,303 specialized secondary schools enrolling 4.6 million students of whom more than a million were studying by correspondence and another half million were attending evening courses.

Higher education has expanded greatly. In 1976–1977 there were some 859 institutions of higher learning of which 65 were universities. Some 5 million students were enrolled, more than half in day-time courses, 1½ million were studying by correspondence, and the rest were attending evening courses. . . .

NOTES

1. Nicholas Hans, *The Russian Tradition in Education* (London: Routledge and Kegan Paul, 1963); see also by the same author "Recent Trends in Soviet Education," in *the Annals: The Soviet Union since World War II*, American Academy of Political and Social Science, May 1949; also *The Principles of Educational Policy*, 2nd ed. (London: King and Son, 1933).

2. For an analysis of the language situation in the Soviet Union, see M. I. Isayev, *National Languages in the USSR: Problems and Solutions* (Moscow: Progress, 1977). Language has occupied a central place in Soviet Educational policy see for example D. P. Korzh "Public Education in the Far North of the USSR"; A. Rudakov, "Public Education in Komi Autonomous Soviet Socialist Republic"; and S. J. Savvin, "Education in the Yakut Autonomous Soviet Socialist Republic" all in *The Year Book of Education 1954*, ed. R. K. Hall, N. Hans, J. A. Lauwerys (London: Evans, 1954).

3. Medinsky, *Public Education in the USSR:* "The all-round development of the individual, the training of the fully educated, active and conscious builders of a communist society, their education in the spirit of Communist morality—such is the aim pursued by the Soviet school." p. 13; and A. P. Pinkevitch, *The New Education in the Soviet Republic,* trans. Nucia Perlmutter, ed. George Counts (New York: John Day, 1929), pp. 26–28.

4. See A. V. Petrovosky, "Basic Directions in the Development and Current States of Educational Psychology," *Soviet Education*, 15, No. 5–6 (March-April 1973). The whole volume is devoted to Soviet educational psychology and on p. 109 it is stated that Soviet psychologists "refute psycho-analytical theories and theory of inborn quality and came to the conclusion: the mental development of the child, the formation of his cognitive processes, psychological traits, and personality features are determined by education and upbringing, i.e. by the way in which the adult person directs and organizes his assimilation of social experiences." See also S. Vygotsky, *Thought and Language,* trans. and ed. Eugenie Hanfmann and Gertrude Vakar (Cambridge: MIT Press, and New York: Wiley, 1962) in which the author discusses Piaget's work and rejects one important point made by him, pp. 116–117.

5. See A. Markushevich, "The Problems of the Content of School Education in the USSR," in *Curriculum Development at the Second Level of Education*, Ed. Brian Holmes and Raymond Ryba. Proceedings of the Comparative Education Society in Europe, 4th General Meeting (London, 1969).

6. *Public Education in the USSR: in 1975–1976* (Moscow, 1977) makes the intentions for introducing optional courses clear. "One should see the introduction of optional courses in the senior grades. Over 8.5 million students attend such classes at present. More than 80 optional courses have been devised for classes in the Russian (or the respective native) language, and literature, history, social science, mathematics, physics, biology, chemistry, nature protection, labour training, pedagogics, psychology, ethics, aesthetics, and other

subjects. Most of these courses envisage broader and deeper study of individual aspects or of key problems of the subject in question," p. 58.

7. See V. Strezikozin, "The Soviet Union," in *Examinations, World Year Book of Education*, eds. J. A. Lauwerys, and D. Scanlon (London: Evans, 1969), pp. 152–169; also University of London Institute of Education, *Education in the USSR*, 1976, 1977. For some discussion of factors motivating children see L. I. Bozhovich, "The Personality of School Children and Problems of Education," in *A Handbook of Contemporary Soviet Psychology*, ed. M. Cole and I. Haltzman (New York: Basic, 1969), pp. 224–225.

8. "Decree of the USSR, Council of Ministers, on Part-time Education, April 1964," in *Izvestia*, *23 April 1964*.

9. *Fundamentals of Legislation of the USSR and the Union Republics on Public Education* (Moscow: Novosti, 1975).

10. See University of London Institute of Education, *Education in the USSR*, (Annual reports of Comparative Education tours to the USSR, 1960–1979) for detailed impressions of nursery schools and kindergartens; also Ludwig Liegle, *The Family Role in Soviet Education*, trans. Susan Hecker (New York: Springer, 1975), in which it is reported that 80 percent of working women have preschool age children (p. 57); statistics show (1970) that of the 2.6 million children in nursery schools and kindergartens more than half were two years and under.

11. For much of the information in this section (confirmed by personal visits to Soviet schools) see S. Soloveichik, *Soviet Children at School* (Moscow: Novosti, 1976); see also Spartak Gazaryan, *Children in the USSR* (Moscow: Novosti, 1973); and *USSR Education* (Moscow: Novosti, 1976).

12. For details of curricula and lessons per week see *USSR 77*, and *Public Education in the USSR: in 1975–76* (Moscow, 1977), p. 47.

13. See Liegle, *The Family Role in Soviet Education*, p. 90, for an assessment of plans announced at the 23rd Congress of the party in 1966 to double enrollments in prolonged day schools and his view that the boarding school no longer occupies a prominent position in party policy.

14. See *Soviet Union* for an account, based upon reports presented to the 25th Congress of the Communist party, of future developments in the Soviet Union.

15. Apart from the reports presented at the 24th and 25th Congresses of the Communist party some general lines of development may be gained from M. Prokofyev, *Public Education, USSR, Yesterday, Today, Tomorrow* (Moscow: Novosti, n.d.), and A. M. Arsenyev, *The Soviet School of the Present and Future* (Moscow: Pedagogica, 1971); and from the reports sent to the International Bureau of Education for the biennial conferences held in Geneva attended by delegates from ministries of education of member states. See also the whole volume of *Soviet Education* 19 (November 1976), for a review of policies up to 1980.

16. Seymour M. Rosen, *Education in the USSR—Recent Legislation and Statistics*, U.S. Department of Health, Education and Welfare, Washington, 1975; also *Education and Modernization in the USSR* (Reading, Mass.: Addison Wesley, 1971). See also N. DeWitt, *Soviet Professional Manpower: Its Education, Training and Supply* (Washington: National Science Foundation, 1955).

Socialisation for College Entrance Examinations in Japan

NOBUO K. SHIMAHARA

Rutgers University

The Japanese college entrance examinations (hereinafter CEE) are currently one of the most persistent sources of tension in Japanese life. Pressures for shaping the socialisation of adolescents and secondary schools to meet the requirements of the high-school and college entrance examinations have become a common source of chronic anxiety for students and parents, as well as for teachers. This paper, based upon the author's research in Japan during 1976–1977, will discuss the nature of these pressures and why they exist uniquely in Japanese society. Concomitantly, the paper will analyse the effects of CEE upon secondary schooling and the underlying social and cultural orientation of CEE.

SCHOOLING FOR THE COLLEGE ENTRANCE EXAMINATIONS

Post-World War II education in Japan consists of elementary education for six years, secondary education composed of middle- and high-school education for three years, and college education. Only the first nine years of schooling at the elementary and middle levels are compulsory. In 1975, 38.4% of the 1.6 million eligible age-group (those who reached 18 years of age) entered colleges, and the total enrollment of Japanese college students reached a little more than 2.1 million.

From *Comparative Education* 14 (1978): 253–266. Copyright © 1978, by Carfax Publishing Company. Reprinted with the permission of Carfax Publishing Company and the author.

Approximately 800,000 applicants take CEE every spring from late February to March. There is particularly intense competition among the applicants who seek admission to the national universities. Academically able applicants tend to concentrate upon the less-costly national universities, which are generally regarded as more prestigious and better financed than private institutions. Average rates of competition (number of total applicants divided by number of applicants admitted) in different fields at the national institutions in 1974, for example, were as follows: 8.3 in humanities, 6.8 in social sciences, 5.3 in natural sciences and engineering, 11.6 in medicine and dentistry and 4.8 in education (Ministry of Education, 1976).

Among the private institutions a few are outstanding, but the majority rank lower than the national universities. Entrance competition for the private institutions is equally high, however, because each applicant takes examinations at three to four different institutions and sometimes in different fields within the same university.

Despite such competition, only 30% of the applicants were not admitted to the colleges in 1975. The intense competition reflects the comparative rankings of the universities, in that the applicants compete most fiercely for admission to the universities with the highest prestige. The competition is heightened even more because many applicants (nearly 40% in 1974, excluding those for the two-year colleges) are what is called *rōnin* students (the term *rōnin* was formerly used for the lordless *samurai*). They are high-school graduates who devote a year or more at home or at private preparatory schools to prepare exclusively for CEE for particular colleges because of their failure to gain admission in a previous year. The existence of a large number of *rōnin* students is peculiar to Japanese society and suggests that students regard admission to particular colleges as especially crucial. It goes without saying that the pressure of such post-high-school preparation for CEE increases the psychological and financial stress on the youth and their families.

CEE carries the greatest weight in deciding admissions to colleges. It alone determines admissions to the national and other publicly controlled colleges, since such other kinds of relevant information as high-school scholastic records, teachers' recommendations, and aptitude, are little considered although the submission of carefully prepared high-school reports is required. Thus the applicant has no alternative but to concentrate upon preparing for the CEE which takes place only once a year. In addition, during the whole examination period, the applicant is forced to cope with accumulated pressures that culminate in enormous tension during the examination itself. The applicant's tension is heightened because (OECD, 1971, pp. 88–89):

> In the popular mind, universities are ranked in a strict hierarchy of prestige, secondary schools are ranked in terms of the number of students they can place in prestigious institutions, and graduates are judged by many employers and others in terms of the university, and faculty of a university, into which they win admission through the examination system, rather than in terms of what they know and are able to do. Thus there is a general belief that a student's performance

TABLE 1 Japanese Universities and College and Student Enrolment (1975)

	National University and College	Prefectural and City College	Private University and College	2-year College (National, Pref., City, Private)	Technical School (Private and National)	National School for Special Education	Total
Number of Institutions	81	34	305	513	—	—	933
Male	279,881	36,304	1,049,639	48,658	72,219	0	1,461,701
Female	77,891	14,576	275,971	305,124	736	1976	675,194

Source: Japanese Ministry of Education, *The Educational Standard of Our Nation* (*Wagakunino Kyoiku Suijun*) (Tokyo: Okurasho Insatsukyoku, 1976).

in one crucial examination at about the age of 18 is likely to determine the rest of his life. In other words: the university entrance examination is the primary sorting device for careers in Japanese society.

Generally private colleges follow the criteria for admission established by the national and other publicly controlled colleges, although other variables, such as the ability of the applicant's family to contribute financially, sometimes become important factors. The financial contribution is very important in private medical schools.

CEE has a powerful effect upon secondary and even elementary education. The very orientation of secondary education is defined by the pressures of the CEE, which imposes a particular framework upon the socialisation and schooling of adolescents, according to which their cognitive and motivational orientations to schooling are developed. In other words, a majority of adolescents are conditioned to view schooling as truly relevant when it promotes preparation for the CEE, and as only marginally useful when it does not contribute to their ultimate goal—university admission. Obviously adolescents experience a great deal of self-denial and a lack of intrinsic motivation for learning. It is within this framework that most non-vocational high schools, constituting two-thirds of all high schools, serve as preparatory agents for CEE by orientating their entire educational processes toward its demands.

Meanwhile, in the middle schools (12–15 years), education has also become increasingly aimed at preparing for the high-school entrance examinations. A common assumption is that the degree of academic competitiveness at a given high school ultimately determines the rank of the college to which its students can gain entry. This assumption clearly leads to competition for admission to high schools that are highly ranked academically. Therefore most middle schools are invariably orientated toward preparing students to compete successfully for entrance to high schools.

At nearly all high schools (excluding the vocational high schools), teaching methods and curricula are designed largely to meet the requirements for the CEE. Hence they have been turned into cramming systems in one way or another. Many schools, for example, adopt a system whereby text-based teaching in major subjects such as mathematics and English is shortened and completed by the end of the second year or early in the third year in order to devote the remaining time to CEE drilling. Drill books consisting of examination questions given in the past are often used in place of texts. In addition, most students, particularly seniors, are required to take a number of exercise tests, including several tests designed by particular schools expressly for CEE, a half-dozen national mock entrance examinations (usually called *moshi* in Japanese) given by private corporations, and term and mid-term tests. Most of these tests, other than term tests, are taken only to improve the ability of the students to take examinations.

Such examination-centred schooling is often criticised by the Japan Teachers Union (*Nikkyoso*), the largest national teachers' organisation. Union leaders attack the distortion of secondary education at the cost of personal, social and intellectual maturity. Yet, most union teachers not only acquiesce in such schooling, but reinforce it by responding to examination pressures. Underlying such a contradiction is the overwhelming fact that the reputations of schools and teachers are largely determined by their success in preparing students for entrance examinations. Pressures from parents and the general public for drilling students are exerted constantly.

It is also worth noting that numerous private tutoring services, tutoring schools that operate in parallel with the middle and high schools, and college preparatory schools (all of which are generally called *juku*) exist today in order to respond to examination pressures. According to a survey conducted by the Ministry of Education (*Asahi Shinbun*, March 12, 1977), for example, there are nearly 50 000 *juku* in Japan offering services to middle- and elementary-school students. The survey reports that about 27% of all sixth graders and 38% of all middle school students attend *juku*. In the urban areas with a population of more than 100 000, nearly 50% of the middle school students go to *juku*. The increasing demand for *juku* is exhibited by the fact that 60% of them have been established since 1966, although their growth has also been promoted by private educational industries and retired teachers who have capitalised upon the potential demand for preparatory and sometimes compensatory schooling and tutoring. The *juku*, in their turn, further stimulate the competition among students.

Furthermore, a large proportion of high-school students, about the same as for middle-school students, attend *juku* after school and on Sundays to receive examination drilling. The scale of these *juku* varies from mammoth preparatory schools accommodating more than 10 000 to small ones for half a dozen students. Large *juku* have full-time instructors and handsome dormitories for *rōnin* who come from distant towns and cities. Some of them have staffs that conduct nation-wide exercise examinations and also publish drill books.

Following a similar orientation, a number of publishing firms specialise in drill books, magazines, tests and references related to entrance examinations. These published materials occupy probably one-fourth of the bookshelves in a typical Japanese bookstore. Apparently the more these firms can create anxiety on the part of students and their parents the more materials they can sell.

Another effect of CEE is the formation of a hierarchy of *high schools*. As alluded to above, the number of students that high schools are able to place in universities with good reputations determines the high school's rank. Hence, high-ranking schools are selective and admit only those students with good scholastic records and excellent examination skills. The quality of teaching staff and the school environment have relatively little influence on ranking. Every prefecture and major city has a hierarchy of high schools determined solely by the above criterion.

In 1977, 92.6% of the middle-school graduates entered the high schools. Yet the way middle-school teachers influence who goes to which high schools is revealing and also reinforces the ranking order. Senior students in the middle schools take prefecturewide mock high-school entrance tests (high school *moshi*) five to eight times a year. These tests are either recommended or required by middle-school teachers who need the students' data to determine the level of performance in tests. The results of each test, which are translated into T-scores, are sent to participating schools.

After repeated *moshi*, teachers assume that the level of a student's performance has become so predictable that they can safely decide the rank of the high school to which he may aspire. Hence most teachers use the results of *moshi* to identify the appropriate high schools for their graduates. This practice has resulted in a pattern of apparent polarisation in high-school education, in which academically able applicants concentrate upon admission to high-ranking schools and relatively incompetent applicants have no other choice but the low-ranking schools.

SAIGŌ—A CASE STUDY

A case study will shed light upon the preceding general analysis. The school to be described briefly is Saigō (fictitious name), a 10-year old prefectural high school located outside the city limits of Nagoya, Aichi Prefecture, the fourth largest city in Japan—one of five schools this author studied.

Established in 1968, it has beautiful suburban surroundings. Saigō has the best audio-visual and other learning laboratory facilities in the entire prefecture. It enrols students from Nagoya and its neighbouring communities who come from approximately the 50th percentile of their respective middle schools; thus they were rejected by the more competitive prefectural high schools in Nagoya. Teachers at Saigō characterise many of its 10th-grade students as lacking basic cognitive skills essential to their grade level and especially lacking a habit of sustained learning when they first enter the school. Teachers admit that many students at Saigō suffer from feelings of inferiority.

Yet every year Saigō places 95% of its graduates in various colleges, one-third of them in local national universities. In sharp contrast to the high percentage of *rōnin* on the national level, only 8% of the senior students at Saigō become *rōnin*, as a result of Saigō's special effort to reduce *rōnin*. It has outdistanced other recently established schools in the prefecture in placing students in relatively good universities, and begins to challenge more traditional and competitive schools in Nagoya.

Since its inception, Saigō has been launching unique programmes in which students are trained for three years to develop a pattern of disciplined behaviour. The school emphasises self-denial, strict conformity to the group, endurance, prompt response to external expectations, and acceptance of teachers as the source of moral and academic authority. A social studies teacher at Saigō suggests that their underlying principle is the 'Confucian ethic'. These programmes are part of the group-orientated *seikatsushidō* (guidance for living). Saigō contends that its students can be trained through these programmes to meet CEE requirements. Saigō is now seen as a model for over 60 recently established public high schools in the prefecture. It is also judged nationally to provide a unique direction for high-school education, and thus teachers as well as administrators all over Japan visit Saigō every year to observe its educational programme.

Group training begins from the first day of attendance for the 10th-grade students. Under the supervision of teachers and senior students, they participate for half a day in a strict physical training programme that requires swift and precise coordinated movement and quick response to authority, as in military training. Individual error is regarded as a responsibility of the entire group. Subsequently this training forms the model for various athletic contests, club activities and other kinds of events. Visitors to the school are invariably impressed with the orderliness, promptness and control of behaviour the students show.

The freshman students undergo an intensive four-day 'initiation ritual' (*genpukushiki*), conducted early in the summer, before they develop sufficient sensitivity to the teachers' expectations. They spend these days with their teachers in a distant mountainous area, staying in local inns at night in order to facilitate the internalisation of the teachers' expectations and the development of disciplined group behaviour. This programme is an extension of the aforementioned physical training programme, but is more intensive and 'shocking' and involves more varied activities, such as mountain climbing, building camp-fires, visiting temples and group-living. Students are punished when they are not orderly and obedient. Punishments include admonition, pushing, ridiculing and 'rabbit-hopping' (students are told to hop like a rabbit for a period of time). Each day begins very early in the morning when teachers whistle to signal all students to get up. Students are required to line up immediately on the specified assembly area without the opportunity to take care of personal needs. Teachers stress promptness and punctuality.

Teachers admit that most 10th-grade students become docile, obedient and persevering, as well as very sensitive to the group norms imposed upon them through this training, even though prior to the experience many students resisted *seikatsushidō* as foreign to them. These students did not receive such unyielding *seikatsushidō* at the middle school level. In fact, Saigō students acknowledged that they remained scared, restless and nervous at least for most of the first year at the school and that they were always alert throughout the three years lest they may be called to the faculty office for admonition. They are concerned that individual failure to meet the faculty's expectations may cause terrible embarrassment, since not only individuals but entire groups are often punished.

The faculty apply the fundamental orientation of the afore-mentioned training to the classroom situation, and discipline the students to develop a habit of sustained learning. Since the senior year (12th grade) is most crucial for CEE, most of the 350 senior students are expected to receive *hoshū*, a supplementary drilling, nearly every day for one hour before regular morning class and for two hours after regular afternoon class—an intensive group exercise not seen at prefectural schools in Nagoya.

During the humid midsummer, Saigō conducts a condensed cramming session for the senior students during four days and three nights at the school, which is also used for sleeping. Designed to prepare for CEE, the session requires the participants to rise at 6:00 in the morning and retire at 11:30 at night. Teachers explain that its major objective is to build the students' habit of concentrating on study for many hours and enduring difficulties related to such concentration. Whether or not this is actually effective, teachers consider it important to the students' success in CEE.

These exercises are not part of the prefectural schools in the city. Unlike many students at those schools who attend *juku*, few students at Saigō go to *juku*. Group-orientated *hoshū* appears sufficient to fulfill a function of *juku* for the students at Saigō.

Saigō students are not only strictly guided by their teachers, but also motivated to depend upon them. Faculty members expect students to study as intensely as those attending schools in Nagoya. A study profile of an above-average senior obtained three months prior to CEE reveals this phenomenon well. The student gets up at 6:30 A.M. and reaches school at 7:30. From 7:45 to 8:30 he receives morning *hoshū* (four times a week) followed by regular morning class at 8:50. Classes end at 3:10 and are followed by afternoon *hoshū* (twice a week) from 3:40 to 5:00. He returns home at 6:00. After supper he begins study at 8:00 and continues until 1:00 in the morning. In his senior year, the student takes four term tests and 11 exercise examinations given by private corporations and Saigō. Test scores are periodically posted on a bulletin board.

In order to make CEE preparatory studies effective. Saigō divides students at the beginning of their junior year into different tracks, as other schools do: the humanities and social sciences group for private universities and colleges; the same categorical group for national universities; and the natural science and engineering group for both private and national universities and colleges. Each group has optional courses to stress particular subjects central to the framework of the group's examinations. Most senior students take nationally administered *moshi* five or six times a year as do many students elsewhere. The student referred to above took five such tests given by three different corporations. At Saigō there is an emphasis upon cramming by way of repeating the same texts over and over again, but drill books are also introduced extensively during *hoshū*. This author's observation suggests that though students at Saigō study hard by adherence to group norms, a majority of them are extrinsically motivated to prepare dilligently for CEE because of external pressures exerted by their group, teachers, parents and the mass media. This is particularly true, for example, in the case of *hoshū*. While many students do not wish to participate in *hoshū*, teachers and parents demand that they do.

According to teachers at Saigō, given the average academic qualities of their students, and the wish of nearly all parents that their children attend college, Saigō's approach to the training of students is probably most conducive to achieving students' goals for winning college admissions. In fact, the parents interviewed are more or less pleased with *seikatsushidō* and *hoshū* at Saigō. Nevertheless, one teacher reported that objections to *seikatsushidō* are often raised by a small number of parents. The faculty at Saigō is also aware that the Japan Teachers Union and some intellectuals in Nagoya frequently criticise it for its 'authoritarianism'.

Meanwhile, Saigō teachers are expected to work much harder than faculties in most other schools. They arrive at the school by 7:30 in the morning and leave after 6:00 in the evening. While much of their time is committed to regular teaching, *hoshū* and *seikatsushidō*, they frequently meet late in the afternoon to coordinate their activities. Most of their spring and summer vacations are also devoted to *hoshū*, the summer initiation programme, the summer cramming session and for planning. One of the factors most crucial to the operation of Saigō, according to the director of academic affairs, is the homogeneity of the teachers' attitudes toward education at the school. Hence teachers, he says, often gather after school and during vacation periods for dinner and drinks to promote a group feeling among them. When new teachers are appointed they are taken to a distant inn or hotel overnight where they are 'initiated' into the Saigō group, which acquaints them with its group orientation and expectations.

Saigō has a reputation in the Nagoya area for conducting 'Spartan' schooling, forcing students to study without due consideration for their individual characteristics and motivations. The other two high schools studied in Nagoya by this author provide more relaxed environments. Group-oriented *seikatsushidō*, as emphasized by Saigō, is absent from these schools, and their students are better scholastically than students at Saigō. Whether or not Saigō's schooling is typical, it elucidates one response to the pressures of CEE.

ECONOMIC AND CULTURAL CONDITIONS FOR CEE

A variety of factors contribute to the intensification of CEE in Japan. The most influential ones will be discussed here: namely, economic and cultural factors.

Economic Factors

The current proportion of eligible youth who attend institutions of higher education represents an enormous increase in the past 20 years. In 1960, when Japan had restored economic stability after the devastating destruction of Japanese economic and social life during World War II, only 10.3% of the eligible youth were admitted to college; in 1965 the percentage rose to 22.7, in 1970, to 24; in 1975, to 38.4 (Ministry of Education, 1976). Japanese per-capita income, meanwhile, has risen constantly: $458 in 1960; $1050 in 1967; $1887 in 1970; $4400 in 1975 (United Nations, 1976). In the 1970s, in terms of GNP, Japan surpassed West Germany and took a position second to the USA, among non-Communist nations. Certainly there is an unequivocal correlation between Japan's economic growth and the growth of college enrolment.

Let us look at income differentials among males in the first year of their first employment for three groups: college, high-school and middle-school graduates. When the index for the college graduate is held constant at 100, the indices of high-school and middle-school graduates are shown in Table II.

Though the intervals among these indices have been considerably narrowed in the 15 years between 1960 and 1975, the college graduate has an undoubtedly greater advantage over the other two groups. Let us observe differences among the three groups on terms of longitudinally computed career income. When the index for the college graduate is held constant at 100, the indices of the high-school and middle-school graduates are: 71.4 and

TABLE II   Index of income differentials among males in the first
year of first employment

	College graduates	High-school graduates	Middle-school graduates
1960	100	62.4	45.2
1965	100	71.8	57.2
1970	100	75.8	63.7
1975	100	84	69.4

Source: Based upon Ministry of Education, *The Educational Standard of Our Nation* (*Wagakunino Kyoiku Suijun*) (Tokyo, Okurasho Insatsukyoku, 1976).

61.5 in 1966, 73.9 and 66.7 in 1970, 77.2 and 69.2 in 1974 (Ministry of Labour, 1976). What these statistics demonstrate is that the differentials among the three groups in terms of their initial incomes are by and large reflected in their career incomes.

With regard to allocation of jobs, a majority of the college graduates are predominantly employed in white-collar office, engineering and managerial functions. In 1975, 51% of these jobs were allocated to college graduates whereas 48.3% went to high-school graduates. Nearly three-fourths of the blue-collar jobs in the primary and secondary industries were allocated to high-school graduates, while the rest were largely allocated to middle-school graduates (Ministry of Education, 1976).

In short, it is advantageous from an economic point of view for Japanese youth to receive higher education if they can afford it. In other words, college education is a means for social mobility. The current trend is toward a progressively greater number of families being able to afford sending young sons and daughters to college as long as they can win admissions. The economic variables referred to here help to explain the sharp rise in college enrolment, and, in turn, the competitive pressure for college admission. When the Japanese economy was growing at a rapid pace in the 1960s and early 1970s, higher education responded to the demands of industries to expand. The number of four-year colleges and universities increased 71% in the 15 years between 1960 and 1975, reaching a total of 420, and the number of two-year colleges expanded from 280 to 513, an increase of 83%.

Despite the mushrooming of institutions of higher education in one and a half decades, there are currently about 30% more applicants than these institutions can admit. This surplus of applicants, however, is not a major variable in accounting for the fierce competition in CEE. A more influential factor must be sought in the orientation of Japanese culture.

Cultural Factors

The Japanese cultural orientation dominant in the eighteenth and nine-teenth centuries has been relatively unaltered, though Japan has become a modern complex society that has undergone extensive structural changes since the Meiji Restoration (1868). To put it another way, structural changes that have resulted from the development of industrialism in the past century have not significantly modified vital aspects of the traditional cultural orientation that provides a rationale for social relations. It is these aspects of the orientation that underlie a dominant pattern of Japanese adaptation to rapid social transformation since the inception of Japanese modernisation.

The aspects of Japanese culture to which special attention is given here is the pattern of Japanese behaviour for which the group functions as its framework. As observed By Chie Nakane (1973), the group is most fundamental to all vital aspects of Japanese behaviour including the social, economic, political and educational. It constitutes the pervasive basis of contemporary social relations and mediates the relationship between individuals and their larger society and, thus, is vital not only in a functional sense, but also a general framework that defines an individual's personal identity and social participation (Nakane, 1967, 1973; Ishida, 1970; Dore, 1973; Hsu, 1975; Hazama, 1976; Tsuda, 1977; Clark, 1977). Hence the group takes precedence over the individual.

The concept of group refers to the social organisation. The Japanese group emphasises its 'frame', in Nakane's term (1973, p. 1) which constitutes its boundary and common identification by which its members are bound and seek social and personal anchorage. Anthropological and sociological studies to date (e.g. Kawashima, 1957; Nakane, 1967, 1973; Ariga, 1969, 1971; Kitano, 1976) identify the archetype of the contemporary Japanese group in terms of *ie*, the traditional household developed during the Tokugawa Era (1603–1868) and *dōzoku*, an extension of the *ie* institution that evolved since the middle of the Tokugawa Era through the Meiji. *Dōzoku* came into existence as an entity of households based upon both genealogical and economic relations among them, and it functioned as one of the corporate groups in the village community. Contemporary social organisations in Japan exhibit distinct characteristics of *ie* and *dōzoku* though they are structurally more complex and differentiated than these traditional institutions. Some of these characteristics are: stress on the conformity of motivational orientation, inclusiveness as applied to all group members, vertical social relations within the group, and a strong tendency toward exclusiveness vis-à-vis other groups.

Given such emphasis on the group, it is a paramount need to an individual that he not only belongs to a group, but also becomes a permanent member so as to establish his lasting identity with it and, in turn, to receive life-long protection rendered by it. That need is ordinarily met by life-long employment generally practised by private corporations and governmental institutions. Hence Japanese are often permanently locked into given organisations. This has led to a two-fold consequence: the relative lack of interorganisational mobility on the part of individuals among different groups; and the evolution of Japanese social stratification by the institutions rather than by individuals crossing group boundaries (Nakane, 1973, pp. 90–107). Japanese social structure, in other words, lacks the flexibility of horizontal mobility of individuals.

Returning to the problems of CEE, the group orientation of Japanese culture serves as a primary motivational force that drives Japanese adolescents to compete fiercely in CEE. CEE sorts out adolescents to place them in institutions of higher education that vary greatly in their access to the work organisations they can provide for graduates. Hence applicants tend to concentrate on universities and colleges that guarantee them access to secure firms and governmental institutions ranked highly in the Japanese social stratification system. Since Japanese favour life-time employment in such organisations, whether or not they are able to secure employment in these organisations immediately following university graduation becomes highly crucial to their social mobility. From the viewpoint of an organisation, it is vital for a job applicant to be the latest graduate, since he is expected to be enculturated into the organisation from the bottom of its hierarchy.

Access to big firms and governmental institutions is determined not only by the level of a young person's educational training, but more importantly by the reputation of the university from which he graduated. In other words, major employers regard the level of institutional prestige as a major criterion for judging the qualifications of job applicants. It is interesting to note that university prestige is associated with the rating of entrance examinations on an 'easy-difficult' scale developed by private educational industries (Ehara, 1977, pp. 96–98). One study further reveals that large firms determine the quality of university graduates in terms of such ratings of entrance examinations regardless of their performance at their universities (Nippon Rikurūto Center, 1975, p. 19). Hence, qualifications for employment in such organisations are often determined at the point of entry into universities via CEE.

Major employers also use level of prestige as the criterion for patronising universities for recruitment purposes. This employment practice is called *shiteikōsei*. According to a recent survey, 35% of the sample of major employers subscribe to *shiteikōsei* to recruit applicants for office personnel and 43% of the sample, to recruit engineering personnel (*Keizai Doyūkai*, 1975, p. 20). Still another survey indicated that 300 major firms depend in varying degrees on this employment practice (Nippon Rikuruto Center, 1971, pp. 17–43). Sixty-five universities are often patronised by these major firms including seven formerly imperial, two non-imperial national universities, and two large private universities, which are regarded as the most prestigious in Japan. These 11 universities, particularly Tokyo University, also serve as the source of institutions placing graduates in 'elites' in politics, business, medicine, law and academia (Takane, 1976; Mannari, 1974).

It is evident that admission to these prestigious universities and other patronised universities is vital to youth in order to gain access to groups of their own choice—work organisations with security and prestige. Once applicants are admitted to these universities, university education is relatively easy since, unlike the extremely rigorous entrance examinations, it does not generally require rigorous training. After students enter universities they are more often than not treated as if they are members of exclusive groups receiving secure status without fear of competition or great pressure for academic work. A guarantee of graduation in four years is implicit. Universities consider it their social responsibility to graduate those they admitted. Undoubtedly this is a reflection of the cultural orientation discussed earlier. Thus, most intensely competitive pressure is exerted at the time of CEE.

FUNCTIONS AND DYSFUNCTIONS OF COLLEGE ENTRANCE EXAMINATIONS

Social and Political Functions of CEE

Let us summarise some of the central functions performed by CEE:

(1) CEE serves as a major sorting device for social placement. It is a rite of passage required for adolescents at the age of 18 to secure future membership in certain groups via college. The permanent placement of individuals in given organisations provides individuals security and lasting social and personal identification. At the same time, CEE contributes to the stability of Japanese society, which rests on social stratification by institutions rather than individuals. Despite the tensions it creates for adolescents, parents and teachers, CEE is an acceptable device since it reinforces the Japanese cultural orientation with its emphasis on the group and provision for future group membership.

(2) By implication CEE contributes to political stability. It determines, to a great extent, a narrowly defined motivational and cognitive framework within which adolescents' activities (learning) are legitimated. Such a framework is conducive to the development of students' conformity in motivational and cognitive activities. From the viewpoint of controlling people within a given political system, conformity is a crucial factor since it fosters a convergent and cohesive force. Hence, one of the chief reasons for the perpetuation of CEE may be that needs of the Japanese political system are indirectly or covertly served by CEE. In fact, CEE has never become a major controversial political issue in the post-war era, even though cyclical tension generated every year by CEE is one of the main sources of anxiety in Japanese life. Individuals are expected to deny their divergent needs and interests, and to be diligent and obedient with the hope that self-sacrifice will be rewarded when they gain access to colleges. Since the demand for self-sacrifice is imposed upon adolescents during crucial, formative years of life (13–18 years of age), its effect is great. In other words, during these years adolescents internalise the cultural, technical and economic ideology of Japanese society.

(3) Intensive drilling contributes to the inculcation of basic knowledge at both the elementary and secondary school level. Japanese students are diligent and disciplined.

(4) CEE has created social conditions for: the mushrooming of tutoring and preparatory services that provide thousands upon thousands of school teachers, retired teachers and college students with opportunities for part-time employment and a significant source of supplementary income; a development of private profit-orientated educational institutions (*juku*); and

industries that have made millions of children the consumers of their services—drilling, drill-books, exercise examinations and magazines.

(5) CEE places a high value on achievement. It promotes adolescents' orientation toward achievement. But that orientation recedes after they gain access to universities, and is blended with an ascriptive orientation of organisations when they gain membership in them.

Dysfunctions
Some of the major dysfunctions of CEE include:

(1) Japanese secondary education suffers from a dualism of educational purposes. While overt purposes of education stated in the Manual of the Courses of Study (the official guidebook issued by the Ministry of Education) emphasise each student's personal, social and intellectual maturity, actual curricula and teaching are designed to respond to the requirements of the entrance examination. Similarly, extracurricular activities are subjected to such requirements. Hence, in the actual processes of schooling, little attention is given to students' needs at their current level of maturity. Students are more interested in examination techniques than in substantive learning and growth. The emphasis on conformity in motivational and cognitive orientations required by the entrance examinations suffocates students' potential creativity and diversity of interest, i.e. their development of individuality.

(2) Contrary to the assumption that CEE provides all adolescents with a fair opportunity for open competition based upon the criterion of achievement, CEE gives undue advantage to students who have received intensive and costly drilling in examination-taking. CEE, therefore, discriminates against the economically disadvantaged.

(3) CEE is not capable of diagnosing latent abilities of adolescents, particularly abilities of the disadvantaged and those not adept in examination-taking—potential that might be stimulated and developed later. Hence, it is an arbitrary device for social placement rather than a pedagogical instrument.

(4) Coupled with the above point is the rigidity of the Japanese social structure, which does not allow requisite horizontal mobility—a pattern of mobility that encourages individuals to seek work opportunities that contribute to the maximal development of individual potentials. CEE amounts to an institutional expression of the inflexible social structure, and thus reinforces it by serving as a central mechanism for determining adolescents' future memberships in work organisations via colleges.

(5) CEE requires undue sacrifices of adolescents and their families. Students are expected to regard diverse interests and activities as illegitimate. Their legitimate activities must be centred around requirements of the entrance examinations. They are subjected to drilling and passive absorption of knowledge at school and *juku* day and night. Families of college-bound adolescents often organise their activities to fit the examination-centred needs of children, at the cost of other members' interests and needs. Particularly the economic cost for *rōnin* children, drilling and attendance at *juku* constitutes a large amount of family expenditure.

AN ALTERNATIVE: OLD WINE IN A NEW BOTTLE

In order to ameliorate distortions resulting from the college entrance examinations, in 1971 the Association of National Universities and Colleges, an organisation of the presidents of the national institutions of higher education, proposed an alternative approach to the conventional CEE. Its original proposal outlined two-step entrance examinations to be taken primarily by the applicants for the national institutions (excluding applicants for 305 private colleges). Subsequently, an *ad hoc* committee was constituted to design a new structure and new procedures for entrance examinations. Based on its recommendations, endorsed by the Ministry of Education, the Association decided to implement the two-step examinations beginning in 1979.

Unlike the current CEE prepared by each institution, the first examination will be prepared and administered by the College Entrance Examination Center operated under the supervision of the Association, for all national universities and colleges, as well as for other publicly controlled colleges interested in participating in the uniform examination. The examination will cover all (seven) major subjects and will try to evaluate the high-school achievement level of applicants. The second entrance examination will be prepared by each institution and will be designed to select applicants on the basis of their test performance. Depending upon colleges, the number of subjects will range generally from two to four, and interviews with applicants will be conducted.

It is claimed that the two-step examinations will provide applicants with opportunities to be tested twice instead of once, as in the current practice, and to be evaluated comprehensively. According to the Association, these entrance examinations will lead to a fair selection of applicants and, hence, to the 'normalisation' of high-school education. The Association assumes that the results of those two examinations will be used by colleges to decide admission. Yet, a recent survey indicates that 60% of the institutions participating in the first common examination are planning to use its results to screen applicants eligible for the second examination rather than to obtain data on the high-school achievement level of applicants for the purpose of deciding admission (*Asahi Shinbun*, May 3, 1977).

In the view of the Association, the two-step approach represents an improvement over the current CEE, but high schools are reluctant to admit such improvement. To begin with, the views of high schools are hardly reflected in the Association's decision to implement the two-step examinations since high schools have never been invited to take part in shaping them. High schools all over Japan were given briefings on it, but never encouraged to present counter-proposals. In this respect high schools view the two-step approach as arbitrary and as an imposition upon them. Secondly, they fear that this approach would impose a double burden upon high-school students since they must prepare for two types of entrance examinations to gain admission to national universities. The National Association of High School Principals, prefectural associations of high school principals, and high-school guidance teachers have frequently issued protests over the implementation of the two-step approach. They have requested that the second examination be eliminated and, instead, that high-school reports be used. They have charged that Japanese universities and colleges are self-serving and insensitive to the 'infernal' examination pressures imposed upon adolescents and distortions of high-school education created by them. Thirdly, since the two-step examinations do not involve private institutions, it is argued that the lack of uniformity in entrance examinations would make it difficult for high-school students to prepare for them. Nonetheless, the dates for the two-step examinations are firmly set and high schools have no alternative but to acquiesce.

The *nōken* test, somewhat similar to the first examination, had been given to college applicants on a nation-wide basis during 1963–1968. It was proposed by the Central Council of Education, an agency advisory to the Ministry of Education, and a governmental corporation was subsequently created to implement it. It was short-lived, however, for universities and colleges did not fully use it and eventually ignored it.

Japanese universities and colleges generally insist on their exclusive right to screen applicants by the examinations and criteria they make individually—territorial rights to determine membership. They deny, by and large, the reliability of the high-school reports of applicants, for they claim that these reports lack objectivity. Once applicants gain admission to college through rigorous examinations, however, they are treated inclusively as members of groups immune to competition and rigorous objective evaluation. Characteristics of the group referred to earlier are also evidently attributable to Japanese academic institutions. Critical screening is required when group membership is extended to new members. Therefore student moves from one college to another are very difficult and also rare. Again this phenomenon reflects the rigidity of the Japanese social structure where horizontal mobility between different social organisations is limited.

Given these backgrounds, the success of the two-step examinations is quite uncertain.

A WORD IN CONCLUSION

CEE is an institutionalised practice compatible with the group orientation of Japanese society, which gives precedence to the group—the institution—over the individual. It is a device for social placement that functions to reinforce the existing social stratification. It is not a pedagogical practice designed to promote the personal growth and social maturity of Japanese adolescents. It subjects them to prolonged drilling for the sake of entry to college.

Japanese adolescents are highly disciplined and diligent—an attribute essential to a healthy and productive society. But the crucial problem is how to foster this attribute without resorting to the current CEE and to combine it with the development of independent and critical thinking, creativity and maturity of personality. Due to lack of space, recommendations for the improvement of the CEE and college education are not offered here. This article, however, points out abundant critical problems deriving from the CEE, which may serve as a basis for making recommendations.

REFERENCES

Ariga, K. (1969) *Ariga Kizaemon Chosakushū VII (Collection of Ariga Kizaemon's Works VII)* (Tokyo, Miraisha).

Ariga, K. (1971) *Ariga Kizaemon Chosakushū X (Collection of Ariga Kizaemon's Works X)* (Tokyo, Miraisha).

Asahi-Shinbun, Japanese Daily Newspaper.

Clark, G. (1977) *The Japanese tribe* (Tokyo, Simul).

Dore, R. (1973) *British factory-Japanese factory* (University of California, Berkeley).

Ehara, T. (1977) 'Kigyoga Motomeru Gakureki' ('academic credentials sought by corporations') in: Aso, & Ushiogi, M. (Eds.) *Gakureki Koyoron (Utility of Academic Credentials)* (Tokyo, Yuhitaku).

Hazama, H. (1976) *Nipponteki Keiei (Japanese management)* (Tokyo, Nippon Keizai Shinbunsha).

Hsu, F. (1975) *Iemoto* (Cambridge, Massachusetts, Schenkman).

Ishida, T. (1970) *Nippon Seiji Bunka (Political culture in Japan)* (Tokyo University).

Kawashima, T. (1957) *Ideorogii Toshiteno Kazokuseido (Familial institution as an ideology)* (Tokyo, Iwanami).

Keizai, Doyukai (1975) *Kigyonai Shugyoshano Gakurekini Kansuru Jitai Chosa (Survey on employees and educational credentials in corporations)* (Tokyo, Keizai Doyukai).

Kitano, S. (1976) *Ieto Dozokuno Kisoriron (Fundamental theory of ie and dozoku)* (Tokyo, Miraisha).

Mannari, H. (1974) *Bizinesu Eriito* (Business elite) (Tokyo, Chuokoronsha).

Ministry of Education (1976) *Wagakunino Kyoiku Suijun (The educational standard of our nation)* (Tokyo, Okurasho Insatsukyoku).

Ministry of Labour (1976) *Keizai Hakusho (Economic white paper)* (Tokyo, Okurasho Insatsukyoku).

Nakane, C. (1967) *Kinship and economic organisation in rural Japan* (London, London School of Economics).

Nakane, C. (1973) *Japanese Society* (Harmondsworth, Penguin).

Nippon Rikuruto Center (1971) *Shushoku Jaanaru (Journal of employment).*

Nippon Rikuruto Center (1975) *Gakurekini Kansuru Kigyono Iken Chosa (Survey of corporations' opinions on educational credentials)* (Tokyo, Nippon Rikuruto Center).

Takane, M. (1976) *Nipponno Seiji Eriito (Political elite in Japan)* (Tokyo, Chuokoronsha).

Tsuda, M. (1977) *Nipponteki Keieino Riron (Theory of Japanese management)* (Tokyo, Chuokeizaisha).

OECD (1971) *Reviews of national policies for education: Japan* (Paris, OECD).

United Nations (1976) *Statistical yearbook* (New York, United Nations).

The Structure of American Elementary and Secondary Education

FLOYD M. HAMMACK
New York University

Although education is found in all societies, it is different in every society. Unique historical factors and different stages of economic and social development affect the kind of education each society provides its citizens. This article will highlight two broad aspects of the structure of education: the political mechanisms by which education is governed and the ways in which it is organized into schools and instructional activities. In discussing each of these two facets of schooling, this article will emphasize the distinctive aspects of education in the United States.

GOVERNANCE OF EDUCATION

As Coletta's article (in this section) demonstrates, education in traditional societies hardly has a separate structure. Children learn in the ebb and flow of daily family and village life. But such a description would be inaccurate for a society such as the United States. While education does continue to occur in the midst of everyday life, much is now provided through schools that are separate from family and economic life, and that in some respects constitute a world of their own.[1]

The United States is like other industrial societies in separating much of its education from home and economic life. But we are virtually unique among modern societies in that the education is not mentioned in our national constitution (Ramirez and Boli-Bennett, 1982). In many societies, education is

This article appears here for the first time.

147

a right of citizenship and an obligation of the national government explicitly specified by the constitution.[2] As the introduction to this section notes, most other countries have national government agencies responsible for education and local interests have few means of expressing themselves. Teachers in these countries are appointed and evaluated nationally, as are administrators, and there is usually no equivalent of an elected school board with real responsibility for conducting schools. Moreover, most other countries have a national curriculum developed and overseen by the national education ministry. This curriculum is often tied to national examinations that determine the awarding of diplomas and, in turn, access to higher levels of education.[3]

However, schooling in the United States is not a national responsibility but a state and local one. Because the federal constitution does not mention it, education is entirely a state-controlled function. The federal government has little authority over education. Unless an educational activity (such as racially segregating schools) violates the constitution, the federal government is unable to require change. It does, however, have the ability to recommend, fund, cajole, and in other nonbinding ways influence what states and localities do. And since most states and school districts are short of funds, federal aid is indeed powerful in influencing change in education.

All school districts operate within the confines of the relevant state education law, which specifies requirements for diplomas, certification of teachers, and the like. Private schools too must conform to state education law, but are less restricted than are public schools. For example, in most states the regulations governing the conditions under which one may teach are less strict if one teaches in a private school than if one teaches in a public school. Financial support is almost entirely up to the private school and its sponsors to generate; no tax-derived funds may be used to support private schooling unless special conditions are met (for example, aid for handicapped students enrolled in private schools may come from public sources).[4] Tuition at elementary day schools (not boarding schools) can reach $8000 and more, and it is usually higher for secondary schools.

The control of public education at the elementary and secondary level largely rests with the local school district. School district boundaries are usually quite similar to local political boundaries, but elected school boards are rarely identified with a political party. In 1986 there were about 15,400 separate school districts in the nation, each with its own school board, superintendent, and schools (U.S. Department of Education, 1987: 77). Although smaller school districts have often been consolidated into larger ones, many states still have hundreds and in some cases well over a thousand separate districts. For example, Texas had 1072 operating districts during the 1982–1983 school year (U.S. Department of Education, 1987).

Funding for public schools largely comes from local property taxes and state funds. During the 1984–1985 school year, local sources accounted for 45 percent of revenues, while 49 percent came from state sources and 6 percent came from the federal government (U.S. Department of Education, 1987). The fraction paid for by state sources has been steadily rising, largely due to legal challenges to relying on local property taxes for funding. Reliance on local property taxes generates great disparities in the funds available per student across property-rich and property-poor districts. As states have begun to provide a greater fraction of educational expenses, these disparities have not necessarily been lessened although the poorest districts have received the resources to provide higher levels of educational expenditures. Rich districts have increased their taxation to increase funds, so the differences in funding levels remains, though without the very low levels some districts had maintained (Johns, Morphet, and Alexander, 1983).[5]

Despite local control, U.S. schools do share many similarities across the country. A number of factors contribute to this relative homogeneity. A system of regional, nongovernmental accrediting agencies has developed over the years to define what are proper educational practices. In addition, although admissions requirements vary among colleges, they are similar enough to influence the course offerings of secondary schools. Textbook writers and publishers, who provide instructional material for schools nationwide, influence what is taught and often how it is taught by marketing the same instructional materials nationwide. And a highly mobile student and teacher population have helped reduce the isolation and diversity that might otherwise have developed. Finally, the influence of federal government funding and national professional associations of educators have helped limit local differences. Thus, there is less diversity in curriculum and instruction than in authority and instruction.

An important consequence of the United States' pattern of mixed local and state control is that local concerns are more likely to be reflected in school policies and practices than is common in countries with more centralized educational systems. Citizen participation is direct and often decisive because funds for schools are in part from local sources. The opportunity for local influence is provided through the election of boards and the frequent budget and bond approval elections held within each district.[6] Moreover, parent involvement, whether through parent-teacher associations or informal parent conferences, is expected by school authorities.

THE ORGANIZATION OF SCHOOLS AND INSTRUCTION

Formal public schooling generally begins at age six, although preschool and kindergarten programs are widespread and growing. In 1985 about 39 percent of three- and four-year-olds were enrolled part- or full-time in nursery schools or kindergartens, compared to under 11 percent in 1965 (U.S. Department of Education, 1987). Elementary schools are smaller in scale than schools for older children and are internally less differentiated in the sense that they have essentially the same curriculum and organization. The curriculum is one that all students are expected to master, and most students are exposed to the same subject matter through courses taught by their "homeroom" teacher. However, within the homeroom groups often are formed for specific learning tasks (see the introduction to Chapter 6 for further information on this practice). Grouping by achievement level is very common and early on introduces one of the important lessons of schooling: that schools acknowledge and reward achievement. However, this use of grouping may be an important source of race and class differences in achievement.

But while elementary schools are generally alike in organization and curriculum, they differ widely in student composition. They draw from neighborhoods differing in racial and class composition and thus come to differ from each other in their student composition.

By the time junior high or high school is reached, that is, by age 13 or so, secondary school begins. Our comprehensive secondary schools are models of a kind for the world, where secondary education is more restricted. Since the *Cardinal Principles of Secondary Education* report (National Education Association, 1918), secondary schools have been viewed as important for all students: those who will not attend college as well as those who will (Clark, 1985; Krug, 1964; Trow, 1961). While most 19th-century secondary schools had stiff entrance examinations and were only concerned with preparing students for college entry, by the early 1900s, secondary schools were expected to educate *all* students until they graduated or reached 18 years of age. A major reason they have responded to the educational aspirations of many more students than is the case in many other countries is that school systems in the United States have been so open to local influence.

One significant consequence of this openness is the size of our educational system. A larger percentage of youth are in school longer in this country than in any other (King, 1979). This fact is especially striking at the upper secondary and higher education levels. Over a quarter (28 percent) of those 18 to 24 years old in 1985 had graduated from high school and entered college (U.S. Department of Education, 1987: 155). This figure is much higher than in other countries.

Another important consequence of our commitment to keeping students in school is the organizational form the U.S. high school has taken. The comprehensive high school which provides college preparation, vocational education programs, and general secondary education under one roof has become the most common form of the U.S. secondary school. The explanation for its success as an organizational form rests, in part, on its political and social appeal as well as its educational and economic purposes. The authors of the *Cardinal Principles of Secondary Education* report assert that

> the comprehensive school is the prototype of a democracy in which various groups have a degree of self-consciousness as groups and yet be federated into a larger whole through the recognition of common interests and ideals. Life in such a school is a natural and valuable preparation for life in a democracy. (National Education Association, 1918: 26)

This philosophy for secondary schools was new. In most other countries, secondary schools were not (and many still are not) comprehensive, but are exclusively academic or vocational.[7]

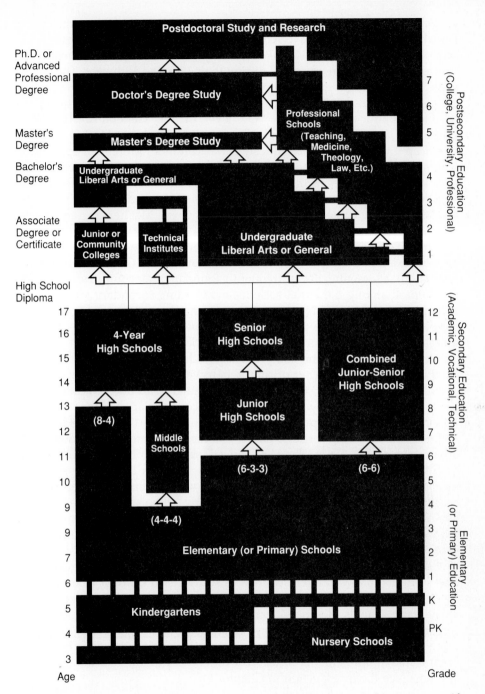

NOTE—Adult education programs, while not separately delineated above, may provide instruction at the elementary, secondary, or higher education level.

Source: Digest of Education Statistics, 1987.

Only in 1972, for example, did Britain increase its "school leaving" age to 16, when most students leave school. In 1978, under 30 percent continued in school after age 16 (King, 1979: 206). Only those attempting to qualify for university entrance are in school during their 17th and 18th year. Those who leave at 16 do so without a diploma, and may not carry any credentials unless they pass one or more national examinations (a "Certificate of Secondary Education" or the "O" level of the General Certificate of Education). But, since most people do not go to school past 16, this is not the handicap it would be if more education was common. Moreover, apprenticeship and part-time vocational programs are widely available.[8] There are, in addition, many colleges of further education available for academic and vocational study beyond age 16. The options are much wider than those available in the United States (King, 1979; Grey, McPherson, and Raffe, 1983).

English university entrance depends on how well one scores on a series of national examinations (the "A," or advanced level of the General Certificate of Education), a screening device frequently found in other countries as well. We are atypical among industrial societies in awarding secondary school diplomas qualifying their holders for college entrance by only assessing the kinds of courses taken and the number of hours spent in school and not through assessment of what is learned during those classroom hours.[9]

Despite its success, the comprehensive school has its problems. Widely cited is the diffuse character of comprehensive secondary schools. As many recent critics have noted, the variety of curricular goals and educational and social purposes served by these schools reduces the clarity of their academic mission. When large proportions of students are not particularly academically inclined, the rigor and sense of purpose necessary to motivate student effort are missing (Trow, 1961). The U.S. educational system lacks the diversity of organizational alternatives for those over 16 found in Britain, for example, and thus must accommodate students of widely differing interests and accomplishments. Moreover, the size of many schools makes them impersonal and adds to the problems of maintaining involvement and commitment among students (Cusick, 1983; Goodlad, 1985; Powell, Farrer, and Cohen, 1985; Sizer, 1985).

Second, comprehensive secondary schools are almost always "tracked" in that students follow different courses of study based on their prior achievement and interests. It is the secondary equivalent of the grouping in elementary schools described earlier. Tracking has been seen by some researchers as a way to restrict opportunity for some while assuring it for more privileged students; others see such curricular alternatives as important organizational adjustments to the real differences among secondary school students (see the introduction to Chapter 6).

While most U.S. secondary schools are comprehensive, there is still great variation among them. First, the characteristics of students at different high schools vary considerably because neighborhood is so closely associated with socioeconomic status. This can be especially pronounced when comparing an inner city school with one in a nearby affluent suburb. College-going rates in the former may not be much higher than 10 to 20 percent, while 80 percent or greater is not uncommon among the latter.

Second, many school districts maintain separate secondary vocational and academic schools, and many ostensibly comprehensive schools are so dominantly serving one educational purpose that they cannot in a meaningful way be called comprehensive (implying as this term does a variety of purposes for a wide range of students). New York City's secondary schools provide a good example of how a system can become highly differentiated. There are over 110 separate high schools in New York. Four grant entry solely on the basis of an examination or audition. Eight more are special ("educational opportunity") high schools organized around vocational themes (such as health careers, business careers, aviation, and so forth), and enrolling students on the basis of prior achievement and selected other characteristics (gender, race, place of residence). Twenty more are ordinary vocational schools, admitting students citywide or boroughwide. Another group of 15 schools is composed of alternative schools, which may be minischools within larger schools or entirely separate. These schools are small and enroll students who have had difficulty in ordinary secondary schools. Finally, 77 schools are general, "academic/comprehensive neighborhood schools." Within many of these schools, however, there are "academies" or other magnet programs, which have some degree of freedom to select their students from wider attendance areas and which constitute schools within schools (Board of Education of the City of New York, 1986).[10]

A third deviation from the comprehensive school is the large private school sector. About one-eighth of all students attend private schools. These schools vary enormously, from one-room "academies" in the basement of Christian fundamentalist churches, to systems of parochial elementary and secondary schools, to exclusive boarding "prep" schools. Most private schools have a religious rationale: they exist to reinforce in children the family's faith.[11] Many of these schools were founded to escape the larger society's intolerance toward the faith's adherents. Thus, Catholic and other religiously sponsored schools were founded to both reinforce students' faith and to protect them from discrimination. A number of schools were started to avoid desegregated education mandated by the courts. Nonreligiously affiliated schools were frequently begun by religiously oriented sponsors, but dropped any formal affiliation they may have had. They exist today as an alternative to public schools providing a moral and educational climate parents seek for their children. In addition, these schools are often more socially homogeneous than public schools and have a single educational mission.

The elite private elementary and secondary schools carry great prestige and importance, outdistancing their numbers or enrollment. Most areas of the United States have these elite schools, which are variously termed "prep" or "boarding" or "country day" schools. The most famous, however, are the boarding schools of New England: for example, Phillips Exeter, Choate/Rosemary Hall, Groton, Hotchkiss and St. Paul's. These schools have enrolled such famous Americans as John F. Kennedy, Adlai Stevenson, George Bush, and Nelson Rockefeller. The importance of these schools lies not only in the fact that they heavily enroll the sons and daughters of the upper class and upper middle class, particularly those of long established wealth and prominence, but also in the fact that they provide their students with privileged access to the top universities and, in turn, corporate and governmental leadership (Cookson and Persell, 1985; Hammack and Cookson, 1980; Useem and Karabel, 1986).[12]

CONCLUSIONS

Public elementary and secondary schools in the United States are heavily influenced by local interests, which provide a significant but declining proportion of their financing. Because of their local origins, the authority of the national government is weak, although it does have the power to financially encourage states and districts to provide the kind of schooling it desires. Especially at the secondary and postsecondary levels, our schools are more inclusive than those of most other countries.

The comprehensive secondary school, though sometimes more an ideal than a reality, is the organizational form that has evolved to serve the high proportion of young people still in school during their late adolescence. However, these schools are strongly differentiated internally, through tracking. Moreover, as a result of the relative homogeneity generated by attendance zones and patterns of discrimination, many of the schools are differentiated according to the students they serve: Racial and economic class segregation is far too frequent. The open school system found in the United States, while keeping more students in school for a longer period than in other countries, is not without its barriers to educational achievement. The practices of grouping, tracking, and secondary school differentiation reduce the degree to which students flow easily from one part of the educational system to the next in ways consistent with students' social background. Finally, although we are currently in a period of criticism and reform in education, our educational system provides a degree of opportunity not found in other countries.

NOTES

1. This does not mean, however, that schools are not intimately connected to the rest of society, as the introduction to this book shows.
2. An important reason why education is not mentioned in our constitution is the date (1789) it was adopted. By world standards, ours is a very old constitution, and dates from a time when formal education hardly existed and was very far from being as critical as it is today. An amendment has not been added to the constitution making education a right of citizenship or an obligation of the national government largely because the states have provided free education and guard their control over it.
3. France provides a good example of a national educational system. Teachers are employees of the national government, and are assigned to schools throughout the country by the national education ministry. They are evaluated both locally, by principals and other staff of the local

school, and also by visiting "inspectors" from the national ministry whose judgments determine the career of teachers. The culminating college degree, the *baccalauréat*, is granted only when a student passes a nationally administered examination.

4. There has been an active movement to provide support for private schooling through tuition tax credits or educational vouchers—which every student in a district would use to gain entrance to public or private schools. Specific plans vary, but none has been implemented in the United States except for a few experiments.

5. An important measure of local property taxation is the amount of tax "effort" a district makes. Effort refers to the rate of taxation per unit of assessed property value. For example, to raise the same amount of money, a district with very high property valuation (with, say, a big industrial plant as well as houses and commercial property), needs to make a smaller effort (less tax per $1000 of assessed value) than a district with less value in its property. In effect, the tax rate needs to be higher (greater effort) the lower the value of the property in a district. The poor pay relatively more.

6. School budgets, like most others, are composed of two basic parts: an operating budget and a capital budget. The operating budget allocates funds for running the school, salaries, supplies, heating, and so on. The capital budget allocates resources for building projects. As these costs are large and not regular (districts do not build new schools every year), funds for them are often raised through special bond or borrowing elections where citizens of the district vote on whether the school district is to be allowed to borrow money to build. The borrowed money will, of course, have to be paid back through higher taxes. These elections, like those for approval of an operating budget, are required in some states for each new capital budget, and are often lost by districts. When this happens, the school board must decide how to proceed to get the budget approved.

7. As other countries have increased the proportion of youth attending secondary schools, the comprehensive high school has been widely adopted (Levin, 1982).

8. Although apprenticeship programs have declined in this country, they still remain a common form of vocational initiation in other countries, including Britain and especially Germany. See the articles by Benavot (1983) and Hamilton (1987) for more on vocational education and apprenticeship systems.

9. This is changing, however. A large number of states, 23 in 1984, use or expect to use minimum competency examinations for awarding high school graduation (U.S. Department of Education, 1985: 69–70). Airasian (1987) provides an up-to-date discussion of this testing movement. However, we still do not have European-style national examinations. The Scholastic Aptitude Test (SAT) and the American College Testing Program (ACT) tests are voluntary for both colleges and students: Not all colleges require them and students do not have to apply to colleges that do require them. In addition, both of these tests are privately administered.

10. An increasing number of educators are advocating choice in education. See Metz (1986), Murnane (1986), and Raywid (1985) for discussions of magnet schools and the philosophy underlying this effort.

11. Almost 80 percent of the enrollment of private schools is in religiously affiliated schools, of which 70 percent is in Catholic schools (U.S. Department of Education, 1986: 48). The research of Alan Peshkin is especially relevant to religious private education. See his article in Chapter 7.

12. For more on the impact of attending an elite secondary school on admission to highly selective colleges, see the article by David Karen in Chapter 5.

REFERENCES

Airasian, Peter W. 1987. "State Mandated Testing and Educational Reform: Context and Consequences." *American Journal of Education* 95 (May): 393–412.

Benavot, Aaron. 1983. "The Rise and Decline of Vocational Education." *Sociology of Education* 56 (April): 63–76.

Cambron-McCabe, Neida H., and Allan Odden (eds.). 1982. *The Changing Politics of School Finance*. New York: Ballinger.

Campbell, Roald F. et al. 1985. *The Organization and Control of American Schools.* Columbus, OH: Merrill.

Clark, Burton R. 1985. "The High School and the University: What Went Wrong in America, Parts 1, 2." *Phi Delta Kappan* (February and March): 391–397; 472–475.

Cookson, Peter W., Jr., and Caroline Hodges Persell. 1985. *Preparing for Power: America's Elite Boarding Schools.* New York: Basic Books.

Cusick, Philip. 1983. *The Egalitarian Ideal and the American High School.* New York: Longman.

Goodlad, John. 1985. *A Place Called School: Prospects for the Future.* New York: McGraw-Hill.

Grey, J., A. F. McPherson, and D. Raffe. 1983. *Reconstructions of Secondary Education: Theory, Myth and Practice Since the War.* London: Routledge and Kegan Paul.

Hamilton, Stephen F. 1987. "Apprenticeship as a Transition to Adulthood in West Germany." *American Journal of Education* 95 (February): 314–345.

Hammack, Floyd Morgan, and Peter W. Cookson, Jr. 1980. "Colleges Attended by Graduates of Elite Secondary Schools." *The Educational Forum* 44 (May): 483–490.

Johns, Roe L., Edgar L. Morphet, and Kern Alexander. 1983. "Human Capital Benefits and the Economics of Education." In Roe L. Johns, et al., *The Economics and Financing of Education.* 4th ed. Englewood Cliffs, NJ: Prentice-Hall.

King, Edmund J. 1979. *Other Schools and Ours: Comparative Studies For Today.* 5th ed. London: Holt, Rinehart and Winston.

Krug, Edward. 1964. *The Shaping of the American High School.* Vol. 1. New York: Harper & Row.

————. 1972. *The Shaping of the American High School.* Vol. 2. Madison: University of Wisconsin Press.

Levin, Henry M. 1982. "The Dilemma of Comprehensive Secondary School Reforms in Western Europe." In Philip G. Altbach, Robert F. Arnove, and Gail P. Kelly (eds.), *Comparative Education,* pp. 319–335. New York: Macmillan.

Metz, Mary Haywood. 1986. *Different By Design: The Context and Character of Three Magnet Schools.* New York: Methuen / Routledge and Kegan Paul.

Murnane, Richard J. 1986. "Family Choice in Public Education: The Roles of Students, Teachers, and System Designers." *Teachers College Record* 88 (winter): 169–189.

National Educational Association. 1918. *Cardinal Principles of Secondary Education.* Washington, DC: Department of the Interior, Bureau of Education.

National Education Association Commission on the Reorganization of Secondary Education. 1918. *Cardinal Principles of Secondary Education.* Washington, DC: U.S. Bureau of Education.

New York City Board of Education. 1986. *High School Admission and the Improvement of Schooling:* A Report of the University Consultants. New York: Author.

New York City Board of Education. 1987. *Directory of the Public High Schools, 1987–1988.* New York: Author.

Plisko, Valena White, and Joyce D. Stern. 1985. *The Condition of Education, 1985: A Statistical Report.* Washington, DC: National Center for Education Statistics.

Powell, Arthur, Eleanor Farrar, and David Cohen. 1985. *The Shopping Mall High School: Winners and Losers in the Educational Marketplace.* Boston: Houghton Mifflin.

Ramirez, Francisco O., and John Boli-Bennett. 1982. "Global Patterns of Educational Institutionalization." In Philip G. Altbach, Robert F. Arnove, and Gail P. Kelly (eds.), *Comparative Education,* pp. 15–36. New York: Macmillan.

Raywid, Mary Ann. 1985. "Family Choice Arrangements in Public Schools: A Review of Literature." *Review of Educational Research* 55: 435–467.

Sizer, Theodore. 1985. *Horace's Compromise: The Dilemma of the American High School.* rev. ed. Boston: Houghton Mifflin.

Trow, Martin. 1961. "The Second Transformation of American Secondary Education." *International Journal of Comparative Sociology* 2: 144–166. Reprinted in Jerome Karabel and A. H. Halsey (eds.), *Power and Ideology in Education,* pp. 105–118. New York: Oxford University Press, 1977.

U.S. Department of Education. Center for Education Statistics. 1986. *Digest of Education Statistics, 1985–86.* Washington, D.C.: Government Printing Office.

_____. 1987. *Digest of Education Statistics, 1987.* Washington, DC: Government Printing Office.

Useem, Michael, and Jerome Karabel. 1986. "Pathways to Top Corporate Management." *American Sociological Review* 51 (April): 184–200.

Wirt, Fredrick, and Michael Kirst. 1988. *Schools in Conflict.* 2nd Edition. Berkeley, CA: McCutchan.

The Higher Education System in the United States

KEVIN J. DOUGHERTY*
Manhattan College

The U.S. higher education system is, in many respects, one of the most unusual in the world. It is much larger than, and organized very differently from, most other nations' systems. The task of this paper is to analyze this unusual system. The paper describes the American higher education system's size, structure, and mode of operation. It analyzes how the higher education system developed over the course of American history. And it compares the American system to the higher education systems in comparable nations, such as Japan, Britain, and the Soviet Union.

BASIC STRUCTURES OF THE U.S. SYSTEM

The United States now has 3340 institutions of higher education enrolling a little over 12.5 million students (U.S. Department of Education, 1988a: 142, 182). Clearly, U.S. colleges enroll a very large proportion of American youth and a sizable proportion of older adults. Over a quarter (28 percent) of all youth age 18 to 24 are enrolled in college (U.S. Department of Education, 1988a: 174). All these numbers are far larger than those for any comparable industrial society. (See below for further discussion.)

Given their number, it is not surprising that colleges in the United States are quite varied. They range from elite public and private universities such as the University of California and Harvard University to liberal arts colleges such as Franklin and Marshall, Liberty University, and Spelman College, two-year junior colleges such as the Chicago City Colleges and Pine Manor Junior College, and one- or two-year business and trade schools such as the American Business Institute.

---

*I wish to thank Floyd M. Hammack and David Riesman for their comments on this paper. This article appears here for the first time.

In fact, the variety is so great as to make it hard to see any pattern. Yet, U.S. colleges can be quite usefully categorized along four axes:

- degrees and programs offered
- control
- student body characteristics
- prestige

Let us examine how U.S. colleges array themselves along each of these four axes.

Degrees and Programs Offered

The U.S. Department of Education defines five kinds of colleges according to the degrees and programs they offer.[1] These five kinds of colleges, their proportion of all colleges, and their share of all college enrollments are shown in Table 1.

The first group is the 171 "doctoral" institutions that offer doctoral and professional programs and produce a large number of graduates with either Ph.Ds or medical and dental degrees. Belonging in this group are the leading private and public universities such as Yale, Stanford, the University of Texas, and Ohio State University.[2]

"Comprehensive" institutions numbering about 420 make up the second category. They offer graduate programs but graduate few people with doctorate or medical degrees. Rather, they specialize in undergraduate, master's, and law programs. Quite often these institutions are former teacher training colleges that expanded into general liberal arts schools and added graduate programs (Dunham, 1969). They include institutions such as the campuses of the California State University system, Western Illinois University, the State University of New York at Oneonta, and Manhattan College.

The third category of colleges emphasize undergraduate education and have very few, if any, graduate programs. These 706 "general baccalaureate" or "liberal arts" colleges vary greatly in program and student composition,

TABLE 1 U.S. Higher Education Institutions Classified by Degrees and Types of Programs Offered (1985)

	Number	% of Institutions	% of enrollments
Doctoral	171	5	25
Comprehensive	418	13	23
General baccalaureate (liberal arts)	706	22	9
Specialized (art, business, etc.)	582	19	5
Two-year	1264	41	38

Source: U.S. Department of Education (1988a: 145, 185).

including institutions as diverse as Morehouse College, Bennington College, the College of Mount Saint Vincent, and Southeastern Bible College.[3]

"Specialized" colleges make up the fourth category. These 600 or so colleges emphasize one field, such as engineering or the arts, offering either a baccalaureate or postbaccalaureate training. They include such institutions as Meharry Medical College, the Rhode Island School of Design, and Rose Polytechnic Institute.

The 1264 "two-year colleges" make up the final category. They specialize in subbaccalaureate degrees such as associate of arts and various kinds of vocational certificates, whether in dental assisting or auto repair (Cohen and Brawer, 1982). These colleges are quite varied, ranging from Orange County Community College to the Tri-County Technical Institute and the Latter-Day Saints Business College.[4]

Control

Another way of approaching the variety of U.S. colleges is in terms of who owns them. U.S. colleges are legally owned by a wide variety of bodies, as can be seen in Table 2. Some 1500 colleges are public, owned by local, state, and federal governmental bodies. They account for 45 percent of all colleges, but 77 percent of all college enrollments.

The best-known federal colleges are, of course, the armed service academies. The state institutions range from huge doctoral-granting "flagship" universities such as the Universities of Texas or Illinois to small colleges such as the State University of New York at Purchase.[5]

The remaining 1840 colleges are private, owned either by religious groups, profit-making corporations, or nonsectarian, nonprofit boards. The nonsectarian, nonprofit private institutions include both many prestigious doctoral

TABLE 2   U.S. Higher Education Institutions Classified by Control (1985)

	Number	% of institutions	% of enrollments
PUBLIC INSTITUTIONS	1498	45	77
Local	173	5	
State/local	398	12	
State	914	27	
Federal	13	<1	
PRIVATE INSTITUTIONS	1842	55	23
Independent, nonprofit	828	25	
Profit making	220	7	
Religious	794	24	
Protestant	(524)	(16)	
Catholic	(235)	(7)	
Other	(35)	(1)	

Source: U.S. Department of Education (1988a: 142, 185).

granting universities, such as the Ivy League universities, and many very small and unprestigious liberal arts colleges. The majority of religious colleges are Protestant, with the remainder largely made up of Catholic colleges.[6] The profit-making institutions range from trade schools to such well-known institutions as the Berklee College of Music.

Ownership is clearly central to control, but it does not exhaust it. Many different actors influence higher educational institutions without necessarily owning them. For example, state agencies, such as boards of higher education, not only own and operate a large number of state universities and colleges but they also exert considerable control over private colleges through financial aid and administrative regulations.[7] Similarly, the federal government owns very few institutions, but it influences other institutions through its student aid, funds for research and development, and so forth.[8] In addition, faculty members can exert control over colleges both internally and externally. Internally, faculty usually have the dominant voice in setting the curriculum and other academic policies. Externally, faculty can influence colleges through college ratings issued by the American Association of University Professors and accrediting associations and through the ideas they develop regarding the proper purposes and methods of higher education.[9] And students, finally, exert control over colleges through their decisions over which colleges and majors to enroll in (Riesman, 1980). As a result of these many different forms of control—ownership, federal aid, state regulation, academic evaluation, and student choice—the American higher education system is actually more homogeneous than would be expected on the basis of its very disparate pattern of ownership. Public and private institutions of different kinds are more similar than one would expect on the basis of their often quite different structures of ownership.

Student Body Composition

Colleges differ not only in their programs and control but also in the characteristics of their student body. While most colleges do not draw exclusively on students of one sex, race, social class, or ability level, colleges still differ considerably in their student mix. For the most part, as one moves from universities to four-year colleges to two-year colleges, the proportion of students who are male, white, upper class, or academically high performing drops. This can be seen in Table 3, which presents the sexual, racial, social class, and academic achievement composition of different kinds of colleges.

In addition, a certain number of colleges specialize in certain kinds of students. There are still 214 single-sex colleges (6 percent of all colleges) (U.S. Department of Education, 1985: 168).[10] Similarly, there is a sizable number of single-race colleges. Perhaps the most notable are the 99 all-black public and private colleges. Located primarily in the South and the border states, these colleges—which include such well-known institutions as Howard, Fisk, and Grambling—play a key role in black education. While they enroll only 20 percent of all black college students, they graduate a majority of all black doctors and lawyers (U.S. Department of Education, 1987a: 122, 151, 157).[11]

TABLE 3   Student Body Composition of Various Types of U.S. Colleges

	(1) Sex: % male (1986)	(2) Race: % white (1986)	(3) Social Class: % with family income above $50,000 (1986)	(4) Academic Ability: % in top fifth of high school class (1986)
Four-Year Institutions	48	81	33	44
Two-Year Institutions	44	76	19	24

Note: The source of the data in columns 1 and 2 is U.S Department of Education (1988a: 170; 1988b: 40). The source for columns 3 and 4 is American Council on Education (1986: 47–48). The figures for sex and race composition are for all students, while the figures for social class and academic ability composition are for freshmen.

Prestige

Colleges are ranked in prestige by students, faculty, the government, and employers. A college's prestige is compounded of the range and level of its degree offerings, its history, its student body composition (particularly its social class and academic composition), and the career success of its graduates. This prestige is important in securing funding, attracting faculty, and enhancing the career outcomes for students. For example, there is evidence that more prestigious schools—particularly those marked by more selective admissions policies—tend to have a more positive impact on their students' economic success than do less prestigious schools, even when one compares students with similar entering characteristics.[12]

No hard-and-fast categorization of colleges by prestige is possible. But the most prestigious institutions tend to be universities—particularly the Ivy League universities and the "Public Ivy" universities such as California and Wisconsin—and the least prestigious institutions tend to be two-year colleges.[13] And within each group, public institutions and private nonprofit nonsectarian institutions tend to be more prestigious than religious and, even more so, proprietary institutions.

THE DEVELOPMENT OF THE U.S. HIGHER EDUCATION SYSTEM

The U.S. higher education system only gradually took on its present diversity of types of institutions. Before the Civil War, some states founded state universities, but U.S. colleges were almost exclusively small colleges, offering either training for the ministry or a general liberal arts education. The training they offered was essentially at the secondary level, because the high school had not yet emerged. These colleges rapidly multiplied, soon exceeding the number in any comparable European country. This multiplication was stimulated by our decentralized governmental system, which allowed states and localities to strive to have their own colleges, and the combination of church-state separation and great religious diversity, which led to denominational competition in establishing colleges (Collins, 1979: 118–121; Jencks and Riesman, 1968: 1–8, 185–186; Rudolph, 1962: 51–55, 275–277).

The next major change in the structure of the U.S. higher education system came in the 80-year stretch between the Civil War and World War II. This era witnessed the higher education system's accommodation to the education of women, Catholics, and blacks, as colleges were founded to meet the educational needs of these groups (Jencks and Riesman, 1968: chaps. 7, 9–10; Rudolph, 1962: chap. 15; Solomon, 1985).

In addition, state universities rapidly multiplied as state governments in the Midwest and West took advantage of federal land grants under the Morrill Act (1862) to finance "land grant" universities. State governments were motivated largely by the traditional desire of wanting an institution to represent one's own regional culture (Jencks and Riesman, 1968: 157–158; Rudolph, 1962: 277–280).

Meanwhile, many private colleges, such as Harvard and Yale, converted themselves into universities, in part as a solution to the problem of declining enrollments due to the oversupply of colleges in the mid-19th century. At the same time, several new private universities were founded, such as Johns Hopkins University (1876), the University of Chicago (1892), and Stanford University (1885). The new universities, whether public or private, proved more attractive than the traditional college. They provided an alternative to the traditional classical curriculum (emphasizing required courses in the humanities and knowledge of Greek and Latin) by offering science and modern foreign languages and elective courses. And they provided superior access to the professions through university graduate and professional schools that were being founded in the late 19th and early 20th century (Collins, 1979: 121–127; Rudolph, 1962: 348–354; Veysey, 1965).

The final restructuring of U.S. higher education came in the post–World War II era and, more particularly, since the 1960s. Although they had appeared much earlier, two-year colleges exploded in number in the last 25 years. Their development can be traced to a complex mix of forces: the growing number of students desiring college access; business and government officials' interest in postsecondary vocational education; state government officials' desire to curb state higher education budgets and promote economic growth by diverting students away from universities toward the cheaper and more vocationally oriented community colleges; state universities' desire to remain academically selective by diverting less able students to two-year colleges; and local educators' desire for the prestige and opportunities attendant with founding a local college (Dougherty, 1988).

Another major phenomenon of the post–World War II era has been the consolidation of what has been called the "multiversities"—vast universities combining research, teaching, and public service—under the impetus of the huge growth of federal spending on research and development (Kerr, 1963).[14] In recent years, the multiversities have taken on a new feature, as many become "entrepreneurial universities" that establish profit-making companies to cash in on their research capacity. The most notable example is in the areas of computer science, electronics, and microbiology research involving recombinant DNA techniques (Etzkowitz, 1983).

COMPARISON TO THE HIGHER EDUCATIONAL SYSTEMS OF OTHER SOCIETIES

The U.S. higher education system differs from those of other industrial societies in both size, structure, and operation. As we discussed earlier, the U.S. system is much larger in both absolute and relative size than other systems. No country comes close to our 12.5 million students. And no country enrolls as large a proportion of its population as ours does. For example, 5.4 percent of all Americans are in college. The comparable figures are 2.3 percent in West Germany, 2.2 percent in France, 2.0 percent in Japan and the Soviet Union, and 1.6 percent in Great Britain (United Nations Economic, Scientific, and Cultural Organization, 1985, III: 241, 243–245).[15]

Moreover, the U.S. system has a much larger private component, comprising half of all colleges and enrolling a quarter of all students (U.S. Department of Education, 1987a: 122, 168). But the other advanced industrial societies, with the notable exception of Japan, largely do not have private colleges (Clark, 1983: 53–62).

Similarly, the United States has institutions that are virtually unknown in other systems. The four-year liberal arts college without any graduate program is rare outside the United States, and the two-year public or private junior college, which represents 40 percent of all American colleges, is an American invention.[16]

In addition, U.S. colleges are organized in a manner different from non-American colleges. The basic unit of instruction in the American college is the department, made up of teachers holding roughly equal status and engaged in both teaching and research. But the European university is organized on the basis of chairs, who then hire and supervise subordinate faculty. Research is often handled outside the university, through independent research institutes (Clark, 1983: 46–49, 110–116).

Finally, the U.S. higher education system is also much less directed by the national government than are the higher education systems of other industrial societies, in which a Ministry of Education typically finances the institutions and appoints their directors.[17] Instead, American higher education is governed by state and local governments and private boards, and federal funds make up only a small proportion of all higher education revenues (Clark, 1983: 53–62, 137–145).[18]

CONCLUSIONS

On reflection, the U.S. higher education system is much more complicated than it appears at first glance. Its component institutions are quite varied in their curricula and degrees, type of control, student body composition, and prestige. The U.S. system is also, in comparative terms, quite unusual. It is much larger than other higher education systems and has a quite different structure. These features of the U.S. higher education system bring both strength and weaknesses. Because it is so varied and decentralized, the U.S. system is very open to change, adapting fairly rapidly to new demands. But the U.S. system's decentralization also makes it hard to produce equality of educational treatment and results because it is so hard to enforce common policies across the various, highly autonomous institutions (Clark, 1983: 66–67, 190–192).

NOTES

1. The Department's classification originated with the Carnegie Commission on Higher Education (1973). These five categories are often subdivided further.

2. The doctoral institutions can be subdivided further. The Carnegie Foundation for the Advancement of Teaching distinguishes between "research universities" such as M.I.T. and the University of Michigan, which take in the largest amounts of federal funds and produce the largest number of doctoral and professional graduates, and less research-oriented and degree-productive institutions such as Clark University and Western Michigan University (Carnegie Foundation for the Advancement of Teaching, 1987).

3. For an analysis of the more distinctive private liberal arts colleges such as Mills, Sarah Lawrence, and the Claremont Colleges, see Keeton (1971).

4. The number of two-year institutions would be far greater if we were to include the many for-profit colleges offering technical and vocational training. Such colleges numbered 7645 in 1986 (U.S. Department of Education, 1987b: viii).

5. State control used to be exercised through a combination of legislative appropriations and supervision through boards of trustees attached to each college. The result was a great deal of independence for each college. Today, many states have state higher education systems presided over by state higher education boards. As a result, state colleges have gained in coordination but have also lost in autonomy and distinctiveness.

6. For a discussion of the history of religious colleges, see Jencks and Riesman (1968: chaps. 8–9). The Protestant religious colleges are enjoying a strong revival now due to the upsurge of membership and activism among Protestant evangelical denominations (Riesman, 1980: chap. 5).

7. The most striking example is the New York State Board of Regents and its staff arm, the New York State Department of Education. The Regents can order private colleges, and not just public colleges, to eliminate programs or even to shut down if they do not think that their enrollments or quality warrant continuation.

8. For example, the federal government has been able to push colleges to institute affirmative action programs to hire women and minorities and to open up their athletic programs to women by raising the threat of withdrawing federal funds.

9. The faculty's power is largely a 20th century phenomenon in the United States. However, in Europe, the faculty has long been very powerful (Clark, 1983: chaps. 4–5). For an analysis of the American faculty's rise to power, see Jencks and Riesman (1968).

10. For a history and critical analysis of women's colleges, see Rudolph (1962: chap. 15) and Jencks and Riesman (1968: chap. 7). Not all scholars are entirely sold on the benefits of the shift toward coeducation. David Riesman (1979) has raised the question of whether female students might do better academically and personally in all-female schools.

11. For a history and critical analysis of the Black colleges, see Jencks and Riesman (1968: chap. 10). It should be pointed out that the black colleges are not the only single-race colleges. Many colleges have so few nonwhites as to be "white" colleges. These all-white colleges have a considerably different nature than all-black colleges. They are not havens for a subordinate group and, in fact, are sometimes exclusive bastions for the dominant racial group.

12. For evidence of a college quality effect, see Dougherty (1987); Jencks and others (1979: 186–187); Karabel and McClelland (1987); Solmon and Taubman (1973); and Useem and Karabel (1986).

13. Clearly, there are many exceptions to this generalization. There are a fair number of liberal arts colleges—such as Swarthmore, Bryn Mawr, and Grinnell—that are more prestigious than most universities. And similar, although far less numerous, exceptions can be found among two-year colleges.

14. This combination has existed ever since the late 19th century, embodied in the state universities in Michigan, Wisconsin, California, and other states. But this combination was consolidated in the post–World War II period as the pioneering state multiversities were joined by other state universities and many private universities under the impetus of rapidly rising federal aid for research and development.

15. The far larger proportion of students that the United States keeps on after the end of compulsory schooling—around age 16 in most industrial societies—makes hazardous and even invalid any simple contrast between American and foreign college students' characteristics and accomplishments. Yet such invidious comparisons have become a staple of current criticisms of the American educational system. See Chapter 10.

16. Japan imported the American two-year college and now has around 500 (Clark, 1983: 60). Moreover, other countries are increasingly emulating the American two-year college in such forms as the British "college of further education" or "technical college" (King, 1976).

17. Again, Japan is a partial exception. A large portion of its higher education system is privately operated, although substantially funded by the national government (Clark, 1983: 60, 131).

18. However, for the research universities, federal funds make up a very large proportion of their revenues. For example, M.I.T. receives the bulk of its revenues from the federal government.

REFERENCES

American Council on Education. 1986. *The American Freshman: National Norms for Fall 1986.* ERIC ED 278 296. Los Angeles: Higher Education Research Institute, University of California, Los Angeles.

Carnegie Commission on Higher Education. 1973. *A Classification of Institutions of Higher Education.* Berkeley, CA: Carnegie Commission on Higher Education.

Carnegie Foundation for the Advancement of Teaching. 1987. *A Classification of Institutions of Higher Education.* Princeton, NJ: Author.

Clark, Burton. 1983. *The Higher Education System.* Berkeley: University of California Press.

———(ed.) 1985. *The School and the University: An International Perspective.* Berkeley: University of California Press.

Cohen, Arthur, M., and Florence Brawer. 1982. *The American Community College.* San Francisco: Jossey-Bass.

Collins, Randall. 1979. *The Credential Society.* New York: Academic Press.

Dougherty, Kevin J. 1987. "The Effects of Community Colleges: Aid or Hindrance to Socioeconomic Attainment?" *Sociology of Education* 60 (April): 86–103. (See Chapter 5 of this book.)

———. 1988. "The Politics of Community College Expansion." *American Journal of Education* 96 (May): 351–393.

Dunham, E. Alden. 1969. *Colleges of the Forgotten Americans: A Profile of State Colleges and Regional Universities.* New York: McGraw-Hill.

Etzkowitz, Henry. 1983. "Entrepreneurial Scientists and Entrepreneurial Universities in American Academic Science." *Minerva* (autumn): 198–233.

Jencks, Christopher S., and David Riesman. 1968. *The Academic Revolution.* New York: Doubleday.

_____, Susan Bartlett, Mary Corcoran, James Crouse, David Eaglesfield, Gregory Jackson, Kent McClelland, Peter Mueser, Michael Olneck, Joseph Schwartz, Sherry Ward, Jill Williams. 1979. *Who Gets Ahead?* New York: Basic Books.

Karabel, Jerome, and Katherine McClelland. 1987. "Occupational Advantage and the Impact of College Rank on Labor Market Outcomes." *Sociological Inquiry* 57 (fall): 323–347.

Keeton, Morris T. 1971. *Models and Mavericks: A Profile of Private Liberal Arts Colleges.* New York: McGraw-Hill.

Kerr, Clark. 1963. *The Uses of the University.* New York: Harper & Row.

King, Ronald. 1976. *Schools and College: Studies of Post-Sixteen Education.* London: Routledge and Kegan Paul.

Riesman, David. 1979. "A Conversation with Simmons College." *Journal of General Education* 31 (summer): 79–108.

_____. 1980. *On Higher Education.* San Francisco: Jossey-Bass.

Rudolph, Frederick. 1962. *The American College and University.* New York: Vintage.

Solmon, Lewis, and Paul Taubman (eds.). 1973. *Does College Matter?* New York: Academic Press.

Solomon, Barbara Miller. 1985. *In the Company of Educated Women.* New Haven, CT: Yale University Press.

United Nations Educational, Scientific, and Cultural Organization (UNESCO). 1985. *Statistical Yearbook, 1985.* Paris: UNESCO.

U.S. Department of Education. Center for Education Statistics. 1985. *Fall Enrollment in Colleges and Universities, 1983.* Washington, DC: Government Printing Office.

_____. 1987a. *Digest of Educational Statistics, 1987.* Washington, DC: Government Printing Office.

_____. 1987b. *1986 Directory of Postsecondary Institutions.* ASI 1987 4844-3. Washington, DC: Government Printing Office.

_____. 1988a. *Digest of Educational Statistics, 1988.* Washington, DC: Government Printing Office.

_____. 1988b. *Postsecondary Fall Enrollment, 1986.* ASI 1988 4844-2. Washington, DC: Government Printing Office.

Useem, Michael, and Jerome Karabel. 1986. "Pathways to Top Corporate Management." *American Sociological Review* 51 (April): 184–200.

Veysey, Laurence. 1965. *The Emergence of the American University.* Chicago: University of Chicago Press.

4

Teachers, Teaching, and the Organizational Dynamics of Education in the United States

Chapter 3 has made clear that education varies dramatically across nations. The level of economic development characteristic of a society, as well as its history and cultural patterns, affects the nature of the education it provides its citizens. Clearly, education does not exist separate from other aspects of the society. This chapter takes the structural perspective one step closer to the classroom, where education actually takes place. Here, we examine the organization of schools, how it came to take the shape it does, its implications for teachers' work lives and for instruction. The organization of schools has changed over time; yet, whatever shape it has taken, it dramatically affects those who work and learn within it.

Schools are places of employment for teachers as well as places of learning for students. Like many work organizations, schools have several types of authority structures, and relationships between them are not always easy or smooth. Because schools are complex work organizations, we first ask what kind of organization a school has and what the consequences of that form or organization for teachers are. Next, we discuss alternative ways teaching is organized as an occupation, particularly the degree to which it has become professionalized. The barriers to full professional standing are explored, setting the stage for analyzing the alternative of unionization. Of particular interest is how the development of teaching as an occupation has been affected by teachers' characteristics and the organization of schools. Finally, a variety of barriers to proposed improvements in the education and standing of teachers will be identified and related to enduring problems in education. The readings that follow serve to expand in greater detail the themes of organization and occupation discussed in this introduction.

168

THE ORGANIZATION OF SCHOOLS

In the starkest outline, most schools are composed of at least several hundred children grouped generally by age into classrooms of 20 to as many as 40 students overseen by a teacher. This general form has been dominant for many years and has proved very resilient. Despite efforts to change the basic form of classrooms and of schools, the high school, in particular, has been virtually impervious to such reforms. As Cuban (1984: 260) notes, while some change has taken place in curricula, in how teachers relate with students and conduct lessons, these changes are small in comparison to the unchanged, persistent behavior of teachers. Sirotnik (1983) has demonstrated how surprisingly little variety of a classroom activity and organization is produced by our widely decentralized educational system. Across the United States, in elementary and some middle schools, there is little organizational differentiation among teachers; departments are not usually found until high school. Among teachers there are few formal acknowledgments of differences in age or expertise or experience; ranks as among professors in higher education are absent and most unionized districts pay teachers only according to their education and years of experience (Clark, 1985). Merit-pay schemes, a frequently mentioned reform, are still very rare. Inside their classrooms, teachers are dominant and often exercise a high degree of autonomy, but seldom do they control issues affecting the school at large, such as criteria for pupil promotion from one grade to another, testing policies, and general curricular decisions. These decisions are the province of administrators and the school board. A good example of this is provided by the statewide book selection committee in Texas that prepares a list of all books that can be used in Texas schools. School district personnel can only chose from among the books on the list.

All organizations rely on a central principle of authority to govern the relations between their members. Schools rely on three different principles: bureaucratic, professional, and democratic (Hurn, 1985). The incompatibilities and resulting problems created by these different principles in schools will be a major theme of this introduction. We now turn to exploring each of the principles.

Bureaucratic Authority

Organizations with bureaucratic authority systems are governed by legal-rational principles that rest on law and on assessments of the "best" way to delegate responsibility and authority to achieve the required tasks. A hierarchy of authority results that requires employees at lower levels to obey the legitimate (within the legal limits of the job description) requests of superiors. Individual classroom teachers, as we will see, are usually told what the curriculum will include, what books to use, and what objectives they should strive to achieve. School boards, central school district authorities, and state education authorities make these decisions, along with many others. These goals and the means to achieve them descend to school-level principals and curriculum leaders and then to teachers. The authority at each level is supposed to be vested in those who are best able to exercise it; that is, organizational control is supposed to be "rational" in that there is an explicit means/ends rationale. This is a statement of the principle and does not always match the reality of organizational life. Yet, the very fact that we notice the irrationality of some organizational practices is evidence of our expectation that bureaucracies will act rationally.

Schools are bureaucratic organizations because they serve explicit goals and are composed of a variety of people who do specialized work and whose efforts need to be coordinated. Formal rules specify which jobs are to be done within the organization, and there are explicit differences in the authority of members according to their place in the school's hierarchy (Bidwell, 1965; Corwin, 1970; Katz, 1964).[1]

It is hard to overemphasize the importance of size in determining the bureaucratic characteristics of schools. As research on many kinds of organizations has shown (Hall, 1987), greater organization size almost always brings formalization of rules and relationships. In large groups, individuals do not get the opportunity to know each other well and, even more important, if a hierarchy of authority exists, the equality necessary for easy informal relations is missing. Greater school size also brings diversity among students, because large size entails a more heterogeneous student body.[2] Such diversity reinforces the effects of size, resulting in more formal relationships than are encouraged by smaller size and greater hemogeneity.

Professional Authority

In organizations with professional authority, control over decisions is based primarily on expertise and on equality of those qualified by education and achievement. Organizations based on professional authority—such as universities and colleges, partnership law firms, and certain aspects of hospitals—distribute authority equally, without elaborate hierarchies, among their professional members. As with bureaucracies, the power of individual members to participate in collective decision making and in the conduct of their professional activities may be rooted in law, but need not be. The expertise of professionals is translated in these organizations into rules that assert that only their peers are competent to participate in decisions affecting the professional practice. When professionals are employed in bureaucratic settings, their free exercise of professional practice may be limited by bureaucratic hierarchy.

We should not draw the distinction between bureaucratic and professional bases of authority too tightly, however. In an important respect the two forms are compatible: They both respect expertise. What separates them is how and to what degree they protect the freedom of professionals to practice their

---

[1]At least as important, these rules are often violated and serve more as public announcements of the intentions of the organization and its sponsors than as realistic descriptions of the actual behavior within it.

[2]Early urban school organizers saw large size as a more efficient use of educational resources than would be provided by smaller schools. See Tyack (1974) for more on this topic.

expertise. For organizations run by professionals, the protection of professional autonomy is second only to economic viability. For bureaucratically run organizations, other concerns may interfere. We will return to this theme of similarities and differences between these two bases of organizational authority. There is, however, one more which is also found in schools.

Democratic Authority

Finally, some organizations are governed by democratic principles. Democratic organizations distribute authority even more equally, among all members, giving it not to just administrators or experts, but to members generally. Decisions are arrived at through mechanisms like elections where rights are equally distributed.

Although there are few examples of such organizations outside of overtly political party organizations and many labor unions, schools are partly democratic. While students do not have a vote, all adults can elect school board members and, in referenda, vote directly for school budgets. And, in some alternative schools, even students have a vote (Swidler, 1979). Our tradition of local control of public schools is inherently suspicious of educational decisions being made by authorities who are not directly accountable to the local citizens who are largely financing the schools. Highly bureaucratized or professionalized educational organizations are held to be undemocratic. For example, we accept such organizational forms in colleges and universities, where professional control is strong, but have found them unacceptable at lower levels.

We need to explore how each of these three principles of organization and authority operates in the schools and how they interact. The combination of bureaucratic, professional, and democratic forms of organization makes schools distinctive organizations, with distinctive problems. These different and sometimes competing bases of organizational authority cause consequences that are the subject of the readings in this chapter and are often picked up in subsequent chapters.

The Consequences of Multiple Forms of Authority in Schools

The selections by Metz and by Lieberman and Miller illuminate the educational consequences of teachers' peculiar bureaucratic yet professional and democratic work setting. Teachers operate under bureaucratic controls, but as Metz points out, often the board of education has no clear consensus on what "educate" means (or what the central goals are), though there usually are explicit tests students must pass and for which teachers must prepare students. On the other hand, teachers are supposed to be professionals, but the technology of teaching is relatively primitive, without "magic bullets" or drugs that can "heal" the patients or eradicate ignorance (Meyer and Rowan, 1978). Moreover, teachers depend more on the clients than do other professionals. To be successful, teachers need students to actively participate in their own education (Mehan, 1980; Willis, 1981). Therefore, teachers must be centrally concerned with encouraging students to desire what teachers have to offer, to motivate them to value school achievement and to conform to the essential requirements of the classroom.[3] As Metz points out, the teacher's authority to conduct class is always problematic and requires continuous effort to maintain. The organization of schools, the nature of teachers' clients, and the work to be accomplished make success as a teacher far more difficult than for other professionals.

Lieberman and Miller provide a window into the teacher's world not only by describing many of the operative social norms, but also by describing the "dailiness" of teaching. Using extensive quotes from teachers, this selection connects many of the problems (and satisfactions) of teaching with the partial bureaucratization and partial professionalization of schools described here.

TEACHING'S DIFFICULTY IN PROFESSIONALIZING

Among the most important correlates of the multiple forms of authority in schools has been the failure of teaching to become fully professionalized. As a principle of occupational organization, professionalization is distinctive and highly attractive. What distinguishes a profession from occupations has been a source of considerable debate (Hall, 1987; Metzger, 1987). But it is clear, as we noted above in distinguishing among types of organizational authority, that an essential feature is greater autonomy in carrying out their work than is generally the case for other occupations. Professionals argue for this autonomy on the basis of the nonroutine nature of their work and the complex knowledge base and advanced skills that must be mastered (Freidson, 1970, 1985; Larson, 1977). In addition, professional occupations are characterized by lengthy preparation and close supervision by more senior colleagues during early years of professional practice. Furthermore, the most fully developed professional groups have been given by the state a monopoly over the work they perform. In order to protect citizens from unqualified and unscrupulous practitioners, state legislatures pass laws regulating who can practice, what credentials they must present to obtain a license to practice, and what the nature of the practice itself is. In return, those who meet these requirements are free from unlicensed competition.[4]

Teachers have long wanted to emulate the prestige, power, and income of such professions as law and medicine (Lieberman, 1956). Yet they have never been able to, with the result that teaching is often classified a "semiprofession" (Lortie, 1969, 1975). Furthermore, as we noted earlier, teachers seldom have control over the curriculum they are expected to teach. State education authorities and local lay school district officials determine not only broad curriculum objectives but also the very means (materials, books, and so on) to achieve them.[5]

---

[3]Blase (1986) provides a fascinating discussion of how students influence teachers as well.

[4]It is important to note here that professional occupations are not the only ones that are regulated in this way by the state. New York State, for example, regulates 31 occupations, ranging from lawyers to barbers.

[5]Depending on the preferences of school principals and union contracts, individual classroom teachers may have autonomy regarding the exact use of materials and the pacing of the

Furthermore, in a growing number of states, including New Jersey and Arkansas, students must pass statewide, standardized tests to move from one grade to the next. To the degree that the methods or materials of teaching are codified in state or district law and rules, teachers and administrators are both constrained and limited in their ability to develop patterns of educational practice most appropriate to their local conditions (Rosenholtz, 1987). Since the right of relatively autonomous practice is a hallmark of professional standing for an occupation, the imposition of systemwide standards (such as minimum competency tests for promotion or graduation) on schools has the consequence of restricting the possibilities for professionalization of teachers.[6]

Teachers are licensed, but only recently, and only in a minority of states have beginning teachers been required to pass a licensing test, which is the final barrier students must pass in medicine, law, and engineering, for example.[7] Moreover, the strength of licensing provisions for teachers is not very strong. Teacher shortages in many areas have led teachers to be assigned to teach in fields for which they are unprepared ("out-of-license").[8] The flexibility of administrators and boards of education to staff their schools and assign teachers has been protected in most states' education law and in many teacher union contracts.

Several reasons account for teaching's incomplete professionalization. First, an occupation's ability to professionalize is dependent on a variety of factors, including the demand for its services or products. There must be a market for the work of the profession, and it must be one for which a monopoly can be obtained. Beyond this, an occupation's growth depends in part on its own internal organization, which in turn is strongly influenced by the setting in which the work is performed. Solo or small-group practice has given doctors and lawyers a control over their work that is unavailable to those who must practice their occupation within large, bureaucratic organizations (Larson, 1977). Even though some teachers do engage in private, solo practice, as in the case of many music teachers, most teachers find an independent existence as a teacher impossible. The "group" practice in which most teachers engage takes place in a school. As employees of school authorities—instead of being solo practitioners or partners in jointly owned businesses like most law firms and medical practices—teachers encounter dramatically different relations to their work than do other professionals.

---

curriculum. But even though they are not often directly supervised and are usually alone with students for long periods during the school day, many teachers have little real autonomy in how they do their work.

[6]See Chapter 10 for a more extensive discussion of educational reform proposals and the contradiction between those proposals for stricter bureaucratic control over education and those encouraging the professionalization of teachers.

[7]See Shepard and Kreitzer (1987) for a recent discussion of the attempt by Texas to test all practicing teachers.

[8]Lieberman (1956) and Lortie (1969) both give good, if early, reviews of teacher professionalism.

They are employees subject to a level of external and lay control that would not exist within a medical or legal partnership.

Second, characteristics of teaching limit its ability to professionalize. Because the clients are children, many adults think working with them requires no special skills, especially in the early grades when the curriculum is not beyond the intellectual mastery of most citizens. Hence, the expertise and special skills teachers do possess are often discounted (Lortie, 1975).

Third, teaching has also been hampered in its professionalization by the fact that it has long been a predominantly female occupation. With the expansion of elementary schooling in the middle and latter half of the 19th century, teaching emerged as a large-scale occupation. While the earliest teachers were predominantly male, females came to outnumber males during the rapid expansion of schools after the Civil War. There are a number of explanations for this gender shift, but it seems clear that a major factor was women's willingness to accept lower wages than men due to their lack of alternatives for "respectable," middle-class employment (Rury, 1986). Secondary schools—which were mostly concerned with college preparation until well into the 20th century (Trow, 1961)—were initially staffed largely by males. As secondary schools grew in size, diversity, and number, female teachers came to dominate their teaching staff as well, but not to the degree they did (and still do) at the elementary level (Tyack and Hansot, 1982: 183).

The gender pattern of teaching had two important consequences for teaching's ability to professionalize. To begin with, because middle-class women had few alternatives in the labor market, their leverage or bargaining power over school administrators and local boards of education was low. This lack of power led to lower wages and constrained the development of career paths within teaching. In addition, teaching provided females with a flexibility available in no other form of middle-class employment. One could move into and out of teaching as family obligations dictated. Work hours were shorter than for most other full-time jobs—even other female-dominated occupations like nursing—and holidays and summer vacations were longer than other employment provided. These attributes made teaching attractive to individual women with domestic responsibilities, but they also inhibited its development as a profession. Moving in and out of teaching symbolized teachers' commitments to pursuits in addition to teaching and thus lessened their ability to devote all their energies to moving the occupation to a profession.

Teaching's attractiveness has been its flexibility and the middle-class status teachers enjoyed as one of the best-educated occupations in society. Until recently, the labor market offered women few middle-class occupations (nursing, social work, secretarial work). One important way the labor market remained closed to women was that many undergraduate and graduate programs and schools discouraged women from seeking admission. Without the necessary training, credentials required for professional license were unavailable, and, without the credentials, many of the most attractive occupations were closed. However, with the passage of civil rights legislation during the mid-1960s and the rise of the women's movement, previously closed labor market options opened up. An important result is that teaching today has very strong competition from occupations newly opened to women. In fact, as Darling-Hammond (1984) has shown, few well-prepared women are currently preparing for or entering teaching.

Fourth, the lack of a scientifically well-established technology of teaching has been a barrier to the professionalization of teaching. The ability to deliver a predictable result from professional intervention has been central to medicine's professional growth. As Freidson (1970) and Larson (1977) have noted, it is the monopoly of the application of science to health care that is largely responsible for the great power medicine achieved. Because science has provided physicians with powerful tools (X-rays and drugs, for example), the ability of the profession to improve our health has been greatly increased and has helped further the profession's claims for autonomy. But, as we pointed out in the first chapter, social science has not provided teachers with similarly powerful educational tools. Therefore, teachers have not been able to produce equivalent results among their students and the ability of teachers to professionalize has suffered.

Fifth, the tradition of local control of education has limited the ability of teachers to achieve professional standing. As Chapter 3 elaborated,[9] the local community's involvement in financing and governing education has limited teaching's ability to successfully make claims for autonomy. Lay control, virtually by definition, contradicts professional control.

Finally, the strength of educational administrators inside of schools also restricted professionalization. Educational administrators try to keep careful control over teachers. Administrators usually serve at the pleasure of the board, which often views administrators' primary job as keeping the schools running smoothly and avoiding conflict.[10] Closely controlling teachers is one way to attempt to assure the smooth operation of the school (Callahan, 1962; Tyack and Hansot, 1982).

Of course, unionization has discouraged cooperative relations between administrators and teachers. Administrators are often not unionized or are members of a union different from the teachers, but are always expected by the local board of education to represent the employer in relations with teachers. At the same time, the requirements of accountability laid down by state authorities restrict even administrators in their flexibility and, importantly, in their exercise of expertise.

Unionization as a Response to the Limits of Teacher Professionalization

Their status as employees has encouraged teachers to consider other ways of developing an occupational organization and improving the conditions of their employment. Although there were earlier examples of unionization,

---

[9]See the introduction and the article by Hammack for more on our tradition of local control of education.

[10]See the Kerr article in this chapter for more on the attempts by educational administrators—in this case superintendents—to keep control of schools and the local boards of education.

teaching became largely unionized during the 1960s and 1970s. If professional recognition and autonomy are not available, other ways to influence conditions of employment become attractive. Unionization offered the power to negotiate with school districts over working conditions and compensation (Rosenthal, 1969; Johnson, 1983). Of course, there are costs to collective action, especially a loss of individual choice, which can be seen to contradict the spirit of the professional argument for individual autonomy and judgment. Nevertheless, teachers in most public and many private school systems have unionized.

Both unionization and professionalization require motivated workers who see their individual prospects as dependent on joining with others to gain control over critical aspects of the work they do. As long as most teachers were female, confronted with a labor market offering very few alternatives and attracted to teaching because it did not demand continuous employment, it was unlikely that teachers would become either professionalized or unionized.

The selection by Warren, giving an historical analysis of teachers, teaching, and teacher education, adds depth to the brief review presented above and emphasizes the continuities faced by teaching and its efforts to reform. First, according to Warren, teachers' ability to control qualifications for entry has been low. Because teachers do not control their market, the number of employed teachers is determined by what boards of education decide they can afford. Second, conflict over the responsibility for teacher education has been common. Colleges, school districts, and unions all vie for the teacher education market. Finally, he argues that teacher preparation focused on instruction has isolated teachers from the broader social and political issues of education. Teaching, he asserts, needs to become professional.

The prospects for teaching's professionalization may be greater now than in the past. Today, women are far more likely to be in the labor force during their child-rearing years, and are likely to have a consequently stronger commitment to career advancement as well as a much wider range of occupations from which to choose. These circumstances, along with the prospects of a significant teacher shortage, may force some of organizational and political barriers to professionalization to fall. Only when teaching becomes more professional and better compensated, the argument goes, will teaching attract the highly able students required to carry out the broader educational reforms now being implemented (Carnegie Forum, 1986; Case, Lanier, and Miskel, 1986).

THE CHALLENGES OF LOCAL CONTROL

The professionalization of teaching is thwarted not only by the fact it alters the relationships between teachers, students, and administrators, but also because it clearly changes the role of the local community. The tradition of local control of schools by elected lay boards of education whose policies are administered by full-time administrators is one of the important ways teacher professionalization is impeded.

Schools are not only workplaces for teachers but also places where communities try to pass on their ways of life to their children. In many places schools are the primary agency of community continuity and pride. This is perhaps especially the case in communities feeling threatened either by changes in racial or ethnic housing patterns (as is common in cities) or economic and demographic decline (as in smaller and rural communities).[11] In such circumstances the local schools are often seen as one of the primary tools by which a community may defend itself. Of course, such a defense is threatened by desegregation or consolidation. But this community reproduction is also threatened by state regulation (which may cause consolidation, as the process of merging small, previously independent school districts is known) and teacher professionalization. Both have the same consequences as far as citizens are concerned: less control over the more distant schools that educate their children. The states often require schools to have resources that small, local schools cannot afford, and thus force consolidation and the loss of the local school as a focus of town life. Professionalization threatens by shifting authority from community lay people to educational experts, who do not necessarily have the promotion of local community values as their top priority.

The importance of local control throws into question the recently fashionable idea of the teacher as a "transformative intellectual." Aronowitz and Giroux (1985) have envisioned a new role for teachers that would combine teachers' intellectual autonomy with a conscious effort to increase their political activity aimed at transforming the larger society. "In effect, we are arguing that teachers as transformative intellectuals need to become a movement marked by an active involvement in oppositional public spheres in which the primacy of the political is asserted anew" (1985: 42). How such advocacy will fit with the wide community accountability that local control fosters is not clear and not explored by Aronowitz and Giroux.

Close community control is also a problem for schools and for students. The Peshkin selection, "Whom Shall the Schools Serve?", reminds us of how central schools are in maintaining a sense of belonging among members of a community. This selection, moreover, points out the logic of democratic, or local, control of the schools. By most states' law, local citizens are required to tax themselves for most of their schools' expenses and are provided, through the principle of "no taxation without representation," with the right to elect members of the boards of education responsible for expending tax money for schooling. At the same time, local control can be so tight as to not prepare youth for the society outside of the home community and may severly restrict teacher and administrator autonomy.

There is no question, however, as Coleman (1987) has recently emphasized, about the size of the academic and social benefits for students and the surrounding society derived from close relations between schools and their environing communities. His research on Catholic schools, where close

---

[11]Fein (1971) and Altschuler (1970) offer particularly good discussions of the complex issues of community control in large, urban settings.

religious, moral, and often ethnic ties link schools and families, shows how students are more likely to stay in school and to academically achieve.

The selection by Norman Kerr illuminates one of administrators' main solutions to the constraints set by local popular control. Because of their access to and control over information and their full-time staff, superintendents are often able to control the boards of education they serve. Since Kerr's article was written, teacher unionization and complex district politics are more common. Nevertheless, Kerr's research points to the tensions between lay and professional control over education prevalent today. How do professional educators, in this case administrators, maintain their professional aspirations while employed in at least partially bureaucratic settings controlled by state-level authorities and local laypersons? For illumination, we need to look at the history of teacher professionalization.

CONCLUSIONS

This introduction has emphasized how aspects of the structure of schooling influence and interact with the occupational roles available within it. The problems arising from differing goals for schools, from significantly different principles of organizational authority, and from the history and current status of teaching as an occupation have been linked together and explored.

The discussion here points to a conflict between those who seek the improvement of education through state regulation and control and those who see this improvement through the widening of teachers' ability to exercise their expertise more autonomously (Borrowman, 1956: Carnegie Forum, 1986; Murray, Chapter 10 in this book). Reformers are moving in different directions at the same time: more bureaucratization or more professionalization. Warren shows how such issues have characterized education and influenced debate about the preparation of teachers since the 19th century. The organization of schools is influenced by how communities and their leaders view this question. If professionalization of teachers is the route to educational reform and improvement, then schools need to be organized in such a way as to facilitate teachers' exercise of professional autonomy and judgment. If, on the other hand, learning is seen to a greater degree to be a function of the schools' upholding standards set by those outside of schools, then a very different orientation results: one that restricts teacher autonomy and reinforces existing bureaucratic tendencies within schools. Finally, the democratic aspect of schooling places limits on bureaucratic reforms as well as on increased teacher professionalism. For local parents and community leaders to continue to have a dominant role in running schools, the power both of teachers and administrators and of state authorities must be restricted.

The legacy of older staffing patterns, including fairly low salaries for a mostly female work force, helped to sustain strong administration and the rigid rules and relationships implied in the largely bureaucratic form of organization common in schools, especially in public schools. For if teachers were a captive work force (without many comparable occupational options) and if many of them did find in teaching the flexibility to maintain a family as well as work, administrators and local boards did not have to address sharing authority outside the classroom with teachers. But as Warren and other reformers argue, if education is to meet current expectations, such a realignment of power and authority may be required.

The focus of this chapter on how the organizational features of schools affect teachers provides the basis for a similar organizational analysis of students' access to education (Chapter 5) and the learning that takes place in classrooms (Chapter 6).

REFERENCES

Altschuler, Alan A. 1970. *Community Control: The Black Demand for Participation in Large American Cities.* Indianapolis, IN: Pegasus.

Apple, Michael. 1987. *Teachers and Texts.* Boston: Routledge and Kegan Paul.

Aronowitz, Stanley, and Henry A. Giroux. 1985. *Education Under Siege: The Conservative, Liberal, and Radical Debate Over Schooling.* Boston: Bergin and Garvey.

Bidwell, Charles. 1965. "The School as a Formal Organization." In James G. March (ed.), *Handbook of Organizations*, pp. 994–1003. Chicago: Rand McNally.

Blase, Joseph J. 1986. "Socialization as Humanization: One Side of Becoming a Teacher." *Sociology of Education* 59 (April): 100–113.

Borrowman, Merle L. 1956. *The Liberal and Technical in Teacher Education.* New York: Teachers College, Columbia University, Bureau of Publications.

Boyer, Ernest. 1983. *High School.* New York: Harper & Row.

Callahan, Raymond E. 1962. *Education and the Cult of Efficiency.* Chicago: University of Chicago Press.

Carnegie Forum on Education and the Economy. 1986. *A Nation Prepared: Teachers for the 21st Century.* Princeton, NJ: Author.

Case, Charles W., Judith Lanier, and Cecil G. Miskel, 1986. "The Holmes Group Report: Impetus for Gaining Professional Status for Teachers. *Journal of Teacher Education.* 37 (July-August): 36–43.

Clark, Burton. 1985. "The High School and the University: What Went Wrong in America, Part 1, 2." *Phi Delta Kappan* 66 (February and March): 391–397; 472–475.

Coleman, James S. 1987. "Families and Schools." *Educational Researcher* 16 (August-September): 32–38.

Corwin, Ronald. 1970. *Militant Professionalism: A Study of Organizational Conflict in High Schools.* New York: Appleton-Century-Crofts.

Cuban, Larry. 1984. *How Teachers Taught: Constancy and Change in American Classrooms, 1890–1980.* New York: Longman.

Darling-Hammond, Linda. 1984. *Beyond the Commission Reports: The Coming Crisis in Teaching.* Santa Monica, CA: Rand.

Fein, Leonard J. 1971. *The Ecology of the Public Schools: An Inquiry into Community Control.* Indianapolis, IN: Pegasus.

Freidson, Eliot. 1970. *Profession of Medicine.* Boston: Dodd, Mead.

_____. 1985. *Professional Powers: A Study of the Institutionalization of Formal Knowledge.* Chicago: University of Chicago Press.

Hall, Richard. 1987. *Organizations: Structures, Process, and Outcomes.* Fourth Edition. Englewood Cliffs, NJ: Prentice-Hall.

Holmes Group. 1986. *Tomorrow's Teachers: A Report of the Holmes Group.* East Lansing, MI: Author.

Hurn, Christopher J. 1985. *The Limits and Possibilities of Schooling: An Introduction to the Sociology of Education,* 2d ed. Boston: Allyn and Bacon.

Johnson, Susan Moore. 1983. "Teacher Unions in Schools: Authority and Accommodation." *Harvard Educational Review* 53 (August): 309–326.

Katz, Fred E. 1964. "The School as a Social Organization." *Harvard Educational Review* 34 (summer): 428–455.

Larson, M. S. 1977. *The Rise of Professionalism: A Sociological Analysis.* Berkeley: University of California Press.

Lieberman, Myron. 1956. *Education as a Profession.* Englewood Cliffs, NJ: Prentice-Hall.

Lortie, Dan. 1969. "The Partial Professionalization of Elementary Teaching." In Amitai Etzioni (ed.), *The Semi-Professions and Their Organization,* pp. 15–30. New York: Free Press.

_____. 1975. *School Teacher: A Sociological Study.* Chicago: University of Chicago Press.

Mehan, Hugh. 1980. "The Competent Student." *Anthropology and Education Quarterly* 11 (fall): 131–152.

Metzger, Walter. 1987. "A Spectre Haunts American Scholars: The Spectre of 'Professionalism.' " *Educational Researcher* 16 (August-September): 10–19.

Meyer, John W., and Brian Rowan. 1978. "The Structure of Educational Organizations." In Marshall W. Meyer and Associates, *Environments and Organizations,* pp. 78–109. San Francisco: Jossey-Bass.

Murray, Frank. "Goals for the Reform of Teacher Education: An Executive Summary of the Holmes Group Report." *Phi Delta Kappan* (Sept. 1986): 28–32.

Rosenholtz, Susan. 1987. "Education Reform Strategies: Will They Increase Teacher Commitment?" *American Journal of Education* 95 (August): 534–562.

Rosenthal, Alan. 1969. *Pedagogues and Power: Teacher Groups in School Politics.* Syracuse, N.Y.: Syracuse University Press.

Rury, John L. 1986. "Gender, Salaries and Career: American Teachers, 1900–1910." *Issues in Education* 4 (winter): 215–235.

Shepard, Lorrie A., and Amelia E. Kreitzer. 1987. "The Texas Teacher Test." *Educational Researcher* 16 (August-September): 22–31.

Sirotnik, Kenneth A. 1983. "What You See is What You Get—Consistency, Persistency, and Mediocrity in Classrooms." *Harvard Educational Review* 53 (February): 16–31.

Sizer, Theodore. 1985. *Horace's Compromise: The Dilemma of the American High School.* Boston: Houghton Mifflin.

Swidler, Ann. 1979. *Organizations Without Authority: Dilemmas of Social Control in Free Schools.* Cambridge: Harvard University Press.

Trow, Martin. 1961. "The Second Transformation of American Secondary Education." *International Journal of Comparative Sociology* 2:144–166. Reprinted in Jerome Karabel and A. H. Halsey (eds.), *Power and Ideology in Education,* pp. 105–118. New York: Oxford University Press, 1977.

Tyack, David. 1974. *The One Best System.* Cambridge: Harvard University Press.

_____, and Elizabeth Hansot. 1982. *Managers of Virtue: Public School Leadership in America, 1820–1980.* New York: Basic Books.

Willis, Paul. 1981. *Learning to Labor: How Working Class Kids Get Working Class Jobs.* New York: Columbia University Press.

Wirt, Frederick, and Michael Kirst. 1982. *Schools in Conflict.* San Francisco: McCutchan.

Organizational Tensions and Authority in Public Schools

MARY HAYWOOD METZ

University of Wisconsin, Madison

Schools are formal organizations. So are ITT, the local laundromat, prisons, churches, and the Republican Party. One can learn a good deal by analyzing schools' characteristics and conflicts in terms sociologists have developed in the study of other kinds of organizations. These have been but scantily applied in the study of schools.[1]

This chapter introduces the major elements of organizations which sociologists have found to be useful in explaining their form and their activities. It describes the distinctive character of these elements in schools. While I arrived at this formulation as a product of the study of Canton's schools, for the reader it provides an orientation at the outset. The analysis which follows in the rest of the book uses the theory of formal organizations as the dominant framework for explanation. This relatively focused theoretical approach is used in preference to the eclectic one which is more common in the sociological study of schools for the sake of analytical coherence.

GOALS

Formal organizations exist for the accomplishment of formally stated goals. People enter an organization with an obligation to contribute to those goals; those who fail to do so may be disciplined. Outside groups which support an organization may punish it as an entity for failure to meet its announced goals. Thus production and profit for business, the glorification of God and fostering of Christian community for churches, and the winning of elections and responsible governing of the country for parties are the touchstone by which thousands of daily activities and decisions are—or are supposed to be—measured.

But many, if not most, organizations have goals which upon close inspection are varied or diffuse and difficult to measure. When this happens

From *Classrooms and Corridors*: 15–32 by Mary Haywood Metz. Copyright © 1978 by the Regents of the University of California. Reprinted with permission of the publishers.

the different goals or different aspects of a diffuse goal will be in competition for scarce resources. They may contradict one another directly, or means which are most appropriate for reaching one may tend to subvert another.

In one sense there is remarkable clarity about the goals for which public schools are established. Each is created to educate the children of a given geographic area. But as soon as one asks what it means to educate the young, unanimity turns to debate. Educational goals are endless in their variety and subtle in their complexity. Most have a kind of halo which makes them hard to reject outright, even though any two of them may require conflicting attitudes and activities. For example, it is important to have children master a good deal of specific information and to teach children to follow instructions, but it is also important to stimulate their curiosity and teach them to follow out their own lines of questioning. In a given course or a given class these goals will frequently conflict. Consequently, in simply "educating" the children the public schools are usually seeking multiple and pragmatically contradictory ends.

Furthermore, every organization has to seek other goals besides the formal goals which provide its reason for being. If it is to remain an instrument capable of performing its formal goals, it has to insure its own healthy functioning and its own survival in the face of threats from without. It therefore has an array of instrumental goals which are as important as the formal goals to the accomplishment of its official task. These goals attract little notice when they are satisfactorily met, but when their attainment becomes difficult they can absorb more energy than the original purpose of the organization. Arrangements for meeting them can change or subvert the formal goals which an organization actually pursues. The overt or covert sacrifice of an organization's declared purposes for the sake of its survival or smooth functioning has been repeatedly documented in settings as diverse as government agencies, junior colleges, churches, prisons, and mental hospitals.[2]

For schools the most difficult instrumental goal is the maintenance of order among a student body which is only half socialized, comes and remains by legal compulsion, and frequently includes persons with radically different educational and social expectations.

Almost as difficult is the task of maintaining freedom from attack, let alone obtaining support or assistance, from the surrounding community. This community has a license to run the affairs of the schools with fairly close fiscal and policy supervision through local school taxes and elected local school boards. Yet parents and other interested members of the community may have a knowledge of the complexities of pedagogy and the practical necessities of running a school based primarily on memories of their childhood participation in schools. Their educational goals and social outlook may vary enormously as they bring their influence to bear on a single school or set of schools.

In Canton the schools' problem of conflicting goals was clearly visible. The teachers espoused a considerable variety of educational priorities, and many were passionate both in supporting their own and in criticizing others'. The problem of maintaining order among a diverse and skeptical set of students was preoccupying in one form or another for the staff at all the schools. And the community exerted unremitting pressures on the schools.

Schools in general, and in Canton dramatically so, are forced to make choices among their formal goals or to exist with managed or unmanaged conflict. And they must reconcile the requirements of these formal goals with the requirements of maintaining order among the students and support from the community, a task which . . . often requires sacrifices of the formal goals.

TECHNOLOGY

The study of formal organizations more generally directs us to look for other conflicts in schools. It teaches that the character of the technology, the work process,[3] which an organization uses to accomplish its primary tasks tends to be a fundamental characteristic of the organization to which other characteristics must conform.[4] Whether or not there exists a technological process which reliably accomplishes one or another of the organization's goals affects the practical, if not the rhetorical, priorities among those goals.[5]

In the school, the question of technology is of central importance. The raw material of the school's work process, the students, is variable. Differences in cultural background, social position, and individual emotional and cognitive characteristics have an enormous impact on the educational process appropriate to a given child. Yet the process of learning in general, let alone in a given case, is poorly understood.[6]

A considerable range of technological approaches has been and is being used in schools without any incontrovertible demonstration that one is much superior to another, even with a given group of children.[7] It is rarely even claimed that a given approach is reliably appropriate with all students in the way that a chemical manufacturing process may be successful with all properly processed batches of ingredients.

Further, it is almost impossible to know when the school's technology has been successful and when it has not. Teachers have no way of checking on their students' memory of material even a year later, much less when they come to need it in the vicissitudes of adult life. Much learning is intended not as an end in itself but as a basis for developing broad capacities. It is expected that one develops a more logical mind from learning algebra or gains creativity from writing free-form poetry. But how can one assess such capacities reliably, let alone trace their origins? If education is supposed to impart strength of character or richness of personality, the problem of measurement defies description.

Technology, then, is a major problem for the public schools. They are faced with the task of creating changes in diverse raw material through processes which are poorly understood, in the absence of any universally effective means, and without any trustworthy way of measuring the success or failure of whatever methods they finally apply. These technological problems combine with the vague and conflicting goals of education to create a perfect setting for endless controversy. People can disagree forever about the accomplishment of vaguely stated purposes through inadequate means which create results that cannot be satisfactorily measured.[8]

The character of the school's technology thus compounds the tendency to conflict over diverse educational goals. It also makes it easy for a school to sacrifice elusive instructional goals to pressing ones for the maintenance of order. This is especially the case in those schools where students are hard to teach and given to resistance to adults and interference with one another. Thus the weakness of the school's technology makes educational goals most vulnerable where they are most needed.[9]

In Canton disagreements about teaching goals were often intertwined with disagreements about technological effectiveness. Everyone wanted the children "to learn." But teachers' (and students') differing beliefs about the relative importance of different kinds of learning were inextricably mixed with their ideas about the nature and progression of the learning process.[10] And since it was very difficult to measure learning under different systems which were also different in their goals, the arguments had no solid external reference point. In such a situation, conflict cannot be objectively resolved and tensions can mount very high indeed, as they did at one of the schools.

STRUCTURE

Technology shapes an organization not only in its interaction with multiple goals but in its impact on social structure. If the major technological processes of an organization are well understood and routine so that they can be broken into small standardized operations, the organization can be centralized and hierarchical with decisions made at the top and carried out by a large work force of persons with little skill. But when, as in the case of the school, the technology is not well understood and the variable character of the material prevents standardized operations, then the organization is most appropriately decentralized and "flat." The persons who perform the actual work of the organization need to be given relatively large and diffuse tasks with the right to make important decisions independently as they use their intuition to adjust their methods to the requirements of each specific instance.[11]

The spatial and temporal structure of the average American public secondary school is in many ways constructed for the pursuit of a non-routine technology. A single teacher works alone with a group of children for a whole school year. He works out of the sight and hearing of other adults and needs to co-ordinate his efforts with those of other teachers only in minimal ways. Each teacher has a comprehensive task in teaching the whole of a given subject to a constant group of children for a year and he is free to use his intuition and his personality as he goes about it.

In some school systems this isolation is accompanied by a larger autonomy. Teachers are given significant prerogatives in deciding both the content and the style of their teaching without fundamental questioning from colleagues or administrators. Such a situation can also alleviate strains arising from the school's multiple goals. Differences within a faculty need not be carried to the point of open debate leading to victory or defeat, but rather each teacher quietly follows his own ideas in his own classroom.

A model like this is followed—roughly at least—at the university level. But anyone familiar with a range of public schools knows that it is not typical. Teachers' autonomy is limited. In some districts, it is almost non-existent, as standardized curriculum guides prescribe not only the content but much of the method for each class. Two-way intercoms or directives to leave doors open may vitiate the physical isolation of the classroom, as they allow intrusions without warning. There may even be exact rules for teachers' treatment of a large range of classroom situations. These measures are extremes, but their existence underscores the fact that teachers' autonomy is a variable and not a constant factor in public schools. Constraints upon teachers' autonomy reflect fundamental organizational pressures which work upon school structure in direct contradiction to the pressures of the technological requirements of teaching.

ENVIRONMENT

The most important of these pressures come from the students' attacks upon order and from the unfriendly intrusion of parents or community into the school's daily activities. Comparative studies of organizations have found that they cope most easily with environments likely to attack their practices if their structure is centralized and hierarchical and their technological procedures routinized and unambiguous.[12] This strategy is dramatically clear in the response of organizations with subordinates most prone to disorder: prisons.[13] Thus, the most pressing instrumental goals of the school, those of coping with a hostile environment of students or of parents (or other influential community members), suggest a social structure and a technological style diametrically opposed to that most suitable for furthering educational goals.

Typical public school structure reflects these contradictory pressures. The physical, temporal, and social separation of each class with the teacher is contradicted by the formal social structure of the school. Most are formally hierarchical bureaucracies, with the teachers directly responsible to a principal who is in turn responsible and accountable to superiors in the school district administration. The structure of the school is thus ambivalent.[14]

Districts vary in the way that practice shapes the actual operation of the organization. The teachers' independence with their classes may be both proclaimed and generally practiced, or the chain of command may be firmly emphasized. These variations will in each case be the result of a multitude of pressures coming from dominant conceptions of educational goals, from the technological requirements of teaching given kinds of students, and from pressures in the environment.[15] Still, each particular pattern constitutes a way of coping with a set of contradictory organizational imperatives, not a way of exorcising them. The potentiality for strain can be expected to remain, even though compromises blunt the effects of inherent tensions.

The severity of the conflict will vary considerably from district to district depending on the character of the students and community and the strategy of the school. Some student bodies offer only relatively mild problems of disorder, others severe ones. Parents vary in their interest in the schools and in their predisposition to be aggressive or cooperative in addressing what they perceive to be problems. School staffs vary in the diversity and the kind of educational goals which they seriously pursue. Some goals require more technological flexibility than others. Some student bodies respond to standardized techniques while others require the teachers to experiment and explore to the maximum as they go about the pedagogical process.

These differences in student body, community and staffs will appear in a plethora of particular constellations which will affect the daily life of the schools as total configurations. To say that it is necessary to look at the interplay of educational goals, technology, structure, and environmental pressures in order to understand events in the schools is thus to make only the barest beginning toward an analysis of any one school.

In Canton the contradictory pressures described here were especially severe. Both the lower class black children and the affluent white children resisted cooperation with the schools' routines. Order was chronically problematic. Furthermore, the black parents and the professional white parents watched the schools closely to maintain their children's rights and integrity in the face of school discipline. Both were ready to mount a vigorous attack on any practices they considered inappropriate. These pressures encouraged the schools to use protective measures and structures.

At the same time, both sets of parents insisted that the schools pursue effective academic education with their fullest energies. They monitored the schools' performance in this context as best they could. The character of the children at both ends of the academic scale was such as to present a technological challenge in accomplishing such education. To succeed the teachers often needed imaginative, unconventional, and flexible methods. These pressures encouraged the schools to allow teachers and students freedom to work out their methods together in a variety of ways. Flexible structures were required.

Canton's schools thus needed opposed methods and structures in pursuing instrumental and formal goals where both were especially difficult to achieve. They suffered from strain as a consequence.

At the level of formal policy, the school board and district administration stressed educational goals before all else. Following the expectations of the parents and the temper of the times, they encouraged varied and flexible technological approaches and established a decentralized structure which gave principals and classroom teachers a very large measure of autonomy in choosing their means and ends within the context of general policy. They therefore made a set of consistent choices for one set of goals and supporting organizational arrangements.

However, when problems of order or parental attacks did occur, the board and the district staff expected the staffs of the schools to be expeditious in dealing with them. The tensions arising from the contradictions the district faced thus were passed on to the individual schools. It was there that they were felt in strains upon daily activity and acted out in a variety of conflicts. . . .

At both schools, district policy granting the teacher curricular flexibility and autonomy in the conduct of the class made the classroom a unit with significant independence from the wider school. . . . To understand the interaction of teachers and students as they went about defining their common purpose and procedures in the classroom, it is necessary to understand one more element of organizational life.

AUTHORITY

In a formal organization authority provides the major means for carrying goals, technology, and structure from ideals into action. Especially in the classroom context, it is in closely studying relationships of authority that we will see the tensions of the school expressed in daily action. Principals and teachers fulfill their goals by directing others to participate in activities designed to accomplish them. Since principals and teachers have the formal responsibility for carrying out the school's goals and the right to see that others do their part, they possess authority.

Authority is distinguished from other relationships of command and obedience by the superordinate's *right* to command and the subordinate's *duty* to obey. This right and duty stem from the crucial fact that the interacting persons share a relationship which exists for the service of a *moral order to which both owe allegiance.* This moral order may be as diffuse as the way of life of a traditional society or as specific as the pragmatic goals of a manufacturing organization. But in any case, all participants have a duty to help realize the moral order through their actions. This duty may arise from emotional or moral attachment to the order itself, but may be as unsentimental as the manual worker's obligation to give a fair day's work in exchange for a fair day's pay.[16]

Authority exists to further the moral order. It exists because a person in a given position is more able than others to perceive the kinds of actions which will serve the interests of the moral order. On the basis of this capacity he has the right to issue commands which others have the duty to obey. For the sake of generality it is helpful to call persons who give commands superordinates and those who receive them subordinates. The same individual may be simultaneously a superordinate and a subordinate as he acts out different aspects of a single role. Teachers are superordinates in interacting with students but subordinates in interacting with their principal.

Authority is a formal and continuing relationship, an institutionalized one. Strictly speaking it is a relationship of roles, not of persons. The superordinate's right to command rests both upon his occupancy of a role and his presumed ability to translate the needs of the moral order into specific activities which will support it. This ability may stem from several kinds of sources, ranging from the mystic endowments which let a Pope speak infallibly ex cathedra to the pragmatic knowledge of an executive who receives reports from several divisions of a company. The subordinate's duty to obey the superordinate rests upon the superordinate's claim to be acting for the moral order. If this claim is valid, then obedience to the superordinate is obedience to the needs of the moral order.

These characteristics of authority can be summarized in a formal definition. *Authority is the right of a person in a specified role to give commands to which a person in another specified role has a duty to render obedience. This right and duty rest upon the superordinate's recognized status as the legitimate representative of a moral order to which both superordinate and subordinate owe allegiance.*

Authority can thus be graphically represented by a triangle as in Figure 1. This model makes it clear that in every instance of authority one must consider not only the roles of superordinate and subordinate and their relationship but also the moral order and the relationship of both superordinate and subordinate to it. Any one of these elements or relationships affects the shape of every other.

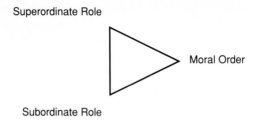

FIGURE 1   The Elements of Authority

Despite the crucial importance of the moral order as the basis of the relationship of superordinate and subordinate, they may not make reference to it in most of their transactions. Under ordinary circumstances, the subordinate *trusts* the superordinate's competence and good faith in the service of the moral order sufficiently to assume that the superordinate's specific commands further its requirements. The fact that the superordinate has given the command is sufficient guaranty of its validity. The act of obedience discharges the subordinate's obligation to the moral order.

In the give-and-take of daily contact, then, the position of the superordinate comes to be the immediate source of his right to command. And indeed the man in the street, even the semiprofessional subordinate,[17] commonly comes to identify authority with the person of the superordinate. So long as events go along smoothly this model suffices. But when trouble arises, when the superordinate has to make unconventional or heavy demands, or when the subordinate grows restive, then both will tend to call upon the moral order directly to sustain—or object to—a command.

Social scientists have also concentrated upon the role of the superordinate in their investigations of variations in authority and the complexities which attend its practice. But also relevant are other questions asked less often by either social scientists or laymen. These revolve around the role of the subordinate, and around *his understanding* of his relationship with his superordinate and of his relationship with the moral order, and indeed around his understanding of the very nature of the moral order.[18]

These questions are less often addressed in considerations of authority, because the answers to them are frequently taken for granted. Much of the time authority works because subordinates never seriously analyze the character of their own role or its relationship to any of the other elements of authority. They accept the definitions of these matters supplied to them by superordinates. They usually do this because they are subordinates as a result of ascriptive positions which they have always held. They are of a race, social class, sex, or age which has traditionally held subordinate status and accepted commands from above in participating in the society's institutions. Alternatively, and often at the same time, they do not question these matters because they have no significant stake in most of them. In organizations, people who work at routine jobs are generally not very interested in their contribution to the organization's overall goals—so long as the company can meet its payroll.

Schools deal with the young, whose experience has traditionally been designed to re-enforce their assumption that they should trust all their elders by virtue of a difference in age. Children belong to an ascriptively subordinate group. However, the assumption of elders' wisdom and good will was radically undermined during the sixties for large numbers of upper middle class children. Poor black children, often already skeptical of these qualities in the school staff, be came much more openly challenging. While many of the children of all the races attending Chauncey and Hamilton still accepted adults' trustworthiness, a large minority did not. They were therefore primed to ask pointed questions about justifications for commands given to them in relationships of authority.

One can in any case generally expect more close scrutiny of the moral order and its relationship to specific commands from subordinates in schools than in many other kinds of organizations. Diffuse goals and a non-routine technology require subordinates independently to understand and apply the principles inherent in a moral order. The more a school emphasizes these qualities in its goals and technology, the more subordinates will routinely make independent reference to the school's moral order.

Further, the distinctive, though not unique, place of students in schools encourages them to be independently attached to a moral order. First, students are themselves the material to be transformed. Even more than professional workers, they have every reason to feel intimately interested in both the overall character of the organization's product and the processes used to transform it.[19]

Secondly, students receive no pay for compliant participation. Other extrinsic rewards are meager. A high school diploma is valuable for almost anyone. But this is a distant and abstract reward for an eighth grader, and one he is likely to think will be his whether he is cooperative or not. Ambitious students for whom good grades and a good record will be useful in gaining access to higher education and other selective postsecondary options receive some extrinsic rewards for cooperation. But these too are relatively abstract. And if high grades are to have meaning for some students, others must receive low grades.[20] There will necessarily be a large number of students who do not expect much return for their work. Thus since students receive little extrinsic reward for their cooperation, the intrinsic rewards must be heightened proportionately if they are to have reason to be voluntarily cooperative with the school's program.

The school's task is infinitely complicated in this context by the existence of compulsory attendance. Students must go to school whether they want to or not, by compulsion of law. In most cases they must go to a particular school and even sit in the class of a particular teacher without any possibility of choice in the matter.

In such a context, students who reflect upon their situation are likely to move in one of two opposite directions. They may become intensely involved in the intrinsic character of their education, taking it for its own reward and thus caring about its nature. Or they may become thoroughly alienated from a context which compels participation but offers neither extrinsic nor intrinsic rewards which are of value to them.[21]

In Canton a sizable group went to each extreme. The most able students from professional families were not under pressure to obtain outstanding grades because most would enter the highly respected state university rather than more selective private colleges. They looked to the intrinsic character of their education for reward. The least able or least conforming of the black students found the school to offer neither intrinsic rewards nor practical assistance. They withdrew from commitment to its moral order.

In this perspective, it is not surprising that the staffs of many schools try to prevent their students from reflecting upon their situation. They try instead to present them with a consistent pattern of expectations which is so widely taken for granted that students do not think to ask what rewards they are receiving. But in such schools the potential for the kinds of questioning of authority which occurred in Canton is still always present. . . .

NOTES

1. In the mid-sixties an article on the school as an organization in a landmark compilation of theoretical and empirical knowledge about organizations emphasized the scanty body of knowledge to review. (See Charles Bidwell, "The School as a Formal Organization," p. 972.) A decade later, in a book summarizing our knowledge of "educational organizations," Ronald Corwin reviewed a significantly larger corpus of research but one still slim compared with that on a variety of other kinds of organizations. (See Ronald Corwin, *Education in Crisis*, especially Chapter 1.)

2. For examples in these categories see the following studies: Philip Selznick, *TVA and the Grassroots;* Burton R. Clark, *The Open Door College;* Donald L. Metz, *New Congregations;* Gresham Sykes, *The Society of Captives;* Charles Perrow, "Hospitals, Technology, Structure, and Goals."

3. The goals of an organization can be perceived as end states of a raw material which the organization exists to transform. This raw material need not be inanimate matter changed in physical or chemical ways; it may be a person or even a symbol. Technology is the process which transforms it. Technology in this sense need include no physical hardware. Salesmanship and non-directive psychotherapy are technologies. So is teaching.

4. Recent studies which treat the effect of technology upon organizational structure are: Joan Woodward, *Industrial Organization;* James Thompson, *Organizations in Action;* Charles Perrow, "A Framework for the Comparative Analysis of Organizations"; and Stanley Udy, *Organization of Work.* My treatment here follows Perrow most closely, but it also draws directly upon Udy.

5. For a cogent argument along these lines in the case of the mental hospital see Perrow, "Hospitals, Technology, Structure, and Goals."

6. In a review article, Boocock concludes that we do not know "what the effective teacher is or does." (See Sarane Boocock, "The School as a Social Environment for Learning," p. 44.) Jackson also makes this point in an empirically based discussion of teachers' strategies for inducing learning and for assessing their success in this effort. (See Philip Jackson, *Life in Classrooms*, pp. 159–63.)

7. There are of course many reports of dramatic improvements in given situations with a change of methods, but one has to remain skeptical, wondering about the probability of a "Hawthorne effect." Writers such as Herbert Kohl, Sylvia Ashton-Warner, and A. S. Neill, who report great improvements with their methods, may create their effects less through their actual techniques than through their own belief in the efficacy of the method and their expectation that their children will learn though others expect them to fail. (See Herbert Kohl, *Thirty-Six Children;* Sylvia Ashton-Warner, *Teacher;* and A. S. Neill, *Summerhill.*) Indeed, one of the most effective tools at a teacher's disposal may be an expectation that his pupils will do well, regardless of the reason for his expectation. (See Robert Rosenthal and Lenore Jackson, *Pygmalion in the Classroom.*) Brophy and Good summarize the recent literature stimulated by the controversy over this study on the effects of teachers' expectations on pupils. (See Jere E. Brophy and Thomas L. Good, *Teacher–Student Relationships.*)

8. Or they may become ritualistic, asking no questions about the benefits of their daily efforts but mechanically following local practice and then disclaiming responsibility for the results. For a detailed description of the bases of this adjustment see Gertrude H. McPherson, *Small Town Teacher.*

9. Compulsory education, requiring all students to attend school and the public school to accept all comers, compounds the technological problems of the school by recruiting diverse and partially resistant raw material. At the same time—as Carlson points out—compulsory education ensures the public school at least minimal public support whether or not it is as effective or efficient as it could potentially be. (See Richard O. Carlson, "Environmental Constraints and Organizational Consequences.")

10. Lortie describes in detail the way that the technological conditions of teaching, along with the structure of the school and the reward system for teachers, interact with processes of recruitment and training of teachers to create prevalent occupational attitudes and behaviors. (See Dan C. Lortie, *Schoolteacher.*)

11. Stanley Udy, "The Comparative Analysis of Organizations," pp. 690–691.

12. Ibid.

13. For a discussion of relevant organizational processes and conflicts, see for example: Donald Cressey, "Prison Organizations"; Richard McCleery, *Policy Change in Prison Management;* and Sykes, *Society of Captives.* Erving Goffman documents similar processes in a variety of "total institutions" which process large "batches" of people, prone to resist the desires of the organization. Such institutions vary from public mental hospitals to conscript armies. See his *Asylums,* especially Part I.

14. Most of the available analysis of schools which calls systematically upon the study of organizations deals with contradictions between schools' bureaucratic structures and teachers' need for autonomy in dealing with their technological problems. See James Anderson, *Bureaucracy in Education* for an extended discussion of these problems along with a review of the relevant educational and organizational literature. The book also reports a study of the effects of differential use of bureaucratic rules upon the staffs of ten junior high schools.

15. The expectations, or demands, of staff members for one kind of structure over another are an important element in this equation. Formally, personal preferences of particular staff members as whole persons—rather than as role players—are conceptualized as part of the organization's environment by students of organizations.

16. There is no acknowledgment of moral responsibility at all from subordinates in many organizations. Inmates in prisons are the most extreme examples. Many students in public schools also do not make such an acknowledgement of duty to educational ends. But it is my argument that failing such attachment, a genuine relationship of authority does not exist.

17. For example, Robert Peabody asked employees in a police department, a social work agency, and an elementary school for a definition of authority. At least one-fourth of each group responded by naming their superior. And a majority of those giving other defining qualities responded in some variation of the general phraseology, "authority is a person who. . . ." However, supervisors were less likely than subordinates to define authority in personal terms. (See Robert Peabody, *Organizational Authority,* pp. 87–90.)

18. The analysis of authority I am using here combines the approaches of Max Weber and Chester I. Barnard. Weber's classic analysis and his three types of authority—charismatic, traditional, and rational legal—stress the moral order, the role of the superordinate, and the relationship between these two. Weber gives relatively minor attention to the role of the subordinate and its relationship to the other elements of authority. (See Max Weber, *From Max Weber,* pp. 96–252.) Barnard, on the other hand, defines authority as the acceptance of a command by the subordinate. He argues that a subordinate gives such acceptance if the command is in accordance with the needs of a shared moral order as *the subordinate understands* those needs. (See Chester I. Barnard, *The Functions of the Executive,* pp. 163–74.) In the context of the school, where compliance depends heavily on students' intrinsic rewards, Barnard's insights are especially relevant. For a fuller discussion of the derivation and details of the model of authority used here see Mary Haywood Metz, "Authority in the Junior High School," Chapter One.

19. Indeed the best analogy for students in schools is in many respects not that of other organizational subordinates but that of clients interacting with free professionals. However, this relationship is altered by the necessity to regulate their activities for the sake of organizational routine as well as education. For an exploration in detail of the differences between professional–client relations and those of students and schools see Charles Bidwell, "Students and Schools."

20. Dreeben analyzes the process by which teachers in the elementary grades teach children to value grades as inherent rewards. (See Robert Dreeben, *On What is Learned in School*, pp. 37–39.)
21. For a somewhat different perspective on the same set of problems see William Spady, "The Authority System of the School and Student Unrest."

REFERENCES

Anderson, J. G. *Bureaucracy in Education.* Baltimore: Johns Hopkins Univ. Press, 1968.

Ashton-Warner, Sylvia. *Teacher.* New York: Bantam Books, 1964.

Barnard, C. I. *The Functions of the Executive.* Cambridge, MA: Harvard Univ. Press, 1962.

Bidwell, C. "The School as a Formal Organization." In *Handbook of Organizations*, J. March, ed., pp. 972–1022. Chicago: Rand McNally, 1965.

———— . "Students and Schools." In *Organizations and Clients*, W. R. Rosengren and M. Lefton, ed., pp. 37–70. Columbus, OH: Merrill, 1970.

Boocock, S. S. "The School as a Social Environment for Learning." *Sociology of Education* 46 (1973): 15–50.

Brophy, J. E., and Good, T. L. *Teacher-Student Relationships.* New York: Holt, Rinehart & Winston, 1974.

Carlson, Richard O. "Environmental Constraints and Organizational Consequences." In *Behavioral Science and Educational Administration Yearbook, Part II*, Daniel Griffiths, ed., pp. 262–76. Chicago: Univ. of Chicago Press, 1964.

Clark, Burton R. *The Open Door College.* New York: McGraw-Hill, 1960.

Corwin, Ronald G. *Education in Crisis.* New York: Wiley, 1974.

Cressey, Donald, "Prison Organizations," In *Handbook of Organizations*, J. March, ed., pp. 1023–70. Chicago: Rand McNally, 1965.

Dreeben, Robert. *On What Is Learned in School.* Reading, MA: Addison-Wesley, 1968.

Goffman, Erving. *Asylums.* Garden City, NY: Anchor Books, 1961.

Jackson, Philip. *Life in Classrooms.* New York: Holt, Rinehart & Winston, 1968.

Kohl, Herbert. *36 Children.* New York: The New American Library, 1967.

Lortie, Dan C. *Schoolteacher.* Chicago: Univ. of Chicago Press, 1975.

McCleery, Richard. *Policy Change in Prison Management.* East Lansing: Governmental Research Bureau, Michigan State Univ., 1957.

McPherson, G. *Small Town Teacher.* Cambridge, MA: Harvard Univ. Press, 1972.

Metz, Donald L. *New Congregations.* Philadelphia: Westminster Press, 1967.

Metz, Mary Haywood. "Authority in the Junior High School." Unpublished doctoral dissertation, University of California, Berkeley, 1971.

Neill, A. S. *Summerhill.* New York: Hart Publishing Co., 1960.

Peabody, Robert. *Organizational Authority.* New York: Atherton Press, 1964.

Perrow, C. "Hospitals, Technology, Structure, and Goals." In *Handbook of Organizations*, J. March, ed., pp. 910–71. Chicago: Rand McNally, 1965.

———— . "A Framework for the Comparative Analysis of Organizations." *American Sociological Review* 32 (April 1967): 194–208.

Rosenthal, R. and Jacobson, L. *Pygmalion in the Classroom.* New York: Holt, Rinehart & Winston, 1968.

Selznick, P. *TVA and the Grassroots.* Berkeley: University of California Press, 1949.

Sykes, Gresham. *The Society of Captives.* Princeton: Princeton University Press, 1958.

Thompson, James. *Organizations in Action.* New York: McGraw-Hill, 1967.

Udy, S. H., Jr. "The Comparative Analysis of Organizations." In *Handbook of Organizations*, J. March, ed., pp. 678–709. Chicago: Rand McNally, 1965.

———— . *Organization of Work.* New Haven: Human Relations Area Files Press, 1959.

Weber, M. *From Max Weber: Essays in Sociology.* Trans., edit, and intro. by H. H. Gerth and C. W. Mills. New York: Oxford Univ. Press, 1958.

Woodward, Joan. *Industrial Organization.* New York: Oxford University Press, 1965.

The Social Realities of Teaching

ANN LIEBERMAN
University of Washington

LYNNE MILLER
University of Maine

Whatever contributes to understanding also contributes to reconstruction.
—Willard Waller, 1967

In this chapter, we develop a set of understandings about the nature of teaching and explore themes that capture some of the dailiness of working in schools. Our intention here is to begin to describe, in a general sense, what it is like to be a teacher. . . .

THE NATURE OF TEACHING

We begin our discussion with a set of understandings about the nature of teaching as a profession. We have developed these understandings over time; they are based on the literature, current research, our work with teachers, and reflections on our own experiences. We label the set of phenomena we are about to describe as "social system understandings" because they reflect the interplay between individual teacher experiences and the social context of schools. These understandings serve as a basis for discussing generalizations about the way teachers learn their jobs, become teachers, and forge a professional identity.

From *Teachers, Their World, and Their Work* (1984): 1–15. Copyright © 1984, by ASCD. Reprinted with permission of the Association for Supervision and Curriculum Development, Ann Lieberman and Lynne Miller. All rights reserved.

Style is Personalized

Teachers are faced with a central contradiction in their work, a contradiction that makes it incumbent upon each one of them to develop a style that is individual and personal. The contradiction stated simply is this: teachers have to deal with a group of students and teach them something and, at the same time, deal with each child as an individual. The teachers, then, have two missions: one universal and cognitive, and the other particular and affective. The cognitive mission demands a repertoire of skills in moving a group and making sure that knowledge builds, extends, and is learned. The affective mission requires that teachers somehow make friends with their students, motivate them, arouse their interest, and engage them on a personal level. In order to deal with this contradiction, teachers develop all kinds of strategies and then meld them together into a style that is highly personal, if not plain idiosyncratic. This style, forged in the dailiness of work developed from trial and error, becomes one's professional identity and, as such, may be militantly protected and defended.

Rewards are Derived from Students

The greatest satisfaction for a teacher is the feeling of being rewarded by one's students. In fact, most of the time the students are the *only* source of rewards for most teachers. Isolated in their own classrooms, teachers receive feedback for their efforts from the words, expressions, behaviors, and suggestions of the students. By doing well on a test, sharing a confidence, performing a task, indicating an interest, and reporting the effects of a teacher's influence, students let teachers know that they are doing a good job and are appreciated. Unlike other professionals who look to colleagues and supervisors for such feedback, teachers can only turn to children.

Teaching and Learning Links are Uncertain

Dan Lortie (1965) has said that teaching is fraught with "endemic uncertainties." No uncertainty is greater than the one that surrounds the connection between teaching and learning. A teacher does his or her best, develops curricula, tries new approaches, works with individuals and groups, and yet never knows for sure what are the effects. One hopes the children will get it, but one is never sure. A teacher operates out of a kind of blind faith that with enough in the way of planning, rational schemes, objectives, and learning activities some learning will take place. But a teacher also knows that some learnings happen that are significant and never planned for and that other learnings never take hold, despite the best of professional intentions.

The Knowledge Base is Weak

Throughout their careers, teachers seek professional knowledge. In preparation, a teacher-to-be takes numerous courses in the theory and the practice of education—most of which are judged as irrelevant upon entering teaching. As a bonafide teacher, one takes even more courses to earn permanent certification. In addition there is a plethora of "staff development" offerings made available and often mandated on the district level. With some exceptions, this inservice work is given the same low grades for relevance and helpfulness as is early pre-professional preparation. The sad fact is that, as a profession, we have not been able to codify teaching under a variety of contingencies in a way that is satisfying to practitioners. The knowledge base in teaching is weak; there is simply no consensus (as there is in medicine and law) about what is basic to the practice of the profession.

Goals are Vague and Conflicting

Although there is much talk of late about goal specificity and accountability, it is still the case that the goals of education are vague and often in conflict. Are we out to impart basic skills or to enrich lives? Do we concentrate on the individual or concern ourselves with the development of the group? Are we teaching to minimal levels of competence, or are we working to develop a wide range of talents and possibilities? Do we most value discipline or learning, order and control or intellectual curiosity? Are we socializing students, or are we educating them? The answer to these questions and to others like them is usually, "Yes, we are doing both." The result is that individual teachers make their own translations of policy and that, in general, the profession is riddled by vagueness and conflict.

Control Norms are Necessary

Daily teachers make an assault on gaining some sense of direction, control, and movement of their classes. Teachers work hard to develop a set of norms and rules that both they and their students can live with. This happens as teachers move through a cycle of giving orders, threatening, being tested, and finally reaching some standards that are accepted and move the class along. While this is being carried out in individual classrooms, schoolwide norms are also being tried and established. The setting of control norms is a necessary part of teaching; it satisfies the need for certainty in an otherwise ambiguous and uncertain world. It also assures teachers of their place in the organization of the school. No matter how effective teachers are in the classroom, all that is ever really known about them in the general organization of the school is whether they keep their classes in line or whether the students are in control. Control precedes instruction; this is a major shibboleth of teaching.

Professional Support is Lacking

Seymour Sarason has written that "Teaching is a Lonely Profession" (1966), a characterization that is indeed apt. Unlike other professions, teaching does not provide for a shared culture based on the movement from knowledge to experience in the company of one's peers. Doctors, for instance, learn their profession through a graduated set of experiences, all shared with others. Not so the teacher. Once graduated from a preparation program, teachers find themselves alone in the classroom with a group of students without a peer or supervisor in sight. The neophyte teacher is left with degree in hand, high expectations internalized, a fistful of untried methodologies, and few adults with whom to share, grow, and learn.

Teaching is an Art

Teaching is an art, despite current efforts to scientize it. Some parts of teaching may lend themselves to programming and rationalization, but in the long haul more artistry than science or technology is practiced as teachers struggle to adjust and readjust, to make routines, and establish patterns, only to recast what has been done in a new form to meet a new need or a new vision. Teachers are best viewed as craftspeople; the reality of teaching is of a craft learned on the job. This understanding is perhaps our most important; that is why we saved it for last. When viewed as a craft, teaching makes sense as a messy and highly personal enterprise, for it concerns itself with the making and remaking of an object until it satisfies the standards of its creator.

In codifying what we have called the "social system understandings" of teaching, we have attempted to impose some order on what is admittedly a disorderly landscape. As we do this, we are well aware that generalizations—no matter how grounded in the realities of practice—somehow always "miss the mark." While useful as guidelines for discussion about our craft, they fail to capture the flesh and blood of teaching, to call up its dailiness. In the section that follows we try to capture some of that dailiness as it is experienced by public school teachers and to build on some of the understandings we have presented here.

THE DAILINESS OF TEACHING

In this section, we move from understandings to themes. Specifically, we explore notions of *rhythms, rules, interactions,* and *feelings* as they are played out in the day-to-day work of teachers in public schools.

Rhythms

A teacher's professional life is measured in terms of years of service. Each of those years is cyclical, mediated by the rhythms of days, of weeks, of months, and of seasons. Let's begin by talking about teachers' days. Days begin early, before the din of the rush hour has peaked, often before the sun has risen. Once sign-in procedures are completed, greetings exchanged with colleagues, the last sip of coffee downed in the teachers' room, and the warning bell sounded, the classroom becomes a teacher's total world. It is a world that is unique and separate from the world of other adults. For six hours a day, five days a week, teachers live in an exclusive and totally controlled environment. For the majority of the day they are bound in space and time. In most instances, teachers need the permission of the principal to leave the building during school hours.

> *"Whoever heard of a profession where you can't even go the bathroom when you have to?"*

Each day has its rhythm. For elementary teachers, the lunch hour divides the day into morning and afternoon activities, each marked by a recess and perhaps some instructional time with an itinerant teacher. They may spend an entire day in one classroom with one group of students. They create routines and patterns that give the day form and meaning.

> *"I live in my own little world in my classroom. Sometimes I think that my children and I share a secret life that is off limits to anyone else. We just go about our business, like so many peas in a pod."*

For secondary teachers, the daily rhythm is more externally determined. Bells ring to signal the passing of classes, each of which will spend some parcel of time with the teacher in his or her classroom. Though students may move throughout the building, high school teachers often never leave their rooms in the course of a day. For every "period" or "hour," there is a routine: taking attendance, continuing from yesterday, introducing today's material, winding down, and making an assignment for tomorrow. Repeated five times a day, such routines become fixed and life becomes predictable.

In the course of a day, activities and interactions multiply, energy fluctuates. Elementary teachers may organize activities to accommodate the ebb and flow of the students' and their own energies. There are quiet times and active times, times set aside for individual attention, large-group instruction, small-group work, and seatwork. Secondary teachers may acknowledge that they are less effective during the first and last hours and more energetic during the middle of the day. The pace and depth of instruction are altered accordingly. For both elementary and secondary teachers, the school day is punctuated by interruptions: PA announcements, telephone calls and messages from the office, minor crises that need attending. All these become incorporated into the pattern of the day. Without missing a step, experienced teachers pick up where they left off.

Days merge into weeks. Monday is always difficult. So is Friday, but the difficulties are softened by the promise of the weekend. Midweek is optimal for teaching. The process—review, teach, test—fits neatly into the natural pace of weeks. Weeks become months and months become seasons. And each has its rhythms. Fall is the time of promise; new beginnings always bring hope. As the seasons progress, there is a downward spiral of energy until Thanksgiving, a perfectly timed and well-deserved break from the routine. There is a resurgence of sorts between Thanksgiving and Christmas, the most harried three weeks on any calendar. The Christmas break brings relief and buoys teachers and students for the final onslaught of the semester's end. January is brief. February is not; it is by far the longest month by any emotional measure.

> *"I always think of changing professions in February."*

By March, the end is within sight and energies surge until the spring break, anticipated as much as the Christmas holiday and well appreciated. Then time passes quickly. There is the last-minute rush to get everything in and to meet the promises made in September by early June. The final weeks are filled with activities—final testing and grading, promotions, graduation, end-of-the-year events. And then, quite arbitrarily, on a Friday in June it all stops. Teachers and students go their separate ways. For ten weeks, there are no routines, no shared rituals, no school. The patterns that were learned and shared rudely come to an end, to be recreated in the fall when the cycle begins again. Such are the rhythms of teaching.

Rules

Like any profession, teaching has its rules—some codified and formal, others tacitly accepted and informal "rules of thumb." Two such rules may be simply stated: *Be practical. Be private.* Some further elaboration aids us in understanding the effect of these simple rules of behavior for teachers.

After years of formal academic preparation, most teachers enter teaching and experience a common jolt. Equipped with theoretical understandings, they lack the practical knowledge that they need for survival.

> Education courses in and of themselves are quite theoretical. To be sure, they are helpful as far as background material goes, but there is no substitute for actual *practical* experience . . . My three year stint of duty as a housemaster and teacher . . . gave me a great deal of *practical* experience in learning more about young people and how to handle young people (Lortie, 1965).

Practical knowledge in schools is defined in terms of its opposites. Being practical is the opposite of being theoretical; being practical is the opposite of being idealistic. University professors are theoretical; inexperienced teachers are idealistic. New teachers in search of practical knowledge, then, must reject the university professors who trained them as well as their own tendencies to seek ideal solutions to difficult problems. Practical knowledge is lodged in the experiences and practices of teachers at work in their class-rooms. It is to other teachers and to oneself that the novice must turn for practical ideas.

What makes an idea practical? First, it develops from the circumstance of the school. Second, it has immediate application. Third, it is offered by practical people. Finally, it addresses practical problems. Practical people are those who are or have recently been teachers. Practical school problems include discipline, attendance, order, and achievement. Practical ideas re-quire little additional work or preparation; they fit into the existing rhythms of the school. Practical ideas are immediate and concrete and can be effected with the resources and structures that currently exist.

> *"No teacher ever does what he or she thinks is best. We do the best we can in the circumstances. What you think is a good idea from the outside turns out to be impossible in the classroom."*

To be practical means to concentrate on products and processes; to draw on experience rather than research; to be short-range and not predictive in thinking or planning.

As an opposite to idealism, practicality values adjustment, accommodation, and adaptation. Idealism is identified with youth; it does not wear well in the adult "real world" of teaching. New teachers are initiated into the practicality ethic during their first year on the job. They learn their "place" in the school organization, to keep quiet when private principles are violated by public practices, and to be politic about what they say and to whom they say it. To be practical, in this sense, is to accept the school as it is and to adapt. Striving to change the system is idealistic; striving to make do is practical. Concern for each student's well-being and optimal learning is idealistic; acceptance of limitations of student potential and teacher influence is practical. Reflective self-criticism is idealistic; expressing the belief "I do the best I can; it's just that the kids don't try" is practical. Being open to change and to outside influences is idealistic; being self-sufficient is practical. Being practical saves one from shame and doubt. It is a useful rule to follow.

The practicality rule has a corollary; that is, be private. In effect, it is practical to be private. What does being private mean? It means not sharing experiences about teaching, about classes, about students, about perceptions.

> "I don't know what it's like in business or industry. It may be the same. I don't know how friendly co-workers are, how honest they are. It just seems that in teaching, teachers really are unwilling to be honest with each other, I think, to confide with each other about professional things and personal things."

By following the privacy rule, teachers forfeit the opportunity to display their successes; but they also gain. They gain the security of not having to face their failures publicly and losing face.

Being private also means staking out a territory and making it one's own. For most teachers, that territory is the individual classroom.

> Teachers have a sense of "territoriality" and an "ideology" [which] includes a belief of the inviolability of a teacher's classroom (McPherson, 1972).

To ensure their claim, teachers seldom invite each other into their classes. Observation is equated with evaluation, and evaluation violates one's sense of place and position in the world.

In being private, each teacher makes an individual and conscious choice to go it alone.

> "Me? You get to a point. I made a personal decision. I know a lot of teachers have done the same thing. You seal off the room and you deal with the students. You say, 'you and me and let's see what we can do alone.' "

Most schools do not provide meaningful supervision, and most teachers do not ask for it. The very act of teaching is invisible to one's peers.

> "It is safer to be private. There is some safety in the tradition, even though it keeps you lonely."

Loneliness and isolation are high prices to pay, but teachers willingly pay them when the alternatives are seen as exposure and censure. When asked in whom he confides about his days, one man replied with some sense of irony and sadness, "My wife."

Interactions

Given the power of classroom territoriality, it comes as no surprise that the most important and immediate interactions that teachers have are with their students.

> *"You work with kids. That's what you do. And a school is a place that will allow you to do that."*

Since, as noted earlier, almost all rewards come from students, relationships with them are primary in the constellation of interactions in a school. For elementary teachers, the focus on children is a taken-for-granted phenomenon.

> *"I'm with my children all day long. I watch them change by the moment. Some days they'll tell me all of their secrets. Other days, they withdraw into their own little shells. Whatever they do, I'm there to see and hear it, and I take it all to heart."*

For secondary teachers, relationships with students are more fragmented and are mediated through the subject matter.

> *"It is the subject matter and the kids. I love the subject matter and naturally you need an audience for that. The kids are the audience and they're important to me. I can't teach my subject matter without touching the kids in some way."*

In either case, relationships with students are daily, direct, sometimes conflictual, but always central.

> *"I dream about them. I have nightmares about them. I can't lose them. It is worse on vacation. When I'm in school and it's late October and I've accepted that I'm really back, then the dreams finally stop."*

For most, it is the personal interaction rather than instructional interaction that is most valued. This is true on the secondary level as well as on the elementary level.

> *"If someone told me that my job is just to teach math, I would quit. I couldn't stand to see myself as someone who teaches skills and nothing else. I have to feel that I am doing something more lasting."*

What is that "something more lasting"? It has to do with influencing and guiding children toward adulthood, with serving as a moral presence, with having a stake in the future.

> *"When you realize that what you say in the classroom—even though you think no one is listening—has an effect on your students, you realize that you are a role model, even if you don't see yourself that way. The kids take what I have to say, think about it, and make decisions based on it. I have that kind of influence . . . it's scary but it makes me feel good. It's a big responsibility."*

Such involvement has its rewards both in the present and in the future.

> *"I like to see them when they come back, so I can see how they're doing, how they're turning out. I love to watch them grow. It's terrific. It's true with any age group—you can see the growth and development. Let's hope it continues. They're so cute. They are all individuals and they bubble about certain things. Some of them, my God, are so brave. . . ."*

We cannot overstate the importance of teacher-student interactions. When the rewards from these interactions are plentiful, teachers are energized and thrive. When the rewards from these interactions are diminished, teachers lose that part of themselves that is most self-sustaining and most central to the well-being of the profession.

If teaching is to be understood as a "lonely profession," then the source of that loneliness lies outside of the realm of children. It is posited in the realm of interactions with other adults, especially one's peers. While relations with students tend to be immediate, direct, and engaging, relations with peers may be characterized as remote, oblique, and defensively protective. The rule of privacy governs peer interactions in a school. It is all right to talk about the news, the weather, sports, and sex. It is all right to complain in general about the school and the students. However, it is not acceptable to discuss instruction and what happens in classrooms as colleagues.

> *"If I were to go into the lounge and say, 'I've had a great class. The kids are really interesting. They were on the board, asking great questions, and they really got from me what I wanted them to,' no one would respond."*

> *"I have never heard another teacher say, 'I have a problem.' You just don't do it. You solve the problem on your own, or you pretend that you don't have one. You never open up to anyone about anything important."*

For most teachers in most schools, teaching is indeed a lonely enterprise. With so many people engaged in so common a mission in so compact a space and time, it is perhaps the greatest irony—and the greatest tragedy of teaching—that so much is carried on in self-imposed and professionally sanctioned isolation.

Our discussion of interactions is not complete until we consider the relation between teachers and principal in a building. Although face-to-face interactions with the principal may not be all that common, especially in a large urban high school, the relationship with one's principal is of paramount importance in a teacher's work life. A principal sets a tone.

> *"I think a principal can make or break a school in terms of—not even the day-to-day functioning—but in terms of the umbrella of attitudes and emotions."*

That umbrella covers a wide area. The principal has the power to make working in a school pleasant or unbearable; that is quite a bit of power. A principal who makes teaching pleasant is one who trusts the staff to perform classroom duties with competence, and who deals with parents and the community in a way that supports teachers' decisions and safeguards against personal attacks.

Teachers avoid "getting on the bad side" of a principal; such a position makes life unbearable. The principal has the power to make extra duty assignments, to criticize classroom practices, to assign undesirable class schedules. More importantly, on an informal level, being disliked by the principal carries with it distinct psychological disadvantages.

> "If I see him in the hall and he doesn't smile or look at me, I'm upset all day. What did I do wrong? Why doesn't he like me? Will he listen to me if there's a problem? I know it shouldn't affect me, but it does."

When teachers view a principal as critical or punishing, they are less likely to take risks and try new approaches. When teachers view a principal as supporting and rewarding, they are more able to approach the principal for support in trying something new, in securing resources, in gaining permission for special undertakings.

The relationship of teacher to principal is one of gaining access to privilege, and almost all privileges are arbitrarily in the hands of the principal. This is especially true for teachers who themselves aspire to administrative positions. The principal's recommendation about the administrative potential of teachers is taken seriously. While many teachers profess that they avoid the principal and learn to work around him or her, the importance of that office is always felt in the daily life of the school.

Feelings

Strong feelings accompany intense and varied interactions. The feelings of teachers about their work and their lives are complex, characterized by conflict, frustration, satisfaction, and joy.

When we characterized teacher-student interactions as the major source of rewards for teachers, we placed great emphasis on feelings of genuine satisfaction that accrue from these relationships. The other side of those feelings, of living one's professional life always in the company of children, is also quite powerful for teachers. These other feelings are more negative and often come to light in the company of other adults who work in "the real world," not the world of schools.

> "I had a disagreement with my mother-in-law the other day. I don't remember what it was about—taxes or something that is being voted on. Every time I started to talk, she would disagree and then tell me that I didn't live in the real world, that I spent all of my time with kids, and that I just didn't know about business and other things. I felt very angry. That kind of thing happens now and again. I feel that I do live in the real world, but people who don't teach don't think that's true."

To the rest of the world, teachers often seem to be living in a child's reality and are viewed as not being able to function as adults in an adult world. This perception leaves teachers uneasy at best, defensive at worse, almost always self-doubting, and characteristically ambivalent about their roles and their constant relationship with young people.

Feelings of self-doubt are exacerbated by the absence of a standard by which one can measure one's professional competence. The lack of peer support and interaction makes it difficult to develop a clear sense of the quality of one's own teaching. Teaching skills are evaluated by the students, whose judgment is not always trustworthy, and by oneself.

> "It took me ten years to feel that I was a good teacher. In fact, I would try very hard not to miss a day of school. I thought if a substitute came in and taught my classes that all the students would find out how bad I was and how good someone else was."

There is a general lack of confidence, a pervasive feeling of vulnerability, a fear of being "found out." Such feelings are made worse because of the privacy ethic. There is no safe place to air one's uncertainties and to get the kind of feedback necessary to reduce the anxiety about being a good teacher, or at least an adequate one.

One way a teacher may gain some confidence is to define a sphere of control. For most, that is the classroom. It becomes essential to gain and maintain dominance if one is to survive.

> "When I'm in my classroom, I know I'm in control. I can teach the way I want to teach, do what I want to do."

Once inside the classroom, a teacher knows that all control is tenuous. It depends on a negotiated agreement between students and the teacher. If that agreement is violated, a teacher will subordinate all teaching activities to one primary goal: to regain and maintain control. Keeping a class in order is the only visible indication to one's colleagues and principal that one is, in fact, a good teacher. When one loses control, one loses everything.

Feelings about control are made more problematic by the awareness on the part of teachers that once outside the classroom, their control is severely limited. Within the formal organization of the school, teachers have little authority in making decisions that affect their environment. Teachers, then, move from a level of almost complete authority to a level of powerlessness. This being in-and-out-of-control leads to feelings of frustration and resignation to the ways things are and will always be.

The feelings that surround issues of always being with children, of professional competence, and of being in-and-out-of-control are highly charged and little acknowledged. They should not be underestimated; these feelings often block a teacher's impulse to work to improve one's teaching or to influence what happens in the school.

Rhythms, Rules, Interactions, and Feelings

In this section, we have tried to present a view of some of the day-to-day realities of schools for the teachers who work there. We have concentrated on rhythms, rules, interactions, and feelings as a way to gain some insight into schools and how to make them better. We may summarize by saying:

- By understanding rhythms, we come to realize that years are cyclical; that patterns often supplant purpose; that what has been done may be undone in the seasons that follow; and that what has not yet been done is still in the realm of the possible.

- By understanding rules, we come to accept the limits of rational plans, the inevitability of resistance, the power of collective sanctions, and the inviolability of individuals and their classrooms.

- By understanding interactions, we come to an awareness of the centrality of children in teachers' lives, of the unrealized potential of colleagueship, and of the power of a principal to make a school better or worse.

- By understanding feelings, we appreciate ambiguity, vulnerability, and defensiveness as camouflages for commitment, concern, and hope; and we come to value patience and realism as guideposts for our own actions.

REFERENCES

Bentzen, Mary. *Changing: The Magic Feather Principle.* New York: McGraw-Hill, 1975.

Doyle, Walter, and Ponder, Gerald A. "The Practicality Ethic in Teacher Decision Making," *Interchange* 8, 3 (1977–78).

Emrick, John, and Peterson, Susan. *A Synthesis of Findings: Five Recent Studies of Educational Dissemination and Change.* San Francisco: Far West Laboratories, 1978.

Geoffrey, William. *Complexities of an Urban Classroom.* New York: Holt, Rinehart & Winston, 1968.

Goodlad, John I. *The Dynamics of Educational Change.* New York: McGraw-Hill, 1975.

Gross, Neal; Giacquinta, Joseph B.; and Bernstein, Marilyn. *Implementing Organizational Innovations.* New York: Basic Books, 1971.

Jackson, Philip. *Life in Classrooms.* New York: Holt, Rinehart & Winston, 1968.

Lortie, Dan C. "Teacher Socialization: The Robinson Crusoe Model." In *The Real World of the Classroom Teacher,* Report of the 1965 National TEPS Conference. Washington, D.C.: National Education Association, 1965.

McPherson, Gertrude. *Small Town Teacher.* Cambridge: Harvard University Press, 1972.

Sarason, S. B.; Levine, M.; Goldenberg, I.; Cherlin, D.; and Bennett, E. *Psychology in Community Settings.* New York: John Wiley & Sons, 1966.

Shiman, David A., and Lieberman, Ann. "Non-Model for Schools." *Educational Forum* 38, 4 (May 1974).

Smith, Louis, and Keith, Pat. *Anatomy of an Educational Innovation.* New York: Wiley, 1971.

Sussman, Leila. *Tales Out of School: Implementing Organizational Change in the Elementary Grades.* Philadelphia: Temple University Press, 1977.

Waller, Willard. *The Sociology of Teaching.* New York: John Wiley, 1967.

Learning from Experience:
History and Teacher Education

DONALD WARREN
University of Maryland

The criticism that focused on American schools 2 years ago has come to rest on teacher education. Given the pattern of educational reform sentiment that has been repeated several times since the mid-1940s, the shift of attention was predictable. If the pattern holds, general interest in the ways teachers prepare for their professional roles will be temporary. The pressure to make changes quickly is thus understandable, if not reassuring. The point surely is to improve teacher education, but some aspects of the current emphasis weaken that possibility. In the hands of traveling in-service trainers, an important and instructive research literature is reduced to a "knowledge base" that is optimistically portrayed as promising more generalized practical applicability than social or behavioral science research can deliver. Overstatement in the other direction comes from the current round of complaints about teachers and their professional preparation. One report announces that "never before in the nation's history has the caliber of those entering the teaching profession been as low as it is today" (Feistritzer, 1983, p. 112). Colorado Governor Richard Lamm comments, "List the ten most somnolent courses in a university, and nine of them will be teacher courses." That remark pales in quotability next to Gary Sykes' characterization of teacher preparation as "higher education's dirty little secret." H. Ross Perot, the Texas industrialist credited with the recent passage of that state's school reform bill, likens teacher education to a fire drill. (Peirce, 1985). The hyperbole borders on silliness, but it gives historians something to chew on.

Current proposals offer strategies for raising the quality of those entering the teaching profession. Teacher shortages in mathematics and the sciences

From *Educational Researcher* 14 (December 1985). Copyright © 1985 by American Educational Research Associaiton, Washington, D.C. Reprinted by permission of the publisher.

are to be reduced, for example, by appointing retired people and housewives with appropriate academic degrees to teaching positions. Others can become teachers by completing an undergraduate major in a standard discipline and an extended apprenticeship in the "real world" of the classroom. People will be encouraged to view teaching as a temporary commitment, not necessarily a lifelong profession. Formal teacher education will not be the exclusive province of schools, colleges, or departments of education; other academic units will assume major roles in teacher preparation. Certification will reflect tested academic achievement and instructional competence, not an array of education courses. As states adopt such proposals, they reverse developments of the past 150 years that were intended to professionalize teaching and teacher education. Whatever the value or wisdom of the proposed changes, they are appropriate subjects of historical investigation.

Earnest and single-minded approaches to the history of teacher education, however, are apt to miss some its ironic and truly delightful developments. As Merle Borrowman (1956) observed almost three decades ago, this is a history that has no notable beginning. Put another way, before there was teacher education—or, from one perspective, even teachers—there was teaching or, in Cubberley's (1934) derisive term, "schoolkeeping." By 1860, almost 7 million American children were attending school, all but about 100,000 in what we call today the elementary grades. The vast majority lived in rural areas; even by the turn of the century most students went to schools located in districts and communities of less than 5,000 people. These general demographic characteristics reflected not only the success of the public school in the United States but also the emergence of a pervasive sector of the American labor market: teaching. The existence of new positions in considerable numbers drew people to the job, prepared or not. Given this order of development, it is helpful to understand the history of teacher education experientially, by starting at the beginning, as it were, with sketches of teaching and of those who taught during the period before teacher education became institutionalized or widespread.

TEACHING

To call teaching a career in the nineteenth century would be misleading, although some of the young people who entered teaching applied precisely that term to their work. For most, it was a part-time job taken up temporarily. School terms could be measured in weeks, and those who taught tended to move on to other occupations or to marriage after a few years. The job centered on the school, and because the school was essentially a classroom, the most visible assignment was instruction. Throughout most of the nineteenth century, teachers in rural and urban schools alike drilled their students in individual or class recitations with ritualistic precision (Finkelstein, 1970). Learning was thought to have occurred when the child could reiterate the information or emulate the skill. Lucia Downing followed the procedure in her rural Vermont school in 1882, and she had only four students (Hoffman,

1981). She relied on memorization, in part, out of expediency. Lacking textbooks, she created materials for her charges from her own recollections. Here was an example of, and a reason for, teaching as one had been taught. After all, Downing's students had few books at home. Memorization could be as useful to them as it had been to her.

Research by Geraldine Clifford (1978, 1982) and Barbara Finkelstein (1970) and a wealth of primary materials made available through women's studies help us interpret the conflicting testimony about teaching methods during the last century. Surveying the evidence, Larry Cuban (1984) concluded that well into the twentieth century, the American classroom remained essentially teacher-centered. In the role of teacher resided the authority over student learning and deportment. The teacher initiated and was held accountable for whatever classroom educational dynamics occurred. Both forms of school-based behavior—learning and deportment—tended to become routinized. Recent research on the teaching role has shown that such modes of instruction—inflexible pedagogy, preoccupation with classroom order, and commitment to lesson plans—are characteristic of new teachers (Koehler, 1985). Nineteenth-century American communities frequently had only new teachers, year after year. Classroom overseers and disciplinarians abounded, but we can also document inductive pedagogies and sheer wonderment at youthful imagination. Downing recalled "one *big* boy who was *peeved* because I would not allow him the same privilege as the little ones who always wanted to kiss 'Teacher' good night" (quoted in Hoffman, 1981, p. 34). She was 14 years old at the time. Other teachers also recorded the delights and frustrations of their jobs and their efforts to teach well. Such personal accounts do not permit us to generalize about teaching during this early period, but they allow glimpses of a nascent, largely untrained profession thinking about its work.

Qualifications for teaching jobs ranged from nonexistent to formally specified. Many candidates acquired positions through family connections or simply lack of competition. Typically, school committees and local superintendents sought assurances on two fronts: candidates' moral character, and their knowledge of subject matters and of the "theory of teaching." The latter could mean little more than the teacher's resolve to act as disciplinarian. Where candidates were numerous, their qualifications received greater attention, but faced with few choices, local officials might select the best applicant, hoping if all else failed that new teacher would be an "upright" person. In some cases the best candidate was the one who required the lowest salary. Crude and informal reviews of teaching candidates occurred in all sorts of school districts. Other urban and rural communities, however, employed more formal procedures. Some used structured interviews, but as early as the 1840s candidates qualified for their moral and academic instructional roles by passing written examinations. (See, e.g., the sample questions reprinted in the *Common School Journal of the State of Pennsylvania*, 1844.)

Teaching in the nineteenth century involved more than classroom instruction, as it has ever since. The teacher's community role was visible and presumed to be powerful. Titles were important, as was the way teachers dressed; the younger ones worked at looking older. Classroom discipline brought order to the school and also established the wider authority and social standing of the teacher, who was frequently an outsider within the community. The symbolic realm of teaching—its effective jurisdiction— extended beyond the schoolhouse. When teaching failed, an entire community, not merely the young, was left wanting. Yet Samuel Hall's (1829) complaint remained—and remains—stubbornly true. The job, he observed, offered little more respectability "than manual labor" (p. 16).

On a more mundane level, teaching involved cleaning the school, chopping wood, and making sure the room was warm in the winter—literally, schoolkeeping. Clever teachers managed to delegate the work to their older students, but they could not delegate the responsibility. Teaching contracts could be quite explicit about that. Ventilation and hygiene were practical worries; a backed up flue could empty the school on a cold day. In villages and rural areas especially, teachers worried about their own health. If they became ill overnight, the students would arrive at school the next day regardless, and if a teacher "took sick" during the day, students would have to be dismissed early. Often parents sent young children to school with their older siblings, leaving teachers to cope with 3- and 4-year-olds as best they could. As Clifford (1978, 1982) found, the job included a fair amount of child care. In addition, parents had to be visited, and even in districts that had abandoned the practice of "boarding around," teachers might live with a family during the school term. Justifiably, they felt permanently caught in the public eye. Their interactions with parents and other community adults tended to be immediate and frequent.

Several historians in recent years have stressed the unbureaucratic character of teaching in rural schools and in most nineteenth-century settings (Clifford, 1978; Tyack & Hansot, 1982). However, in curbing a misguided inclination to view all schools from the perspective of twentieth-century experience with urban, bureaucratized schools, we may overlook earlier forms of paperwork required of teachers. After the Civil War period, even those in one-room rural schools probably kept ledgers that enabled them to submit through prescribed channels the complicated average attendance data that eventually appeared in state reports. Teaching, in short, involved conceptualizing, preparing for, and managing more than lessons.

A complex, if diffuse, policy environment filtered and shaped expectations of teaching in the nineteenth century. Positions were relatively plentiful, which allowed interested candidates to shop around among districts and communities. State officials regularly reported shortages. The problem was twofold. Worry about preparation and qualifications was common (Lewis, 1857; Snarr, 1946), but demand for teachers could overwhelm qualms about teachers' "moral and intellectual status." The opening of new schools and the frequent movement of teachers to new jobs or out of teaching altogether combined to create absolute shortages. Thus, the number of teaching positions in Illinois doubled during the 1850s and doubled again in the next decade. During this period, other midwestern states reported average annual increases in the number of new teaching positions ranging from 150 to 800. These data came from state education officials anxious for additional school funding from their legislatures. We can assume the numbers have been inflated, but there is no denying the demand for teachers was great, especially in the rural areas. The shortages touched every region of the country, far exceeding the number of people prepared in the newly emerging teacher training programs.

Salaries, of course, largely determined who responded to these job opportunities. Downing earned $20 for her 10-week term in rural Vermont and could expect to double that amount in a year by teaching two terms (Hoffman, 1981). Her salary was below average. White teachers in 1870 received an average annual salary of $190. The average income earned by white teachers increased gradually over the years, reaching $1,050 in the early 1930s. Salaries for black teachers were considerably lower. The worry voiced by New Hampshire's superintendent in the 1850s remained well-founded for some time:

> The compensation and reputation connected with what are termed the learned professions are strong incitements to effort in aspiring candidates, while a situation in the district school has associated with it none of these motives. The charms of the school are few and dim in the estimation of the talented . . . (quoted in Brown, 1937, p. 19)

The combined effects of available positions and low pay explained why teachers moved from district to district with such frequency. In addition, salaries and working conditions encouraged them to leave teaching for other pursuits. Even though they had few other employment opportunities, the women who were drawn to teaching in increasing numbers could not be counted on to stay put. The tentativeness of their professional commitment was reasonable; it was not surprising that efforts to institutionalize and require professional training failed to attract much response from would-be teachers. Why spend time and money in preparation when the job itself neither required nor rewarded the investment? People prepared for teaching by attending a common school, by self-directed study, or both; they learned how and what to teach from their own teachers. The major incentive for many to become teachers undoubtedly was that they could find no other work to do, at least for the time being.

The grand claims for the importance of teaching voiced by nineteenth-century school reformers must be read with the policy environment firmly in mind. Individual idealists, servants of God and the nation, have left records of their hopes and their labors. However, a mass educational system was arising and few communities or states had the resources or the will to finance their part of it; rural communities, where most teaching occurred, were notoriously cash poor. In this policy environment, teaching positions could be acquired with relative ease, but given the demands and the meager rewards of the job, who would want it?

TEACHERS

In truth, we know more about teaching in the nineteenth and early twentieth centuries than we know about those who taught. We can be relatively confident only about matters of size and general characteristics. Between 1870 and 1900, the number of teachers grew from 200,000 to 425,000, increasing approximately 80,000 each decade. For the next 30 years the growth per decade was in the neighborhood of 150,000; by 1930 there were close to 800,000 teachers. Most worked in elementary schools, although the proportion of high school teachers rose dramatically after 1910. By 1930, women outnumbered men in the teaching force by more than 5 to 1. From numerous studies of teaching, state reports, and local surveys, we can construct a picture of American teachers during this period. Their formal training was uneven and the total years of schooling they brought to their work remained low. An impression prevailed that as a group they lacked impressive intellectual abilities and academic interests. On all these points, considerable variation existed among regions and within states. The sharpest differences occurred between teachers in large cities and those in farming areas. Urban teachers were better prepared, held their positions longer, and earned higher salaries than their counterparts in villages and rural communities.

David Angus (1983) notes the dearth of historical studies of the social origins of teachers. As he suggests, the topic requires quantitative approaches, and a number of data bases and resource materials invite analyses using contemporary techniques. One difficulty is the unreliability of education-related statistics in early state and U.S. Bureau of Education reports. Some of these weaknesses can be circumvented, however, and there are important reasons for doing so. Needed is the kind of quantitative basis that social class research can provide for examining historically teachers' frames of reference and loyalties.

A tentative beginning of such a project appeared as part of the *National Survey of the Education of Teachers* (Evenden, Gamble, & Blue, 1935) conducted early in the 1930s. Mandated by Congress, the *Survey* was published in six volumes of findings and recommendations in the middle of the decade.[1] It remains the most comprehensive empirical study of the effects, status, and prospects of teacher education in the United States, although by current standards it contains bothersome technical flaws. Oddly enough, the *Survey* did not collect data on teachers' social backgrounds. However, returns on a questionnaire that was distributed to teacher college and liberal arts college students in the midwest permitted the staff to construct general descriptions of the two student populations. The assumption that teacher college students could be safely classified as prospective teachers proved to be wrong. Fewer of these students than liberal arts college students intended to earn degrees. They were more likely to interrupt their studies, usually to take temporary teaching positions, and more of them needed financial assistance. Their parents and siblings were less educated. More of them were born in rural communities and villages, and their families were more likely to be involved in farming. They were clearer, more precise and fixed, about their vocational goals. They attended colleges closer to their homes. The *Survey* staff was shocked to learn that over 10% of the teacher college students had no plans to become teachers, whereas almost 50% of the liberal arts college students thought they might. The latter were seen as posing a threat to teacher professionalization—they could claim the necessary academic preparation, but they would have missed the education courses needed to help them be effective in the classroom. The "marked provincialism" of teacher college students observed by the *Survey* staff has been noted in studies of active teachers (see, e.g., the review in *Elsbree,* 1939). Tyack and Hansot (1982) found small-town, pietistic backgrounds to be prevalent among nineteenth- and early twentieth-century school administrators and other educational leaders. However, the available data are sketchy and, like those gathered by the *Survey,* tend to be regionally specific. It may also be noted that the *Survey* tells us more about the social class differences of those attending the two types of colleges than about the social class characteristics of prospective teachers.

Sources reviewed by Finkelstein (1970) and Cuban (1984) reflect long-held negative views of teacher effectiveness and instructional styles. Nineteenth-century state superintendents despaired of attracting and holding able, committed teachers in their schools. Their messages to state legislatures regularly reported dissatisfaction with the quality and stability of the teaching force. Rural teachers apparently longed to live and work in cities, whereas teachers in large cities seemed to prefer working in less urban settings. The professional behavior of teachers generally impressed observers as inflexible, unimaginative, insecure, and often uncaring. Such negative assessments were pervasive and consistent—so much so that they inspire doubt. How can we reconcile this portrait of failure and low public regard of teachers with steadily increasing school enrollments? Teachers must have been doing something right, or else parents valued the schooling of their children for reasons other than the perceived quality of teachers.

Susan B. Anthony thought she understood why teaching was held in such low esteem: It was a female job. In her now familiar speech to a gathering of predominantly male educators in Rochester, New York in 1853, she reasoned that because women were viewed as incompetent for any other profession, men choosing to become teachers tacitly admitted they had "no more brains than a woman." Furthermore, they should expect low salaries because they competed "with the cheap labor of women" (quoted in Lerner, 1977, pp. 235–236). The rationales offered for bringing women into teaching in greater numbers stressed economic and pedagogical benefits. Paying women teachers less than men promised absolute savings. In addition, women helped to solve the teacher shortage problem. Finally, they were seen as having natural and special abilities to inculcate morality and to lead the educational development of children. There was a dark side to these explanations as well. Calvin Stowe, who later married Harriet Beecher, thought that bringing women into teaching might deflect feminist urges to speak at public meetings and hold elective office, "notwithstanding the exhortations of Harriet Martineau, Fanny Wright, and some other[s]" (quoted in Knight & Hall, 1951,

p. 415). In light of such testimony, the feminization of teaching can be viewed not only as a step toward independence, if not greater social equality, for women, but also as a process of defusing women's quest for larger roles in public affairs. If Anthony was correct, the teaching profession paid a heavy price for the fresh, inexpensive female recruits it gained. Teachers now had to do battle with bias against women as well as against their profession.

Teachers inevitably found themselves thrust into public roles, and several sources have stressed the importance of teachers' relations with the communities in which they worked. Much depended on their ability to fit in. In one study, Clifford (1982) concluded that young female teachers tended to work in districts close to their homes. Elsewhere (1978) she commented on the migratory habits of nineteenth-century teachers generally. We know also of Catharine Beecher's effort to draw eastern women to teaching positions in the West. By mid-century, state superintendents in this region were complaining about the number of "outsiders" teaching in their schools (Snarr, 1946). One could argue that because these states were largely populated by recent settlers, new teachers should have had little difficulty being accepted by their communities. But the influx offended regional sensibilities. A general impression prevailed that the able teachers remained in the East, whereas the unfit and the adventurers moved west. Illinois superintendent David Gregg thought "there would be great advantage in having a body of intelligent teachers educated in our midst, who are well acquainted with western habits, customs, and feelings" (quoted in Snarr, p. 20). The notion that local teachers should be locally trained eventually gained favor among legislators, who invoked it in supporting the establishment of regional state normal schools.

Primary sources confirm Gregg's implied criticism. Teachers in rural areas wrote, often bitterly, of their loneliness, the absence of cultural resources, and the crudeness of local residents. Some remained aloof; others threw themselves into church and community activities. Even those who closed the social and cultural gap might yet confront a more resistant form of alienation by virtue of their roles as teachers. Unlettered parents apparently pushed their children into schooling, however rudimentary; but if the process took hold, strains within the family could follow. Personal reminiscences, from women in particular, tell of family tension and parental resentment over a child's awakened educational aspirations (see, e.g., Lerner, 1977). By simply doing their instructional work well, teachers could set themselves apart from their communities. Loneliness resulting from this sort of alienation would not be erased by locally oriented teacher training.

TEACHER EDUCATION

The familiar history of teacher education in the United States was a Hegelian account of successive and successful reforms. Moving upward from the founding of the first normal school, this history tended to treat institutions, key leaders, goals, and legislation as a cluster of independent phenomena. It was a history of and for teacher training.

The actual story has been more lively and important. Some colleges and schools provided teacher education unintentionally; others, as Herbst (1980) noted, intended to offer only teacher preparation and found themselves serving students with different destinations in mind. Self-conscious teacher education programs existed early in the nineteenth century, for example, Lancasterian training schools and Mary Lyon's effort at Mount Holyoke (Kaestle, 1973; Green, 1979). Later, some district schools, even in rural areas, offered teacher training for those who would become teachers in the level of schooling they were just completing. Urban high schools added "normal departments." Teacher institutes, financed locally or by the states, attracted large followings. Reformers spoke longingly and frequently of the need for normal schools throughout the century, but those institutions were founded slowly. Toward the end of the century, universities began to establish schools or colleges of pedagogy. The effect of these efforts on the great body of teachers came later. In the meantime, for reasons having little relation to the quality or availability of teacher education, teachers either received no formal training at all, received modest amounts of training after they began teaching, or had recourse to a great variety of sometimes fleeting institutional arrangements. Throughout the nineteenth century, most programs offered high-school level preparation. In the twentieth century we find a steady lengthening and upgrading of teacher education. Four-year degree programs differentiated by teaching specialty became commonplace. This long-term development in teacher training actually occurred—it was no Hegelian fairy tale. It was punctuated by periodic pedagogical reform efforts, just as Cubberley (1934) said. He is as good a source as any for the chronology of isolated developments.

So constructed, the story nevertheless offers little reason for celebration. By 1931, over 65% of the white elementary school teachers had preparation ranging from only 6 weeks to 2 years of college work. Even fewer black elementary school teachers received this level of preparation: 22% had only 4 years or less of high school. Black and white high school teachers tended to have 3 to 4 years of college. Rural teachers as a group had less preparation than urban teachers. These general descriptions are based on data collected from teachers in the *Survey* cited previously. Except by level, the questionnaire distributed by the *Survey* staff permitted no distinctions among types of institutions. A normal school was assumed to offer college level work.

Conclusions drawn by the *Survey* staff were consistent with the teacher education reform agenda that had been operative for over 75 years. The major objective was to increase the amount of teacher preparation in the now traditional curricular areas of academic studies, professional studies, and practice. The reform strategy also remained unchanged. If more preparation was assumed to be better preparation, the way to success was enforcement. Minimum age requirements for teachers were necessary. A high school diploma was a prerequisite for admission to teacher education. Certification criteria should specify amounts of preparation required in particular subjects. As the *Survey* staff admitted, however, little convincing evidence available in 1930 showed the quantity of teacher preparation could be correlated with student achievement. The relationship between teacher effectiveness and type of preparatory institution—for example, teacher college, liberal arts college, or university—remained a matter of conjecture. No one could be confident that greater amounts of teacher education, including supervised practice teaching, had a positive impact on teachers' performance in the classroom. Unwilling to end on an uncertain note, the *Survey* staff concluded by calling for more research on teacher education and pressing for preparation programs that would reflect the proven characteristics of effective teaching.

Given nineteenth-century teaching conditions and what we know about the history of teachers, the focus on quantitative reforms of teacher education is understandable. Blaming a defensive professional culture, Church and Sedlak (1976) found that programmatic reforms reflecting enthusiasm for a particular pedagogy or a new teacher education curriculum tended to atrophy over time. In addition, no durable, pervasive institutional structure existed to house pedagogical reforms of teacher education and keep them lively through use and experimentation. In 1930, creating and strengthening the institutional framework of teacher education superseded concern about its quality. In fact, reformers perceived structural growth as qualitative improvement.

In 1985, a mature structure exists. We no longer debate whether its level should be that of higher education or whether preservice preparation should require at minimum a bachelor's degree. A guild of teacher educators or teachers of teachers, to use Mary Lyon's term, is in place, its work supported by an accumulation of social and behavioral science research. The talk throughout the nineteenth century about a science of education sounds pretentious and quaint compared to twentieth-century confidence and sophistication.

BASIC PATTERNS

In many respects the history of teacher education cannot be read as prologue to the present; it seems so different from current realities as to be irrelevant. Yet, persistence of basic patterns should give us pause. Consider, for example, the following. First, from the early nineteenth century forward, market considerations have driven both the policies and the curricula in teacher education, as both have responded to shortages and surpluses of teachers. The size of the teaching force nationally, the differing pressures it has exerted on the states over time, and the fluctuating demand for teachers have rendered meaningless envious comparisons between teacher education and preparation for other professions, such as law or medicine, that aspired to operate at graduate levels. The teacher economy continues to function independently of professional judgment about teacher education, as it did in the nineteenth century, and independently of research findings, as it does in our time. To be effective, imposed standards in teacher education have required the availability of candidates with restricted employment opportunities or strong altruistic commitments, preferably both.

Second, attempts to clarify responsibility for teacher education reflect a long history of controversy over the separateness of teacher preparation programs. The early advocates of normal schools wanted single-purpose institutions (Learned, Bagley, McMurry, Dearborn, & Strayer, 1920) and complained that students headed for careers other than teaching diluted the professional focus of their schools. Nevertheless, normal schools and, later, teacher colleges served general, nonprofessional educational purposes, one reason being the happy congruence of a growing demand for accessible higher education and the need of teacher training institutions for students. Harold Rugg (1952) thought the reasons for such contradictory attitudes and policies were fairly obvious. He argued that no college curriculum could be effective unless it was controlled by the faculty responsible for it. Teacher education, like other higher education programs, has felt the effects of academic politics, that is, the faculty's competition for enrollments, budgets, and prestige. Such factors have determined a program's existence, quite apart from its quality; controlling them has been an issue of some consequence for teacher education. Cremin (1965) saw the influence of these factors on relations between Teachers College and Columbia University. Powell (1980) found them at work in conflicts between the Harvard Graduate School of Education faculty and the Arts and Sciences faculty, many of whom argued against education as an appropriate university program while trying to lay claim to education students.

Third, from the outset, teacher education has been viewed as virtually synonymous with instructional preparation. As a result, courses in practice teaching, in professional studies such as history of education and school economy (class management), and in academic studies have received a particular practical slant. This focus has tended to organize and to reinforce a limited conception of teaching as classroom activity. Subtly or overtly, the classroom has been depicted as appropriately teacher-centered, and this view has served to anchor teachers' professional lives. To the extent that the emphasis on methodological practice has prevailed, teacher education ironically has grown increasingly remote from the conditions of teaching and the experience of teachers, neither of which have been confinable to classrooms. Offered in isolation, preparation for instruction has left teachers unprepared for their more difficult responsibilities, which are to conceptualize, innovate, and analyze disparate educational and policy phenomena.

The intrusion of policy on pedagogy in teacher education has left the purposes of teacher education both fixed and fluid. There have not been any unadulterated philosophies at work, and thus temporary passions have mixed with institutional structures and social arrangements in determining how teachers acquire preparation and what they have become prepared to do and to be. Despite changes over the past two centuries, teacher education has seemed to be in perpetual disfavor. The programs were misguided, too short, or superficial; the candidates unpromising. Yet, the persistence of basic patterns of influence and policy suggests that the zeal for improvement has been narrowly focused. Enforced alterations of teacher education programs satisfy an urge for action, but the inseparable histories of teaching, teachers, and teacher education offer resources for more effective strategies. Teachers deserve preparation that conceptualizes and builds upon the broad scope of their actual responsibilities. In addition, assuming reform is the goal, teacher training programs require improvement in the conditions under which teachers work.

NOTES

1. The *National survey of the education of teachers* (Washington, DC: U.S. Government Printing Office) was published in six volumes as follows:
   Betts, G. L., Frazier, B. W., & Gamble, G. C. (1932). *Selected bibliography on the education of teachers* (Vol. 1).
   Evenden, E. S., Gamble, G. C., & Blue, H. G. (1935). *Teacher personnel in the United States* (Vol. 2).
   Rugg, E. U. et al. (1935). *Teacher education curricula* (Vol. 3).
   Caliver, A. (1933). *Education of Negro teachers* (Vol. 4).
   Frazier, B. W. et al. (1935). *Special survey studies* (Vol. 5).
   Evenden, E. S. (1935). *Summary and interpretation* (Vol. 6).

REFERENCES

Angus, D. L. (1983). The empirical mode: Quantitative history. In J. H. Best (Ed.), *Historical inquiry in education: A research agenda.* Washington, DC: American Educational Research Association.

Borrowman, M. L. (1956). *The liberal and technical in teacher education: A historical survey of American thought.* New York: Bureau of Publications, Teachers College, Columbia University.

Brown, H. A. (1937). *Certain basic teacher-education policies and their development and significance in a selected state* [New Hampshire]. New York: Bureau of Publications, Teachers College, Columbia University.

Church, R. L., & Sedlak, M. W. (1976). *Education in the United States: An interpretive history.* New York: The Free Press.

Clifford, G. J. (1978). Home and school in 19th-century America: Some personal history reports from the United States. *History of Education Quarterly, 18,* 3–34.

Clifford, G. J. (1982). "Marry, stitch, die, or do worse": Educating women for work. In H. Kantor & D. B. Tyack (Eds.), *Youth, work, and schooling: Historical perspectives on vocationalism in American education.* Stanford, CA: Stanford University Press.

Common School Journal of the State of Pennsylvania. (1844). Volume 1 [Entire Volume].

Cremin, L. A. (1965). *The wonderful world of Ellwood Patterson Cubberley: An essay on the historiography of American education.* New York: Bureau of Publications, Teachers College, Columbia University.

Cuban, L. (1984). *How teachers taught: Constancy and change in American classrooms, 1890–1980.* New York: Longman.

Cubberley, E. P. (1934). *Public education in the United States: A study and interpretation of American educational history.* Boston: Houghton Mifflin.

Elsbree, W. S. (1939). *The American teacher: Evolution of a profession in a democracy.* New York: American Book Company.

Evenden, E. S., Gamble, G. C., & Blue, H. G. (1935). Teacher personnel in the United States. In *National survey of the education of teachers* (Vol. 2). Washington, DC: U.S. Government Printing Office.

Feistritzer, C. E. (1983). *The condition of teaching: A state by state analysis.* Princeton, NJ: The Carnegie Foundation for the Advancement of Teaching.

Finkelstein, B. J. (1970). *Governing the young: Teacher behavior in American primary schools, 1820–1880.* Unpublished doctoral dissertation, Teachers College, Columbia University.

Green, E. A. (1979). *Mary Lyon and Mount Holyoke: Opening the gates.* Hanover, NH: University Press of New England.

Hall, S. (1829). *Lectures on schoolkeeping.* Boston: Richardson, Lord & Holbrook.

Herbst, J. (1980). Beyond the debate over revisionism: Three educational pasts writ large. *History of Education Quarterly, 20,* 131–145.

Hoffman, N. (Ed.). (1981). *Woman's "true" profession: Voices from the history of teaching.* Old Westbury, NY: The Feminist Press.

Kaestle, C. F. (Ed.). (1973). *Joseph Lancaster and the monitorial school movement: A documentary history.* New York: Teachers College Press.

Knight, E. W., & Hall, C. L. (Eds.). (1951). *Readings in American educational history.* New York: Greenwood Press.

Koehler, V. (1985). Research on preservice teacher education. *Journal of Teacher Education, 36,* 23–30.

Learned, W. S., Bagley, W. C., McMurry, C. A., Dearborn, N., & Strayer, G. D. (1920). *The professional preparation of teachers for American public schools: A study based upon an examination of tax-supported normal schools in the State of Missouri.* New York: Carnegie Foundation for the Advancement of Teaching.

Lerner, G. (Ed.). (1977). *The female experience.* Indianapolis, IN: Bobbs-Merrill.

Lewis, W. G. (1857). *Biography of Samuel Lewis.* Cincinnati, OH: The Methodist Book Concern.

Peirce, N. (1985, March 26). Putting teachers to the test. *The Philadelphia Inquirer,* p. 9A.

Powell, A. G. (1980). *The uncertain profession: Harvard and the search for educational authority.* Cambridge, MA: Harvard University Press.

Rugg, H. (1952). *The teacher of teachers: Frontiers of theory and practice in teacher education.* New York: Harper & Brothers.

Snarr, O. W. (1946). *The education of teachers in the middle states.* Moorhead, MN: Moorhead State Teachers College.

Tyack, D., & Hansot, E. (1982). *Managers of virtue: Public school leadership in America, 1820–1980.* New York: Basic Books.

Whom Shall the Schools Serve? Some Dilemmas of Local Control in a Rural School District

ALAN PESHKIN

University of Illinois

Local control of their schools provides American communities with a substantial measure of freedom to teach what they wish. And who will gainsay the right of local communities to determine how and by whom their children will be educated?

Yet, adherence to the principle of local control can result in controversial educational policy. Through conformity to the will of the local community, schools may teach bigotry in place of tolerance or contempt for learning in place of the love of it. And who then is well served? The community? The students? The nation? Consider the case of Mansfield.[1]

Corn and soybean fields make an island of Mansfield village. Here, in the heart of America's agricultural Midwest, live 1,500 people. Few of them are farmers. Some run stores, others do maintenance for the village, still others teach school. Because there is no local industry, the majority of working villagers commute to the factories of Stanton, twenty-five miles away.

Around the town, in an area of seventy-five square miles, live another 800 people—mostly farmers and their families. In common with the villagers they patronize the stores, attend the churches, and pay their taxes in Mansfield. Some exercise considerable influence, for the farm families of the community are also its residents of longest standing and hold offices in local organizations. Hence they bring their own concerns to bear on the lives of the villagers.

From *Curriculum Inquiry* Vol. 6 No. 3 (1977): 181–204. Copyright © 1977 by John Wiley and Sons, Inc. Reprinted by permission of John Wiley and Sons, Inc, and the author.

Together the residents of the village and of the countryside make up the Mansfield community. It is a modestly prosperous one; the median family income in 1970 was $9,500, which exceeded somewhat the median for the state as a whole. At the same time, only 5.6 percent of the residents had an annual income of less than $3,000, the poverty level designated for the 1970 census. Mansfield is also a homogeneous community. None of its residents is black, and nearly every one was born in the United States to English-speaking parents.

Like American communities of all sorts, Mansfield supports a school system. There are two schools in the district: an elementary school consisting of kindergarten through sixth grade, and a secondary school—Mansfield High School—consisting of seventh through twelfth grade. In 1973, the system enrolled 500 students and employed thirty-five teachers.[2]

These were the characteristics of Mansfield and its school that had drawn my interest. Initially I had gone there to investigate the relation between school and community in a rural setting.[3] The study of rural schooling has been relatively neglected in recent decades; and yet, with the continued growth of urban society, small-town life has increasingly become an endangered species. Of late, small towns located near places of work have attracted migrants from the cities, refugees from the discontents of urban life. Because Mansfield has not had the housing to accommodate many urban migrants, it has retained the features of rural life that I had come to study.

For two years, then, and with the help of six research assistants, I directed fieldwork in Mansfield, studying the high school and the community that supports it. We began with the school, interviewing teachers, school board members, and students; attending classes, school-sponsored events, teachers' meetings, school board meetings; reading through school documents of all sorts.[4] From the school we turned to the community, interviewing the mayor and the village board, whose meetings we also attended. We took part in local church and organizational activities. I myself lived in Mansfield during most of the second year of fieldwork. Like any Mansfielder I shopped, paid my bills, maintained a bank account, and frequented the post office there. Yet, though I lived and worked in the community steadily for a year, though I associated daily with Mansfielders, they for their part continued to regard me as a visitor. I remained the professor who had come to conduct research. Perhaps it was because they knew I did not plan to stay, perhaps because I had not brought my family. In any case, I was never viewed as a member of the community, not even as a sometime resident. For Mansfielders maintain a vital and exclusive *sense of community*, and that sense may be crucial to maintaining the community itself.[5] Hence my study, which had started as a general inquiry into the relation between Mansfield and its high school, came to center on the role of the high school in maintaining Mansfield's sense of community and, conversely, on the interest of the community in maintaining Mansfield High School.

THE COMMUNITY THROUGH THE EYES
OF ITS MEMBERS

That Mansfield possesses a sense of community was first suggested by Mansfielders themselves, many of whom spoke positively about small-town and country life. To discover the extent of this feeling, we surveyed the views of Mansfielders concerning Mansfield itself, their opinions on various contemporary issues, and the extent of their identification with the community.[6] . . . Though my initial impressions were not all borne out in the survey findings, the sense of community is evident and its basis is suggested.

Mansfield's sense of community reveals itself most clearly in the tendency of Mansfielders to affirm statements suggesting comfort and solidarity. These respondents believe that they are safe in Mansfield, that others in the community can be counted on to help in times of trouble, that Mansfield is a good community of its sort. Most are distinctly satisfied with Mansfield's churches, its schools, its fitness as a place to rear children. . . .

But the sense of community does not signify unanimity. In the first place, there are some residents who are not caught up in the communal web. Newcomers and outsiders, among others, may feel alienated, unwelcome to share in the feeling of collective well-being. They are not part of the Mansfield mainstream. But then mainstream Mansfield itself cannot be regarded as homogeneous. Certain areas of disagreement appear in the survey responses. On most of the items, . . . for example, more than half the respondents appear to hold a positive view of Mansfield; but to items that invite a comment on the communal intimacy of Mansfield life—statements about the need for privacy and the familiar character of the community—responses are plainly divided. Still, the modal view of Mansfield life is decidedly favorable.

Judging by their opinions on contemporary issues, . . . Mansfield's adults subscribe mostly to conservative values. They respond less conservatively than one might suppose to such issues as abortion, gun control, and the women's liberation movement; yet the pattern of responses in each case suggests disparity among individuals rather than general disagreement with the conservative position. But then the conservative stance is plain on such other matters as welfare, capital punishment, foreign aid, race, patriotism, the American way of life, and belief in God. Many of these views are manifest in the classroom, as will be shown. In any event, though Mansfielders are not of one mind on a number of current issues, the conservative drift of the mainstream is evident.

What stands out . . . is the Mansfielders' strong identification with their own community. They manifest communal feelings despite their links to mass society through communication and transportation networks, and despite their dependency on nearby cities for jobs, recreation, shopping, and medical services.[7] Their community not only suits them; it is also a part of them. The identity of mainstream Mansfielders is supplied, in part, by the feeling that they belong in Mansfield. More than 50 percent affirmed that they "feel more at home in Mansfield than [they] ever could someplace outside the Mansfield community."

This mainstream group, then, with its conservative inclinations and its strong community identification, is the one that controls the schools. The manner of its control became evident as we continued our research. Through several years of data collection, an image of Mansfield High School emerged, as though from the pieces of a puzzle. Findings from the early interviews with teachers fit together with those from observing in classrooms, interviewing students, and examining documents. The resulting picture is shown below in the words of the various actors whose decisions govern school policy and whose behavior constitutes educational practice at Mansfield High School.

THE SUPERINTENDENT AND THE SCHOOL BOARD

Superintendent Tate welcomed me and my project to Mansfield, promised and delivered his full cooperation, and stipulated only that we do nothing to disturb the routine of the school. This condition on our work embodied a concern of considerable importance to him and to the school board. A substantial part of a teacher's esteem depends on his capacity to maintain order. The school leadership recently was pleased to learn of the resignation of an otherwise good teacher who "couldn't cut the mustard with the kids" (keep them quiet).

At the time my study began, Tate had been at Mansfield High School for twenty-one years, five as coach and industrial arts teacher and sixteen as superintendent. Though not of local origin, nor in fact of rural background, he was most comfortable with country life. He had been content to confine his career to Mansfield despite job offers from larger school systems. In their turn, Mansfielders and the school board were very pleased with him; he became a person of consequence in community life and an accepted agent of community values in his capacity as educational leader. The school board, guardians of the community, trusted him on matters of fact and judgment, secure in the knowledge that he served their interests.

The seven-member board was presided over by a Mansfield-born farmer. Five of the other six members also were native Mansfielders and farmers, notwithstanding that most school district residents work in factories and live in town. In fact, over the twenty years this school board has existed, the president has always been a farmer and at least five of seven members have been Mansfield-born farmers.[8] Because school board elections generally inspire a good turnout—about two hundred of a possible seven hundred eligible voters—the "right" candidates continue to get elected. (The right candidates are those without the kind of "axe to grind" that might disturb the status quo.) The credentials of the newest board member were his status as a native and the well-known fact that he loved Mansfield and had a deep regard for its traditions. He replaced a man of demonstrated skill, a six-year veteran on the board who had lived in Mansfield only ten years.

One year after my study began, Superintendent Tate died. This misfortune required the school board to undertake a task they had long dreaded—selecting a new superintendent. They assembled in special session one hot

August week to interview five candidates. Afterward, as they sat together to make a choice, their desiderata emerged.

"Should we talk about Hagedorn to see why we don't want him?"

"Yes, let's get the feeling of the board on him. I believe we have better men. Not quality-wise, though. He could handle the job and the P. R. [Public Relations]. I don't think he's the type we're looking for."

"I hate to say it, but his physical appearance is against him. You need to call a spade a spade."

"He's not stable like some of the others."

"I'm afraid he'd be the butt of behind-the-back jokes."

"He's carrying far too much weight. That's a strain on the heart."

"He was tired. A man that size gets physically tired. We shouldn't kid ourselves. Image is very important. That size is against him."

"The next one is Dargan."

"I was impressed, but I feel he is too big for our town and school. His ideas are for the city, for bigger schools. We're not ready for all that."

"I felt he would probably be anxious to start a lot of things I don't know if we're ready for. He's definitely for a nongraded system. He said he'd start slow but he wanted it pretty bad. Knocking down walls scares you just a bit."

"I was impressed. But then we had more fellows in. We learned more about this nongraded idea. He would be a pusher, I'm sure."

"He had too many ideas to start off with. You need to see what a school has before jumping in."

"I thought he might be a little slow with discipline problems."

"I saw dollar signs clicking around in my head when he talked. He may be too intelligent for this community. He may talk over the heads of the community."

"Another thing. He was emphatic about four weeks vacation."

"Salary-wise he asked for the most."

"Well, this Dargan, he said he wanted to come to a small community. I think he may want to bring too many ideas from the city with him. He may be more than we want."

"What did you like about Morgan? These next three are a hard pick."

"He gave a nice impression here, I believe, of getting along with the public and the kids. This impressed me more than anything."

"To me he talked generalities."

"He had a tremendous speaking voice. He's young."

"His voice got very nasal at the end when he got relaxed."

"He wouldn't stay."

"He's on his way up."

"I believe he'd be a forceful individual."

"Take this other man, Rogers. I had a feeling about him. He said, 'If you hired me and I accepted it . . . ' I don't think he's too anxious for the job."

"I can see why he was offered a job selling real estate. He's got the voice. He'd have your name on the line. I'm inclined to believe he'd talk himself out of most situations. Getting down to brass tacks, he spoke in generalities. He admitted he didn't know too much about new things in education. We need more specific answers."

"More or less this leaves us with Reynolds."

"He's the man to put on top."

"I'd hate to pick any one of the top three over the others."

"Both Reynolds and Rogers said that they have no hours. They work by the job. Reynolds worked his way through college."

"He was on ground floor as far as salary goes."

"And he's country."

After rejecting candidates for adverse physical appearance and for holding city and big-school ideas, they selected Reynolds, who worked hard like a farmer, would settle for a "reasonable" salary, and was "country"—a designation that had never before been mentioned as a criterion for selecting their new superintendent, or anything else, for that matter. Perhaps it should have been self-evident that no one could be chosen superintendent of school in Mansfield who did not appear "country," the board's shorthand description of a suitable candidate for their rural-dominated, traditionally oriented school district.

TEACHERS AND THE SCHOOL EXPERIENCE

The central fact characterizing Mansfield's teachers is their small-town origin. Of the eighteen teachers in the high school, six had fathers who farmed; but ten were born and raised in or around towns of under 2,000, three in towns of under 4,500, four in towns of under 15,000, and only one in a city of 800,000. Indeed, the teachers not only grew up in small towns; they generally studied at the smallest of the state universities, Central State,[9] and after graduation taught in schools very much like the ones they themselves had attended. From all indications they are at home in Mansfield; when asked about their ideal place to live, 75 percent indicated a preference for towns of 4,500 or less.

To get some idea of teacher views about education, we asked what changes they would like to see made. They generally confined their responses to the redress of particular grievances. A few wanted a new building; others, a chance to teach only their special subject, better discipline, more vocational courses, or less money spent on athletic programs. Most frequently they wished to eliminate poor teachers, the "dead weight" who had been in the system for too many years. There were no grand schemes, no innovations proposed by the group, 81.7 percent of whom had agreed that one of the most important things in Mansfield was its good school system.

The apparent comfort of the teachers with the education they provide may be attributed to their own upbringing in communities much like Mansfield and their generally expressed satisfaction with small-town life. The reasons for this satisfaction strikingly accord with those offered by Mansfield's adults and students—the security, absence of anonymity, open doors, friendliness, and uncrowded feeling of living in a slower-paced atmosphere. "We'll be here when we die, I'm sure," said Mrs. Adams, a native Mansfielder; "I can't imagine living anywhere else," concluded Mr. Shirley, an adopted Mans-fielder.

Some teachers held modest expectations about what the school could accomplish but acknowledged their hope of reaching at least one or two students in a serious way. None was truly doubtful about his own and his colleagues' opportunity to do something of value. Mr. Thompson, the biology teacher, noted that teachers tended to maintain a close relationship with students and parents. Because of the intimacy of this small stable community, some teachers admitted to being less than objective in their judgment of students. One suggested that Mansfield teachers are "more lenient because we're more familiar with [students] and their families," meaning by this that the teachers are "not as strict academically as maybe we should be." Yet Mansfield would hardly have it otherwise. "The schools are just about what the people want," observed Mr. Shirley. "They do what they are expected to do." In this Mr. Cahill concurred. "The high school does a better than average job of socializing the students for this community."

On entering high school, the children of Mansfield's farmers and factory workers are given a handbook. Like so many other documents cluttering the drawers of Mansfield and other schools, this one contains a mixture of specific statements to guide the behavior of the students (for example, regulations that relate to the prom, detentions, driving one's car at noon) and more general, usually unread, statements. The handbook's list of "General Behavior Principles for Students" suggests how Mansfield's educational leaders believe students should behave. The attention of students is directed to:

- Regular attendance
- Punctuality in all matters
- Careful preparation and learning of assignments
- Orderly classrooms
- Courtesy
- A relaxed but business-like atmosphere
- Acceptance of the authority of teachers
- Pride and concern for school property
- Personal appearance
- The desire to be a contributing member of society

These are norms that reflect an emphasis on social control. Clearly, the ideal student is one who would make life easy for teachers and administrators.

A further clue to the nature of a school is provided by its objectives. To be sure, statements of objectives often originate in requests from outsiders (the state visiting team, for example) and serve only ceremonial purposes. Teacher and student conduct in class tells more about the academic experience than do statements of objectives, but the latter may be valuable for suggesting not so much what really happens in schools as what ideals undergird the behavior of its educators.

The most recent occasion to prepare objectives was provided in 1972 by the State Office of Instruction's request that each school system prepare a document called "Goals for Tomorrow." Excerpts from the document that was submitted to the state are included below.

A. The Instructional Program

Provide for such quality education that should help every student acquire to the fullest extent possible for his mastery of a good basic education and to open further channels of study to him as an adult . . .

B. Suggested Student Goals (Desired Learner Outcomes)

I. Develop growth in their ability to think rationally, to express their thoughts clearly, and to read and listen with understanding.

II. Develop salable skills . . .

III. Develop the ability and desire to understand the rights and duties of a citizen of a democratic society, and to be diligent and competent in their performance of their obligations as members of the community and citizens of the state, the nation, and the world.

IV. Acquire good health habits . . .

V. Develop a better understanding of the methods of science and man's environment . . .

VI. Develop areas of concern that include responsibility, honesty, self-respect, justice, courtesy and kindness, discrimination between right and wrong, respect for individual differences, obedience to parents, and respect for authority and laws. [An earlier version of this goal included "loyalty, patriotism, and nondiscriminatory behavior," but was omitted from the final statement submitted to the state office.]

VII. Provide opportunities to develop their capacities to appreciate beauty in literature, art, music, and nature.

VIII. To provide opportunities to learn to use leisure time well and budget it wisely . . .

When we compare Mansfield's "Goals for Tomorrow" with those prepared by other schools from neighboring districts of approximately the same size, we find many similarities. A number of broad categories dominate the goals of all the school districts: (1) basic skills, (2) vocational training, (3) consumerism, (4) leisure time, (5) democratic citizenship, (6) health, (7) the arts, (8) thinking ability, (9) family, and (10) personal qualities. In addition to these shared categories, however, are several which Mansfield omits from its lists, as either oversights or ideas to which Mansfield is not committed. For example, a number of school systems, usually somewhat larger ones, mentioned that they planned to enable each student to: "develop . . . the ability to identify problems and to apply clear, critical, reflective, and creative thinking . . . to reach their solutions"; "develop an awareness of the history, influence, and interrelationships of all cultures"; "be . . . acquainted with his rights and responsibilities . . . as a member of a pluralistic society"; "develop intellectual curiosity and eagerness for lifelong learning." My impression is that in Mansfield these latter goals are not so much disapproved as they are unimportant; they do not occupy the foreground of concern.

In contrast, the provision of "a good basic education" is of major concern. It is mentioned under the Instructional Program and voiced frequently by Mansfield's school board members and administrators. It is one of three fundamental points that bear on the academic aspects of the school. The second is the development of "salable skills," listed under Suggested Student Goals, and the third is the provision of courses that will enable students to attend post-secondary institutions.

The emphasis on the "basics" is not readily observable in the classroom. It is used more as a slogan, a conventional way of affirming that the board and administration do not concern themselves with lofty intellectual goals, that they do not have pretensions of sophistication, and that they mean to keep down the costs of schooling—for money spent on the basics is by definition money well spent. Mansfield's investment in the development of "salable skills" is evident in the variety of courses offered in home economics, business education, industrial arts, vocational agriculture, and auto mechanics.

Notwithstanding the curriculum-oriented meetings held in preparation for state and North Central Association visitations, Mansfield teachers neither plan nor coordinate the value orientation of their instruction. To be sure, they attempt cooperative planning when a subject has a sequential basis—English, for example. But there is no party line, no deliberate effort to endorse a particular view of religion, politics, patriotism, or community. Perhaps no such efforts are necessary if the process of selecting teachers and administrators has already ensured their suitability for service in Mansfield. In any case, the classroom behavior of Mansfield's teachers rather consistently displays the value orientation of the school board and the community. But other sorts of aims that go unstated in Mansfield's official documents also go unpursued in its classrooms. There, the discourse, while often provocative, is not distinctly critical or reflective. Examinations tend to focus on recall. And traditional American attitudes toward God, country, and self-reliance are manifest and unchallenged, as we see in many different classes. . . .

Outside School

At Mansfield High School, sports and extracurricular activities more than hold their own in competition with academic matters. Indeed, at times they almost overwhelm academics.[10] Football practice begins before school opens in fall and the final baseball game is not played until May. In between falls an avalanche of athletic events played by varsity and junior varsity teams, male and female, spurred on by the cheerleaders who are backed up by the pep club.

No less overwhelming are the money-raising activities of clubs and classes, which introduce students to American voluntarism through magazine and newspaper subscription drives, bake sales, cake walks, car washes, soup suppers, ad infinitum. Each day students are thus drawn out of their classrooms and the school by a round of events which provide the main school attraction for many students and a major source of recreation for the community. Mansfield High School's balance of curricular and extracurricular activities appears to serve Mansfielders well. They are not distressed with what could be interpreted by some critics as a disproportionate investment of student and educator time, money, and energy in nonacademic pursuits. From their perspective, Mansfield High School, like a good shoe, fits Mansfield.

PARENT AND STUDENT EXPECTATIONS

In the absence of a formal survey of what Mansfielders want their school to accomplish and whether they believe they get what they want, we must depend on several different indicators of the community adults' agreement with the teachers' assessment of schooling in Mansfield. Data from 239 Mansfield adults, representing perhaps one-third the number of families in the school district, show that 69 percent believe Mansfield has a good school system (7 percent disagreed and 23 percent neither agreed nor disagreed). This fairly high figure,[11] the paucity of complaints presented at school board meetings or to the administrators, the dearth of responses (less than thirty) to the superintendent's invitation to react to the new "Goals for Tomorrow" (sent to every boxholder in the school district), the disbanding of the PTA some years ago—all suggest that the community is essentially satisfied with its school system. These facts do not indicate parental apathy so much as an absence of contentious issues. The parents clearly are interested in education. In 1969 they voted to build a new grade school; in 1975 they voted to increase their education tax levy at a time when that was a rare occurrence; and throughout each year they demonstrate their affection for the high school by attending its many activities—from football games to the Christmas program to the graduation exercises. In two recent years, more than 40 percent of the school district population attended *each* of the football team's five home games.

I conclude, accordingly, that while Mansfield adults might be unhappy with a particular teacher, a losing football season, or some incident, they are basically content with what they perceive the school to be doing to Mansfield's youth, with the shape, though not necessarily with every detail, of their children's education. Thus, when a teacher observed that the school gives the community what it wants, her judgment appeared sound.

Students basically join their parents in affirming their esteem for Mansfield High School and Mansfield. A recent class of graduating seniors was interviewed to explore their views.

Some of the college-bound students entertained thoughts of eventually moving away from the community, though not to towns either too distant from or even much larger than Mansfield.[12] Places like Chicago and St. Louis appeared attractive in the way that a fantasy does. ("You know, having never lived there [Chicago] it's kind of the ideal place right now." This same student, now at college, is homesick and hopes to transfer to a school closer to Mansfield.) Seldom, however, did seniors refer to settling in places much larger than Auburn (approximately 5,000); even Stanton (approximately 100,000) is too large. In fact, as of fall, 1972, more than 50 percent of the seven hundred graduates from the period 1947 to 1972 lived in Mansfield or the surrounding twenty-five-mile region which constitutes the effective home area for all resident Mansfielders—the area where they shop, date, get medical attention, and seek recreation. Those few seniors who perceived Mansfield school and community as providing unduly restricted social and academic opportunity were more than matched by many others who feared the dangers and seeming anonymity of larger places, and even doubted that they could master driving in city traffic. They were reasonably realistic about what Mansfield offered, though less so about urban schools and communities.

In their characterization of Mansfield, the seniors show the impact of having grown up in a small rural setting. Some express a desire to get out ("seems like people who stay in Mansfield don't get anywhere") and others express pleasure at staying home. Wayne reflects the distress of many adults who oppose the possible consolidation of Mansfield High School into one large county school. He shares the sentiments of Elmer, who better than most students conveyed the special quality of life in Mansfield as experienced by those who belong. Elmer felt that "deep down the people of Mansfield care for everybody. I think that it's really a good town . . . that everybody cares for each other and . . . if something big came up . . . everybody would join in and help each other." These views, frequently expressed by community adults, are not shared by all Mansfielders, but they represent a salient characteristic of life in the town.

Teachers, as previously indicated, acknowledged that they were "not as strict academically as we should be." Students also acknowledged this fact but did not seem troubled by it. Both teachers and students implicitly concur in a level of academic expectation they find comfortable. Even capable students fail to perceive value in the more abstract aspects of education, and their speech often reflects a casual style that has its counterpart among the adults. ("You're not supposed to use 'ain't,' but I say it all the time.") With the exception of Maryann, who meant to maximize the academic possibilities of high school and got encouragement to do so from her father, students disdain the need for hard work, even if one hopes to achieve acceptably high grades—that is, to make the B honor roll. Wayne, now a university student, admits he could have worked harder, but, he observes, "Who wants to sit at a book for each class an hour a night? It's no fun. There are too many other things going on." Mike imagines that the people who get *A*s stay at home so much they don't learn to communicate with others, rationalizing his own modest efforts with the thought that "there is more to life besides grades." Marge finished near the top of her class but regrets, as she contemplates her questionable preparedness for college, that she did not try harder. "It wasn't that important to me," she concludes. And students in the National Honor Society are accused of putting on airs "They act like they're higher than everybody else," says Helen, who preferred fun to study and settled for being on the B honor roll rather than seeming a "real brain."

From the views of these seniors, it seems that the school experience offers more than students without college plans want, but no more than the college-bound want to work for. Somewhere between these modest points Mansfield's teachers pitch their intellectual tents, accommodating themselves to a level of aspiration that threatens few.

LOCAL CONTROL AND ITS DILEMMAS

Community control of the schools flourishes in Mansfield. The community's elected school board chooses a superintendent who selects the teachers and supervises the operation of the schools. If the board trusts him, as it trusted Superintendent Tate, then it often rubber-stamps his decisions, confident that he knows what the community wants. Nevertheless, though it defers to his expertise, the board also keeps an eye on his work. And this is the evident, the officially constituted machinery of community control in Mansfield.

Yet, as we have seen, a great deal of the machinery is neither evident nor officially constituted. Such features of Mansfield High School as the level of academic expectation that guides classroom practice and the relative importance of curricular and extracurricular activities are also determined by the local community, though not by deliberate choice. When we asked board members and administrators directly about their criteria for selecting teachers and instructional materials, they did not mention maintaining the community and its values. They said they preferred teachers who had both curricular and extracurricular strengths, liked children, and were good disciplinarians. Not until the school board met to select a superintendent did someone voice a criterion that explicitly reflected the community's ethos. He is "country," they said of Reynolds. Judging from recent appointments to the teaching staff, the board liked to hire local people, though its members did not acknowledge that they gave preference to such persons. After the meeting at which Reynolds was chosen superintendent, one board member regretted that the ideal person for the job could not apply because he lacked the appropriate credentials. This ideal person happened to be a local man, now working elsewhere in the state.

Mansfield's educators do not decide the level of academic discourse in classrooms or the relative importance of academic and nonacademic matters. Rather, the prevalent academic standards are determined by the district's hiring practices and are put into effect as those whom the board has hired interact with one another, the students, and the parents of the community. The result is an academic posture well suited to the concerns of a small rural community.

School policy is not calculated to promote this outcome. To be sure, there are policy statements in several district documents, but they are consulted only in exceptional cases (involving, for example, expulsion) and are couched in typically grand language. One item in the board's *Rules, Precedents, and Procedures* explicitly requires the sort of congruence between school and community that we have been discussing: "The teacher should have a respectful attitude toward the standards and the accepted patterns of behavior of the community in which he is employed." But the fact that teachers actually possess a respectful attitude is attributable not to this regulation but to the process of recruitment and selection. Mansfield's teachers do not need to be taught what behavior is acceptable in Mansfield.

Over the years there has been little active participation by the community-at-large in educational policy making. Nothing has arisen to demand it. The community itself has not changed much. The migration rates during most of this century have been moderate, and many local families have remained in residence from generation to generation. Likeminded people replace one another on the school board, and they comfortably reflect the school district's stability. Hence factional dispute is rare and particular instances of displeasure with the school can be dealt with informally. A telephone call to one of the board members, or a remark in the restaurant or the post office, is sufficient.

Whatever its benefits, the close fit between school and community in Mansfield results in four dilemmas.

Although the school experience of Mansfield students does not preclude occupational and educational success, it is still comparatively limited. In other school districts, parents, students, and teachers place more emphasis on academic achievement and press for more resources to be directed toward intellectual goals. Consequently, there are children in the state and nation who are taught better mathematics and science, and who are better informed about their nation's political and economic complexities. Mansfielders strive to hire, not the best teacher in an intellectual sense, but the teacher who will best serve Mansfield. This is an important distinction. They would dismiss as unsuitable teachers who were "too intelligent for this community" and therefore "more than we want," just as they dismissed the candidacy of Dargan for the superintendency. Thus the first dilemma: If education is thought best when it attempts to maximize the intellectual potential of a child, then Mansfield High School may be faulted; but if under the conditions of places like Mansfield the schools contribute to a sense of personal identity and low alienation,[13] then something of possibly compensating value has been gained. I suggest that Mansfield's children do not have educational opportunities equal to those available in larger cities and their suburbs. They are denied equal opportunity not because of their race, religion, or national origin, but rather because they are being schooled in the prevalent ethos of Mansfield. Yet if different standards were instituted for academic performance, the selection of educators, and the balance between academic and nonacademic activities, Mansfield High School would no longer suit its community. Such standards would have to be imposed from the outside, for they find little support in Mansfield. Indeed, they might threaten the community.

The close fit discussed here promotes generational stability in Mansfield. Neither by learning nor by aspiration are the community's children sharply distinguished from their parents. Their shared feelings about where to live and what to believe suggest a second dilemma: In Mansfield, maximizing intellectual achievement and high intergenerational stability are probably incompatible.

Though Mansfield has no black residents, it sustains anti-black sentiment and thus socializes its children into attitudes that conflict with national ideals. No school policy supports this sentiment, but the school is a forum for its expression and its reinforcement by peers. This points to a third dilemma: Mansfield's harmonious relation of school and community is maintained at the cost of compromising some national ideals. In this dilemma, *particularism*, in the form of the local community's sense of the good, is pitted against *universalism*, in the form of the nation's sense of the good—both of which inspire essential activity, the former to human dignity and the latter to national unity.[14] Plainly, the interests of any individual community may differ from those of the nation as a whole. It is unpleasant, however, to contemplate a national society so insecure that it cannot believe itself the richer for its subgroup enclaves, each with its own identity. Yet if the outlook of some subgroups became dominant, then social justice and national integration would be threatened.

These dilemmas of local control suggest that there is no good social organization without a boundary to its goodness. That local autonomy has limits was made clear by the 1954 desegregation decision of the U.S. Supreme Court. Thus, at the same time that we see virtue in the intimacy of Mansfield school and community, we must be prepared to appeal to principles of justice and equality and condemn what we have praised if the price exacted by their harmony is judged intolerable. Who is to judge? And when is it to be declared that the cost of goodness for some has become intolerable for others? These are especially complex and controversial questions. For example, F. A. Rodgers (1975) discusses the preintegration high school in North Carolina. He concludes that, as a result of desegregation, not only did many black educators lose their jobs, but the black community lost a critical factor in the facilitation and development of its political and social activities. Rodgers's doubt about the outcome of the 1954 Supreme Court decision suggests that one may question whether or not local community gains and losses should take priority over national ideals.

Rodgers's conclusions bring us to the final dilemma. To those with roots in Mansfield's past, to those who resonate with their little school's special balance of academic, athletic, and other nonacademic activities, school reorganization is anathema.[15] Yet, reorganization is an increasingly likely solution to the problems of the Mansfields of America, as lower enrollments necessitate the closing of classes and small schools fall victim to declining economies of scale. "Over my dead body" was the response of a Mansfielder to consolidation. He is one of many who react to the proposed loss of their school with a passion comparable to that of people who feel that their cultural survival is in jeopardy when their native language is threatened. The continued existence in Mansfield of a school that can contribute to subgroup maintenance, to the integration of its community, is inversely related to the application of two universalistic principles: fiscal rationality, which argues for school reorganization; and academic excellence, which supports the employment of educators and promotes curricular reform that would not be suitable for Mansfield as presently constituted. These principles are espoused by educational organizations ranging from state teachers' unions to state school board associations.[16] They are therefore strongly supported. Countervailing arguments are just beginning to gather force among diverse groups which urge resistance to the increasing scale of contemporary society.

I have tried to resist the allure of romanticism here. Mansfield is not a paradise either to me or to those of its inhabitants who for different reasons remain outside the charmed circle of acceptability. It is a community in a psychological sense and, like all such communities, somewhat exclusive. While not everyone does feel or can feel he belongs there, I find Mansfield appealing because it is able to embrace, to attach, those who, in a manner of speaking, will submit to it. Believing that such rewards are uncommon, I value places where they are available.

With its particular brand of instruction, its ideological orientation, and its stress on sports and money-raising activities, Mansfield High School is not a school for everyone or everyplace. Given local control, it was not meant to be, nor could it be. But it does belong in Mansfield. As one teacher observed after reflecting on the school's strengths and weaknesses, "I guess it's as good a school as you can expect Mansfield to have." Under circumstances of local control, her comments are essentially accurate. She did not intend to be patronizing. As a native of the area, she knew what kind of school the desires and expectations of Mansfield's adults would support. Given the people, the school is appropriate.

Based on external perspectives, Mansfield High School may be judged more harshly than my comments suggest. But as I assured my Mansfield hosts, I had not come to conduct an evaluation. I planned, rather, to examine the relationship between school and community in a rural setting. I found the relationship to be mutually beneficial. The two are joined in the maintenance of an American subgroup which I do not see as prototypical for all of us, which is flawed, but which is worth treasuring—if the price paid by Mansfield and the nation is not too high.

In 1975, at the height of the resistance to busing in Boston, a journalist reported the bitter observations of a former Bostonian:

> "I'll never forgive them for this. Forcing me out."
> "Why?" I asked. "Most people who have the money *want* to live in the suburbs."
> "You could never understand," he said. "I'm a townie. I lived all my life in Charlestown. You know, we got something special here. There's only one Bunker Hill in the whole country." [Klein 1975, p. 82]

And they've got something special in Mansfield, too. Keeping that something special depends upon whom Mansfield High School serves.

NOTES

1. To preserve the anonymity of my informants, the name of their community has been altered, as have all other names.
2. Since 1967, enrollment in the school district has declined each year. In 1975, the salary offered a beginning teacher was $8,336 and the maximum teacher salary was $13,144. (For the state as a whole, in 1974, the median salary for a beginning teacher with a B.A. was $8,400 and the median maximum salary $14,350.) On the basis of *effort rank* (which is the correlation between a district's potential wealth, as measured by its assessed valuation per pupil, and the degree to which it draws upon its wealth for the support of its schools, as measured by its total tax rate), Mansfield is an above-average school system.
3. In many respects, this study is in the tradition of such earlier community studies as West (1945), Vidich and Bensman (1958), Lynd and Lynd (1929), and Hollingshead (1959). The first three focus on the community, and schooling is an essential but subordinate concern of these studies; the fourth centers on the school, but views schooling chiefly through the concept of social class. Though my own fieldwork encompassed the entire community, I intended to center my inquiry on the school, considering its function within the community.
4. In approaching the school, we moved very slowly to establish ourselves as unthreatening observers who would participate upon request in the life of the school but whose prime interest was in finding out about the school in all its aspects. We believed it important to establish that we had not come to evaluate the quality of instruction or administration. In time our data collection came to include: (1) observing and tape recording lessons; (2) interviewing all of the teachers and school board members, and many of the students; (3) reading student diaries; (4) analyzing documents such as statements of course objectives, teacher-made tests and student homework, school board policy statements and minutes, etc.; (5) administering a questionnaire. We attended all school events, teachers' meetings, and school board meetings. We moved into the community through introductions provided by the superintendent. There we met and interviewed the mayor and his village board. We attended village board meetings, collected all available documents, and became part of community life through participation in local church and organizational activities. Data collection culminated with the administration of a questionnaire, which was followed up by in-depth interviews. These were the formal activities. But since I lived in Mansfield during most of the second year of fieldwork, I was an informal participant as well. Because I did not bring my family, I was unable to learn about the community through their experiences.
5. MacIver and Page define *sense of community* as "common living with its *awareness* of sharing a way of life as well as the common earth" (1961, p. 10). As a result of "sharing a way of life," a subgroup has developed in Mansfield whose members share "some common quality that makes them distinguishable from other members of a major group to which they belong" (*Webster's Third International*, s.v. "subgroup"). To be sure, the Mansfielder is readily recognized as an American, but the outcomes of growing up in Mansfield and places like it differ from those produced in other social settings in the United States.
6. The questionnaire was sent by mail to every other male and female listed in a special commercial phone directory, excluding any person whose nuclear family was already included in the sample. The return rate was slightly more than 50 percent, with females outnumbering males by almost two to one. Comparing the responses of males and females revealed no differences of consequence between the groups.
7. The people of Mansfield, unlike those of Springdale (Vidich and Bensman 1958), generally deal with mass society in conscious, rational terms. It is a reality to be taken account of, though one often feared and abused as the source of complications in village life. Its denial is arguably evident in the localistic orientation of its school system. Yet this may be the natural outcome of people's doing what appears appropriate and desirable rather than of their avoiding the reality that confronts them in the media, nearby cities, and state and national government. In express terms, the school intends to contribute to the academic and occupational mobility of its students; that it does more than this is not the result of policy.
8. The grade and high schools were organized into a unit district about twenty years ago.
9. This is a neighborhood-type institution which serves, though not exclusively, small-town graduates in the central part of the state.

10. The investment in sports is substantial, certainly consonant with the level of expenditure made by other schools in Mansfield's athletic conference. One hears grumbling about an overemphasis on sports, but at no time did teachers state that they were deprived of what they needed for instructional purposes. Mansfield considers itself a football town, turns out in large numbers for most athletic events, but by no means neglects the school's musical and dramatic events. The school's laboratory equipment acceptably serves the needs of biology (the only required science), chemistry, and physics, which is occasionally offered depending on enrollment. Mansfield High School has one laboratory for all of its science courses.

11. According to a 1971 Gallup Poll (1972, p. 17) conducted in communities of 2,500 or less, 64 percent were satisfied with their children's education; 26 percent were not, and 10 percent did not know. Comparable statistics for the nation as a whole were 60, 20, and 12 percent. I cite these figures with diffidence since, unlike for Gallup Poll election outcomes, I am uncertain of their accuracy for the groups they supposedly represent. Moreover, I did not ask if people in Mansfield were pleased with their children's education, but if they thought the school system was one of the most important things in Mansfield.

12. From 1947 to 1972, approximately 40 percent of all graduates continued their education after graduation. In the 1947–65 period, for which the data are most complete, 46 percent of the graduates in the top half of their class were living in or around Mansfield as of 1972. This group includes most of those who attended college.

13. These data are not fully persuasive, but they tend to confirm my sense of Mansfielders' low level of alienation, particularly among the mainstream vis-à-vis non-Mansfielders (see table 4, p. 203).

14. See Fein's (1971) excellent book for further discussion of universalism.

15. Reorganization, while much discussed, is not necessarily imminent. Many residents fear that their high school will be consolidated with the other county schools to create one large system. Their shrinking enrollments and the disposition of educators to prefer larger systems suggest that Mansfielders' fears have some warrant.

16. See the *Illinois Education News* (February 1975) section on school reorganization which shows the heads of the Illinois Education Association, Illinois Federation of Teachers, Illinois Association of School Administrators, and Illinois Association of School Boards favoring the universalistic principles that support school reorganization.

REFERENCES

Fein, Leonard J. *The ecology of the public schools: An inquiry into community control.* New York: Pegasus, 1971.

Hollingshead, August De Belmont. *Elmstown's youth: The impact of social classes on adolescents.* New York: John Wiley & Sons, 1959 [1949].

_____. "The issue is: School district reorganization." *Illinois Education News* 4, no. 5 (1975): 2,14.

Klein, Joe. "The Boston busing crisis." *Rolling Stone* (23 October 1975): 32-82 passim.

Lynd, Robert S., and Lynd, Helen Merrell. *Middletown: A study in American culture.* New York: Harcourt, Brace and World, 1929.

Maciver, Robert Morrison, and Page, Charles H. *Society: An introductory analysis.* New York: Holt, Rinehart & Winston, 1961 [1949].

National Opinion Research Center. *National data program for the social sciences.* Principal investigator, James Davis, Chicago: University of Chicago Press, July 1974; July 1975.

Rodgers, Frederick A. *The black high school and its community.* Lexington, Mass.: Lexington Books, 1975.

"Satisfaction Index—Education." *The Gallup Opinion Index*, report 81, March 1972.

Vidich, Arthur J., and Bensman, Joseph. *Small town in mass society.* Garden City, N.Y.: Doubleday, 1958.

West, James. *Plainville, U.S.A.* New York: Columbia University Press, 1945.

The School Board as an Agency of Legitimation

NORMAN D. KERR

. . . It will be argued that under some conditions, which may not be uncommon, school boards chiefly perform the function of *legitimating* the policies of the school system to the community, rather than *representing* the various segments of the community to the school administration, especially with regard to the educational program. This unintended function of school boards may be viewed as an organizational defense which counteracts the threat to the school system's institutional security inherent in local control by laymen.

METHODS AND RESEARCH SITES

While other studies will be cited for supporting evidence, our conclusions will be drawn mainly from intensive observations and interviews carried out in 1962–63 in two suburban school districts located about 25 miles from a large northern city.*

School districts were selected which were adjacent to each other and located within the same county and township. One of the districts was undergoing rapid expansion due to the influx of former city dwellers, and was almost three times the size of the other in terms of enrollment. The percentage increase in enrollment over the previous year had been 18 per cent. This district also attracted a large proportion of Jewish residents as a consequence

The American Sociological Association, from "The School Board as an Agency of Legitimation" by Norman D. Kerr from *Sociology of Education*, vol 38, 1964. Reprinted by permission of the publisher and the author.

*A residency stipend from the Russell Sage Foundation for an investigation of the problems of education in the light of sociological theory and prior research made it possible to carry out the study.

of having once been a Jewish resort area. (It was estimated that 55 per cent of the high school students were Jewish.

The smaller system was growing much less rapidly due to its location a few miles farther from the city. The percentage increase in enrollment over the previous year was 5 per cent. The population was predominately Protestant, with a large Catholic minority. Both districts contained a high proportion of commuters, and both contained nuclear villages around which commuters tended to locate their homes.

The terms of office of the two superintendents were fairly typical for the type of succession represented by each of them. The superintendent of the smaller district had held the position for 11 years, and had formerly been the high school principal. The superintendent of the larger district had held the position for 6 years after moving from another suburban district. According to a national study of the succession of school superintendents, the mean time in office of "insiders," or individuals who have moved up within the system, is 10 years; for "outsiders" it is 8 years.[1] . . .

ANALYSIS AND INTERPRETATIONS

The main forces shaping school board members' attitudes and performance will be dealt with under the following headings: (A) school board politics, (B) pressures for conformity throughout the process of socialization on the board, and (C) community pressures generated by the school system's impact on the public.

A. School Board Politics

There were two major features of school board politics in the two districts which seemingly had considerable effect on the role behavior of board members: (1) the relative absence of clear-cut constituencies, and (2) the candidates' lack of familiarity with school board activities and with the educational program.

1. *The absence of constituencies.* If candidates for the school board do not represent visible constituencies which support their candidacy, ensure their election, and watch the behavior of their representatives after election, then the mandate which board members receive permits considerable freedom in adjusting to the expectations of school administrators and older board members.

That only a minority of school board candidates obtain the backing of particular groups in the community is suggested by one of the findings in Gross' study. Drawing on the replies of a sample of superintendents in Massachusetts, Gross found that only 29 per cent of the school board members represented some group when they sought election. The motive of "gaining political experience" was attributed to 21 per cent of the board members by the superintendents, while the motive of "civic duty" was attributed to 64 per cent.[2]

The notorious paucity of issues in school board elections also testifies to the absence of constituencies. This situation perplexed a candidate in the larger district who was searching earnestly for a platform. During a meeting in which the local Citizens Council for Better Schools was planning a campaign for one of their members, the candidate grew exasperated because no one could supply him with an issue: "I can't just say I'm for better schools—that's what everybody says." The kinds of issues which finally emerged in this campaign, and the doubtful validity of most of them, will be mentioned later on. What was striking about this particular candidate, however, was that even though he had the backing of a citizens' organization, he was at a loss to provide a cogent issue for his campaign. . . .

Because of the absence of visible constituencies, new board members are highly receptive to the pressures for conformity which stem from the incumbent board members and from school administrators. . . .

2. *Unfamiliarity with school board activities and with the school program.* The candidates' ignorance about the school program is difficult to document because of the lack of studies which have measured this factor. We know a great deal about the knowledge of the public in general, however, and the evidence points to considerable ignorance and apathy about the local schools.[3] For suggestive evidence of the candidates' ignorance, we shall have to rely on our observations in the two suburban districts.

a. *Unfamiliarity with the school program.* . . .

There is not space here to document in detail the knowledge of the school program possessed by the ten candidates who ran for the board in the larger district (two additional candidates were incumbents seeking re-election.) An indirect measure of their familiarity with the program was attempted by means of a content analysis of the platforms written by all the candidates at the request of the local League of Women Voters and published in the newspapers.

On the basis of this material, all of the new candidates devoted greatest attention to non-educational issues, such as financing new buildings, setting up citizens' advisory groups for the building program, improving school bus transportation, and exploring the possibility of a statewide purchasing system. All but one of the candidates made general statements about the needs of a good educational program, such as "I would try for a real breakthrough in curriculum," or "(we should) utilize a sound philosophy of education to meet the needs of each individual child." But a total of only 15 concrete recommendations was made. And most significant is the fact that 12 of these 15 recommendations were already being implemented in the school system. These included a syllabus for advanced students, special classes for the retarded and for the emotionally disturbed, a low drop-out rate (12 per cent), and guidance for college-going students. Moreover, the candidates failed to mention several innovations which had *not* been incorporated into the program, such as foreign languages in the elementary schools, the ungraded primary school, teaching machines, and educational television. These omissions suggest that the candidates' recommendations for the school program were gleaned randomly from popular articles about education with little reference to the needs of their particular school system. To the voting public, who may have been only a little less informed than the candidates, the irrelevance of the recommendations was not always apparent.

b. *Unfamiliarity with school board activities.* The candidates probably possessed greater knowledge of the school program than of school board activities. They could at least draw upon their children's experiences in the schools, and they could exploit their relationships with teachers, either through PTA meetings or through more personal contacts. But they seldom attended public school board meetings. None of the ten candidates in the larger district attended a single school board meeting during the preceding year, and only one of the four candidates in the smaller district attended a meeting.

Further, many meetings of school boards are executive sessions from which the public is barred. . . .

The real work of weighing alternative goals, referring to state laws and local board policies, consulting with the administration, and persuading one another to adopt a course of action is carried out in these closed meetings. Public meetings in the two districts were usually reserved for formal action; but during my period of observation, almost none of the considerations that actually produced the boards' decisions were revealed in public meetings. Consequently, public meetings were typically routine and dull. . . .

In sum, owing to the policy of holding executive meetings to deal with "delicate matters," it was impossible for aspiring board members to learn much in advance about the intricate and often exciting business of decision-making which took place on the school boards. Therefore, freshmen board members were very dependent upon the school administration and the incumbent board for information about the goals and means of the system, and they were also unprepared to resist the pressures for conformity which stemmed from the superintendent and from older board members.

B. Socialization and Pressures for Conformity

1. *The induction phase.* It is impossible to draw a sharp line between the induction phase and later socialization on the board. We have simply defined this phase as comprising the early contacts of the new board member with school authorities. Our observations suggest that this is a crucial stage in the process of defining the role of new board members.

a. *Induction by the administration.* The superintendent in the larger district invited new board members to an "orientation" in his office before the new members were exposed to the incumbent board. In these orientations the conversation focussed on legal and financial affairs of the school. In one case, however, the new member interrupted the superintendent to mention a recommendation which Conant had made about suburban school programs. Since he could only vaguely recall the idea, he asked the superintendent if a copy of Conant's book were available in the office. The superintendent replied that it was, but that it was more important for him to explain the legal aspects of board membership. He then continued to pile a great deal of legal and financial material in front of the new board member, advising him to spend the next few weeks studying it. Finally, at the close of the meeting, the superintendent firmly directed the new member to refer all complaints about the school program to his office or to the principal of the school which was involved before attempting to reply to anyone. Nothing more was said about the school program, even though this member had been outstandingly articulate and inquisitive about the educational program during his campaign. As he left the superintendent's office, he only expressed dismay about the mountain of material which he was obliged to master. In the smaller district, measures were taken to indoctrinate only those candidates who appeared to be especially threatening. For example, the candidate of the taxpayers association was inducted by means of guided tours of the school plant. These tours were conducted by the assistant superintendent for buildings and grounds, and lasted several days. In the course of the tours, the new member was impressed by the numerous maintenance and construction problems and by the economies which had been achieved in handling these problems. As a result of common occupational interests and mutual respect for one another's competence, the assistant superintendent and the new board member became close friends. We have already mentioned that this board member never did initiate the economy drive that the school authorities had feared. When I asked the assistant superintendent about the member's influence on school expenditures, he replied:

> It hasn't changed. As a matter of fact, it's increased. When you put on a new project, you automatically get an increase, and John saw the need. . . . Our tax rate has gone up each year. . . .

   . . . b. *Induction by incumbent board members.* The board members in the two districts were equally adept at defining role behavior for new members in a way which reduced the new members' threat to the ongoing system. In the first place, new members are seldom unknown quantities to older board members, for the latter follow the campaign very closely. In fact, they discuss the candidates privately among themselves and pick their favorites. This makes them better prepared to deal with the new member. And as the president of the school board in the larger district informed me, "There's usually some fear when a new member comes on the board, but usually we're able to make them see our policies."

There were several means by which the two school boards sought to obtain the conformity of new members. First, the new member was assigned to a freshman status with the clear implication that he was to be a learner rather than a spokesman for an indefinite period of time. Condescension, paternalism, chiding, and even humiliation were sanctions which kept the new member in his freshman status. The success of these methods depended upon the greater familiarity of older members with technical matters and past board policies. Success also depended upon the greater power of the board president who shared with the superintendent the responsibility for guiding the discussions.[4] . . .

   2. *Later socialization and control.* The indoctrination of new board members did not end with their initial contacts with the administration or with the

incumbent board members. There was still a great deal to learn about state laws, financial practices, the school program, and school board policies, written and unwritten. It was also important to discover the best way to influence other members of the board without antagonizing them. Thus, the later period of socialization was prolonged over several months.

Owing to their unfamiliarity with the work of the school boards, the self-confidence of new members was sometimes severely strained. As one of the board members in the smaller district confessed in a meeting with the public for the selection of board candidates:

> *It takes almost a year to understand the language. It's like speaking another language—like aid for each child, the language of the administration. There's a period of adjustment that you have to go through, and sometimes you feel like you ought to quit. I know that Mr. Adams, when he first came, wasn't sure if he was at a school board meeting or some other kind of meeting.*

Thus, ignorance of school board activities may plague new members for a considerable period of time, thereby prolonging their exposure to pressures for conformity. When the new members began to demonstrate their grasp of board functions and their willingness to conform to the ground rules, the manipulative measures of the president or of the superintendent were relaxed. If a member remained critical of the board or the administration, however, pressure continued. . . .

Occasional deviations of a less extreme nature were handled more gently, but firmly nevertheless. In contrast with the controls exercised during the phase of induction, when the initial ignorance and lack of confidence of the new members rendered them more pliable, the controls that normally operated during the later phase drew their power from the affective relationships which emerged among the members. Meeting as frequently as they did, and sharing common problems and criticisms from the public, the board members tended to develop affective ties. As the relationships became more intimate, the sanctions became more subtle and more personal. The way in which the former candidate for the taxpayers association was restrained is illustrative. As an older member remarked in an interview:

> *There was quite a lot of concern about that—that he would be a pennypincher. But he's turned out to be a cooperative member of the board. . . . We've gotten* close enough *to where I* laugh him out of some of those things.

The superintendent in the district was keenly aware that a congenial atmosphere on the board produced greater cohesion, and consequently, from his point of view, greater malleability. He described a special annual supper for the members as follows:

> Superintendent—*This is one of the ways I* weld the school board together. *They get to know one another personally.*
> Interviewer—*But aren't there other school board suppers during the year?*
> Superintendent—*Yes, but this is the only one to which their wives are invited. So they don't talk business, and get to know one another socially.*

One of the most striking characteristics of the boards' discussions was the relative absence of concern with the educational program. Because this sub-cultural "trait" was so obvious, it is worthwhile examining the way in which new board members were indoctrinated with the attitude that education was the province solely of the school administration.

In order to determine the amount of time that was devoted to various topics during board meetings, a careful record was kept of almost all regular, special, and executive meetings for the entire year. . . . In thirteen meetings of the board in the smaller district, 58 per cent of the time was devoted to financial affairs, while only 10 per cent of the time was devoted to the educational program. In the larger district the respective figures were 45 per cent and 13 per cent. Even if we eliminate the time spent preparing the bond issue referenda, . . . far more attention was devoted to non-educational than to educational matters in both districts.

The omission of the education program from the boards' deliberations was sustained by several mechanisms. Some of these involved manipulation by the administration; others derived from fundamental features of the structure of the relationship between a professional educator and laymen.

One means by which the administration manipulated the visibility of the educational program involved the school board agenda. In both districts the agenda was prepared by the superintendent, with occasional suggestions from the board members. Items concerning the educational program were conspicuously absent from the agenda. In addition to following the agenda, the superintendents were adept at directing the discussion by means of tactical silence or outright diversion. Once when I remarked to the superintendent in the smaller district that the school board seemed to devote very little time to education, he replied:

They don't know anything about it; but the things they know they talk about, like sidewalks, sites, and so forth. I let them go on sometimes because I don't want them to talk about curriculum. This is another thing they don't put in the books.

Another method of diverting attention from the school program was to anticipate the board's interest in a manner which disarmed them. This was achieved mainly by detailed reports on the school program. With rare exceptions, the educational program was discussed in both districts only when the superintendents presented a report, either personally or through one of their administrative assistants.[5] These reports invariably displayed the achievements of the program rather than the unresolved problems. By casting a favorable light, they signified that further attention from the board was superfluous. (One example from the smaller district was a report on the low drop-out rate and how the administration felt it had been achieved. An example from the larger district was a report on curriculum guides which had been written by the staff, printed, and already distributed.)

Sometimes a board member requested a report on some aspect of the school program. It was usual, however, for several weeks to elapse before the report was presented, during which time steps were taken to insure that it would be favorable. (When I asked the superintendent in the larger district what he would do if a board member insisted on a change in the school program, he replied that he would implement the request "only if I could get agreement on a more important matter." Upon further inquiry he admitted that the board had not once caused him to change a decision about the educational program during the six years of his superintendency.)[6]

In addition to these manipulative measures of the administration, there were structural features of the school board–superintendent relationship which facilitated the superintendent's autonomy. Perhaps the most important feature of this relationship was the board's dependence upon the superintendent's performance as an educator. School board members are held accountable by the community for the superintendent's performance because the board members are by definition his superiors, at least in the eyes of the public. And since there is the danger that the superintendent's commitment to effective performance will be undermined if he is forced to abandon his professional goals, it is important for board members to confer on the superintendent a goodly portion of the autonomy which the latter considers his prerogative as a professional.

Gross' study suggests that the willingness of school boards to allocate educational decisions to superintendents is widespread. The highest degree of consensus on different aspects of the division of labor between board members and superintendents concerned the professional educational tasks of the superintendents, such as the selection of new textbooks and the shaping of instructional policy.[7]

What deserves emphasis here, however, is that the school board's attitudes often originate in the socialization process, rather than in a uniform predisposition on the part of candidates regarding the professional prerogatives of the superintendent. There are two pieces of evidence for this proposition. First, as we have already seen, the school board candidates in the two districts paid a fair amount of attention to needed reforms in the educational program during their campaigns, despite their ignorance of the current program. The contrast between this behavior and their performance as board members must be attributed to the socialization process which we have delineated.

Second, it was observed that older board members occasionally warned freshmen members not to invade the domain of educational policy. The following exchange, which took place in a closed meeting in the smaller district is illustrative. The topic was teachers' salaries, and the question arose whether the merit plan (which had been administered chiefly by the superintendent) was sound. Knudsen, the freshman board member, spoke with authority since he was a professor of education and had formerly taught in the school system.

> Knudsen—*This all comes down to the fact that we don't have clearcut criteria for merit.*
> Vinson—*I disagree with that very strongly.*
> Arnold—*That's not something that school boards should get into. That's for the administration.*

Arnold, the president, and Vinson were among the three oldest members of the board. A similar warning was issued by an older board member in the larger district when a new member sought to inquire into educational policy.

Thus far we have presented an essentially passive picture of the school boards' role in legitimating the school systems and the administrators. There were also occasions when the board members actively justified the superintendents' decisions to the public. In order to understand how a formally representative body may be converted into an active agency of legitimation, we need to examine the board's relationship with the community.

C. Community Pressures

School boards operate in a context of potential crisis owing to the pervasive effect which their decisions have on the community. As a consequence, school boards sometimes undergo (1) alienation from the public, and (2) concealment. This was the case in both suburban districts.

1. *Alienation from the public.* Since the issues which came before the school boards were often quite complex, they were only partially understood by the community. In the two districts, considerable ignorance of financial and legal affairs was demonstrated by the uninformed questions, the unrealistic proposals, and the misguided criticisms which flowed from public assemblies. But the school board members were obliged to note that the public's ignorance did not deter them from drawing conclusions about the school boards' competence. The following cases are examples.

> *A local builder took ten minutes of a board meeting to present a proposal that local residents build the three million dollar high school with their own labors "the old church raising type of idea."*
>
> *Hundreds of residents claimed vociferously that a two-story school building was cheaper than a one-story building, despite public testimony to the contrary by architects, and evidence from studies made by building experts throughout the nation. . . .*

Every one of these criticisms required tactful and exhaustive explanations in public meetings of the board or in public assemblies attended by hundreds of residents. But an explanation at a single meeting seldom sufficed, and so the board repeated the same explanations continually but with mounting impatience. . . .

Under these circumstances, it was not surprising that the school board members grew increasingly cynical about the value of representing the public's wishes. At one time or another, most of the school board members in the larger district expressed their alienation from the community. . . .

. . . The board's alienation from the community developed from the members' greater understanding of the needs of the system, combined with the community's unwillingness to grant them superior knowledge. As a consequence, the board members in the larger district were further released from community restraints and more exposed to the values of the administration. They therefore became preoccupied with the task of explaining and justifying the needs of the system to the community. Since this process was mainly observed in the larger, more rapidly growing district, it seems that a school board's alienation is closely related to the public's lack of understanding.

2. *Concealment from the public.* As Vidich and Bensman have pointed out, the visibility of the consequences of school board decisions generates a need for the board to conceal itself from the public.[8] One way in which this need is met is by maintaining unanimity. In effect, a unanimous vote reduces the visibility of arguments against the decision.

The two suburban school boards were no exception to the rule of unanimity. There had been only one split vote in the past two years in the smaller district, and the board members attributed the only budget defeat they had suffered in the ten years since centralization to this lapse in observing the principle of unanimity. The following statement by the board president in the larger district, urging the members to reach a decision on the school bond referendum, reveals the pressures that promote agreement:

> I would hate like the dickens for our vote to be hung up like this at that time (i.e., when the public is admitted), because there are people in the community who will take note. That's why I want to reach a consensus now.

It should be noted, however, that the superintendents had to be included in any consensus that was reached. . . .

The superintendent's support seems to be important for two reasons. First, he has to join the board in selling the decision to the public. If the superintendent failed to demonstrate his support for the board's decision, then the members were exposed to suspicion no less than if a board member had dissented. The second reason concerns a factor which we have already mentioned, namely, that the school is judged by the effectiveness with which the superintendent performs his duties. The board must therefore be careful not to force their views upon him lest they undermine his professional motivation. As a consequence, it was largely the decisions of the administration which were legitimated through recurrent expressions of unanimity among board members.[9]

There were also occasions when board members played an even more active role in presenting the views of the administration to the community. The members appeared before PTA meetings and other public gatherings to promote the budget or the bond issue. And there were innumerable opportunities for them to urge support of the school system through more personal contact.

The importance of personal contacts was strikingly demonstrated by the board member in the smaller district who received the support of the taxpayers association. In fact, the career of this board member illustrates several points made earlier. During an interview three years after his first election, and immediately following his re-election he stated:

> A school trustee has to support the superintendent. If he didn't, it would be terrible with the staff and the public. You've got to back up the superintendent.

When I asked if the board had ever turned down the superintendent's recommendation for a new teacher, he answered: "Never. On what grounds could we? We aren't qualified." Finally, it was plain from the comments of the assistant superintendent who had introduced the board member to the school plant, and of a board member who had served with him for three years, that the former taxpayers' representative had become very useful in legitimating the school system to the most economy-minded sector of the community. As the assistant superintendent noted:

> *Maybe we have a person now who can communicate with some people we were missing before. They can ask him questions and get direct answers. Now they feel they have a representative.*

And as the school board member pointed out:

> *He reaches people on the street who don't have children in the school—old timers, part of the old community whose parents were here.*

SUMMARY AND CONCLUSION

. . . In conclusion, our analysis has sought to identify a number of influences which act upon school board members in such a way as to deflect behavior from formally prescribed goals, and even from the candidates' own goals for the system. Thus, we have argued that under certain conditions the chief contribution of school boards to the continuance of our educational system is their legitimation of the schools' policies, rather than their representation of the community.

Within the framework of a more general theory of organizations, the function of legitimation may be regarded as arising from the organizational prerequisite of attaining security in the environment.[10] Due to the "openness" of American school systems at the *top*—because of school boards—and at the *bottom*—because of the presence of students inside the organization—the system is threatened with loss of professional control. Our attention has therefore focussed upon one set of organizational mechanisms which tends to restore security and maintain this control.

NOTES

1. Richard O. Carlson, "Succession and Performance among School Superintendents," *Administrative Science Quarterly*, 6, 2 (Sept. 1961), p. 223.
2. Neal Gross, *Who Runs Our Schools?* New York: Wiley and Sons, 1958, ch. 7.
3. Cf. Roscoe C. Martin, *Government and the Suburban School*, Syracuse, N.Y.: Syracuse University Press, 1962, p. 56.
4. The imposition of a freshman status on the new board members is similar to what Michels has called a "quarantine" of the new recruits to the leadership cadre of a political party. *Political Parties*, New York: Dover Publications, Inc., 1959, p. 170.
5. Only once was a report presented by an instructor in the smaller district; and this person was actually the administrator of the physical education program and a close friend of the superintendent. Likewise, in the larger district, a group of older high school teachers once presented a report during the year.

6. The superintendents were not the only administrators in the two districts who disapproved of the boards' intervention in professional matters which legally came under the boards' jurisdiction. For example, a questionnaire survey in the two districts included a question concerning the role that the school board should play in hiring teachers: "To what extent do you think the following persons or groups *should* influence the selection of new teachers?" Eight out of 13 administrators in the larger district and 5 out of 8 in the smaller district replied that the school board should be "not at all" involved in selecting teachers.

7. Neal Gross, Ward Mason, and Alexander McEachern, *Explorations in Role Analysis*, New York: Wiley and Sons, 1958, ch. 8.

8. Arthur J. Vidich and Joseph Bensman, *Small Town in Mass Society*, Garden City, New York: Doubleday and Co., 1960, pp. 176–8.

9. Roberto Michels has put the issue of unanimity more concisely, if less analytically: "When there is a struggle between the leaders and the masses, the former are always victorious if only they remain united," *op. cit.*, p. 157.

   Another means of concealment advocated by board members in both districts was the omission of certain statistics from brochures which described the building program. Still another means, of course, was executive or closed sessions. The intense pressures for conformity exerted by the board while socializing new members were probably also dictated by the need to achieve unanimity on specific decisions.

10. Philip Selznick, *TVA and the Grass Roots*, (Berkeley and Los Angeles: University of California Press, 1949). Selznick's concept of "formal cooptation" as practiced by the TVA in response to organizational insecurity is, of course, extremely pertinent to our analysis of school boards. In the case of school boards, however, an inherent feature of school systems is converted into a legitimating agency; while in the case of the TVA, the structure of local representation was initiated for purposes of legitimation.

5

Access and Opportunity
in Education

Chapters 3 and 4 have laid out the overall structure of U.S. schooling and the organization of districts and schools. In Chapters 5 through 9, we now move in a more interactional direction. We trace students' careers in the schools: observing who goes to school and for how long, tracking students' experiences while in school, and picking students up as they emerge from school and go into the labor force.

Chapter 5 provides an overall map of students' educational careers. It describes how family background (especially class, sex, and race) affects educational access and opportunity: how much schooling they get and where they go to school. Its concern is to trace patterns that will then be filled in in Chapters 6 through 9.

CLASS AND EDUCATION: SOCIAL MOBILITY
OR REPRODUCTION?

The question of equality of educational access and opportunity is of vital interest to virtually all the theories of the social role of education that we covered in Chapter 2. All the theories agree that education has expanded enormously, with many more people graduating from high school and going on to college. (For more on this, see the essays by Hammack and Dougherty in Chapter 3.) All agree, as well, that advanced education has become crucial in determining which occupations people enter. Many jobs are closed to those who do not have a certain level of education. And the greater a person's education is, generally the more prestigious and highly paying their job. (For further discussion, see Chapter 9.) But the various theories of the social role of education disagree sharply on the implications of these changes for social mobility: that is, children's movement away from their parents' class position.

247

Functionalists argue that social mobility has been huge, and the key to this has been an enormous equalization of educational opportunity. Differences by family background in educational access have gotten steadily smaller. Marxists, Weberians, and Bourdieuians, meanwhile, argue that while education has become more available, it has become no more equally distributed. Children from advantaged families still get more education than children from disadvantaged families. As a result, education does not so much provide social mobility as "reproduce" or transmit inequality from one generation to another.[1]

Each position has evidence in its favor, but the weight of evidence lies with the critics of functionalism. In functionalism's favor, there is the evidence of considerable social mobility in our society (Blau and Duncan, 1967; Featherman and Hauser, 1978). For example, Featherman and Hauser (1978: 93) calculate that, among American men surveyed in 1973, 51 percent were in a higher occupational stratum than their fathers, while 17 percent were lower.[2] Furthermore, education does play a key role in this social mobility: It has a powerful impact on income and occupational prestige, with a majority of this effect being unconnected to family background (Jencks and others, 1979; Sewell and Hauser, 1975).[3]

But arguing against the functionalist position are other findings. First, while considerable social mobility does exist, it still does not ensure equality of opportunity. People who are nonwhite, female, or from working-class backgrounds do not have the same economic opportunities as do others. For example, only 26 percent of sons of manual workers enter professional and managerial occupations, while the comparable figure for sons of managers or professionals is 59 percent (Featherman and Hauser, 1978: 89).

Second, while education does provide social mobility, it is also a major cause of social class reproduction. Children of the upper and middle classes accumulate more and better education than working-class children. For example, Table 1 shows that high school graduates who are in the top quartile in socioeconomic status are nearly twice as likely to go on to college as those who are in the bottom quartile.[4] And there is a similar, although smaller, gap

---

[1]Among these critics, Pierre Bourdieu stands out for the originality and thoroughness of his attempt to explain this paradox about education: that "plus ça change, plus la même chose" (the more things change, the more they stay the same).

[2]They define five strata, ranked socioeconomically as follows: upper nonmanual (professionals, managers, nonretail sales); lower nonmanual (proprietors, clerks, retail sales); upper manual (crafts workers); lower manual (operatives, laborers, service); and farm (farmers and farm laborers). It should be noted that this ranking of occupations—for example, putting proprietors in a lower stratum than managers and farmers lower than laborers—is debatable.

[3]For example, Jencks and others (1979: 224, 227) calculate that about two-thirds of the impact of educational attainment on occupational prestige and income is independent of the association of both education and occupational prestige or income with family background and test scores. Sewell and Hauser (1975: 72, 80), meanwhile, find the independent impact of education to be, if anything, higher.

[4]This gap is only partly explained by differences in test scores. If we restrict the comparison to high school graduates scoring in the top quarter in academic ability, the gap actually widens: 85 percent versus 53 percent. Socioeconomic status is measured by a composite of father's occupation and education, mother's education, and family income.

TABLE 1 Educational Attainment in Relation to Social Background

	% of 20–21 Year Olds Without High School Diploma	% of 18–24 Year Olds in College	% of High School Graduates Reaching College
TOTAL	14	28	
RACE			
Whites	13	29	55
Blacks	18	20	43
Hispanics	28	17	52
SOCIAL CLASS			
Top ¼			56
Bottom ¼			32
SEX			
Males			55
Females			53

Source: U.S. Department of Education (1987: 86, 155).

in college access between whites and blacks (but not Hispanics).[5] Moreover, these gaps in educational attainment play a major role in the transmission of inequality. Studies find that nearly half of the reason that upper-class students tend to get higher-status jobs than working-class students is because they get more education (Jencks and others, 1972, 1979).[6]

Finally, the enormous expansion of education over the last few decades has not resulted in a great equalization of economic opportunity. Many who have recognized the great inequalities in educational and occupational opportunity have hoped that they would gradually disappear with the expansion of education.[7] But social science research gives little hope that this will be the case. The association between family background and adult success has changed very little since the beginning of this century, despite a massive expansion of education (Blau and Duncan, 1967: 178; Featherman

[5]Sex differences in educational attainment have largely disappeared in the last 10 years. As Table 1 shows, women are as likely as men to go on to college. However, women are still less likely to enter graduate and professional school and to major in programs leading to the better-paying jobs.

[6]For example, Jencks and others find that about 40 percent of the association between men's childhood family background and adult occupational status is due to their educational attainment, even after controlling for the effect of IQ test scores. The comparable percentage for men's adult income is lower, however (Jencks and others, 1972: 201, note 17, 215; 1979: 74, 214–215, 218).

[7]The United States has been unusual in its degree of reliance on education as a means of income redistribution. Other societies have relied more on extensive social welfare programs (such as family allowances and national health-care systems) coupled with steeply progressive taxes or the nationalization of private wealth (Heidenheimer, 1981).

and Hauser, 1978: 73–74, 93).[8] This stability in rates of social mobility is tied to a similar stability in the relationship between family background and educational attainment. Social scientists have found that the statistical association between family background and educational attainment has changed very little over the course of this century, despite the enormous expansion of high schools and colleges (Blau and Duncan, 1967; 178; Featherman and Hauser, 1978: 242–243, 251).[9]

These surprising findings on the role of education in social mobility indicates the importance of carefully exploring the impact of social class, race, and sex on educational attainment in order to determine why educational access has remained sharply unequal. The selections in this chapter take on that task of exploration, highlighting three important points. First, while sex and (less so) race differences in educational access have contracted, this has not been the case for social class differences. Sharp class differences still exist in rates of dropout, college going, and college graduation. Second, access to particular institutions is becoming as important as access to higher education per se. Differences in college type—whether between elite private universities or middling four-year colleges or public community colleges—have a significant impact on students' success. Finally, how much access is provided to education is not just a matter of student demand or the availability of able students. It is also determined by political struggle, a struggle often taking place under the opposing banners of equality and excellence. These three points are explored in the following pages.

FAMILY BACKGROUND AND EDUCATIONAL ACCESS AND SUCCESS

A key form in which social class and race (but not sex) differences in educational attainment appear is in differential rates of high school dropout. Rates of high school dropout are notoriously difficult to determine, because schools and scholars vary greatly in how they define dropout. For example, school districts differ in whether they count as dropouts learning disabled children who have not gotten a high school diploma by the time they leave school (Hammack, 1986). But as a rough measure, about one-seventh of students fail to get a high school diploma. As Table 1 shows, 14 percent of all

---

[8]Featherman and Hauser do find that the correlation between fathers' occupation and sons' first full-time occupation dropped from 0.56 (on a scale from 0 to 1, which is a perfect correlation) for those born between 1909 and 1913 to 0.42 for those born between 1949 and 1953. However, almost all of this drop was due to the movement of farmers' sons out of farming. Hence, with so few farmers left, there is little reason to think that the correlation will continue to drop in the future (Featherman and Hauser, 1978: 73–74).

[9]Featherman and Hauser find that the correlation between family background and years of education attained dropped very slightly, from 0.58 for those born between 1907 and 1911 to 0.50 for those born between 1947 and 1951. Most of this equalization of education was confined to a sharp reduction in social class differences in high school graduation. Meanwhile, the correlation between family background and college access stayed the same: 0.44 for the 1907–1911 birth cohort and 0.46 for the 1947–1951 cohort (Featherman and Hauser, 1978: 242–243, 251).

people age 20 to 21 in 1985 had failed to get a regular or GED high school diploma. But this overall figure obscures even larger rates for certain racial, ethnic, and social class groups. Hispanics and, less so, blacks are much less likely to receive a diploma than whites (28 percent and 18 percent versus 13 percent) (U.S. Department of Education, 1987: 86). And similar differences exist between students low and high in social class (Rumberger, 1983). In fact, Rumberger (1983: 211) finds that race and ethnic differences in dropout are largely class differences: the high dropout rates of blacks and Hispanics are largely due to the fact that a greater proportion of blacks and Hispanics than of whites are of working-class background.[10]

The selection by Deborah Strother reviews recent research on the dropout problem. She briefly lists the dominant characteristics of dropouts, examines the reasons dropouts give for leaving schools, and weighs the school factors that are associated with high dropout rates. A factor that emerges as highly important is whether students are exposed to teachers who are inexpert, bored, and have little commitment to successfully teaching their students. Strother's article alerts us to the fact that dropping out of high school should not be seen simply as students' fault but rather as a problem arising out of a bad interaction between working-class and minority students and schools that are dispirited and dismissive of such students. (This interaction is the subject of Chapter 6.)

Another key form in which differences in educational attainment appear is in differences in college access. As Table 1 shows, there are major differences in college access by race and social class, although no longer by sex. These differences in social background are examined in the selection by David Karen, "Access to Higher Education in the United States, 1900 to the Present." Karen shows that the once large sex differentials in access to higher education have essentially disappeared. But race and class differences, which had narrowed going into the 1970s, started to widen again in the late 1970s and 1980s. In fact, black access to higher education has dropped back to the levels of the early 1960s.[11] An especially valuable feature of Karen's article is that he goes beyond simply tracing patterns of college access to analyze how the admissions process really works, using a particularly intriguing case: undergraduate admissions to Harvard University.

SCHOOL QUALITY AS WELL AS QUANTITY

David Karen's article makes the point that where one goes to college can be nearly as important as whether one goes to college. This point is analyzed at

---

[10]The importance of social class in explaining race and ethnic differences in dropout indicates that, to explain the higher dropout rates of blacks and Hispanics, our focus should not be on factors unique to black and Hispanic culture but rather on factors common to working-class life, whether nonwhite or white.

[11]It should be pointed out, however, that college access by Hispanics and Asians has improved in recent years (U.S. Department of Education, 1987).

length in the selection by Kevin Dougherty, "The Effects of Community Colleges: Aid or Hindrance to Socioeconomic Attainment?". Dougherty shows that students entering community colleges with a desire to eventually attain a bachelor's degree are significantly less likely to secure one than students of similar academic ability, educational ambition, and social background who go to four-year colleges. He traces this result to the community college's difficulty in retaining students, the obstacles community college students encounter when they try to transfer to four-year colleges, and the high attrition at the four-year college among even those community college students who do successfully transfer.

The effects of differences in school type or quality are not restricted to the distinction between community colleges and four-year colleges. Even among four-year colleges there are differences in "college quality" that affect student outcomes. Students who attend more academically selective and prestigious four-year colleges are more successful than similar students attending less selective and prestigious four-year colleges (Jencks and others, 1979: 186; Karabel and McClelland, 1987; Solmon, 1973; Wachtel, 1975).[12]

THE POLITICS OF EDUCATIONAL EQUALITY

The importance of education in adult success makes it likely that—like all other valued resources—it would be the object of competition and conflict. In fact, this is argued by the Marxist class conflict or resistance school discussed in Chapter 2. This school has stressed how the amount and quality of education provided to students has ebbed and flowed with the fluctuating strength of groups committed to greater equality—especially the labor, civil rights, and women's movements—and competing groups who have opposed greater equality in the name of higher standards. In fact, in this battle we can see again the recurrent American tug of war between competing goals for education that we discussed in Chapter 1.

David Karen's article fits this perspective. As he shows, sex and race differentials in college access narrowed in the 1960s in part because subordinate groups mobilized politically—in the form of the women's, civil rights, and labor movements—to demand fairer admissions and greater financial aid. But these successes were not irreversible. Karen describes how the gains won by the civil rights movement were eroded in the 1970s and 1980s by what he calls the "conservative countermobilization," which reached its apex with the election of Ronald Reagan. This countermobilization raised the argument that too many unqualified and unmotivated students were entering higher education.[13]

---

[12]Sewell and Hauser (1975: chap. 5), however, find no significant college quality effect. This debate over college quality resembles the debate over "effective schools" that we will address in Chapter 6.

[13]For examples of this concern with "excellence" at the expense of equality, see the excerpts from the reports by the National Commission on Excellence in Education and the Heritage Foundation in Chapter 10.

The selection by Richard Alba and David Lavin, "Open Admissions: Is Higher Education a Right or a Privilege?", finds a similar dynamic of subordinate-group mobilization and conservative reaction in the case of open admissions at the City University of New York (CUNY). CUNY inaugurated its open admissions policy in 1969 because of strong pressure from black students and because it realized the increasing importance of wider access to college in an increasingly postindustrial New York City. Under this policy, all graduates of New York City high schools were guaranteed access to a CUNY college: either a community college or, if their grades were high enough, a four-year college.[14] But in 1975, New York City's brush with bankruptcy strengthened conservative forces and allowed them to trim back, although not eliminate, open admissions. Despite its controversial history, Alba and Lavin show that CUNY's open admissions policy has greatly expanded rates of college access and graduation, not only for nonwhites but also for working-class whites. In fact, they gained even more from open admissions than did minority students.

Such clashes over access to education have been a fundamental feature of U.S. educational history. From the very beginning of American history, racial and ethnic minorities, working-class people, and women have fought for equal access to education. The selection by Meyer Weinberg, "To Educate All the Children of All the People," focuses on racial and ethnic conflict over access to education in American history.[15] He shows that, for over 150 years, blacks, Native Americans, and Mexican-Americans have struggled with the white, Anglo majority to ensure greater access to education for their children. The struggle began in the early 19th century as one for access to any schooling. But in this century the struggle has become one for equal schooling. The most notable symbol of this struggle was, of course, the Supreme Court's landmark case, *Brown v. Topeka Board of Education* (1954), in which it ordered the desegregation of schools nationwide. This decision by no means ended contention over educational opportunity. In fact, it ushered in that contentious and energizing era—which has come to be called "the Sixties"—in which not only blacks but also women, Hispanics, Native Americans, Asians, and working-class people fought for greater access to education. And this fight goes on today, with such new protagonists as Asians and the handicapped. (For more on these various groups "with special needs," see Chapter 8.)

The politics of educational access are going to change greatly in the coming years as a result of major changes in the character of the American population, according to the selection by Harold Hodgkinson, "All One System:

---

[14]CUNY's open admissions policy is considerably more open that California's famed "master plan," which guarantees college access to all California high school graduates. CUNY's plan allows far more students to enter four-year colleges straight from high school and makes transfer from community colleges to four-year colleges considerably easier (Lavin and Alba, 1981; Karabel, 1983).

[15]The study of the working-class's and women's struggle for equality of educational access is much less developed than the study of the educational struggle of blacks and other nonwhites. But for important contributions to the history of the working-class struggle, see Katznelson and Weir (1985) and Wrigley (1982).

Demographics of Education—Kindergarten Through Graduate School." Elementary and secondary schools are increasingly attended by students who are poor, members of minority groups, live in single-parent families, or come home to empty houses because their parents are working and unable to afford day care ("latchkey" children). These children are going to encounter greater obstacles than other students in securing a good education, graduating from high school, and gaining access to education. As a result, their needs will increasingly set the agenda for educational policy and politics in the coming years.

CONCLUSIONS

Given the importance of education in U.S. life, educational access and opportunity will remain one of the most important issues in both politics and scholarly research. Until such a day that education ceases to have its current importance as a gateway to economic success or educational access becomes truly equal, both laypeople and scholars will be debating the extent, causes, and implications of inequality of educational opportunity.

These questions are the subject of the readings following this introduction. They review the extent of class, race, and sex differences in high school dropout, college entrance, and college graduation and the history of struggles to open up access to education. With this background, Chapters 6 and 7 can take us into the school in order to explain how schools and students interact to produce educational outcomes.

REFERENCES

Blau, Peter, and Otis D. Duncan. 1967. *The American Occupational Structure.* New York: Wiley.

Featherman, David L., and Robert M. Hauser, 1978. *Opportunity and Change.* New York: Academic Press.

Hammack, Floyd M. 1986. "Large School Systems' Dropout Reports: An Analysis of Definitions, Procedures, and Findings." *Teachers College Record* (spring): 324–341.

Heidenheimer, Arnold J. 1981. "Education and Social Security Entitlements in Europe and America." In Peter Flora and Arnold J. Heidenheimer (eds.), *The Development of Welfare States in Europe and America,* pp. 269–304. New Brunswick, NJ: Transaction Books.

Jencks, Christopher S., Marshall Smith, Henry Acland, Mary Jo Bane, David Cohen, Herbert Gintis, Barbara Hayns, Stephan Michelson. 1972. *Inequality.* New York: Basic Books.

———, Susan Bartlett, Mary Corcoran, James Crouse, David Eaglesfield, Gregory Jackson, Kent McClelland, Peter Mueser, Michael Olneck, Joseph Schwartz, Sherry Ward, Jill Williams. 1979. *Who Gets Ahead?* New York: Basic Books.

Karabel, Jerome. 1983. "The Politics of Structural Change in American Higher Education: The Case of Open Admissions at the City University of New York." In Harry Hermanns, Ulrich Teichler, and Henry Wasser (eds.), *The Compleat University,* pp. 21–58. Cambridge, MA: Schenkman.

_____, and Katherine McClelland. 1987. "Occupational Advantage and the Impact of College Rank on Labor Market Outcomes." *Sociological Inquiry* 57 (fall): 323–347.

Katznelson, Ira, and Margaret Weir. 1985. *Schooling for All.* New York: Basic Books.

Lavin, David E., and Richard D. Alba. 1981. *Right versus Privilege: The Open Admissions Experiment at the City University of New York.* New York: Free Press.

Rumberger, Russell. 1983. "Dropping Out of High High School: The Influence of Race, Sex, and Family Background." *American Educational Research Journal* 20: 199–220.

Sewell, William, and Robert M. Hauser. 1975. *Education, Occupation, and Earnings.* New York: Academic Press.

Solmon, Lewis. 1973. "The Definition and Impact of College Quality." In Lewis Solmon and Paul Taubman (eds.), *Does College Matter?* New York: Academic Press.

U.S. Department of Education. Center for Education Statistics. 1987. *Digest of Education Statistics, 1987.* Washington, DC: Government Printing Office.

Wachtel, Paul. 1975. "The Return to Investment in Higher Education: Another View." In F. Thomas Juster (ed.), *Education, Income, and Human Behavior.* New York: McGraw-Hill.

Wrigley, Julia. 1982. *Class Politics and Public Schools: Chicago, 1900–1950.* New Brunswick, NJ: Rutgers University Press.

Dropping Out

DEBORAH BURNETT STROTHER

Phi Delta Kappa, CEDR

During the 1960s, *dropping out* meant turning on, tuning in, growing into a new awareness of self. Today, *dropping out* has resumed its traditional meaning, and people who drop out are losers—especially high schoolers, who suffer tremendous disadvantages when they leave school without earning a diploma. Instead of flower power, the dropouts of the Eighties can look forward only to diminishing power over their own destinies as an increasingly sophisticated world leaves them farther and farther behind.

If anything, the dropout problem is growing worse. In cities such as New York, Philadelphia, and Chicago, the high school dropout rate now exceeds 40%.[1] In recent years, over 25% of potential high school graduates—more than one million young people—quit school before graduation.[2] This means that more than a million young people joined the ranks of Americans who are poorly equipped to face the demands of an increasingly complex society.

High dropout rates generate public alarm. National leaders call the dropout situation a tragedy that the U.S. cannot afford; concerned citizens claim that dropouts will cost billions of dollars in welfare benefits and lost revenue. Secretary of Education William Bennett proposed that schools be paid a bounty for rescuing dropouts,[3] and Rep. Charles Hayes (D-Ill.) proposed a bill that the Senate failed to act on, which would have authorized $50 million to fund programs to deal with the dropout problem.

Many educators are worried that higher standards in the public schools will cause students who already perform poorly to drop out. A year ago Anne Lewis wrote: "The 'excellence movement,' in many instances, changed the rules for millions of minority and disadvantaged students. But it didn't change a system that was already practically incapable of motivating them."[4] Nathan Quinones, chancellor of the New York City Board of Education, said

From *Phi Delta Kappan* 68 (December 1986): 325–328. Copyright © Phi Delta Kappa. Reprinted by permission of the publisher.

that "if we are to take credit for improving academic achievement without considering the dropout rate, then we are undermining that achievement. And if we don't do something, we are going to sap the strength of this country."[5]

DEFINING THE PROBLEM

Most of the school districts in the U.S. monitor the enrollment and attendance of students until they graduate or drop out. The records these school districts keep suggest that dropping out is a serious problem but that there is little agreement on the definition of a *dropout*. Some districts change the definition from year to year, and many districts define *dropout* to match the purpose for which the statistics are being kept. Cities or states sometimes put pressure on school districts to keep records in such a way as to make the dropout rate appear low.[6]

Moreover, school districts calculate the dropout rate in different ways. Many of them count only high school students; few of them keep data on elementary, junior high school, or special education dropouts. Nor does a standard system exist for keeping records on dropouts.

Because the definitions vary, estimates of the number of dropouts also vary. Generally speaking, a dropout is an individual whose natural progression toward graduation from high school has been interrupted. It is the length of this interruption and the reasons for it that create the problem.

WHO DROPS OUT?

In High School and Beyond, a longitudinal study of U.S. high school students sponsored by the National Center for Education Statistics, dropouts were systematically questioned before and after they decided to leave school. Ruth Ekstrom and her colleagues at the Educational Testing Service used data from the High School and Beyond study to analyze the characteristics of dropouts.[7]

The researchers found that a disproportionate number of dropouts were male, older than average for their grade level, and members of racial or ethnic minorities. They were likely to attend urban public schools in the South or West. They came from low-income—often single-parent—families; many had mothers who worked outside the home, who lacked formal education, and who had low educational expectations for their children. These young people had few study aids available to them at home, and their parents were not interested in monitoring their school or nonschool activities. They had fewer opportunities than their classmates for learning outside of school; their grades and test scores were lower; they read less, did less homework, and reported having more disciplinary problems in school. They also reported that they were unpopular with other students and alienated from school life. They tended not to take part in extracurricular activities, and they said that their jobs were more important to them than school.

Ekstrom and her colleagues concluded that the findings have important implications for policy makers who seek to deal with the dropout problem.

No single program or policy can meet the needs of the diverse dropout population. Three major types of programs are needed: 1) programs to help pregnant teenagers remain in school; 2) programs to help youth with economic needs combine work and education; and 3) programs directed toward students who perform poorly because they are dissatisfied with the school environment.[8]

The researchers also noted that students' home environments have a critical, but indirect, impact on their decision to drop out. They advocated new policies to help parents monitor their children's progress in school more closely and to make early intervention for high-risk children available more readily.

AND WHY?

Although the characteristics that dropouts tend to share have been identified, few studies have focused on students who displayed the same characteristics but who graduated from high school nonetheless. Thus we don't know whether the identified characteristics of dropouts are causes of their dropping out.

Not surprisingly, studies in which dropouts have been asked directly, "Why did you drop out?," provide some of the best answers to that question. According to Walter Hathaway, director of research and evaluation for the Portland Public Schools, the following reasons for leaving school early were most commonly given by Oregon dropouts in 1980: dissatisfaction with teachers (19.3%), dislike of school in general (15.3%), lack of credits (13.1%), dislike of a specific school (13.1%), boredom/lack of interest (11.7%), pregnancy (11.4% of females), and desire to attend an alternative education program or institution (11.2%).[9] Other studies point to some of the same factors, Hathaway notes, as well as to the existence of academic difficulties or disciplinary problems in school and to the desire of dropouts to work full-time.

In 1984 Michelle Fine asked dropouts from a high school in upper Manhattan why they had left school before graduation.[10] The school they had attended was large and underfunded, with a staff that was organized along stereotypical racial lines (white administrators, a predominantly white teaching staff, and black female aides).

The reasons these New York students gave for dropping out included: specific complaints about the organization and staffing of the school; family, social, or economic obligations (including pregnancy) that took precedence over schooling; and pressure from the school staff to leave. Fine discovered that many dropouts were really pushed out—and they did not realize that they have a legal right to a high school education.

In reporting her findings, Fine also alluded to some startling statistics that complicate the dropout picture: the estimated monetary return on education for women is only 40% that for men, and the estimated monetary return on education for blacks is only 63% that for whites. Noted Fine, "With the same level of education—the high school diploma—whites, men, and upper-middle-class students reap consistently more per additional year of education than do blacks, women, and working-class/low-income students, respectively."[11]

Although not a study of dropouts per se, *Voices from the Classroom*, by Laurie Olsen and Melinda Moore, presents additional information on why some vulnerable or marginal students choose to drop out of school.[12] This information came from interviews with students about their classroom interactions with teachers. Most of the students viewed their teachers as unhappy with their jobs, disgruntled, bored, and boring. Olsen and Moore pointed out that

> poor teachers erode students' confidence, their fragile sense of acceptability to their peers, and can contribute to truancy, dropping out, and acting out. Students go to great lengths to avoid teachers they feel put them in uncomfortable or humiliating positions—and if unable to avoid them, students can be affected for a long time by classroom situations they feel undermine, degrade, or humiliate them.[13]

In *Voices from the Classroom* many students speak with anger or embarrassment about such interactions with teachers. The specific findings of the study include the following.

- The larger the school, the more problems that students and teachers reported with the quality of teaching. Large classes and overcrowded schools increased every teacher's workload and made it difficult for them to respond to individual needs.
- Students said that their prime concerns were teachers' knowledge of subject matter and their accessibility.
- Students said that good teachers were characterized by accessibility and willingness to provide extra help. (The students emphasized that they relied on their teachers to answer questions, to discuss their work, and to provide one-to-one help.)
- Students reported that the better teachers went out of their way to follow up on students who had fallen behind, to reach out to those who seemed to be having trouble, and to give all students opportunities to ask questions and receive help in class.
- Teachers who embarrassed students were roundly disliked, and some students said that they would do anything to avoid the classes of such teachers. Students—particularly those in the early teens—also expressed ager and hurt over teachers who showed favoritism to certain youngsters.

SCHOOL-RELATED CAUSES

How much do schools contribute to the dropout problem? Several recent studies have sought answers to this question.

Gary Wehlage and Robert Rutter looked for answers in the data from the High School and Beyond study.[14] They found that students are more likely to drop out if school is a place where "teachers are not particularly interested in all students, and the discipline system is perceived as neither effective nor fair"—if school is a place where "one gets into trouble."[15]

Wehlage and Rutter acknowledge that some children may be more difficult to teach than others. But schools are nonetheless mandated to provide schooling from which all children can profit. To reduce the number of dropouts, Wehlage and Rutter advise schools to put an end to truancy, to provide caring and personalized teaching, to offer structured programs, to establish clear and demanding (but attainable) expectations for students, and to adapt schoolwork to children's individual needs. Youngsters should also have access, these researchers say, to community-based educational programs and other alternatives to the public schools.

Meanwhile, Matthew Schulz and his colleagues examined the records of 98,000 students enrolled as ninth-graders in Chicago public high schools between 1978 and 1980 who later graduated or dropped out.[16] They found that reading achievement and age on entering high school—not race or gender—were the best predictors of dropping out. However, 78% of the black students in the sample demonstrated low reading achievement, and 31% of the Hispanic students in the sample were older than their classmates when they entered high school because they had been retained in the earlier grades. Schulz and his colleagues recommend that school districts develop policies focused on increasing students' reading achievement (without retention) *before* they enter high school.

Some of these same Chicago researchers have tried to separate the effects of *high schools* on dropout rates from the effects of *student characteristics*.[17] By removing the effects of student attributes, they were able to obtain an unbiased ranking of school performance. When they compared this ranking with a ranking of the same schools based on their dropout rates, they noticed that some schools were characterized by low dropout rates and poor performance, while other schools had high dropout rates and good performance.

Ronald Toles has suggested that the differences between dropout rank and performance rank could be used to select schools for a comparative study aimed at identifying the characteristics that make high schools effective. A comparative study could examine such variables as community support, school safety, school discipline, grading policies, amount of homework assigned, and type and degree of support available for less able students.

POLICIES AND PROGRAMS

David Doss and his colleagues in the Austin (Texas) Independent School District followed a group of students from age 14 until they dropped out or graduated from high school. The researchers interviewed 100 of those youngsters in the group who dropped out.[18] The interviews revealed that many decisions to leave school early may have been reasonable responses—especially in those cases in which the students were disrupting the learning of others and getting little out of attending school themselves.

If dropout prevention programs are to succeed at keeping such students in school, Doss recommends that the programs focus on two things. First, they should insure that all capable students actually develop some minimum number of useful basic skills. Second, they should attract and hold students by including components that meet students' economic needs and by providing activities that students find valuable and engaging.

Doss suggests, in addition, that dropout prevention programs should have clear plans of action and serve small groups of students. The teachers in such programs should expect their students to succeed, the students should support the program goals, and the curriculum should focus on real-life problems and situations. Such programs, Doss adds, should provide students with successful work experiences in the community.

Meanwhile, in Los Angeles a special task force on dropouts reported back to the Board of Education in February 1985, according to Floraline Stevens, director of research and evaluation for the Los Angeles Unified School District (LAUSD). Among other things, the task force recommended that the school district:

- adopt a practical (i.e., operational) definition of *dropout;*
- identify successful local, state, and national efforts to retain potential dropouts and recover actual dropouts; and
- implement short- and long-range programs, practices, and organizational and instructional changes aimed at reducing the district's dropout rate and enticing dropouts to return to school.

In the months since the task force report, the LAUSD has established a computer file of potential dropouts. The district has also chosen 24 senior high schools—those with the highest dropout rates—to take part in a pilot program focused on dropout prevention and recovery, and it has provided the necessary resources to implement the program.

The program at each of the 24 schools must include a dropout prevention component, which provides information to all students and special counseling and educational resources to any student who is identified as exhibiting attendance and behavioral problems that may lead to dropping out. The program at each of the schools must also include a recovery component, which coordinates efforts on the part of students, the school, the home, and the community to encourage dropouts to complete the requirements for a high school diploma.

The new LAUSD program has already had one positive spinoff. In the fall of 1986 the state of California required statistics on dropouts from every school district in the state. With its computerized system for tracking potential and actual dropouts, the LAUSD will be able to give the state accurate data on the dropout situation in Los Angeles.

There have always been dropouts. But the plight of those who leave school before graduation is worsening in this era of high unemployment.

Moreover, dropouts are often a burden on the society. Mary Hatwood Futrell, president of the National Education Association, has pointed out that 60% of all prison inmates in the U.S. are high school dropouts. "In New York, taxpayers are billed $30,000 a year for each inmate," Futrell notes. That amount is nearly "10 times the amount necessary to pay for one year of schooling."[19] Dropouts also cost taxpayers $75 billion annually in welfare benefits and lost revenues, according to Futrell.

Practitioners need to communicate to the public the fact that a high dropout rate is not just a problem for the schools to solve, according to Floraline Stevens. Serving vulnerable and marginal students effectively will require a financial commitment from Congress, state legislatures, the business community, and other institutions in both the public and the private sectors.

If schools are able to address four factors through policy, program development, and fiscal enhancement, Stevens predicts a decrease in the number of dropouts. Those factors are: 1) alienation from teachers, administrators, and peers; 2) poor attendance and high truancy rates; 3) low academic achievement, especially in reading; and 4) negative economic and social pressures at home or in school.

The identification of potential dropouts before they reach high school is essential, Stevens says. Schools should also examine their policies and services to make certain that they are not pushing students out of school and discouraging dropouts from reentry.

Well-planned programs for dropouts will require additional funding, Stevens adds. The money would pay for counselors to work with students at risk of dropping out, workers to canvass communities for dropouts and entice them back to school, and special teachers to work with at-risk students and with dropouts who return to school.

NOTES

1. ECS Business Advisory Commission, *Reconnecting Youth* (Denver: Education Commission of the States, October 1985), p. 10.
2. Samuel S. Peng, "High School Dropouts: A National Concern," paper prepared for the Business Advisory Commission, Education Commission of the States, March 1985, p. 4.
3. William J. Bennett, "Pay Schools a Bounty for Rescuing Dropouts," *USA Today*, 29 April 1986, p. 8-A.
4. Anne C. Lewis, "Washington Report: Young and Poor in America," *Phi Delta Kappan*, December 1985, p. 252.
5. Lucia Solorzano, "The Campaign to Lure Kids Back to Class." *U.S. News & World Report*, 3 March 1986, p. 77.
6. Floyd Morgan Hammack, "Large School Systems' Dropout Reports: An Analysis of Definitions, Procedures, and Findings," *Teachers College Record*, Spring 1986, pp. 324–41.
7. Ruth B. Ekstrom, Margaret E. Goertz, Judith M. Pollack, and Donald A. Rock, "Who Drops Out of High School and Why? Findings from a National Study," *Teachers College Record*, Spring 1986, pp. 356–73.

8. Ibid., p. 371.

9. Verne Duncan, *Oregon Early School Leavers Study* (Salem: Oregon Department of Education, 1980).

10. Michelle Fine, "Why Urban Adolescents Drop Into and Out of Public High School," *Teachers College Record*, Spring 1986, pp. 393–409.

11. Ibid., p. 395.

12. Laurie Olsen and Melinda Moore, *Voices from the Classroom: Students and Teachers Speak Out on the Quality of Teaching in Our Schools* (Oakland, Calif.: Citizens Policy Center, 1982).

13. Ibid., p. 20.

14. Gary G. Wehlage and Robert A. Rutter, "Dropping Out: How Much Do Schools Contribute to the Problem?," *Teachers College Record*, Spring 1986, pp. 374–92.

15. Ibid., p. 385.

16. E. Matthew Schulz, Ronald Toles, William K. Rice, Jr., Irving Brauer, and Jaqueline Harvey, "The Association of Dropout Rates with Student Attributes," paper presented at the annual meeting of the American Educational Research Association, San Francisco, April 1986.

17. Ronald Toles, E. Matthew Schulz, and William K. Rice, Jr., "A Study of Variation in Dropout Rates Attributable to Effects of High Schools," paper presented at the annual meeting of the American Educational Research Association, San Francisco, April 1986.

18. David A. Doss. *Mother Got Tired of Taking Care of My Baby* (Austin, Tex.: Office of Research and Evaluation, Austin Independent School District, Pub. No. 82.44. 1983).

19. Mary Hatwood Futrell, "It's a Tragedy We Cannot Afford," *USA Today*, 29 April 1986, p. 8-A.

Access to Higher Education in the United States, 1900 to the Present*

DAVID KAREN
Bryn Mawr College

Early in this century, it was possible to ascend to the heights of the economy without ever having set foot in college. The corporate magnates of that era moved to the top through their guile, wits, and, most importantly, money. Due, in part, to their success, it is difficult nowadays to follow their path without having a baccalaureate. In fact, higher education has become *the* sorting machine for employers hiring professionals and managers. As of 1985, college graduates earned one-third more than high school graduates and were one-third less likely to be unemployed (U.S. Department of Education, 1987a: 112). There are, then, concrete economic benefits that follow from participation in higher education. The question is who has been able to gain access to this path to economic success and in what way.

In this paper, I examine patterns of access to higher education during this century. I begin with an overview of these trends, focusing on the degree to which women, blacks, and working-class students have increased their participation in higher education. I then look at class, race, and sex differences in how students are distributed across different kinds of colleges: two-year, four-year, elite universities, and so forth. Besides tracing these patterns of access, this paper also provides an explanation of how they developed. I argue that blacks' and women's political mobilization during the 1960s contributed to the expansion of the system, thus enabling them to enter top-tier institutions at rates higher than ever before. To illuminate precisely

This article appears here for the first time.

*I would like to thank Katherine McClelland and the editors of this volume for their helpful comments on this paper.

how this happened, I report on the admissions process at Harvard College. Finally, I suggest that political mobilization—this time from the Right—has led to declines in black enrollments.

A NOTE ON POLITICAL MOBILIZATION AND COUNTERMOBILIZATION

Political mobilization involves the joining together of individuals who are excluded from some critical resource (for example, decision-making power, valued goods and services, and so on) for action directed at changing patterns of institutionalized behavior. The particular form that political mobilization takes (ranging from making a request to a power center to massive urban revolts) depends on the perceived nature and extent of resistance to the subordinate group's demands and the resources available for the struggle. Political mobilization usually begins with relatively unthreatening encounters between participants and may lead eventually to violent demonstrations. In terms of how political mobilization exerts effects, many mediating mechanisms may be at work. There may be a direct response by a specific administrator who, recognizing the legitimacy of the complainants and having the power to do so, takes steps to ameliorate the situation. Alternatively, there may be long-term protests by excluded groups that lead, through fear of major disruptions, to government responses that then affect the behavior of even private institutions toward these groups. Finally, political mobilization may lead to increasing the availability of overall resources (as occurred with expanding the number of places in higher education as a whole), thus making possible increases in access to that resource across the population.

Countermobilization involves the assertion of power on the part of dominant groups to reestablish the *status quo ante*. This assertion of power may, through the government, take the form of nonenforcement of affirmative action laws, rollbacks of programs that disproportionately benefited excluded groups, or even the encouragement of discriminatory attitudes and practices, such as stricter use of standardized tests for admission to elite colleges. We may see the New Right and the Reagan presidency as primary actors in the post-1976 countermobilization.

TRENDS IN ACCESS TO HIGHER EDUCATION AS A WHOLE

The most remarkable fact about higher education in the United States is its great size and openness, relative to other countries (Dougherty, Chapter 3 above) and relative to its recent past. While in the last 15 years the system's previously rapid rate of growth has given way to stasis, the system is maintaining itself at a very high rate of enrollment.

Table 1 shows the remarkable growth of higher education in this century. We have moved during this century from a country in which one out of fifty young people attends college to one where one out of four attends college.[1] What has accounted for this phenomenal growth?

Higher growth benefited from the perception of the United States as the land of opportunity (Kluegel and Smith, 1986), although intergenerational social mobility does not appear to be significantly higher in the United States than in other industrial societies (Miller, 1960). The emergence of a national economy in the early 20th century consolidated patterns of access to upper-class positions (Collins, 1979; Levine, 1980). By the 1920s, the idea that college was necessary for gaining access to high-status and well-paying occupations had become well established (Jencks and Riesman, 1968: 94). With the increased size and bureaucratization of businesses, owners could no longer rely on their own families and personal networks to staff management; colleges increasingly came to play this role. In addition, between approximately 1880 and 1920, professional education was radically revamped in law (Auerbach, 1976), medicine (Starr, 1982), and business (Hofstadter, 1962). Higher education was coming to be perceived as a place where knowledge and expertise were being produced and transmitted. As high-status positions in the occupational structure became more closely associated with attendance at an institution of higher education, more and more people attempted to gain access. For example, relatively successful, mobility-conscious immigrants—perhaps especially Jews (Gorelick, 1981)—increasingly demanded higher education. In addition, since many institutions were under private control, they relied on increases in enrollments to make ends meet. Early in the century, in fact, institutional prestige was rather strongly tied to size of institution, so colleges eagerly pursued new students (Jencks and Riesman, 1968). Thus, as college attendance increasingly came to be tied to occupational success both in perception and actuality, institutions of higher education took advantage of this situation and actively attempted to increase enrollments.

TABLE 1   Enrollment Rates of Young People, 1900–1985

Year	Enrollment as a % of 18- to 24-Year-Olds
1900	2.2
1920	4.6
1940	8.5
1946	9.3
1950	15.0
1960	18.3
1967	25.5
1970	25.7
1975	26.3
1980	25.6
1985	27.8

Sources: U.S. Bureau of the Census (1975); U.S. Department of Education (1987b).

During the pre–World War II period, the college-eligible population increased as high school graduation rates rose precipitously. Federal funds were increasingly directed toward higher education both during World War I and during the Depression, thus providing a new source of revenues during times of crisis. And with increases in the number of and enrollments in community colleges, the types of institutions that called themselves "colleges" expanded. Higher education as a whole, then, showed itself to be a remarkably adaptable institution during this period as it fulfilled a variety of roles: terminal vocational programs, preprofessional education, warehouses for the potentially unemployed, training grounds for soldiers, and managerial training grounds for industry.

The changes observed in the higher educational system in the United States during the first four decades of the 20th century were notable, but they did not approach the truly revolutionary changes that were to come. The 1944 G.I. Bill (Servicemen's Readjustment Act) began this revolutionary change. As the end of World War II approached, national leaders feared a return to Depression-level unemployment after demobilization. The enactment of the G.I. Bill addressed this concern directly. Making college easily accessible would provide the economy time to readjust to peacetime production and, perhaps, to train the veterans for secure, well-paying jobs. As a student of the G.I. Bill makes clear, "anxiety over economics preceded and dominated altruism toward veterans" (Olson, 1974: 24).

The response by veterans to the opportunities created by the G.I. Bill far surpassed expectations. Male enrollment in higher education increased from a low of 5.6 percent of 18- to 21-year-olds in 1943 to a high of over 38 percent in 1949 (Ferriss, 1969: 387). With so many veterans attending college and their academic performance hailed by the media, it is fair to say that "the G.I. Bill established the idea that a college education might become not a privilege for the few but a right for the many" (Hodgson, 1978: 54). Middle-class groups increasingly came to depend on higher education as a means of ensuring that their children would do as well or better than themselves, instead of relying on inherited wealth or on family, union, or personal contacts.

Once the veterans finished college, enrollment rates dropped, reaching a nadir in 1951. From then until the 1970s, however, male and female enrollments as a percentage of the 18- to 21-year-old population virtually never failed to register an annual increase. What was behind this tremendous post-War expansion? A number of key factors played a role, most notably the Cold War, the coming of age of the baby boom cohort, the war in Vietnam, and the civil rights movement and women's movement and their legislative consequences. I will briefly discuss the relationship of each of these to higher education.

After World War II, the United States emerged as the economic, political, and military leader of the world. Before the end of the 1950s, the U.S. government's links to higher education had become even closer than those forged immediately after the War. Most important, perhaps, for issues of access was that in 1958, in response to the Soviet Union's Sputnik launching, the federal government initially appropriated over a billion dollars for colleges through the National Defense Education Act (Hodgson, 1978). This commitment was continued in response to black mobilization, with appropriations in 1963 and 1965 as well (Morris, 1979). But probably most important in increasing male enrollments in the mid- to late 1960s was the war in Vietnam and the availability of 2-S deferments for students. Perhaps for the first time since the G.I. Bill, students who might not otherwise have gone to college were streaming into institutions of higher education at an unprecedented rate. This, combined with the fact that the 1945–1957 baby boom cohort was now of college age, made the absolute increases even more extraordinary.[2]

One final contextual point must be made. In moving from World War II to the 1960s, we move to a society in which the agricultural sector was in rapid decline and the white collar (and especially professional) sector was rapidly increasing. Insofar as there has been an increasing number of occupational positions that have traditionally required a college education, more and more people will have been oriented toward higher education. As competition for those jobs increased, even greater amounts of education became necessary to be eligible for those positions (see Collins, 1979). Expanding enrollments, then, must be seen in relationship to larger economic processes.

Access by Particular Groups

In this section, I argue that as a result of the civil rights movement and the women's movement, minority and female access to higher education has increased, even to prestigious institutions. To examine this argument, I will discuss the timing and extent to which subordinate groups[3] have gained access to higher education in this century. I will focus on the more recent period, since there are very few studies of access done before World War II and since the issue of subordinate-group access has been posed seriously and massively only since then.[4]

Probably the most important factor in increasing black and working-class representation in higher education has been the huge increase in high school graduation rates. If we examine high school graduation rates among blacks and whites, ages 25 to 29, we find a process of convergence over the last 40 years. In 1940, 41 percent of whites had at least graduated from high school, while only 12 percent of blacks had gone as far (U.S. Bureau of the Census, 1948); in 1985, the white rate was 87 percent and the black rate was 81 percent (U.S. Bureau of the Census, 1987).

A similar process is evident with respect to social class. Among sons of fathers who completed seven or fewer years of schooling, the percentage who at least graduated from high school increased from 34 percent in 1943 to 45 percent in 1953 to 54 percent in 1963 to 58 percent in 1973.[5] Sons of fathers who had had at least some college attained this level of education in the following percentages for these four cohorts: 86, 93, 94, and 96. During these years, then, we see that "class" differences in attaining high school graduation have been reduced.

Women's participation in higher education follows a different path from that of other subordinate groups. As early as 1870, more women than men graduated from high school in any given year. Despite this graduation advantage, however, women's higher education enrollments did not surpass men's until 1979. In 1985, the last year for which data are available, women comprised 52 percent of total enrollment in institutions of higher education (U.S. Department of Education, 1987b, 122).

Looking more closely at the last 30 years, we can see how women and blacks were able to lessen their disadvantages in access relative to dominant groups. Between 1960 and 1975, the percentage of students who were female rose from 37 to 45 percent. Black enrollments also increased tremendously during the late 1960s and early 1970s, almost reaching the same level as the black share of the population: 12 percent (Astin and others, 1982; Morris, 1979). Finally, social class differentials in access have been reduced. Looking at the college enrollment rates of dependent family members, aged 18–24, we see that students from families earning less than $5000 (in 1967 dollars) raised their enrollment rates from 20 to 22 percent, while those in the $15,000 and over category dropped from 68 to 58 percent (U.S. Bureau of the Census, 1978). Overall, then, due to increases in rates of high school graduation and because top socioeconomic groups had reached a ceiling in their rates of college entrance, it appears that class differentials in access to higher education have diminished.[6] During this time of expansion, then, relatively excluded groups were able to increase their presence in the system of higher education.

To anticipate what will follow, I argue that the tremendous overall expansion of higher education has narrowed overall differentials in access between dominant and subordinate groups. However, subordinate groups that mobilized politically and gained official recognition as social categories (especially women and blacks) have been able to make inroads into the better institutions of higher education. Working-class students, who did not mobilize politically and who have not been officially recognized as a social category, have not been able to increase their access to the more prestigious institutions. Finally, within the decade 1976–1985, a countermobilization arose that has led to a decline in black enrollments. Because of the particular ways in which women have been subordinated, they have been largely able to avoid the effects of this countermobilization.

TRENDS IN ACCESS TO PARTICULAR
INSTITUTIONS OF HIGHER EDUCATION

It is important to examine subordinate groups' patterns of access to different levels of the higher educational hierarchy and to elite institutions in particular, because, at a time when so many young people are attending college, *where* one goes to college is consequential for various economic outcomes (see for example Karabel and McClelland, 1987). Though somewhat sketchy, the data are very suggestive.

With respect to access to elite institutions of higher education, blacks and women increased their access through different routes, although both benefited from political mobilization. Black increases flowed from a combination of governmental response, local on-campus protests that administrators were reluctant to repress violently, and elite college competition to attract the highest SAT-scoring blacks so as to comply with federal guidelines. Women, on the other hand, gained access to prestigious institutions through a series of administrative decisions to admit women at individual universities in response to the women's movement in general and to government incentives (as provided, for example, by the Education Amendments of 1972). A key difference between blacks' and women's mobilization is that young whites and blacks differ greatly in their social origins—and thus their test scores—while young men and women do not. Thus, for women, strict application of academic/meritocratic guidelines would lead to increased female access to given institutions; for blacks, this would not be enough. To increase black access, then, the mobilization had to be more extensive—after all, it was attacking a traditional exclusionary factor: standardized tests. As we will see below, since black demands called into question more entrenched selection mechanisms, a reassertion of traditional sorting criteria would affect blacks more than women.

Table 2 compares the distribution of women in different kinds of institutions in 1960 and in 1978. The table therefore allows us to examine whether during women's political mobilization in the last 20 years there has been an increase in access to "elite" rather than "mass" institutions. The data indicate that women's representation increased most in Ivy League colleges, followed by "other prestigious" institutions. However, it is noteworthy that female enrollments also rose sharply at community colleges. In fact, in terms of absolute numbers, community colleges absorbed the bulk of enrollment increases over the past 30 years.

This pattern of access is consistent with a "cooptation" response by privileged groups to subordinate groups' demands. In this pattern, institutional elites individually allow for some increases in subordinate-group enrollment at the top institutions, but, overall, the greatest absolute increase is at the bottom of the system. Thus, access to higher education in general and to elite institutions in particular increases, but the lion's share of the change is concentrated in lowest-tier institutions.

TABLE 2 Percentage Female of Total Degee-Credit Enrollment at Different Types of Institutions, 1960 and 1978

Institutional Type	1960	1978	% Increase
Ivy League	22	38	71
Other Prestigious*	26	41	54
Four-year Institutions	37	48	30
Two-year Institutions	38	53	39

*"Other Prestigious" are those colleges ranked "most selective" or "highly selective" by Cass and Birnbaum in *The Comparative Guide to American Colleges* (1979).

Sources: U.S. Bureau of the Census (1978); U.S. Office of Education (1960); American Council on Education (1987).

Through their political mobilization, blacks too were able to make inroads into the top institutions during the 1960s and 1970s. Certain institutions, particularly upper-tier institutions, responded to black political mobilization and the federal government's linkage of institutional subsidies to affirmative action plans by instituting extensive black recruitment programs (Stadtman, 1980: 128–130). In fact, during the early 1970s competition for "highly able" black students became intense, with some prestigious colleges even offering all-expense-paid campus visits (Weinberg, 1977: 34).

The information that most directly addresses the issue of the distribution of blacks within higher education is the American Council on Education's annual *National Norms for Entering Freshmen*. Though they have limitations, the data in Table 3 show that black two-year, four-year, and private university enrollments rose through the mid-1970s. Other data sources also chart the increases in black attendance at top institutions during the same period. Blacks comprised 2.3 percent of Ivy League enrollment in 1967, 5.1 percent in 1970, 6.7 percent in 1974, and 6.3 percent in 1976. For "other prestigious" colleges, the figures were 3.9 in 1970, 4.5 in 1974, and 4.8 in 1976 (Karen, 1983; Levitan, Johnston, and Taggart, 1975: 101; U.S. Department of Health, Education, and Welfare, 1974, 1976). Linking these figures to our hypothesis about the impact on enrollments of subordinate-group political mobilization, we may note that blacks made inroads into top institutions at precisely the time that black political mobilization was at its height and federal affirmative action enforcement was strongest. While as noted in Table 3 the 1969 black enrollment in private universities was 15.2 percent of their total enrollment, this is no doubt largely due to sampling error. It is perhaps not coincidental, however, that the sampling error occurred in the year after Martin Luther King's assassination and major outbursts of campus activism (see below).

To further underline the effect of political mobilization, let us examine the college destinations of students of working-class or lower socioeconomic

TABLE 3   Black Percentage of First-Time Full-Time Freshmen in Two-Year and Four-Year Colleges and Private Universities: 1966–1987

Year	Two-Year Colleges (%)	Four-Year Colleges (%)	Private Universities (%)
1966	4.1	7.7	2.1
1969	3.8	8.3	15.2
1972	8.7	11.9	4.8
1975	8.5	11.9	4.6
1978	6.1	11.3	9.6
1981	7.5	11.3	5.1
1984	7.3	14.2	10.4
1987	7.3	12.3	4.4

Source: American Council on Education (1966–1987).

background. If the political mobilization hypothesis is correct, this group, which did not mobilize politically, should not have made any relative gains in access to prestigious colleges. As Table 4 indicates, at private universities, students from families with incomes less than half the national median comprised 8 percent of all students in 1966 and 7 percent in 1975. Students from families with incomes more than twice the national median increased their representation from 32 to 36 percent between 1966 and 1975. At the other end of the higher educational spectrum, at public two-year colleges, the students from poorer families increased their representation from 17 to 20 percent, while the students from well-off homes decreased their representation from 11 to 9 (McPherson, 1978: 172).

We have seen, then, that two subordinate groups that mobilized politically—blacks and women—increased their access to higher education in general and to elite institutions in particular during the 1960s and 1970s. By contrast, another subordinate group that did not mobilize—the working class—showed no similar pattern of increased access to elite institutions. Although aggregate statistics show us the overall relationship between political mobilization and college access, they cannot show *how* these changes were accomplished. To examine the *process* by which mobilization affects access, we must look at the admissions process at particular institutions. Hence, I turn now to a study I have conducted of access to Harvard College (Karen, 1985).

ACCESS TO HARVARD COLLEGE

During the late 1970s and early 1980s, Harvard College—the undergraduate component of Harvard University—received approximately 13,000 to 14,000 applications annually to fill the 2000 slots it has available each year. The overall admission rate is approximately 15 percent. However, certain groups have secured much higher admission rates. Some of the major factors that

TABLE 4   Percentage of Students Attending Private Universities and Public Two-Year Colleges by Family Income: 1966 and 1975

	1966 (%)	1975 (%)	% Change
Private Universities			
Low Family Income	8	7	−12.5
High Family Income	32	36	+12.5
Public Two-Year Colleges			
Low Family Income	17	20	+17.6
High Family Income	11	9	−18.2

Note: Low family income is defined as less than half the median family income; high family income is defined as more than twice the median family income.

Source: McPherson (1978: 172).

increase likelihood of admission are: having very high scores on standardized tests; being a potential varsity athlete; having parents who attended Harvard/Radcliffe; attending certain elite high schools; and being black, Hispanic, or Native American, but *not* Asian. How have these factors affected admissions decisions and what role have political and organizational factors played in this process? We will examine three of these factors: test scores, alumni advantage, and race/ethnicity.

High-Test-Scores Advantage

While it may come as no surprise that Harvard favors students who score well on standardized tests, this factor actually became consequential only relatively recently. While M.I.T. has always been oriented to the highest scorers, Harvard has long admitted not just high test scorers but also students with other characteristics: creativity, alumni background, and so forth. However, in the late 1950s the natural sciences faculty at Harvard led a protest in favor of the selection of high scorers on standardized tests and against Harvard's policy of admitting virtually all alumni sons. A report issued in response to this protest noted that Harvard could no longer "view the problem of admissions as essentially one of combining minimum academic requirements with a modest selectivity designed, as one uncommonly indiscreet dean of the College had said not many years before, 'to bring us as many as possible of the very rich and the very bright' " (Harvard University, 1960: 5). Harvard now had to stress intellectual promise in its entering classes. The result of this protest was that the bottom decile of Scholastic Aptitude Test (SAT) scores for Harvard admits the very following year were the highest they have ever been—before or since. Thus, even the use of ability measures in admissions decisions has been affected by political mobilization.[7] Another factor that has led to greater attention to test scores is the fact that graduate and professional schools have increasingly relied on test scores for selection. Hence, to maintain its position as an institution that produces national leaders in many fields, Harvard has given greater weight to test scores in its undergraduate admissions.

Alumni Child Advantage

Alumni children have admission rates in the 35 to 40 percent range, compared to 15 percent for the applicant pool as a whole. Alumni children's advantage derives primarily from the fact that they have highly educated parents who send them to good schools, are involved in interesting and challenging extracurricular activities, score well on standardized tests, and so forth. Thus, all of the things that Harvard looks for are more likely to be found in its graduates' progeny than in the general population. But alumni children also benefit from the fact that being an alumni child is a recognized advantaged *category* in the admissions process. Admissions officials are always aware of whether or not a given applicant is an alumni child. This categoric advantage stems in part from alumni power. They play an important role in the admissions process, interviewing applicants and making recommendations to the Admissions Office. Most important, though, is the financial contribution that alumni may make. This is evidenced by the fact that if one's parents were not able to parlay their Harvard/Radcliffe degrees into incomes sufficient to finance a stint at Harvard for the next generation, the Admissions Office is less likely to present the family another opportunity. For those without Harvard connections, aid-blind admission is the rule. But among alumni-related applicants, once academic and other factors are taken into account, those who apply for financial aid have admission rates eight percentage points below those who do not apply for financial aid (Karen, 1985).

Racial and Ethnic Identification

Through the mid-1960s, Harvard regularly admitted approximately 50 blacks per year. But following Martin Luther King's assassination in 1968, student protesters at Harvard demanded the hiring of black admissions officers and an increase in recruitment and admission of blacks. Within one year, the number of admitted black applicants shot up to 109, with 91 matriculating. Such an immediate and direct response to political mobilization is rarely seen, but the conditions both on campus and nationally (ghetto revolts were occurring on a large scale following King's assassination) produced a swift response.

So successful was the black political mobilization that Native Americans and Hispanics also mobilized, resulting in higher rates of admission as well. Asian-Americans did not do as well, however. Asian-Americans' admission rates were far lower than other minorities and even lower than whites. For the class of 1984, the combined admission rate for Native Americans, blacks, and Hispanics was 27.3 percent and the white rate was 15.2 percent, but the Asian-American rate was 13.4 percent.[8] However, the Harvard Asian-American Association recently has been able to pressure the Admissions Office to increase its recruitment and acceptance of working-class Asian applicants.

How have women fared in the formerly all-male admissions process? In 1976, the Harvard and Radcliffe Admissions Offices for the first time joined forces and considered all applicants together. It would be difficult to explain this occurrence without reference both to the women's movement and to Yale's and Princeton's inclusion of women in 1969. While the committee considering the merger could have called for a policy requiring an equal ratio of men and women in each class, it chose to recommend a policy of "equal access," which means that the Admissions Committee should treat applications on a sex-blind basis (this has resulted in a 60:40 ratio of men:women). The reason cited for equal access rather than equal ratio was that "for the foreseeable future, men will continue to dominate the leadership of most activities, that Harvard has traditionally trained a significant fraction of these leaders, and that both for reasons of service to society and essential financial support of the University, the number of men cannot be reduced" (Strauch, 1975: 14). This illustrates how, even when subordinate groups successfully mobilize and gain certain benefits, traditional elites often still control the levers of power.

COUNTERMOBILIZATION AGAINST GREATER ACCESS: 1975 TO 1985

The phenomenal growth in higher education enrollments slowed considerably in the 1975–1985 period. During this period of slowdown, subordinate groups weakened in their mobilization and there has been a countermobilization by dominant groups. How have subordinate groups fared during this period of slowed expansion? As Table 5 shows, the black share of enrollments has decreased significantly during the past decade. At the same time, however, Asian-American and Hispanic enrollments have increased. This difference can be attributed to several factors: a sharp increase in the number of young Asian-Americans and Hispanics, an increase in the average social class standing of the Asian-American community, and political mobilization of the Hispanic community. With respect to the latter, 71 percent of all Hispanic college students came from four states—California, Florida, New York, and Texas—in which Hispanics constitute an important voting bloc and have established themselves as a political presence.

The decline in black representation can be seen as an outgrowth of a process of countermobilization operating at several levels. The fiscal crisis of many state and local governments in the mid-1970s led to severe cutbacks in social programs, many of which had benefited the black community. The quality of inner-city schools declined, and cuts in compensatory education and similar programs led to declines in the college-oriented pool of students (Staples, 1986: 50). Perhaps most important, by 1976–77, five of the six major federal student aid programs had peaked in terms of their highest average awards, with significant declines thereafter (U.S. Department of Education, 1987a: 208). These cuts were all the more devastating in that during this time the cost of higher education rose considerably more rapidly than the rate of inflation.

Women, on the other hand, have continued to increase their enrollments. As noted above, because the class distribution of school-aged females is the same as that of males, women are less susceptible than other subordinate groups to the negative effects of class-based countermobilization. However,

TABLE 5 Race and Ethnic Background of College Students: 1976–1986

RACE/ETHNICITY	1976 (%)	1980 (%)	1986 (%)	% change 1976–1986
Asian-American	1.8	2.4	3.7	+105.6%
Black	9.6	9.4	8.9	−7.3%
Hispanic	3.6	4.0	5.1	+41.7%
Native American	0.7	0.7	0.7	0
White	84.3	83.5	81.5	−3.3%
Total Enrollment (in millions)	10.8	11.8	12.2	+9.3%

Source: "Enrollment Since 1976" (1988)

men's enrollments in first professional and doctoral degree programs continue to be higher than women's. Thus, while women's political mobilization has raised expectations for women's educational attainment, it has not entirely overcome the persistence of male advantage in the sector that leads most directly to elite occupational positions.

With respect to working-class access, little change has occurred in recent years. Data comparing college enrollments for 1972 and 1980 high school seniors indicate virtually no change in the percentages going on to college among those in the low, medium, and high socioeconomic status categories (U.S. Department of Education, 1985: 224).

In summary, the last decade has seen declines in black enrollment, increases in women's enrollments, and relative stability in working-class enrollments. The timing of the black enrollment decline seems especially strongly related to declines in federal funding and thus lends support to the countermobilization hypothesis. Women, because their class distribution mirrors men's during school-attendance years, have not been affected by the cutbacks. Working-class students, among high school graduates at least, have maintained their relative position in higher education enrollments.

CONCLUSION

This paper shows that the unique nature of the U.S. higher education system has led to a tremendous expansion in the 20th century, which has increased the access of subordinate groups in the society. Political mobilization by subordinate groups has affected not only whether people gain access to college but also access to particular institutions, particularly elite institutions. But enrollment gains due to political mobilization are not irreversible. During the 1975–1985 period, as funding cuts have been instituted, blacks have lost some of the ground they had previously gained. Future action of mobilized groups must address not only the availability of funds but the standards that are used to evaluate applicants, if the gains that have been achieved are to be maintained and extended. As we have seen, the relative importance of specific criteria in admissions decisions is a historical result of political mobilization and reactions to it.

NOTES

1. The figures for enrollments as a percentage of the 18- to 21-year-old population provide an even more striking impression: They indicate that almost half of the college-age population is enrolled in higher education.

2. Note that both supply and demand factors must be present for enrollment increases to have occurred. Demand for college does not necessarily produce increased numbers of available places, nor does increased supply necessarily yield more bodies on college campuses.

3. I use the term *subordinate group,* following Parkin (1979), to refer to women, racial/ethnic minorities, and those of working-class background (blue collar, lower-class, or low socioeconomic status). The lack of specificity for the working-class group is a function of the varied

designations applied to it in the collection of statistics and in the sociological literature. Advances in subordinate groups' access to elite colleges usually take the form of official recognition of a group as a social category to be reckoned with, following the group's constitution of itself through political mobilization. It is symptomatic of the working class's lack of access to elite institutions that it has no *official* label in college admissions and other areas of life. For more on group formation and official recognition, see Przeworski (1977) and Bourdieu (1984).

4. For more on the pre-1940 period, see Karen (1988).

5. These figures are based on unpublished tabulations from the Census Bureau's 1973 survey, *Occupational Changes in a Generation.* They are taken from the reports of the 25- to 34-, 35- to 44-, 45- to 54-, and 55- to 64-year-old cohorts. While there are problems with these data (overreporting, underreporting, subsequent completions), they actually underestimate the class differences in educational attainment, thus providing a conservative test of whether these differences decreased over time.

6. For further discussion, see Karen (1988).

7. To refer to the actions of Harvard professors as political mobilization might seem odd. However, within the university, the faculty are excluded from decision-making power over critical decisions. In this particular case, they mobilized against alumni who, until this point, were virtually guaranteed that their sons would be offered admission to Harvard.

8. This is not to say that Asians are not relatively well-represented at Harvard. In 1981, approximately 11 percent of those admitted were Asian-American; this represented almost half of all minority students (Harvard University, 1982).

REFERENCES

American Council on Education. 1987. *Fact Book on Higher Education, 1986–87.* New York: Macmillan.

Astin, Alexander W., Helen S. Astin, Kenneth C. Green, Laura Kent, Patricia McNamara, and Melanie R. Williams. 1982. *Minorities in American Higher Education.* San Francisco: Jossey-Bass.

Astin, Alexander W., and others. 1966–1987. *The American Freshman: National Norms for Entering Freshmen.* Los Angeles: Cooperative Institutional Research Program, University of California, Los Angeles.

Auerbach, Jerrold S. 1976. *Unequal Justice: Lawyers and Social Change in Modern America.* New York: Oxford University Press.

Bourdieu, Pierre. 1984. *Distinction: A Social Critique of the Judgment of Taste.* Cambridge, MA: Harvard University Press.

Cass, James, and Max Birnbaum. 1979. *Comparative Guide to American Colleges.* 9th ed. New York: Harper & Row.

Collins, Randall. 1979. *The Credential Society.* New York: Academic Press.

"Enrollment Since 1976." *Chronicle of Higher Education.* March 9, 1988, p. A36.

Ferriss, Abbott L. 1969. *Indicators of Trends in American Education.* New York: Russell Sage Foundation.

Gorelick, Sherry. 1981. *City College and the Jewish Poor.* New Brunswick, NJ: Rutgers University Press.

Harvard University, Faculty of Arts and Sciences. 1960. *Admission to Harvard College: A Report by the Special Committee on College Admissions Policy.* Cambridge, MA: Harvard University.

Harvard University. 1982. *Office of Admissions and Financial Aids, Annual Report.* Cambridge, MA: Harvard University.

Henry, David D. 1975. *Challenges Past, Challenges Present: An Analysis of American Higher Education Since 1930.* San Francisco: Jossey-Bass.

Hodgson, Godfrey. 1978. *America In Our Time: From World War II to Nixon, What Happened and Why.* New York: Vintage.

Hofstadter, Richard. 1962. *Anti-Intellectualism in American Life.* New York: Vintage.

Jencks, Christopher, and David Riesman. 1968. *The Academic Revolution.* Garden City, N.Y.: Doubleday.

Karabel, Jerome, and Katherine E. McClelland. 1987. "Occupational Advantage and the Impact of College Rank on Labor Market Outcomes." *Sociological Inquiry* 57: 323–347.

Karen, David. 1983. "Trends in Access to Higher Education: Race, Class, and Sex." Paper presented at the annual meeting of the American Sociological Association.

———. 1985. "Who Gets Into Harvard: Selection and Exclusion at an Elite College." Unpublished Ph.D. dissertation, Harvard University. (University Microfilms International #8520225.)

———. 1988. "Higher Education Enrollments and Political Mobilization in the Twentieth Century." Unpublished paper, Bryn Mawr College, Department of Sociology.

Kluegel, James R., and Eliot R. Smith. 1986. *Beliefs About Inequality: Americans' Views About What Is and What Ought to Be.* New York: de Gruyter.

Levine, Steven B. 1980. "The Rise of American Boarding Schools and the Development of a National Upper Class." *Social Problems* 28: 63–94.

Levitan, Sar A., William B. Johnston, and Robert Taggart. 1975. *Still A Dream: The Changing Status of Blacks Since 1960.* Cambridge, MA: Harvard University Press.

McPherson, Michael S. 1978. "The Demand for Higher Education." In David W. Breneman and Chester E. Finn, Jr., *Public Policy and Private Higher Education,* pp. 143–196. Washington, DC: Brookings.

Miller, S. M. 1960. "Comparative Social Mobility." *Current Sociology* 9: 81–89.

Morris, Lorenzo. 1979. *Elusive Equality: The Status of Black Americans in Higher Education.* Washington, DC: Howard University Press.

Olson, Keith W. 1974. *The GI Bill, the Veterans, and the Colleges.* Lexington: University of Kentucky Press.

Parkin, Frank. 1979. *Marxism and Class Theory: A Bourgeois Critique,* New York: Columbia University Press.

Przeworski, Adam. 1977. "Proletariat into Class: The Process of Class Formation from Karl Kautsky's *The Class Struggle* to Recent Controversies." *Politics and Society* 7 (4): 343–401.

Stadtman, Verne A. 1980. *Academic Adaptations: Higher Education Prepares for the 1980's and 1990's.* San Francisco: Jossey-Bass, 1980.

Staples, Brent. 1986. "The Dwindling Black Presence on Campus." *New York Times Magazine,* April 27, 1986, pp. 46ff.

Starr, Paul E. 1982. *The Social Transformation of American Medicine.* New York: Basic Books.

Strauch, Karl. 1975. *Report of the Committee to Consider Aspects of the Harvard-Radcliffe Relationship That Affect Administrative Arrangements, Admissions, Financial Aids, and Educational Policy.* Cambridge, MA: Harvard University.

U.S. Bureau of the Census. 1948. *Current Population Reports,* Series P-20, No. 15, "Educational Attainment of the Civilian Population: April 1947." Washington, DC: Government Printing Office.

_____. 1975. *Historical Statistics of the United States, Colonial Times to 1970, Bicentennial Edition. Part Two.* Washington, DC: Government Printing Office.

_____. 1978. *Current Population Reports,* Series P-20, "School Enrollment—Social and Economic Characteristics of Students." Washington, DC: Government Printing Office.

_____. 1987. *Current Population Reports,* Series P-20, No. 415, "Educational Attainment in the United States: March 1982 to 1985." Washington, DC: Government Printing Office.

U.S. Department of Education, Center for Education Statistics. 1985. *The Condition of Education, 1985 Edition.* Washington, DC: Government Printing Office.

_____. 1987a. *The Condition of Education, 1987 Edition.* Washington, DC: Government Printing Office.

_____. 1987b. *Digest of Education Statistics, 1987.* Washington, DC: Government Printing Office.

U.S. Department of Health, Education, and Welfare, Office of Civil Rights. 1974. *Racial and Ethnic Enrollments in Institutions of Higher Education.* Washington, DC: Government Printing Office.

_____. 1976. *Racial and Ethnic Enrollments in Institutions of Higher Education.* Washington, DC: Government Printing Office.

U.S. Office of Education, Educational Statistics Branch, Division of Statistics and Research Services. 1960. *Opening (Fall) Enrollment In Higher Education, 1960: Institutional Data.* Circular No. 637 (OE-544003-60). Washington, DC: Government Printing Office.

Weinberg, Meyer. 1977. *A Chance to Learn: A History of Race and Education in the United States.* New York: Cambridge University Press.

The Effects of Community Colleges: Aid or Hindrance to Socioeconomic Attainment?

KEVIN DOUGHERTY

Manhattan College

In this century, the community college has emerged as one of the central elements of the U.S. higher education system.[1] Totally absent until 1900, community colleges now number nearly one thousand and enroll 36 percent of all students in higher education (National Center for Education Statistics [NCES] 1985, p. 14). Moreover, community colleges have become a central artery into higher education for working-class and minority students. Students in public two-year colleges are considerably more likely than students in four-year colleges to be nonwhite and to have parents who hold working-class jobs, make less than the median family income, and have not gone to college. For example, 41.4 percent of students in public two-year colleges have family incomes of less than $20,000, and 20.8 percent are nonwhite. The comparable percentages for students in four-year colleges are 31.0 percent and 16.6 percent, respectively (U.S. Bureau of the Census 1985, pp. 58–59; NCES 1984, p. 65).

Community-college supporters and activists have argued that these colleges serve society by providing social mobility and teaching the technical skills needed by a complex industrial economy (Cohen and Brawer 1982, p. 1; Eells 1931, p. 93; Medsker 1960, p. 4; Monroe 1972, pp. 32–37). Medsker articulates this group's functionalist view of the community college:

From *Sociology of Education* 60 (April 1987): 86–103. Copyright © 1987 by American Sociological Association. Reprinted by the permission of Kevin J. Dougherty.

I thank Steven Brint, Jerome Karabel, David Lavin, Frances Rust, Beth Stevens, and several anonymous reviewers for their comments on this paper. I also thank Carolle Thomas for her diligent research assistance. An earlier version of this paper was presented at the 1986 meetings of the American Educational Research Association, San Francisco.

[The two-year college] is perhaps the most effective democratizing agent in higher education. It decentralizes post-high school opportunities by placing them within reach of a large number of students. It makes higher education available at low cost to the student and at moderate cost to society. . . .Furthermore, the American technological economy requires many persons trained at an intermediate level—not full-fledged engineers or scientists but high-level technicians or semi-professionals. [1960, p. 4]

In the last fifteen years, however, the community college has come under intense criticism from several scholars who constitute what I call the class-reproduction school of community-college scholarship. This school argues that community colleges reproduce the class structure of our capitalist society by producing graduates trained and socialized for work in capitalist enterprises and by insuring that children inherit their parents' social-class positions (Bowles and Gintis 1976, pp. 208, 212; Karabel 1972, pp. 523–24; Nasaw 1979, p. 235; Pincus 1974, p. 18; Zwerling 1976, p. xix). Karabel states,

Hailed as the "democratizers of higher education," community colleges are, in reality, a vital component of the class-based tracking system. The modal junior college student, though aspiring to a four-year diploma upon entrance, receives neither an associate nor a bachelor's degree. The likelihood of his persisting in higher education is *negatively* influenced by attending a community college. [1972, p. 555]

This clash of perspectives has produced a vigorous, even vitriolic, debate over the merits of the community college (Vaughan 1980; Zwerling 1976). But despite its vigor, the debate has not yet been settled. There is still no agreement on the effects of community colleges, and there is very little discussion of how those effects are produced. One reason, discussed below, is that the contending parties use very different measurements of the community college's effectiveness. Moreover, most of the debaters have relied on weak, often anecdotal data to make their cases.

This paper advances the debate over the effects of community colleges in two ways. First, it critically reviews the results of several different studies of the relative impact of community colleges, four-year colleges, and other postsecondary schools on the educational and economic attainment of their entrants. This critical review leads to the conclusion that community-college entrance definitely hinders both the educational and economic attainment of students who aspire to a baccalaureate but probably aids the educational attainment of students who aspire to a vocational degree. However, we cannot determine the effects of community-college entrance on the economic success of vocationally oriented students. Second, the paper synthesizes a wide variety of research to explain why entrance into a community college hinders the educational attainment of students who aspire to a baccalaureate.[2]

RESEARCH DESIGN

The first objective—to measure the relative impact of community colleges on the educational and economic attainment of their entrants—is by no means easy. Community-college commentators have advanced quite different standards to judge the effectiveness of community colleges. The class-reproduction school gauges the success of the community college primarily by comparing the proportions of community-college entrants and four-year-college entrants who eventually secure bachelor's degree.[3] Their focus on baccalaureate attainment stems from their belief that about three fourths of community-college students aspire to a bachelor's degree (Karabel 1972, pp. 530–36; Pincus 1974, p. 21; Zwerling 1976, p. 81). The functionalist school, on the other hand, rejects the use of baccalaureate attainment as the main standard of community-college effectiveness. Instead, they measure the community college's contribution to occupational and income attainment and the degree to which it broadens access to higher education (Cohen and Brawer 1982, pp. 356–57). Their competing standard is grounded in the belief that most community-college students do not wish a baccalaureate. Cohen and Brawer (1982, p. 46), for example, argue that only 15 to 33 percent of all community-college entrants aspire to a bachelor's degree.

Neither the class-reproduction nor the functionalist school is correct in its assessment of community-college entrants' aspirations and in the standards it consequently proposes. The real number of baccalaureate aspirants lies between their two estimates. I estimate that 30 to 40 percent of all community-college entrants aspire to a baccalaureate. Another 30 to 40 percent want an associate's degree but not a baccalaureate. The remaining 20 to 30 percent seek adult or community education courses (for purposes of recreation, personal development, or remedial education). The class-reproduction school's estimate that two thirds of community-college entrants aspire to a baccalaureate is too high; as Cohen and Brawer (1982, p. 46) note, it comes from the American Council of Education-Cooperative Institutional Research Program (ACE-CIRP) freshman national norms, which ignore part-time entrants, who are numerous and have lower aspirations than full-time entrants (Sheldon 1982). On the other hand, the functionalist school's figure of 15 to 33 percent, which is based on flawed data, is too low.[4]

This paper addresses the following questions:[5]

1. How do students entering community colleges compare with students entering four-year colleges and other kinds of colleges in baccalaureates attained? How do these three kinds of entrants compare in years of education attained? The first question pertains to the one third of community-college entrants who aspire to a baccalaureate; the second pertains to all community-college entrants.

2. How do community-college entrants compare with other college entrants in the prestige and income of the jobs they enter? How do they compare in rates of unemployment? These questions are particularly pertinent to students who do not aspire to a baccalaureate.

3. What particular aspects of the community college's organization and relationship to other higher educational institutions explain the lower educational attainment of community-college entrants, particularly those aspiring to a baccalaureate?

The first two sets of questions will be answered by examining several different quantitative studies of student outcomes. These studies analyze a variety of surveys, including the National Longitudinal Survey of the High School Class of 1972 (NLS-72), the National Longitudinal Survey of Labor Market Experience (NLSLME), the ACE-CIRP annual survey of college freshmen, and several more specialized surveys. These studies were chosen because they are the most recent and the most methodologically rigorous studies available. In particular, they allow us to compare the attainments of community-college entrants and other college entrants and to control for key differences in prematriculation characteristics, most notably, family background, high school academic record, and educational and occupational aspirations. In addition, these studies use longer follow-up periods than other broadly based studies of student outcomes. One follows up its respondents ten years after college entrance, another nine years, and two others seven years.

To answer the third question, I sort the obstacles that community-college entrance puts to educational attainment into three main processes that fit together in a funnel-like structure: attrition within the community college, difficulty transferring to four-year colleges, and attrition after transfer. I then marshall findings from a wide variety of quantitative and qualitative studies to illuminate how these three processes operate. These studies range from the nationwide surveys used to answer the first two questions to quantitative studies of state community-college systems and ethnographic studies of individual community colleges.

THE EVIDENCE ON COMMUNITY-COLLEGE EFFECTS

Educational Attainment

There are several careful quantitative studies describing the impact on educational attainment of entering a community college rather than a four-year college or postsecondary vocational school. Despite differences in sampling, follow-up periods, and analytic methods, these studies arrive at the same findings. Baccalaureate aspirants who enter community colleges attain significantly fewer bachelor's degrees and years of education than similar students who enter four-year colleges. However, vocational aspirants seem to do better if they enter a community college rather than a four-year college or postsecondary vocational school. . . .

Using the NLS-72,[6] Velez (1985) examined students who entered the *academic* programs of community colleges and four-year colleges in fall 1972 and who were followed up in fall 1979.[7] He found that seven years after college entrance, 79 percent of the students who had entered an academic program in a four-year college, but only 31 percent of the students who had entered an academic program in a two-year college, received a bachelor's degree—a difference of 48 percent (p. 197).[8] And the *net* difference (i.e., that remaining after controlling for the prematriculation differences in student composition) is still large—18.7 percent (p. 199). . . .Using the same sample, follow-up period, and controls, Anderson (1984) found that students who entered community colleges lagged behind students who entered state four-year colleges by 13.4 percent in bachelor's degrees attained (pp. 33–34).[9]

The finding that community-college entrants are considerably less likely to receive a bachelor's degree than similar four-year-college entrants is not restricted to studies using the NLS-72. Alba and Lavin (1981) also found a significant net difference among 1970 baccalaureate aspirants entering the community colleges and four-year colleges of the City University of New York who were followed up in 1975. Although the CUNY community colleges promote the pursuit of a baccalaureate more than most, Alba and Lavin still found that the senior-college entrants received 11.2 percent more bachelor's degrees than the community-college entrants, even net of differences in prematriculation characteristics. Astin (1982, pp. 98–100) examined a nation-wide sample of 1971 full-time college entrants aspiring to at least a bachelor's degree and found that by 1980, the community-college entrants were uniformly less likely to have baccalaureates than the four-year-college entrants, even net of entering student characteristics. For example, for whites, the partial correlation between the percentage attaining a bachelor's degree and community-college entrance was -0.14; but the partial correlation between the percentage attaining a bachelor's degree and entrance to different types of four-year colleges was between -0.04 and 0.15. The pattern was similar for blacks, Chicanos, and Indians but not for Puerto Ricans.

Anderson (1984) examined years of education attained and found that students who entered academic programs in community colleges attained 0.25 year less schooling than similar students who entered academic programs in four-year state colleges (pp. 33–34). Breneman and Nelson (1981) report a similar difference in a study not restricted to baccalaureate aspirants. They found that four years after college entrance, community-college entrants had attained 0.3 year less schooling than four-year-college entrants (and 11.3 percent fewer baccalaureates), net of differences in pre-enrollment characteristics (pp. 82–83).

Baccalaureate aspirants clearly fare better if they enter a four-year college, but this may not be true of college entrants with lower aspirations. Breneman and Nelson (p. 90) estimate that 44 percent of community-college entrants (and 20 percent of four-year-college entrants) attain more education if they enter a community college rather than a four-year college. These students are more likely to be nonacademically oriented, nonwhite, and of low socioeconomic status than students who benefit more from entering a four-year college.[10] This finding is reinforced by another analysis of the NLS-72, which shows that fall 1972 college entrants who aspired to *less* than a bachelor's degree were less likely to have dropped out of higher education by fall 1974 if they had entered a two-year college rather than a four-year college (NCES 1977*b*, pp. 71, 74).

Somers, Sharpe, and Myint (1971) reached a similar conclusion when they compared the impact on vocational students of entering a community college with the impact of entering a postsecondary vocational-technical school. In a nationwide 1969 follow-up of 1966 graduates of vocational programs, they found that community-college vocational graduates were more likely to pursue education after graduation than postsecondary vocational-school graduates, even after controlling for pre-enrollment differences (Somers et al. 1971, pp. 168–75).

In sum, baccalaureate aspirants who enter community colleges attain fewer bachelor's degrees and less years of education than students who enter four-year colleges. However, students who aspire to a vocational degree seem to do better (though the evidence is weak) if they enter a community college rather than a four-year college or postsecondary vocational school.

Economic Attainment

Several different kinds of studies allow us to measure the relative economic benefit of entering a community college: studies comparing the economic attainments of community-college entrants and four-year-college entrants, studies comparing community-college vocational students and students entering postsecondary vocational-technical schools, and studies comparing graduates and dropouts of community-college vocational-education programs. . . . They lead to the conclusion that among students who aspire to a baccalaureate, those entering community colleges fare less well economically than those entering four-year colleges. However, we do not know if this finding holds for students who do not aspire to a baccalaureate, particularly older students. Moreover, we cannot determine whether community-college education is superior to postsecondary vocational-technical education or to no postsecondary education at all.

Anderson (1984), Monk-Turner (1983), and Breneman and Nelson (1981) exemplify the first type of study. They compared community-college entrants with four-year-college entrants and found statistically significant differences in occupational attainment but no clear difference in earnings, net of differences in pre-enrollment characteristics. . . . This finding clearly holds for baccalaureate aspirants; Anderson's sample was restricted to academic-program entrants, most of whom were baccalaureate aspirants, and her findings were replicated by Breneman and Nelson and by Monk-Turner.

Anderson found that among NLS-72 fall 1972 entrants to two-year and four-year *academic programs* followed up in 1979, those who had entered community colleges secured jobs that were 2.4 points lower on the Duncan index but that paid 5 cents more an hour than the jobs secured by those who had entered four-year colleges (p. 36).[11] Monk-Turner, however, found a net difference of 3.5 points on the Duncan index in favor of four-year-college entrants among NLSLME respondents who were working full time ten years after high school graduation (pp. 395, 401).[12] Finally, Breneman and Nelson found that among NLS-72 men employed full time in October 1976, those who had entered community colleges secured jobs that were significantly lower in status, but essentially the same in income, than the jobs secured by those who had entered four-year colleges. However, they argue that this parity in income is likely to break down in the long run because of the significant advantage four-year-college entrants have in occupational attainment, which is strongly correlated with income.

The second group of studies—comparisons between community-college vocational students and similar students in postsecondary vocational-technical schools—partially address the limitations of the studies above. They examine vocationally oriented students, they are not restricted to recent high school graduates, and they look at postsecondary vocational-technical schools as well as community colleges, although they ignore four-year colleges. In February 1976, Wilms (1980) followed up several thousand students who had entered 21 community colleges and 29 proprietary vocational schools in four major cities in fall 1973. He found that the proprietary-school attenders had significantly higher beginning weekly salaries than the community-college attenders, even when he controlled for various pre- and postmatriculation differences (pp. 117–118). However, Somers et al. (1971), in a 1969 nationwide survey of 1966 graduates of vocational-education programs in community colleges and postsecondary vocational-technical schools, found that graduates of community-college vocational-education programs secured more prestigious and remunerative jobs and suffered less unemployment than graduates of postsecondary vocational-technical schools, net of differences in various student characteristics. Unfortunately, the contradiction between the two studies cannot be resolved, since neither study has a clear edge in methodological rigor. Though Wilms did not control for occupation prepared for, he did follow up nongraduates as well as graduates of vocational programs; Somers et al. did not.

Pincus (1980) exemplifies the last kind of study—comparisons between graduates and dropouts of community-college vocational-education programs. After reviewing reports by community-college agencies in several different states, he concluded that the vocational graduates were more often employed than the nongraduates, but they fared no better and perhaps worse in income (pp. 350–53). The ultimate meaning of this finding is in question, however. As Pincus noted, it would have been preferable to control for differences in background and academic performance between graduates and nongraduates, but the data that would have allowed this were unavailable.

In sum, among students who aspire to a baccalaureate, students who enter community colleges fare less well economically than comparable students who enter four-year colleges. However, we do not know if this finding holds for students who do not aspire to a baccalaureate, particularly older students. Also, because the evidence is contradictory or of poor quality, we also do not know whether community-college education is superior to postsecondary vocational-technical education or to no postsecondary education in economic benefits for students who do not aspire to a baccalaureate.

Summary

The evidence on the effectiveness of community colleges provides support for both supporters and critics of the community college. But on balance, the evidence lies more on the side of the critics.

The evidence supports the class-reproduction theory that community colleges are inferior to four-year colleges in facilitating both the educational and the economic attainment of students who aspire to a baccalaureate.

But the functionalist supporters of the community college are partially vindicated: Community colleges do seem to be more effective than both four-year colleges and postsecondary vocational-technical schools in facilitating the educational attainment of students who do not aspire to a baccalaureate. However, the evidence on the relative effectiveness of community colleges promoting the economic success of these students is contradictory and quite sparse.

CAUSES OF COMMUNITY-COLLEGE EFFECTS

In this section, I develop a model to explain why community-college entrance interferes with baccalaureate aspirants' educational attainment. I focus on educational attainment because it is an important outcome in its own right and because it constitutes the principal medium through which community colleges affect their entrants' economic success. Breneman and Nelson (1981, pp. 84–85) found that when years of education attained are controlled, the direct effect of community-college entrance on occupational status falls to insignificance and the direct effect of community-college entrance on income drops sharply.

Many different factors explain why community-college entrance hinders the educational attainment of students. The interrelationships among these factors constitute three main processes:

1. In the first two years of college, institutional factors produce a higher dropout rate among community-college entrants than among comparable four-year-college entrants. The key institutional factors underlying this process are community colleges' low academic selectivity and lack of dormitories.

2. Among students who survive the first two years of college, community-college entrants encounter greater institutional obstacles to continuation into the upper division of four-year colleges than comparable four-year-college entrants. The key factors here are community colleges' strong vocational orientation, the distaste of four-year colleges for community-college transfers, the scarcity of financial aid for community-college transfers, and the simple fact that movement to the upper division requires movement to a new and unfamiliar school.

3. Among students who do enter the upper division of four-year colleges, community-college entrants encounter greater institutional hindrances to continuation in the upper division of four-year colleges than com-

parable four-year-college entrants. These factors include frequent loss of credits, difficulty securing financial aid, difficulty becoming socially integrated into the four-year college, and poorer preparation for upper-division work and consequent difficulty becoming academically integrated into the four-year college.

These three processes are articulated in a funnel-like structure that operates like the tournament mobility system conceived by Rosenbaum (1976). In such a system, which is a variant of the contest mobility system described by Turner (1960), students go through a series of tests. If they survive one test, they pass on to the next: if they fail at any point, they drop out of the contest.

Attrition in the Freshman and Sophomore Years

Of the students in the NLS-72 who entered college in fall 1972, 39.3 percent of those who entered two-year colleges dropped out of higher education by fall 1974. The dropout rate for students who entered four-year colleges was 23.5 percent. By fall 1974, then, 15.8 percent more two-year-college entrants than four-year-college entrants had dropped out of higher education (NCES 1977b, pp. 135–36).[13]

Unfortunately, the NCES did not estimate the net difference in dropout rates—controlling for differences in pre-enrollment characteristics—between two-year-college and four-year-college entrants. However, Astin (1972), using a national sample of 1966 college entrants, estimated equations to predict separately the dropout rates by 1970 of two-year-college and four-year-college entrants. He found that when the two-year-college equation was applied to four-year-college entrants, it *overestimated* the dropout rate at 151 of 194 four-year colleges. Conversely, the four-year-college equation *underestimated* the dropout rate at 14 of 23 two-year colleges (pp. 10, 47–48).[14]

But how do community colleges contribute to their entrants' higher dropout rate? Research on this question is still rather primitive; almost all research on dropouts has focused on four-year-college dropouts (Tinto 1975; Pantages and Creedon 1978). But two factors stand out: the community colleges' lack of residential facilities and their lower academic selectivity and prestige.

A number of scholars have pointed to community colleges' lack of residential facilities as an important *institutional* cause of higher dropout rates (Anderson 1981, p. 12; Astin 1977a, pp. 109, 217, 1977b, pp. 91–92, 165–68; Karabel 1972, pp. 533n; Velez 1985, pp. 196–97). Community colleges virtually never maintain dormitories; most four-year colleges do.[15] On-campus residence powerfully contributes to student persistence. It promotes student success in college by fostering contact with faculty and other students, participation in extracurricular activities, and satisfaction with campus life. At the same time, on-campus residence weakens the influences of the home and neighborhood, which create obligations and allegiances that divert time and energy from school work (Astin 1977a, Tinto 1975, pp. 107, 109–10; Velez 1985, pp. 198–199).

Community colleges also adversely affect their entrants' persistence rates by being less selective academically and less prestigious. Several studies have found that academic selectivity has a significant positive impact on persistence, independent of other college characteristics and student characteristics (Anderson 1984, pp. 33, 36; Astin 1982, pp. 101–102; Tinto 1975, pp. 114–15). The community college's low academic selectivity impinges on its students' academic achievement, and thus dropout rates, in two ways.

Because community colleges are less selective, community-college entrants more often find themselves surrounded by peers who are not interested in or good at academic work and who discourage those who are. This anti-academic student culture is rooted in the fundamental ambivalence of working-class and minority students toward education. Most of these students want to do well, but they are also afraid of failing. Furthermore, they believe academic success requires them to take on the culture of an alien group and to repudiate (and be repudiated by) their family and peers. Hence, working-class and minority students develop powerful norms against academic success (London 1978, chaps. 3–4; Neumann and Riesman 1980, p. 58; Weis 1985, pp. 102, 122, 134–37, 153–54).[16]

At the same time, community-college entrants seem to receive less academic support from their teachers than four-year-college entrants (London 1978, chaps. 2, 5; Neumann and Riesman 1980, p. 61; Weis 1985, pp. 84, 89–90, 93). On the whole, community-college teachers seem to have lower expectations of their students. They perceive their students as less academically able and motivated, so they concentrate on reaching a few and largely ignore the rest. This process sets up a vicious circle; students and faculty each find that their prejudices toward the other are powerfully confirmed. Community-college teachers' diminished expectations of their students reflect the difficulty of teaching students who arrive at college bereft of many of the skills that colleges traditionally expect and that make teaching go smoothly. They also reflect the unhappiness of community-college teachers, particularly those in the liberal arts, who find themselves in low-status colleges teaching nontraditional students. Moreover, many community-college teachers often differ greatly in background from their working-class and minority students; thus, they find it hard to appreciate their students' world views, motivations, and real strengths.

Problems in Transferring to Four-Year Colleges

Even when community-college entrants do persist in college, they move on to the upper division of four-year colleges at a lower rate than four-year-college entrants.[17] For example, 24.4 percent of students who entered two-year colleges in fall 1972 transferred to four-year colleges by fall 1974.[18] Meanwhile, 76.4 percent of students who entered four-year colleges were still enrolled in four-year colleges in fall 1974 (NCES 1977a, pp. 6–9, 72–74, 1977b, pp. 22–26, 191–92). These differences stand up even when pre-existing student characteristics and differential attrition are controlled. For example, NLS-72 data indicate that 49.3 percent of two-year-college entrants who aspired to a baccalaureate *and* who survived the first two years of college transferred to a four-year college by their third year. Meanwhile, 96.2 percent of similar four-year-college entrants were still in four-year schools in their third year (NCES 1977a, pp. 8–13, 1977b, pp. 50–51, 135–36).[19]

Attending a community college hinders students' transfer to four-year schools in two ways. Many students lose their desire to transfer. And students who still wish to transfer find it difficult to do so.

Students lose their desire to transfer for various reasons. Transfer involves a difficult readjustment. Community-college entrants have to move to a new school, perhaps in a different community, where they might stay only two or three years. Four-year-college entrants find no such chasm lying between their sophomore and junior years. Hence, they need less encouragement from their college teachers and counselors to continue into the junior year.

Moreover, community colleges fail to provide adequate support for transfer. Community colleges are less interested today in their transfer programs than in their vocational programs. This vocational orientation has created lower transfer rates. The California state community college board found that vocationally oriented community colleges have significantly lower transfer rates to the University of California than more transfer-oriented community colleges, even net of differences between community colleges in student-body composition (race and grades) and proximity to the university (California Community Colleges 1984, pp. 17–19). Similarly, Anderson (1984, pp. 33–34) found that—net of differences in student-body characteristics, academic selectivity, etc.—NLS-72 college entrants were significantly less likely to receive a bachelor's degree if they entered vocationally oriented two-year or four-year colleges.

Community-college vocational-education programs weaken their students' desire to transfer because their goal is to move their students directly into the labor market. The teachers in these programs are often recruited from the trades for which they train students and have relatively little interest in and knowledge about how students can be aided in transferring to four-year colleges.

Of course, many community-college entrants enroll in vocational programs because this is their original desire. But many become vocational students because the community college shunts them in this direction. Community colleges exert a vocationalizing influence through several channels. They spread before students a vast array of attractively packaged vocational programs. They give vocational-education programs new and attractive facilities and blur the distinction between academic and vocational-education programs. They proclaim that vocational-education graduates do as well as baccalaureates. Finally, community colleges develop elaborate counseling programs to reconcile their supply of and students' demand for vocational education (Dougherty 1988b, Brint and Karabel forthcoming; Clark 1960).

But even if community-college entrants retain a desire to transfer, they encounter problems in being admitted to four-year colleges and in securing financial aid. Community colleges do not control an upper division to which they can pass on students as they wish. Rather, they depend on four-year colleges to accept students. And there is evidence that four-year colleges are less willing to take in community-college transfers than to pass on their own native students. Willingham and Findikyan (1969, pp. 5–6) found that among a varied sample of 146 four-year colleges, 27 percent of all students wishing to transfer from two-year colleges and 62 percent of vocational students were rejected. Many of these transfer applicants are rejected because of academic deficiencies. Still, there is evidence that four-year colleges have a definite distaste for community-college transfer applicants, particularly those from vocational programs. Willingham and Findikyan (1969, p. 25) found that among the 146 four-year colleges they surveyed, only 26 percent encouraged transfers in their publications, only 17 percent prepared special material for transfers, and only 27 percent visited junior colleges (Willingham and Findikyan 1969, pp. 5–6).[20]

Community colleges also have little control over whether transfer applicants will receive financial aid, and many applicants do not. The NLS-72 found that students who transferred from two-year colleges received fewer scholarships and other grants than students who initially entered four-year colleges (19.3 percent versus 38.9 percent), although they received as many loans (22.1 percent versus 23.8 percent).[21] A study of accepted transfer applicants to the University of California who did not matriculate (19 percent of those accepted) found that a major reason was finances (Baratta and Apodaca 1984, p. 6).

Attrition After Transfer

Even after transferring to four-year colleges, community-college entrants are still at greater risk of dropping out because of factors that are tied to the community college. Community-college transfers to four-year colleges are significantly more likely than comparable four-year-college natives to drop out of four-year college. . . . Several studies—some national and some state-specific—have found that three to five years after transferring, about a third of all transfers have dropped out. After a few more years, even more are felled. By comparison, four-year-college natives in California and New York who are also entering the junior year have a considerably lower dropout rate.

How much of this difference in dropout rates is due to institutional factors rooted in the awkward coupling of four-year and two-year colleges and how much is due to the lower ability and lack of motivation of two-year-college transfers? (NCES 1977a, pp. 32, 75). Unfortunately, there are no studies comparing the educational attainments of community-college transfers and four-year-college natives net of differences in their pre-college characteristics and experiences.

In any case, there is evidence that four institutional factors do contribute significantly to transfer students' greater dropout rate: credit loss, difficulty getting financial aid, lack of social integration into the four-year college, and sharp drops in grades. First, a fair number of transfer students lose credits in transit to four-year colleges. This credit loss harms transfer students' educational attainment by slowing them down and making them vulnerable to competing demands and attractions. A study of transfers from Maryland community colleges found that 6 percent lost 13 or more credit hours, i.e., at least one semester (Maryland State Board for Community Colleges 1983, p. 12). Several national studies conducted during the 1960s discovered that 10 to 12 percent of two-year-college transfers lost at least a semester's worth of credits (Godfrey and Holmstrom 1970, p. 167; Knoell and Medsker 1965, p. 61; Willingham and Findikyan 1969, p. 30). Several factors cause credit loss. Most four-year colleges refuse to give more than two years' credit. They also routinely disallow credit for community-college courses that have no equivalent in their own curriculum or that are upper-division courses in their eyes. And four-year colleges often give no credit or only partial credit for community-college courses in which the student received a D, although four-year-college natives usually receive credit for D's (Kintzer and Wattenbarger 1985, chap. 2; Knoell and Medsker 1965, p. 61; Maryland State Board for Community Colleges 1983, p. 12; Winandy and McGrath 1970, pp. 189–90).

Transfer students also have difficulty getting financial aid. As noted above, they receive financial aid less often than four-year natives. This lack of financial aid increases the chances that transfer students will withdraw or flunk out. Transfer students who drop out of college usually give lack of money as their main reason (Knoell and Medsker 1965, p. 71). Lack of financial aid causes students to drop out because it forces them to take jobs, which interfere with their social and academic integration into the four-year institution.

Third, transfer students find it difficult to become socially integrated into the four-year institutions they have entered; thus, their grades, commitment to college, and ultimately, persistence suffer (Astin 1977b, pp. 154, 168; Knoell and Medsker 1965, p. 68). For example, among Los Angeles community-college transfers to UCLA, those who dropped out were significantly more likely to have most of their friends outside UCLA (Kissler, Lara, and Cardinal 1981, pp. 9–10). Among the reasons that transfers find it harder than natives to integrate themselves socially are their greater need to work to support themselves, the greater pressure they are under to get good grades so that they can validate their admission, the lack of orientation programs directed specifically to transfer students, and the fact that clubs and other extracurricular activities at four-year colleges usually focus their recruitment of new members on freshmen.

Finally, transfer students find it hard to perform well academically at four-year colleges. Studies repeatedly find that they tend to suffer rather sharp drops in their grades in the first year after transfer (Cohen and Brawer 1982, pp. 349–50; Hills 1965; Kintzer and Wattenbarger 1985; Knoell and Medsker 1965, pp. 27–28). For example, the median GPA of fall 1982 community-college transfers to the University of California and California State University systems dropped one-half point at UC and one-third point at CSU on a five-point scale (California Community Colleges 1984, pp. 26, 30, F-2). Similarly, fall 1979 Illinois community-college transfers to Illinois public and private universities suffered an average drop of about one-third grade point between their community-college GPA and their first-year university

GPA (Illinois Community College Board 1984, p. 11).[22] In turn, bad grades are significantly associated with greater attrition. Among Los Angeles community-college transfers to UCLA, those who dropped out had significantly lower grades at UCLA than those who continued (Kissler et al. 1981, pp. 9–10). Transfer students' grade drop leads to attrition quite directly when students are simply dismissed or put on academic probation. Additionally, poor grades lead many to voluntarily withdraw.

Clearly, a good part of the grade shock that community-college students encounter stems from the disparity between their abilities and the tougher standards of the four-year colleges. But it also stems from institutional factors, particularly, less access to financial aid and poorer academic preparation in the community college. As discussed in the previous section, transfer students are less likely to receive financial aid than four-year-college natives. And this disability significantly and independently depresses their upper division grades and persistence rates. A study of fall 1977 transfers from Los Angeles community colleges to UCLA found that the students' grades at UCLA were significantly and negatively associated with their amount of unmet financial need, even when their community-college GPAs and quality of preparation were controlled (Kissler et al. 1981, pp. 6–8). Moreover, community-college transfers get poorer grades than four-year-college natives because their lower-division preparation, on the average, is inferior (Aulston 1974, pp. 116–118; Kissler et al. 1981, pp. 6–8; Knoell and Medsker 1965, pp. 60, 98). For example, the fall 1977 transfers to UCLA received much less writing instruction in the lower division than the UCLA natives. Two thirds of the transfers said that at UCLA they frequently had to write papers integrating ideas from various parts of a course, but only one third said they had done this frequently at the community college. The transfers' lack of writing experience had a significant and independent effect on their upper-division grades and persistence rates, even when their demographic characteristics, community-college grades, community-college courses, and study habits were controlled (Lara 1981, pp. 2, 8–9).

SUMMARY AND CONCLUSIONS

This paper has a two-fold task: to determine the effects of community colleges on educational and economic attainment and to determine how the community college produces those effects. The first section of this paper critically reviews the findings of a wide range of studies that compare the impacts of community colleges and other kinds of postsecondary institutions on their entrants' educational attainment and economic success. It concludes that the critics from the class-reproduction school somewhat more accurately characterize the community colleges' effects than do the supporters of the functionalist school.[23] Community colleges are significantly less able than four-year colleges to facilitate the educational and economic attainment of the approximately 30 to 40 percent of community-college entrants seeking bachelor's degrees. Generally, baccalaureate aspirants entering community colleges secure significantly fewer bachelor's degrees, fewer years of education, less prestigious jobs, and in the long run, poorer paying jobs than comparable students entering four-year colleges. On the other hand, community colleges may be superior—but here the data are much weaker—to four-year colleges for the 30 to 40 percent of community-college entrants who seek a subbaccalaureate degree. Vocational-education aspirants seem to attain more years of education if they enter a community college rather than a four-year college or postsecondary vocational school. However, the data are too sparse and contradictory to be conclusive on which type of institution best promotes the *economic* success of students who do not aspire to a baccalaureate.

The second section of the paper develops a model to explain why entrance into a community college hinders the educational attainment of baccalaureate aspirants. This model states that the factors hindering community-college entrants' educational attainment constitute three main processes that are linked in a funnel-like structure: attrition in the community college, difficulty transferring to four-year colleges, and attrition after transfer. Within each process, several mechanisms are at work. The greater attrition in the community college is significantly and independently associated with the community colleges' low academic selectivity and prestige and lack of dormitories. Second, community-college entrants find it difficult to transfer because their desire to transfer is weakened by the community college's vocational emphasis and the need to enter a new college. Moreover, even if their desire to transfer remains strong, they are less able to secure acceptance and financial aid from four-year colleges. Finally, attrition after transfer is precipitated by the sharp drop in grades that many students suffer, lack of financial aid, difficulty becoming socially integrated into the new school, and frequent loss of credits.

My conclusions are based on the convergence of a wide variety of studies. Still, there is a considerable need for further research on the extent and nature of the effects of community colleges. Such research is urgently needed because of the central role community colleges play in our higher education system and therefore in our system of social stratification.

We particularly need research oriented to three main tasks. The first task is to refine our estimates of the magnitude of community-college effects in several different areas. To begin, it would be useful to determine the transfer rates of community-college entrants and the continuation rates of four-year-college entrants net of differences in family background, educational aspirations, academic ability, and several other variables. In such a study, it would be illuminating to determine the number of community-college students, particularly vocational majors, who initially plan to transfer to a four-year school but either fail to apply or apply but fail to go on.

Another area in which refined estimates are needed involves attrition in the upper division. We need a systematic comparison of the upper-division attrition rates of four-year-college natives, community-college transfers, and transfers from other types of institutions net of precollege and lower-division characteristics.

Third, we need to move beyond the two-way comparison of community colleges with four-year colleges and examine the effects of community colleges relative to both four-year colleges and public and private postsecondary vocational-technical schools. It would be especially illuminating to compare the effects of community colleges with the effects of other types of colleges that share varying combinations of the characteristics typical of community colleges: low tuition, accessibility, unselectiveness, and vocational emphasis. Through such a study, we can more precisely determine the relative impact of the community college and the particular characteristics—which may not be peculiar to the community college—that contribute to that impact.

The second main task is to contextualize these effects by examining how they interact with variations in student characteristics. We need to carefully explore how community-college effects shift in magnitude and direction as students vary in social class, sex, race, educational aspirations, type of program, and age. As we have seen, there is intriguing, although somewhat weak, evidence that community-college effects differ greatly by students' aspirations. Two interactions of community-college effects with age are particulary worth exploring. One concerns the effect of community colleges on students entering college many years after high school. All the major studies on community-college effects focus on college students who are just out of high school. But this is problematic in the case of community colleges; only about half of community-college students enter within a year or two of high school graduation (U.S. Bureau of the Census 1985, p. 54).[24] The second interaction involving age concerns time elapsed since leaving college. We need to examine whether follow-up periods longer than the seven to ten years that now dominate in studies of community-college effects yield different results.[25]

The third task is to test the relative importance of the various components of the model of community-college effects developed in the second section of this paper. That model was constructed by piecing together findings from various narrow-gauged studies. This procedure, which was dictated by the current state of research, does not allow us to determine what mechanisms are particularly lethal to the academic and economic life chances of community-college entrants. Hence, we need studies that examine the simultaneous impact of many, if not all, of the factors identified above.

NOTES

1. The term *community college* is used here to denote public two-year institutions that offer both academic and vocational education. Community colleges make up the bulk of two-year colleges in both number and enrollment.
2. The purposes and causes (i.e., the motives and actors) behind the expansion of the community college are addressed in Dougherty (1988a, 1988b).
3. However, members of the class-reproduction school have recently begun to consider the economic returns to a community-college education. See Pincus (1980, 1986) and Karabel (1986).

4. There are no national figures on the distribution of aspirations among community-college entrants. The figures presented here are estimated from studies of the aspirations of community-college entrants in California, Maryland, and Virginia (Adams and Roesler 1977, p. 15; Beaver and Kruckenburg 1985, pp. 66–70; McConochie 1983, p. 10; Sheldon 1982, pp. 1–34). My estimate is higher than Cohen and Brawer's (1982) principally because they mistakenly based their estimate in part on a Washington study that measures the aspirations of community-college students enrolled at all levels, rather than the aspirations of community-college *entrants* alone (Meier 1979).

5. Because of the lack of current data, I was unable to consider two additional standards. One was the effect of relative availability of various types of college on college-entrance rates for different localities and kinds of students. Unfortunately, the studies on this subject are few and, given the enormous growth of community colleges in the last twenty years, out of date (Medsker and Trent 1964; Tinto 1973, 1974). The other standard that could not be applied was success in adult and community education. The issue of how one defines success in this area has been given little attention, and in any case, the main surveys of student outcomes ignore adult students.

6. The NLS-72 questioned over 20,000 spring 1972 high school seniors nationwide and followed them up in fall 1973, 1974, 1976, and 1979.

7. Velez (1985) and Anderson (1984) sampled only community-college entrants who enrolled in academic programs and excluded those who enrolled in vocational and other programs. In essence, they concentrated on the community-college and four-year-college students most likely to pursue a baccalaureate.

8. Velez's data are from two-year colleges generally rather than just community colleges. That is, he included data from private junior colleges and two-year branches of state universities. However, community colleges enroll the vast majority of two-year-college students, so the data should apply with little distortion to community colleges in particular.

9. Unfortunately, Anderson compared community-college entrants with entrants to six different kinds of institutions: public and private two-year colleges, four-year colleges, and universities. I compare community colleges to state four-year colleges because public four-year nondoctoral-level colleges enroll 22.5 percent of all students in higher education, more than public universities (19.3 percent) and all private institutions (22.3 percent) (NCES 1985, p. 8).

10. Breneman and Nelson obtained this figure by estimating separate regression equations for the educational attainment of four-year-college entrants and the attainment of public two-year-college entrants. They then applied the coefficients from each regression equation to the values for each student and determined which students would benefit more from the application of the regression weights for the community-college equation than from the application of the weights for the four-year-college equation.

11. Anderson's figures might underestimate the real success of four-year-college entrants, however. She included in her sample respondents still in school, as long as they had some job. Since four-year-college entrants are more often still in school and working part-time seven years after first entering college, her analysis tends to deflate their occupational prestige and income.

12. Monk-Turner undoubtedly underestimated the real impact of college type on occupational attainment because she controlled for educational attainment and type of college entered at the same time. Breneman and Nelson (1981, pp. 84–85) found that much of the effect of college type on economic attainment is mediated by years of education attained.

13. Not surprisingly, community-college attrition rates are higher for the socioeconomically and academically disadvantaged. Nonwhite students of low socioeconomic status with poor high school records have higher community-college attrition rates than students with the obverse characteristics (Astin 1972; NCES 1977b, pp. 22, 135–36, 150).

14. For two-year-college and four-year-college entrants separately, Astin (1972, pp. 10, 47–48) regressed students' continuation into the second year of college on a host of characteristics, including sex, race, socioeconomic status, high school test scores and grades, and respondents' and parents' educational aspirations at the beginning of college.

15. Anderson (1981, p. 14) found that 59 percent of the four-year-college entrants in the NLS-72 lived on campus.

16. For generalizations of this point to education as a whole, see Apple (1982), Giroux (1981), and Willis (1977).

17. The transfer rates reported above are based on a two-year follow-up of students who entered college directly out of high school. Unfortunately, transfer rates based on the NLS-72 seven-year (1979) follow-up have not been reported. And other data on transfer rates are much poorer. Cohen, Brawer, and Bensimon (1985, p. 3) estimated, with no clear evidence, that 13 to 15 percent of all community-college entrants eventually go on to four-year schools. Very few states publish data on the proportion of an entering cohort that eventually transfers. Those studies that do report such data report quite different transfer rates: e.g., 9.5 percent in California in a three-year follow-up of all entrants and 24.3 percent in Maryland in a four-year follow-up of degree-credit entrants (Sheldon 1982; McConochie 1983, pp. 18–19).

18. As with attrition rates, transfer rates for community-college entrants vary systematically by the major demographic variables. White male community-college entrants of high socioeconomic status with good high school records have higher transfer rates than students with the obverse characteristics (Holmstrom and Bisconti 1974, pp. 71–86; NCES 1977a pp. 28, 32, 70–73; Van Alstyne et al. 1973, pp. 1–5).

19. Even if the 38.3 percent of two-year-college entrants who aspired to a baccalaureate and who were still enrolled in two-year colleges in fall 1974 did eventually transfer—which is quite unlikely—the community-college transfer rate would total only 87.6 percent, well below the 96.2 percent continuation rate for four-year-college entrants who aspired to a baccalaureate and who survived the first two years of college (NCES 1977b, pp. 191–92).

20. During the 1970s, four-year colleges' distaste for community-college transfers seemingly weakened as higher education enrollments hit a plateau and state governments moved to ease transfer from the community colleges to state universities (Kintzer and Wattenbarger 1985, pp. 36–38). However, we have no firm data on the extent of this reorientation of sentiment.

21. The gap is probably smaller today, since transfer students are more numerous and colleges compete vigorously for students. Yet, there is still no federal program specifically for transfer students, and many states have taken little initiative in this area. Again, more research is needed.

22. It is often claimed that transfers' upper-division grades soon recover from "transfer shock." However, this claim is based on a comparison of the mean GPA of students who are two or three years past transfer with the GPA of students who transferred within the previous year. This cross-sectional approximation of a longitudinal analysis does not correct for the fact that the older transfer students no longer include the many transfer students who did badly the first year and dropped out.

23. This does not mean that the class reproductionists' assessment of the *motives* behind this effect is also correct. The desire to hinder students' mobility played a very small role in the rise of the community college (Dougherty 1988a, 1988b).

24. This restriction of survey data to younger entrants may not greatly bias the estimates for baccalaureate aspirants, since older community-college entrants are largely uninterested in pursuing a baccalaureate (Sheldon 1982). On the other hand, the restriction in age may affect the estimates for economic attainment to a significant, but unknown, degree.

25. In fact, studies with different follow-up periods may well find different effects, but they will probably be in the same direction as those found so far. For example, for CUNY, Lavin et al. (1986) found that fourteen years after college entrance, 62.4 percent of four-year-college entrants, but only 27.6 percent of community-college entrants, had attained bachelor's degrees. Thus, the gap at CUNY increased from 18 percent after five years to 25 percent after fourteen years. Similarly, studies using longer follow-up periods may find even greater differences in economic attainment because they will not have to exclude, as shorter-range studies do, large numbers of four-year-college entrants who are still in college, attending professional and graduate schools.

REFERENCES

Adams, June J., and Elmo Roesler, 1977. *A Profile of First-Time Students at Virginia Community Colleges, 1975–76.* Richmond: Virginia Community College System. (ERIC No. ED 153 694)

Alba, Richard, and David Lavin. 1981. "Community Colleges and Tracking in Higher Education." *Sociology of Education* 54:223–47.

Anderson, Kristine. 1981. "Post-High School Experiences and College Attrition." *Sociology of Education* 54:1–15.

———. 1984. *Institutional Differences in College Effects*. Boca Raton: Florida Atlantic University. (ERIC No. ED 256 204)

Apple, Michael. 1982. *Education and Power*. New York: Routledge and Kegan Paul.

Astin, Alexander. 1972. *College Dropouts: A National Study*. Report No. 7(1). Washington, DC: American Council on Education.

———. 1977a. *Four Critical Years*. San Francisco: Jossey-Bass.

———. 1977b. *Preventing Students from Dropping Out*. San Francisco: Jossey-Bass.

———. 1982 *Minorities in American Higher Education*. San Francisco: Jossey-Bass.

Aulston, M.D. 1974. "Black Transfer Students in White Colleges." *NASPA Journal* 12:116–23.

Baratta, Frank, and Ed Apodaca. 1984. *A Profile of California Community College Transfer Students at the University of California*. Berkeley: University of California. (ERIC No. ED 260 754)

Beaver, Evelyn, and Joanne Kruchenburg. 1985. *Annual Report of Enrollment, Fall 1985*. Sacramento: California Community Colleges. (ERIC No. ED 261 740)

Bowles, Samuel, and Herbert Gintis, 1976. *Schooling in Capitalist America*. New York: Basic Books.

Breneman, David, and Susan Nelson. 1981. *Financing Community Colleges*. Washington, DC: Brookings Institution.

Brint, Steven, and Jerome Karabel. Forthcoming. *The Diverted Dream*.

California Community Colleges. 1984. *Transfer Education*. Sacramento: Office of the Chancellor. (ERIC No. ED 250 025)

Clark, Burton. 1960. *The Open Door College*. New York: McGraw-Hill.

Cohen, Arthur M., and Florence B. Brawer. 1982. *The American Community College*. San Francisco: Jossey-Bass.

Cohen, Arthur M., Florence B. Brawer, and Estela Bensimon. 1985. *Transfer Education in American Community Colleges*. Los Angeles: UCLA, Center for the Study of Community Colleges. (ERIC No. ED 255 250)

Dougherty, Kevin 1988a. "The Politics of Community College Expansion: Beyond the Functionalist and Class Reproduction Theories." *American Journal of Education* 96 (May): 351–393.

———. 1988b. "Educational Policymaking and the Relative Autonomy of the State: The Case of Occupational Education in the Community College." *Sociological Forum* 3 (summer): 400–432.

Eells. Walter C. 1931. *The Junior College*. Boston: Houghton-Mifflin.

Florida State Education Department. 1983. *A Longitudinal Study Comparing University Native and Community College Transfer Students in the State University System of Florida*. Tallahassee: Florida State Education Department. (ERIC No. ED 256 405)

Folger, John, Helen Astin, and Alan Bayer. 1970. *Human Resources and Higher Education*. New York: Russell Sage.

Giroux, Henry. 1981. *Ideology, Culture, and the Process of Schooling*. Philadelphia: Temple University Press.

Godfrey, Eleanor P., and Engin L. Holmstrom. 1970. *Study of Community Colleges and Vocational Technical Centers*. Washington, DC: Bureau of Social Science Research. (ERIC No. ED 053 718)

Hills, J. R. 1965. "Transfer Shock: The Academic Performance of the Junior College Transfer," *Journal of Experimental Education* 33:201–15.

Holmstrom, Engin, and Ann S. Bisconti. 1974.*Transfers from Junior Colleges to Senior Colleges*. Washington, DC: American Council on Education.

Illinois Community College Board. 1984. *Fall 1979 Transfer Study, Report 4: Third and Fourth Year Persistence and Achievement*. Springfield: Illinois Community College Board. (ERIC No. ED 254 275)

Karabel, Jerome. 1972. "Community Colleges and Social Stratification." *Harvard Educational Review* 42:521–62.

_____. 1986. "Community Colleges and Social Stratification in the 1980s." Pp. 13–30 in *The Community College and its Critics*, edited by L. Steven Zwerling. New Directions in Community Colleges No. 54. San Francisco: Jossey-Bass.

Kintzer, Frederick, and James L. Wattenbarger. 1985. *The Articulation/Transfer Phenomenon*. Washington, DC: American Association of Community and Junior Colleges, (ERIC No. ED 257 539)

Kissler, Gerald, Juan Lara, and Judith Cardinal. 1981. *Factors Contributing to the Academic Difficulties Encountered by Students who Transfer from Community Colleges to Four-Year Institutions*. Los Angeles: UCLA. (ERIC No. ED 203 920)

Knoell, Dorothy, and Leland L. Medsker. 1965. *From Junior College to Senior College*. Washington, DC: American Council on Education.

Lara, Juan. 1981. *Differences in Quality of Academic Effort between Successful and Unsuccessful Community College Transfer Students*. Los Angeles: UCLA. (ERIC No. ED 201 359)

Lavin, David, James Murtha, Barry Kaufman, and David Hyllegard, 1986. "Long-Term Educational Attainment in an Open-Access University System: Effects of Ethnicity, Economic Status, and College Type." Paper presented at the annual meetings of the American Educational Research Association, San Francisco.

London, Howard. 1978. *The Culture of a Community College*. New York: Praeger.

Maryland State Board for Community Colleges. 1983. *The Role of Community Colleges in Preparing Students for Transfer to Four-Year Colleges and Universities*. Annapolis: Maryland State Board for Community Colleges. (ERIC No. ED 230 255)

McConochie, Daniel. 1983. *Four Years Later: Follow-up of 1978 Entrants, Maryland Community Colleges*. Annapolis: Maryland State Board for Community Colleges. (ERIC No. ED 234 850)

Medsker, Leland L. 1960. *The Junior College*. New York: McGraw-Hill.

Medsker, Leland L., and James Trent. 1964. *The Influence of Different Types of Public Higher Education Institutions on College Attendance from Varying Socioeconomic and Ability Levels*. Berkeley: University of California, Center for the Study of Higher Education. (ERIC No. ED 002 875)

Meier, Terre. 1979. *Washington Community College Factbook. Addendum A: Student Enrollments, Academic Year 1978–79*. Olympia: State Board for Community College Education. (ERIC No. ED 184 616)

Monk-Turner, Elizabeth. 1983. "Sex, Educational Differentiation, and Occupational Status." *Sociological Quarterly* 24:393–404.

Monroe, Charles R. 1972. *A Profile of the Community College*. San Francisco: Jossey-Bass.

Nasaw, David. 1979. *Schooled to Order*. New York: Oxford University Press.

National Center for Education Statistics. 1977a. *Transfer Students in Institutions of Higher Education*. Washington, DC: U.S. Government Printing Office.

_____. 1977b. *Withdrawal from Institutions of Higher Education*. Washington, DC: U.S. Government Printing Office.

_____. 1984. *Fall Enrollment in Colleges and Universities, 1982*. Washington, DC: U.S. Government Printing Office.

_____. 1985. *Fall Enrollment in Colleges and Universities, 1983*. Washington, DC: U.S. Government Printing Office.

Neumann, William, and David Riesman. 1980. "The Community College Elite." Pp. 53–71 in *Questioning the Community College Role*, edited by George Vaughan. New Directions in Community Colleges No. 32. San Francisco: Jossey-Bass.

Pantages, T. J., and C. F. Creedon. 1978. "Studies of College Attrition: 1950–1975." *Review of Education Research* 48:49–101.

Pincus, Fred L. 1974. "Tracking in Community Colleges." *Insurgent Sociologist* 4:17–35.

_____. 1980. "The False Promises of Community Colleges: Class Conflict and Vocational Education." *Harvard Educational Review* 50:332–61.

_____. 1986. "Vocational Education: More False Promises." Pp. 41–52 in *The Community College and its Critics*, edited by L. Steven Zwerling. New Directions in Community Colleges No. 54. San Francisco: Jossey-Bass.

Rosenbaum, James. 1976. *Making Inequality*. New York: Wiley.

Sheldon, Stephen. 1982. *Statewide Longitudinal Study: Report on Academic Year 1978–1981. Part 5, Final Report*. Los Angeles: Pierce College. (ERIC No. ED 217 917)

Somers, Gerald, Laure Sharpe, and Thelma Myint. 1971. *The Effectiveness of Vocational and Technical Programs*. Madison: University of Wisconsin, Center for Studies in Vocational and Technical Education. (ERIC No. ED 055 190)

Tinto, Vincent. 1973. "College Proximity and Rates of College Attendance," *American Educational Research Journal* 10:273–93.

_____. 1974. "Public Junior Colleges and the Substitution Effect in Higher Education." Paper presented at the annual meetings of the American Educational Research Association. (ERIC No. ED 089 808)

_____. 1975. "Dropout from Higher Education: A Theoretical Synthesis of Recent Research." *Review of Educational Research* 45:89–125.

Trent, James, and Leland L. Medsker. 1968. *Beyond High School*. San Francisco: Jossey-Bass.

Turner, Ralph. 1960. "Modes of Social Ascent Through Education." *American Sociological Review* 25:855–67.

U.S. Bureau of the Census. 1985. "School Enrollment—Social and Economic Characteristics of Students: October 1981 and 1980." *Current Population Reports*, ser. P-20, no. 400. Washington, DC: U.S. Government Printing Office.

Van Alstyne, Carol, Cathy Henderson, Charles Fletcher, and Yi Sien. 1973. *Comparison of the Characteristics of Transfer and Nontransfer College Students*. Washington, DC: American Council on Education. (ERIC No. ED 085 028)

Vaughan, George, ed. 1980. *Questioning the Community College Role*. New Directions in Community Colleges No. 32. San Francisco: Jossey-Bass.

Velez, William. 1985. "Finishing College: The Effects of College Type." *Sociology of Education* 58:191–200.

Weis, Lois. 1985. *Between Two Worlds: Black Students in an Urban Community College*. Boston: Routledge and Kegan Paul.

Willingham, Warren, and Nurhan Findikyan. 1969. *Patterns of Admission for Transfer Students.* New York: College Entrance Examination Board.

Willis, Paul. 1977. *Learning to Labour.* New York: Schocken.

Wilms, Wellford. 1980. *Vocational Education and Social Mobility.* Los Angeles: UCLA. (ERIC No. ED 183 966)

Winandy, Donald, and Robert McGrath. 1970. "A Study of Admissions Policies and Practices for Transfer Students in Illinois." *College and University* 45:186–92.

Zwerling, L. Steven. 1976. *Second Best: The Crisis of the Junior College.* New York: McGraw-Hill.

Open Admissions: Is Higher Education a Right or a Privilege?

―――――

RICHARD D. ALBA
State University of New York at Albany

DAVID E. LAVIN
City University of New York

The open-admissions policy at the City University of New York (CUNY) may be the most misunderstood innovation in the history of American higher education. Controversial from its inception, the policy was initiated as a response to a series of confrontations in the spring of 1969 on the campus of the City College of New York (CCNY), the oldest and most famous of the 15 two- and four-year colleges then comprising the City University. The confrontations focused on a set of demands made by groups wanting increased access to City College for educationally disadvantaged students, notably Blacks and Hispanics. The demands had a forceful logic, not only in the egalitarian concerns of the 1960s but also in the history of City University.

The university had been in the vanguard of the development of public higher education for the urban poor. Its origins lay in the middle of the nineteenth century, when the citizens of New York City voted by referendum to establish the Free Academy (renamed the College of the City of New York in 1866). Its mission was set forth by the head of the new institution at opening ceremonies in 1849:

The Free Academy is now to go into operation. The experiment is to be tried, whether the highest education can be given to the masses; whether the children of the whole people can be educated; and whether an institution of learning, of the highest grade, can be successfully controlled by the popular will, not by the privileged few, but by the privileged many.

Although City College was destined to provide a broad avenue for the social mobility of ethnic minorities, that role was not apparent at first. In the early years the student body consisted largely of native-born Protestants. However, beginning in the 1880s and gaining momentum in the ensuing few decades, there was a vast immigration of poor Jews from Eastern Europe, especially from Russia. They and their children were drawn to City College in substantial numbers. By 1905 Jews constituted about 75 percent of the student body.

By the 1920s and the 1930s, City College students were regarded as among the most able in the nation, and the college was often referred to as the "proletarian Harvard." The list of its graduates' accomplishments in academia, business, and in public life read like a selection from *Who's Who in America*, contributing to faith in the college as an open door to the middle class.

By this time, other colleges had been added, resulting in a municipal college system. Hunter College was established at the end of the nineteenth century as a teacher-training school for women, and in the 1920s and 1930s three more four-year schools were added. This expansion responded to the growing demand for college, and led in time to further diversity in the student body of New York's public colleges. After World War II Catholics of Irish and Italian descent began to attend in larger numbers, and by the late 1960s comprised about a third of the entering classes.

But despite the expansions, the municipal colleges could not meet the growing demand for higher education, especially after World War II. In an effort to maintain a balance between enrollments and facilities, entrance requirements were stiffened. Even with the addition of three community colleges in the 1950s, the system was unable to accommodate many of those who wanted to attend. At the same time, the occupational structure of the city was changing, increasing the need for workers with at least some college education. Serious questions were raised about the appropriateness of increasingly selective admissions standards in a publicly supported university.

These questions were particularly relevant with respect to the newest arrivals in New York City, from the American South and the Caribbean. During the 1950s the population of New York City remained almost constant, but more than 700,000 Blacks and Hispanics (largely Puerto Ricans) replaced a similar number of whites who left the city over that decade. Typically the members of the new groups were unskilled and educationally disadvantaged. Relative to their proportions in high school graduating classes, minorities were sharply underrepresented in the municipal colleges at the end of the

1950s. In the 1960s, entrance requirements at the four-year colleges stiffened even more, requiring in some years a high school average of almost 90. Even in the community colleges the admissions requirements were stringent.

Minority students were at a great disadvantage in the competition for places at CUNY by the time they finished high school. By 1965 half of the Black and Puerto Rican students in the city's public school system attended segregated schools, where, generally, the grades tended to be quite low. In addition, minority students were much more likely than whites to attend vocational high schools or to be placed in nonacademic tracks within general high schools. A 1967 census showed that only 8 percent of the City University's matriculated students were Black or Hispanic.

The access of minority students to the university became an issue during the 1960s, a time of rising expectations and growing militancy among minority groups throughout the nation. With Albert H. Bowker's assumption of the CUNY chancellorship in 1963, a move toward expanded access was begun. Having come from California, where the public sector already had a system of universal access to higher education, and possessing a strong liberal consciousness, Bowker understood the opportunities the CUNY situation provided and also its exigencies. Recognizing the major demographic changes that had taken place in the city, he believed that the university's highly selective admissions policies might erode its political support.

The greater centralization of the municipal college system that had taken place in 1961 when the system was designated the City University of New York provided Bowker with considerable power to forge policies applicable to all the component institutions. In the short run, he developed special admissions programs, outside the normal admissions standards, designed to bring more minority students into the university's colleges. By 1966 he had committed the university to a longer-term plan to offer 100 percent admission. The university proposed that by 1975 a place be provided for every high school graduate who applied. These programs and plans provoked increasing controversy. On the one hand, minorities were dissatisfied, feeling that not enough was being done and that progress was too slow. On the other hand, traditional clients of the university, especially Jewish groups, felt that in a situation of limited fiscal resources, increased admission of minorities outside the regular admissions procedures was taking away the college seats of students who were qualified under the regular criteria. A perceived tension between "merit" and "quotas" became a major theme of conflict in the university.

Matters came to a head in the spring of 1969, when a group of minority students succeeded in sealing off a large part of the campus of City College, effectively closing down the school. The campus seizure precipitated a series of events that eventually led the university to accelerate its timetable for the 100 percent admissions plan. Universal admissions seemed the only way to avoid the political and moral impasse that would have been created by a massive special-admissions program only for minority students. In July 1969 the CUNY trustees resolved to initiate an open-admissions policy beginning in the fall of 1970. The plan ultimately agreed upon was far less stratified than the initial model developed earlier by Bowker and his staff, which consisted primarily of an expansion of community college enrollments. It was now clear that the access issue was focused primarily on the four-year senior colleges.

Despite what its name seems to imply, the open-admissions policy did not guarantee that every applicant could attend the college he or she preferred, but rather that every high school graduate could attend a college somewhere in the university. In terms of admissions, its central features were (a) to make the type of the student's high school diploma irrelevant for the admissions process and (b) to create, in effect, two admissions pools, one for the senior colleges and the other for the two-year schools. Eligibility for the senior-college pool was created by either a high school average of at least 80 *or* ranking in the top half of a high school graduating class. The two criteria were a marriage of a traditional admissions standard with one intended to provide greater access. The high school average criterion meant that students who would have qualified for some senior college before the policy would continue to do so; the primary aim of the rank criterion was to increase minority representation in the senior colleges by creating a pathway for students from ghetto high schools where averages tended to be low. Students not eligible for the senior-college pool were placed in the community-college one. Within these pools, admission to a particular college was competitive, with students competing against others who sought admission to that college on the basis of their high school average.

While open-access policies have a long tradition in American higher education, the CUNY model introduced elements not seen in other systems. For one, the admissions plan was designed to generate far less sorting between senior and community colleges than did other such systems, notably California's. CUNY's goal of increased opportunity was apparent in a second feature of the policy: mobility between two- and four-year colleges. To ease the transfer route, a place in one of the senior colleges was guaranteed for any graduate of a community college.

There was a third unique aspect to the CUNY plan. Other open-enrollment systems have been characterized by early and high dropout rates. These programs have defined their obligation as the creation of access, but the responsibility for academic success lies with the students. In contrast, the CUNY concept of opportunity embraced the full course of student academic careers, encompassing not only access but also outcome. As the CUNY board put it in its open-admissions resolution, "We do not want to provide the illusion of an open door to higher education which in reality is only a revolving door, admitting everyone but leading to a high proportion of failure after one semester." The primary means for achieving this aim was the development of large programs of remediation, supportive counseling, and related services. In addition, the university decided that students should not be dismissed for academic reasons during the grace period of the freshman year.

CUNY's open-admissions model exhibited the features of a system of universal higher education. Like the primary and secondary schools, it was free and publicly supported, and it provided a next rung on the educational ladder for all those who had completed the earlier steps. In effect, the policy attempted to lay to rest the often debated questions about who was "college material" and who should be educated. At least on paper, the university went further than any other in defining higher education as a right, rather than as a privilege restricted to the academically or socially select.

ACCESS TO HIGHER EDUCATION UNDER OPEN ADMISSIONS, 1970–75

The open-admissions policy had an immediate impact on enrollment at the City University. The freshman class admitted for the fall of 1970, the first under the new policy, jumped to 35,000 from 20,000 the year before—a 75 percent increase.

The policy had its intended effect of allowing students to enter schools to which they would not have been admitted before. As we have already noted, students with high school averages below 80 generally would not have been admitted to any senior college just before the program took effect. By this criterion, 40 percent of the 1970 senior-college freshmen were open-admissions students. Further, students with high school averages below 75 usually would not have been admitted anywhere within the university before the new program. But in 1970, students with such averages accounted for two-thirds of the freshmen in the community colleges. Indeed, of the total group of 1970 freshmen, over a third would not have been admitted at all before the open-admissions policy.

Nonetheless, not every college was deluged with the new students. Within the public perception, there has been a very important distinction between the four older, well-established colleges (Brooklyn, City, Hunter, and Queens Colleges) and the remaining senior colleges. These four often are thought of as more elite institutions, and because of the increased competition for them, they had far fewer places for open-admissions students. In 1970, open-admissions students were only a quarter of the students entering the four older colleges, whereas they made up two-thirds of the students entering the others. They did, however, increase over time, forming 40 percent of the freshmen at the elite schools in 1975. In that year, open-admissions students made up half of the class entering all the senior colleges.

As one might expect, the open-admissions students came with weaker academic skills than the students who entered before 1970. A sense of the educational task facing CUNY is given by the proportions defined by the university as needing improvement in the verbal and mathematics skills required for college work. Among the open-admissions freshmen entering senior colleges in 1970, 53 percent were deemed underprepared in language skills (reading and/or writing), and the same percentage were considered below par in math. Corresponding figures for regular students were 19 percent and 16 percent. Among community-college freshmen, three-fourths of open-admissions students needed more work in language skills and 77 percent needed more work in math, although half or more of the regular students were also underprepared in these areas. So overall, with the launching of open admissions, abrupt changes took place, especially in the senior colleges. Not only was there a massive influx of previously ineligible students, but they were far more likely than the traditional students to need special educational services.

But perhaps the most profound effect of the policy was on the ethnic composition of the university. Among students entering in 1969, just before the open-admissions program took effect, minority students were about 20 percent of the community colleges, and they were just 15 percent of the students entering the four-year schools. Indeed, the situation was more serious than these numbers convey. Before the open-admissions policy, the university had developed special admissions programs, bypassing the regular admissions channels, for minority students. In the senior colleges the special admissions program was known as SEEK (Search for Education, Elevation, and Knowledge); in the community colleges it was called College Discovery. Surprisingly few minority students were admitted outside these programs. In fact, before open admissions, the SEEK program was virtually the only mechanism by which Black and Hispanic students could attend the senior colleges. In 1969, about 75 percent of the minority students enrolled in the senior colleges were in the SEEK program; in the community colleges about 45 percent of all minority students were in College Discovery.

The numbers of minority students rose sharply as soon as open admissions began. Their representation among all entering students increased from 20 percent in the 1969 class to 27 percent in 1970. This 1970 figure approximated for the first time the proportion of minority students in that year's high school graduating class. In absolute terms, given the increased size of the freshman class, the numbers of Black and Hispanic freshmen more than doubled in this first year, and more than tripled if admissions due to SEEK and College Discovery are excluded. The proportion of minority freshmen continued to rise in subsequent years, leveling off at around 40 percent by 1973.

The minority presence shot up at the senior colleges as well. Only 15 percent of the freshmen at these schools in 1969, minority students made up 22 percent in 1970 and 40 percent by 1975. The increase was nearly as strong at the four elite schools, where minority students had become a third of the freshmen by 1975. But it is only after the exclusion of the special-program students that one really sees the effect of the new policy. Among senior-college freshmen admitted outside the SEEK program, the proportion of minority students increased eightfold between 1969 and 1975; at the elite schools, this proportion went up sixfold.

As a consequence of these changes, the policy lessened the ethnic stratification at the university, the concentration of different groups at different levels. Before 1970, minority students were found disproportionately in the community colleges. In 1969, for example, the proportion of minority students among freshmen in the senior colleges was only 76 percent of what would be expected on the basis of their enrollment in the university. In 1970, this proportion leapt to 83 percent of what would be expected and by

1975 it had further increased to over 90 percent. Open admissions, in other words, brought about a distribution of minority students between the university's two major levels that was more like the distribution of white students. However, this equalization was not true in relation to the four elite senior colleges. In 1975, the proportion of minority students among freshmen at these schools was still only 78 percent of what would be expected on the basis of overall minority enrollment, and their underrepresentation was no different from what it had been in 1969.

None of this is very surprising. Yet the open-admissions program had paradoxical effects: minority students were not the sole beneficiaries of open admissions; indeed, in a purely numerical sense, they may not have been the most important beneficiaries of the program, as large numbers of white ethnic students from the Jewish and Catholic groups traditionally served by the university were also admitted under the new criteria. To be sure, as the changes in the racial composition of CUNY imply, larger proportions of Blacks and Hispanics than of Jews and Catholics were admitted to CUNY and to its senior-college system under open admissions. The differences between minority groups and the traditional beneficiaries of CUNY education were largest at the elite senior colleges, where more than half of the Black students in each cohort were admitted under the new criteria as compared with 20 percent or less of Jews and Catholics. (These figures do not include special-program students, who were not included in the study on which our tabulations are based.) The disparity is smaller at the other senior colleges, where large percentages of every group were admitted under open admissions, and it disappears at the community colleges where the proportion of Jews admitted by the new criteria was one of the two largest.

But when we consider the absolute numbers of students from each group who were admitted under the policy, or alternatively the percentage of beneficiaries each group represents, a very different picture emerges. At least for the freshman cohorts of 1970, 1971, and 1972, the ones we have been able to analyze in detail, open-admissions white ethnic students generally outnumbered open-admissions Blacks and Hispanics throughout the system. For example, in the 1970 cohort, under a quarter of the open-admissions students at the senior colleges were Black or Hispanic, while nearly two-thirds were Jewish or non-Hispanic Catholic. One aspect of the extent to which white ethnics benefited is especially striking. Those who have recognized that whites have been important beneficiaries have—with considerable unanimity—singled out Catholic groups, the Irish and Italians, as the chief white beneficiaries. But Jewish students also benefited in a major way from open admissions, even at the senior-college levels: roughly a quarter or more of the 1970 freshmen at the senior colleges who would not have been admitted under the old requirements were Jewish.

It is important to emphasize that these white ethnic beneficiaries of the open-admissions program were *not*, for the most part, students who would have gone to college somewhere anyway. According to one question asked in a survey of the 1970 freshmen, substantial proportions of these white students felt that the policy made it possible for them, or at least encouraged them, to attend college. Yet oddly, the white ethnic open-admissions students were not, with the exception of their high school records, different from the white students who would have been admitted without the policy. They were not, in other words, from socially disadvantaged backgrounds, at least by comparison with the students who traditionally attended CUNY. The minority beneficiaries, on the other hand, were different. They were quite likely to have come from impoverished families.

Undoubtedly, the absolute numbers of white ethnic and minority beneficiaries of the policy were modified in the freshman cohorts of 1973, 1974, and 1975, since these contained larger proportions of minority students. But the key point is that the benefits of the controversial program were not confined to one or two groups but were spread broadly throughout the major ethnic groupings in the city. Despite the general public perception of open admissions, minority students and open-admissions students were not one and the same.

ON THE MATTER OF ACADEMIC STANDARDS

The most controversial aspect of the open-admissions policy has been the question of its effect on the quality of education at the university. Critics charged that the academic processes became so watered down after the deluge of underprepared students that they were rendered virtually meaningless. The university was savaged by articles in local and national media that stated, or at least implied, that nearly illiterate students were moving successfully toward graduation at CUNY colleges.

There is no simple way of answering these charges. It is difficult to know whether, or how much, academic standards changed as a result of open admissions. We lack the kind of data that would allow us to determine, for example, whether the intellectual content of courses was softened after open admissions. In fact, we can't be sure whether grading standards changed because we lack the data about the pre-open-admissions period necessary for determining whether students with similar high school records received similar grades at CUNY before and after the program. Even if we had this information, it would be difficult to draw a firm conclusion. It should be remembered that since the 1960s there has been a grade inflation at colleges and universities throughout the nation. It would be difficult to disentangle the effects of open admissions from these broader currents.

Still, it is clearly reasonable to expect that open admissions had some sort of effect. On the matter of grades, this expectation receives indirect support from one university study of grading patterns, which found that, in the aggregate, the grades handed out by faculty were lower at some campuses after open admissions began but higher at others. Since many students with weak high school backgrounds were admitted under the policy, we would have expected to see a more definite pattern of lower grades if standards had been maintained.

But one should not be misled into believing that academic standards had become so porous as a result of the policy that they let nearly anyone through.

Quite the reverse is true. By the evidence of the grades students received and the credits they earned, standards remained fairly rigorous. Consider, for example, the freshman year of the 1972 cohort, which was the third year after the program had begun, long enough for patterns to have stabilized. Over half of the open-admissions students in both the senior and community colleges earned below a C average, which was required for graduation. Few of the open-admissions students earned credits at a rate that would allow them to graduate on time (at least 30 credits a year). In fact, among students completing both semesters of the freshman year, only about 30 percent of the open-admissions students at both levels earned as many as 24 credits, and about the same number earned less than 12 for the year.

ACADEMIC ACHIEVEMENT UNDER OPEN ADMISSIONS

Still, over the long haul, many of the open-admissions students stuck it through. Few, of course, graduated on time. Only 13 percent of the 1970 open-admissions students at the senior colleges had graduated by the end of their fourth year. But in the slowness of their progress toward graduation, open-admissions students were not so different from many of the students who had attended CUNY before 1970. The City University has always served a large number of poor students, who have had to divide their energies between school and a part- or full-time job. Making allowance for their slower progress, open-admissions students did at least as well as students with similar high school records who attended colleges and universities elsewhere in the nation. Five years after their entry, over a quarter of the open-admissions students who entered senior colleges in 1970 had graduated, and 16 percent were still in attendance. (The national figures are lower than these.) At the end of this period, over 20 percent of the open-admissions students who entered community colleges had graduated, another 11 percent had transferred to four-year schools without earning the associate degree, and 5 percent were still attending the two-year colleges.

The opportunity for a college education that open admissions provided on a mass scale is especially critical for New York City's minority communities. According to a survey of the class that graduated from the city's high schools in 1970, about 70 percent of the minority graduates who went on to college (about two-thirds of the total) enrolled in the City University schools. Hence, any contribution of open admissions to the pool of college graduates was bound to be a substantial one. According to our analysis of the fate of this graduating class, Black open-admissions graduates from the university's colleges outnumbered Black graduates who would have been admitted without the policy, so that the policy more than doubled the number of Black students who received a degree of some kind from the university. It more than doubled as well the number of Black baccalaureates and, if one assumes that a student who graduates with at least a B average is likely to qualify for a postbaccalaureate program, then it nearly doubled the number of Black students placed on the threshold of graduate or professional school. Its impact on the number of Hispanic graduates was not quite as large, but still it increased the numbers of Hispanic graduates by about two-thirds. As a result of those sorts of calculations, it can be said that the first five years of entering classes under the open-admissions program produced thousands of minority college graduates.

The importance of this contribution should not blind one to the advantages that fell to white groups under this same open-admissions system. These advantages are to be expected, because white students had on average superior high school records. But even in this group of students who would not have qualified for the colleges they entered without the open-admissions program, white students had noticeably stronger high school backgrounds (they were more likely to have been in college preparatory high school tracks, for example).

Hence, even though the ratio of white to minority individuals in the city's college-age population was roughly 1.5 to 1, there were four white ethnic graduates for every minority graduate among the students who entered the university in 1970. In the same group, there were six white ethnic students who graduated with a baccalaureate for every such minority student; and there were ten white ethnic students who graduated with records likely to qualify them for graduate or professional school for every such minority student.

The same point is made by ethnic disparities in the proportions of graduates from each group. For example, among the open-admissions students who entered the senior colleges in 1970, 37 percent of the Jews and 29 percent of the non-Hispanic Catholics had graduated after five years, compared with 23 percent of the Blacks and 19 percent of the Hispanics. Among open-admissions freshmen at the community colleges, 25 percent of the Jewish students and 24 percent of the Catholic students received the associate degree, compared with 18 percent of the Black and 19 percent of the Hispanic students. These differences are not profound, but they take on a somewhat different coloration when one realizes that non-open-admissions students were considerably more likely to earn a degree than were open-admissions students, and whites were more likely to be non-open-admissions students. Also, students who began at the senior colleges were more successful than those who began at the community colleges, and minority students were more likely to enter the two-year schools. Hence, when we ignore students' high school records and their levels of entry, ethnic disparities reach dramatic levels. Of the 1970 cohort, close to half the Jewish students and nearly 40 percent of the Catholic ethnics received a degree of some kind. By contrast, only a quarter of the Blacks and Hispanics did. Moreover, over 40 percent of *all* Jewish entrants and nearly a quarter of the Catholic entrants graduated with a baccalaureate; only 13 percent of Black entrants and 14 percent of Hispanic entrants did so. And, once again, the minority students were more dependent on the City University for a college education than were the white ethnic students. (The Catholics, for example, could avail themselves of the extensive Catholic college system in and around the city.)

The 1970 figures are, to be sure, extreme, because they are based only on the first class to enter under the new policy. Subsequent cohorts contained larger proportions of minority students, and over time their chances of being placed in senior colleges improved. Unfortunately, we lack the data about those entering the university from 1973 to '75, when minority representation grew to over 40 percent among freshmen, to calculate with precision the relative weight of ethnic advantages and disadvantages in the later groups. Our projections for the 1975 cohort suggest that the gains for whites may have been reduced dramatically in this group, although they will not have disappeared. However, these calculations hinge on the assumption that student careers in this cohort will have developed in the same fashion as in the 1970 group. This is a large assumption, as the education of students in the later cohorts was severely disrupted by the events of the fiscal crisis.

NEW YORK CITY'S FISCAL CRISIS AND ITS REPERCUSSIONS FOR OPEN ADMISSIONS

In the spring of 1975, New York City teetered on the edge of bankruptcy. As it strove to contain the crisis, all municipal services experienced substantial cutbacks, but by far the heaviest buffeting was received by the City University. Within a very short period, the university found its budget for the 1975–76 academic year cut by over 20 percent, from $650 million to $510 million. How the university could deal with this sudden cut was the focal point around which a paralyzing crisis developed. It was a crisis that reawakened many of the conflicts that had accompanied the birth of open admissions and that brought into question the very mission of the university. Eventually, it brought about major changes in the structure and functioning of the open-admissions policy.

The toll taken by the university's crisis was a grim one. Between the fall of 1975 and the fall of 1976 the size of the entering freshman classes at CUNY plummeted from 40 thousand to 29 thousand. Overall enrollment shrank from about 250,000 students to 200,000. Full-time staff decreased by more than 5,000, or 25 percent, of whom about 2,000 were instructional staff. More than half of the 9,000 part-time teaching positions were eliminated.

These drastic changes occurred at least in part because, as CUNY entered an era of scarcity, the conflicts that preceded open admissions, still smoldering, ignited with renewed intensity. The most important of these was the conflict that many perceived as that between broader educational opportunity on the one hand and the preservation of academic standards on the other. This conflict between equity and excellence had never entirely disappeared during open admissions, though for a time there appeared to be an uneasy coexistence between the two goals. But when the conflict between them burst forth again, it contributed to the paralysis that prevented the university from dealing forthrightly with its financial crisis. As a result, CUNY defaulted on its financial obligations in the spring of 1976 and was forced to close—just at the period of final exams and commencement.

The crisis precipitated many changes in the university's policies, including the open-admissions policy. In short order, CUNY's century-old tradition of free tuition was abolished. Admission to its senior colleges was made more difficult, and more stringent criteria for student retention were put in place. Faculty retrenchment was severe and hit hardest at those staff providing the remedial and counseling services so important to the open-admissions effort. At the same time, a program of basic skills proficiency testing was introduced in the areas of math, reading, and writing, and entry to the junior year of college was made contingent upon passing these tests.

The crisis and its aftermath left the university a different place. It is now an institution where enrollments are more centered around its two-year colleges. In 1975, the last year the original open-admissions criteria were in force, 53 percent of the freshmen were placed in a senior college. In 1976, when the new admissions criteria took effect, only 37 percent were placed. The changes at the university probably hinder minority students more than whites, since white students have on average better high school records and are more likely to be able to afford the alternative of attending a state or private college. In fact, students with strong high school records, especially whites, now appear less likely to enroll in the university.

CONCLUSION

The open-admissions experience gives new meaning to the question, Is access to higher education a privilege or a right? In contemporary American society, as elsewhere, higher education is distinguished from the preceding stages of the educational system because it is a selective stage, to which only some should have the privilege of access. In the general view, this privilege is extended to those who qualify on the basis of previous academic achievements, although the American system has always had places somewhere for those with the financial means to pay tuition, regardless of their academic qualifications. In practice, the combination of academic and financial barriers has tended to exclude youth of lower socioeconomic status and of minority origins despite the growth in rates of college attendance after World War II and the great importance a college education has assumed for the future occupational and financial situations of individuals. As a consequence, the view of higher education as a privilege has had strong ideological overtones, legitimating the increasingly significant role of higher education in overall inequality of opportunity.

Open admissions was based on a new premise: college education is a right, just as grammar school and high school education have come to be accepted. The policy assumed that anyone possessing a high school diploma could benefit from the chance to attend college. Under open admissions, CUNY exhibited the features of a system of universal higher education: like the primary and secondary schools, it was free and publicly supported and it provided a next rung on the educational ladder for those who had advanced beyond the earlier steps. Since it was located in a major population center, students from poor families could attend without burdening their families with the need to support them away from home.

But the view of higher education as a privilege did not die under open admissions: it merely faded into the background. Six years after open admissions began, the question of who should be educated acquired again a legitimacy derived from older notions of privilege. The assault on open admissions as undermining academic standards emerged from the premise that not all students are "college material." That premise was widely enough shared so that the direction of change in response to the fiscal crisis was in favor of selectivity: more stringent requirements for admission to four-year colleges; skills proficiency tests as the gateway to the upper levels of the four-year colleges: and the imposition of tuition, whose effects were not fully offset by financial aid to those who could not afford to pay.

If, under the pressures of the fiscal crisis, the view of college as a privilege has regained its ascendancy, it is likely that this change is the result of attempts by socially more advantaged groups to maintain their position. One consequence of coming from an advantaged family is the greater chance such origins give to attain the educational credentials necessary for socioeconomic success. The democratization of educational opportunity that the open-admissions program signified threatened to reduce this competitive edge. Thus, while CUNY is still a more open institution than other systems of higher education, such as that of California, the legacy of the fiscal crisis has been a narrowing of the mission to which the university committed itself in 1969. In the end, it has moved closer to the older view, that higher education is a privilege, not a right.

To Educate All the Children of All the People

MEYER WEINBERG

University of Massachusetts, Amherst

. . . The first significant numbers of black students entered public schools after the Civil War. There they pursued the same curricula available elsewhere. No distinctive black education was available either in the private or the public schools. The communal element in black education consisted not so much in this or that aspect of instruction as in the determination to gain a just share of the community's educational resources. Nothing buoyed that spirit as much as the Civil War. This conflict was the greatest shared experience of Afro-American history. Without it, the slave songs would have been merely dolorous reminders of a hard past. With it, the songs are constant reminders of the capacity of the Negro people to participate in their own emancipation. In other lands, such a profound, pervasive movement customarily formed the core of nationalistic memories. Here, it played a similar role, only within a biracial framework.

Until the past decade or so, black culture failed to become an integral part of schools attended by Negro children. Whether in North or South, instruction depended almost wholly on efforts by individual teachers. Traditional black colleges failed to deal with Afro-American culture in a central way, wishing to establish further their similarity to white colleges. Apparently, it was not until 1936 that a traditional black college first required students to take a course in black studies.[1] In the North, public schools shied away from the field. Permission to teach about black life was granted as a concession. Thus, the legislature of Illinois amended the state school code in 1931 as follows: "History of the Negro race may be taught in all public schools." Thirty years later, the law remained unchanged. During the early post-World

War II years, several northern states began to require fairer treatment of blacks and other minorities in textbooks. The enactments were not enforced. As a consequence, the unprecedentedly large public school enrollments after 1945 depended on textbooks that ranged from racist to condescending in their discussion of the Negro.

The public schools were systematically inhospitable to Spanish-speaking minorities as well. In the Southwest, the very presence—let alone the culture—of Mexican-Americans in the schools was resented. Yet the Spanish language continued as a vigorous element of community life. Its persistence was attacked by school officials, who transformed a language difference into a learning handicap.

Neither Puerto Ricans nor Mexican-Americans could turn to the Roman Catholic parochial school as a protector of their language and culture. Both in Puerto Rico and Mexico the Church was an upper-class institution with little regard for either the social or cultural interests of the people. Parochial schools tended to serve a narrow circle of children. In the United States, too, the Catholic Church organized few schools for Puerto Ricans and Mexican-Americans. Polish immigrants in Buffalo or Chicago sent their children to Polish-language church schools; yet no such option ordinarily existed for the Spanish-speaking minorities.

For these groups especially, traditional culture was nurtured in the family and the home. Their ethnic awareness depended, too, on a proliferation of hometown clubs organized in the new land. The outright rejection by the schools of the Spanish language did little to shake the devotion of the people. Middle-class elements in the Spanish-speaking communities were readier than others to forsake the traditions.

Only during the 1960s did the schools begin an accommodation to Afro-American and Spanish-speaking cultures. In both cases, sharp community conflict preceded even those modest moves. The public schools resisted significantly modifying their standard of cultural assimilation.

Even these stirrings of change, however, failed to disturb the denigrative impact of the schools upon Indian-American children. The schools, both federal and local, thoroughly excluded Indian content from the curriculum. Even where many thousand Indian children attended schools in a relatively compact area—as on the Navajo Reservation—only a tiny proportion of the teachers were themselves Indian, and the curriculum was culturally estranged from the students.

The rebirth of ethnic consciousness among the four minorities during the 1960s was epochal in one special respect. In each case, demands were made that the public schools take on responsibility for ethnic education. This was another evidence of growing self-confidence by the groups. Ethnic autonomy lost some of its private character and became more a public fact.

COMMUNITY AND SCHOOLS

In a geographical sense, American public education has been state controlled and locally administered. This feature resulted in localism becoming the mechanism for directly misappropriating funds designed for the benefit of Negro, Mexican-American, and Indian children. State governments were conscious partners in this educational plunder of the minorities. State governments in the North as well as the South refused to exercise educational superintendence over their public schools. Again and again they turned aside complaints by minority parents. In states containing large cities, state educational agencies abdicated regulatory functions in such cities. As a result, racial discrimination and deprivation in large cities were countenanced and encouraged.

State and local government fostered a distorted sense of the public interest wherever ethnic and economic differences separated children in the same school systems. Failure to challenge the existence of clear inequalities allowed them to be accepted as legitimate. The object for parents then became how they could maintain their advantage or lose their disadvantage. Parents whose children received a discriminatorily higher allotment became wedded to the unequal system. Their primary concern was that their children continue to receive a larger share. Parents of the deprived children worked to obtain for them an education somehow equal to that enjoyed by the privileged children. The system of unequal expenditures thus bred among parents a mentality of "more than" and "as much as." As a result, there was little room for considering whether the system achieved a good education for either group of children. The continuation of the system inevitably crowded out considerations of improving the education of all. With the pressure of the system oriented away from improvement, it came to be regarded as a positive virtue if the system simply maintained the existing level of quality. A vested interest has been described as an institutionalized right to something for nothing. This applied to the public schools even when the "something" was not much.

Attempts by minority communities to control the schools their children attended rarely succeeded. Too often, this goal was pursued by use of private schools. The utter poverty of the group usually doomed the effort or condemned the children to a second-rate education. In one case, however, outright community control on an ethnic basis was highly successful; the schools set up by the five southern tribes, preeminently the Cherokees, attained a level of quality which at times surpassed that of public school systems in neighboring states. Very special circumstances made this possible.

During the 1820s and 1830s, the federal government chose to buy the Cherokee lands east of the Mississippi. In return for the lands, the Cherokees received money, among other things, to be used to set up bilingual schools. While force and fraud finally pushed the Indian into the desolate plains across the Mississippi, schools were built under the agreed-upon arrangement. Forty years later, the situation had changed. When federal authorities in 1868 dictated peace treaties to the Navajo and Sioux Indians, no provision was made for Indian-controlled schools or for bilingual instruction. Indeed, no actual schools were provided for a number of years. The Indian-controlled Cherokee schools operated in all for some eighty years. They were closed down and placed under state authority in 1906, the year when, by act of

Congress, the Cherokee Nation ceased to exist. Community control of schools had been possible because a minority possessed actual sovereignty over a definite territory. Once that sovereignty was destroyed, the basis for an independent Cherokee culture was gravely weakened. The language and customs of the Cherokees lost their protective framework. Thirty years later, the University of Oklahoma refused to teach any courses in Indian culture.

Black and Mexican-American communities never exercised territorial sovereignty within the borders of the United States. A small number of all-black towns that did arise in Oklahoma and elsewhere were exceedingly poor and could not support an adequate school system. In Texas, separate school districts for Mexican-Americans were organized, but this was a means of cutting off minority children from the benefits of the schools the Anglos had built in adjacent districts.

During the 1960s, a movement for community control arose in New York City and a few other urban centers. Its appeal had two factors: (1) it expressed the historical demand of minority parents to control the education of their children, and (2) it expressed profound dissatisfaction of minority parents with the low quality of education provided by urban school systems. On one hand, the movement was a declaration of self-confidence by black and Puerto Rican parents in their ability to act on behalf of their children. On the other, it was an announcement of political import—if mostly for future realization—about the disillusionment of minority parents with the established institutions of school governance. Teachers' unions, administrators' organizations, and political parties combined to oppose calls for community controls. It was not, however, the localism but the transfer of power involved in community control that aroused the greatest opposition. Since power was not concentrated in the communities themselves, the problem of controlling citywide centers of power swiftly became a critical concern of minority communities. The pace of political organization quickened accordingly, especially where cooperation developed between two or more minorities.

SCHOOL STAFFS

Historically, school staffs enforced the system of exclusion and discrimination. Zealous white teachers and principals frequently initiated exclusory actions. Occasionally, white voices were raised in defense of black children's education. In 1856, for example, at a convention of the New York state teachers' organization, Susan B. Anthony, the feminist leader and a teacher in Rochester, strongly condemned the exclusion of Negro children from many schools in the state. When delegates failed to take up the challenge, Miss Anthony pledged to raise the issue again the next year.[2] This she did. Four separate resolutions were presented. One read: "Resolved, that the exclusion of colored children from our public schools, academies, colleges and universities, is the result of a wicked prejudice against color." Another resolved that "*all* proscription from educational advantages and honors, on account of color, is in perfect harmony with the infamous decision of Judge Taney [in the

Dred Scott case], that 'black men have no rights which white men are bound to respect.' " While the majority of a committee approved the resolutions, the convention adopted the minority report which stated limply that "the colored children of the state should enjoy equal advantages of education with the whites."[3]

Equivocation marked the outer bound of professional willingness to defend equal educational opportunities. After the Civil War and the subsequent rise of national professional organizations, the situation did not change in its essentials for nearly a century. University schools of education, intimately interlocked with local school systems, also failed to oppose racially discriminatory features of the schools. Both the National Education Association and the American Federation of Teachers organized separate locals for black teachers. The AFT abolished such locals in 1956, the NEA more than a decade later.[4]

National teachers' organizations cooperated in legislative and fund-raising efforts on behalf of general civil rights goals during the 1960s. In few local areas, however, could the groups be found actively cooperating with minority group movements for desegregation. In cities like Chicago, the teachers' union followed the lead offered by a school board and superintendent who were notorious for their opposition to desegregation. In New York City, the teachers' union became the leading defender of the racial status quo. From time to time, it actively manipulated racial issues for partisan purposes. The rising militancy of teachers' groups was limited to the benefit of the material interests of their members. Local teachers' organizations have proved no more sensitive to the needs of minority children than organized administrators, teachers colleges, and state and local school officials.

Black teachers' and administrators' organizations were in an equivocal position. They were primarily concerned with their own material well-being. Yet they found themselves, willy-nilly, in the public arena as the spokesmen for black educational interests. Since they lacked a significant power base of their own and in fact were at the mercy of white political authorities, they hesitated to risk dismissal. At the level of the individual school, however, Negro teachers and principals were often bolder. More informal avenues of influence enabled them to press for additional funds or personnel. Examples were not lacking, to be sure, of near-complete acquiescence to the barest budgets. Yet black teachers' organizations in the South laid the basis for fundamental educational change when they took to the courts in the late 1930s and early 1940s.

NONEDUCATIONAL MOVEMENT

The history of American education includes a history of affirmative efforts not to educate. During much of Mexican and Puerto Rican history, the lower classes—including Indians and blacks—were excluded from educational facilities. Upper-class representatives were frank to argue—when they bothered to at all—that only a select few deserved an education. Nor can it be said that any mass protests arose at such exclusion through much of the nine-teenth century. In the United States, similar aristocratic views dogged the supporters of public schooling.

Compulsory ignorance, however, was a distinctive American policy of noneducation. It was based on a positive fear by the southern ruling classes that blacks were all too educable. The policy of forbidding the education of slaves or free Negroes was an affirmation of the ability of blacks to learn rather than of the conviction argued by many theologians, scientists, and educators that blacks could not learn. The laws were also a peculiar acknowledgment of the attractions of freedom.

In the pre-Civil War North, most black children were either excluded altogether from school or segregated. In certain areas, they attended schools in common with white children. Objections to nonsegregated education were often couched in unembarrassed racist terms. Yet the very success of nonsegregated schools encouraged the thought that common schools for all would benefit the entire community.

The Boston school committee, seeking to establish a psychological theory to justify its persistent policy of segregation, in 1846, at a time when most towns in Massachusetts had desegregated their schools, insisted that black children could not benefit from a common education. It contended that black students were competent in instructional matters dependent on memory but would fall behind in the use of "the faculties of invention, compassion, and reasoning."[5] The absence of similar complaints in other towns where schools were not segregated suggested a factual weakness of the argument. Nor did Boston authorities point to any specific schools. At this time, all but a few Negro children in Boston were assigned to one school. For two years, black parents had conducted a running battle with the principal of the Smith School. In 1844, after a careful, exhaustive study, they had concluded the principal believed in the inferiority of his pupils. "If a man conscientiously imbibes a belief that a race of persons, with whom he is thrown in contact, are an inferior class," the parents declared, "will he not begin imperceptibly to himself, to treat them as such?"[6] It could well have been the discredited principal of the Smith School who provided the school committee with the psychological theory of inferiority two years later.

A general racism infected the North before the Civil War. Even Horace Mann shared the belief in inborn inferiority of blacks. But it must be emphasized that the broader educational segregation and deprivation of minority children were based on power and status arguments. Unlike the Bostonians, most partisans of segregation defended its attractions without trying to justify exclusion of black children on intellectual grounds. Blacks were to be discriminated against simply because they did not share in the power arrangements. But they had no power, after all, because they were black. The advent of intelligence tests early in the twentieth century provided a new basis for an intellectual defense of exclusion or invidious distinctions. By the close of World War I, leading psychologists had constructed theories of intellectual worth that equated minority status with low academic ability. The public shcools obliged by adopting the same line of reasoning. It was accomplished effortlessly because it was consonant with the general exclusionary trends developed over the previous decades. Having lived so long by the practice of inequality, the schools easily slipped into accepting the pseudoscientific theory of inferior intellectual ability.

When academic sensibilities began to prohibit linking low ability with race—as was the case during the 1940s and 1950s—social class became the culprit. Not since John Calvin had so many plain human beings been consigned to the nether regions. Predestination by social class became the new orthodoxy. In the 1960s, a stage was reached when a psychologist appropriated the reasoning if not the words of the Boston school committee of a century earlier. Jensen held black children to be less capable than white children in abstract or conceptual thinking but equal or superior in learning dependent on memory. He attributed an intelligence quotient lag of blacks overwhelmingly to genetic inheritance rather than environmental discrimination.[7] Investigators were unable to produce experimental data or direct empirical evidence from school settings in which academic performance of black and white children as such could be distinguished by strict racial criteria. Instead, analogies were offered with test differences between individual white children. Ability differences between individuals within a single race were asserted without evidence to explain differences of a similar magnitude between races.

Much of the force of public debate about racial differentials in intelligence derived from a fundamental confusion. Involved were two separate questions, neither capable of immediate scientific demonstration. The first issue concerned the practical social capacity of large groups of people ("races") to conduct civilized life including specific careers, problematic life situations, in family and community, in the creation of artistic products, and other practical challenges. To find any race inferior in this sense would require evidence of incapacity that persisted *even when the opportunity had been made available*. No such evidence was brought forward that held for blacks *but not for members of any other race*. The second issue involved a judgment whether any racial differences in intellectual ability would persist in the absence of all social discrimination. Having mistakenly thought they settled the first issue, it was further assumed by many that the second was thereby also resolved. To "settle" the second question would require an absolute equality of social conditions. Nobody seriously claimed this already obtained. Nor were any of the adherents of the inherently inferior school of thought perceptibly active in community movements to equalize conditions. Guesses about the eventual outcome ranged widely. Anthropologist Washburn, for example, thought it just as likely that blacks would perform in a superior way under equal conditions.[8]

The debate evaded educational issues. Both sides tended to accept declarations that lacked the most elementary documentation. For example, Jensen had written that compensatory education was tried and found wanting. The only controversy involved the explanation of the failure. In fact, however, the practice of compensatory education was exceedingly defective in most basic respects. Much of the money designed for such use was misappropriated for ineligible middle-class children. Neither federal nor state government supervised expenditures. Exceedingly unimaginative instructional approaches were employed, thus repeating the failures of noncompensatory education. Racial isolation was the context of most compensatory efforts.

The debate was interminable because of the confusion of historical questions with questions of the future. Gross unrealism led many participants in the debate to treat premises as facts. Schools were thus relieved of a share of the responsibility for educational failure. Two foundations of public noneducation were race and social class, the former immutable by virtue of biology, the second irremediable in the absence of major social changes. This ideology, couched in the language of science, dominated educational practice. A search for highly talented minority and poor white youth, sporadic and ill-financed as it was, implied that these young people were merely "exceptional." For the great mass of the remaining children, a norm of nonachievement was tolerated.

Historically, the significance of race in education has been underestimated. More recently, many analysts of right and left persuasions have interpreted minority children as essentially poor children, defining their plight as economic rather than racial. Another view is that the four minorities discussed in this book are not unlike all other minority children so that their problems are those of any ethnic group. Both these views evade the dominant role of race in American education.

Race continues to be one of the most basic political issues in American life. Governmental authorities and educators may indeed wish to avoid direct consideration of this fact and continue to speak of education as a nonpolitical area. One is reminded of the Wendell Phillips-Horace Mann debate. When Phillips accused Mann of ignoring racial discrimination in the Boston schools, he also observed that Mann concerned himself with technical educational innovations. Immersion in the pedagogical dimension of education was a tested means of avoiding political conflict. But, Phillips charged, Mann was was not so much avoiding conflict as refusing to declare his own contribution to that conflict.

In pre-Civil War America, educational philosophizing did not reach the issue of race as such; race was not considered a problem but a condition of life. American educators persisted in this analysis for nearly a century more. Except for black educators and social critics, and the rarest white educator, race was immune from discussion as a problem. Even a philosopher such as John Dewey, who made democracy in education a central point of his analysis, apparently never wrote an article dealing with race in education. A social scientist such as Thorstein Veblen, who spared little in American society, also seems never to have discussed race as an issue. Race was admitted into the select circle of scientific problems only when the impingement of minority peoples in practical affairs stirred new political discontents. Only a century after the Civil War were racial and ethnic concerns finally permitted to assume the status of "problems." The political element was still dominant, but it was a new politics. For the first time in American history, through a more democratic politics than ever before, American education was forced to contemplate the requirements of a system to educate all the children of all the people.

The study of history perfects the art of looking forward, not backward. In the perspective of several centuries, the future cannot but be influenced by a novel feature: millions of minority parents and children are self-aware of their rights and increasingly skilled in contending for those rights. The schools cannot long resist such a momentous fact.

NOTES

1. For offerings in courses in black life and history since 1921, see Nick Aaron Ford, *Black Studies: Threat or Challenge?* (Port Washington, N.Y.: Kennikat Press, 1973), p. 52.

2. *Liberator*, August 22, 1856.

3. *Liberator*, August 21, 1857.

4. See Michael J. Schultz, "The Desegregation Effort of the National Education Association," *Integrated Education*, 8 (March-April 1970), pp. 37–44.

5. *Liberator*, August 21, 1846.

6. *Liberator*, August 2, 1844.

7. Arthur R. Jensen, "How Much Can We Boost I.Q. and Scholastic Achievement?" *Harvard Educational Review* (winter 1969). Cf. A. G. Davey, "Teachers, Race and Intelligence," *Race*, 15 (October 1973), pp. 195–211.

8. Sherwood L. Washburn, "The Study of Race," in Melvin M. Tumin (ed.), *Race and Intelligence* (New York: Anti-Defamation League of B'nai B'rith, 1963), pp. 54–55.

All One System: Demographics of Education—Kindergarten Through Graduate School

HAROLD L. HODGKINSON

Institute for Educational Leadership

INTRODUCTION

In the beginning of this report, it is important to inform the reader of one of the major perceptual assumptions behind it. Almost everyone who works in education perceives it as a set of discrete institutions working in isolation from each other. These institutions restrict the age range of their students:

Nursery schools
Day care centers
Kindergartens
Elementary schools
Junior High Schools
Senior High Schools
Two Year Colleges
Four Year Undergraduate Colleges
Universities with Graduate Programs
Post-Graduate Institutions

People working in each of the above institutions have virtually no connection with all the others and little awareness of educational activity provided by the total. Because of this, the school is defined as the unit, not THE PEOPLE WHO MOVE THROUGH IT. The only people who see these institutions as a system are the students—because some of them see it all.

Striking as it seems, virtually all graduate students completed the third grade at an earlier time in their lives. It is our conviction that we need to begin seeing the educational system from the perspective of the people who move through it. This is because changes in the composition of the group moving through the educational system will change the system faster than anything else except nuclear war. . . .

Many changes are taking place now in the numbers and composition of the birth and immigrant groups that are beginning to enter elementary schools. These changes will necessarily occupy the educational system for at least the next twenty years. By knowing who is entering the system, and how well they are progressing, everyone at all levels will have time to develop effective programs for the maximum educational gains of all students. . . .

BRIEFING ON MAJOR DEMOGRAPHIC TRENDS

. . . It may be useful to describe the demographic changes that form the framework of our analysis.

1. BIRTHS: One of the major tools of demography is differential fertility—some groups have a lot more children than others, and thus are over-represented in the next generations. For example, it is clear that Cubans (1.3 children per female) and whites (1.7 children per female) will be LESS numerous in our future—a group needs about 2.1 just to stay even, which is the case for Puerto Ricans. However, Blacks (2.4), and Mexican-Americans (2.9) will be a larger part of our population in the future. All these young people have to do is GROW OLDER and we have the future. In attempting to explain differences in birth rates by region, we need to keep in mind that these regional differences are mostly ethnic—increased birth rates in the "Sun Belt" are due to a large degree by minority births, while "Frost Belt" declines are caused by the white populations. . . .

2. AGE: Mostly because of varying birth rates, the average age of groups in the U.S. is increasingly various—the 1980 Census reveals that the average white in America is 31 years old, the average Black 25, and the AVERAGE Hispanic only 22! It should be easy to see that age produces population momentum for minorities, as the typical Hispanic female is just moving into the peak childbearing years, while the average white female is moving out of them. This is why California now has a "majority of minorities" in its elementary schools, while Texas schools are 46% minority, and half the states have public school populations that are more than 25% nonwhite, while all of our 25 largest city school systems have "minority majorities."

By the year 2020, most of the Baby Boom will be retired, its retirement income provided by the much smaller age groups that follow it. This is a demographic argument, not an economic one. But if larger numbers are taking out, and much smaller numbers are putting in, the economics are rather clear. For example, in 1950 seventeen workers paid the benefits of each retiree. By 1992, only three workers will provide the funds for each retiree and one of the three workers will be minority.

It is also clear that for the next decade, the only growth area in education will be in adult and continuing education, with increases in elementary schools in certain regions. Perhaps more important is that in 1983 there were more people over 65 in America than there were teen-agers, and (because of the Baby Boom growing old) that condition remains a constant for as long as any of us live. America will simply not be a nation of youth in our lifetime. This is why by 1992, half of all college students will be over 25 and 20% will be over 35.

The mostly white Baby Boom, on the other hand, represents 70 million people who are middle-aged during the 1980's. . . .

3. FAMILY STATUS: Major changes have taken place in the ways we live together. In 1955, 60% of the households in the U.S. consisted of a working father, a housewife mother and two or more school age children. In 1980, that family unit was only 11% of our homes, and in 1985 it is 7%, an astonishing change.

More than 50% of women are in the work force, and that percentage will undoubtedly increase. Of our 80 million households, almost 20 million consist of people living alone. The Census tells us that 59% of the children born in 1983 will live with only one parent before reaching age 18—this now becomes the NORMAL childhood experience. Of every 100 children born today:

- 12 will be born out of wedlock
- 40 will be born to parents who divorce before the child is 18
- 5 will be born to parents who separate
- 2 will be born to parents of whom one will die before the child reaches 18
- 41 will reach age 18 "normally"

The U.S. is confronted today with an epidemic increase in the number of children born outside of marriage—and 50% of such children are born to teen-age mothers. Although the percentage of Black teen-age girls who have children outside of marriage is higher than that of white girls, comparisons with other nations indicate that a white teen-age female is twice as likely to give birth outside of marriage as in any other nation studied. The situation is most striking with very young mothers, age 13 and 14. Indeed, every day in America, 40 teen-age girls give birth to their THIRD child. To be the third child of a child is to be very much "at risk" in terms of one's future. It appears that sexual activity among the young is no more frequent here than elsewhere; the major difference is the inability of American youth to get access to information about contraception. Information about abortion is similarly restricted, although the variations across states are wide—Mississippi reports 4 abortions per 1,000 teen-age live births, while New York reports 1,200 abortions compared to 1,000 teen-age live births.

There is a particular aspect of this situation that is vital—teen-age mothers tend to give birth to children who are premature, due mostly to a lack of physical examinations and to their very poor diet while pregnant. Prematurity leads to low birth weight, which increases these infants' chances of major health problems due to the lack of development of the child's immune system. Low birth weight is a good predictor of major learning difficulties when the child gets to school. This means that about 700,000 babies of the annual cohort of around 3.3 million births are almost assured of being either educationally retarded or "difficult to teach." This group is entering the educational continuum in rapidly increasing numbers.

Several other family factors are important to cite—first, with over half of the females in the work force (and almost 70% if you only consider "working age" women), the number of "latch-key children"—those who are home alone after school when adults are not present—has shown a major increase and will continue to do so, as women increasingly opt for work AND children. (Of those mothers of one-year-olds, half have already returned to work.) The typical pattern for women today is (1) get settled in a job, (2) get married, and (3) have children, as opposed to the previous pattern of entering the work force only after the children were mature enough to fend for themselves. There are at least four million "latch-key" children in the U.S. of school age. Many of them think of home as a dangerous, frightening place, particularly if there are no other children in the home. They "check in" with parents by phone. They spend many hours watching TV and talking to their friends on the phone, and have to make decisions about knocks on the door and phone calls from strangers. The evidence is not yet in, and some children may benefit from having family responsibilities while home alone, but many others become problems at school.

There is some very good news also—there is today a solid and relatively well-established Black middle class family structure in the U.S. Access to the political structure has yielded 247 Black mayors in the U.S., and 5,606 Black elected officials in 1984, along with 3,128 elected Hispanic officials. Forty-four percent of the entering freshman class at the University of California, Berkeley in fall, 1984 was minority, while Harvard's entering class was 20% minority. In some major American cities, Blacks have been able to move to the suburbs. Here are the ten highest rates:

	Blacks in Metro Area	Blacks in Core City	Blacks in Suburbs	
Miami	281,000	87,000	194,000	(69%)*
Newark	406,000	191,000	215,000	(52.9%)
D.C.	870,000	448,000	422,000	(48.5%)
L.A.	943,000	504,000	439,000	(46.5%)
Atlanta	525,000	283,000	242,000	(46%)
Oakland	263,000	159,000	104,000	(39.5%)
St. Louis	319,000	206,000	113,000	(35.4%)
Birmingham	240,000	158,000	82,000	(34.1%)
Philadelphia	883,000	638,000	245,000	(27.7%)
Cleveland	345,000	251,000	94,000	(27.2%)

Editors' Note: This column gives the percentage of metro area Black residents who live in suburbs.

This is not to say that suburban housing is not segregated, but simply that there is more choice available in the system today. One unfortunate thing is that the percentage of Black two-income families is declining as a percent of all Black households, meaning that Blacks now distribute themselves over a much wider socioeconomic range than in the past. (Politicians seeking "The Black Vote" will have to be very careful in the future, as will politicians courting any supposedly "special interest group.") Between 1970 and 1980, the percentage of women, as well as minorities, in professional and managerial jobs virtually doubled.

There can be little doubt that affirmative action programs were responsible for at least some of these grains—firms doing business with the Federal government increased their minority work force by a fifth, while firms not doing business with the government increased minorities by only an eighth.

The other side of this coin is the rapid increase in the number of poor households headed by a female Black or Hispanic. Ninety percent of the increase in children born into poverty is from these households. Although two of three poor children are white, the percentage of Black children living with one parent who are poor is much higher, and those children who stay in poverty for more than four years (only one in three poor children does) are heavily Black. A child under six today is six times more likely to be poor than a person over 65. This is because we have increased support for the elderly, and government spending for poor children has actually DECLINED during the past decade. The result is an increase of over two million children during the decade who are "at risk" from birth. Almost half of the poor in the U.S. are children.

Today, we are a nation of 14.6 million Hispanics and 26.5 million Blacks. But by 2020 we will be a nation of 44 million Blacks and 47 million Hispanics—even more if Hispanic immigration rates increase. The total U.S. population for 2020 will be about 265 million people, a very small increase from our current 238 million—and more than 91 million of that figure will be minorities (and mostly young, while the mostly white Baby Boom moves out of the childrearing years by 1990, creating a "Baby Bust" that will again be mostly white, while minority births continue to increase).

We need to say a word about the third growing non-white sector of our nation, Asian-Americans. At the moment they are a much smaller group than Blacks and Hispanics (about 3.7 million in 1980), but their growth potential from immigration is very great for the next decade—they currently represent 44% of all immigrants admitted to the US. However, their diversity is very great:

- Sixty percent of Asian-Americans are foreign-born, yet the average Japanese-American speaks English as his/her native language, while almost no Indochinese do.

- Almost 30% of Asian-Americans arrive in the U.S. with four years of college already completed—39% of all Asian-American adults are college graduates.

- Their SAT verbal scores are far below white averages; their math SAT scores are equally far above whites.
- Because of increased Indochinese immigration, language problems among Asian-American youth will increase.
- Asian-American youth are heavily enrolled in public schools; a high percentage graduate and attend college. (Although access to college is wide-spread, hiring and promotion discrimination against Asian-Americans is also common.)
- Because of their competence in math and the physical sciences, Asian-Americans represent a disproportionate share of minority students at many of the highest rated universities.

As we review this material, it is easy to be comforted by the data on increased access for minorities to good jobs, to political leadership, and to owning their own businesses. However, it is equally clear that what is coming toward the educational system is a group of children who will be poorer, more ethnically and linguistically diverse, and who will have more handicaps that will affect their learning. Most important, by around the year 2000, America will be a nation in which one of every THREE of us will be non-white. And minorities will cover a broader socioeconomic range than ever before, making simplistic treatment of their needs even less useful.

4. REGION: Although the "Sunbelt" has shown high increases in growth percentage, the U.S. is very much an Eastern-dominated nation and will remain so well past the year 2000. An easy way to see this is to look at the percentage of our 237 million population who reside in each of the four time zones.

In 1985, we can see that the declines in the Middle Atlantic and New England states that were characteristic of the 70's have now been slowed—outmigration from most of these states has been matched by inmigration, leaving us with a new question: how do the people moving out compare with the people moving in? For example, Colorado is now the state with the highest percentage of its population possessing a college degree, but a very large number of these degrees were acquired in another state, at that state's expense, while Colorado has enjoyed the talents of the college graduates moving in.

In addition, the national decline of about 13% in public school students of the 1970–1980 decade breaks down to zero decline in about 12 "Sunbelt" states and over 25% in some "Frostbelt" states. There will be two major education agendas in the next decade: (1) planning for growth (kindergarten through graduate school) in 12 states, and (2) planning for continuing declines in secondary school populations in most of the rest. But few states with growth projections have noticed that the increased youth cohort is an increased MINORITY pool—"minority majorities" are possible in the next decade in the public schools of ten states.

5. EDUCATION: The higher education system is facing some major problems in terms of the work which will be done by its graduates. For example, over 18,000 doctorates will be awarded in the humanities during the 1980's with only a "handful" of jobs available for them in teaching. Doctoral scientists and engineers are more employable, and their numbers have grown since 1973 by 52%, to 364,000. However, only one in eight is female, and they are mainly in biology (20%), sociology/anthropology (27%), and psychology (28%). Few minorities are represented: Blacks are only 1.3% of doctoral scientists, Hispanics 0.6%, while Asians were 7.7% although they are only 1.5% of the U.S. population. (And in all U.S. graduate engineering programs, 43% of the students are foreign students. Thirty-six percent of all math and computer science graduate students are foreign students.)

In addition, the Bureau of Labor Statistics has stated that of the current group of college students, one in five will graduate and work in a job that requires no college education at all. In 1972, one in seven workers had a college degree, while in 1982 one worker in four did. Our economy is very good at generating new jobs—but most of them are low-paying service jobs which require little education. The problem is not a decline in "quality" jobs, but rather an increase in the number of college graduates, from 575,000 per year entering the work force annually during the 1960's to 1.4 million college graduates going to work annually during the 1970's. The problem may be alleviated in the next decade due to the decline of about 5 million youth in the 18–24 year old cohort, which may bring educational supply and job demand into better balance.

Our public schools have about finished a major season of state-based educational reforms. As of February, 1985:

- 43 states have strengthened high school graduation requirements, including 15 that require "exit tests" of high school seniors
- 14 states have adopted some version of "merit pay"
- 37 will lure the best college students into teaching through scholarships and other incentives
- Although standards have been made "tougher," only a handful of states have appropriated additional moneys for counselling and remediation for those who will need assistance in reaching the standards.

With the increased percentage of women (especially mothers) in the work force, the issues surrounding day care and early childhood education are coming to the fore. The successes of Head Start and similar programs have focussed new energy on the potential of early intervention programs for solving some of the educational and social problems that crop up later.

The number of youth eligible for Head Start type programs will increase in the next decade, as the number of children in poverty continues to expand. Poverty is more common among children than any other age group. . . .

In 1983, 14 million children lived in poverty—about 40% of the poor population. We have already seen that children in poverty come from certain kinds of households. In 1983, childhood poverty was 40% among ethnic minorities, but 14% among non-minority children. Fifty percent of children in female-headed households were in poverty compared to 12% in male-present households. Thirty percent of children in central cities were in poverty in 1983, but only 13% of children in non-central portions of cities. From 1959 to 1969, childhood poverty fell sharply, declining by about 6.5 million, despite an increase of 9% in the child population during the decade. From 1969 to 1979, childhood poverty increased, but slightly and erratically. From 1979 to 1983, however, the number of children in poverty grew by 3.7 million, and the rate grew from 16 to 22 percent, the highest level in 21 years. Although there was no decline in childhood poverty in 1983, such rates are quite dependent on economic conditions; if the present recovery continues it may be that childhood poverty will be reduced. The only thing we know with certainty is that the number of children eligible for Head Start type programs has increased by at least 1/3rd, while the programs are being level-funded in 1985.

Given the fact that only around 400,000 children are actually in Head Start, while at least three million are eligible, one of the best state strategies for improving their future would be the establishment of a state-wide Head Start system. Phasing in such a system might take a number of years, but no innovation could assure greater cost savings in terms of future services (prisons, drug control centers) that would not be needed. Head Start programs work.

To summarize the education consequences of demographic changes:

1. More children entering school from poverty households.
2. More children entering school from single-parent households.
3. More children from minority backgrounds.
4. A smaller percentage of children who have had Head Start and similar programs, even though more are eligible.
5. A larger number of children who were premature babies, leading to more learning difficulties in school.
6. More children whose parents were not married, now 12 of every 100 births.
7. More "latch-key" children and children from "blended" families as a result of remarriage of one original parent.
8. More children from teen-age mothers.
9. Fewer white, middle-class, suburban children, with day care (once the province of the poor) becoming a middle class norm as well, as more women enter the work force.
10. A continuing decline in the level of retention to high school graduation in virtually all states, except for minorities.
11. A continued drop in the number of minority high school graduates who apply for college.
12. A continued drop in the number of high school graduates, concentrated most heavily in the Northeast.
13. A continuing increase in the number of Black middle class students in the entire system.

14. Increased number of Asian-American students, but with more from Indonesia, and with increasing language difficulties.

15. Continuing high drop-outs among Hispanics, currently about 40% of whom complete high school.

16. A decline in the number of college graduates who pursue graduate studies in arts and sciences.

17. A major increase in part-time college students, and a decline of about 1 million in full time students. (Of our 12 million students, only about 2 million are full time, in residence, and 18–22 years of age.)

18. A major increase in college students who need BOTH financial and academic assistance. A great liaison between the offices of student financial aid and counseling will be essential.

19. A continuing increase in the number of college graduates who will get a job which requires no college degree. (Currently 20% of all college graduates.)

20. Continued increases in graduate enrollments in business, increased undergraduate enrollments in arts and sciences COURSES but not majors.

21. Increasing numbers of talented minority youth choosing the military as their educational route, both due to cost and direct access to "high technology."

22. Major increases in adult and continuing education outside of college and university settings—by business, by government, by other non-profits such as United Way, and by for-profit "franchise" groups such as Bell and Howell Schools and The Learning Annex.

23. Increased percentage of workers with a college degree. (From one in seven to one in four today.)

6

Factors Influencing
Academic Learning

The process of education is one of both success and failure. Many learn much and acquire advanced degrees; many do not. Those who do not succeed in school tend to be, as Chapter 5 shows, disproportionately working class and nonwhite.[1] This strong association between students' family background and their school success arouses the concern of most observers of education, although for different reasons. For policymakers, teachers, citizens, and scholars of a functionalist orientation, inequality in educational attainment is worrisome because it contravenes what they take to be education's function of providing equality of opportunity and social mobility. On the other hand, Marxists, Weberians, and Bourdieuians are also bothered, but not surprised, by the impact of family background on educational success. They see differences in educational attainment as in keeping with what they take to be education's real, although unfortunate, role of preserving inequality in society: the perpetuation of social inequality. In either case, both sides wish to understand the roots of educational success and failure and the role of family background in this process.

In order to explain educational success and failure, we need to move in an interactional direction, following students into and through the school. Chapters 6 and 7 do this tracing. Chapter 6 examines how "academic" or "cognitive" learning is produced: how students come to differ in how many years of education they get, how good their grades are, and how well they score on tests of reading, writing, arithmetic, and other such skills. Chapter 7, meanwhile, analyzes the creation of "nonacademic" or "noncognitive" learning: how basic social and political beliefs and attitudes such as individualism, obedience to authority, and religiosity are inculcated.

---

[1]Women have caught up with men in rates of college going. However, they still get fewer years of graduate education (Heyns and Bird, 1982; Karen, this book).

Scholars have advanced a host of explanations to explain class, race, and sex inequality in academic learning. These explanations fall into two main camps, which we can term the student-centered and the school-centered explanations. Generally, functionalists and political conservatives tend to advance student-centered explanations, while Weberians and Marxists and political liberals and radicals tend to give school-centered explanations. The student-centered explanations focus on how the traits students bring to school—for example, their intellectual ability and their desire for education—affect how much they get out of school. The school-centered explanations, on the other hand, focus on how schools differ in how they treat students of different backgrounds, with working-class or minority students more often getting poorly equipped schools or being assigned to the lower track. We will give considerable attention to the school-centered explanations. They are at the center of current debate over the causes of academic learning. And they recognize the point, which we have emphasized in earlier chapters, that the school's structure and organization shape interactions within it.

SCHOOL-CENTERED EXPLANATIONS

School-centered explanations argue in common that the reason working-class or nonwhite students get less education is because they go to inferior schools or are ineffectively taught. The specific school deficiencies that are highlighted vary greatly across different school-centered explanations.

School Resources

Until the mid-1960s, the dominant school-centered explanation was one that we can term the "school resources" argument. This explanation focused on differences between the social classes and races in the quality of the schools they attended.[2] Adherents of this position believed that working-class and nonwhite students received less education because they attended schools that spent little on students and lacked well-endowed facilities and experienced teachers (Sexton, 1961).

The school resources explanation seems almost self-evident. But in the late 1960s and early 1970s, it was shattered by two studies: one by James Coleman and his colleagues (1966) and another by Christopher Jencks and his colleagues (1972). They found that across the nation working-class and nonwhite students on the average did not attend schools that spent significantly less money, had less experienced teachers, or were less well equipped than the schools attended by more privileged students. Moreover, what differences there were in these particular school resources had little impact on class

---

[2]Until the late 1960s, sex differences in educational attainment were not seen as problematic. It was well known that women typically got less education, but this was widely held as acceptable, given that they did not enter the same occupations as men. Hence, little effort was expended to explain why women received less education.

and racial differences in educational attainment. In fact, school differences of whatever sort seemed to have little impact: the greatest test score gap was not between average students at two different schools but between good and bad students in the same school.[3] This unexpected finding was replicated by a host of reanalyses of the very same data used by Coleman and Jencks (Mosteller and Moynihan, 1972) and by evaluations of compensatory education programs, such as Head Start, that found that they did not seem to produce any striking benefits.[4]

These findings largely destroyed the school resources explanation and, along with it, much of the rationale liberals of the time gave for educational reform.[5] Within a few years, however, a variety of new school-centered explanations of educational inequality appeared. These new explanations were more attentive to within-school differences in student achievement. Moreover, rather than focusing on gross school features such as per capita school spending and average experience of teachers, these new explanations focused on the precise interactional factors that account for how schools affect students. These factors—most notably, the amount of time students actually engage in learning ("academic learning time"), curriculum grouping or tracking, and the climate of expectations in a school—are discussed below. Finally, these new explanations had a more sophisticated view of schools. Rather than seeing them as simply spots where students and teachers come together, they saw schools more as organizations that are comprised of different levels, each of which has its own unique processes and impact on students (Barr and Dreeben, 1983).

Academic Learning Time[6]

The kernel of this concept is the idea that how much time you spend learning determines how much you learn. This idea has a rather long lineage. John Carroll (1963) was a key early proponent of the importance of learning time. His argument was then picked up and refined in Benjamin Bloom's (1976) idea of "mastery learning," Harnischfeger and Wiley's (1978) concern with quantity of schooling, Fisher and others' (1980) concept of "academic learning time," and Barr and Dreeben's (1983) concern with the impact of amount of material covered.[7]

---

[3]Put in technical terms, most of the difference between students was "within schools" rather than "between schools."

[4]Later research, however, found that the pessimistic initial evaluations of Head Start may have been far off the mark. See, for example, Weikart and Schweinhart (1984).

[5]This explanation is still offered by some scholars and by many policymakers and parents, as witness the fact that a common element of virtually any call for educational reform is a recommendation for more spending on schools, better educated teachers, and more modern facilities. See Chapter 10 for more on this.

[6]The sources cited with respect to "academic learning time" are listed under this title in the reference section.

[7]For a nice summary of this conceptual development, see Barr and Dreeben (1983: 34–40) and Levin (1984).

The selection by Charles Fisher, Richard Marliave, and Nikola Filby, "Improving Teaching by Increasing 'Academic Learning Time'," argues that how much students learn is affected by how much time they actually spend learning ("academic learning time" or "time on task") as versus running around the classroom or engaging in classroom housekeeping tasks. Fisher and others argue that "academic learning time" is dependent on how much time is allocated for a certain learning task, how much of the allocated time students are actually engaged in working on the task, and the match between the task's difficulty and the student's ability at the moment. These factors are in turn dependent on yet another set of factors: teachers' ability to diagnose whether the tasks are appropriate to the lesson and to students' abilities; the amount of substantive academic contact between teachers and students (especially feedback by the teachers on whether students are correctly grasping the lesson); how clear teachers are in specifying the tasks students are to do; and finally, teachers' degree of emphasis on academic goals and student achievement as versus concern with students' attitudes and feelings.[8]

Many scholars and policymakers put great stock in the importance of academic learning time. It is a major basis for the recommendation of the National Commission on Excellence in Education (1983) and other recent educational commissions that the school day and the school year be extended.[9] And there is reason to believe that academic learning time may explain part of the seeming gap in effectiveness between American and Japanese schools. Japanese schools not only have a longer school day and year; but more important, less school time is wasted in students failing to concentrate on learning and instead engaging in inappropriate activities (Gordon, 1987: 7).

Despite its attractiveness, however, the academic learning time concept must be approached with a degree of caution. The policy implications of the concept are by no means clear. Simply increasing the amount of time students spend in class or on homework may not necessarily translate into more learning. Students may not want to spend more time on schoolwork and may respond by dropping out or putting in less effort.[10] Furthermore, the research foundation for the academic learning time argument is not entirely secure. Studies comparing American schools to each other and American to foreign schools do not find that differences in instructional time translate into large differences in amount learned, once one adequately controls for differences in the characteristics of students and teachers (Karweit, 1981; Levin, 1984).[11]

---

[8]These more basic factors are discussed in Charles Fisher and others (1980). Recent studies buttressing and extending the argument by Fisher and others include Barr and Dreeben (1983), Brophy and Good (1986), and Dreeben and Gamoran (1986).

[9]See Chapter 10 of this book for excerpts from and commentary on the recent reports by the education commissions.

[10]To be sure, advocates of the academic learning time argument acknowledge that the key is how much "engaged" time is achieved. But they are still hazy on how one gets this.

[11]Specifically, Levin (1984) criticizes the well-known studies by Harnischfeger and Wiley (1978)—which found a very large impact of instructional time on learning—for having inadequate

Curriculum Grouping

"Curriculum grouping" or tracking has also interested scholars concerned with explaining differences in educational attainment. By curriculum grouping we mean the breaking up of students into different classes or groups within classes and teaching them different material or at different paces. This differentiation of students is made on the basis not only of students' test scores but also other factors, such as the number of students in the class and their distribution of ability (Barr and Dreeben, 1983: chap. 4). Hence, curriculum or instructional groups are often rather heterogeneous in test scores and only partially approach being ability groups, a term that is often, but mistakenly, used as a synonym for curriculum groups.

Many scholars argue that curriculum grouping plays a key role in producing class and race differences in educational attainment for two reasons. First, curriculum grouping, particularly in the elementary school, has a significant impact on educational attainment that is independent of the characteristics of students.[12] And second, students differing in social class and race tend to be assigned to different curriculum groups (Alexander and Cook, 1982; Dreeben and Gamoran, 1986; Hallinan, 1984; Rosenbaum, 1980a, 1980b).[13]

Researchers are now pointing to two major factors in order to explain how assignment to different curriculum groups leads to differential educational achievement. One factor is that students in different groups are exposed to different *amounts* of instruction (Barr and Dreeben, 1983; Dreeben and Gamoran, 1986; Grant and Rothenberg, 1986; Rowan and Miracle, 1983). (Note the tieback to the academic learning time argument.) Lower-track students seemingly receive less academic learning time because their teachers expect them to learn less and because they are more likely to be interrupted by the teacher and by each other (Eder, 1981; Grant and Rothenberg, 1986; Haskins, Walden, and Ramey, 1983; Rist, 1970; Schwartz, 1981). The second major factor is that lower-track students are exposed to lower *quality* instruction: their curriculum is more oriented to rote skills than comprehension and higher order reasoning; and their teachers are less enthusiastic and prepared (Hiebert, 1983; McDermott, 1978; Oakes, 1985; Persell, 1977; Rosenbaum, 1980a).

---

controls for student and school characteristics. Because of this, the difference in achievement that they found might be largely due *not* to differences in instructional time but to differences in such factors as student body composition.

[12]The effects of elementary school ability grouping seem to be considerably greater than those of high school tracking. However, even high school track placement has significant effects, independent of student characteristics, on important student outcomes, such as whether students plan to attend college (Alexander and Cook, 1982).

[13]The sources cited are listed in the reference section under the title "Curriculum Grouping." Typically, the association of class and race with curriculum-group or track assignment drops considerably and even becomes insignificant once class and race differences in test scores are controlled for. However, this does not mean that students' social class or race does not affect which curriculum group they are placed in. Rather, it indicates that much of the relationship between students' social class and race and their curriculum-group assignment may be due to class and race differences in academic achievement.

The selection by Frances Schwartz, "Supporting or Subverting Learning: Peer Group Patterns in Four Tracked Schools," provides an ethnographic analysis that illustrates these points. Schwartz contrasts the educational process in lower-track and upper-track classrooms and examines the sources of these differences. She notes that lower-track pupils are more disruptive than higher-track pupils. But Schwartz argues that this difference occurs because lower-track pupils feel ashamed about the low status of their track and their teachers' lack of interest in their progress. This lack of teacher interest is expressed in pushing lower-track students less hard and reprimanding them less often than high-track students. Teachers are less interested in lower-track students because they do not fit teachers' model of the good student; so to avoid disappointment, teachers reduce their expectations.[14]

Most educational researchers are now advocating that curriculum grouping should be used much more carefully (Hallinan, 1984), and some argue that it should be entirely abandoned (Oakes, 1985). Numerous teachers find this suggestion utopian given the difficulties of running heterogeneous classrooms. However, a variety of scholars are pioneering various methods for effectively teaching heterogeneous groups (Sharan, 1980; Slavin, 1980, 1987).

Effective Schools

The theoretical and research current that has been loosely labeled the "effective schools" approach draws together many of the elements of the new school-centered explanations described above: especially the concern with academic learning time and teachers' expectations. Moreover, with its concern with how school organization and climate contribute to effective education, the effective schools movement ties in nicely with our interest in how the structural features of schools condition teacher behavior and student success.

The selection by Gilbert Austin, "Exemplary Schools and the Search for Effectiveness," summarizes the tenets of the effective schools approach.[15] Researchers using this approach have identified schools whose students perform much better than is typical for such students. They then have tried to isolate the characteristics that distinguish such unusually effective schools. What emerges is that these effective schools are characterized by the following: a climate of high expectations for students on the part of teachers and principals; principals who carefully plan the educational program, strongly support teachers and secure their loyalty, but also hold teachers accountable; teachers who spend most of their time actually teaching and who monitor their students closely; and teachers and principals who feel they

---

[14]For discussions as to how teachers come to form reduced expectations in the face of the wear and tear of teaching, see Becker (1952), Cusick (1983), and Sizer (1984).

[15]Other well-known exponents of the effective schools approach include Edmonds (1979), Brookover and others (1979), and Austin and Garber (1985). Works supporting the effective schools movement are cited under "Effective Schools" in the references.

have room to experiment and adapt school procedures to the actual circumstances they encounter.[16]

These claims about effective schools resonate with other bodies of research that are not normally connected. The effective schools movement has much in common with the back-to-basics movement of the 1970s, which also emphasized the importance of order and discipline, attention to basic skills, and increased testing (Stedman, 1987: 218). Moreover, the effective schools approach has much in common with the much publicized research on the benefits of private schooling by James Coleman, whose 1966 report did so much to call into question the school resources approach. In recent research, Coleman has argued that Catholic schools provide a significantly better education than do public schools, due to particular features such as stricter discipline and higher educational standards (Coleman, Hoffer, and Kilgore, 1982; Coleman and Hoffer, 1987; and Hoffer, Greeley, and Coleman, 1985).[17]

The effective schools approach has generated great enthusiasm among educators, researchers, and policymakers. Many of its ideas show up in the report of the highly influential National Commission on Excellence in Education (1983) (see Chapter 10). Moreover, many states have rushed to implement effective schools programs (Stedman, 1987).

While the effective schools argument opens up very attractive vistas for educational research and policy, it is by no means solidly founded. Questions have been raised over whether the putative effects are anywhere as strong or as solidly backed up by evidence as claimed.[18] Moreover, even if the effective schools impact proves to be sizable, it is often unclear how effective schools could be intentionally produced. For example, partisans of the effective schools approach have not yet made clear how precisely one creates a school-wide climate of expectations for high achievement. This question about implementation is made more troubling by the fact that most studies of effective schools have been conducted on inner city elementary schools, raising questions about their generalizability to other schools. Finally, the effective schools program may generate negative side effects. It may lead to excessive standardization, leaving little room to tailor the curriculum to the needs of different students. And it may result in focusing too much attention on raising test scores, at the expense of other goals such as developing artistic ability or appreciation (Cuban, 1983; Purkey and Smith, 1983; Rowan, Bossert, and Dwyer, 1983; Stedman, 1985, 1987).

---

[16]The effective schools movement has emphasized the importance of leadership by principals. However, it has been argued that the important thing is school-based leadership, and this can come as well from committees of teachers, school/parent councils, or some other similar source (Stedman, 1987: 218).

[17]The extent, sources, and policy implications of these findings have, however, been challenged by a wide variety of scholars. See the special issues on Coleman's research in *Sociology of Education* (April/July 1982, October 1983, and April 1985) and the *Harvard Educational Review* (November 1981).

[18]In particular, it is unclear to what degree the effective schools movement may be overemphasizing differences *between* schools in quality, when the most important differences in student achievement are within the same schools, as between the college preparatory and vocational tracks (Coleman and others, 1966; Jencks and others, 1972).

STUDENT-CENTERED EXPLANATIONS

Student-centered explanations have coexisted with school-centered ones, either as complements or competitors. They emphasize the impact on student learning not of what schools do but of what students bring to school. As with the school-centered explanations, student-centered explanations come in a variety of forms. "Geneticist" arguments trace the lower educational attainment of working-class or minority pupils largely to a lack of genes contributing to intelligence. "Cultural deprivation" or "culture deficit" arguments, meanwhile, attribute the educational difficulties of working-class or nonwhite pupils to a lack, due to an inadequate home life, of those skills and attitudes that aid school success. "Culture difference" arguments, however, attribute disadvantaged students' educational difficulties to students' rebellion against schools or schools' intolerance of pupils who come with skills and attitudes that are different from white upper-class or middle-class culture.

Functionalists and political conservatives are more prone to offer student-centered explanations than are liberals and radicals. Moreover, when the latter do offer student-centered explanations, they tend to be less individualistic than conservative or functionalist explanations. Rather than attributing differences in learning to family upbringing, liberals and radicals root them in large-scale social structures, such as race differences in position in the economy. The Ogbu reading in this chapter is an example of a liberal or radical student-centered explanation.

Genetic Differences

The geneticist argument was advanced most prominently by the educational psychologist Arthur Jensen (1969), who had begun his career as a partisan of cultural deprivation theory. Noting the seeming failure of compensatory education, Jensen argued that scholars now had to take seriously the argument that working-class or minority students do less well educationally because they have less intelligence and that deficit in intelligence is largely due to an inferior genetic makeup. This argument is not new. The geneticist explanation had been around since the turn of the century, but it had been in eclipse since the 1940s (Kamin, 1974). The novelty of Jensen's article lay in his vigorous restatement of an old argument and the wide range of studies he used to try to substantiate it.[19]

The geneticist argument has been vigorously attacked by many different scholars on a variety of grounds. First, antigeneticists argue that race and social class differences in average test scores are largely due to cultural biases in the content of tests and in the conditions under which they are given. They agree that nonwhite or working-class students on the average get lower test scores than do white or upper-class students, but they argue that this reflects a difference not in intelligence but in knowledge of white or upper-class culture. Second, the antigeneticists argue that any remaining real differences in test scores are largely not due to genetic factors but to social factors,

[19]A concise and readable defense of Jensen's argument can be found in Herrnstein (1980).

including both family upbringing and schooling (Bowles and Gintis, 1976: chap. 4; Jencks and others, 1972; Kamin, 1974; Persell, 1977: 58–75).[20]

Cultural Deprivation

The argument that student differences are due to social factors has taken two main forms: cultural deprivation theory and, more recently, cultural difference theory. Cultural deprivation theory, which was in its heyday in the mid-1960s, is represented by the selection by Martin Deutsch, "The Disadvantaged Child and the Learning Process." Deutsch argues that working-class and nonwhite students perform poorly because their families do not raise them in such a fashion as to develop the skills and attitudes that contribute to school success. Disadvantaged children come to school without adequate skills in using the English language, making adequate visual and auditory discriminations, and asking informational questions of adults. Moreover, he asserts, disadvantaged children have low educational and occupational aspirations, a poor sense of time, and less ability to work without immediate reward. These deficiencies in skill and attitude are rooted in parents' poor socialization practices, the absence of the father, and the family's frequent poverty and unemployment.[21]

Many scholars have bitterly attacked the cultural deficit theory as letting schools and other social institutions escape criticism by focusing blame on the supposed deficiencies of working-class and minority school children. They argue that this attitude of "blaming the victim" permeates much of social policy because it provides policymakers and concerned citizens with an apparent solution to social problems that deflects blame from themselves and obviates the need for fundamental social change (Baratz and Baratz, 1970; Ryan, 1969).[22] The cultural deprivation argument was also undermined by the seeming failure of one of its key policy recommendations: compensatory education. The first evaluations of compensatory education seemed to indicate that it did not work (Jensen, 1969). (However, see footnote 4.)

In the face of cultural deprivation theory's flaws, scholars emphasizing a student-centered explanation of educational outcomes went in two different directions: some, like Jensen, toward a geneticist argument; and some toward a culture difference argument.

---

[20]Recently, the geneticist/antigeneticist controversy has begun to break down as certain proponents of the genetic interpretation stake positions midway between Jensen and the antigeneticists. For example, Sandra Scarr (1981: 447–464) agrees that IQ tests do not measure intelligence in any final sense, but rather the intellectual skills demanded by white, upper-class culture; and she agrees that racial differences in IQ test scores are almost entirely due to environmental factors.

[21]Other statements of cultural deprivation theory can be found in Banfield (1968); Bloom, Davis, and Hess (1965); and Lewis (1965). See the category "Cultural Deprivation/Cultural Difference" in the references.

[22]This criticism is particularly on target in the case of Banfield (1968), but it is less fair to other statements of cultural deprivation theory, which are more open to social change and recommend extensive programs of compensatory education.

Culture Differences

The "cultural difference" argument rejects cultural deprivation theory from a very different angle from the geneticist school. The cultural difference argument acknowledges that working-class and nonwhite youth arrive at school lacking the attitudes and skills that schools expect, but it rejects the claim that this lack is due to any deficiency on the part of working-class or minority students or their parents. However, culture difference theorists disagree among themselves in the explanations they offer for the student/school cultural mismatch. Two main arguments have been made.

Some partisans of the culture difference position agree that working-class and minority students do often lack educationally important skills and attitudes. However, they attribute this lack not to inadequate parenting (as argued by the cultural deprivation school) but to the problem of being raised within an oppressed subculture.

The selection by John Ogbu, "Social Stratification and the Socialization of Competence," argues this particular culture difference position. Ogbu criticizes the cultural deprivation school's "failure of socialization" argument.[23] Instead, Ogbu argues that black parents (and predominantly black schools) have *effectively* socialized black children. The reason their children differ from white children in their attitudes and skills is because black socialization has a different goal. Blacks and whites still differ considerably in the opportunities they face: Blacks face a "job ceiling" in how far they can rise that whites do not face. Black parents therefore socialize their children to have the attitudes and skills that will allow them to cope with inferior positions. These skills and attitudes tend to differ from those that whites acquire and expect, because whites face a different future.

Ogbu's argument is very similar to Bowles and Gintis's (1976) "correspondence principle" and Bourdieu's (1974) notion of "habitus." All of them view the low educational aspirations of working-class and minority students as due to parents' and children's unhappy accommodation to the realities of an unequal class structure. (See Chapter 2 for more on Bowles and Gintis and Bourdieu.)

Other culture difference theorists take a position quite different from the above. They simply deny that working-class and nonwhite youth have inferior or problematic skills. The problem lies instead in the fact that students refuse to use their skills or schools fail to recognize and build on them. Paul Willis (1981) and Joseph Kahl (1953) argue that the problem lies in students' refusal. Kahl (1953) describes many working-class students as having low aspirations and not trying hard because they positively want to be working class. Willis (1981) makes a similar, but more pungent, argument: He states that working-class students not only prefer working-class life but contemp-

---

[23]Ogbu's characterization of the cultural deprivation argument as one of "failure of socialization" is not entirely fair. The more sophisticated versions of the cultural deprivation argument—particularly Lewis (1965)—agree that working-class and minority-group cultures are an adaptation to oppressive life circumstances. However, unlike Ogbu, they tend to veer off into treating minority culture as due to a defective family life and as more the cause, than the consequence, of working-class and minority-group poverty.

tuously reject the school because they correctly perceive it to be wedded to middle-class values of intellectualism and emotional control. Other scholars argue that the problem lies not in pupil rejection of the school but rather in schools' failure to recognize and build on disadvantaged pupils' real skills (Baratz and Baratz, 1970; Labov, 1970). For example, the sociolinguist William Labov (1970) shows that blacks, far from speaking a substandard form of English, speak a distinct dialect that operates on different rules and is quite complex. Blacks' educational problem therefore rests not on blacks' supposed lack of command of English but the fact that schools react negatively to black English. One solution, therefore, is to provide instruction, at least initially, in black English (Baratz and Baratz, 1970: 41).

CONCLUSIONS

The variety of explanations for school success and failure that we have reviewed is bewildering. Which, if any, are right? We argue that several of these explanations hold great promise for educational policy, especially when used in conjunction in order to make up for their individual one-sidedness.

There is no reason to choose between a school-centered and a student-centered explanation. Both sides of the student/school relationship must be incorporated in any complete explanation of why some students do better educationally than others. For example, the school-centered explanations make virtually no reference to how students' backgrounds affect their schooling; yet the student-centered explanations show that students' backgrounds have a profound impact on their ability and willingness to benefit from schools. Many studies are showing that the success of schools' efforts to motivate students depends in good part on receiving support from parents and members of the local community (Coleman and Hoffer, 1987; Stedman, 1987: 218–219). On the other hand, the new student-centered explanations need the supplement of school-centered explanations. Student-centered explanations describe the mismatches between the characteristics that students bring to school and those that schools demand, but they largely fail to explain in detail how the school can reduce this mismatch.

The area of educational expectations provides a good example of the importance of both student-centered and school-centered explanations. Quantitative sociologists studying student careers have found that student aspirations are affected by such student-centered variables as parents' aspirations and students' ability. But those studies have also found a strong impact of school-centered variables: in this case teachers' aspirations for students (Sewell and Hauser, 1975: 98–105).[24]

[24]It should be noted that schools' impact on student aspirations is not restricted to elementary or secondary school. Colleges also have a significant impact in shaping student hopes (McClelland, forthcoming).

Our recommendation of detente and synthesis between warring positions applies not just to the conflict between the school-centered and student-centered explanations, but also to the conflicts within each of these positions. For example, there is reason to believe that both the cultural difference and cultural deprivation arguments are partially correct. As the culture difference school claims, working-class and black students do come to school with abilities and motivations that school can build on. At the same time, as the cultural deprivation school argues, these students do tend to lack some of the skills and attitudes that schooling requires and this lack is not simply a product of discrimination but also to some degree family breakdown and economic deprivation (Hurn, 1985: 163–166).[25]

While a more complete theory of educational outcomes must combine the best of available explanations, it should not simply rest here. There are many areas in which the available explanations are seriously defective or incomplete. First, these explanations are often not clear on their precise policy implications. For example, as discussed above, the proponents of academic learning time and effective schools have not yet fully spelled out precisely how one would utilize their research finding to improve schools. Second, the explanations above, particularly the school-centered arguments, come close to arguing that the school alone can solve the problem of class and race inequality in educational performance and attainment. But, as several scholars have forcefully pointed out, schools cannot by themselves eliminate educational inequality, for it arises in good part from economic and political inequalities in the larger society (Bowles and Gintis, 1976; Jencks and others, 1972). However, schools can certainly mitigate educational inequality.[26] And by doing that, they lay the basis for addressing the more fundamental structures of inequality. These questions about the policy implications of the explanations reviewed here are pursued in greater detail in the introduction to Chapter 10, which concerns the current movement for educational reform.

REFERENCES

General References

Becker, Howard S. 1952. "Social Class Variations in the Teacher-Pupil Relationship." *Journal of Educational Sociology* 25 (April): 451–465.

Bourdieu, Pierre. 1974. "The School as a Conservative Force. Scholastic and Cultural Inequalities." In John Eggleston (ed.), *Contemporary Research in the Sociology of Education*, pp. 32–46. London: Methuen.

---

[25]One scholar who has tried to reconcile the culture difference and cultural deprivation approaches has been the British sociologist of education Basil Bernstein (Bernstein, 1974–1976; Karabel and Halsey, 1977: 62–71). Within the sociology of race relations, William J. Wilson (1987) has been making a similar attempt to avoid the cultural deprivation/cultural difference polarization.

[26]The utility of schools in reducing class inequality is highlighted by Heyns (1978), who finds that working-class and nonwhite students keep pace educationally with their more privileged classmates much better during the school year than during the summer.

Bowles, Samuel, and Herbert Gintis. 1976. *Schooling in Capitalist America*. New York: Basic Books.

Coleman, James S., Ernest Q. Campbell, Carol J. Hobson, James McPartland, Alexander M. Mood, Frederic D. Weinfeld, and Robert L. York. 1966. *Equality of Educational Opportunity*. Washington, DC: Government Printing Office.

Cusick, Philip A. 1983. *The Egalitarian Ideal and the American High School*. New York: Longman.

Gordon, Bonnie. 1987. "Cultural Comparisons of Schooling." *Educational Researcher* (August-September): 4–7.

Herrnstein, Richard. 1980. "In Defense of Intelligence Tests." *Commentary* 69 (February): 40–51.

Heyns, Barbara. 1978. *Summer Learning and the Effects of Schooling*. New York: Academic Press.

————, and Joyce Adair Bird. 1982. "Recent Trends in the Higher Education of Women." In Pamela Perun (ed.), *The Undergraduate Woman*, pp. 43–69. Lexington, MA: Lexington Books.

Hurn, Christopher. 1985. *The Limits and Possibilities of Schooling*. 2nd ed. Boston: Allyn and Bacon.

Jencks, Christopher, Marshall S. Smith, Henry Acland, Mary Jo Bane, David Cohen, Herbert Gintis, Barbara Heyns, and Stephan Michelson. 1972. *Inequality*. New York: Basic Books.

Jensen, Arthur R. 1969. "How Much Can We Boost I.Q. and Scholastic Achievement?". *Harvard Educational Review* 39: 1–123.

Kahl, Joseph. 1953. "Educational and Occupational Aspirations of 'Common Man' Boys." *Harvard Educational Review* 23: 186–203.

Kamin, Leon. 1974. *The Science and Politics of IQ*. Hillsdale, NJ: Erlbaum.

Karabel, Jerome, and A. H. Halsey (eds.). 1977. *Power and Ideology in Education*. New York: Oxford University Press.

Karen, David. 1989. "Access to Higher Education in the United States, 1900 to the Present." (Reprinted in Chapter 5 of this book.)

McClelland, Katherine. Forthcoming. "Cumulative Disadvantage Among the Highly Ambitious: The Effects of Social Origins, Gender, Marriage, and College Quality on Early Educational Attainments and Occupational Expectations." *Sociology of Education*.

Mosteller, Frederick, and Daniel P. Moynihan. 1972. *On Equality of Educational Opportunity*. New York: Vintage Books.

National Commission on Excellence in Education. 1983. *A Nation At Risk*. Washington, DC: Government Printing Office.

Persell, Caroline H. 1977. *Education and Inequality*. New York: Free Press.

Scarr, Sandra. 1981. *Race, Social Class, and Individual Differences in I.Q.* Hillsdale, NJ: Erlbaum.

Sewell, William H., and Robert M. Hauser. 1975. *Education, Occupation, and Earnings*. New York: Academic Press.

Sexton, Patricia C. 1961. *Education and Income*. New York: Viking.

Sharan, Shalom. 1980. "Cooperative Learning in Small Groups." *Review of Educational Research* 50: 241–271.

Sizer, Theodore. 1984. *Horace's Compromise*. Boston: Houghton-Mifflin. (See the Sizer article in Chapter 10 of this book.)

Slavin, Robert. 1980. "Cooperative Learning." *Review of Educational Research* 50: 315–342.

_____. 1987. "Cooperative Learning and the Cooperative School." *Educational Leadership* 45 (November): 7–13.

Weikart, David, and Lawrence J. Schweinhart. 1984. *Changed Lives: The Effects of the Perry Preschool Program on Youths through Age 19.* Ypsilanti, MI: High Scope.

Willis, Paul. 1981. *Learning to Labour.* New York: Columbia University Press.

Wilson, William J. 1987. *The Truly Disadvantaged.* Chicago: University of Chicago Press.

Academic Learning Time/Time on Task

Barr, Rebecca, and Robert Dreeben. 1983. *How Schools Work.* Chicago: University of Chicago Press.

Bloom, Benjamin, 1976. *Human Characteristics and School Learning.* New York: McGraw-Hill.

Brophy, Jere, and Thomas L. Good. 1986. "Teacher Behavior and Student Achievement." In M. C. Wittrock (ed.), *Handbook of Research on Teaching.* New York: Macmillan.

Carroll, John B. 1963. "A Model of School Learning." *Teachers College Record* 64: 723–733.

Fisher, Charles W., David C. Berliner, Nikola N. Filby, Richard Marliave, Leonard S. Cahen, and Marilyn M. Dishaw. 1980. "Teaching Behaviors, Academic Learning Time, and Student Achievement." In Carolyn Denham and Ann Lieberson (eds.), *Time to Learn,* pp. 7–32. Washington, DC: Government Printing Office.

Harnischfeger, Annagret, and David Wiley. 1978. "Conceptual Issues in Models of School Learning." *Journal of Curriculum Studies* 3: 215–231.

Karweit, Nancy. 1981. "Time in School." In Ronald Corwin (ed.), *Research in the Sociology of Education and Socialization.* vol. 2. Greenwich, CT: JAI Press.

Levin, Henry. 1984. "About Time for Educational Reform." *Educational Evaluation and Policy Analysis* 6 (summer): 151–164.

Curriculum Grouping

Alexander, Karl, and Martha Cook. 1982. "Curriculum and Coursework." *American Sociological Review* 47: 626–640.

Dreeben, Robert, and Adam Gamoran. 1986. "Race, Instruction, and Learning." *American Sociological Review* 51: 660–669.

Eder, Donna. 1981. "Ability Grouping as a Self-Fulfilling Prophecy." *Sociology of Education* 54: 151–162.

Grant, Linda, and James Rothenberg. 1986. "The Social Enhancement of Ability Differences." *Elementary School Journal* 87 (spring): 28–37.

Hallinan, Maureen. 1984. "Summary and Implications." In Penelope Peterson, Louise Cherry Wilkinson, and Maureen Hallinan (eds.), *The Social Context of Instruction,* pp. 229–240. New York: Academic Press.

Haskins, Ron, Tedra Walden, and Craig Ramey. 1983. "Teacher and Student Behavior in High and Low Ability Groups." *Journal of Educational Psychology* 75: 865–876.

Hiebert, Elfrieda. 1983. "An Examination of Ability Grouping for Reading Instruction." *Reading Research Quarterly* 18 (winter): 231–255.

Oakes, Jeannie. 1985. *Keeping Track.* New Haven, CT: Yale University Press.

Persell, Caroline H. 1977. *Education and Inequality.* New York: Free Press.

Rist, Ray C. 1970. "Student Social Class and Teacher Expectations: The Self-Fulfilling Prophecy in Ghetto Education." *Harvard Educational Review* 40: 411–451.

Rosenbaum, James. 1980a. "Social Implications of Educational Grouping." In David Berliner (ed.), *Review of Research in Education,* pp. 361–401. Washington, DC: American Educational Research Association.

_____. 1980b. "Track Misperceptions and Frustrated College Plans." *Sociology of Education* 53: 74–87.

Rowan, Brian, and Andrew Miracle. 1983. "Systems of Ability Grouping and the Stratification of Achievement in Elementary School." *Sociology of Education* 56: 133–144.

Schwartz, Frances. 1981. "Supporting or Subverting Learning: Peer Group Patterns in Four Tracked Schools." *Anthropology and Education Quarterly* 12: 99–121. (An excerpt is included in this chapter.)

Effective Schools

Austin, Gilbert R., and Herbert Garber (eds.). 1985. *Research on Exemplary Schools.* Orlando, FL: Academic Press.

Brookover, Wilbur, Charles Beady, Patricia Flood, John Schweitzer, and Joe Wisenbaker. 1979. *School Social Systems and Student Achievement.* New York: Praeger.

Coleman, James S., Thomas Hoffer, and Sally Kilgore. 1982. *High School Achievement.* New York: Basic Books.

_____and Thomas Hoffer. 1987. *Public and Private Schools: The Impact of Communities.* New York: Basic Books.

Cuban, Larry. 1983. "Effective Schools: A Friendly but Cautionary Note." *Phi Delta Kappan* 64: 695–696.

Edmonds, Ron. 1979. "Effective Schools for the Urban Poor." *Educational Leadership* 37: 15–27.

Hoffer, Thomas, Andrew M. Greeley, and James S. Coleman. 1985. "Achievement Growth in Public and Catholic Schools." *Sociology of Education* 58 (April): 74–97.

Pallas, Aaron M., Doris R. Entwisle, Karl L. Alexander, and Doris Cadigan. 1987. "Children Who Do Exceptionally Well in First Grade." *Sociology of Education* 60: 257–271.

Purkey, Sherman, and Marshall S. Smith. 1983. "Effective Schools: A Review." *Elementary School Journal* 83: 426–452.

Rowan, Brian, Steven Bossert, and David Dwyer. 1983. "Research on Effective Schools: A Cautionary Note." *Educational Researcher* 12 (April): 24–31.

Stedman, Lawrence. 1985. "A New Look at the Effective Schools Literature." *Urban Education* 20: 295–326.

_____. 1987. "It's Time We Changed the Effective Schools Formula." *Phi Delta Kappan* 69 (November): 215–224.

Cultural Deprivation/Cultural Difference

Banfield, Edward. 1968. *The Unheavenly City.* Boston: Little, Brown.

Baratz, Stephen S., and Joan C. Baratz. 1970. "Early Childhood Intervention: The Social-Science Base of Institutional Racism." *Harvard Educational Review* 40: 29–50.

Bernstein, Basil. 1974–1976. *Class, Codes, and Control.* 3 vols. London: Routledge and Kegan Paul.

Bloom, Benjamin S., Allison Davis, and Robert Hess. 1965. *Compensatory Education for Cultural Deprivation.* New York: Holt.

Deutsch, Martin, and Associates. 1964. *The Disadvantaged Child.* New York: Basic Books. (A chapter is excerpted in this book.)

Labov, William. 1970. "The Logic of Non-Standard English." In Frederick Williams (ed.), *Language and Poverty,* pp. 153–189. Chicago: Markham.

Lewis, Oscar. 1965. "The Culture of Poverty." *Scientific American* 215 (October): 19–25.

Ryan, William. 1969. *Blaming the Victim.* New York: Vintage Books.

Improving Teaching by Increasing "Academic Learning Time"*

CHARLES FISHER
University of Colorado, Boulder

RICHARD MARLIAVE

NIKOLA N. FILBY
Far West Laboratory for Educational Research and Development

Research on teaching effectiveness[1] has produced a concept that teachers and supervisors can use to improve student learning. It is Academic Learning Time, defined as the amount of time a student spends engaged in an academic task that he/she performs with high success.

The basic components of Academic Learning Time are *allocated time, student engagement,* and *student success rate.* In grade two mathematics instruction, for example, a certain amount of time is set aside for work on addition. There may be a block of time each day for addition, or addition tasks may be interwoven with other activities. In any case, the time *allocated* for addition constitutes an upper limit on the school time available for learning that

From Educational Leadership (1979):52–54. Copyright © 1979 by ASCD. Reprinted with permission of the Association for Supervision and Curriculum Development and the author.

*This article is based on some of the findings of the Beginning Teacher Evaluation Study (Fisher, Filby, Marliave, Cahen, Dishaw, Moore, Berliner, 1978). The study was sponsored by the California Commission for Teacher Preparation and Licensing and funded by the National Institute of Education. The latter portion of the article describes current work being conducted at the Far West Laboratory as part of the Program on Teacher Development and Academic Learning Time.

subject. Decisions about time allocation are usually made by the teacher, but in some classes they may be made by individual students or jointly by students and teacher. Allocations may be different for different students in the same classroom.

For some portion of the allocated time, a student will be actively engaged in working on the task. Depending on the task, the student will be manipulating something, reading, thinking, interacting with other students, or in some way processing information about the task. Hence, *engaged time* is that portion of allocated time during which the student is paying attention.

The amount of student learning is influenced not only by the amount of engaged time, but also by the "match" between the task and the particular student. If the task is so difficult that the student produces few correct responses, then not much learning will result. On the other hand, if the student produces many correct responses, he/she is more likely to be learning.

Academic Learning Time occurs when all three of these conditions apply simultaneously; that is, when time is allocated to a task, the student is engaged in the task, and the student has a high rate of success.

THE STUDY

As part of The Beginning Teacher Evaluation Study[2] (Fisher, Filby, Marliave, Cahen, Dishaw, Moore, and Berliner, 1978), the amount of Academic Learning Time accumulated by students in reading and mathematics instruction at grades two and five was compared with changes in student achievement. Six students from each of 25 grade two classes and 21 grade five classes were given extensive reading and mathematics achievement batteries in October, December, and May. In the two interest periods, measures of allocated time, engagement rates, and success rates[3] were obtained for individual students by extensive direct observation and teacher logs. Measured differences in the basic elements of Academic Learning Time for a particular intertest period were then analyzed statistically for relationships with the change in student achievement scores from the beginning to the end of the period. These analyses were carried out separately at each grade level for reading and mathematics, and for many subcontent areas within reading and mathematics.

THE FINDINGS

Very large differences in time allocation were observed between classes. For example, the average amount of time allocated to mathematics in second-grade classes varied from around 25 minutes per day in one class to around 60 minutes per day in another class. In fifth-grade reading and reading-related instruction, the average amount of allocated time was found to vary from about 60 minutes per day in some classes to about 140 minutes per day in other classes. Similar differences were found in the amount of time allocated to specific topics within a subject (for example, addition and subtraction without regrouping). Teachers who allocated more time to a particular content area or topic had students who achieved at higher levels than teachers who allocated less time to that content area or topic.

Without attention, little can be learned. However, the data revealed that the average rate of engagement varied widely across classes and across individual students. For example, during reading and mathematics instruction there were classes that had an average engagement rate of about 50 percent. This means that students were attending to their work only half of the time. In other classes, the average engagement rate approached 90 percent. Two classes might have allocated the same amount of time to reading instruction, but one class had almost twice as much real engaged learning time as the other. The proportion of allocated time in which students were actively engaged in the assigned task was positively associated with learning.

Students also varied in their success rates. The average student in the study spent about half the time working on tasks that provided high success. In grade five mathematics, the average was somewhat less. Students who spend more time than the average in high success activities had higher achievement scores in the spring, better retention of learning over the summer, and more positive attitudes toward school. An independent finding stated that the proportion of time that reading or mathematics tasks provided a low success rate for a student was negatively associated with student learning.

Allocated time, engagement rate, and success rate—the three ingredients of Academic Learning Time—are all associated with student achievement. Students who accumulate more Academic Learning Time generally have higher scores on achievement tests. This means that Academic Learning Time can be interpreted as an immediate, ongoing measure of student learning.

STAFF DEVELOPMENT APPLICATIONS

During the last year, elementary school teachers have collaborated with Far West Laboratory staff to develop practical procedures for monitoring the elements of Academic Learning Time in their classrooms. Once a procedure has been developed that is appropriate for that particular classroom, it is used to gather descriptive information on the elements of Academic Learning Time. This initial period yields baseline data on the classroom and also provides time to build a positive relationship between teacher and staff developer.

The teacher then identifies a classroom situation he/she would like to work on. For example, the teacher may choose to reduce transition time from one activity to another, try more small group activities, change the reading materials for a particular child, or integrate a transfer student into the class. The teacher can now use the Academic Learning Time information as feedback to analyze the situation and to assess the impact of the intervention. Depending upon the issue, feedback information might be obtained on only one element of Academic Learning Time, on only one group of students, on a single student during work on a specific curriculum content area, or on a specific grouping of students.

This procedure allows teachers to examine particularly relevant pieces of their everyday classroom life in terms of practical classroom variables that are related to learning and over which they have some degree of control. Using such a system, teachers modify their teaching so that students learn more and build their own capacity to change.

NOTES

1. The use of time variables to conceptualize factors in school learning was first proposed by Carroll (1963). Most recently, Harnischfeger and Wiley (1976) and Bloom (1976) have done extensive work on time and learning in an educational context.
2. See, in this issue: Marjorie Powell. "New Evidence for Old Truths," pp. 49–51.
3. Many other variables were measured as well.

REFERENCES

Bloom, B. S. *Human Characteristics and School Learning.* New York: McGraw-Hill, 1976.

Carroll, J. B. "A Model for School Learning." *Teachers College Record* 64:723–33; 1963.

Dunkin, M. J. and B. J. Biddle. *The Study of Teaching.* New York: Holt, Rinehart and Winston, 1974.

Fisher, C. W., N. N. Filby, R. S. Marliave, L. S. Cahen, M. M. Dishaw, J. E. Moore, and D. C. Berliner. "Teaching Behaviors, Academic Learning Time and Student Achievement." Final report of Phase III-B, Beginning Teacher Evaluation Study. San Francisco, California: Technical Report V-1, Beginning Teacher Evaluation Study, Far West Laboratory for Educational Research and Development, 1978.

Gage, N. L., editor. *Handbook of Research on Teaching.* Chicago: Rand McNally, 1963.

Harnischfeger, A. and D. E. Wiley. "The Teaching-Learning Process in Elementary Schools: A Synoptic View." *Curriculum Inquiry* 76 (6):5–43.

Travers, R. M. W., editor. *Second Handbook of Research on Teaching.* Chicago: Rand McNally, 1973.

Supporting or Subverting Learning: Peer Group Patterns in Four Tracked Schools[1]

FRANCES SCHWARTZ
Philadelphia Child Guidance Clinic

I. INTRODUCTION

The scene is an inner-city school. Classroom 314 is quiet as students listen attentively to the teacher's questions about a recent lesson. Suddenly, eager hands begin to wave and bodies twist out of their seats amidst shouts of "ooh me," "I know," "ooh-oh." Quiet returns when one student is chosen to answer. As soon as she has responded, others begin to yell out refutations or additions and compete again for teacher recognition. As they participate wholeheartedly in class, several students are simultaneously but secretly passing notes and candy and signaling to each other in sign and face language. When the questions end and seat work begins, some students offer to help others who are unsure of how to proceed.

But across the hall in room 315, chaos reigns. The room is noisy with the shouting, laughter, and movement of many children. Though most students are seated, many are walking or running aimlessly around the classroom. Some stop at others' desks, provoke them briefly, and move on. Several students who are lining up textbooks as "race courses" for toy cars laugh when the teacher demands their attention. As the teacher struggles to ask a question over the noise, few if any students volunteer to answer. When one student does respond correctly, others yell out "You think you're so smart."

What accounts for the striking contrast between these two classes? Relations among students promote academic performance in room 314 but hinder it in room 315. Why do proeducational patterns emerge in one

From *Anthropology and Education Quarterly* 12:2 (1981). Reproduced by permission of the American Anthropological Association and the author. Not for further reproduction.

classroom and antieducational student relationships in another? The explanation is undoubtedly complex, relying on home environment and school characteristics, as well as many cultural and psychological factors. Focusing on the school's role in generating these differences, this paper will argue that such contrasts in student social organization are not random or coincidental. Explanations for contrasting peer group patterns rest not at the individual but at the institutional level. While not denying the impact of a particular teacher or a certain mix of students on peer relationships, this paper contends that the behavior of both the students and the teacher can be more profitably understood in the broader institutional context. Both are embedded in a specific educational structure that influences what they expect of each other and themselves and, consequently, how they behave. By viewing the peer group's academic orientation as a reaction to the expectations and constraints of a specific position in the educational structure, we can begin to systematically and predictably understand the differences between classrooms.

As anthropologists with an emphasis on culture, we have tended to ignore the impact of a specific instructional structure on students' interaction patterns. Instead we have looked more to the link between home and school than to factors within the school itself for explanations of student performance. Now we need to ask, What is the educational structure of the school? What are the mechanisms and criteria for student assignment to a particular classroom? What is the instructional approach of the school?

This paper will analyze the impact of one controversial system, tracking (or the hierarchical placement of students on the basis of ability), on student social organization. Drawing on ethnographic data from inner-city schools, we will first identify consistent differences in high- and low-track peer group interaction patterns. Then, more speculatively, we will attempt to explain the emergence of the specific patterns. We will suggest that students' positions in the academic hierarchy correspond to contrasting peer and teacher expectations. As students in high and low tracks respond to these positive and negative expectations, respectively, they devise behavioral patterns that perpetuate and solidify spirals of academic success or failure. We will speculate that tracking becomes the organizational and expectational framework that shapes the educational activities and priorities of teachers and students alike, and influences the utilization of educational facilities and resources.

There is a circular relationship between expectations and behavior. Behavior that may develop initially in response to the contrasting social climates of high- and low-tracked classrooms eventually itself becomes an independent influence on institutional expectations (see Metz 1978). However, in its attempt to clarify the impact of the instructional system on students' educational orientation, this paper speculates exclusively about the link from expectations to behavior and not the obverse. . . .

II. PEER GROUP INTERACTION PATTERNS

In its analysis of academic placement and students' social relationships, this paper draws on ethnographic data from four inner-city schools where students are tracked on the basis of standardized test scores. Research reported here was conducted initially at one New York City elementary school and secondarily at three Philadelphia schools, one junior high and two elementary. Initial investigations at the New York City school, the King School,[2] disclosed dramatic differences in the social organization and educational attitudes of high- and low-tracked students. While high-track peer groups appeared to endorse academic activity, low-track social ties hindered and subverted participation in classwork. Yet further research was required to ascertain the generalizability of these patterns. Later, in conjunction with an applied research project in the Philadelphia schools, we had the opportunity to observe the impact of tracking in greater depth. This investigation not only confirmed King School findings, but also suggested tentative explanations for the specific patterns observed previously.

Research methods at both the King and Philadelphia schools consisted primarily of intensive observation of student-student and student-teacher interaction. Observations were conducted several times a week for six months in both cities. (An assistant worked with me at the junior high school.) At the King School, three fourth grades, a high , middle, and low class, were observed. Observations in the Philadelphia elementary schools focused primarily on high and low, third and fourth grade classes—six classes in all. Moreover, we had already observed fourth grade peer group patterns at one of the schools during a previous school year. At the junior high school, one high- and one low-tracked seventh and ninth grade class were studied. In addition, the same major subject area teachers were observed with classes of different rank.

Additional research techniques at the King School included the following: interviews with parents of each class to determine their knowledge of and involvement in children's education, and examination of students' permanent school record files. In all three Philadelphia schools, interviews were conducted with students to determine their understanding and assessment of their own placement. At both elementary schools, sociograms were conducted with all fourth grade students to clarify possible links between popularity and rank.

The four schools studied differed in size and ethnic composition. The King School, with a student population of 1,100, is located in the midst of a vast low-income housing project. Ethnically, the school is composed of 51 percent Hispanic, 44 percent black, and 5 percent other students. Unlike the King School, two of the three schools in Philadelphia were ethnically homogeneous. However, like the King School, all three serve predominantly working- or lower-class populations. With a student population of 500, the Waverly Elementary School, located in an old, entrenched working-class neighborhood, is 99 + percent white. The Schooner Junior High School, located in a once lower middle class but rapidly declining black neighborhood, has a population of 1,400 students who are almost all black. The third school, the Potts Elementary School, is located on the ethnically diverse borders of the Waverly School neighborhood. Its student body of 350 pupils is approximately 33 percent black, 33 percent white, and 33 percent Hispanic.

The interaction patterns of students in each of these schools will be described in two situations typical of children's school experiences—formal and informal classtime. The two vary both in the degree and type of adult control exerted and in the extent and nature of the academic work demanded. The first situation, formal class time, occurs when the teacher dominates the class and demands the attention of all the students for an academic lesson. The second situation, informal class time, occurs when the children work independently and are permitted to interact with peers. For both elementary and junior high school students, informal time might include periods in specialty classes, as well as time in academic classes when the teacher is working with one group and the rest of the class is assigned independent seat work. Students in high and low tracks respond to each of these situations in different ways. While high-track students' reactions endorse academic performance, low-track students' responses hinder it.

Formal Classtime

While top-track students interact covertly with peers during teacher-centered lessons and lectures, low-track pupils relate to peers in an overt and disruptive manner. Overtly, like the top-stream students studied by Lacey (1970), top-track students appear to accept school goals and to adhere to the teacher's behavioral standards. Yet, at the same time that they display appropriate formal behavior, unbeknownst to the teacher, the entire class is often involved in an intricate network of secretive interaction, or "sneaking." It is so well disguised, in fact, that this behavior can be observed only by sitting in the midst as opposed to the rear of the classroom.

Various forms of sneaking are practiced. One is secret communication. Students talk by putting their heads down on the desk (as if resting) and then turning around discreetly and whispering to a friend. To pass food, candy, and notes, students lean back in their chairs and hand a neighbor the item in a book or pencil case. Another form of sneaking is secretive amusements. During each lesson, at least two or three children secretly read library or comic books. A child places the reading material on his or her lap, keeping the correct school book open on the desk and looking up from time to time. Children also play games of tic, tac, toe and knit or crochet under their desks.

During 15 minutes of one junior high school English class, the following sneaking occurred:

> The room is quiet as the teacher instructs the students in the difference between adverbs and adjectives: "O.K., some of you seem to be confused about what an adverb does, and how it differs from an adjective. Several of you made mistakes on the test. An adjective describes what? Who can tell me?" As students raise their hands to answer the questions, a number (4 girls and 3 boys) are circulating notes to each other. When one student secretly receives a note, several around him ask to see it, and it is passed along to his neighbors.
>
> At least three students are finishing homework from other classes. Several are passing gum and potato chips to one another. The teacher

continues with her questions: "O.K., who can tell me where the adverbs and adjectives are in this sentence?"

A girl who has volunteered to respond busily taps another girl to tell her that a third friend is trying to signal to her. The first girl is called on by the teacher, answers the question correctly and then returns to the note she was writing before she raised her hand.

By contrast with the scheming of the top tracks, the low tracks display overt antischool and antiteacher behavior similar to that identified among low-stream students by Lacey (1970). These students are well aware of and frequently allude to their academic status in their discussions:

Well I never got left back. Last year I was a dumb-dumb. This year I'm better. Lillion [another girl in the class] is such a dumb-dumb now. She can't even read.

Their classroom behavior is characterized by challenging and teasing the teacher, obstructing academic activity, and misusing educational resources.

These students directly undermine the teacher's authority. Using their academic position to legitimate their misbehavior, they respond when confronted by the teacher, "What do you expect from me, I'm only in the dumb class?" Sometimes they provoke the teacher outright. Two boys began to taunt the teacher. One says "pow." The other says "pow, teacher, pow." A student walks into a junior high classroom late and slams open the door. His peers start to laugh as he shouts, "O.K. teach, I'm here. Go ahead and teach." Then others begin to taunt the teacher, yelling, "Yeah, teacher, teach, teach."

Low-track students react to academic lessons by teasing each other, by using academic resources inappropriately, by moving continually around the classroom, and by sabotaging the activity at hand. In elementary school classrooms, many students spend more time misusing academic materials, by turning books upside down, dropping materials on the floor, pinning pencils together end to end, and falling backward in their chairs, than attending to their classwork. In the King School, pairs of students paint their clothing and faces, run around the classroom, stopping to wrestle on the floor, and stand up and dance during lessons. Two boys who are asked to obtain paper go to the supply closet and pull reams of paper onto the floor. When a third boy mounts the closet, shouting and laughing, the other two begin throwing pieces of paper at him. Junior high school students often skip class and/or arrive late. Once there, they get out of their seats, throw books, tease each other, and ignore the teacher's questions or directions.

In testing situations, students blatantly defy accepted rules of conduct. By exposing everyone in the class as a cheater, grade school students prevent a spelling test from occurring. As the teacher passes out papers, two boys start to spell words to each other. Another child announces to the teacher that the boys are cheating. A girl turns around in her seat and questions her neighbor about a word. Soon many of the students in the class claim that others are copying words and the test is canceled.

In one junior high school English class, students disrupt a test by openly exchanging papers and calling out answers to each other. The teacher's efforts to regain control and proceed with the test fail, and the test is aborted.

T: O.K. Number 10.
Karl: Why you keep messin? You ain't said number 9.
T: Close that book!
Karl: You giving words ain't in the book.
T: Turn around please. . . .
A girl turns around and spells the word out loud to a student behind her. Another girl shows her paper to her neighbor. A boy yells out the correct spelling of the word and others laugh. . . .
T: Number 15. Commercial.
A girl moves her desk next to a friend's and begins to copy her words.
T: Don't show her your paper.
By this time, several students are openly exchanging papers or spelling words for each other.
T: If I knew the test would be like this, I wouldn't have given it.
Eventually she halts the test and destroys the test paper.

Thus students in high and low tracks respond to formal classtime not only in contrasting ways, but also in different social units. As a single unit, students in top classes share an open academic life with the teacher, but rely on each other to sustain a secretive social life. By contrast, mostly as pairs, the low-track students use their relationships with each other to obstruct the academic enterprise.

Informal Classtime
By contrast with formal instructional periods, during informal classtime, there is no immediate pressure for public performance and little threat of academic evaluation. As the teacher becomes less central, either observing or working with a small group as students work on their own, students' classroom opportunities and priorities shift. As they react to the constraints and possibilities of this situation, students alter their classroom organization. High-track students utilize the opportunity to experiment with antischool activity toward nonacademic teachers and to work cooperatively with peers in academic settings. Although low-track students react less wildly and destructively toward the teacher, they continue to undermine each other's academic efforts.

In high-track classes during noninstructional time, the sneaking networks comprised of the entire class dissolve. Students interact openly with each other in smaller groups. In elementary classes with specialist teachers and in nonacademic junior high school classes like music, art, and shop, students adopt language and behavior typical of low tracks during formal time. Boys and girls often exhibit different behavioral patterns. The girls verbally abuse the school and the teachers, and the boys prove themselves physically. The girls openly express hostility to and about teachers and chastise each other for relating nicely to a teacher. In the King School library, for instance:

Alice: The teacher just wants to make you cry. He thinks he's gonna take away those books. Shoot!
Carole: That's what he did to Anita.
Tanya: I won't cry for anything.
Alice: I don't know how she could talk to the teacher and how she could like him. I would make the student teacher wipe the floor with my hat.

Too, they laughingly use profanities ordinarily barred from the classroom. The boys attack each other physically and talk back to nonclassroom teachers. They brag about running wildly in the hallways, throwing objects at each other and the teacher, and fighting and wrestling.

A top ninth grade section bursts into the Art room noisily laughing, slamming drawers and chasing each other around the room. They threaten to paint each other and put chalk and crayon on their faces. Several students refuse to sit down when the teacher calls for order. The teacher yells angrily: "Do you act like this in other classes? I am shocked at a top class behaving like this. Now sit down and get quiet immediately."

During independent work periods in academic classes, particularly reading, students continue to work seriously. Many volunteer to help each other and respond positively to peers' requests for academic help. In the Waverly School, high-track fourth grade students are working on math problems:

Ronald is helping David. Bob watches and says: "Don't tell him, help him figure it out." Steven tells Rick that he doesn't understand one of the problems. "Here, I'll help you."

During reading at Potts:

David: What page do you want to do now?
Tommy: I don't know, let's take a little breather. Then we can keep going.
The boys briefly stop work. Then Tommy suggests they turn to the next page and they begin to work cooperatively.

Frequent comparison and competition about grades do not seem to diminish student willingness to provide assistance.

Eric: What page are you on?
Joe: 12.
Eric: Oh. I'm ahead of you. I'm on 15.
Joe: Must have been when I was absent. I'll help you anyway.

Students' academic weaknesses or poor showings on a test are not equated with a lack of intelligence. A poor grade seems to be seen less as a reflection of a person's innate capabilities than as an indication of his or her lack of preparation.

Teddy: David, you're a bad speller. Might be a good reader but a bad speller. Need to study words more.

In a junior high math class, student papers are returned. Students ask each other, "What did you get? What did you get?" When one boy admits that he did poorly, another looks over his paper and remarks: "Boy, you didn't even study for this test? You got to get yourself together, man."

Students' comments as they work reveal a positive identification with the group and others in it. They often comment humorously about their math and reading groups as they cooperate. Several students remarked laughingly, "Hey, this is a crazy group!" Others note, "What a group. The best!"

By contrast, during informal periods in nonacademic settings, low-track students shift their activities to discussion of their real and imagined life outside school. Their taunting is replaced by conversations about a world where they know more and can be more. In small groups they discuss neighborhood and family events and share their fantasies about the future.

In music class a group of seventh grade low-track students discuss a recent neighborhood incident, a robbery in a local grocery store. Several of the same students who sit silently through formal classtime except to challenge the teacher describe their versions of the robbery.

In their fantasies, elementary school students' future success depends on age and wealth, *not* on education:

Linda: We can't talk about that stuff now. Only when we're teenagers.
Claude: I won't be around here when I get old.
Kevin: I'm going down South.
James: I'm going to get $100 and a car when I go down South.
Kevin: If I want money all I have to do is ask my grandmother.

During independent work time in academic classes, low-track students are caught in a no-win contradictory situation. On the one hand they undermine those who make academic efforts.

A fourth grade teacher asks a low reading group to put test papers on the bulletin board. When one boy goes to the board, others around him comment, "You think you're so great. There you go showin off." Others comment that another student, who got 100, copied.

Yet on the other hand they accuse each other of cheating and being stupid, and compete continually about their work.

As they begin independent work, two girls cover their workbook pages with books. Catherine to girl next to her: "You can't copy off me." Nancy: "I'm not. You're the one that's copying." A boy announces that he has gotten the answer right and others say, "You copied off her." A boy points to another's paper: "You got it wrong, did it wrong. You stupid."

Rather than identify positively with their groups, like the top tracks, these students attempt to differentiate themselves from their peers. They distinguish themselves as "smart" from others whom they label as "stupid." In a fourth grade reading period:

Kelvin: What page you on?
Sandra: 47.
Kelvin: I'm way ahead of you. I'm smarter than all of them.
Sandra: No, I'm smarter than you.
Kelvin: No you ain't.
Sandra: You didn't even pass your test.
Kelvin: So, you can't catch up to me.
Sandra: Yes I could, little boy.

Thus these students are undercut by peers if they do succeed and belittled by them if they do not. By contrast with the cooperation among high-track students during informal classtime, low-track students fail to support each other's academic efforts.

Thus, with the relative easing of adult control, high- and low-track students continue to react divergently. High-track pupils utilize the absence of immediate academic consequences to experiment with misbehavior. By contrast, free from the necessity to defend themselves against academic humiliation and failure, low-track students focus on life outside the school. Although they compete during independent work situations, the high-track students facilitate each other's academic efforts. In their interactions they emphasize their shared group status and collective identity. By contrast, low-track students' interactions with peers focus more on the mechanics and organization of activity than on substance. They spend more time accusing each other of doing work incorrectly and cheating than actually dealing with content. Their preoccupation with form and competition about relative "smartness" appear to obfuscate attending to the task at hand.

III. SPECULATIVE EXPLANATIONS

In Section II, we demonstrated that students in the same structural position in four inner-city schools display remarkably similar educational attitudes and peer group interaction patterns. But can we explain why these *particular* patterns emerge within a tracked school? Some possible explanations are outlined later. . . .

Rank and Social Standing with Peers[3]

In the classroom, students' peers become their social and potentially educational resources. Their perception of the worth and attractiveness of these peers determines if and how they choose to interact with them. It becomes a key constraint that shapes their behavioral options. For elementary students in top tracks, classmates are valued as individuals with whom interaction is desirable. By contrast, among low-track students, classmates are viewed as social outcasts to be avoided. Instead, these students prefer to associate with high-track peers. Sociogrammatic data from the Potts and Waverly elementary schools indicate that, while high-track students choose others of the same rank as friends, low-rank students tend to choose those of high rank. In fact, the lower the rank is, the fewer the reciprocal ties between classmates. Multidimensional sociograms required all fourth grade students in each school to group a stack of cards representing each individual in the fourth grade into three piles: (1) Those you hang around with the most, (2) Those you hang around with some of the time, and (3) Those you hardly hang around with or don't know.

Results indicate that 50 percent of lower–rank students choose more high- than low-rank peers to "hang around with most." By contrast, less than 1 percent of high-track students choose those of low rank as much or more than their own classmates for this category. Low-rank students have fewer than one half as many reciprocal friendship choices as high-rank pupils at Potts and one eighth as many at Waverly. The grouping patterns that emerge as a result of those choices indicate that top-track students cluster into reciprocal groups and exclusive cliques, while low-track students tend to be linked in less dense reciprocal pairs.

Overall, the higher his or her academic rank, the greater is the student's popularity. Results indicate that academic placement corresponds to the number of times a student was chosen in the top category, "hang around with most." With a mean of 6.5 top-category choices for each child in both schools, three times as many high as low students received 8 to 9 choices and two times as many high as low students received 10 or more choices.

Rank and Satisfaction with the Classroom Situation

Students' feelings about their academic situations further inform their behavior. If one associates his or her classroom activities with academic stigmatization and "dumbness," he or she is likely to react against and avoid "involvement" in them. Conversely, if one equates classroom placement with superior intelligence, one is likely to willingly engage in activities that reinforce status.

Data indicate that, while top-tracked students view their positions positively, most low-ranked students do not. Looking up to their top-ranked peers, many low-track students view their own situations with disdain and dismay. Interviews with fourth grade students at Potts and Waverly and with seventh graders at Schooner reveal that almost all students (98 + percent at all three schools) know their academic rank and understand the basis for this placement. Low-rank students almost unanimously express dissatisfaction with their placements and know far more about the activities in the higher tracks than those in high-tracks know about them. While over 95 percent of the low-rank students would like to be in another class or track, less than 1 percent of high-track students express a similar desire. Indicative of the comparative value they assign to their respective tracks, 70 percent of the low groups can name the Basal readers and other books used in high tracks. Additionally, 46 percent can accurately describe high-track academic activities. By contrast, only one top-track student at Potts, three at Waverly, and two at Schooner can describe the material used in the low track. Virtually none can describe low-track classroom activities. Most note only that they do "easy work."

Rank and Teacher Expectations

The institutional structure that colors students' perceptions shapes those of teachers as well. Previous research has demonstrated that teachers, faced with institutional pressures to upgrade achievement, develop a common-sense strategy for dealing with differentially tracked students (see Schutz 1962; Sharp and Green 1975). High-rank pupils who are likely to succeed and contribute positively to the teachers' professional image are perceived as ideal pupils whose specific educational needs the teacher is capable of meeting (Becker 1952; Rist 1973). By contrast, teachers tend to distance themselves from low-ranked pupils, viewing them more as an unreachable group than as a series of individuals with distinctive educational problems. Rather than risk professional failure with pupils whom they fear they will be unable to motivate, teachers often make fewer demands on low-rank pupils and apply less exacting standards to their own performance with them (Keddie 1971; Leacock 1969).

Like the patterns suggested by previous research, teachers at the four schools studied here displayed contrasting expectations of and modes of interacting with high- and low-track students. Their differential norms are demonstrated both in written comments about students and in their interaction with them. Year-end comments on King School students' permanent record cards from kindergarten to the fourth grade indicate that, by the time a student reaches the fourth grade, academic rank is likely to determine teachers' apparent educational interest in him or her. Over this four-year period, record cards reveal a progressive polarization in the length and nature of teachers' year-end comments about high- and low-track students. While in kindergarten, most students received either positive, diagnostic, or constructive comments; by the third grade, many of the low-track students were negatively labeled with a single phrase. In kindergarten, many of the high-rank students were described as eager, ready to learn, and cooperative. However, many low-track students were described as needing more reading readiness work, more training in classroom participation, or more socialization for school. By the third grade, only eight of the high-track students received even mildly negative comments about behavior, such as "talks too much" or "does not talk enough" The rest were cited as academically excellent and cooperative. Their strengths in a variety of academic subjects, their interests, and their personal characteristics were detailed. By contrast, six students in low tracks were characterized only as N.E. (non-English speakers), and the rest were cited as "disruptive," "nonconformists," "withdrawn," "day-dreamers," and "nonparticipants," with no fuller explanations.

It is impossible to determine whether the predominantly negative comments about low-rank students and the largely positive statements about the high-track students are accurate descriptions of their behavior or a reflection of teachers' expectations about and characterizations of high- and low-track students. However, whatever their accuracy, these comments do reveal differences in the attention and detail with which teachers describe high and low tracks. By the third grade, top-rank students were clearly afforded more particularistic and elaborate evaluations than the low-tracked pupils.

Observational data confirm and elaborate teachers' use of contrasting standards. Observations of the same junior high school teachers with both high- and low-track students, as well as ethnographic analysis of King, Potts, and Waverly school classrooms, reveal consistent differences in teachers' behavior toward high and low classes. From their initial modes of address through their questioning and disciplinary procedures, teachers structure their interaction with high- and low-tracked students in markedly different ways.

At the beginning of class periods, teachers of high groups tend to emphasize students' shared, superior status. They require that all students be seated and prepared to work before they begin classwork. They emphasize the class's exclusive status by challenging them to live up to their image of a top group and chiding them not to act like "9–9" (the lowest ninth grade track).

> As a noisy high-track 9th grade enters its math class the teachers says, "Am I in the wrong class? Is this academic or axademic?"

> Another teacher says to a top 7th grade: "We will sit here and wait 'til everyone is ready. And I mean everyone. I'm not in competition with you. I'm not answering any questions 'til it's quiet and you show me you're ready."

By contrast, with low tracks, teachers tend to begin the period without waiting for the students' undivided attention. Rather, as soon as one half to three quarters of the students are quiet, the teacher begins.

> As a low 7th grade enters English class the teacher says, "I saw a lot of you come into the room too noisy. I do not want to hear anyone. I know what to expect of you and a lot of you are paying attention so let's begin." As she begins to review the previous day's quiz at least 8 of the 26 students present are out of their seats, talking to friends, or misusing academic supplies.

Once teachers begin classwork, their instructional patterns differ as well. As a group, students in lower sections receive half as many directions about classroom activities and one-third fewer explanations, lectures, or demonstrations by teachers than higher-track students. Teachers tend to review or correct homework assignments 20 percent more with the high- than low-tracked students. Teachers adopt different questioning strategies with high and low tracks, also. High-track students are encouraged to volunteer, either individually or collectively, to respond to questions as often as they are called on by name. When they answer incorrectly, the teacher tends to either correct them, push them until they obtain the correct answer, or indicate that they are wrong and question someone else. By contrast, low-track students are rarely asked to volunteer. Instead they are questioned by name. Often teachers announce that they want to see who is misbehaving or is inattentive and direct questions to those students:

> In a low seventh grade social studies section, the teacher begins to question students: "O.K. No more talking. James, sit down. Derrick, turn around. I don't want to see that again, Troy, if you're so smart. If you know it all and don't have to pay attention, tell me the definition of latitude." Troy does not answer. The teacher scans the class and says, "Let's see who else is too smart to pay attention!"

When one student fails to respond, or responds incorrectly, teachers question another, often without indicating whether the first answer was correct or not.

In their instructional patterns, teachers apply different standards to high- and low-track performance. Rather than gear work to the ability level of the class, many junior high school teachers present the same material with different emphases to both tracks. High-track students are praised for their intelligence and pushed to excel. With high tracks, teachers stress achievement and the need for perfection:

> I expect you all to do an excellent job on this assignment.

With low-track students, however, they tend to stress behavior more than achievement. These students are reminded that they can compensate for poor academic work with neatness and good manners:

> Some people were disappointed with their grade. Remember notebook is an easy way to get a good grade. Neatness, accuracy, indentation, and completeness.

> I guarantee you'll do well if you put forth effort in behavior. . . .

Teachers are less demanding and more lax with low groups. Some teachers explicitly express their differential standards with high and low tracks. One junior high math teacher, who was exacting with the top classes, explained the absence of academic activity with his lowest group. "I play the role of Godfather and father-confessor to these kids. Tell me their problems and I help them out. It takes a while to get started. First I let them do errands around the school building."

Teachers also tend to establish different reward and punishment systems with high and low classes. Students in high-ranked sectors are touched and praised for their behavior and their performance twice as much as low-ranked peers:

> During the first 10 minutes of top-group reading class the teacher calls five students darling or babe, affectionately touches two students, and jokes with three others. With a low-track section, the same teacher touches no one affectionately, and calls two students darling.

> Teachers remark to high tracks as they work, "What a smart group this is" or "I'm really proud of you," or "This class is making me very happy."

Moreover, teachers tend to personalize their interaction with high-track students, discussing noncritically their own and the student's interests and home lives.

Although teachers complain about low-rank students' behavior more frequently, they actually punish high sections more. While low-ranked students are threatened with punishment twice as much as high sections, high-ranked students are *actually punished* three times more than their low-ranked peers. Their threats and the rules they enforce differ from high to low section as well.[4] Top-track students are admonished for their personal conduct:

> What did I tell you about gum chewing.
> Get rid of it.
> There is to be no eating in this class.
> For the last time throw out the potato chips.
> Sit up like a lady and get busy. Now.
> Cut the talking 9–1.

And they are threatened with punishment primarily for failure to complete their classwork.

> This is classwork, not homework. If you do not finish it in class, you will be late to lunch.

> No one leaves this classroom until he has finished the assignment. I'm serious. Either it's done now or you stay in.

When students fail to complete assignments, teachers' threats are often carried out. For instance, one group of students from a seventh grade math class miss 20 minutes of their 40-minute lunch period, and several top ninth graders are detained a half hour after school in order to finish incomplete assignments.

By contrast, low groups are reprimanded primarily for disrupting the class and moving without permission:

> Get in your seat, who said you could get up.
> Daniel, what did I tell you yesterday. Face the front of the room.
> George, shut up.
> Tyrell, turn around, the front of the room's this way. Move your desk back into the row and leave Sandra alone.

Students are threatened not with academically related punishments but instead with exclusion from the learning environment:

> Felicia, I've had it with you. You're going to the office.
> O.K., who's going to get detention.
> Daniel, any minute now I'm sending you out of class.

Thus year after year students in high and low tracks interact with teachers who approach them in dramatically different ways as both students and people. When one views the classroom situation from the teachers' perspective, it is not difficult to understand how the demands of their role and their experiences with differentially ranked students promote these contrasting styles (see Metz 1978). Yet, the fact remains that, whatever its source, this behavior does emerge and contributes to the perpetuation of students' existing academic labels. Unfortunately, most teachers (and students) are too enmeshed in their respective institutional positions to either see the situation from the other's perspective or to be able to actively change it. As Keddie (1971) notes, once inside the classroom, even those teachers who most vehemently oppose tracking in the abstract become unwittingly ensnared in its expectational and behavioral patterns.

Student Behavior and the Classroom Social Climate

In a tracked school, then, rank shapes students' social and educational experiences. To obtain a fuller understanding of the way in which institutional expectations encourage the particular behavior and academic orientation of each track, we can integrate the preceding data into a composite picture of the classroom as students experience it. We can speculate about the way in which teacher and peer expectations converge to support the specific social patterns and educational priorities we observed among high- and low-track students.

Summarizing the influences on top-track behavior, we can suggest that their peer group endorsement of academic participation through cooperation and sneaking is prompted by the following:

1. Teachers' and peers' treatment of these students as an exclusive group.
2. Teachers' careful and constant monitoring of their classroom participation and performance.
3. Students' personalized interaction with the teacher.
4. Students' unwillingness to jeopardize their high status by risking predictable punishment for overt misbehavior.

From the moment they enter the classroom, the top tracks are treated collectively as a special and superior group and individually as students with distinctive personalities, interests, and educational needs by peers and teachers alike. High-tracked students come to view their classmates as individuals whose high social status is linked to their own academic success. Group identification and solidarity become equated with academic superiority. Popularity with peers and their treatment by teachers set them apart from others socially as well as academically. Students see themselves collectively as individuals whose prized position is both demonstrated and maintained by their social grouping into exclusive cliques.

While the source of the high track's group orientation becomes apparent, their formal classtime sneaking requires further explanation. One could characterize the classroom message these students receive as, "You can't slide. We are watching you." These students learn that they are closely and carefully monitored by the teacher, and that almost every time they perform an academic task, there will be consequences. When they answer a question, they can expect the teacher to listen to their response, to indicate if it is correct, and either to push them to obtain the right answer or turn to someone else. Any evidence of misbehavior or failure to complete homework or class-work is likely to result in punishment and, perhaps more seriously, to threaten their educational position. These students also learn that because they have the flexibility of participating in class voluntarily, they can shape classroom discourse and pace their own involvement in it. When they are prepared with an answer or comment, they can volunteer and gain teacher recognition.

Hence students devise a means of differentiating themselves from teachers who care about them without directly challenging their authority. Rather, sneaking constitutes an indirect way of maintaining peer ties without jeopardizing academic standing. As long as students function academically, inserting themselves into classroom activities and completing their written work, they can simultaneously pursue their surreptitious social relationships. Ironically, these students establish a system outside the teacher's domain that reinforces the very norms she or he has conveyed to them. Sneaking confirms not only their shared group status, but also the need to be vigilant and attentive.

During informal classtime, when student behavior is less closely monitored, the classroom constraints shift. For these students there seems to be a direct relationship between the academic authority of an adult and the degree to which they feel they must behave. The greater the official power of the individual teacher to control their educational rank, the less these students act out. Although these students retain their collective focus during informal time, their activities change. With nonacademic or specialty teachers other than their own, students can risk experimentation with overt misbehavior. In these settings their behavior is less likely to result in punishment or to affect their academic reputations. Too, since students rely on the entire class to misbehave, it would be most unlikely for all of them to be threatened with academic demotion. By contrast, during informal periods with academic instructors or classroom teachers, there is no basis for sneaking. Students learn that they can interact with peers as long as they continue to work. While they do compete, they also sustain their group identification by helping and cooperating with each other on academic tasks.

By contrast, for low-tracked students we can speculate that lack of popularity with even their own classmates and negative teacher expectations promote their competitive, disruptive, and largely dyadic interaction. We can suggest that this antieducational pattern is supported by the following:

1. Student and teacher devaluation of low-track standing.
2. Teachers' use of academic participation more as punishment for misbehavior than as recognition for effort.
3. Students' lack of personalized interaction with the teacher.
4. Students' repeated exposure to teachers' failure to follow through with threats for misbehavior.

Through their interactions with teachers and peers, low-track students learn that academic and social worth rest not on solidarity with, but rather on differentiation from, their classmates. The segmented approach of their teachers and lack of esteem from their peers foster competition and frag-mented patterns of interaction. As they come to devalue their academic label and classroom activities, they opt not to pursue friendships with others who remind them of that status. Instead, they find one person with whom they can identify and set themselves apart from others. Group activity would belie the very label they seek to deny.

The classroom message conveyed to the low class could be summarized as, "It doesn't matter what you do. Nothing counts." They are subject to classical patterns of low expectation conveying behavior (Rosenthal and Jacobson 1968). Classroom organization discourages students from either taking themselves, their work, or their teachers seriously. Little work is adequately explained or demanded from them. They learn that, despite repeated threats, misbehavior is *not* likely to be punished, and effort is *not* likely to be rewarded. There is an inverse relationship between student motivation and teacher recognition. If one behaves correctly, one is ignored academically. When one volunteers, one is not often called on, and when one tries to do seat work, one is often unclear about directions. Further, when the student is finally called on, she or he often gets confusing feedback about the accuracy of the answer. Unlike top tracks, these students have little sense of the teacher as a person who is interested in them as individuals.

Thus these students have little to lose academically and run little risk of punishment for wild behavior. By taunting teachers to whom they are not personally attached and mocking classroom activities, they react against reminders of their inferior status. By jeering at peers who attempt to perform publically in class, they effectively restrict academic activity in general and their own participation in particular. In fact, their one collective action is cooperation to actively sabotage tests and undermine teachers' academic authority.

During informal periods in their own or academic classes, these students turn their negativity about their status onto each other. When the teacher is no longer a target for their reactions, they vie with each other to deny their shared status. Left to their own devices without the threat of public performance and without the confusion of teacher questioning and correction procedures, many students at least try to do their seat work. Yet, caught in a dilemma by their academic label, it becomes more important to compete with and differentiate oneself from like-ranked peers than to complete the task at hand. By downgrading others' efforts and intelligence, one can set oneself apart from classmates and ensure that they do not succeed where one might fail. Though the teacher is not actively involved in these independent activities, students seem to incorporate her or his negative messages into their interactions with each other. As they work, they continually repeat the teacher's explicit and implicit expectations. During informal time, then, they seem to defend themselves against their label by imposing it onto others.

By contrast, during informal time with teachers other than their own or with nonacademic specialists, it is no longer necessary to defend themselves against possible failure and humiliation. During these periods when they are not confronted by their academic inferiority, they have less of a motive and focus for misbehavior. Instead they escape their role in the school context by discussing their lives outside that setting and their activities outside the classroom.

IV. CONCLUSIONS

In the classroom, student peer group relationships can be an educational resource or an academic impediment. In this study we have attempted to demonstrate how the educational structure influences these relationships. In our analysis of the impact of tracking on peer group interaction patterns, we have argued that students' educational orientation is determined more by institutional than individual factors. We have attempted to demonstrate that classroom behavior of students and teachers alike is organized by a powerful system of institutional expectations in which rank predominates. Educational and social assumptions about students in different academic positions shape divergent classroom social climates for high- and low-tracked students. As individual students in different tracks react to these contrasting expectations and constraints, they come to share different views of themselves, their teachers, and their peers. These understandings in turn promote different social priorities and markedly contrasting strategies for coping with their academic label and classroom situations. High-track students utilize peer ties to preserve their academic status as they simultaneously create their own social domain. Low-track students, however, use peer ties to react against the situation that has negatively labeled them. . . .

NOTES

1. This research was funded in part by a grant from the Hazen Foundation (New Haven, Connecticut) to the Affective Education Program of the School District of Philadelphia. Kathy Connors, Earlene Sloan, and Hank Kopple of the Affective Education Program helped to formulate the research problem and strategies. Carole Joffe, Marc Ross, and Michael Weinstein offered many insightful comments and suggestions about earlier drafts of this paper.

2. The names of all four schools have been altered in order to disguise the research site.

3. Sociograms on which these findings are based were not administered to junior high school students. Given Lacey's finding that, once secondary school students are assigned to tracks, they tend to develop divergent high- and low-track norms for popularity, it may be that this discussion about peers applies primarily to elementary school students.

4. In enforcing different rules, teachers may well be reacting to differences in student behavior. As previously stated, student patterns themselves become an independent influence on teacher behavior. However, regardless of the type of misbehavior, teachers do differ in their willingness to actually follow through and punish high and low tracks and in the punishment they assign.

REFERENCES

Barker, Lunn, J. C. 1970 Streaming in the Primary School. Slough, England: National Foundation.

Becker, Howard. 1952. Social Class Variations in the Teacher-Pupil Relationship. Journal of Educational Sociology, 25:451–465.

Becker, Howard, and Blanche Geer 1968 Making the Grade. New York: Wiley.

Finn, Jeremy 1972 Expectations and the Educational Environment. Review of Educational Research 43(3).

Hargreaves, David 1967 Social Relations in a Secondary Modern School. London: Routledge & Kegan Paul.

Keddie, Nell 1971 Classroom Knowledge. In Knowledge and Control. Michael Young, ed. London: Collier Macmillan Publishers.

Lacey, Colin 1970 Hightown Grammar. Manchester, England: University of Manchester.

Leacock, Eleanor 1969 Teaching and Learning in City Schools. New York: Basic Books.

Metz, Mary H. 1978 Classrooms and Corridors. Berkeley: University of California Press.

Rist, Ray 1973 The Urban School: Factory for Failure. Boston: MIT Press.

Rosenthal, R., and R. Jacobson 1968 Pygmalion in the Classroom. New York: Holt, Rinehart and Winston.

Schaefer, W. E., and C. Olexa 1971 Tracking and Opportunity. New York: Harper & Row.

Schutz, Alfred 1962 Collected Papers, Vol. I. The Problem of Social Reality. The Hague: Martinus Nijhoff.

Schwartz, Frances 1976 Continuity and Change in Student Adaptation to One Alternative School: The Transformation of Academic Behavior. Unpublished Ph.D. dissertation. New York: Columbia University.

Sexton, Patricia C. 1961 Education and Income: Inequality of Opportunity in the Public Schools. New York: Viking Press.

_____ . 1967 The American School: A Sociological Analysis. Englewood Cliffs, N.J.: Prentice-Hall.

Sharp, Rachel, and Anthony Green, with Jacqueline Lewis 1975 Education and Social Control: A Study in Progressive Primary Education. Boston: Routledge & Kegan Paul.

Van Velsen, J. 1964 The Politics of Kinship. Manchester, England: University of Manchester Press.

Exemplary Schools and the
Search for Effectiveness

GILBERT R. AUSTIN
University of Maryland, Baltimore County

Until the mid-1960s, educators were confident they were capable of teaching children from all backgrounds, given adequate resources. This confidence was shared by the public, as evidenced by the widespread support given to the Elementary and Secondary Education Act of 1965 (ESEA). However, in the past decade, people have begun questioning the values of traditional education due to a number of new studies (Coleman and others, 1966; Jencks and others, 1972; Plowden, 1967; Husen, 1967). One example is the Coleman Report, a vital document in the annals of educational research.

WHAT MAKES A DIFFERENCE?

The Department of Justice initiated this survey apparently so that they could document willful discrimination in education. This is one of the few examples in our country's history of a specific request made by Congress for social research that might provide a basis for policy. The Office of Education asked James S. Coleman of Johns Hopkins University and Ernest Q. Campbell of Vanderbilt University to direct the $1.5 million project.

These were its main conclusions:

1. Family background is important for achievement.
2. The relationship of family background to achievement does not diminish over years of schooling.

3. Variations in school facilities, curriculum, and staff have little effect on achievement independent of family background.

4. School factors that have the greatest influence (independent of family background) are the teacher's characteristics, not the facilities and curriculum.

5. Attitudes, such as sense of control of the environment or a belief in the responsiveness of the environment, were found to be highly related to achievement . . . (Mayeske, 1973).

Coleman is *not* saying schools don't make a difference. His report indicates that if you compare children who have had no schooling with those who have had schooling, schooling has a *great* and important effect at all socioeconomic levels. His writing indicates that when you look for differences in the effect of schooling between schools, it is difficult to identify school-related variables that account for the observed differences. This is different from saying schooling has no effect. The only place where school versus no school achievement has been studied is in Prince Edward County, Virginia, in 1959, when the county closed its public school system to avoid the Supreme Court's racial desegregation decree. In that situation, all children who went to volunteer schools learned a great deal more than children who did not attend school (Green, 1979).

The findings of the Coleman Report were supported by the results of many early evaluations of the Elementary and Secondary Education Act—Tempo (General Electric, 1968); Technomics, Inc. (1968); Scientific Educational Systems (1970); Kirst (1967); Ginsberg (1970); Evans (1969); Hanushek (1972); McLaughlin (1975).

After a careful review of the extensive research on educational effectiveness, the Rand Corporation in a report to the President's Commission on School Finance concluded, "Research has not identified a variant of the existing system that is consistently related to students' educational outcomes." The report continues, "We must emphasize that we are not suggesting that nothing makes a difference, or that nothing 'works.' Rather we are saying that research has found nothing that consistently and unambiguously makes a difference in students' outcomes." This exhaustive review of the research and evaluation literature also stated that ". . . in every type of school the principal appears to be essential to making the school operate effectively, but also shows that a principal's effectiveness depends in part on the amount of support he or she receives from higher administrative levels" (Averch, 1972).

VARIABLES OUTSIDE THE SCHOOL

During this time, other researchers were taking a different approach. They tended to accept that many programs had not lived up to their expectations, but they were more interested in identifying those exemplary schools that met their goals. Henry Dyer (1972) proposed a general model that takes into consideration the variables that cannot be manipulated by the schools. The Dyer model involved predicting student performance from hard-to-change surrounding conditions and student input performance. The hard-to-change surrounding conditions included student, home, and community character-istics that were related to achievement and were not under the direct control of the school. The input variable was a measure of the students' performance at the beginning phase of schooling which was to be evaluated. The most common method of implementing the general model is regression analysis using mean values of the predictor variable to predict mean output achieve-ment. For example, to examine the effectiveness of teaching reading in grade six to grade nine, the sixth-grade reading achievement mean and mean values of demographic variables could be used to predict the mean score for ninth-grade reading achievement. The discrepancy between a school's pre-dicted performance and the actual performance is interpreted as a measure of its relative effectiveness for the time period studied. Schools are usually classified into effectiveness categories based upon the size of the discrepancy between observed and predicted scores. Hawkridge (1968, 1969) identified a number of ESEA programs that worked. The U.S. Office of Education published descriptions of those programs in pamphlet form under the title, *The "It Works" Series.* Wargo (1971) continued Hawkridge's work.

EXEMPLARY SCHOOLS

A study by Robert Klitgaard and George Hall (1973) builds on the work of Dyer, Hawkridge, and Wargo and raises a question of central concern to the author of this article.

> "Perhaps educational research has looked in the wrong places for evidence of effectiveness. Previous studies have indicated that, on average, school policies do not greatly affect measurable student scholastic and occupational performance. Suppose this is true. Might there remain, nevertheless, a group of schools that are different? Are there any exceptions to small average tendencies and insignificant regression coefficients? The mathematics of previous studies allow for such a possibility, as long as the number of exceptions is not large" (Klitgaard and Hall, 1973).

Klitgaard and Hall examined six data sets for outliers: Michigan schools; New York City elementary schools; Project Talent data; New York State school districts; New York State schools; and Project Yardstick data. They identified groups of overachieving schools that made up between two and nine percent of various samples. From a policy standpoint they characterized these schools as being "statistically 'unusual'," but whether they can be considered unusually effective depends on one's subjective scale of magnitude. They conclude:

> "Nonetheless, moving away from average effects in educational re-search and policy making does seem worthwhile. We have located

schools and districts that consistently perform better than their peers. It is probably worthwhile to continue such research, and to begin looking for unusually effective classrooms and programs" (Klitgaard and Hall (1973).

Following the ideas advanced by Klitgaard, a number of states have designed and completed studies of outlier or exemplary schools. Four states—New York, Pennsylvania, Delaware, and Maryland—have completed longitudinal or case studies of exceptional schools.

The major finding of these studies is that there is no one single factor that accounts for a school being classified as exceptional. These schools appear to have a critical mass of positive factors which, when put together, make the difference. All of these factors were not found in each school in the studies but are characteristic of the group as a whole.

- Strong principal leadership (for example, schools "being run" for a purpose rather than "running" from force of habit);
- Strong principal participation in the classroom instructional program and in actual teaching;
- Higher expectations on the part of the principal for student and teacher performance advancement;
- Principals felt that they had more control over the functioning of the school, the curriculum and program, and their staff;
- Greater experience and more pertinent education in the roles of principals, teachers, and teacher aides;
- Teachers were rated as warmer, more responsive, and showing more emphasis on cognitive development in classes that did not involve direct reading instruction as well as in reading classes;
- Teachers expected more children to graduate from high school, to go to college, to become good readers, and to become good citizens;
- Teachers were more satisfied with opportunities to try new things; they were free to choose teaching techniques in response to individual pupil needs;
- More satisfactory parent-teacher relationships;
- Job responsibilities for the teacher aides included working across all grades with primarily small, low-ability groups; close involvement of teachers and paraprofessionals with pupils;
- On several measures, differences seemed to be more pronounced in grades one to three than in grades four to six;
- Schools had a longer instruction day;
- In evaluation, the teachers relied almost completely on teacher-developed tests and teacher judgments of student achievement;
- More positive self-concept and a feeling of controlling their own destiny observable as early as grade three on part of children.

THE PRINCIPAL AND LEADERSHIP

These characteristics show that school characteristics are related to mean school achievement. Also, a school that performs in unusually successful ways has a principal or a leader who is an exceptional person. Recent research by Guditus and Zirkel (1979) indicates that this kind of leadership comes to a principal as a result of what is called expert power as compared with legitimate power, coercive power, referent power, or reward power. The principals in these studies were viewed by the teachers and the pupils as persons who are expert in a wide variety of areas concerning education. In these studies, the principal is identified as an expert instructional leader, instead of an administrative leader, and the level of instructional expertise falls in the area of reading or arithmetic. The second characteristic that emerged from these studies is that the levels of expectations for the children held by the principals and teachers were unusually high, and the children tended to rise to these expectations in their performance levels. We also find, in agreement with Brookover (1978), that the major reasons why a school is identified as performing above expectation or below are most pronounced in the early grades of the school. This is perhaps because their instructional day is longer, and more of the day, particularly in the early grades, is spent on student-oriented instruction in the area of reading and mathematics.

This research does not, however, demonstrate how these school characteristics develop in the school. The atypical school demonstrates that a favorable climate can exist in low-SES as well as high-SES or minority schools, but the process by which the climate and associated higher achievement came to exist is not documented by this research.

Smith and Tucker (1977) say "that a decade of research and evaluation has taught us that the effectiveness of educational treatments, programs, or technologies varies greatly from one school to the next. No one curriculum or instructional practice has been found to be consistently superior to others over time in a variety of different settings." We continue to believe, however, that local schools do make a difference. The individual characteristics of principals, teachers, schools, neighborhoods, and home influence a pupil's achievement far more than particular instructional models. Thus, research confirms the faith of those who believe that no improvement in the quality of schooling is likely unless the people in individual schools, in concert with the parents and children they serve, agree on what they want to accomplish. They then must be given the freedom to orchestrate resources to accomplish it. The school climate must provide stimulating ideas and facilitate the exchange of ideas with colleagues. Teachers must have the opportunity to work together over time to achieve common objectives, and—not least important—have the sense that they are sufficiently free of administrative intervention that it is worth investing time and energy in the effort to improve the education offered in their school. When the teachers and other school personnel feel successful about education in their school, children also believe they can achieve and they do.

AUTHOR'S NOTE

Since the original article was published, the author has continued to pursue research on effective schools. Many of the characteristics of exemplary schools identified as important have stood up over time. An excellent listing of these characteristics was made by Purkey and Smith (1983). The most important characteristics that have emerged in the last five years are: leadership; maximized learning time; widespread recognition of success; a sense of community (school climate); high expectations shared by the principal, teachers, parents, and students; and a shared concern for order and discipline in the school.

Effective schools research has gained major support from the U.S. Department of Education. Two centers have been funded to study excellence in education. The Center for Research on Elementary and Middle Schools is located at Johns Hopkins University and directed by James McPartland. The National Center for Effective Secondary Schools is located at the University of Wisconsin and is directed by Fred Newman. Each center is funded for over $1 million a year. The Office for Educational Research and Improvement has recently released an RFP to fund a Research and Development Center for School Leadership.

The National Directory of Principals' Centers now lists 107 centers in the United States and other countries. Reflecting this growing international interest, the first International Congress on Effective Schools was held in London in January 1988. Nineteen countries were represented. In the 47 papers presented, many of the exemplary school characteristics mentioned in the original article were emphasized.

Leadership, particularly on the part of the principal, was identified as a key factor. Every exceptional school identified had this ingredient. Leadership quality in the best schools is not only given by the principal but is reinforced and sustained by the teaching faculty.

A common characteristic of effective schools reported at the conference is that there is widespread recognition of success. The children are led to believe that their academic, social, and personal accomplishments are important and will be recognized by the school.

The one characteristic that was most often mentioned in the reports was school climate. The attitude of the students toward the school has a great impact on their performance. The best way to describe a successful school's climate is to think of the term "family," a successful family.

Finally, in an exemplary school, one finds great respect for the individual, commitment to order and discipline, and high expectations on the part of administration, faculty, and parents.

REFERENCES

Averch, Harvey A. and others. *How Effective is Schooling? A Critical Review and Synthesis of Research Findings.* Prepared for President's Commission on School Finance. Santa Monica: The Rand Corporation, 1972.

Brookover, Wilbur B. and others. "Elementary School Social Climate and School Achievement." *American Educational Research Journal* 15(2): Spring 1978.

Coleman, James S. and others. *Equality of Educational Opportunity*. Washington, D.C.: United States Government Printing Office, 1966.

Dyer, Henry S. "Some Thoughts About Future Studies." *On Equality of Educational Opportunity*. F. Mosteller and D. Moynihan, editors. New York: Vintage Press, 1972.

Evans, John. "Evaluating Social Action Programs." Washington, D.C.: USOE/HEW, June 1969.

Ginsberg, Alan and others. "Title I of ESEA—Problems and Prospects." Washington, D.C.: HEW, 1970.

Green, Joseph. "Desegregation in Prince Edward County, Virginia." In: Kathleen Burk. *A Comparison of School Effectiveness Measures Based on Regression Models with Different Types of Predictors and Several Classification Procedures*. San Francisco: Paper Presented at American Educational Research Association Conference, April 1979.

Guditis, Charles W. and Perry A. Zirkel. "Basis of Supervisory Power of Public School Principals." San Francisco: Paper Presented at American Educational Research Association Conference, April 1979.

Hanushek, Eric A. *Longitudinal Surveys of Educational Effects*. Washington, D.C.: Council of Economic Advisers, 1972.

Hawkridge, D. G., P. Campeau, and P. Trickett. *A Guide for Authors of Evaluation Reports of Educational Programs*. Palo Alto, California: American Institutes for Research in the Behavioral Sciences, 1969.

Hawkridge, D. G., A. B. Chalupsky, and A. O. H. Roberts. *A Study of Selected Exemplary Programs for the Education of Disadvantaged Children, Parts I and II*. Palo Alto, California: American Institutes for Research in the Behavioral Sciences, September 1968.

Husen, Torsten. *International Study of Achievement in Mathematics: A Comparison of Twelve Countries*, Volume I. New York: John Wiley and Sons, 1967.

Jencks, Christopher and others. *Inequality: An Assessment of the Effect of Family and Schooling in America*. New York: Basic Books, 1972.

Kirst, Michael W. "What Types of Compensatory Education Programs are Effective." Washington, D.C.: Paper Presented for The National Conference on Equal Educational Opportunity in America's Cities, sponsored by the U.S. Commission on Civil Rights, November 16–18, 1967.

Klitgaard, Robert E. and George Hall. *A Statistical Search for Unusually Effective Schools*. Santa Monica, CA: The Rand Corporation, 1973.

Mayeske, George and others. *A Study of the Achievement of Our Nation's Students*. Washington, D.C.: HEW, 1973.

McLaughlin, Milbrey W. *Evaluation and Reform: The Elementary and Secondary Education Act of 1965/Title I*. Cambridge, Massachusetts: Ballinger Publishing Company, 1975.

Plowden Report. *Children and Their Primary Schools*. Central Advisory Council for Education. HMSO 1967, Vol I and II.

Scientific Educational Systems, Inc. *Joint Federal/State Task Force on Evaluation—Comprehensive Evaluation System: Current Status and Development Requirements*. 1970.

Smith, M. and M. Tucker. *A Research Perspective on Educational Improvement*. Washington, D.C.: USOE/HEW, October 1977.

Technomics, Inc. "A Study of Cost/Effectiveness in Title I Schools." February 1968.

TEMPO. *Survey and Analyses of Results from Title I Funding for Compensatory Education.* Santa Barbara, CA: General Electric Co., 1968.

Wargo, Michael J. and others. *Further Examination of Exemplary Programs for Educating Disadvantaged Children.* Palo Alto, California: American Institutes for Research in the Behavioral Sciences, July 1971.

ADDITIONAL REFERENCES

Austin, G. and H. Garber (eds.) *Research on Exemplary Schools.* New York: Academic Press, Inc., 1985.

Brookover, W. et al. *Creating Effective Schools.* Holmes Beach, Florida: Learning Publications, Inc., 1982.

Dalin, P. and V. Rust. 1982. *Can Schools Learn?* Windsor, Berks., Great Britain: Nfer-Nelson Publishing Company, Ltd., 1983.

Greenfield, W. (ed.) *Instructional Leadership: Concepts, Issues, and Controversies.* Newton, Massachusetts: Allyn and Bacon, Inc., 1987.

Lane, J. and Walberg, H. (eds.) *Effective School Leadership.* Berkeley, California: McCutchan Publishing Corp., 1987.

Purkey, S. and Smith, M. "Effective Schools: A Review." *The Elementary School Journal,* 83: 427–452, 1983.

Reynolds, D. (ed.) *Studying School Effectiveness.* Lewes, East Sussex, Great Britain: The Falmer Press, 1985.

Sergiovanni, T. *The Principalship: A Reflective Practice.* Newton, Massachusetts: Allyn and Bacon, Inc., 1987.

The Disadvantaged Child and
the Learning Process

MARTIN DEUTSCH
New York University

. . . Among children who come from lower-class socially impoverished circumstances, there is a high proportion of school failure, school dropouts, reading and learning disabilities, as well as life-adjustment problems. This means not only that these children grow up poorly equipped academically, but also that the effectiveness of the school as a major institution for socialization is diminished. The effect of this process is underlined by the fact that this same segment of the population contributes disproportionately to the delinquency and other social-deviancy statistics.

The thesis here is that the lower-class child enters the school situation so poorly prepared to produce what the school demands that initial failures are almost inevitable and that the school experience becomes negatively rather than positively reinforced. Thus the child's experience in school does nothing to counteract the invidious influences to which he is exposed in his slum, and sometimes segregated, neighborhood.

We know that children from underprivileged environments tend to come to school with a qualitatively different preparation for the demands of both the learning process and the behavioral requirements of the classroom. There are various differences in the kinds of socializing experiences these children have had, as contrasted with the middle-class child. The culture of their environment is a different one from the culture that has molded the school and its educational techniques and theory.

We know that it is difficult for all peoples to span cultural discontinuities, and yet we make little if any effort to prepare administrative personnel or

From *Education in Depressed Areas*, A. Harry Passow, ed. (New York: Teachers College Press, Copyright © 1963 by Teachers College Press, Columbia University. All rights reserved.) Reprinted with permission of the publisher.

teachers and guidance staff to assist the child in this transition from one cultural context to another. This transition must have serious psychological consequences for the child, and probably plays a major role in influencing his later perceptions of other social institutions as he is introduced to them.

It must be pointed out that the relationship between social background and school performance is not a simple one. Rather, evidence which is accumulating points more and more to the influence of background variables on the patterns of perceptual, language, and cognitive development of the child and the subsequent diffusion of the effects of such patterns into all areas of the child's academic and psychological performance. To understand these effects requires delineating the underlying skills in which these children are not sufficiently proficient. A related problem is that of defining what aspects of the background are most influential in producing what kinds of deficits in skills.

ENVIRONMENTAL FACTORS

Let us begin with the most macroscopic background factors. While it is likely that slum life might have delimited areas that allow for positive growth and that the middle-class community has attributes which might retard healthy development, generally the combination of circumstances in middle-class life is considerably more likely to furnish opportunities for normal growth of the child. At the same time, slum conditions are more likely to have deleterious effects on physical and mental development. This is not to say that middle-class life furnishes a really adequate milieu for the maximum development of individual potential: it does not. The fact that we often speak as though it does is a function of viewing the middle-class environment in comparison to the slum. Middle-class people who work and teach across social-class lines often are unable to be aware of the negative aspects of the middle-class background because of its apparent superiority over the less advantageous background provided by lower-class life. We really have no external criterion for evaluating the characteristics of a milieu in terms of how well it is designed to foster development; as a result, we might actually be measuring one area of social failure with the yardstick of social catastrophe. . . .

In the lower-class Negro group there still exist the sequelae of the conditions of slavery. Although a hundred years have passed, this is a short time in the life of a people. And the extension of tendrils of the effects of slavery into modern life has been effectively discouraged only in the last few decades, when there have been some real attempts to integrate the Negro fully into American life. It is often difficult for teachers and the personnel of other community agencies to understand the Negro lower-class child— particularly the child who has come, or whose parents have come, from the rural South. There is a whole set of implicit and explicit value systems which determine our educational philosophies, and the institutional expectation is that all children participate in these systems. Yet for these expectations to be met, the child must experience some continuity of sociocultural participation in and sharing of these value systems before he comes to school. This is often just not the case for the child who comes from an encapsulated community, particularly when the walls have been built by the dominant social and cultural forces that have also determined the value systems relating to learning. . . .

The Negro family was first broken deliberately by the slave traders and the plantation owners for their own purposes. As was pointed out earlier, the hundred years since slavery is not a very long time for a total social metamorphosis even under fostering conditions—and during that period the Negro community has been for the most part economically marginal and isolated from the contacts which would have accelerated change. The thirteen depressions and recessions we have had since Emancipation have been devastating to this community. These marginal economic and encapsulated social circumstances have been particularly harsh on the Negro male. The chronic instability has greatly influenced the Negro male's concept of himself and his general motivation to succeed in competitive areas of society where the rewards are greatest. All these circumstances have contributed to the instability of the Negro family, and particularly to the fact that it is most often broken by the absence of the father. As a result, the lower-class Negro child entering school often has had no experience with a "successful" male model or thereby with the corresponding psychological framework in which effort can result in at least the possibility of achievement. Yet the value system of the school and of the learning process is predicated on the assumption that effort will result in achievement.

To a large extent, much of this is true not only for the Negro child but for all children who come from impoverished and marginal social and economic conditions. These living conditions are characterized by great overcrowding in substandard housing, often lacking adequate sanitary and other facilities. While we do not know the actual importance, for example, of moments of privacy, we do know that the opportunity frequently does not exist. In addition, there are likely to be large numbers of siblings and half-siblings, again with there being little opportunity for individuation. At the same time, the child tends to be restricted to his immediate environment, with conducted explorations of the "outside" world being infrequent and sometimes nonexistent. In the slums, and to an unfortunately large extent in many other areas of our largest cities, there is little opportunity to observe natural beauty, clean landscapes, or other pleasant and aesthetically pleasing surroundings.

In the child's home, there is a scarcity of objects of all types, but especially of books, toys, puzzles, pencils, and scribbling paper. It is not that the mere presence of such materials would necessarily result in their productive use, but it would increase the child's familiarity with the tools that will confront him in school. Actually, for the most effective utilization of these tools, guidance and explanations are necessary from the earliest time of exposure. Such guidance requires not only the presence of aware and educated adults, but also time—a rare commodity in these marginal circumstances. Though many parents will share in the larger value system of having high aspirations for their children, they are unaware of the operational steps required for the preparation of the child to use optimally the learning opportunities in the school. Individual potential is one of the most unmarketable properties if the child acquires no means for its development, or if no means exist for measuring it objectively. It is here that we must understand the consequences of all these aspects of the slum matrix for the psychological and cognitive development of the child.

PSYCHOLOGICAL FACTORS

A child from any circumstance who has been deprived of a substantial portion of the variety of stimuli which he is maturationally capable of responding to is likely to be deficient in the equipment required for learning. . . .

This emphasis on the importance of variety in the environment implies the detrimental effects of lack of variety. This in turn leads to a concept of "stimulus deprivation." But it is important that it be correctly understood. By this is not necessarily meant any restriction of the quantity of stimulation, but, rather, a restriction to a segment of the spectrum of stimulation potentially available. In addition to the restriction in variety, from what is known of the slum environment it might be postulated that the segments made available to these children tend to have poorer and less systematic ordering of stimulation sequences, and would thereby be less useful to the growth and activation of cognitive potential. . . .

In individual terms, a child is probably farther away from his maturational ceiling as a result of this experiential poverty. This might well be a crucial factor in the poorer performance of the lower socioeconomic children on standardized tests of intelligence. On such tests, the child is compared with others of his own age. But if his point of development in relation to the maturational ceiling for his age group is influenced by his experience, then the child with restricted experience may actually be developed to a proportionately lower level of his own actual ceiling. If a certain quantum of fostering experience is necessary to activate the achievement of particular maturational levels, then perhaps the child who is deficient in this experience will take longer to achieve these levels, even though his potential may be the same as the more advantaged child. It might be that in order to achieve a realistic appraisal of the ability levels of children, an "experience" age rather than the chronological age should be used to arrive at norms. . . .

Visually, the urban slum and its overcrowded apartments offer the child a minimal range of stimuli. There are usually few if any pictures on the wall, and the objects in the household, be they toys, furniture, or utensils, tend to be sparse, repetitious, and lacking in form and color variations. The sparsity of objects and lack of diversity of home artifacts which are available and meaningful to the child, in addition to the unavailability of individualized training, gives the child few opportunities to manipulate and organize the visual properties of his environment and thus perceptually to organize and discriminate the nuances of that environment. These would include figure-ground relationships and the spatial organization of the visual field. The sparsity of manipulable objects probably also hampers the development of these functions in the tactile area. For example, while these children have broomsticks and usually a ball, possibly a doll or a discarded kitchen pot to play with, they do not have the different shapes and colors and sizes to manipulate which the middle-class child has in the form of blocks which are bought just for him, or even in the variety of sizes and shapes of cooking utensils which might be available to him as playthings. . . .

The effect of sparsity of manipulable objects on visual perception is, of course, quite speculative, as few data now exist. However, it is an important area, as among skills necessary for reading are form discrimination and visual spatial organization. Children from depressed areas, because of inadequate training and stimulation, may not have developed the requisite skiils by the time they enter first grade, and the assumption that they do possess these skills may thus add to the frustration these children experience on entering school.

The lower-class home is not a verbally oriented environment. The implications of this for language development will be considered below in the discussion of the contentual systems. Here let us consider its implication for the development of auditory discrimination skills. While the environment is a noisy one, the noise is not, for the most part, meaningful in relation to the child, and for him most of it is background. In the crowded apartments, with all the daily living stresses, there is a minimum of non-instructional conversation directed toward the child. In actuality, the situation is ideal for the child to learn inattention. Furthermore, he does not get practice in auditory discrimination or feedback from adults correcting his enunciation, pronunciation, and grammar. In studies at the Institute for Developmental Studies we have found significant differences in auditory discrimination between lower-class and middle-class children in the first grade. These differences seem to diminish markedly as the children get older, though the effects of their early existence on other functioning remain to be investigated. Here again we are dealing with a skill very important to reading. Our data indicate too that poor readers within social-class groups have significantly more difficulty in auditory discrimination than do good readers. Further, this difference between good and poor readers is greater for the lower-class group.

If the child learns to be inattentive in the preschool environment, as has been postulated, this further diminishes incoming stimulation. Further, if this trained inattention comes about as a result of his being insufficiently called upon to respond to particular stimuli, then his general level of responsiveness will also be diminished. The nature of the total environment and the child-adult interaction is such that reinforcement is too infrequent, and, as a result, the quantity of response is diminished. The implications of this for the structured learning situation in the school are quite obvious.

Related to attentivity is memory. Here also we would postulate the dependence of the child, particularly in the preschool period, on interaction with the parent. It is adults who link the past and the present by calling to mind prior shared experiences. The combination of the constriction in the use of language and in shared activity results, for the lower-class child, in much less stimulation of the early memory function. Although I know of no data supporting this thesis, from my observations it would seem that there is a tendency for these children to be proportionately more present-oriented and less aware of past-present sequences than the middle-class child. This is consistent with anthropological research and thinking. While this could be a function of the poorer time orientation of these children or of their difficulty in verbal expression, both of which will be discussed below, it could also relate to a greater difficulty in seeing themselves in the past or in a different context. Another area which points up the home-school discontinuity is that of time. Anthropologists have pointed out that, from culture to culture, time concepts differ and that time as life's governor is a relatively modern phenomenon and one which finds most of its slaves in the lower-middle, middle-middle, and upper-middle classes. It might not even be an important factor in learning, but it is an essential feature in the measurement of children's performance by testing and in the adjustment of children to the organizational demands of the school. The middle-class teacher organizes the day by allowing a certain amount of time for each activity. Psychologists have long noticed that American Indian children, mountain children, and children from other non-industrial groups have great difficulty organizing their response tempo to meet time limitations. In the Orientation Scale developed at the Institute, we have found that lower-class children in the first grade had significantly greater difficulty than did middle-class children in handling items related to time judgments.

Another area in which the lower-class child lacks preschool orientation is the well-inculcated expectation of reward for performance, especially for successful task completion. The lack of such expectation, of course, reduces motivation for beginning a task and, therefore, also makes less likely the self-reinforcement of activity through the gaining of feelings of competence. In these impoverished, broken homes there is very little of the type of interaction seen so commonly in middle-class homes, in which the parent sets a task for the child, observes its performance, and in some way rewards its completion. Neither, for most tasks, is there the disapproval which the middle-class child incurs when he does not perform properly or when he leaves something unfinished. Again, much of the organization of the classroom is based on the assumption that children anticipate rewards for performance and that they will respond in these terms to tasks which are set for them. This is not to imply that the young lower-class child is not given assignments in his home, nor that he is never given approval or punishment. Rather, the assignments tend to be motoric in character, have a short time span, and are more likely to relate to very concrete objects or services for people. The tasks given to preschool children of the middle class are more likely to involve language and conceptual processes, and are thereby more attuned to the later school setting.

Related to the whole issue of the adult-child dynamic in establishing a basis for the later learning process is the ability of the child to use the adult as a source for information, correction, and the reality testing involved in problem solving and the absorption of new knowledge. When free adult time is greatly limited, homes vastly overcrowded, economic stress chronic, and the general educational level very low—and, in addition, when adults in our media culture are aware of the inadequacy of their education—questions from children are not encouraged, as the adults might be embarrassed by their own limitations and are in any case too preoccupied with the business of just living and surviving. In the child's formulation of concepts of the world, the ability to formulate questions is an essential step in data gathering. If questions are not encouraged or if they are not responded to, this is a function which does not mature. . . .

In order for a child to handle multiple attributes of words and to associate words with their proper referents, a great deal of exposure to language is presupposed. Such exposure involves training, experimenting with identifying objects and having corrective feedback, listening to a variety of verbal material, and just observing adult language usage. Exposure of children to this type of experience is one of the great strengths of the middle-class home, and concomitantly represents a weakness in the lower-class home. In a middle-class home, also, the availability of a great range of objects to be labeled and verbally related to each other strengthens the overall language fluency of the child and gives him a basis for both understanding the teacher and for being able to communicate with her on various levels. An implicit hypothesis in a recent Institute survey of verbal skills is that verbal fluency is strongly related to reading skills and to other highly organized integrative and conceptual verbal activity.

The acquisition of language facility and fluency and experience with the multiple attributes of words is particularly important in view of the estimate that only 60 to 80 percent of any sustained communication is usually heard. Knowledge of context and of the syntactical regularities of a language makes correct completion and comprehension of the speech sequence possible. This completion occurs as a result of the correct anticipation of the sequence of language and thought. The child who has not achieved these anticipatory language skills is greatly handicapped in school. Thus, for the child who already is deficient in auditory discrimination and in ability to sustain attention, it becomes increasingly important that he have the very skills he lacks most. . . .

In observations of lower-class homes, it appears that speech sequences seem to be temporally very limited and poorly structured syntactically. It is thus not surprising to find that a major focus of deficit in the children's language development is syntactical organization and subject continuity. In preliminary analysis of expressive and receptive language data on samples of middle- and lower-class children at the first- and fifth-grade levels, there are indications that the lower-class child has more expressive language ability than is generally recognized or than emerges in the classroom. The main differences between the social classes seem to lie in the level of syntactical organization. If, as is indicated in this research, with proper stimulation a surprisingly high level of expressive language functioning is available to the same children who show syntactical deficits, then we might conclude that the language variables we are dealing with here are by-products of social experience rather than indices of basic ability or intellectual level. This again suggests another possibly vital area to be included in an enrichment or a remedial program: training in the use of word sequences to relate and unify cognitions.

Also on the basis of preliminary analysis of data, it appears that retarded readers have the most difficulty with the organization of expressive language.

Differences between middle- and lower-class language usage have been defined by Bernstein.[1] He reports that the middle class tends to use a more formal language, oriented to relating concepts, while the lower class uses a more informal language, whose referents are more likely to be concrete tasks or objects. This difference might explain why we have found that the middle-class fifth-grade child has an advantage over the lower-class fifth-grader in tasks where precise and somewhat abstract language is required for solution. Further, Bernstein's reasoning would again emphasize the communication gap which exists between the middle-class teacher and the lower-class child. . . .

The other contentual factors that so often result in a poorly prepared child being brought to the school situation are closely interrelated with language. Briefly, they revolve around the child's understanding and knowledge of the physical, geographic, and geometric characteristics of the world around him, as well as information about his self-identity and some of the more macroscopic items of general information. It could be reasonably expected, for example, that a kindergarten or first-grade child who is not mentally defective would know both his first and last names, his address or the city he lives in, would have a rudimentary concept of number relationships, and would know something about the differences between near and far, high and low, and similar relational concepts. Much of what happens in school is predicated on the prior availability of this basic information. We know that educational procedures frequently proceed without establishing the actual existence of such a baseline. Again, in the lower-class child it cannot be taken for granted that the home experience has supplied this information or that it has tested the child for this knowledge. In facilitating the learning process in these children, the school must expect frequently to do a portion of the job traditionally assigned to the home and curriculum must be reorganized to provide for establishing a good base. This type of basic information is essential so that the child can relate the input of new information to some stable core.

From all of the foregoing, it is obvious that the lower-class child, when he enters school, has as many problems in understanding what it is all about and why he is there as school personnel have in relating traditional curriculum and learning procedures to this child. Some reorientation is really necessary, as discussion of these problems almost always focuses on the problems the school has, rather than on the enormous confusion, hesitations, and frustrations the child experiences and does not have the language to articulate when he meets an essentially rigid set of academic expectations. Again, from all the foregoing, the child, from the time he enters school and is exposed to assumptions about him derived from experience with the middle-class child, has few success experiences and much failure and generalized frustration, and thus begins the alienating process in the direction of the apathetic and disgruntled fifth-grader described earlier.

The frustration inherent in not understanding, not succeeding, and not being stimulated in the school—although being regulated by it—creates a basis for the further development of negative self-images and low evaluations of individual competencies. This would be especially true for the Negro child who, as we know from doll play and other studies, starts reflecting the social bias in his own self-image at very early ages. No matter how the parents might aspire to a higher achievement level for their child, their lack of knowledge as to the operational implementation, combined with the child's early failure experiences in school, can so effectively attenuate confidence in his ability ever to handle competently challenge in the academic area, that the child loses all motivation. . . .

SCHOOL CONDITIONS

Educational factors have of course been interlaced throughout this discussion, but there are some special features that need separate delineation.

The lower-class child probably enters school with a nebulous and essentially neutral attitude. His home rarely, if ever, negatively predisposes him toward the school situation, though it might not offer positive motivation and correct interpretation of the school experience. It is in the school situation that the highly charged negative attitudes toward learning evolve, and the responsibility for such large groups of normal children showing great scholastic retardation, the high dropout rate, and to some extent the delinquency problem, must rest with the failure of the school to promote the proper acculturation of these children. Though some of the responsibility may be shared by the larger society, the school, as the institution of that society, offers the only mechanism by which the job can be done.

It is unfair to imply that the school has all the appropriate methods at its disposal and has somehow chosen not to apply them. On the contrary, what is called for is flexible experimentation in the development of new methods, the clear delineation of the problem, and the training and retraining of administrative and teaching personnel in the educational philosophy and the learning procedures that this problem requires.

In addition, the school should assume responsibility for a systematic plan for the education of the child in the areas that have been delineated here by the time the child reaches kindergarten or first grade. This does not mean that the school will abrogate the family's role with regard to the child, but rather that the school will insure both the intellectual and the attitudinal receptivity of each child to its requirements. Part of a hypothesis now being tested in a new preschool program is based on the assumption that early intervention by well-structured programs will significantly reduce the attenuating influence of the socially marginal environment.

What might be necessary to establish the required base to assure the eventual full participation of these children in the opportunity structure offered by the educational system is an ungraded sequence from age three or four through eight, with a low teacher-pupil ratio. Perhaps, also, the school system should make full use of anthropologists, sociologists, and social psychologists for description and interpretation of the cultural discontinuities which face the individual child when he enters school. In addition, the previously discussed patterning of deficits and strengths should be evaluated for each child and placed in a format which the teacher can use as a guide. In the early years this would enable diagnostic reviews of the intellectual functioning of each child, so that learning procedures, to whatever extent possible, could be appropriate to a particular child's needs. New evaluation techniques must be developed for this purpose, as the standardized procedures generally cannot produce accurate evaluation of the functioning level or achievement potential of these children.

Possibly most important would be the greater utilization by educators in both curriculum development and teacher training of the new and enormous knowledge, techniques, and researches in the social and behavioral sciences. Similarly, social and behavioral scientists have in the school a wonderful laboratory to study the interpenetration and interaction of fundamental social, cognitive, psychological, and developmental processes. Close and continuing collaboration, thus, should be mutually productive and satisfying, and is strongly indicated.

REFERENCES

1. Bernstein, B. Language and social class. *Brit. J. Psychol.*, 1960, **11**, 271–276.
2. Hunt, J. McV. *Intelligence and experience.* New York: Ronald, 1961.

Social Stratification and the Socialization of Competence[1]

JOHN U. OGBU
University of California, Berkeley

. . .

SUBORDINATE-GROUP COMPETENCE IN THE CLASSROOM: A CRITICAL LOOK AT THEORY, RESEARCH AND POLICY

Since the late 1950s social scientists have used what I call the failure-of-socialization hypothesis to explain differences between blacks and whites in social competence as well as in cognitive, language, and motivational competences (see Bereiter et al. 1966; Bloom, Davis, and Hess 1965; Denenberg 1970; Deutsch et al. 1967; Goldberg 1971; Gordon 1968; Hess and Shipman 1967; Hunt 1969; Inkeles 1968a; Katz 1967; Little and Smith 1971; Passow 1963, 1971; Rees 1968). These differences were assumed to be responsible for black school failure. The failure-of-socialization hypothesis basically states that blacks and similar "disadvantaged groups" deviate from the white middle-class socialization pattern and consequently do not transmit to their children white middle-class competences which promote white middle-class school success. The hypothesis assumes that a child's acquisition of such school-relevant skills as language, cognition, motivation, and social competences are determined primarily by the nature of parent-child interaction, especially mother-child interaction (see Clarke-Stewart 1977; Gordon 1968; Hunt 1969). It therefore directs researchers to focus on patterns of parent-child interaction and on how these vary according to sex, race, socioeconomic status, and structure of the family. These studies show beyond doubt that blacks, especially lower-class blacks, differ significantly from white middle-class parents in the way they raise their children.

As to why black parents differ in their methods, the hypothesis suggests that blacks are culturally deprived or, in some versions of it, that blacks are culturally different. The cultural-deprivation version says that blacks do not have the skills or abilities to teach their children white middle-class competences and values which lead to white middle-class school success (for critical reviews of this perspective, see Clement and Johnson 1973:5–6; Ogbu 1978). This version of the hypothesis also stresses that black parents do not teach their children the middle-class learning style or "learning-to-learn" which facilitates white middle-class type of school success (Bloom, Davis, and Hess 1965:15; Passow 1963:337).

The cultural-difference version of the hypothesis states that blacks socialize their children differently because they have a different culture which requires social and other competences different from those valued in the white middle-class culture and school. Consequently black children fail in school because they bring with them competences different from those relevant to school success (Cole and Bruner 1972; Connolly and Bruner 1974; Inkeles 1968a).

The failure-of-socialization hypothesis greatly influenced certain aspects of the social policies that were begun in the late 1950s and were intended ultimately to improve black school performance. The immediate objective of these policies was in part to compensate black children for the competences they had not acquired in their early socialization. Some programs were devised to assist children already in school to make up for the competences they had not acquired earlier. Although these early programs were not particularly successful, similar programs were introduced on a more massive scale in the mid-1960s following the passage of the federal Elementary and Secondary Education Act of 1965 (see Ogbu 1978 for a summary of the early and later compensatory education programs). By the early 1960s it was, of course, known to social scientists and policymakers alike that this method of compensation was not working. This knowledge, however, did not result in rejection of the failure-of-socialization hypothesis. Instead, the hypothesis was elaborated to include the assumption that the harmful effects of cultural deprivation and cultural differences established themselves so early that it was necessary to intervene during the preschool years to ensure that black children would develop the appropriate white middle-class types of social, language, cognitive, and motivational competences required for white middle-class types of school success (see Bloom, Davis, and Hess 1965; Kerber and Bommarito 1965:345–46).

One of the earliest of these *preventive preschool programs* was jointly sponsored by the Institute of Developmental Studies and the New York City Board of Education under the leadership of Martin Deutsch in 1962 (Deutsch et al 1967; Powledge 1967). Similar programs were begun about the same time in Baltimore, Md., in Philadelphia, Pa., and in Nashville, Tenn. Early evaluations of the programs indicated that children who participated in them scored higher than children who had not taken part in the programs when tested on cognitive skills (Little and Smith 1971; Gottfried 1973; Rees 1968). The early reports of such gains greatly influenced two important conferences on the problem of school failure of blacks and other subordinate groups. Both the Conference on Curriculum and Teaching in the Urban Ghettoes at Columbia University in 1962 and the Conference on Compensatory Education for the Culturally Deprived at the University of Chicago in 1964 concluded that early intervention on a massive scale was necessary because subordinate-group parents had failed to socialize their children adequately. As the Chicago Conference put it: "While we would advocate that the intellectual training of the child be in the home and by the parent, if they [the parents] cannot do it adequately, the school is the logical social agency to do it" (Bloom, Davis, and Hess 1965:17; see also Passow 1963). Both conferences made several recommendations, many of which were later incorporated into the Head Start in 1965 and other preschool programs as well as into much later parent-education programs. In the main, these programs are designed either to resocialize black children to acquire white middle-class social, language, cognitive, and motivational competences or to teach black mothers to transmit these competences to their children.

As is well known by now, these programs have not been particularly successful in helping black children acquire white middle-class competences. Although there are many reports that children in the programs score higher on IQ tests than do other children who do not take part in the programs, their higher scores are also reported to disappear or "fade out" after they leave the programs for regular schooling (Goldberg 1971: 79–81; Little and Smith 1971: 52–53; Miller 1967:146; Passow 1971:13–14; Stanley 1973; Wilkerson 1970:28; but see Brazziel 1974 and Bronfenbrenner 1975 for a different assessment.) This "fade-out" problem has not led to the abandonment of the failure-of-socialization hypothesis; on the contrary, it has further reinforced it, for the hypothesis now asserts that the adverse influences of the children's home environment on their ability to develop white middle-class competences for later school success establish themselves much earlier than was previously thought and that intervention at the age of five, four, or three is too late; what is needed, according to the newest version, is to intervene at the birth or even before the birth of the child (see Goldberg 1971; White 1970).

The programs designed to transmit to black children the competences of the white middle class fail largely because they are based on an inadequate or a wrong theory of *why* people in a given society develop certain types of competences. The failure-of-socialization hypothesis which underlies these programs makes no distinction between the reason *why* white middle-class people are characterized by their patterns of social, language, cognitive, and motivational competences and *how* white middle-class children acquire their competences in the course of socialization. In fact, the failure-of-socialization hypothesis explains the existence of the competences solely in terms of the methods of their acquisition. In other words, it asserts that socialization processes determine competences rather than the other way around. It then proceeds to suggest that the different socialization practices of blacks are *wrong* because they do not enable black children to acquire white middle-class competences. Yet the hypothesis does not even suggest that blacks and middle-class whites have the same access to the same social, occupational, and political roles requiring the same social, language, cognitive, and motivational competences. Such access would justify the evaluation of black childrearing practices as right or wrong on the basis of their deviation from the childrearing practices of the dominant whites.

In the next section I intend to show that blacks and whites have traditionally had differential access to social, economic, political, and other roles; consequently the two racial groups are characterized by different patterns of competences which may require different techniques of childrearing for successful transmission.

RACIAL STRATIFICATION AND THE SOCIALIZATION OF COMPETENCE: AN ALTERNATIVE PERSPECTIVE

1. *Racial Stratification and Role Stratification:* A racially stratified society is a society in which two or more racial groups are organized into dominant and subordinate groups. Those who have access to high-status social, occupational, and political roles are primarily members of the dominant racial group; members of the subordinate racial group or groups have access mainly to the low-status, menial roles.

Racial stratification may coexist with class stratification, as it does in the United States, but the two systems have different consequences for the socialization of competence. Gerald Berreman (1972, 1977) has presented a succinct summary of the distinction between the two systems of stratification. Briefly, he states that class stratification is based on economic relations and that the attributes (such as education, occupation, income, and the like) that determine a person's class membership can be acquired during the lifetime of the individual. Furthermore, class stratification legitimatizes social mobility and prescribes the means of achieving it. In contrast, racial stratification is not based on acquired characteristics such as education, occupation, and income, but on "status honor." The individual is born with the attributes (e.g., skin color) that determine his racial-group membership, and racial stratification forbids upward mobility from one major ranked group to the other.

More pertinent to the theme of the present essay is that class and racial stratification differ in what Berreman calls *status summation*, that is, in the extent to which social, economic, political, and other socially valued roles in society are distributed among members of society according to the rank-order of their groups of origin, rather than on the basis of their individual training and abilities. In a relatively open-class system, people who originate from a given social class can be found distributed among a wide range of social, occupational, and political roles on the basis of their education and abilities; in such a system the status summation is low. Status summation in a racially stratified system is usually very high because of the tendency of members of the subordinate racial group to be restricted to those social, occupational, political, and other roles which members of the dominant group consider appropriate for the subordinate group, rather than to be distributed on the basis of their individual training and abilities.

Members of the lower class and members of racially subordinate groups also differ in the way they *perceive* and *interpret* their low social, economic, and political status. Lower-class members tend to "accept the social definition of the legitimacy of their status and to feel individually inadequate or unfortunate." Consequently, their "class injuries" are "hidden." That is, they have no clear conception of the possible external sources of their low status (Berreman 1977:23; see also Sennett and Cobb 1972). The injuries of members of a racially subordinate group are not, however, hidden; they are generally aware of the external barriers imposed on them because of their race. They do not accept the social definition of the legitimacy of their menial status, nor do they blame themselves for such low status.

Finally, racially stratified groups are themselves internally stratified by class, but the classes within the subordinate and dominant racial groups are not equal because, as noted earlier, members of the two racial groups do not have equal opportunity to acquire the education, occupation, income, and other attributes for higher class status. The class systems of the racially stratified groups also tend to differ in their patterns of social mobility: the system of the dominant racial group tends to encourage strategies emphasizing individual initiative, industriousness, perseverance, and competitiveness, whereas that of the subordinate racial group tends to encourage strategies of dependence, deference, and manipulation (Ogbu 1978:chap. 4). These differences between racial and class stratifications lead to differences in the distribution of roles in society, to differences in the distribution of competences required by incumbents of these roles, and to differences in methods of acquiring the competences, that is, to differences in socialization practices.

In my attempt to study the educational implications of American racial stratification I have used the concept of *role ceiling*, particularly *job ceiling*, to describe the nature of the social, occupational, and political participation of blacks in American society (Ogbu 1974a, 1974b, 1975, 1977, 1978). In most of my work, however, I have placed a greater emphasis on the job ceiling, because there is more objective data on black occupational history than on their social and political histories (see Bullock 1973; Burkey 1971; Gould 1977; Greene and Woodson 1930; Ladenburg and McFeely 1969; Levitan, Johnston, and Taggart 1975; Ogbu 1978:chap. 5).

In American society a person's job is a very important indicator of his status (see Miller 1971:18; Berg 1969). Americans believe that a person's education determines the kind of job he does; social scientists and policymakers assume that black underrepresentation in high-status jobs and their poverty are due to their lack of education, the latter often being attributed to the failure of black parents to transmit to their children the competences of white middle-class people which promote the white middle-class type of school success.

The concept of *job ceiling* refers to three aspects of the employment experiences of blacks, namely, (1) that blacks have traditionally not been permitted to compete freely as individuals with whites for any types of jobs to which they aspire and for which they are qualified; (2) that they are not allowed to obtain their proportionate share of the more highly desirable jobs primarily because of their race; and (3) that because of these restrictions blacks are largely confined to the least desirable occupations.

A decade-by-decade analysis of the employment history of black Americans in each region shows that this broad division into jobs above and below the job ceiling has existed since blacks first became wage earners after emancipation. The job ceiling has tended to be raised, however, during periods of national crisis or labor shortages, such as the period of economic growth of 1900 to 1908, in the war years, in the period of restriction of foreign immigration (1922 to 1929), and in periods of intense pressure from civil rights groups, such as that which occurred in the 1960s. In general, black occupational advances are not like those of whites, which depend on educational advances and an expanding economy; rather, black occupational advances depend on unpredictable political, economic, and administrative needs and decisions of the dominant white elites. Thus the job ceiling, though raised significantly since the mid-1960s, still exists, restricting most blacks to low-status jobs and keeping many of them underemployed and unemployed.

2. *Role Stratification and Stratification of Competences:* Role stratification by race, as evidenced by role and job ceilings, also results in the stratification of competences associated with the roles. Jobs above the job ceiling tend to require and promote different kinds of competences from those required and fostered by jobs below the job ceiling. This contrast in the competences associated with the two levels of occupations has been pointed out by Kohn (1969), Scrupski (1975), and others (Bowles and Gintis 1976; Levin 1976). Professional, technical, managerial, official, and similar jobs, according to these authors, both require and promote such personal qualities as independent judgment, autonomy, flexibility in thinking, and so on, all of which are related to a sense of self-direction. Low-status jobs below the job ceiling, such as blue-collar operative, domestic workers, and laborers, on the other hand, do not require or promote a sense of self-direction. Instead, they require and encourage obedience to authority, conformity to external rules, and such qualities. Competences which are functional or adaptive for the role incumbents above the job ceiling are not necessarily functional for role incumbents below the job ceiling, and vice versa. This stratification of competences, which in the United States coincides with black-white stratification to a large extent, determines the training or socialization of future incumbents of the stratified roles as well.

3. *Stratification of Competences and Competence Transmission:* My position is that the competences demanded by the high-status roles typical of the white middle class require one kind of childrearing practice, while the competences associated with the low-status roles of blacks require another kind of childrearing practice. Unfortunately, it is difficult to demonstrate the validity of this proposition on the basis of existing data on racial differences in childrearing practices. Most studies of black childrearing practices are oriented primarily toward determining the extent to which they approximate the practices of middle-class whites; they are not designed as studies of transmissions of the competences required by the social, occupational, and political roles of blacks (see extensive reviews of the literature by Hess 1970

and Clarke-Stewart 1977). Thus, I suggest that middle-class white parents socialize their children the way they do because it is probably the technique best suited for transmitting the competences or personal qualities that middle-class children will require for effective high-status participation in adult life, and black parents socialize their children the way they do because that is probably the technique best suited for transmitting the competences that black children will require in their future low-status roles, but I cannot spell out here precisely *how* it happens.

4. *Racial Stratification, Socialization of Competence, and the Classroom:* Many studies of black socialization practices, especially studies in the last two decades, have been conducted out of concern for the kinds of competences that black children bring to the classroom. More specifically, these studies are made to determine how black socialization practices and experiences affect the language, cognitive, motivational, and social competences of black children which are believed to influence their school performance. I indicated earlier in this essay that the general conclusion of these studies is that black children fail in school because their parents do not socialize them to acquire the competences of white middle-class people. Hence black children come to school with competences not relevant to the white middle-class type of school success.

But as I have suggested in a number of writings, most social, occupational, political and other roles traditionally open to blacks did not even require the white middle-class type of school success, nor did they require white middle-class types of social, language, cognitive, and motivational competences (Ogbu 1974a, 1974b, 1975, 1976, 1977, 1978). Moreover, if one examined the classroom situation very closely in the recent past, one might find that the problem was not so much that black children were not able to learn white middle-class skills which the schools were teaching them because the children did not possess white middle-class competences; rather, the problem was that the schools were actually teaching black children skills that reinforced the competences appropriate for their low-status roles in adult life.

In the area of social competence, some recent studies indicate that classroom dynamics are such as to encourage black and white pupils to develop contrasting personal qualities or competences. The best example of such studies is that of Leacock (1969), who studied fifth-grade committee organization in four schools serving predominantly middle-class whites, lower-class whites, middle-class blacks, and lower-class blacks, respectively. Leacock found that the way the committee functioned in each school encouraged the pupils to develop behavioral skills or social competences which more or less reflected the social competences associated with the adult roles of their respective groups of origin. For example, the teacher-pupil relationship in the grade five committee of the black middle-class school reflected the dilemma of black leadership in the wider society where, as in this class committee, "Leadership is formally assigned but devoid of real responsibility" (Leacock:167). In contrast, in the white middle-class school the leadership role assigned to the pupils involved real responsibility, "coupled with a fine sense of when it is appropriate to defer to authority, (and this) parallels the pattern of relationship on professional and administrative levels of organizations (in the wider society)" (Leacock:166; see also Ogbu 1978:chap. 4).

With regard to motivational competence, I have suggested, on the basis of my own study in Stockton, that the classroom reward system for blacks may reflect the way in which local communities reward adult blacks. In analyzing the experiences of one sample of subordinate-group students from the first through the sixth grade, I found that most of them were consistently given the same letter grade of C regardless of their individual efforts or progress as indicated in the teachers' written comments. I also found that in the wider community adult blacks did not appear to be hired, paid, or promoted according to their education and individual abilities (Ogbu 1978). In some other school systems there appears to be a lack of consistency in the way teachers evaluate the classroom accomplishments of black children (Dorothy C. Clement, personal communication). But the general tendency is to underreward black children for their classroom accomplishments, a situation which has also been reported for Mexican-American pupils (see Grebler et al. 1969). The way blacks *perceive* and *interpret* the reward systems of the school and of their local communities (as well as of the nation as a whole) very much influences their schooling efforts or their motivational competences in the classroom.

Other organizational features of the school reinforce black acquisition of those cognitive skills or competences appropriate for their low-status adult roles. The schools frequently shunt black children into the so-called "watered-down curricula" and "dead-end courses," which do not stress development of the cognitive competences required for high-status roles in adult life. Biased intelligence testing, misclassification based on the results of such testing, and unproven assumptions regarding the educational benefits of homogeneous grouping or tracking provide the rationale for black over-representation in courses and curricula that reinforce their acquisition of cognitive competences for low-status social, occupational, and political roles in adult life (see Children's Defense Fund 1974; Findley 1973; Hobbs 1975; Marascuilo and McSweeney 1972; Rothstein 1974; U.S. Commission on Civil Rights 1974; U.S. Senate Select Committee on Equal Educational Opportunity 1972).

CONCLUSIONS

I began this essay by expressing my skepticism about current formulation and interpretation of studies of subordinate-group socialization processes. The prevailing perspective fails to see the goal of socialization of competence in terms of present realities. It tends to judge subordinate-group parents as incompetent socialization agents because they do not transmit to their children the social, cognitive, and other competences adaptive to the social, occupational, and political roles of middle-class whites. Yet the experts who have tried to take over the socialization role of subordinate-group parents have not proved more successful in transmitting middle-class competences to subordinate-group children.

In this essay I have suggested an alternative view of the problem. It is my contention that white middle-class people are characterized by their typical social, cognitive, language, motivational, and other competences because these are required by their roles in society. Blacks lack the white middle-class competences because their own social, occupational, and political roles are different and require different competences. Given the differences in adaptive competences which exist between the stratified racial groups, the two groups use different childrearing practices best suited for the transmission of their respective competences. Parents within each of the two racial groups are to be judged as competent or incompetent agents of socialization on the basis of how well they succeed in transmitting to their children the competences required for the social, occupational, and political roles open to members of their group.

Researchers must continually distinguish their role as social scientists from their role as social reformers. So far not many have been able to do so, especially in the last couple of decades. Many social scientists want blacks and other subordinate groups to do as well in school as middle-class white people do. This goal is commendable. But in their eagerness to bring about change, they often design their studies not so much to understand the total situation as to discover *what is wrong* and how the situation should be changed. I believe this approach leads to the wrong kinds of questions, the wrong kinds of answers, and the wrong kinds of solutions.

NOTES

1. Work on this paper was supported financially by the following: Financial support for this paper came from the Carnegie Council on Children; Faculty Research Funds, University of California, Berkeley; and NIMH (Research Grant 1 RO3 MH25130–01). An earlier version of the paper was presented at a symposium on Social Competence in the Classroom at the 76th annual meeting of the American Anthropological Association, Houston, Texas, December 2, 1977.

REFERENCES

Aberle, David F. 1968 The Influences of Linguistics on Early Culture and Personality Theory. *In* Theory in Anthropology. Robert A. Manners and David Kaplan, eds. Pp. 303–317. Chicago: Aldine.

Adams, Arvil V. 1972 Toward Fair Employment and the E.E.O.C.: A Study of Compliance Procedures Under Title VII of the Civil Rights Act of 1964: A Report. Washington, D.C.: U.S. Government Printing Office.

Bereiter, Carl et al. 1966 An Academically Oriented Preschool for Culturally Deprived Children. *In* Preschool Education Today. Fred M. Hechinger, ed. Pp. 105–135. New York: Doubleday.

Berg, Ivar 1969 Education and Jobs: The Great Training Robbery. New York: Praeger.

Berreman, Gerald D. 1972 Race, Caste, and Other Invidious Distinctions in Social Stratification. Race 23:4.

———. 1977 Social Inequality: A Cross-Cultural Paradigm. Files of the author.

Bloom, Benjamin S., Allison Davis, and Robert Hess, eds. 1965 Compensatory Education for Cultural Deprivation. New York: Holt.

Bowles, Samuel, and Herbert Gintis 1976 Schooling in Capitalist Society: Educational Reform and the Contradictions of Economic Life. New York: Basic Books.

Brazziel, William F. 1974 Quality Education for All Americans: An Assessment of Gains of Black Americans with Proposals for Program Development in American Schools and Colleges for the Next Quarter-Century. Washington, D.C.: Howard University Press.

Brimmer, Andrew F. 1974 Economic Development in the Black Community. In The Great Society: Lessons for the Future. Eli Ginzberg and Robert M. Solow, eds. Pp. 146–163. New York: Basic Books.

Bronfenbrenner, Urie 1975 Is Early Intervention Effective? In Influences on Human Development. Second ed. Urie Bronfenbrenner and Maureen A. Mahoney, eds. Pp. 329–354. Hinsdale, Ill.: Dryden Press.

Bullock, Paul 1973 Aspiration vs. Opportunity: "Careers" in the Inner City. Ann Arbor: University of Michigan Press.

Burkey, Richard M. 1971 Racial Discrimination and Public Policy in the United States. Lexington, Mass.: D.C. Heath.

Children's Defense Fund 1974 Children Out of School in America. Washington, D.C.: Washington Research Project.

Clarke-Stewart, Alison 1977 Child Development in the Family: A Report to the Carnegie Council on Children. New York: Academic Press.

Clement, Dorothy C., and Patricia A. Johnson 1973 The "Cultural Deprivation" Perspective. In Beyond "Compensatory Education": A New Approach to Educating Children. F.S. Rosenau and J. Cheever, eds.: Pp. 1–26. San Francisco: Far West Laboratory for Educational Research and Development.

Cole, Michael, and J.S. Bruner 1972 Preliminaries to a Theory of Cultural Differences. In Early Childhood Education. Ira J. Gordon, ed. Pp. 161–180. Chicago: University of Chicago Press.

Connolly, K.J., and J.S. Bruner 1974 Introduction: Competence: Its Nature and Nurture. In The Growth of Competence. K.J. Connolly and J.S. Bruner, eds. Pp. 3–7. New York: Academic Press.

Denenberg, Victor H. 1970 Education of the Infant and Young Child. New York: Academic Press.

Deutsch, Martin, et al. 1967 The Disadvantaged Child. New York: Basic Books.

Findley, Warren G. 1973 How Ability Grouping Fails. In Inequality in Education, No. 14. Pp. 38–40. July 1973.

Fried, Morton H. 1968 On the Evolution of Social Stratification. In Theory in Anthropology. Robert A. Manners and David Kaplan, eds. Pp. 251–260. Chicago: Aldine.

Goldberg, Miriam L. 1971 Socio-Psychological Issues in the Education of the Disadvantaged. In Urban Education in the 1970's. A. Harry Passow, ed. Pp. 61–93. New York: Teachers College Press.

Gordon, Ira J. 1968 Parent Involvement in Compensatory Education. Urbana: University of Illinois Press.

Gottfried, Nathan W. 1973 Effects of Early Intervention Programs. In Comparative Studies of Blacks and Whites in the United States. Kent S. Miller and Ralph Mason Dreger, eds. Pp. 274–293. New York: Seminar Press.

Gould, William B. 1977 Black Workers in White Unions: Job Discrimination in the United States. Ithaca: Cornell University Press.

Grebler, Leo, J.W. Moore, and Ralph Guzman, eds. 1969 The Mexican-American People, The Nation's Second Largest Minority. New York: Free Press.

Greene, Lorenzo, and Carter G. Woodson 1930 The Negro Wage Earner. Washington, D.C.: Association for the Study of Negro Life and History.

Hess, Robert D. 1970 Class and Ethnic Factors in Socialization. *In* Carmichael'ʃ Manual of Child Psychology. Third ed., Vol. 2. Paul Mussen, ed. Pp. 457–557. New York: Wiley.

Hess, Robert D., and Virginia C. Shipman 1967 Early Experience and the Socialization of Cognitive Modes in Children. *In* Problems of Children and Youth in Modern Society. Gene R. Medinnus, et al., eds. New York: Selected Academic Readings.

Hobbs, Nicholas 1975 The Future of Children. San Francisco: Jossey-Bass.

Hunt, J. McV. 1969 The Challenge of Incompetence and Poverty: Papers on the Role of Early Education. Urbana: University of Illinois Press.

Inkeles, Alex 1968a Social Structure and the Socialization of Competence. *In* Socialization and Schools. Harvard Educational Review, eds. Pp. 50–68. Cambridge, Mass.: Harvard University Press.

_____ . 1968b Society, Social Structure, and Child Socialization. *In* Socialization and Society. John A. Clausen, ed. Pp. 73–129. Boston: Little, Brown.

Kahn, Tom 1968 The Economics of Inequality. *In* Negroes and Jobs: A Book of Readings. Louis A. Ferman et al., eds. Pp. 15–28. Ann Arbor: University of Michigan Press.

Katz, Irwin 1967 The Socialization of Academic Motivation in Minority-Group Children. *In* Nebraska Symposium on Motivation. D. Levine, ed. Pp. 133–191. Lincoln, Nebr.: University of Nebraska Press.

Kerber, August, and Barbara Bommarito 1965 Preschool Education for the Developing Cortex. *In* The Schools and the Urban Crisis. August Kerber and Barbara Bommarito, eds. Pp. 345–349. New York: Holt, Rinehart & Winston.

Killingsworth, Charles C. 1969 Jobs and Income for Negroes. *In* Race and the Social Sciences: A Survey from the Perspectives of Social Psychology, Education, Political Science, Economics and Sociology. Irwin Katz and Patricia Gurin, eds. New York: Basic Books.

Kohn, Melvin L. 1969 Social Class and Parent-Child Relationships: An Interpretation. *In* Life Cycle and Achievement in America. Rose Laub Coser, ed. Pp. 21–48. New York: Harper & Row.

Ladenburg, Thomas J., and William S. McFeely 1969 The Black Man in The Land of Equality. New York: Hayden.

Leacock, Eleanor B. 1969 Teaching and Learning in City Schools: A Comparative Study. New York: Basic Books.

Levin, Henry M. 1976 Educational Reform: Its Meaning? *In* The Limits of Educational Reform. Martin Carnoy and Henry M. Levin, eds. Pp. 23–51. New York: David McKay.

Levitan, Sar A., William B. Johnston, and Robert Taggart 1975 Still a Dream: The Changing Status of Blacks Since 1960. Cambridge, Mass.: Harvard University Press.

Little, Alana, and George Smith 1971 Strategies of Compensatory Education: A Review of Educational Projects for the Disadvantaged in The United States. Paris: Organization for Economic Cooperation and Development.

Marascuilo, Leonard A., and Maryellen McSweeney 1972 Tracking Minority Students Attitudes and Performance. *In* Urban Education. Richard R. Heidenreich, ed. Pp. 82–92. Arlington, Va.: College Readings.

Miller, Harry L., ed. 1967 Education for the Disadvantaged. New York: Free Press.

Miller, Herman P. 1971 Rich Man, Poor Man. New York: Crowell.

Norgren, Paul, and Samuel E. Hill 1964 Toward Fair Employment. New York: Columbia University Press.

Ogbu, John U. 1974a Race, IQ, and Socioeconomic Inequality: A Critique of Jensen's Hypothesis. Paper Read at a Symposium on Race and Intelligence, Anthropology Program, Massachusettes Institute of Technology, Cambridge, Mass. April 30, 1974.

_____ . 1974b Ascribed Inequality and Social Policy. Paper Prepared for a meeting of the Carnegie Council on Children and Social Policy, Jackson, Mississippi, May 4, 1974.

_____ . 1975 Castelike Minorities. In Excluded Children: A Draft Report of the Staff of the Carnegie Council on Children. New Haven, Conn. Unpublished Manuscript.

_____ . 1976 Socialization of Competence in a Double-Track System. Paper presented at a meeting of the Social Anthropology Faculty, Department of Anthropology, University of California, Berkeley. March 1976.

_____ . 1977 Racial Stratification and Education: The Case of Stockton, California. IRCD Bulletin, vol. XII, no. 3, Summer, 1977. pp. 1–27.

_____ . 1978 Minority Education and Caste: The American System in Cross-Cultural Perspective. New York: Academic Press.

Passow, A. Harry, ed. 1963 Education in Depressed Areas. New York: Teachers College Press.

_____ . 1971 Urban Education in the 1970's. Pp. 1–45. New York: Teachers College Press.

Powledge, Fred 1967 To Change a Child: A Report on the Institute for Developmental Studies. Chicago: Quadrangle Books.

Rees, Helen E. 1968 Deprivation and Compensatory Education: A Consideration. Boston: Houghton Mifflin.

Richards, Martin P. M., ed. 1973 The Integration of a Child into a Social World. Introduction. Pp. 1–10. London: Cambridge University Press.

Rothstein, Richard 1974 How Tracking Works. In Demystifying School: Writings and Experiences. Miriam Wasserman, ed. Pp. 61–74. New York: Praeger.

Scrupski, Adam 1975 The Social System of the School. In Social Forces and Schooling: An Anthropological and Sociological Perspective. Nobuo Kenneth Shimahara and Adam Scrupski, eds. Pp. 141–186. New York: David McKay.

Sennett, Richard, and Jonathan Cobb 1972 The Hidden Injuries of Class. New York: Random House.

Stanley, Julian C., ed. 1973 Compensatory Education for Children, Ages 2 to 8: Recent Studies of Educational Intervention. Introduction and Critique. Pp. 1–10. Baltimore: Johns Hopkins University Press.

U.S. Commission on Civil Rights 1974 Bilingual/Bicultural Education: A Privilege or a Right? Washington, D.C.: Government Printing Office.

U.S. Senate Select Committee on Equal Educational Opportunity 1972 Report: Toward Equality of Educational Opportunity. Washington, D.C.: Government Printing Office.

White, Sheldon H. 1970 The National Impact Study of Head Start. In Disadvantaged Child. Jerome Hellmuch, ed. Pp. 163–184. Compensatory Education: A National Debate, Vol. 3. New York: Brunner/Mazel.

Wilkerson, Doxey A. 1970 Compensatory Education: Defining the Issues. In Disadvantaged Child. Jerome Hellmuch, ed. Pp. 24–35. Compensatory Education: A National Debate, Vol. 3. New York: Brunner/Mazel.

7

Factors Influencing Nonacademic Learning

When people think of schooling, they tend to focus on the academic effects discussed in Chapter 6: the knowledge learned in academic disciplines such as mathematics, science, and literature. However, academic learning by no means exhausts the effects of schooling. We must also consider such important nonacademic effects as developing self-esteem, work diligence, tolerance for civil liberties, religiosity, belief in capitalism, and patriotism. These nonacademic effects are important if only because they are crucial to securing desired academic effects: Students' learning depends as much on their motivation and self-esteem as it does on their ability, and good teaching is as much a matter of exciting as informing students. But the nonacademic outcomes of schooling are also important in their own right, because they constitute among the most important outcomes desired by society and powerful patrons of the school.

Whether to be properly socialized workers, citizens, parents, or religious believers, adults must not only be technically qualified but also motivationally prepared to discharge their adult roles. In fact, as we will see in Chapter 9, many argue that employers prefer to hire the better educated more because they are presumed to be better motivated and trainable than because of any specific work-relevant skills that they are supposed to have.

The study of nonacademic learning has taken two main forms: research on what has been called the "hidden curriculum" of elementary and secondary schooling (Apple, 1982; Jackson, 1968; Giroux and Purpel, 1983) and research on the "enduring effects" of college education (Bowen, 1977; Feldman and Newcomb, 1969; Hyman, Wright, and Reed, 1975; Trent and Medsker, 1968). Within these two provinces of nonacademic effects, a wide variety of views have been offered from the perspective of functionalism, Marxism, Weberianism, and the work of Bourdieu and John Meyer. In the following pages, we will explore these various perspectives, observing the conventional division between the nonacademic effects of elementary and secondary education and of higher education, while protesting that this division has had the unfortunate effect of obscuring the common characteristics of nonacademic learning across all levels of education.

NONACADEMIC LEARNING IN ELEMENTARY AND SECONDARY SCHOOLING

Students of education agree on the importance of nonacademic learning in elementary and secondary school. But they disagree strongly on its content and social purpose, largely along the lines of the theories discussed in Chapter 2. On the question of content, many students of education focus on economic outcomes (for example, the teaching of punctuality, work diligence, desire for achievement, and so forth), while others focus on noneconomic outcomes (such as patriotism, religiosity, and respect for high culture). On the question of social purposes, some scholars view nonacademic learning as serving the interests of society as a whole in stability, while others view nonacademic learning as serving the interests of the dominant social class or other group in society. The differing answers to the two questions about the content and social purpose of nonacademic learning generate four different positions that largely conform to the various theories of the role of education discussed in Chapter 2. The cross-cutting of these two questions, which is depicted in Table 1, generates several different positions: functionalists, Marxists, Weberians, and Meyerites. These positions are discussed below.

Functionalism

Functionalists focus on the role of schools in inculcating certain orientations that are deemed basic to effective occupational performance in a modern industrialized society. They identify the beneficiary of this socialization process as society as a whole: Students benefit from moving smoothly into their adult roles; society benefits from having a well-working social order.

The selection by Robert Dreeben, "The Contribution of Schooling to the Learning of Norms: Independence, Achievement, Universalism, and Speci-

TABLE 1   Differing Positions on the Nonacademic Effects of Education

	Content of Nonacademic Learning	
Whose Interests Are Met?	Occupational	Nonoccupational
Society as a Whole	Functionalists	John Meyer
Specific Interest Group	Marxists (capitalist class)	Weberians (status groups) Bourdieuians (capitalist class, upper middle class)

ficity," is representative of the functionalist position. Building on the work of Talcott Parsons (1959), Dreeben discusses the role of schools in inculcating four key social norms, or rules of behavior, that he argues are necessary to the smooth functioning of a modern industrialized and bureaucratized society. He argues that the school is better able to inculcate these norms (independence, achievement, universalism, and specificity) because its structure and operations differ in key ways from other socializing or educational institutions, particularly the family. Independence involves being willing to be self-reliant and responsible, and the school is able to foster this by removing children from their family and by inculcating the idea that some kinds of cooperation are improper (that is, they constitute "cheating"). The norm of achievement requires performing tasks to one's best ability, and schools encourage this norm by providing a range of avenues for achievement, including not only academics but also extracurricular activities such as athletics. Universalism centers on accepting being treated not as a special, individual case but as a member of a category. Schools promote universalism by grouping students, who otherwise differ greatly, into classes homogeneous in age, ability, or subject being studied, in which all the students are treated in much the same way. Finally, specificity involves acceptance of relationships that are narrow and transitory. Schools lead students to accept this by exposing students to many classmates and teachers, thus forcing students to learn to tolerate rather narrow relationships.

The functionalist position has been criticized on several grounds. Some question whether schools do indeed inculcate the values of universalism and individualistic achievement. After all, students often subvert universalism by asking for exceptions in their cases or individualistic achievement by that form of cooperation called cheating. Moreover, many schools deliberately stress cooperation rather than individualism and use teaching methods—such as group learning techniques—that emphasize this alternative value (Slavin, 1980, 1987). In addition, functionalism has been criticized for depicting education's nonacademic effects as applicable to all students and, relatedly, for assuming that these effects are equally beneficial to all members of society. Marxists in particular have argued that schools socialize students of differing class backgrounds very differently and that this differential socialization is in service of the capitalist class's interest in perpetuating the unequal class relations of capitalist society.

Marxism

Marxists agree with functionalists in viewing nonacademic school learning as being mostly concerned with the attitudes and behavior necessary to deal with an industrialized, bureaucratized society.[1] But where functionalists see this learning as of benefit to the whole society, Marxists see it as aiding above all the capitalist class (the owners of businesses). Schools try to produce the

---

[1]The fountainhead of this argument was Bowles and Gintis (1976), with important elaboration and refinement being done by Apple (1979, 1982), Carnoy (1975), and Carnoy and Levin (1976, 1985). For more on this "class reproduction" position, see the introduction to Chapter 2.

work qualities useful to a capitalist economy that divides workers into different classes with varying incomes, power, and responsibility. However, Marxists differ on precisely how schools go about doing this.

Members of the "class reproduction" wing of Marxism argue that schools prepare their graduates for a class-differentiated system through a "correspondence principle" in which the structure of schools mirrors the structure of the workplace. Schools are directed by teachers and administrators who coordinate the work of students, with upper-class and middle-class students enjoying considerable autonomy in their schooling (thus resembling middle managers) and working class students having very little leeway (like workers in a firm).

In "Social Class and the Hidden Curriculum of Work," Jean Anyon explores the nature of class-differentiated schooling by examining the school experiences of four different kinds of students: children of executives, children of professionals, children of lower-middle-class families, and children of working-class families. She argues that students in working-class schools are taught in a way that corresponds to their parents' work conditions: little autonomy and creativity and close supervision. Schoolwork consists of carrying out fragmented tasks, with teachers giving little explanation of their purpose and leaving little leeway for alternative ways of doing them. Schools enrolling lower-middle-class children also drill their students in the right way to do things, but provide a bit more explanation and leeway than the working-class children had. In upper-class, "executive elite" schools, students are taught in a way that corresponds to their parents' jobs, which emphasize taking initiative and understanding the overall purposes of one's work. Teachers urge their students to learn to handle responsibility, to develop their own ideas, and to work out the rationale underlying what they are doing. Finally, schools serving affluent professional families emphasize developing students' abilities of linguistic and artistic expression in order to prepare them for professional, artistic, and scientific occupations like their parents'.

The "class reproduction" position elaborated by Anyon is striking but raises some questions. First, Anyon does not explain how schools come to provide class-specific instruction. She might follow Bowles and Gintis (1976) and argue that it is due to outside demands, whether of business or of working-class parents. But it could be argued instead that much of the rigidity of education in working-class schools is simply due to the fact that these schools are typically very large and must adopt bureaucratic devices as a way of handling large masses of students (Hurn, 1985: 237; Sirotnik, 1983).[2] Second, Anyon treats schools as largely patronized by one class, but in actuality schools are more diverse than this. Even schools with many upper-class or middle-class students often have many working-class stu-

[2]For more discussion, see the introduction to Chapter 4. Also, schools take on bureaucratic traits in part out of a desire to cope with uncertainty by copying a successful organizational model (bureaucracy) and to meet the codes of practice promulgated by professional associations (DiMaggio and Powell, 1983).

dents. If so, wouldn't these working-class students receive a non-working-class education? To salvage her thesis of class-differentiated education, Anyon would need to explore how schools provide a differentiated education within their own walls, through such means as curriculum grouping. A notable start in this direction is provided by Oakes (1982). Finally, Anyon's argument is not all that different from Dreeben's functionalist position. He too would argue that the school's structure mirrors that of the larger society and therefore prepares students for that society. Moreover, the content of working-class and middle-class schooling, as described by Anyon, approximates Dreeben's schooling in the norms of universalism and specificity.

This functionalist aroma of the class reproduction view has prompted criticism by its Marxist sibling, the "resistance" approach (Apple, 1982; Aronowitz and Giroux, 1985).[3] Resistance theorists argue that schools *try* to do what Anyon claims. But resistance theorists question whether schools succeed in getting students to learn capitalist nonacademic attitudes and behaviors. Resistance theorists highlight instances in which students reject, subvert, or otherwise resist those attitudes and behaviors that educators try to impose on them. Hence, resistance theorists would point out how one of the most important nonacademic effects of schools is the creation of antischool youth groups or gangs (Willis, 1981).[4]

Both Marxists schools—class reproduction and resistance—share a problem, however. In their emphasis on social class, they ignore other ways in which the nonacademic outcomes of education are tailored to ethnic or racial groups. Weberians, however, have been very attuned to this.

Weberianism

Weberians certainly do not ignore class-differentiated schooling. But they also bring a unique interest in how schooling serves to pass on the distinctive beliefs, attitudes, and behavior of "status groups," whether religious, ethnic, racial, or occupational groups. As a result, while sharing Marxists' interest in how education serves special interests, Weberians do not share their emphasis on occupationally oriented nonacademic effects. Alan Peshkin's "God's Choice," a study of a fundamentalist Christian school in Illinois, represents the Weberian position. Peshkin's Weberianism lies in noting the role of schools, such as Bethany Baptist Academy, in strengthening the cultural solidarity of a status group, in this case the Christian fundamentalist movement. Peshkin notes how Bethany is a "total institution" that tries to provide the fundamentalist movement with disciplined members who are protected from the temptations of secular society. Bethany Baptist's leaders have some interest in economic behavior and attitudes, because they support

---

[3]Anyon does mention student resistance, but it only constitutes a passing nod to the "resistance" approach. For more on the "class reproduction" and "resistance" approaches within Marxism, see Chapter 2.

[4]Some functionalists have also noted that the school's academic emphasis has the effect of creating an antiacademic backlash, particularly among unsuccessful students (Trow, 1961: 112–113).

capitalism, but their fundamental interest is in inculcating Christian culture. Hence, they try to propagate Christian values and behavior not only through the formal curriculum (in the form of religious instruction) but also through a dress code, church-sponsored youth activities, and so on.

John Meyer

Despite all their disagreements about the content and purpose of nonacademic effects, the previous positions agree that schools create them through particular things they do. John Meyer is unusual because he directly questions this (Meyer, 1977; Meyer and Rowan, 1978). To be sure, he does agree that graduates differ from nongraduates in their nonacademic attitudes, beliefs, and behavior. But he sees this as a product of the fact that we expect graduates to be different and they change to conform to this expectation. It is a case of labeling: If you label someone in a certain fashion, they eventually come to fit the label. The reason that we expect more from educated people, according to Meyer, is because industrial societies give schools the role of selecting people for the most desirable jobs. Meyer argues that colleges create a social category (the college graduate) that is incorporated into the personnel policies of employers. Therefore, people who did not attend college are not eligible for "college-level" jobs, no matter how well they might be able to perform them, because those jobs are restricted to college graduates. We act as though advanced education creates people deserving of those jobs, even if there is little evidence for it. Meyer's perspective alerts us to the importance of credentials as *symbols* of achievement and not just as concrete evidence of it.

THE ENDURING EFFECTS OF COLLEGE EDUCATION

Studies of nonacademic learning in the schools have focused on elementary and secondary schooling. But, beginning with Theodore Newcomb's (1943) pioneering study of Bennington College students, there has also been considerable attention to the effects of college on students' nonacademic attitudes and behavior. These studies typically find that college graduates generally are better informed on general issues, more interested in politics, more tolerant of the rights of others, and more self-confident than those who did not go to college (Astin, 1977; Bowen, 1977; Feldman and Newcomb, 1969; Hyman, Wright, and Reed, 1975; Trent and Medsker, 1968).

The selection by Kevin Dougherty and Floyd Hammack, "The Other Side of College: The Nonacademic Effects of Higher Education," reviews and critiques these findings on college effects. It briefly surveys the main findings in the areas of general knowledge, civic and political attitudes and behavior, personal ambition, self-confidence, and creativity. At the same time, Dougherty and Hammack raise three questions about the validity and meaning of these findings. Many of the studies on college effects suffer from severe methodological problems, leaving questionable how many of the apparent differences between college graduates and nongraduates are properly attributable to college. As part of this discussion, the article reviews typical flaws in the research designs of studies of college effects. Second, even if college effects are present, the article raises the question of whether they are due to particular actions on the part of colleges. The article examines Meyer's (1972, 1977) argument that the apparent effect of college is a product not of what it does but of society's and students' expectations of what a college-educated person should be like. Finally, the article examines the social meaning of colleges' nonacademic effects. The study of these effects has not attracted the same degree of theoretical discussion as has the debate on nonacademic learning in elementary and secondary school. The dominant approach is an implicit functionalism that holds that students' nonacademic learning is largely useful both to them and to society. However, as a useful counterpoint to this vague consensus, the article examines the argument of some Marxists and Weberians that college students are not necessarily more politically and civically enlightened and that college nonacademic learning largely benefits not society as a whole but special interest groups, whether the capitalist class or certain status groups. They argue that undergraduates' seeming shift toward greater liberalism and tolerance involves not a major transformation of attitudes but rather the development of a more sophisticated capacity to either hide or politely express illiberal and intolerant attitudes.

CONCLUSIONS

The selections included in this chapter show that schooling's impact is by no means exhausted by its academic effects, which are assessed by achievement test scores and graduation rates and are largely the product of the formal curriculum. Schooling also has a pronounced impact on a wide variety of nonacademic attitudes and behavior, ranging from work habits to attitudes toward authority figures.

This question of the nonacademic effects of schooling has been approached from different perspectives, ranging from functionalism, class reproduction Marxism, Weberianism, and the work of John Meyer. Each of these perspectives makes a contribution to our understanding of nonacademic learning. The functionalist and Marxist arguments alert us to the economic attitudes and behaviors inculcated by school, while the Weberian approach points out the importance of noneconomic attitudes and behaviors. Furthermore, the functionalist arguments alert us to the usefulness of nonacademic learning to the entire society, while the Marxist and Weberian arguments make us realize its usefulness to furthering the interest of specific interest groups, whether the capitalist class (Marxism) or a status group such as fundamentalist Christians (Weberianism).

While open to combining various theories of the nonacademic role of education, we should not uncritically adopt them. This particularly applies to analyses that put great emphasis on the "hidden curriculum" of schooling (Apple, 1979, 1982; Giroux and Purpel, 1983). These studies have two major flaws. One is their weak empirical basis. The other is their assumption that the "hidden" curriculum is indeed hidden and quite separate from the overt curriculum.

Discussions about nonacademic learning in elementary and secondary school, despite their frequent brilliance, have been erected on a surprisingly weak empirical base. These discussions have proceeded with little reference to empirical research on whether school practices do indeed affect students in the ways that researchers hypothesize (Hurn, 1985: 222). It is not that evidence on the nonacademic effects of schooling is unavailable. Researchers have looked extensively at the impact of schools on students' educational aspirations, self-esteem, political attitudes, and so forth (Hess and Torney, 1967; Persell, 1977). But these studies have not been integrated into the main discussion on the nonacademic impact of schooling. Studies of this nonacademic impact examine how schools try to affect and might affect students' nonacademic attitudes and behavior, but these studies rarely demonstrate in any conclusive manner that schools are indeed successful. This empirical underdevelopment may be due to the fact that there has been much less controversy over the question of nonacademic effects than there has been over academic effects. As we have seen, functionalists and Marxists agree to a surprising degree about the nonacademic effects of schools, although they put very different interpretations on them. Hence, unlike research on academic effects, studies of nonacademic effect have not had to be as careful about proving their arguments about how and to what degree schools shape students' attitudes and behavior.

The second flaw of research on the nonacademic effects of elementary and secondary schooling has been assumption that the "hidden curriculum" is indeed hidden and different from the overt curriculum. In the 19th century, educational leaders were quite explicit about their desire that schools instill good work habits, law-abidingness, and patriotism (Mann, 1848; Vallance, 1983). And this interest has continued to this day. Especially in elementary school, teachers consciously try to instill good work habits and good classroom behavior and grade students on the basis of their conduct (Apple, 1979; Gracey, 1977; Hammack, 1988). Students are quite aware of this, as witness their attempts to get on the good side of teachers. And this overt interest in the nonacademic side of education is, if anything, increasing, with the emphasis put on classroom order by the "back-to-basics" movement and the reports of the National Commission on Excellence in Education (1983) and the Heritage Foundation (Gardner, 1985). (See Chapter 10 for further discussion.)

Not only is the "hidden" curriculum not hidden, it is also not informal. Nonacademic learning does not depend alone on the more or less unintended and unconscious effect of classroom structure, rules, and rituals. To be sure, classroom structures, such as having students' desks bolted down facing toward the front of the room, certainly convey a hierarchical view of the teacher-student relationship. Classroom rules and rituals such as the Pledge of Allegiance do teach students powerful lessons about what behavior is proper in social life. But much of the nonacademic skills, beliefs, and attitudes that students learn comes from the formal curriculum. Much of what they learn about citizenship, family relations, and work skills comes from courses and textbooks in civics, family life, and vocational education.

REFERENCES

Apple, Michael. 1979. *Ideology and the Curriculum.* London: Routledge and Kegan Paul.

_____. 1982. *Education and Power.* London: Routledge and Kegan Paul.

Aronowitz, Stanley, and Henry Giroux. 1985. *Education Under Siege.* South Hadley, MA: Bergin and Garvey.

Astin, Alexander. 1977. *Four Critical Years.* San Francisco: Jossey-Bass.

Bowen, Howard. 1977. *Investment in Learning.* San Francisco: Jossey-Bass.

Bowles, Samuel, and Herbert Gintis. 1976. *Schooling in Capitalist America.* New York: Basic Books.

Carnoy, Martin (ed). 1975. *Schooling in a Corporate Society.* New York: McKay.

_____, and Henry Levin (eds.) 1976. *The Limits of Educational Reform.* New York: Longman.

_____ and _____. 1985. *Schooling and Work in the Democratic State.* Stanford, CA: Stanford University Press.

DiMaggio, Paul J., and Walter W. Powell. 1983. "The Iron Cage Revisited: Institutional Isomorphism and Collective Rationality in Organizational Fields." *American Sociological Review* 48 (April): 147–160.

Dreeben, Robert. 1968. *On What Is Learned in School.* Boston: Addison-Wesley.

Feldman, Kenneth, and Theodore Newcomb. 1969. *The Impact of College on Students.* 2 vols. San Francisco: Jossey-Bass.

Gardner, Eileen. 1985. *A New Agenda for Education.* Washington, DC: Heritage Foundation. (See Chapter 10 for an excerpt.)

Giroux, Henry, and David Purpel. 1983. *The Hidden Curriculum and Moral Education.* Berkeley, CA: McCutchan.

Gracey, Harry. 1977. "Learning the Student Role: Kindergarten as Academic Boot Camp." In Dennis H. Wrong and Harry L. Gracey (eds.), *Readings in Introductory Sociology,* pp. 215–226. New York: Macmillan.

Hammack, Floyd M. 1988. "The Not-So-Hidden Curriculum: A Study of Elementary School Report Cards." Unpublished Manuscript, School of Education, Health, Nursing, and Arts Professions, Department of Organizational and Administrative Studies, New York University.

Hess, Robert D., and Judith V. Torney. 1967. *The Development of Political Attitudes in Children.* New York: Doubleday.

Hurn, Christopher. 1985. *The Limits and Possibilities of Schooling.* 2nd ed. Boston: Allyn and Bacon.

Hyman, Herbert, Charles Wright, and John S. Reed. 1975. *The Enduring Effects of Education.* Chicago: University of Chicago Press.

Jackson, Philip. 1968. *Life in Classrooms.* New York: Holt, Rinehart & Winston.

Mann, Horace. 1848. "Report for 1848." In Mann, *Life and Works of Horace Mann.* vol. 4 (Annual Reports). Boston: Lee and Shepard, 1891.

Meyer, John W. 1972. "The Effects of the Institutionalization of Colleges in Society." In Kenneth Feldman (ed.), *College and Student,* pp. 109–126. New York: Pergamon.

_____. 1977. "The Effects of Education as an Institution." *American Journal of Sociology* 83 (July): 55–77.

_____, and Brian Rowan, 1978. "The Structure of Educational Organizations." In Marshall Meyer and associates, *Environments and Organizations,* pp. 78–109. San Francisco: Jossey-Bass.

National Commission on Excellence in Education. 1983. *A Nation at Risk.* Washington, DC: Government Printing Office. (See Chapter 10 for an excerpt.)

Newcomb, Theodore. 1943. *Personality and Social Change: Attitude Formation in a Student Community.* New York: Holt.

Oakes, Jeannie. 1982. "Classroom Social Relationships: Exploring the Bowles and Gintis Hypothesis." *Sociology of Education* 55 (October): 197–212.

Parsons, Talcott. 1959. "The School Class as a Social System." *Harvard Educational Review* 39: 297–318.

Persell, Caroline. 1977. *Education and Inequality.* New York: Free Press.

Peshkin, Alan. 1986. *God's Choice: The Total World of a Fundamentalist Christian School.* Chicago: University of Chicago Press. (See excerpt in this chapter.)

Sirotnik, Kenneth. 1983. "What You See Is What You Get—Consistency, Persistency, and Mediocrity in Classrooms." *Harvard Educational Review* 53: 16–31.

Slavin, Robert. 1980. "Cooperative Learning." *Review of Educational Research* 50: 315–342.

_____. 1987. "Cooperative Learning and the Cooperative School." *Educational Leadership* 45 (November): 7–13.

Trent, James W., and Leland L. Medsker. 1968. *Beyond High School.* San Francisco: Jossey-Bass.

Trow, Martin. 1961. "The Second Transformation of American Secondary Education." *International Journal of Comparative Sociology* 2: 144–166. Reprinted in Jerome Karabel and A. H. Halsey (eds.), *Power and Ideology in Education,* pp. 105–118. New York: Oxford University Press.

Vallance, Elizabeth. 1973. "Hiding the Hidden Curriculum." *Curriculum Inquiry* 4 (fall): 5–21.

Willis, Paul. 1981. *Learning to Labor.* New York: Columbia University Press.

The Contribution of Schooling to the Learning of Norms: Independence, Achievement, Universalism, and Specificity

ROBERT DREEBEN
University of Chicago

In speaking of these four ideas as norms, I mean that individuals accept them as legitimate standards for governing their own conduct in the appropriate situations. Specifically, they accept the obligations to (1) act by themselves (unless collaborative effort is called for), and accept personal responsibility for their conduct and accountability for its consequences; (2) perform tasks actively and master the environment according to certain standards of excellence; and (3) acknowledge the rights of others to treat them as members of categories (4) on the basis of a few discrete characteristics rather than on the full constellation of them that represent the whole person. I treat these four norms because they are integral parts of public and occupational life in industrial societies, or institutional realms adjacent to the school. . . .

The social properties of schools are such that pupils, by coping with the sequence of classroom tasks and situations, are more likely to learn the principles (i.e., social norms) of independence, achievement, universalism, and specificity than if they had remained full-time members of the household. Although I have spoken thus far only of the similarities and differences between the family and the school, the nature of that comparison is largely determined by the character of public institutions, in particular the economy and the polity. Schools, that is to say, form one of several institutional linkages between the household and the public sphere of adult life, a linkage organized around stages of the life cycle in industrial societies. There is substantial evidence that conduct in the family and conduct on the job are governed by contrasting normative principles. From this we can imply that if the education of children were carried on primarily within the jurisdiction of the family, the nature of experiences available in that setting would not provide conditions appropriate for acquiring those capacities that enable people to participate competently in the public realm. . . .

INDEPENDENCE

One answer to the question, "What is learned in school?" is that pupils learn to acknowledge that there are tasks they must do alone, and to do them that way. Along with this self-imposed obligation goes the idea that others have a legitimate right to expect such independent behavior under certain circumstances. Independence has a widely acknowledged though not unequivocal meaning. In using it here I refer to a cluster of meanings: doing things on one's own, being self-reliant, accepting personal responsibility for one's behavior, acting self-sufficiently,[1] and handling tasks with which, *under different circumstances*, one can rightfully expect the help of others. The pupil, when in school, is separated from family members who have customarily provided help, support, and sustenance, persons on whom he has long been dependent.

A constellation of classroom characteristics, teacher actions, and pupil actions shape experiences in which the norm of independence is learned. In addition to the fact that school children are removed from persons with whom they have already formed strong relationships of dependency, the sheer size of a classroom assemblage limits each pupil's claim to personal contact with the teacher, and more so at the secondary levels than at the elementary. This numerical property of classrooms reduces pupils' opportunities for establishing new relationships of dependency with adults and for receiving help from them.

Parents expect their children to act independently in many situations, but teachers are more systematic in expecting pupils to adhere to standards of independence in performing academic tasks. There are at least two additional aspects of classroom operation that bear directly on learning the norm of independence: rules about cheating and formal testing. Let us consider cheating first. The word itself is condemnatory in its reference to illegal and immoral acts. Most commonly, attention turns to how much cheating occurs, who cheats, and why. But these questions, while of great importance elsewhere, are of no concern here. My interest is in a different problem: to what types of conduct is the pejorative "cheating" assigned?

In school, cheating pertains primarily to instructional activities and usually refers to acts in which two or more parties participate when the unaided action of only one is expected. Illegal or immoral acts such as stealing and vandalism, whether carried out by individuals or groups, are not considered cheating because they have no direct connection with the central academic core of school activities. Nor is joint participation categorically proscribed; joint effort is called cooperation or collusion depending on the teacher's prior definition of the task.

Cheating takes many forms, most of which involve collective effort. A parent and a child may collaborate to produce homework; two pupils can pool their wisdom (or ignorance, as the case may be) in the interest of passing an examination. In both cases the parties join deliberately, although deliberateness is not essential to the definition; one pupil can copy from another without the latter knowing. In the case of plagiarism, of course, the second party is not a person at all, but information compiled by another. The use of crib notes, perhaps a limiting case, involves no collusion; it consists, rather, of an illegitimate form of help. These are the main forms of school cheating, but there are many variations, routine to exotic. Thus actions called cheating are those closely tied to the instructional goals of the school and usually involve assisted performance when unaided performance is expected. As one observer put it: Pupils ". . . *must learn to distinguish between cooperating and cheating.*"[2]

The irony of cheating *in school* is that the same kinds of acts are considered morally acceptable and even commendable in other situations. It is praiseworthy for one friend to assist another in distress, or for a parent to help a child; and if one lacks the information to do a job, the resourceful thing is to look it up. In effect, many school activities called cheating are the customary forms of support and assistance in the family and among friends.

In one obvious sense, school rules against cheating are designed to establish the content of moral standards. In another sense, the school attaches the stigma of immorality to certain types of behavior for social as distinct from ethical reasons; namely, to change the character of prevailing social relationships in which children are involved. In the case of homework, the school, in effect, attempts to redefine the relationship between parents and children by proscribing one kind of parental support, which is not a problem in other circumstances. The teacher has no direct control over parents but tries to influence them at a distance by asking their adherence to a principle clothed in moral language whose violations are punishable. The line between legitimate parental support (encouraged when it takes the form of parents stressing the importance of school and urging their children to do well) and collusion is unclear, but by morally proscribing parental intervention beyond a certain point, the teacher attempts to limit the child's dependence on family members in doing his school work. In other words, he expects the pupil to work independently. The same argument applies to pupils and their friends; the teacher attempts to eliminate those parts of friendship that make it difficult or impossible for him to discover what a pupil can do on his own. In relationships with kin and friends, the customary sources of support in times of adversity, the school intervenes by restricting solidarity and, in the process, determines what the pupil can accomplish unaided. The pupil, for his part, discovers which of his actions he is held accountable for individually within the confines of tasks set by the school. . . .

Second, as to testing, and particularly the use of achievement tests, most important for independence are the social conditions designed for the *administration* of tests, not their content or format. By and large, pupils are tested under more or less rigorously controlled conditions. At one end of the spectrum, formal standardized tests are administered most stringently; pupils are physically separated, and the testing room is patrolled by proctors whose job is to discover contraband and to guarantee that no communication occurs, these arrangements being designed so that each examination paper represents independent work. At the other end, some testing situations are more informal, less elaborately staged, although there is almost always some provision to ensure that each pupil's work represents the product of only his own efforts.

Testing represents an approach to establishing the norm of independence, which is different from the proscription against cheating even though both are designed to reduce the likelihood of joint effort. Whereas the rules against cheating are directed toward delineating the form of appropriate behavior, the restrictions built into the testing situation provide physical constraints intended to guarantee that teachers will receive samples of the work pupils do unassisted. Actually, unless they stipulate otherwise, teachers expect pupils to do most of their everyday work by themselves; daily assignments provide the opportunities for and practice in independent work. Tests, because they occur at less frequent intervals than ordinary assignments, cannot provide comparably frequent opportunities; by the elaborate trappings of their administration, particularly with college entrance exams, and the anxiety they provoke, they symbolize the magnitude of the stakes.

It may be objected that in emphasizing independence I have ignored cooperation, since an important item on the school agenda is the instruction of pupils in the skills of working with others. Teachers do assign work to groups and expect a collaborative product, and to this extent they require the subordination of individual to collective efforts, but judging the product according to collective standards is another question. . . .

ACHIEVEMENT

Pupils come to accept the premise that they should perform their tasks the best they can, and act accordingly. The concept of achievement, like independence, has several referents. It usually denotes activity and mastery, making an impact on the environment rather than fatalistically accepting it, and competing against some standard of excellence. Analytically, the concept should be distinguished from independence, since, among differences, achievement criteria can apply to activities performed collectively.

Much of the recent literature treats achievement in the context of child-rearing within the family as if achievement motivation were primarily a product of parental behavior.[3] Even though there is reason to believe that early childhood experiences in the family do contribute to its development, classroom experiences also contribute through teachers' use of resources beyond those ordinarily at the command of family members.

Classrooms are organized around a set of core activities in which a teacher assigns tasks to pupils and evaluates and compares the quality of their work. In the course of time, pupils differentiate themselves according to how well they perform a variety of tasks, most of which require the use of symbolic skills. Achievement standards are not limited in applicability to the classroom nor is their content restricted to the cognitive areas. Schools afford opportunities for participation in a variety of extra-curricular activities, most conspicuously athletics, but also music, dramatics, and a bewildering array of club and small group activities serving individual interests and talents.

The direct relevance of classroom work in providing task experience judged by achievement criteria is almost self-evident; the experience is built into the assignment-performance-evaluation sequence of the work. Less evident, however, is the fact that these activities force pupils to cope with various degrees of success and failure, both of which can be psychologically problematic. Consistently successful performance requires that pupils deal with the consequences of their own excellence in a context of peer equality in nonacademic areas. For example, they confront the dilemma inherent in having surpassed their age-mates in some respects while depending on their friendship and support in others, particularly in out-of-school social activities. The classroom provides not only the achievement experience itself but by-products of it, taking the form of the dilemma just described.

Similarly, pupils whose work is consistently poor not only must participate in achievement activities leading to their failure, they must also experience living with that failure. They adopt various modes of coping with this, most of which center around maintaining personal self-respect in the face of continuing assaults upon it. Probably a minority succeed or fail consistently; a majority, most likely, do neither one consistently, but nonetheless worry about not doing well. Schooling, then, assures most pupils the experiences of both winning and losing, and to the extent that they gain some modicum of gratification from academic activities, it teaches them to approach their work in a frame of mind conducive to achievement. At the same time they learn how to cope, in a variety of ways and more or less well, with success and failure.

Failure is perhaps the more difficult condition with which to cope because it requires acknowledgment that the premise of achievement, to which failure itself can be attributed in part, is a legitimate principle by which to govern one's actions. Yet situations that constrain people to live with personal failure are endemic to industrial societies in which many facets of public life are based on achievement principles; political defeat and occupational nonpromotion being two cases in point.

As suggested earlier, the school provides a broad range of experiences other than those restricted to the classroom and academic in nature; these experiences are also based on achievement criteria but differ in several important respects. Alternatives to academic performance give the pupil a chance to succeed in achievement-oriented activities even though he may not be able to do well in the classroom.

How these alternative activities differ from those of the classroom is as important as the fact that they do so differ, as evidenced by the case of athletics. Competitive sports resemble classroom activities in that both provide participants with the chance to demonstrate individual excellence. However, the former—and this is more true of team than individual sports— permit collective responsibility for defeat, whereas the latter by and large allow only individual responsibility for failure. That is to say, the chances of receiving personal gratification for success are at least as great in sports as in the classroom, while the assault on personal self-respect for failure is potentially less intense. Athletics should not be written off as a manifestation of mere adolescent nonintellectualism, as recent writers have treated it.[4] . . .

The school provides a wider variety of achievement experiences than does the family, but it also has fewer resources for supporting and protecting pupils' self-respect in the face of failure. As pupils proceed through successive school levels, the rigors of achievement increase, at least for those who continue along the main academic line. Moreover, at the secondary levels the number of activities governed according to achievement principles increases as does the variety of these activities. As preparation for adult public life in which the application of these principles is widespread, schooling contributes to personal development in assuring that the majority of pupils not only will have performed tasks according to the achievement standard, but that they will have had experience in an expanding number of situations in which activities are organized according to it.

UNIVERSALISM AND SPECIFICITY

Unlike independence and achievement, universalism and specificity are not commonly regarded as good things. Parents and teachers admonish children to act independently and do their work well; few of them support the idea that people should willingly acknowledge their similarity to one another in specifically categorical terms while ignoring their obvious differences; that is, in a sense, denying their own individuality.

Ideologically, social critics have deplored the impersonal, ostensibly dehumanizing, aspects of categorization, a principle widely believed to lie at the heart of the problem of human alienation; the attachment of man to machine, the detachment of man from man. Often ignored, however, is the connection between this principle and the idea of fairness, or equity. Seen from this vantage point, categorization is widely regarded as a good thing, especially when contrasted to nepotism, favoritism, and arbitrariness. People resent the principle when they think they have a legitimate reason to receive special consideration, and when their individuality appears to vanish by being "processed." Yet when a newcomer breaks into a long queue of patiently waiting people instead of proceeding to the end of the line, they usually condemn him for acting unfairly (for not following the standard rule for all newcomers to a line). They do *not* react by expressing any sense of their own alienation, since they accept the same categorical principle as binding on themselves. In other words, this is not the occasion to proclaim one's individuality, but to act like everybody else and be sure they do likewise. The contrasts between the two dualities (individuality and dehumanization, fairness and special privilege) are similarly predicated on the principles of universalism and specificity; people differ in their posture toward each duality according to ideological position, situation, and, more cynically, in their conception of self-interest.

The concepts of universalism and specificity have been formulated most comprehensively by Parsons, though only part of his formulation is directly germane to this discussion. As part of his concern with social systems, Parsons views universalism as one horn of a dilemma (the other being particularism) in role definition; under what circumstances does the occupant of one social position govern his actions by adopting one standard or another when dealing with the occupant of another social position? My concern, however, is not with a selection among alternative, conflicting standards, but with the conditions under which individuals learn to impose the standards of universalism and specificity on themselves and to act accordingly.

Defining the central theme of universalism raises problems because the term has been assigned a variety of meanings, not all of them clear. The relevant distinction here is whether individuals are treated in terms of their membership in categories or as special cases. In one respect or another an individual can always be viewed as a member of one or more categories, universalistically; he is viewed particularistically if, considering his similarity to others in the same category, he still receives special treatment. . . .

. . . Thus, *"A man's orientation toward his family,"* according to Blau, *"is considered particularistic because it* singles out for special attention *the members of an ingroup, rather than persons with a certain attribute regardless of whether it makes them part of his ingroup or not."*[5]

The norm of specificity is easily confused with universalism despite its distinctiveness. It refers to the scope of one person's interest in another; to the obligation to confine one's interest to a narrow range of characteristics and concerns, or to extend them to include a broad range.[6] The notion of relevance is implicit; the characteristics and concerns that should be included within the range, whether broad or narrow, are those considered relevant in terms of the activities in which the persons in question are involved. Doctors and storekeepers, for example, differ in the scope of the interest they have in the persons seeking their services, but the content of their interests also varies according to the nature of the needs and desires of those persons.

It is my contention that what the school contributes to the acceptance by children of those norms that penetrate many areas of public life is critical, because children's pre-school experience in the family is weighted heavily on the side of special treatment and parental consideration of the whole child. To say that children learn the norm of universalism means that they come to accept being treated by others as members of categories (in addition to being treated as special cases, as in the family).

Categorization

Schools provide a number of experiences that families cannot readily provide because of limitations in their social composition and structure. One such experience is the systematic establishment and demarcation of membership categories. First, by assigning all pupils in a classroom the same or similar tasks to perform, teachers in effect make them confront the same set of demands. Even if there are variations in task content, class members still confront the same teacher and the obligations he imposes. Second, parity of age creates a condition of homogeneity according to developmental stage, a rough equalization of pupil capacities making it possible for teachers to assign similar tasks. Third, through the process of yearly promotion from grade to grade, pupils cross the boundaries separating one age category from another. With successive boundary crossings comes the knowledge that each age-grade category is associated with a particular set of circumstances (e.g., teachers, difficulty of tasks, subject matter studied). Moreover, pupils learn the relationship between categories and how their present position relates to past and future positions by virtue of having experienced the transitions between them. In these three ways, the grade (more specifically the classroom within the grade) with its age-homogeneous membership and clearly demarcated boundaries provides a basis for categorical grouping that the family cannot readily duplicate. Most important, the experiences of membership in a group of age-equals and repeated boundary crossings makes it possible for pupils to acquire a relativity of perspective, a capacity to view their own circumstances from other vantage points than they themselves have occupied.[7]

Although each child holds membership in the category "children" at home, parents, in raising them, tend to take age differences into account and thereby accentuate the uniqueness of each child's circumstances, thus belying in some measure the categorical aspects of "childhood." However, even if the category "children" breaks into its age-related components within the family, it remains intact when children compare themselves with friends and neighbors of similar age. In typical situations of this kind, children inform their parents that friends of the same age have greater privileges or fewer responsibilities than they. Parents, if they cannot actually equalize the circumstances, often explain or justify the disparity by pointing to the special situation of the neighbor family; they have more money, fewer children, a bigger house. Whatever the reason, that is, parents point out the uniqueness of family circumstances and thereby emphasize the particularities of each child's situation. The school, in contrast, provides the requisite circumstances for making comparisons among pupils in categorical rather than particular terms.

Another school experience fostering the establishment of social categories is the re-equalization of pupils by means of the high school track system after they have differentiated themselves through academic achievement in the lower grades, a mechanism that minimizes the likelihood of teachers having to deal with special cases. Teachers with a variegated batch of pupils must adopt more individualized methods of instruction than those whose pupils are similar in their level of achievement. In so doing, they partially recreate a kinship-type of relationship with pupils, treating segments of the class differently according to differences in capacity, much as parents treat their children differently according to age-related capacities.

As far as level is concerned, the high school is a better place to acquire the principle of universalism than the lower school levels because pupils within each track, who are of roughly similar capacity, move from classroom to classroom, in each one receiving instruction in a different subject area by a different teacher. They discover that over a range of activities, they are treated alike and that relatively uniform demands and criteria of evaluation are applied to them Thus they learn which differences in experience are subordinated to the principle of categorization. The elementary classroom, oriented more to instruction in different subjects by a single teacher, does not provide the necessary variations in persons and subjects for a clear-cut demonstration of the categorical principle.

Persons and Positions

Although the idea of categorization is central to the norm of universalism, it has additional and derivative aspects. One is the crucial distinction, widely relevant in industrial societies, between the person and the social position he occupies. Individuals are often expected to treat one another according to their social position, rather than according to their individual identity. Schooling contributes to the capacity to make the distinction (and to the obligation to do so) by making it possible for pupils to discover that different individuals occupying a single social position often act in ways that are attached to the position rather than to the different persons filling it. Even though all members of a given classroom find themselves in the same circumstances (they are about equal in age and roughly resemble each other in social characteristics related to residence), they still differ in many respects: sex, race, religion, ethnicity, and physical characteristics being among the most obvious. Their situation, therefore, provides the experience of finding that common interests and shared circumstances are assigned a priority that submerges obvious personal differences. The same contention holds for adults. Male and female adults are found in both school and family settings; in school, pupils can discover that an increasingly large number of different adults of both sexes can occupy the same position, that of "teacher." This discovery is not as easily made in the family because it is not possible to determine definitively whether "parent" represents two positions, one occupied by a male, the other by a female, or a single position with two occupants differing in sex. Children are not left completely without clues in this matter since they do have other adult relatives who can be seen as distinct persons occupying the same position: aunts, uncles, grandparents, and the like. Yet even extended families do not provide the frequent and systematic comparisons characteristic of the schools. Schooling, in other words, enables pupils to distinguish between persons and the social positions they occupy (a capacity crucially important in both occupational and political life) by placing them in situations in which the membership of each position is varied in its composition and the similarities between persons in a single position are made evident.

Specificity

The school provides structural arrangements more conducive to the acquisition of the norm of specificity than does the family. First, since the number of persons and the ratio between adults and nonadults is much larger in classrooms than in the household, the school provides large social aggregates in which pupils can form many casual associations (in addition to their close friendships) in which they invest but a small portion of themselves. As both the size and heterogeneity of the student body increase at each successive level, the opportunities for these somewhat fragmented social contacts increase and diversify. The relative shallowness and transiency of these relationships increase the likelihood that pupils will have experiences in which the fullness of their individuality is *not* involved, as it tends to be in their relationships among kin and close friends.

Second, on leaving the elementary school and proceeding through the departmentalized secondary levels, pupils form associations with teachers who have a progressively narrowing and specialized interest in them. (This comes about both because of subject matter specialization itself and because the number of pupils each teacher faces in the course of a day grows larger.) Although it is true that children, as they grow older, tend to form more specific relationships with their parents (symptomatically, this trend manifests itself in adolescents' complaints of parental invasions of privacy), the resources of the school far exceed those of the family in providing the social basis for the establishment of relationships in which only narrow segments of personality are invested. . . .

A CONCEPTUAL CAVEAT

. . . There is no guarantee that pupils will come to accept these four norms simply because these experiences are available, nor should one conclude that these experiences contribute to the learning of only the four discussed here; for example, the pupils may lack the necessary social and psychological support from sources outside the school or sufficient inner resources to cope with the demands of schooling. These are reasons external to the school situation and may be sufficient to preclude both the instructional and normative outcomes. However, forces inherent in the schooling process itself may be equally preclusive, since the same activities and sanctions from which some pupils derive the gratification and enhancement of self-respect necessary for both kinds of outcome may create experiences that threaten the self-respect of others. Potentialities for success *and* failure are inherent in tasks performed according to achievement criteria. Independence manifests itself as competence and autonomy in some, but as a heavy burden of responsibility and inadequacy in others. Universalistic treatment represents fairness for some, cold impersonality to others. Specificity may be seen as situational relevance or personal neglect. Within industrial societies where norms applicable to public life differ markedly from those governing conduct among kin, schools provide a sequence of experiences in which individuals, during the early stages of personality development, acquire new principles of conduct in addition to those already accepted during childhood. For reasons earlier enumerated in detail, the family, as a social setting with its characteristic social arrangements, lacks the resources and the competence[8] to effect the psychological transition. This is not to say that only the school can produce the necessary changes, but of those institutions having some claim over the lives of children and adolescents (e.g., the family, child labor, occupational apprenticeship, tutoring, the church, the mass media[9]), only the schools provide adequate, though not always effective, task experiences and sanctions, and arrangements for the generalization and specification of normative principles throughout many spheres of public life. . . .

AN IDEOLOGICAL CAVEAT

Although I have treated them as norms, independence and achievement have been regarded by many observers of the American scene as dominant cultural themes or values, general standards of what is desirable.[10] In view of this, it is important that the argument of this book not be taken as a defense of national values, although it should not surprise anyone that the normative commitments of individuals who have passed through American schools are generally (though not invariably) consistent with national values. The main purpose of this analysis is to present a formulation, hypothetical in nature, of how schooling contributes to the emergence of certain psychological outcomes, and not to provide an apology or justification for those outcomes on ideological grounds. I have avoided calling universalism and specificity cultural values even though both are norms, since few, if any, observers include them among the broad moral principles considered desirable in American life. Their exclusion from the list of values should further confirm the nonideological intent of this discussion.

Having the means to produce a desired result is not the same as an injunction to use them in producing it. Of the many considerations entering into the decision to employ available resources in creating even widely valued outcomes, the probable costs involved should give pause. For the norms in question here, whose desirability can be affirmed either on ideological grounds or in terms of their relevance to public life in an industrial society, conditions conducive to their development are also conducive to the creation of results widely regarded as undesirable. Thus, a sense of accomplishment and mastery, on the one hand, and a sense of incompetence and ineffectualness, on the other, both represent psychological consequences of continuously coping with tasks on an achievement basis. Similarly with independence: self-confidence and helplessness can each derive from a person's self-imposed obligation to work unaided and accept individual responsibility for his actions. Finally, willingness to acknowledge the rightness of categorical and specific treatment may indicate the capacity to adapt to a variety of social situations in which only a part of one's self is invested, or it may indicate a sense of personal alienation and isolation from human relationships.

From the viewpoint of ideological justification, the process of schooling is problematic in that outcomes morally desireable from one perspective are undesirable from another; and in the making of school policy the price to be paid must be a salient consideration in charting a course of action.

NOTES AND REFERENCES

1. Winterbottom, for example, lumps independence and mastery together; the indices she uses to measure them, however, involve ostensibly different phenomena in that the mastery items refer to tendencies toward activity rather than to independence. Marian R. Winterbottom, "The Relation of Need for Achievement to Learning Experiences in Independence and Mastery," in John T. Atkinson (ed.), *Motives in Fantasy, Action, and Society,* pp. 453–478, Van Nostrand, Princeton (1958). As a definitional guideline for this discussion, I have followed the usage of Bernard C. Rosen and Roy D'Andrade, "The Psychosocial Origins of Achievement Motivation," *Sociometry* **22**, No. 3, 186 (1959) in their discussion of independence training; and of McClelland and his colleagues in a study of independence training, David C. McClelland, A. Rindlisbacher, and Richard DeCharms, "Religious and Other Sources of Parental Attitudes toward Independence Training," in David C. McClelland (ed.), *Studies in Motivation,* pp. 389–397, Appleton-Century-Crofts, New York (1955).

2. Kaspar D. Naegele, "Clergymen, Teachers, and Psychiatrists: A Study in Roles and Socialization," *Canadian Journal of Economics and Political Science* **22,** No. 1, 53 (1956).

3. See, for example, Marian R. Winterbottom, *ibid.;* Bernard C. Rosen and Roy D'Andrade, *op. cit.,* pp. 185–218; and Fred L. Strodtbeck, "Family Interaction, Values, and Achievement," in David C. McClelland *et al., Talent and Society,* pp. 135–191, Van Nostrand, Princeton (1958).

4. For one attempt to treat athletics condescendingly as nonintellectualism, see James S. Coleman, *The Adolescent Society,* Free Press of Glencoe, New York (1961).

5. Peter M. Blau, "Operationalizing a Conceptual Scheme," *American Sociological Review* **27,** No. 2 (1962), p. 164; my emphasis.

6. In the case of specificity, ". . . the burden of proof rests on him who would suggest that ego has obligations vis-à-vis the object in question which transcend this specificity of relevance." Talcott Parsons, *The Social System,* p. 65, Free Press, Glencoe, Ill. (1951). In the case of diffuseness, ". . . the burden of proof is on the side of the exclusion of an interest or mode of orientation as outside the range of obligations defined by the role-expectation." Parsons, *ibid.,* p. 66.

7. For a discussion of relativity of perspective, see Daniel Lerner, *The Passing of Traditional Society,* pp. 43–75, Free Press of Glencoe, Glencoe, Ill. (1958).

8. For a discussion of competence as an organizational characteristic, see Philip Selznick, *Leadership in Administration,* pp. 38–56, Row, Peterson, Evanston, Ill. (1957).

9. Mary Engel, "Saturday's Children: A Study of Working Boys," Cambridge, Mass., Harvard Graduate School of Education, Center for Research in Careers, Harvard Studies in Career Development No. 51, 1966; Carl I. Hovland, "Effects of the Mass Media of Communication," in Gardner Lindzey (ed.), *Handbook of Social Psychology, II,* pp. 1062–1103, Addison-Wesley, Reading, Mass. (1954); Blanche Geer *et al.,* "Learning the Ropes: Situational Learning in Four Occupational Training Programs," in Irwin Deutscher and Elizabeth Thompson (eds.), *Among the People: Studies of the Urban Poor,* Basic Books, New York (1968).

10. For a general discussion of the concept of value and of major American cultural themes, see Robin M. Williams, Jr., *American Society,* pp. 397–470, Alfred A. Knopf, New York (1960).

Social Class and the Hidden Curriculum of Work

JEAN ANYON
Rutgers University, Newark

Scholars in political economy and the sociology of knowledge have recently argued that public schools in complex industrial societies like our own make available different types of educational experience and curriculum knowledge to students in different social classes. Bowles and Gintis (1976), for example, have argued that students from different social class backgrounds are rewarded for classroom behaviors that correspond to personality traits allegedly rewarded in the different occupational strata—the working classes for docility and obedience, the managerial classes for initiative and personal assertiveness. Basil Bernstein (1977), Pierre Bourdieu (Bourdieu and Passeron 1977), and Michael W. Apple (1979), focusing on school knowledge, have argued that knowledge and skills leading to social power and reward (e.g., medical, legal, managerial) are made available to the advantaged social groups but are withheld from the working classes, to whom a more "practical" curriculum is offered (e.g., manual skills, clerical knowledge). While there has been considerable argumentation of these points regarding education in England, France, and North America, there has been little or no attempt to investigate these ideas empirically in elementary or secondary schools and classrooms in this country.[1]

This article offers tentative empirical support (and qualification) of the above arguments by providing illustrative examples of differences in student *work* in classrooms in contrasting social class communities. The examples were gathered as part of an ethnographical study of curricular, pedagogical and pupil evaluation practices in five elementary schools.* The article

Adapted from "Social Class and the Hidden Curriculum of Work" by Jean Anyon from *Journal of Education* 162 (1980): 67–92. Reprinted by permission of the publishers and the author.

*The research was funded by Rutgers University Research Council and will be reported in detail elsewhere.

attempts a theoretical contribution as well, and assesses student work in the light of a theoretical approach to social class analysis. The organization is as follows: the methodology of the ethnographical study is briefly described; a theoretical approach to the definition of social class is offered; income and other characteristics of the parents in each school are provided, and examples from the study that illustrate work tasks and interaction in each school are presented; then the concepts used to define social class are applied to the examples in order to assess the theoretical meaning of classroom events. It will be suggested that there is a "hidden curriculum" in school work that has profound implication for the theory—and consequence—of everyday activity in education.

METHODOLOGY

The methods used to gather data were classroom observation; interviews of students, teachers, principals, and district administrative staff; and assessment of curriculum and other materials in each classroom and school. All classroom events to be discussed here involve the fifth grade in each school. All schools but one departmentalize at the fifth grade level. Except for that school where only one fifth grade teacher could be observed, all the fifth grade teachers (that is, two or three) were observed as the children moved from subject to subject. In all schools the art, music, and gym teachers were also observed and interviewed. All teachers in the study were described as "good" or "excellent" by their principals. All except one new teacher had taught for more than four years. The fifth grade in each school was observed by the investigator for ten three-hour periods between September 15, 1978 and June 20, 1979.

Before providing the occupations, incomes, and other relevant social characteristics of the parents of the children in each school, I will offer a theoretical approach to defining social class. . . .

THE SAMPLE OF SCHOOLS

With the above discussion as a theoretical backdrop, the social class designation of each of the five schools will be identified, and the income, occupation, and other relevant available social characteristics of the students and their parents will be described. The first three schools are in a medium-sized city district in northern New Jersey, and the other two are in a nearby New Jersey suburb.

The first two schools I will call *Working-Class Schools*. Most of the parents have blue-collar jobs. Less than a third of the fathers are skilled, while the majority are in unskilled or semiskilled jobs. During the period of the study (1978–1979) approximately 15 percent of the fathers were unemployed. The large majority (85 percent) of the families are white. . . .

The third school is called the *Middle-Class School*, although because of neighborhood residence patterns, the population is a mixture of several social classes. The parents' occupations can be divided into three groups: a small group of blue-collar "rich," who are skilled, well-paid workers such as printers, carpenters, plumbers, and construction workers. The second group is composed of parents in working-class and middle-class white-collar jobs: women in office jobs, technicians, supervisors in industry, and parents employed by the city (such as firemen, policemen, and several of the school's teachers). The third group is composed of occupations such as personnel directors in local firms, accountants, "middle management," and a few small capitalists (owners of shops in the area). The children of several local doctors attend this school. Most family incomes are between $13,000 and $25,000 with a few higher. This income range is typical of 38.9 percent of the families in the United States (U.S. Bureau of the Census, 1979, p. 2, table A).

The fourth school has a parent population that is at the upper income level of the upper middle class, and is predominantly professional. This school will be called the *Affluent Professional School*. Typical jobs are: cardiologist, interior designer, corporate lawyer or engineer, executive in advertising or television. . . .

In the fifth school the majority of the families belong to the capitalist class. This school will be called the *Executive Elite School* because most of the fathers are top executives, (e.g., presidents and vice presidents) in major U.S.-based multinational corporations—for example, ATT, RCA, City Bank, American Express, U.S. Steel. A sizable group of fathers are top executives in financial firms on Wall Street. . . .

SOCIAL CLASS AND SCHOOL WORK

There are obvious similarities among United States schools and classrooms. There are school and classroom rules, teachers who ask questions and attempt to exercise control and who give work and homework. There are textbooks and tests. All of these were found in the five schools. Indeed, there were other curricular similarities as well: all schools and fifth grades used the same math book and series (*Mathematics Around Us*, Scott Foresman, 1978); all fifth grades had at least one boxed set of an individualized reading program available in the room (although the variety and amounts of teaching materials in the classrooms increased as the social class of the school population increased); and, all fifth grade language arts curricula included aspects of grammar, punctuation and capitalization.[2]. . .

The Working-Class Schools

In the two working-class schools, work is following the steps of a procedure. The procedure is usually mechanical, involving rote behavior and very little decision making or choice. The teachers rarely explain why the work is being assigned, how it might connect to other assignments, or what the idea is that lies behind the procedure or gives it coherence and perhaps meaning or significance. Available textbooks are not always used, and the teachers often prepare their own dittoes or put work examples on the board. Most of the rules regarding work are designations of what the children are to do; the rules are steps to follow. These steps are told to the children by the teachers and often written on the board. The children are usually told to copy the steps as notes. These notes are to be studied. Work is often evaluated not according to whether it is right or wrong, but according to whether the children followed the right steps.

The following examples illustrate these points. In math, when two-digit division was introduced, the teacher in one school gave a four-minute lecture on what the terms are called (i.e., which number is the divisor, dividend, quotient, and remainder). The children were told to copy these names in their notebooks. Then the teacher told them the steps to follow to do the problems, saying, "This is how you do them." The teacher listed the steps on the board, and they appeared several days later as a chart hung in the middle of the front wall: "Divide; Multiply; Subtract; Bring Down." The children often did examples of two-digit division. When the teacher went over the examples with them, he told them for each problem what the procedure was, rarely asking them to conceptualize or explain it themselves: "3 into 22 is 7; do your subtraction and one is left over." During the week that two-digit division was introduced (or at any other time), the investigator did not observe any discussion of the idea of grouping involved in division, any use of manipulables, or any attempt to relate two-digit division to any other mathematical process. Nor was there any attempt to relate the steps to an actual or possible thought process of the children. The observer did not hear the terms dividend, quotient, etc., used again. The math teacher in the other working-class school followed similar procedures regarding two-digit division, and at one point her class seemed confused. She said, "You're confusing yourselves. You're tensing up. Remember, when you do this, it's the same steps over and over again—and that's the way division always is." Several weeks later, after a test, a group of her children "still didn't get it," and she made no attempt to explain the concept of dividing things into groups, or to give them manipulables for their own investigation. Rather, she went over the steps with them again and told them that they "needed more practice."

In other areas of math, work is also carrying out often unexplained, fragmented procedures. For example, one of the teachers led the children through a series of steps to make a one-inch grid on their paper without telling them that they were making a one-inch grid, or that it would be used to study scale. She said, "Take your ruler. Put it across the top. Make a mark at every number. Then move your ruler down to the bottom. No, put it across the bottom. Now make a mark on top of every number. Now draw a line from. . . ." At this point a girl said that she had a faster way to do it and the teacher said, "No, you don't; you don't even know what I'm making yet. Do it this way, or it's wrong." After they had made the lines up and down and across, the teacher told them she wanted them to make a figure by connecting some dots and to measure that, using the scale of one inch equals one mile. Then they were to cut it out. She said, "Don't cut until I check it."

In both working-class schools, work in language arts is mechanics of punctuation (commas, periods, question marks, exclamation points), capitalization, and the four kinds of sentences. One teacher explained to me, "Simple punctuation is all they'll ever use." Regarding punctuation either a teacher or a ditto stated the rules for where, for example, to put commas. The investigator heard no classroom discussion of the aural context of punctuation (which, of course, is what gives each mark its meaning). Nor did the investigator hear any statement or inference that placing a punctuation mark could be a decision-making process, depending, for example, on one's intended meaning. Rather, the children were told to follow the rules. Language arts did not involve creative writing. There were several writing assignments throughout the year, but in each instance the children were given a ditto, and they wrote answers to questions on the sheet. For example, they wrote their "autobiography" by answering such questions as "Where were you born?" "What is your favorite animal?" on a sheet entitled, "All About Me."

In one of the working-class schools the class had a science period several times a week. On the three occasions observed, the children were not called upon to set up experiments or to give explanations for facts or concepts. Rather, on each occasion the teacher told them in his own words what the book said. The children copied the teacher's sentences from the board. Each day that preceded the day they were to do a science experiment, the teacher told them to copy the directions from the book for the procedure they would carry out the next day, and to study the list at home that night. The day after each experiment, the teacher went over what they had "found" (they did the experiments as a class, and each was actually a class demonstration led by the teacher). Then the teacher wrote what they "found" on the board, and the children copied that in their notebooks. Once or twice a year there are science projects. The project is chosen and assigned by the teacher from a box of three-by-five-inch cards. On the card the teacher has written the question to be answered, the books to use, and how much to write. Explaining the cards to the observer, the teacher said, "It tells them exactly what to do, or they couldn't do it."

Social studies in the working-class schools is also largely mechanical, rote work that was given little explanation or connection to larger contexts. In one school, for example, although there was a book available, social studies work was to copy the teacher's notes from the board. Several times a week for a period of several months, the children copied these notes. The fifth grades in the district were to study U.S. history. The teacher used a booklet she had purchased called "The Fabulous Fifty States." Each day she put information from the booklet in outline form on the board and the children copied it. The type of information did not vary: the name of the state, its abbreviation, state capital, nickname of the state, its main products, main business, and a "Fabulous Fact" (e.g., "Idaho grew 27 billion potatoes in one year. That's enough potatoes for each man, woman and . . ."). As the children finished copying the sentences, the teacher erased them and wrote more. Children would occasionally go to the front to pull down the wall map in order to locate the states they were copying, and the teacher did not dissuade them. But the observer never saw her refer to the map; nor did the observer ever hear her make other than perfunctory remarks concerning the information the children were copying. Occasionally the children colored in a ditto and cut it out to make a stand-up figure (representing, for example, a man roping a cow in the Southwest). These were referred to by the teacher as their social studies "projects."

Rote behavior was often called for in classroom oral work. When going over math and language arts skills sheets, for example, as the teacher asked for the answer to each problem, he fired the questions rapidly, staccato, and the scene reminded the observer of a sergeant drilling recruits: above all, the questions demanded that you stay at attention: "The next one? What do I put here? . . . Here? Give us the next." Or "How many commas in this sentence? Where do I put them . . . The next one?"

The (four) fifth grade teachers observed in the working-class schools attempted to control classroom time and space by making decisions without consulting the children and without explaining the basis for their decisions. The teacher's control thus often seemed capricious. Teachers, for instance, very often ignored the bells to switch classes—deciding among themselves to keep the children after the period was officially over, to continue with the work, or for disciplinary reasons, or so they (the teachers) could stand in the hall and talk. There were no clocks in the rooms in either school, and the children often asked, "What period is this?" "When do we go to gym?" The children had no access to materials. These were handed out by teachers and closely guarded. Things in the room "belonged" to the teacher: "Bob, bring me my garbage can." The teachers continually gave the children orders. Only three times did the investigator hear a teacher in either working-class school preface a directive with an unsarcastic "please," or "let's" or "would you." Instead, the teachers said, "Shut up," "Shut your mouth," "Open your books," "Throw your *gum* away—if you want to rot your teeth, do it on your *own* time." Teachers made every effort to control the movement of the children, and often shouted, "Why are you out of your *seat??!!*" If the children got permission to leave the room they had to take a written pass with the date and time.

The control that the teachers have is less than they would like. It is a result of constant struggle with the children. The children continually resist the teachers' orders and the work itself. They do not directly challenge the teachers' authority or legitimacy, but they make indirect attempts to sabotage and resist the flow of assignments:

Teacher:	I will put some problems on the board. You are to divide.
Child:	We got to divide?
Teacher:	Yes.
Several children:	(Groan) Not again. Mr. B., we done this yesterday.
Child:	Do we put the date?

> *Teacher:*   Yes. I hope we remember we work in silence. You're supposed to do it on white paper. I'll explain it later.
>
> *Child:*   Somebody broke my pencil. (Crash—a child falls out of his chair.)
>
> *Child:*   (repeats) Mr. B., somebody broke my *pencil!*
>
> *Child:*   Are we going to be here all morning?

(Teacher comes to the observer, shakes his head and grimaces, then smiles.)

The children are successful enough in their struggle against work that there are long periods where they are not asked to *do* any work, but just to sit and be quiet.[3] Very often the work that the teachers assign is "easy," that is, not demanding, and thus receives less resistance. Sometimes a compromise is reached where, although the teachers insist that the children continue to work, there is a constant murmur of talk. The children will be doing arithmetic examples, copying social studies notes, or doing punctuation or other dittoes, and all the while there is muted but spirited conversation— about somebody's broken arm, an afterschool disturbance of the day before, etc. Sometimes the teachers themselves join in the conversation because, as one teacher explained to me, "It's a relief from the routine."

Middle-Class School

In the middle-class school, work is getting the right answer. If one accumulates enough right answers one gets a good grade. One must follow the directions in order to get the right answers, but the directions often call for some figuring, some choice, some decision making. For example, the children must often figure out by themselves what the directions ask them to do, and how to get the answer: what do you do first, second, and perhaps third? Answers are usually found in books or by listening to the teacher. Answers are usually words, sentences, numbers, or facts and dates; one writes them on paper, and one should be neat. Answers must be in the right order, and one can not make them up. . . .

Affluent Professional School

In the affluent professional school, work is creative activity carried out independently. The students are continually asked to express and apply ideas and concepts. Work involves individual thought and expressiveness, expansion and illustration of ideas, and choice of appropriate method and material. (The class is not considered an open classroom, and the principal explained that because of the large number of discipline problems in the fifth grade this year they did not departmentalize. The teacher who agreed to take part in the study said she is "more structured" this year than she usually is.) The products of work in this class are often written stories, editorials and essays, or representations of ideas in mural, graph, or craft form. The products of work should not be like everybody else's and should show individuality. They should exhibit good design, and (this is important), they must also fit empirical reality. Moreover, one's work should attempt to interpret or "make sense" of reality. The relatively few rules to be followed regarding work are usually criteria for, or limits on, individual activity. One's product is usually evaluated for the quality of its expression and for the appropriateness of its conception to the task. In many cases one's own satisfaction with the product is an important criterion for its evaluation. When right answers are called for, as in commercial materials like SRA (Science Research Associates) and math, it is important that the children decide on an answer as a result of thinking about the idea involved in what they're being asked to do. Teacher's hints are to "think about it some more.". . .

Executive Elite School

In the executive elite school, work is developing one's analytical intellectual powers. Children are continually asked to reason through a problem, to produce intellectual products that are both logically sound and of top academic quality. A primary goal of thought is to conceptualize rules by which elements may fit together in systems, and then to apply these rules in solving a problem. School work helps one to achieve, to excel, to prepare for life.

The following are illustrative. The math teacher teaches area and perimeter by having the children derive formulae for each. First she helps them, through discussion at the board, to arrive at $A = W \times L$ as a formula (not *the* formula) for area. After discussing several, she says, "Can anyone make up a formula for perimeter? Can you figure that out yourselves? (pause) Knowing what we know, can we think of a formula?" She works out three children's suggestions at the board, saying to two, "Yes, that's a good one," and then asks the class if they can think of any more. No one volunteers. To prod them, she says, "If you use rules and good reasoning, you get many ways. Chris, can you think up a formula?"

She discusses two-digit division with the children as a decision-making process. Presenting a new type of problem to them, she asks, "What's the *first* decision you'd make if presented with this kind of example? What is the first thing you'd *think*? Craig?" Craig says, "To find my first partial quotient." She responds, "Yes, that would be your first decision. How would you do that?" Craig explains, and then the teacher says, "OK, we'll see how that works for you." The class tries his way. Subsequently, she comments on the merits and shortcomings of several other children's decisions. Later, she tells the investigator that her goals in math are to develop their reasoning and mathematical thinking and that, unfortunately, "there's no *time* for manipulables."

While right answers are important in math, they are not "given" by the book or by the teacher, but may be challenged by the children. Going over some problems in late September the teacher says, "Raise your hand if you do not agree." A child says, "I don't agree with 64." The teacher responds, "OK, there's a question about 64. (to class) Please check it. Owen, they're disagreeing with you. Kristen, they're checking yours." The teacher emphasized this repeatedly during September and October with statements like, "Don't be afraid to say if you disagree. In the last [math] class, somebody disagreed, and they were right. Before you disagree, check yours, and if you still think we're wrong, then we'll check it out." By Thanksgiving, the children did not often speak in terms of right and wrong math problems, but of whether they agreed with the answer that had been given.

There are complicated math mimeos with many word problems. Whenever they go over the examples, they discuss how each child has set up the problem. The children must explain it precisely. On one occasion the teacher said, "I'm more—just as interested in *how* you set up the problem as in what answer you find. If you set up a problem in a good way, the answer is *easy* to find."

Social studies work is most often reading and discussion of concepts and independent research. There are only occasional artistic, expressive, or illustrative projects. Ancient Athens and Sumer are, rather, societies to analyze. The following questions are typical of those which guide the children's independent research: "What mistakes did Pericles make after the war?" "What mistakes did the citizens of Athens make?" "What are the elements of a civilization?" "How did Greece build an economic empire?" "Compare the way Athens chose its leaders with the way we choose ours." Occasionally the children are asked to make up sample questions for their social studies tests. On an occasion when the investigator was present the social studies teacher rejected a child's question by saying, "That's just fact. If I asked you that question on a test, you'd complain it was just memory! Good questions ask for concepts."

In social studies—but also in reading, science, and health—the teachers initiate classroom discussions of current social issues and problems. These discussions occurred on every one of the investigator's visits, and a teacher told me, "These children's opinions are important—it's important that they learn to reason things through." The classroom discussions always struck the observer as quite realistic and analytical, dealing with concrete social issues like the following: "Why do workers strike?" "Is that right or wrong?" "Why do we have inflation, and what can be done to stop it?" "Why do companies put chemicals in food when the natural ingredients are available?" etc. Usually the children did not have to be prodded to give their opinions. In fact, their statements and the interchanges between them struck the observer as quite sophisticated conceptually and verbally, and well-informed. Occasionally the teachers would prod with statements such as, "Even if you don't know [the answers], if you think logically about it, you can figure it out." And "I'm asking you [these] questions to help you think this through."

Language arts emphasizes language as a complex system, one that should be mastered. The children are asked to diagram sentences of complex grammatical construction, to memorize irregular verb conjugations (he lay, he has lain, etc. . . .), and to use the proper participles, conjunctions,and interjections, in their speech. The teacher (the same one who teaches social studies) told them, "It is not enough to get these right on tests; you must use what you learn [in grammar classes] in your written and oral work. I will grade you on that."

Most writing assignments are either research reports and essays for social studies, or experiment analyses and write-ups for science. There is only an occasional story or other "creative writing" assignment. On the occasion observed by the investigator (the writing of a Halloween story), the points the teacher stressed in preparing the children to write involved the structural aspects of a story rather than the expression of feelings or other ideas. The teacher showed them a filmstrip, "The Seven Parts of a Story," and lectured them on plot development, mood setting, character development, consistency, and the use of a logical or appropriate ending. The stories they subsequently wrote were, in fact, well-structured, but many were also personal and expressive. The teacher's evaluative comments, however, did not refer to the expressiveness or artistry, but were all directed toward whether they had "developed" the story well.

Language arts work also involved a large amount of practice in presentation of the self and in managing situations where the child was expected to be in charge. For example, there was a series of assignments in which each child had to be a "student teacher." The child had to plan a lesson in grammar, outlining, punctuation, or other language arts topic and explain the concept to the class. Each child was to prepare a worksheet or game and a homework assignment as well. After each presentation, the teacher and other children gave a critical appraisal of the "student teacher's" performance. Their criteria were: whether the student spoke clearly; whether the lesson was interesting; whether the student made any mistakes; and whether he or she kept control of the class. On an occasion when a child did not maintain control, the teacher said, "When you're up there, you have authority, and you have to use it. I'll back you up."

The teacher of math and science explained to the observer that she likes the ESS program because "the children can manipulate variables. They generate hypotheses and devise experiments to solve the problem. Then they have to explain what they found."

The executive elite school is the only school where bells do not demarcate the periods of time. The two fifth grade teachers were very strict about changing classes on schedule, however, as specific plans for each session had been made. The teachers attempted to keep tight control over the children during lessons, and the children were sometimes flippant, boisterous, and occasionally rude. However, the children may be brought into line by reminding them that "it is up to you." "You must control yourself," "you are responsible for your work," you must "set your priorities." One teacher told a child, "You are the only driver of your car—and only you can regulate your speed." A new teacher complained to the observer that she had thought "these children" would have more control.

While strict attention to the lesson at hand is required, the teachers make relatively little attempt to regulate the movement of the children at other times. For example, except for the kindergartners, the children in this school do not have to wait for the bell to ring in the morning; they may go to their classroom when they arrive at school. Fifth graders often came early to read, to finish work, or to catch up. After the first two months of school the fifth grade teachers did not line the children up to change classes or to go to gym, etc., but, when the children were ready and quiet, they were told they could go—sometimes without the teachers.

In the classroom, the children could get materials when they needed them and took what they needed from closets and from the teacher's desk. They were in charge of the office at lunchtime. During class they did not have to sign out or ask permission to leave the room; they just got up and left. Because of the pressure to get work done, however, they did not leave the room very often. The teachers were very polite to the children, and the investigator heard no sarcasm, no nasty remarks, and few direct orders. The teacher never called the children "honey," or "dear," but always called them by name. The teachers were expected to be available before school, after school, and for part of their lunch time to provide extra help if needed.

DISCUSSION AND CONCLUSION

. . . What potential relationships to the system of ownership of symbolic and physical capital, to authority and control, and to their own productive activity are being developed in children in each school? What economically relevant knowledge, skills, and predispositions are being transmitted in each class-room, and for what future relationship to the system of production are they appropriate? It is of course true that a student's future relationship to the process of production in society is determined by the combined effects of circumstances beyond elementary schooling. However, by examining ele-mentary school activity in its social class context in the light of our theoretical perspective on social class, we can see certain potential relationships already developing. Moreover, in this structure of developing relationships lies theoretical—and social—significance.

The *working-class* children are developing a potential *conflict* relationship with capital. Their present school work is appropriate preparation for future wage labor that is mechanical and routine. Such work, insofar as it denies the human capacities for creativity and planning, is degrading; moreover, when performed in industry, such work is a source of profit to others. This situation produces industrial conflict over wages, working conditions, and control. However, the children in the working-class schools are not learning to be docile and obedient in the face of present or future degrading conditions or financial exploitation. They are developing abilities and skills of resistance. These methods are highly similar to the "slowdown," subtle sabotage and other modes of indirect resistance carried out by adult workers in the shop, on the department store sales floor, and in some offices.[4] As these types of resistance develop in school, they are highly constrained and limited in their ultimate effectiveness. Just as the children's resistance prevents them from learning socially legitimated knowledge and skills in school and is therefore ultimately debilitating, so is this type of resistance ultimately debilitating in industry. Such resistance in industry does not succeed in producing, nor is it

intended to produce, fundamental changes in the relationships of exploitation or control. Thus, the methods of resistance that the working-class
children are developing in school are only temporarily, and *potentially,*
liberating.

In the *middle-class school* the children are developing somewhat different
potential relationships to capital, authority, and work. In this school the work
tasks and relationships are appropriate for a future relation to capital that is
bureaucratic. Their school work is appropriate for white-collar working-class
and middle-class jobs in the supportive institutions of United States society.
In these jobs one does the paperwork, the technical work, the sales and the
social service in the private and state bureaucracies. Such work does not
usually demand that one be creative, and one is not often rewarded for critical
analysis of the system. One is rewarded, rather, for knowing the answers to
the questions one is asked, for knowing where or how to find the answers,
and for knowing which form, regulation, technique, or procedure is correct.
While such work does not usually satisfy human needs for engagement and
self-expression, one's salary can be exchanged for objects or activities that
attempt to meet these needs.

In the *affluent professional school* the children are developing a potential
relationship to capital that is instrumental and expressive and involves
substantial negotiation. In their schooling these children are acquiring *symbolic capital:* they are being given the opportunity to develop skills of linguistic,
artistic, and scientific expression and creative elaboration of ideas into
concrete form. These skills are those needed to produce, for example, culture
(e.g., artistic, intellectual, and scientific ideas and other "products"). Their
schooling is developing in these children skills necessary to become society's
successful artists, intellectuals, legal, scientific, and technical experts and
other professionals. The developing relation of the children in this school to
their work is creative and relatively autonomous. Although they do not have
control over which ideas they develop or express, the creative act in itself
affirms and utilizes the human potential for conceptualization and design that
is in many cases valued as intrinsically satisfying.

Professional persons in the cultural institutions of society (in, say, academe, publishing, the nonprint media, the arts, and the legal and state
bureaucracies) are in an expressive relationship to the system of ownership in
society because the ideas and other products of their work are often an
important means by which material relationships of society are given ideological (e.g., artistic, intellectual, legal, and scientific) expression. Through
the system of laws, for example, the ownership relations of private property
are elaborated and legitimated in legal form; through individualistic and
meritocratic theories in psychology and sociology, these individualistic economic relations are provided scientific "rationality" and "sense." The relationship to physical capital of those in society who create what counts as the
dominant culture or ideology also involves substantial negotiation. The
producers of symbolic capital often do not control the socially available
physical capital nor the cultural uses to which it is put. They must therefore
negotiate for money for their own projects. However, skillful application of

one's cultural capital may ultimately lead to social (for example, state) power and to financial reward.

The *executive elite school* gives its children something that none of the other schools does: knowledge of and practice in manipulating the socially legitimated tools of analysis of systems. The children are given the opportunity to learn and to utilize the intellectually and socially prestigious grammatical, mathematical, and other vocabularies and rules by which elements are arranged. They are given the opportunity to use these skills in the analysis of society and in control situations. Such knowledge and skills are a most important kind of *symbolic capital*. They are necessary for control of a production system. The developing relationship of the children in this school to their work affirms and develops in them the human capacities for analysis and planning and helps to prepare them for work in society that would demand these skills. Their schooling is helping them to develop the abilities necessary for ownership and control of physical capital and the means of production in society.

The foregoing analysis of differences in school work in contrasting social class contexts suggests the following conclusion: the "hidden curriculum" of school work is tacit preparation for relating to the process of production in a particular way. Differing curricular, pedagogical, and pupil evaluation practices emphasize different cognitive and behavioral skills in each social setting and thus contribute to the development in the children of certain potential relationships to physical and symbolic capital, to authority, and to the process of work. School experience, in the sample of schools discussed here, differed qualitatively by social class. These differences may not only contribute to the development in the children in each social class of certain types of economically significant relationships and not others, but would thereby help to *reproduce* this system of relations in society. In the contribution to the reproduction of unequal social relations lies a theoretical meaning, and social consequence, of classroom practice.

The identification of different emphases in classrooms in a sample of contrasting social class contexts implies that further research should be conducted in a large number of schools to investigate the types of work tasks and interactions in each, to see if they differ in the ways discussed here, and to see if similar potential relationships are uncovered. Such research could have as a product the further elucidation of complex but not readily apparent connections between everyday activity in schools and classrooms and the unequal structure of economic relationships in which we work and live.

NOTES

1. But see, in a related vein, Apple and King (1977) and Rist (1973).
2. For other similarities alleged to characterize United States classrooms and schools, but which will not be discussed here, see Dreeben (1968), Jackson (1968), and Sarason (1971).
3. Indeed, strikingly little teaching occurred in either of the working-class schools; this curtailed the amount that the children were taught. Incidentally, it increased the amount of time that had to be spent by the researcher to collect data on teaching style and interaction.
4. See, for example, discussions in Levison (1974), Aronowitz (1978), and Benson (1978).

REFERENCES

Althusser, L. Ideology and ideological state apparatuses. In L. Althusser, *Lenin and philosophy and other essays*. Ben Brewster, Trans. New York: Monthly Review Press, 1971.

Anyon, J. Elementary social studies textbooks and legitimating knowledge. *Theory and Research in Social Education*, 1978, 6, 40–55.

Anyon, J. Ideology and United States history textbooks. *Harvard Educational Review*, 1979, 49, 361–386.

Apple, M. W. *Ideology and curriculum*. Boston: Routledge and Kegan Paul, 1979.

Apple, M. W., & King, N. What do schools teach? *Curriculum Inquiry*, 1977, 6, 341–358.

Aronowitz, S. Marx, Braverman, and the logic of capital. *The Insurgent Sociologist*, 1978, 8, 126–146.

Benson, S. The clerking sisterhood: rationalization and the work culture of saleswomen in American department stores, 1890–1960. *Radical America*, 1978, 12, 41–55.

Bernstein, B. *Class, codes and control, Vol. 3. Towards a theory of educational transmission*. 2nd ed. London: Routledge and Kegan Paul, 1977.

Bourdieu, P. and Passeron, J. *Reproduction in education, society, and culture*. Beverly Hills, Calif.: Sage, 1977.

Bowles, S. & Gintis, H. *Schooling in capitalist America: educational reform and the contradictions of economic life*. New York: Basic Books, 1976.

Braverman, H. *Labor and monopoly capital: the degradation of work in the twentieth century*. New York: Monthly Review Press, 1974.

Dreeben, R. *On what is learned in school*. Reading, Mass.: Addison-Wesley, 1968.

Jackson, P. *Life in classrooms*. Holt, Rinehart & Winston, 1968.

Lampman, R. J. *The share of top wealth-holders in national wealth, 1922–1956:* A study of the National Bureau of Economic Research. Princeton, N.J.: Princeton University Press, 1962.

Levison, A. *The working-class majority*. New York: Penguin Books, 1974.

New York Stock Exchange. *Census*. New York: New York Stock Exchange, 1975.

Rist, R. C. *The urban school: a factory for failure*. Cambridge, Mass.: MIT Press, 1973.

Sarason, S. *The culture of school and the problem of change*. Boston: Allyn and Bacon, 1971.

Smith, J. D. and Franklin, S. The concentration of personal wealth, 1922–1969. *American Economic Review*, 1974, 64, 162–167.

U.S. Bureau of the Census. *Current population reports*. Series P–60, no. 118. Money income in 1977 of families and persons in the United States. Washington, D.C.: U.S. Government Printing Office, 1979.

U.S. Bureau of the Census. *Statistical abstract of the United States: 1978*. Washington, D.C.: U.S. Government Printing Office, 1978.

Williams, R. *Marxism and literature*. New York: Oxford University Press, 1977.

Wright, E. O. *Class, crisis and the state*. London: New Left Books, 1978.

God's Choice: The Total World of a Fundamentalist Christian School

ALAN PESHKIN

University of Illinois, Chicago Circle

. . . Simultaneous with the expansion of conservative, fundamentalist churches has been the impressive growth of new Christian schools sponsored by these churches.[1] To begin with, private schools of all sorts claim approximately 12 percent (5.3 million) of the nation's 48 million or so school children.[2] As of 1976, churches sponsored 85 percent of these private schools and Roman Catholic schools composed 75 percent of this 85 percent; by 1981, the Catholic percentage had decreased to 65 percent, stabilizing after fifteen years of decline (Heard 1981). So the impressive expansion of Christian schools must be seen in context: their pupils compose a tiny segment of what at best is a small portion of all school-aged children. From 1965 to 1975, Catholic school enrollments plummeted from 5.5 to 3.4 million, a loss of 38.7 percent. At the same time, the number of most other types of religious schools increased, perhaps none more impressively than those associated with the two largest of the conservative national Christian education groups—the Association of Christian Schools International and the American Association of Christian Schools. BBA belongs to the latter group. Since many Christian schools remain unaffiliated and all resist state accreditation, it is difficult to keep precise track of Christian school growth.[3] Erickson et al. estimated that as of 1975 there were about 400,000 students in such schools (1978:84); Nordin and Turner claim 350,000 in 1977 (1980:391); *Time* writers put the total at 450,000 in 1981 (up from 140,000 in 1971), or 1 percent of all school-age children (June 8, 1981). When these figures, modest in absolute terms, are seen in the light of public school enrollment declines—"11 percent in the West while private enrollment [largely but not exclusively in Christian schools] climbed 19 percent. In the South . . . public schools declined 6 percent while private enrollment increased by 31 percent" (*Newsweek*, April 20, 1981)—then we understand the hyperbolic language of "dramatic" growth, "resurgence," and "boom." Such language is most typically used to characterize what invariably is referred to as "the most rapidly expanding segment of American education."

From all indications, the claim is true: the Christian school is a rising star.[4] The vitality of these schools is evident in the increasingly comprehensive services their national organizations provide to members and in the increasing availability of textbook and instructional materials from Christian publishers. Christian schools constitute a market upon which some publishers have banked their success. The schools have grown despite their tuition costs and the shrinking pool of school-aged children. Can it be denied that they are perceived to be doing something very right? Have they found a formula for success in their blend of emphasis on the basics, dress codes, strong discipline, patriotism, and God? "Many parents," observes Christian writer Dorothy Rose, "have become weary of 'innovative' teaching activities. Movies, rap sessions, open classrooms and the 'nongraded' school" (1979:48) are among the innovations she lists. Based both on what they offer and on what they reject, Christian schools have attained a degree of success that cannot be explained, as it has in some places, by racism alone. They are not just *The Schools that Fear Built* (Nevin and Bills 1976). Indeed Christian schools open and thrive in communities where there are no black families.

If many American adults find comfort in the alternative opportunity Christian schools provide, many more have been attracted to the politics of Jesse Helms, Republican Senator from North Carolina, the religion of Jerry Falwell, and "an interlocking set of organizations out to change the politics [and the morals!] of the nation" (Drew 1981:82). Given the "perfect candidate" in Ronald Reagan, Americans in 1980, and again in 1984, heard a great deal about conservatives, right-wing politics, a rejection of our liberal past, the new right, and God and politics. Arthur Schlesinger, Jr., contested this "illusion of conservatism," and postelection polls found that rejection of Carter accounted more for Reagan's victory than a "conservative tide" (Gallup 1980). The defeat in 1980 of congressmen whose voting records had earned them a place on conservative "hit lists," and the burst of attention from the media to this successful juncture of religion and politics, stimulated a reaction against each of the three major domains of conservative effort— education, religion, and politics, although in education and religion the signs of "fighting back" have been apparent for some time.

Theologians and church scholars who place the mainline churches in a pivotal position in American society view the decline of these churches as signifying changes of great and negative consequence. The distinguished historian Martin E. Marty articulates this concern when he laments the decline of the religious center which contained

> theologians and artists, pastors and literary figures, doers and thinkers, who construed reality in light of faith in Christ but who were critically open to the idea of using that faith to transform (not merely to judge) the culture. . . . The collapse of the middle has . . . and will have fateful consequences for religious communication in a pluralistic culture. [1979:12]

Smylie is less temperate when he describes electronic evangelists such as Oral Roberts, Pat Robertson, Jim Bakker, and Jerry Falwell, who epitomize the success of conservative Christian leaders and their mastery of television. "In the American ethos," Smylie writes, "these are the leaders by whom many members of the Protestant congregations measure ministerial effectiveness; at the same time, others suspect them of being manipulative and panderers of 'cheap grace' " (1979:84).

The clergy whose churches have been most negatively affected by the turn toward religious conservatism—Lutherans, Episcopalians, United Methodists, Presbyterians—have struggled to devise a response which keeps their churches faithful to social issues and somehow manages to stop the loss of members. For example, liberal and moderate evangelicals organized the Evangelicals for Social Action. This group is supported by Kenneth Kantzer, the editor of *Christianity Today,* who said he "doesn't like 'to see evangelicalism identified with the extreme right' " (Larson 1980:48). And a strong response to the fundamentalists appeared in the *New Republic,* a journal not ordinarily given to theological stances. Charles Krauthammer denounced the fundamentalists' resort to "secular humanism" as a club to attack everything about American society that violates their sense of propriety. Krauthammer does not reject a place for religion, he rejects this place being dominated by what he calls simplistic "lunacy" (1980:20–25).

After the 1980 defeat of Gaylord Nelson, Birch Bayh, George McGovern, and Edmund Muskie, the political reaction to conservative success also became evident. McGovern established Americans for Common Sense in order to build a "counterforce" (Weissmann 1981:8–9). His colleague Senator Edward Kennedy wrote the liberal faithful in 1981 requesting money for the Fund for a Democratic Majority to be used during the 1982 congressional election. Norman Lear, producer of "All in the Family" and other television shows, created People for the American Way, a "coalition of laymen and ministers" to oppose the conservatives who mix religion and politics.

Reactions in the public school domain relate to but are not invariably caused by Christian school success. Public schools, always easy targets for criticism, have been attacked by many, including Christian fundamentalists. The latter, paradoxically, condemn public schools as centers of secular humanism, and thus unfit for Christian children, at the same time that they concentrate on several issues which, if corrected, might make public schools more acceptable places for Christian children. For example, they criticize the public schools' use of "unacceptable" books like *The Catcher in the Rye, Go Ask*

Alice, The Diary of Anne Frank, and dictionaries that contain words like "bed" used as a verb for sexual intercourse. Their cause is advanced by Mel and Norma Gablers' Educational Research Associates and the Reverend Jack Gambill's Decency in Education Committee. A measure of the prominence of the censorship issue in American life and the role of the Gablers in it can be seen in *People* magazine's three-page article devoted to them. The article, with its pictures of the smiling, determined, praying Gablers, quotes a National School Board Association editor: "What they [the Gablers] are trying to do is purge the schools of all views other than their own. They are trying to kill the concept of pluralism, and that is a danger to our democracy" (Demaret 1981:86).

Fundamentalist-supported censorship relates to the public school's sex-education courses, but more prominently to the creationist-evolution controversy. The creationists want public schools to label evolution a theory, not a fact, and to give equal time to creationist theory so that children are not "misled" by teachers and textbooks which ignore any but the evolutionists' position. This issue has moved well beyond a textbook-control issue to the involvement of concerned professionals on both sides of the controversy,[5] and ultimately to the critical judicial arena of states (California and Arkansas) where antagonists clash in updated versions of the famous 1925 trial of John Scopes, the Tennessee science teacher who taught evolution in his classroom. It also has involved the American Civil Liberties Union, which brought suit against "religious indoctrination [creationism] in the public schools" of Arkansas, and informed its members of its concerns about daily prayer permitted in Louisiana schools; silent prayer permitted in Massachusetts, Arizona, and Connecticut schools; *all* theories of creation being taught in Columbus, Ohio; and school-district approval of the distribution of Bibles in Houston classrooms.

Defenders of the much-maligned, beleaguered public schools have both voice and platform, but defense, in this case, lacks the pizzazz of attack. Throughout the 1970s and lasting until about 1983, when the inquiries of federal government and foundation-supported groups inspired a frenzy of state-led educational reforms, initiative and attack had been seized by the public school antagonists. Nonetheless, the reaction from the education profession was apparent. President Shanker of the American Federation of Teachers cited Gallup poll data to verify that 64 percent of the American public and 84 percent of public school parents gave public schools either an A, B, or C rating. He criticized those who make "unfair targets" of the public schools (1979:8). The National Education Association dramatically established its position with a front-page picture in its *Reporter* of a bulldozer about to engulf a little red school and the headline, "As Attacks on Public Education Multiply . . . NEA FIGHTS—To protect *freedom to teach*" (*NEA Reporter* March 1981:1). Newspaper editorialists reminded readers that though the growth of private schools demonstrates flaws in public education, "public schools must get full and generous public support before any expansion of that public support is considered for 'schools of choice' " (Bloomington [Ill.] *Daily Pantagraph*, May 14, 1980:4). And the American Jewish Committee, ever sensitive to maintaining the separation of church and state, opposed tuition tax credits for private schools while linking viable public schools to the cardinal principle of an "open pluralistic society" (*Jewish Community Journal*, November 1981:5).[6]. . .

BETHANY BAPTIST ACADEMY

On the face of it, the academy is a school much like any other. Of course, it is a voluntary school, a private school, required by the state of Illinois only to register,[7] but as with any school the conventional imperatives regarding the provision of space, instruction, scheduling, and the like, operate.

BBA contains about 350 boys and girls in its kindergarten through twelfth grade. The school building is split, its K–6 section occupying the south wing, built in 1976, and its 7–12 section occupying the north wing, built in 1973. Between stands the gymnasium connecting the two wings. This was built in 1970 as a church activity center. For several years it provided space for religious services as church membership rose from about 130 to about 1,500 in eighteen years. Physical facilities expanded to keep pace with student enrollments, which increased from 88 in 1972, the school's first year, to 358 in 1980. In recent years, enrollments have shown no appreciable change. This pleases Bethany because it suggests a stability won in the face of economic hard times and declining numbers of school-aged children in the local population.

The academy's building is separated from the church by a parking lot that also is used for recess activity and for physical education. In terms of space use and program, the entire church-school complex operates as an organic whole. This is consonant with Bethany's belief that church and school are one: the school is simply the academic expression of the church and no less integral to the church, as Pastor [William] Muller has said, than its Sunday morning services. Bethanyites assume, accordingly, that the autonomy enjoyed by churches under our traditional separation of church and state precludes any level of government having jurisdiction over the school, beyond safety requirements.

BBA's remarkably clean hallways are the pride of Headmaster [Tom] McGraw. The airy, spacious elementary classrooms have the stimuli-cluttered look of elementary classrooms anywhere. By contrast, the secondary classes are relatively dreary, though livened somewhat by bulletin boards displaying pinned and stapled pictures and good thoughts, an administration requirement. The gym, with a stage built at one side, doubles as an assembly hall. Opposite the stage is a small kitchen. To buy lunch, children line up against the gym wall, pick up their trays of food, and enter the lunchroom. The school library and the administrative quarters are in the elementary wing. Headmaster McGraw's well-decorated office is behind that of his secretary, who acts also as a factotum for the entire school—nurse, cheerleader consultant, piano accompanist for vocal soloists, and upholder of school rules. A decorative bookcase containing several books on Abraham Lincoln held in place by Lincoln bookends stands against the office wall; above it are two pictures of Lincoln and the Gettysburg Address framed. A waist-high barrier separates the visitor's sitting area from the offices. On the wall behind the visitor's couch hangs a picture of Theodore Roosevelt with "Thoughts of T.R." printed beneath. Surrounding this picture are plaques: the William Muller Award for high school students; the Anne Muller Award for the senior girl whose life best exemplifies the principles of the founder; the National School Choral Award; etc.

BBA's day begins at 8:00 A.M., when McGraw presides over the daily teachers' meeting. All non-bus-driving, off-duty, K–12 teachers come to hear him read and explicate a brief verse of Scripture. This is followed by announcements and by a prayer offered by a different teacher each day. McGraw always invites prayer requests, and these intentions are incorporated in the daily prayers, which also include, along with the general hope for an effective day in the Lord's service, specific prayers for needy members of the school and church community, as well as thanks for blessings received. After 8:00 A.M., students begin arriving by foot, car, or bus and must go at once to the lunchroom. At 8:25, they begin a ten-minute locker break followed by a ten-minute daily homeroom period. Thereafter, classes begin; each one is forty-three minutes long. Two extracurricular activities—the student newspaper and the yearbook—are incorporated into the school day. Others begin after 3:10 P.M., when classes are done for the day; they are cheerleading and volleyball for girls, and soccer, basketball, baseball, track and field, and wrestling for boys.

BBA's curriculum approximates that of most small public high schools. Students must take four years of English and physical education, three years of social studies, two years each of math and science, and one year of speech; they may take a foreign language, typing, band, choir, journalism, office practice, and drafting. Subjects peculiar to BBA as a Christian school are a required four-year Bible course and an optional soul-winning course; the school also requires attendance at chapel three times a week by all students in grades 7–12.

The rhythm of the school year, as manifest in BBA's scheduled events, also is not far removed from that of public schools. State and national holidays provide respite from the school routine. Summer vacations coincide exactly with Hartney's public schools. In fall, soccer rather than football brings spirit and high hopes to BBA's students, to whom victory means no less than it does to their public school counterparts; wrestling and basketball in winter and baseball and track and field in spring remove students from class for out-of-town games and keep the school buses rolling throughout the state. There are organized competitions and special tournaments aplenty to provide unlimited lunchtime, locker-room, and class-lull chatter. Each season has its special assembly program. Since 1978 BBA has had a yearly graduating class. Now each year is marked by seniors leaving, with all the accompanying ritual of that occasion. And like the public school, BBA's year is marked by days of no school when teachers attend workshops and conventions devoted to in-service training. The single event with no public school counterpart is the week-long evangelistic meetings held each fall and spring.

On principle, BBA does not now—and means never to—receive government funds.[8] To Christian educators, government money connotes government control. Accordingly, they depend completely on other means to finance their enterprise. Bethany Baptist Church covers the school's large, nonrecurring costs. Of the four separate construction projects that went to make up the school's present building, church funds meet the mortgage payments for three of the projects, while BBA pays for the fourth. Tuition fees are the largest source of income in its budget, which amounted to $310,000 in 1981–82. Annual high school fees that year were $900 (up from $750 in 1979–80 and $800 in 1980–81).[9] Approximately 75 percent of the budget goes for teacher salaries. Pastor Muller estimated that BBA's per pupil costs in 1980–81 were $738, compared to the public school's $1,500 to $2,000. Funds are received from four other sources: candy sales—the 1980 sale produced a profit of $10,000 from a gross of $25,000; gifts; matching funds; and monthly donations from members of the Builders Club.

By readily measurable indicators, BBA is a success. It collects sufficient revenue to stay in or near the black. Stable student enrollments maintain the flow of tuition-fee revenues. Staff turnover is minimal. And the school's space and physical facilities accommodate its present student body and instructional program. Whether BBA succeeds by the measure of its most fundamental goal—serving the glory of God—remains to be discussed.

THE AMERICAN ASSOCIATION OF CHRISTIAN SCHOOLS

BBA is part of America's fundamentalist Christian school movement. More particularly, it belongs to the nationwide American Association of Christian Schools (AACS) and to its state branch, the Illinois Association of Christian Schools (IACS).

The AACS began with approximately 125 member schools and 25,000 students in 1972 and grew to more than 1,000 schools and 150,000 students by 1982. It has become a full-service organization for its affiliated schools who must "subscribe without reservation" to the AACS Statement of Faith. This statement holds to the Bible's inerrancy, and emphasizes, among other doctrines, Christ's Virgin Birth and Second Coming, salvation only "by grace through faith," and the necessity of the "New Birth." Mindful of the denominational independence of the churches sponsoring their member schools, the AACS does not establish a large, central bureaucracy, or prescribe standards (beyond its doctrinal statement) for its member schools.

As the AACS has matured, it has expanded the range and adequacy of its services to members, as well as to pastors aspiring to open new schools. To help start a new school, AACS consultants offer specific financial and curricular suggestions.

An AACS flyer, distributed when A. C. Janney, the founder, directed the organization from Hialeah, Florida, clarifies why Christians should avoid public schools. The flyer describes these as institutions that may transport children long distances from their homes; that may hire teachers who are atheists, cultists, or addicts; and that may teach children to be "revolutionists." An undated letter sent from Janney's office to "Christian Friends" aspiring to start a Christian school said:

> There are two major things we must do if our country is to continue as a free nation. . . . Christians must join hands in stopping the floodtide of socialistic-communistic legislation that is now being introduced and we must rescue our Christian youth from the brain-washing socialistic, amoral, and often atheistic public school system to educate them in a Biblical philosophy of life. We welcome you to the ranks of the Christian School Movement.

After a member school has been in operation for at least three years, it may seek AACS accreditation by completion of a long self-evaluation instrument and the visit of an accreditation team. While scorning the legitimation that state offices of education offer through their accreditation process, the AACS lauds its own accreditation process for verifying that proper biblical and academic standards are upheld. "It is time," Janney writes in an AACS tract called "Accreditation," "that we establish God's standards and leave the world out. Accreditation can be a blessing—if it's accreditation by God's people, for God's people . . . with God's stamp of approval on it."

The AACS literature makes clear that the association intends to provide Christian schools with the Christian counterpart of those events and opportunities available to public school educators and students: health insurance and retirement programs; academic, religious, and athletic competition, organized at regional, state, and national levels; a Christian Honor Society; regional, state, and national clinics and conferences; and publications, including *The Administrator*, a quarterly journal; the monthly *AACS Newsletter* (which announces meetings and forthcoming events, news from member schools and states, and legislative alerts); and the infrequent *Christian School Communicator*, a single-page statement on topics such as "Christian Education: Reaching the Heart" and "Christian Education Begins at Home."

Finally, and quite exactly like the national organizations that serve public school teachers, administrators, and school board members, the AACS has an office in Washington and a full-time staff member to monitor legislation and to activate, when necessary, their legislative-alert network. More than this, the AACS is committed to promoting the sensitivity and competence of its "pastors, administrators, and Christian school leaders" to deal with issues in the political domain. To this end, it has sponsored an annual Washington conference since 1974. In 1980 the conference featured Senator Jesse Helms (R., North Carolina) and the two representatives, John Ashbrook (R., Ohio) and Robert Dornan (R., California), who led the fight against the Internal Revenue Service's effort to tax Christian schools. Participants were informed that their meeting in the Senate Office Building would cover "the critical issues facing our movement that need to be communicated to our Congressmen." In 1981 the conference featured Senator William Armstrong (R., Colorado), "a real friend to Christian education"; Senator Charles Grassley

(R., Iowa), "a consistent conservative in Congress" and a "Baptist lay preacher"; and Representative Carrol Campbell (R., South Carolina), "one of the real bright young conservative leaders.". . .

BBA'S DOCTRINAL ORIENTATION

God's School
. . . There is no better starting point for a discussion of the foundation of Bethany's educational enterprise than the fact that its educators believe that their school is God's school and that they are doing God's work, fulfilling his plan for themselves and their students. Repeatedly one hears at meetings of Christian educators and one reads in their documents that they are not merely good men doing good work.[10] Immeasurably more than this, they are godly men doing God's work! Lester Roloff,[11] a Texas pastor and subject of attention in the media for his controversial treatment of the runaway, orphaned, abandoned, wards of his school, literally screams while addressing his AACS brethren in a chandeliered Hilton hotel ballroom: "We're going to win Texas [for Christ] because God says we're going to win. Oh, we've lost some skirmishes, but God will take us to victory. . . . Folks, my work is like shooting chickens in the yard."

In the same glittering Hilton ballroom, at the same meeting, Pastor Jerry Prevo of the Anchorage Baptist Temple faces a large, silent, attentive audience while standing under a three-foot-high red, white, and blue banner that reads, "Christian Education is the Foundation for America's Future." Pastor Prevo's words are as confidently assertive as that of the banner hanging overhead: "Don't get discouraged [when one's state enacts or enforces legislation that threatens the autonomy of Christian schools]. Keep making sacrifices because it is the work of God and he wants us to give our all."

In God's school, taught by God's teachers, it must follow that God's truth is the beginning and end of instruction. The presence of Scripture is not detectable in every moment of classroom activity. In mathematics or physical education or driver training, for example, one often listens in vain for the sound of an overtly religious comment. Nonetheless, whenever knowledge is present, so is God, because "All avenues of knowledge stem from God," as Paul W. Cates writes in an AACS pamphlet. He continues:

> Since God is central in the universe and is the source of all truth, it follows that all subject matter is related to God. . . . The Bible itself becomes the central subject in the school's curriculum. . . . This is not to imply that the Bible is a textbook on anything and everything; but rather that the Bible is to be the point of reference from which we can evaluate all areas and sources of knowledge (1975:3–4).

. . .

Christian Pedagogy
Bethany educators use various images of the nature of children, depending on the point they wish to make. They are lambs, insofar as they are to

submit to the authority of parents, teachers, and God. They are warriors, insofar as they are to relate to the world, forcefully resisting its allures and forcefully presenting the path of salvation to the unsaved. They are sinners and babes in Christ, insofar as they are not fully informed by the Word of God, and therefore must learn to give their problems to God and become strong to prevent the flesh from taking over. As "kids, but not dumb kids," they require adult teachers who reign supreme in their classrooms. Most of all, says McGraw, they need a judicious blend of love and discipline.

Because children love to be disciplined, Bethanyites believe, they will develop psychological problems if they rebel against authority. Moreover, "If a boy runs your classroom," McGraw tells his teachers, "this won't teach him submission to God. If a girl runs your classroom, this won't teach her submission to her husband. As humans, we have a problem in this area of authority."

Corollary to Bethany's view of youth is their view of the teacher as overseer. Given their scriptural commitments (for example, "Train up a child in the way he should go: and when he is old, he will not depart from it" [Proverbs 22:6], teachers must operate according to what McGraw calls "our whole philosophy of supervision":

> We believe in teachers being right on top of things, to where somebody could easily misunderstand what we are doing and accuse us of looking over their [the students'] shoulders all the time. Well, I guess we do that, and we don't apologize for it. We realize that you can't leave kids alone, for instance, in unchaperoned situations, whether it's a youth activity, school activity, or whatever. It just doesn't work.

If many students are traveling to a game or taking a trip, boys and girls ride in separate buses; if few are going, boys sit in the back and girls in the front of the same bus. "We believe that those kinds of arrangements prevent problems; it's a realistic view of the nature of man."

And given the teachers' scriptural commitments, they and their fellow Christian teachers throughout America enjoy a unity of purpose that distinguishes them from most teachers anywhere in the world. They belong to the same church, share a virtually identical view of the Bible, and are directed by leaders who are presistently faithful adherents of the same doctrine. "I can't name a single policy of the school," says McGraw, "that doesn't somewhere fall into a doctrinal statement of the church." He acknowledges differences of opinion regarding nonessentials like the wearing of slacks, use of cosmetics, playing music in the church, etc.

> Most of these disagreements come from misunderstanding. There's a verse in Corinthians [actually, 1 Peter 3:3] dealing with plaiting the hair and wearing brass [gold] and so on. In those days, it was a mark of the harlot.

Regarding essentials, unity prevails. Headmaster McGraw considers BBA's unity of purpose the characteristic which most distinguishes it from the public school. Whereas a diversity of religious and nonreligious views characterize teachers in even the most homogeneous public school, Christian educators are of one mind on the central elements of belief. As true believers, they collectively endeavor to make true believers of their students—that is, persons who perceive the Bible as absolute truth and who believe and mean to live by these truths absolutely. True believers do not conceive of competing, alternative truths. Truth is singular; it is to be possessed, not sought after. To reject the true believer's way is to err and suffer the appropriate consequences. In mundane matters, truth may be pursued; in the critical matters of this life and of the hereafter, Truth is known, revealed by God in his scriptures, and must be acquired. To search for that which already is known, is to give credence to a vain intellectualism which vitiates the integrity of an inerrant Bible. Bethany's Christians reject Lessing's view that

> if God were to hold out enclosed in His right hand all Truth, and in His left hand just the active search for Truth . . . and should say to me: Choose! I should humbly take this left hand and say: Father! Give me this one; absolute truth belongs to Thee alone" (*Wolfenbüttfer Fragmente*).

Obviously, teachers at BBA fulfill both an academic and a religious role, intending to perform in ways that integrate the two. Leading students to the Lord, abetting their efforts to get right with the Lord, edifying them in regard to the Word of the Lord—all these functions merge with more conventional academic ones to shape the teacher's role. For teachers to be fitting agents of the Lord, as McGraw advises them, they must be strong Christians themselves.

> Christians must learn how to resist the devil. He can attack in new areas. Pick friends who are stronger than yourself. Keep your life free from sin. Confess daily both sins of omission and commission. Thoughts are sins if they're wrong; don't let the devil take root. You can't prevent a bird from flying over you, but you can prevent it from building a nest in your hair.

In regard to having impact in their classroom, teachers' lives weigh more heavily than the subjects they teach. The latter, however, are of consequence and have varying priorities. To be sure, the compulsory Bible class, thrice-weekly chapel, and daily devotions are salient, but there remains a full day of experiences to be ordered in some way. Other subjects, whatever their content, are to be integrated with Scripture, not in a necessarily conscious, planned way, but naturally—in fact, quite literally—as the spirit moves them. Thus, when teachers are replete with the Word of God, they become aware of the occasions for integration as these occur in the course of a lesson. Fundamentalist Christian educators commonly use the term "integration" to designate their need to merge Scripture and subject matter in their daily classroom routine. Whatever the subject and activity, they are urged to integrate to the fullest extent possible, although I believe they would accept the warning of the Christian educator A. J. Jacquot that "It's a sin against God to let your class lead you to always discuss doctrine and neglect subject matter."

From Headmaster McGraw's perspective there is a clear order of subject-matter priorities at BBA. Religious instruction is most important, followed by English. McGraw's valuation of English is straightforward: Christianity is based on the Word of God, access to the Word of God is gained through mastery of language, and mastery of language is acquired through instruction in English. He observes that the priest interprets doctrine for the Catholic, but for the fundamentalist "every believer is a priest before God." Thus, to be an effective "priest" the Christian must be literate. Teachers add a vocational argument to the case for four years of compulsory English: the world's employers value workers accomplished in reading, writing, and speaking English.

A one-year required speech course is closely allied to the English program. In support of speech, McGraw quotes Romans 10:17: "So then faith cometh by hearing, and hearing by the word of God." Speech students concentrate on the mechanics of effective oral presentation, using both sacred and secular content. An optional two years of drama instruction, taught as a regular class, not as an extracurricular activity, bolsters the speech option and extends the work students do in speech. A school that values the identification of would-be preachers can easily justify emphasizing the development of verbal skills.

Music belongs in this cluster of core subjects but is not exactly a part of it. In McGraw's view, "music is a universal language. . . . It relates very definitely to the spiritual emphasis by preparing the heart for the overall spiritual impact." In fact, music is much esteemed, and both vocal and instrumental opportunities abound in regular classes offered during the school day. Yet, since no class in music is required of all students, its importance must be inferred from the way BBA treats it in regard to making time for its programs, releasing students from class for practice, and the like. The case for the importance of music at BBA is like the one that can be made for athletics at most public schools.

In considering the position of the rest of his school's curriculum, McGraw refers to Bob Jones University in South Carolina, his alma mater and former employer, and the most preferred school for BBA's graduates "because of their doctrinal position and their position on separation." Bob Jones has many departments and courses of study, but it stresses the training of preachers and teachers, the two notably Christian vocations. Accordingly, BBA stresses those parts of its curriculum which bear on a student's becoming a full-time Christian and entering full-time Christian service. It considers all other subjects—mathematics, social studies, science, etc.—as useful and interesting, though clearly of secondary importance. BBA divides its curriculum into two broad categories, the more valued one containing the core experiences of Bible, chapel, English, speech, drama, and music, and the less valued one containing all other subjects—the periphery.

McGraw's advice to his teachers suggests another way to think about the two categories of instruction. He tells the teachers that they should urge their students "to read the newspapers and watch the news. This won't change their lives—only changing their hearts will do that—but it's still important." In short, the core subjects have a greater capacity to affect the heart and thereby change lives.

McGraw and BBA hold an instrumental view of learning. Many BBA graduates will end up in secular jobs, but when funds and time are limited, and priorities lie elsewhere, instructional opportunities geared to such employment are foregone. In fact, BBA neither means to be geared to non-Christian vocations nor apologizes for their comparative neglect. BBA is most definitely a vocational school, designed to inculcate youth with the desire to become Christian professionals, at the same time that it provides a general education suitable for being a Christian person. "We don't let kids get excused at noon to go to work," says McGraw. "I don't see the sense of kids leaving school early to pump gas or work at K Mart." The view of instruction as instrumental in spiritual terms also applies to the development of Christian intellectuals. Intellectualism is often too much a matter of pride, McGraw believes, rather than of service of the sort which should provide the primary rationale for learning.

> You look at our library . . . we don't have the emphasis [number of books] there to turn out a high school kid who'd say he wants to be a university professor. What we don't want is to worship learning. To a Christian there has to be a goal that is something beyond. We think of scholarship as an avenue of service, as opposed to scholarship for its own sake.

Administrator and teacher commitment to Scripture do not dictate common classroom procedures. To be sure, McGraw and others offer guidelines to teachers for sound instruction, and some of these guidelines are traceable to scriptural views of values, children, and authority. Still, there is the type of diversity that one may find in any school, based on variations in teachers' experience and their personalities, and on the subject matter being taught. Nonetheless, BBA has a common view of ideal teaching practice, as heard in the words of Headmaster McGraw speaking either at preschool or during-the-semester in-service meetings with his teachers.

"Our job is teaching the truth." I don't believe there is a more essential premise for understanding the Christian approach to instruction than this statement which McGraw spoke without the least hint of hubris. BBA believes it can teach the truth, because it believes it possesses the truth, not regarding man's contemporary issues of how to reduce national debt, cure cancer, or prevent acid rain, but regarding his cosmic concerns about the origins of man and earth, life and death, man's ultimate fate, the nature of God, and proper conduct. Moreover, since Christian truth can explain why things are the way they are, Christian teachers can provide answers when public school teachers only shrug with uncertainty: "Why don't the parts of an atom fly apart? Because God holds all things together."

For identifying BBA priorities, it may be useful to note the school's core and peripheral experiences, but this delineation is not useful in characterzing teaching practice. No one advises teachers about how to teach in relationship to either of these two categories, but, rather, in relationship to their notions of truth and authority. If some matter falls within the scriptural domain of truth, it is incumbent upon teachers to present that matter as uncontestably, unequivocally true. Students can wonder why, seek explanations, raise questions on any topic, and, in the end, they can reserve judgment about what to accept as true. What is deemed to be true, however, will never be taught as though it might be open to questions; above all, when teachers have pronounced what is true, students may not question the teachers' authority to do so. For the essence of the proper student response to authority is submission, total and unqualified, as long as the person in authority is not violating scriptural doctrine. Pedagogical variety exists in the context of an essentially teacher-centered classroom, wherein neither student idiosyncrasies nor the textbook should ever dominate, and where all teaching efforts must be directed to shape students' minds to Christ. In McGraw's words "Bethany is a closed system within the biblical framework. We would say that that opens it to everything. The world, of course, would disagree." Students are free to accept or reject this perspective, but it is the only one that BBA sanctions.

McGraw and Donna Reynolds, BBA's elementary school supervisor and a contributor to teacher in-service programs, provide observations on teacher practice. McGraw says:

> The more you do that is student-centered, the more you surrender control of the class. Teacher-directed activity is the key to learning. Lecturing is more important than discussion. We believe strongly in the prepared person and that comes from our preaching heritage. Don't apologize for telling the kids what is right. They should be taught not to question you. Tell them, "This is my classroom and this is what I expect. This classroom is not a democracy. It's a dictatorship. You don't vote on anything!" This is what I tell the kids.

Administrative guidance to teachers extends considerably beyond these points; it extends to the familiar homilies mined from the background of any experienced teacher—know your subject, have a plan, use audiovisual aids, practice reinforcement, avoid sarcasm, motivate—while never forgetting, as Donna Reynolds emphasizes, that

> as a Christian teacher you are concerned with a student's life. You must communicate the subject matter; you must also teach God's principles of right and wrong and show in your life God's standard of Christian living. What do you see when you look at your students? Individuals for whom Christ died! Individual Christian leaders of tomorrow!

Bethany educators take great pride in their school's orderliness. They are committed to firm discipline based on well-established policies and regulations. To this end, they have devised a demerit system which communicates to students a general rank order of infractions, ranging from tardiness and gum-chewing to lying, attending movies, and cheating on tests. Demerits extend to misdeeds committed both in and out of school. Since BBA takes its students to be BBA students at all times and places, there is no limit to the application of school regulations: "Our testimony [as a school] wouldn't be worth five cents if we didn't follow this policy. We're trying to teach these kids how to live all the time—not just from Monday to Friday." Corporal punishment is scripturally sanctioned and may substitute for demerits, but the older a student is the more sparingly it is used. Teachers are urged to manage their classes without frequent recourse to demerits. At the same time, they are urged to apply school rules strictly, and to understand that the world's rejection of authority makes it all the more necessary for them to enforce a strict code of conduct.

About every school it can be asked, "What kind of person does it strive to develop?" Seldom can the question be answered simply, and seldom do schools take pains to articulate an answer which can serve as a blueprint for the educative experiences they should organize. But if pressed, answer they can, or answers can be inferred from classroom practice. They want their students to be vocationally successful, socially adept, good citizens in political terms, and the like. I will discuss classroom practice and other school activities in later chapters, but here, in connection with the general ideas that govern the entire school's operations, it is possible to be definitive about the kind of person BBA means to develop.

The school attends primarily to developing youth to live in God's will and to serve Christ, but it also emphasizes right conduct, such as punctuality, honesty, cleanliness, and forgivingness. The Bible is presented as the handbook for good conduct, so that what is scriptural is allowable, what is unscriptural is shunned, and what is in doubt is best avoided. Christian students are to learn to live separate from the world, as full-time Christians in terms of spirituality and faithfulness, totally submissive to God's will and to the vicars of his will.

All schools have behavioral norms to guide student conduct; they are most often contained in student handbooks and are the subject of occasional talks. Seldom, however, has any American school been as professedly, unabashedly, unremittingly absorbed by normative commitments as the Christian school. It bristles with established norms at both the center and the periphery of its corporate life (notwithstanding . . . tiny, transitory islands of student counterculture . . .). I infer from the exhortations and the behavior of BBA's adult arbiters and practitioners of Christian virtue that the norms are obligatory, absolute, beyond discussion, and good for all occasions. There is right conduct and wrong conduct, without qualification.

With its emphatic normative commitment, BBA can be relatively relaxed about its paucity of instructional technology, its slim curricular and extracurricular offerings, and its truly modest library holdings. The spare quality of its material resources may be remedied in time, but for now it is not a cause for critical comment from within the Bethany community. Laboratory materials and books are valued, as are a broader range of vocational subjects. In fact, however, the dominant goals of BBA can be attained without possessing more of the material things of education. Unsurprisingly, the school is not relaxed about establishing the means to attain those goals which abide at the heart of BBA's existence.

NOTES

1. For example, from 1968 to 1978 Southern Baptists increased (15 percent) from 10.9 to 12.9 million while the United Methodist Church declined (4.36 percent) from 10.3 to 9.8 million (National Council of Churches, 1968 and 1978).

2. See *Digest of Education Statistics* for annual data on nonpublic schools.

3. Nordin and Turner "found that 72 percent of Kentucky and 50 percent of Wisconsin fundamentalist schools did not belong to any national 'Christian' school organization" (1980:392), and Cooper and McLaughlin found that private schools were undercounted by as much as 35 percent (reported by Heard, August 24, 1981:4).

4. Important but lesser degrees of success are being experienced by other types of private schools amidst talk of vouchers that would afford parents the choice of public or private schooling for their children, and talk of James Coleman's instantly controversial study (1981), which purported to demonstrate the superiority of private schools.

5. On the one hand, there is the Creation Science Research Center, and, on the other, groups like the American Anthropological Association, which passes motions beginning: "Whereas evolutionary theory is the indispensible foundation for the understanding of physical anthropology and biology . . ." (*Anthropology Newsletter*, January 1981:1). Similarly opposed, Duane Gish of the Institute for Creation Research debates the famous writer-scientist Isaac Asimov in "The Genesis War" (*Science Digest*, October 1981:82–87).

6. Notwithstanding Jerry Falwell's and other fundamentalists' support for Israel, American Jews in the 1970s and 1980s were alert to and concerned about the signs of anti-Semitism associated with Christian fundamentalism. They were animated not only by the constant efforts to convert Jews, but also by the Reverend Bailey Smith, Southern Baptist Convention president, who within a two-week period informed a meeting of fifteen thousand people that "God almighty does not hear the prayer of a Jew" and then later said Jews have "funny-looking noses" (Champaign-Urbana *News Gazette*, November 15, 1980:8). Tom Driver of Union Theological Seminary coupled with "frightening irony" the pro-Israeli stance of Falwell and others and their anti-Semitism (Champaign-Urbana *News Gazette*, November 15, 1980:8). The same article quoted Rabbi Alexander Schindler, head of the Union of American Hebrew Congregations: It is "no coincidence that the rise of right-wing fundamentalism has been accompanied by the most serious outbreak of anti-Semitism since World War II." The fundamentalists' denials of anti-Semitism are weakened by statements such as the following by Bob Jones. He is editor of *Faith*, a family magazine published by Bob Jones University. Jones observes that Andrew Young, United Nations ambassador, did and said many unworthy things yet managed to keep his position until he "displeased Israel and her American supporters. . . . The point is, he has done and said other things just as detrimental . . . yet the President [Carter] smiled tolerantly and continued publicly to stand by this contemptible and unworthy man until the Israeli pressures were applied. It makes us wonder who, indeed, besides the Communists . . . is running America" (April 1980:2).

7. Registration is the least that a state can require of its private schools. To register in Illinois is "to assure compliance with the federal and state laws regarding attendance, length of term, nondiscrimination and with applicable fire and health safety requirements" (State Board of Education 1978:1). At an IACS workshop, Headmaster McGraw advised his colleagues not to fight the state on its intent to enforce health and safety regulations: "Health and safety are Caesar's and should be rendered unto him." States that try to impose their customary standards for recognition incur legal resistance from Christian schools.

8. On the subject of outside funding, McGraw notes: "Our survival is tied to only one thing—the Word of God. It is not tied to any outside group. That's one of the reasons we fight so hard to refuse state or federal funds. We don't want our survival tied to allegiance to any outside group."

9. In 1978 tuition fees averaged $562 in fourteen Wisconsin Christian schools and $609 in seventeen Kentucky schools (Turner 1979:124).

10. The use of the male gender here and elsewhere in the book derives from the fundamentalist Christians' almost exclusive use of the male gender in both spoken and written language. They do not use plural nouns or a his/her construction to avoid dominance by the male reference.

11. Lester Roloff is so admired at Bethany that when he urged his audience to write letters in his behalf, Headmaster McGraw prepared a reminder to this effect and pinned it to the bulletin board in the teacher's room along with the duty assignment and the other announcements teachers should heed.

REFERENCES

Cates, Paul W. 1975. "Christian Philosophy of Education." Hialeah, Fla.: American Association of Christian Schools.

Coleman, James S., Thomas Hoffer, and Sally Kilgore. 1981. *Public and Private Schools.* Washington, D.C.: National Center for Education Statistics.

Demaret, Kent. 1981. "The House of the Two Gablers Helps Decide What Johnny Can't Read in Texas Schools." *People,* 5 October: 86, 88–89.

Drew, Elizabeth. 1981. "A Reporter at Large: Jesse Helms." *New Yorker,* July 20: 78–95.

Erickson, Donald A., et al. 1978. "Recent Enrollment Trends in U.S. Nonpublic Schools." In *Declining Enrollments: The Challenge of the Coming Decade,* edited by Susan Abramowitz and Stuart Rosenfeld. Washington, D.C.: National Institute of Education.

Gallup, George. 1980. "Little Evidence of Shift to Right Detected in Nation." *Champaign-Urbana News Gazette,* November 14.

Heard, Alex. 1981. "Study Discovers Many Overlooked Private Schools." *Education Week,* August 24:4.

Krauthammer, Charles. 1981. "The Humanist Phantom." *New Republic* 185: 20–25.

Larson, Roy. 1980. "God and Politics 'From Sea to Shining Sea.'" *Chicago Sunday Sun-Times,* March 2.

Marty, Martin E. 1979. Foreword to *Understanding Christian Growth and Decline,* edited by Dean R. Hoge and David A. Roozen. New York: Pilgrim Press.

National Council of Churches. 1968. *Yearbook of American Churches.* New York: Council Press.

————. 1978. *Yearbook of American and Canadian Churches.* Nashville: Abingdon.

Nevin, David, and Bills, Robert E. 1976. *The Schools that Fear Built: Segregationist Academies in the South.* Washington, D.C.: Acropolis Books.

Nordin, V. D., and Turner, W. L. 1980. "More than Segregated Academies: The Growing Protestant Fundamentalist Schools." *Phi Delta Kappan* 61 (February): 391–94.

Rose, Dorothy W. 1979. "Success Story of Christian Schools." *Good News Broadcaster,* September: 48–50.

Shanker, Albert. 1979. "Poll Shows Support for Education." *American Teacher* (November): 8.

Smylie, James H. 1979. "On Growth and Decline in Historical Perspective." In *Understanding Christian Growth and Decline,* edited by Dean R. Hoge and David A. Roozen. New York: Pilgrim Press.

State Board of Education. 1978. *Policies and Guidelines for Registration and Recognition of Nonpublic Elementary and Secondary Schools.* Springfield, Ill.: Illinois Office of Education.

Turner, William L. 1979. "Reasons for Enrollment in Religious Schools: A Case Study of Three Recently Established Fundamentalist Schools in Kentucky and Wisconsin." Ph.D. dissertation, University of Wisconsin—Madison.

Weissmann, Arnie. 1981. "Target McGovern." *Advocate* 15: 8–9.

The Other Side of College:
The Nonacademic Effects of
Higher Education

KEVIN J. DOUGHERTY

Manhattan College

FLOYD M. HAMMACK

New York University

Beginning with Theodore Newcomb's (1943) pioneering study of Bennington College students, social scientists have paid considerable attention to the effects of college on students' nonacademic knowledge, attitudes, and behavior (Astin, 1977; Bowen, 1977; Feldman and Newcomb, 1969; Hyman, Wright, and Reed, 1975; Jackman and Muha, 1984; Trent and Medsker, 1968; Weil, 1985).[1] This research has found that college students undergo important changes in many areas—most notably, general knowledge, civic and political attitudes and behavior, personal ambition, self-confidence, and creativity. This paper has two tasks. It summarizes the main findings of this research on college nonacademic learning. And it then reviews the questions raised about the validity and meaning of college effects.

THE FINDINGS OF COLLEGE EFFECTS RESEARCH

General Knowledge
Not surprisingly, researchers have found that college enhances students' general knowledge, that is, knowledge that is not specific to a particular discipline or occupation. College students gain considerably from freshman

This article appears here for the first time.

to senior year in knowledge of music and the arts, our governmental system, basic science, and so forth (Astin, 1977: 123–126). Furthermore, vocationally important nonacademic learning also occurs in college: for example, work discipline; ability to learn new tasks; and knowledge of how large, bureaucratic organizations work (Bowles and Gintis, 1976; Collins, 1979: chap. 1; Thurow, 1972). College students tend to pick up these general skills not so much through particular formal courses as through the simple experience of taking courses and meeting academic requirements and of working within a bureaucratic organization, namely a college (Bowen, 1977: 157–178; Feldman and Newcomb, 1969: I, 40).

Civic and Political Attitudes and Behavior

College also appears to foster changes in civic and political attitudes and behavior. College-educated people demonstrate considerably greater interest and participation in politics than non-college-educated people, and seniors more than freshman. This interest and participation is made evident in college-educated people's greater involvement in activities such as talking about politics, voting, campaign work, lobbying, and community organizing (Bowen, 1977: 150–155; Campbell and others, 1960: 477–481; Feldman and Newcomb, 1969: I, 21–23; Hyman, Wright, and Reed, 1975: 89–93, 176–179). College graduates also get more involved than do non-college-goers in volunteer work and other forms of community participation (Bowen, 1977: 155–156; Pace, 1974: 60–61).

Studies also repeatedly find that college-goers are less prejudiced toward people of different races, ethnic groups, and religions, are less stereotyped in their thinking about gender roles, and are less authoritarian and dogmatic than non-college-educated people, and similarly for seniors as versus freshmen.[2] This orientation shows up in more favorable attitudes to civil liberties and civil rights and openness to dissenting views (Bowen, 1977: 119, 143–150, 190; Feldman and Newcomb, 1969: I, 31–32, 34; II, 20–24, 49–56, 66–67; Trent and Medsker, 1968: 147–166). College-goers also appear to be more "liberal" in another sense. College graduates and seniors are more concerned about poverty and more supportive of social-welfare programs than are non-college-goers and freshmen (Astin, 1977: 36–40; Bowen, 1977: 143–150; Feldman and Newcomb, 1969: I, 20; II, 19–20). College graduates are also more supportive of nontraditional gender roles than non-college-goers (Funk and Willits, 1987).

These findings are by no means uncontested, however. With regard to prejudice, a number of scholars have found that greater education does not necessarily breed greater tolerance and openmindedness. For example, Jackman and Muha (1984) found very little connection between education and race, class, and sex prejudice in the United States. They examined how the attitudes of men toward women, whites toward blacks, and the nonpoor toward the poor differed by years of education in a 1975 nationwide survey of adults. They found that education explained very little of the variation in answers to 43 questions, whether before or after controlling for the effects of socioeconomic status, family income, class identification, age, region, and size of hometown. Moreover, Weil (1985) finds that, while more educated people are less anti-Semitic in the United States, the better educated in Austria are no less, and perhaps even more, anti-Semitic than the less educated.

College may also fail to make its students more questioning of authority, especially with regard to one particular form of authority: that of the expert. Precisely because this is the kind of authority that college teachers invoke and that colleges train people to utilize, students may not question it as much as those who do not go to college. And this blind spot is increasingly important as our society more and more relies on specialized expertise to conduct its affairs.[3]

Personal Ambition

College has traditionally been seen as a time and place for students to free themselves sufficiently from family influences to be able to set their own life course. This process of self-creation is reflected in changes between freshman and senior year in education and occupation aspired to. In the case of educational and occupational aspirations, many students change their aspirations during college as they encounter people and experiences that challenge these aspirations (Astin, 1977: 135–154; Bowen, 1977: 109, 112; Feldman and Newcomb, 1969: I, 37–38; II, 80–90). Sometimes this change takes the form of a "warming up" of expectations (Astin, 1977: 113). But it often involves a "cooling" of expectations. McClelland (forthcoming) found that 80 percent of students entering college in 1972 aspiring to a high-status occupation had lowered their hopes by 1979 either to a low-status professional occupation (44 percent) or a lower-level white collar occupation (36 percent). This diminishment of hopes in good part reflects the state of the labor market.[4] But it is also affected by the quality of college attended, with the diminishment greater in community colleges and low-status four-year colleges (Dougherty, 1987; McClelland, forthcoming).

Self-Confidence

Another aspect of self-creation is greater confidence. College seems to enhance students' self-confidence and sense of autonomy by allowing them the opportunity to clarify their attitudes, beliefs, and skills and to learn to depend less on others for basic approval (Astin, 1977: 40–42; Feldman and Newcomb, 1969: I, 33; II, 57–60). At the same time, this emancipation from inherited beliefs and values can undermine the confidence of some students. They lose their traditional ties and sources of meaning but are unable to establish new ones.

Creativity

Finally, there is some evidence that there may be a mild effect of college attendance on creativity (Bowen, 1977: 83–85; Feldman and Newcomb, 1969: I, 29; II, 38–39). This trait turns on the ability to distance oneself from conventional structures and practices and be able to posit new ones. Hence, this trait includes not only an artistic dimension but also intellectual and political tolerance and openness.

CAUTIONS ABOUT THE RESEARCH ON COLLEGE EFFECTS

Findings about college nonacademic learning must be approached with considerable caution, because they emerge from research procedures that often leave much to be desired. The most trustworthy findings come from studies that follow college freshmen through graduation and compare how they have changed with a similar group who did not enter college but are also followed up years later.

Yet, most studies of college effects do not use this approach, but rather rely on two other approaches that have deep flaws. A very common technique used to measure the effect of going to college is to compare college graduates against less educated people on some variable of interest: for example, knowledge of and interest in culture. Unfortunately, these comparisons are usually made without at the same time taking into account other factors that may be the actual cause of the difference on the variable of interest (cultural knowledge in this case). College-goers and non-college-goers differ considerably on characteristics other than going to college that also have a powerful effect on attitudes and behavior: for example, gender, class background, race and ethnicity, and educational and occupational aspirations. Hence, in order to isolate the effect of going to college as versus not going to college, a comparison of college-goers and non-college-goers would have to control for these differences between the two groups.

A better, but still flawed, measure of college effects is to compare seniors to freshmen. But this technique assumes that the seniors represent what the freshmen will become in four years, when in fact seniors could differ from freshmen for many reasons other than because college changes students. Seniors can differ from freshmen because many freshmen and sophomores, especially less able ones, drop out. Moreover, students change over the course of college simply because they are maturing and are exposed to noncollege events such as wars, economic prosperity and recession, and social conflict that powerfully shape attitudes.[5] In short, students clearly change over the course of their college years, but much of this change need not be due to something directly related to going to college—for example, college instruction, living in a dormitory with other students, student activities, or athletic programs.[6]

NONFUNCTIONALIST VIEWS OF COLLEGE EFFECTS

The findings that college fosters such attitudes and behaviors as greater tolerance and higher creativity are by no means uncontested, as we saw above. Moreover, even if the findings are true, their meaning is also at issue. The research on college effects just surveyed has largely viewed these findings from a functionalist perspective, assuming that college nonacademic learning benefits both students and society. Moreover, this research on college effects has assumed that these effects are due to the particular things colleges do: provide instruction and student activities and bring students together in the adolescent societies that dormitories constitute. But scholars from various nonfunctionalist perspectives have rejected both assumptions.[7]

These nonfunctionalist scholars question the social benefit of college effects. For example, they argue that rather than producing greater tolerance, education simply fosters greater subtlety in stating and justifying one's interests. Jackman and Muha (1984) argue that college-educated people are essentially no less race, class, and sex prejudiced than less educated people, but they are more subtle in how they state and defend their prejudices. For example, white college-educated people are no more likely than less educated whites to express a desire to live in a neighborhood with equal numbers of blacks and whites. But rather than stating a preference for an all-white neighborhood, they tend to argue for a neighborhood with a few blacks, knowing that such a small number will mean that the neighborhood is still essentially white (Jackman and Muha, 1984: 764).

Bourdieu (1977, 1984) also casts doubt on the benefit to society as a whole of college nonacademic learning (especially about high culture in the arts and humanities). This high culture, he argues, is not necessarily the most intrinsically valuable culture in society. Rather, it is regarded as the highest culture because it is the culture of the dominant class. And because of this connection to the dominant class, the teaching of this culture facilitates and legitimates the transmission of privilege from upper-class parents to upper-class children. Upper-class children pick up high culture more easily, because they have been exposed to it already in their homes. And because of this facility with high culture, upper-class children do better in school than less privileged students.[8]

Second, the nonfunctionalist scholars also question the assumption that the college effects observed are really due to things colleges actually do. Meyer (1972, 1977) argues that, despite the great range of colleges in our society, colleges have surprisingly similar effects on students' attitudes and behavior. He holds that this similarity of effect suggests that simply going to college rather than anything that colleges in particular do is what accounts for how college students change. He argues that our society has very firm ideas about what a college-educated person's attitudes and behavior should be. Hence, once people come to consider themselves college educated (which may happen the day they get their college acceptance or even earlier), they start to transform themselves into what is socially expected of a college-educated person. In short, "college" has an effect on student attitudes and behavior, but this "college" effect is not due to any particular institution but rather to the idea of college held by our society.[9]

SUMMARY

There is little disagreement that colleges do foster changes in students' nonacademic attitudes and behavior. But as we have seen, there is debate over how extensive these changes are, the means by which they occur, and what their social meaning is. The parties to this debate tend to take positions that parallel the different theories that one encounters in discussions of the "hidden curriculum" of elementary and secondary schooling.

NOTES

1. There was much less research on college's contributions to academic learning until recently, when state governments, the U.S. Department of Education, and higher educational associations began to call for greater accountability in higher education (Dougherty, 1988; Ewell, 1987).

2. Although this finding has been repeatedly corroborated, there is some question about its validity and meaning. See below for more.

3. See Habermas (1973: chap. 7).

4. During the 1970s, the labor market demand for college graduates weakened sharply, although they continued to enjoy a strong advantage over high school graduates. Between 1970 and 1978 only 46 percent of college graduates entered professional or technical jobs, while 73 percent of those graduating between 1962 and 1969 entered these jobs (Smith, 1986). See Hammack (1987–1988) for a discussion of the causes and consequences of this shift.

5. For example, student attitudes in recent decades have been powerfully shaped by the war in Vietnam (1964–1975), the Iran hostage crisis, the economic boom of the 1960s and late 1980s, and the repeated economic recessions of the 1970s and early 1980s (Hammack, 1987–1988).

6. For more on this point, see Feldman and Newcomb (1969: I, 52–53, 64–66) and Astin (1977: chap. 1).

7. See the introduction to Chapter 2 for a discussion of these nonfunctionalist perspectives, which draw on the work of Karl Marx, Max Weber, Pierre Bourdieu, and John Meyer.

8. See DiMaggio and Mohr (1985) for evidence on the influence on school attainment of success in acquiring high culture. For more on Bourdieu, see Swartz (1989).

9. Meyer's (1977) hypothesis of the source of college effects recalls Merton's (1968: 319–320) concept of "anticipatory socialization."

REFERENCES

Astin, Alexander. 1977. *Four Critical Years.* San Francisco: Jossey-Bass.

Bourdieu, Pierre. 1977. "Cultural Reproduction and Social Reproduction." In Jerome Karabel and A. H. Halsey (eds.), *Power and Ideology in Education,* pp. 487–511. New York: Oxford University Press.

———. 1984. *Distinction: A Social Critique of the Judgment of Taste.* Cambridge, MA: Harvard University Press.

Bowen, Howard. 1977. *Investment in Learning.* San Francisco: Jossey-Bass.

Bowles, Samuel and Herbert Gintis. 1976. *Schooling in Capitalist America.* New York: Basic Books.

Campbell, Angus, Philip Converse, Warren Miller, and Donald Stokes. 1960. *The American Voter.* New York: Wiley.

Collins, Randall. 1979. *The Credential Society.* New York: Academic Press.

DiMaggio, Paul, and John Mohr. 1985. "Cultural Capital, Educational Attainment, and Marital Selection." *American Journal of Sociology* 90 (May): 1231–1261.

Dougherty, Kevin. 1987. "The Effects of Community Colleges: Aid or Hindrance to Socioeconomic Attainment?" *Sociology of Education* 60 (April): 86–103. (Excerpted in Chapter 5 of this book.)

_____. 1988. "The Politics of Accountability in Higher Education." Unpublished paper, Department of Sociology, Manhattan College.

Ewell, Peter. 1987. "Assessment: Where Are We?" *Change* 19 (January-February): 23–28.

Feldman, Kenneth, and Theodore Newcomb. 1969. *The Impact of College on Students*. 2 vols. San Francisco: Jossey-Bass.

Funk, Richard B., and Fern K. Willits. 1987. "College Attendance and Attitude Change: A Panel Study, 1970–1981." *Sociology of Education* 60 (April): 224–231.

Habermas, Jürgen. 1973. *Theory and Practice*. Boston: Beacon Press.

Hammack, Floyd M. 1987–1988. "The Decline in Critical and Historical Sensibility Among College Students: What Has Changed?" *The Gallatin Review* 7 (winter): 27–33.

Hyman, Herbert H., Charles Wright, and John S. Reed. 1975. *The Enduring Effects of Education*. Chicago: University of Chicago Press.

Jackman, Mary R., and Michael J. Muha. 1984. "Education and Intergroup Attitudes." *American Sociological Review* 49 (December): 751–769.

McClelland, Katherine. Forthcoming. "Cumulative Disadvantage Among the Highly Ambitious: The Effects of Social Origins, Gender, Marriage, and College Quality on Early Educational Attainments and Occupational Expectations." *Sociology of Education*.

Merton, Robert K. 1968. *Social Theory and Social Structure*. Rev. ed. New York: Free Press.

Meyer, John W. 1972. "The Effects of the Institutionalization of Colleges in Society." In Kenneth A. Feldman (ed.), *College and Student: Selected Readings in the Social Psychology of Higher Education*, pp. 109–126. New York: Pergamon.

_____. 1977. "The Effects of Education as an Institution." *American Journal of Sociology* 83: 55–77.

Newcomb, Theodore. 1943. *Personality and Social Change*. New York: Holt.

Pace, C. Robert. 1974. *Evaluating Liberal Education*. Los Angeles, CA: University of California, Los Angeles.

Smith, Herbert. 1986. "Overeducation and Underemployment: An Agnostic Review." *Sociology of Education* 59 (April): 85–99.

Swartz, David. 1989. "Pierre Bourdieu." (See the selection in Chapter 2 of this book.)

Thurow, Lester. 1972. "Education and Economic Inequality." *The Public Interest* 28 (Summer): 66–81. Reprinted in Jerome Karabel and A. H. Halsey (eds.), *Power and Ideology in Education*, pp. 325–335. New York: Oxford University Press.

Trent, James W., and Leland L. Medsker. 1968. *Beyond College*. San Francisco: Jossey-Bass.

Weil, Frederick D. 1985. "The Variable Effects of Education on Liberal Attitudes." *American Sociological Review* 50 (August): 458–474.

8

Students with Special Needs

$\mathbf{W}$e turn now to the analysis of the provisions schools make for students held to have special needs. This introduction will review some of the legal and philosophical grounds on which special needs are defined and will discuss some of the issues surrounding these special categories. All of the categories discussed below represent examples of groups for whom school achievement is particularly problematic and who have successfully argued in courts that the existing educational arrangements have not benefited them. In this respect, they have frequently articulated an educational outlook that is Weberian or Marxist in our theoretical terms, and have illustrated the Weberian and resistance Marxist position that education is a domain of conflict in the society: a setting in which larger social conflicts play themselves out. At the same time, these arguments have rested on a functionalist premise that education *does* matter, and that it should be more equally distributed.[1]

The readings in this chapter are concerned with students for whom typical educational provisions are in some way inadequate. This grouping brings together many different kinds of students—the physically handicapped, those with learning disabilities, students with poor English language skills, females, and black students—for which courts or legislatures have held that a special effort is necessary in order to provide equal educational opportunity.[2] Students in these groups are held to be eligible for services not offered to advantaged students, such as smaller classes, classes taught in the native language and in English, and special care in admissions or recruitment.

This introduction will examine how and why these special obligations exist and what are their consequences for schools and for the eligible

---

[1]Refer back to Chapter 5, where education's role in the processes of social mobility is more fully developed.

[2]This is not to say, of course, that in all respects these groups are not vastly different in their history, their needs and in how schools respond to those needs. However, as the remainder of this introduction will show, there is value in illuminating their commonalities.

students. Central to our perspective is that these services must be seen in political as well as educational terms.

THE POLITICS OF SPECIAL NEEDS

It is important to first examine the ways groups are identified in schools as in need of special services to achieve equal education. Americans have histori- cally been leery of "special treatment." The political theorist Louis Hartz stated: "In the democratic mind, 'special privilege' is the worst of political crimes" (quoted in Dreeben, 1968: 112). Whatever privileges are offered, whatever exemptions from the norm of universalism are made available, each must be very carefully limited and defended. As the Dreeben selection in Chapter 7 notes, one of the strongest school norms is universalism. This norm refers to the belief that schools should evaluate all children and distribute all rewards according to the same criteria. While not infrequently violating it themselves, schools expect students to come to accept this norm of univer- salism as they progress through the early grades and learn what it is to be a student. And indeed students do come to demand that schools treat them as the same; for example, "teacher's pets" are ofttimes objects of derision and can undermine the teacher's authority in the eyes of the rest of the students. The norm of universalism, thus, can empower students in fighting unequal treatment.

The norm of universalism is reflected in the rights of citizenship guaran- teed by the Constitution, especially the Fourteenth Amendment, which prohibits governments from denying to any citizen "the equal protection of the laws." Joining this amendment in providing a legal bulwark against discrimination is the Civil Rights Act of 1964, and especially Title VI of that Act, which states: "No person in the United States shall, on the ground of race, color or national origin, be excluded from participating in, be denied the benefits of, or be subject to discrimination under any program or activity receiving Federal financial assistance" (42 United States Code & 2000d (1970)). As these provisions have come to be applied by the courts, public agencies are prohibited from unequally providing public services to those who qualify for them. However, the fact that law is still being created in this area provides ample evidence that discrimination persists.

The courts have employed the notion of "suspect categories" (race, color, national origins) in deliberations of discrimination cases. Any law, public agency, or publicly supported activity must not act on the basis of a suspect category unless it can be demonstrated that an overriding public benefit is served by the discrimination. "When the government classifies persons according to 'suspect' criteria or invades 'fundamental' interests, its actions are 'strictly scrutinized' and such action can survive only if it is the sole practicable means to a compelling state interest" (Sexton, 1979: 315). A critical aspect of a suspect category is that it refers to an ascribed characteristic, an attribute over which the individual members of the group are held to have no control. This helps to explain why other categories that we know are the basis of differential treatment, such as social class, are not acknowledged by the courts or in legislation. Class discrimination is not intrinsically suspect in court cases because one's class is attributed to behavior, such as educational achievement, that is seen as a matter of individual responsibility.[3]

The equal protection clause of the Fourteenth Amendment and the Civil Rights Act of 1964 have become the primary vehicles for the protection and extension of equal access to education. Since racial segregation of schooling was held unconstitutional by the *Brown v. Board of Education of Topeka, Kansas* (1954) decision, many different groups have raised the issue of discrimination in court. The equal protection argument has been used by groups who feel that they have been either denied access to schooling or discriminated against in programs within schools.

An important element of these cases has been the definition of what constitutes equality of treatment. In *Plessy v. Ferguson* (1896), the Supreme Court held that an equal expenditure on segregated schools was sufficient to meet the expectations of the law. In the 1954 *Brown* decision, however, the Court held that equal treatment required more than equal facilities that happened to be separate: Any segregation based on race alone was held to be inherently illegal and in violation of the Fourteenth Amendment. The 1964 Civil Rights Act went further to assert that race, color, sex, and national origin could not be used as legitimate categories for discrimination in hiring, public accommodations, and so on. In the 1970s, the Supreme Court held that discrimination in participation in or deriving benefits from educational programs was illegal. For example, in the important bilingual education case, *Lau v. Nichols,* the Court ruled: "It seems obvious that the Chinese-speaking minority receives fewer benefits than the English-speaking majority from respondents' school system which denies them a meaningful opportunity to participate in the educational program—all earmarks of discrimination banned by the regulations" (414 U.S. at 568: quoted in Teitelbaum and Hiller, 1977: 143).

As the *Lau* case indicates, blacks have not been the only ones to fight for greater access to schooling under the equal protection clause of the Constitution. For example, physically and psychologically disabled students also benefited from the use of the equal protection guarantee to open access to education, as in the Supreme Court's decisions in *Pennsylvania Association for Retarded Children v. Commonwealth of Pennsylvania* (1972) and *Mills v. Board of Education of District of Columbia* (1972). Until these cases had been successfully argued in court, many school districts refused to provide an education for severely retarded, wheelchair-bound or blind or other handicapped students. The argument against discrimination hostile to these students was that they were not receiving equal protection or equal benefit from the law establishing the schools. Their disability was held to be an invalid reason for school to deny them educational services.

---

[3]However, Chpaters 5 and 6 contain selections that show that much of the class destination of adults is also ascribed. But given the pervasive individualism of our society, there is great reluctance to admit this.

In addition, non-English-speaking students provide an example of the equal protection argument against discrimination *within* schools. Advocates of children who speak a language other than English have argued that the lack of bilingual and English-as-a-second-language classes in schools has effectively discriminated against students whose first language is not English. Advocates for these students argue that they are hindered in competition for the rewards of schooling. Thus, to ensure equality of opportunity to all students, they assert that it is necessary to provide bilingual instructional services to non–English speakers, services not otherwise available to students whose first language is English. The article by Ovando in this chapter provides an example of this argument.

Finally, women too have fought under the banner of equal protection. They have contested the lesser financial support many schools provide the female athletic programs in comparison to that provided the programs for males. In addition, females have not benefited from vocational education programs in the same measure as males have. Cases concerning both of these issues have been successfully argued in court, and the Educational Amendments of 1972 (Title 9) extended to women the protections of equal educational access.

The struggle over access to education has been full of turmoil—educational, political, and religious. Constitutional guarantees to due process and equal protection must be exercised. Although our law provides a variety of rights to every citizen, enforcement of those rights needs vigilance. Especially in the case of long-standing practices—such as racial segregation of schools, monolingualism, sex discrimination, and limited access to the handicapped—the extension of services to new groups has always been resisted by other groups who often see the new arrangements as jeopardizing their education. Because court cases are very expensive, may take years to resolve, and risk public scrutiny of those who bring the suit, individual members of groups with grievances often band together to pursue justice.

It has been estimated that in the years between 1974 and 1984, over 1300 cases decided in federal court affected the public schools (Jarvis, 1984; cited in Stevens and Wood, 1987: 22) This vast number of court cases emphasizes the importance education has attained in our national life and the role litigation has come to play in the struggle for equal protection. As Chapter 9 will show, education has become increasingly important in determining occupational opportunities. Hence, if educational opportunities are not equitably distributed, neither can occupational opportunities.

The number of federal court cases also illustrates how conflictual our public life is today. People and groups have become alert to their rights and are eager to defend them. However, all individuals or groups by no means equally possess the ability to identify and defend their interests and rights. What is necessary is that individuals sharing a common interest or circumstance in schools (or other public institutions) come to recognize their commonality and act on it. Action of this sort is often called collective in that it is group-based, involving the defense of group-based interests. Such action requires organization to bring together disparate individuals into a unity with a single voice. Through organization, a group can accumulate and effectively deploy its resources, financial and human.[4] Virtually all examples of groups whose special needs have become the focus of educators have mobilized themselves for collective action of the kind just described. Their success has resulted in court decisions in their favor and in legislation acknowledging their special circumstances. Without such efforts, their needs might well have not been met.

Court decisions and legislative remedies usually call for stopping the practices held illegal and redressing the negative consequences of the practices. In the case of racial segregation of schools, courts ordered the integration of racially separate schools. Courts also have ordered busing, magnet schools, and voluntary transfer plans among paired or grouped schools. To help non–English speakers, bilingual education, transitional English, and instruction in their native languages have been ordered or recommended. In the case of discrimination against females, the remedies have included encouragement of nontraditional gender enrollment and more equal expenditures for athletics. For handicapped students, special education has been ordered, including separate classes taught by teachers specializing in the education of those with physical and learning difficulties. However, in some of the most important of these cases involving handicapped students, the fact of separate facilities and schooling has been the issue, and main-streaming has been ordered.

In some of these cases, affirmative action plans have been ordered. These plans usually concern admission or eligibility on different criteria for members of groups that have historically been denied access to, or have been unable to qualify for, educational services and benefits available to others. Search committees, today, are often required to make very explicit their criteria and the job requirements, advertise in periodicals aimed at minority populations, and *actively* seek qualified candidates from all backgrounds. However, such plans have been the subject of litigation and political backlash by those claiming they sanction reverse discrimination.[5] This takes us to our next topic.

THE CONSEQUENCES OF SPECIAL NEEDS PROGRAMS

The consequences of special needs programs are as important as their origins. The key question is whether the reforms do, indeed, succeed in more

---

[4]For an introduction to the collective mobilization literature, see Burstein (1985), Gamson (1975), Tilly (1978), and Zald and McCarthy (1987).

[5]The best-known case of this sort is *Bakke* (1978). Alan Bakke, who is white, sued the University of California at Davis when denied admission to their school of medicine while minority students with lower scores on admissions tests and lower grades were accepted. He was admitted on appeal, and has since become a physician. However, the legality of special admissions categories was upheld, providing they conform to very specific guidelines. See the thorough discussion of this case in Sexton (1979).

equitably distributing the benefits of education. An important aspect of this question concerns whether unanticipated consequences, which always occur during social change, undermine the reforms gained.

For example, some school desegregation plans have resulted in a high level of racial tension and white flight, leaving few white students to integrate with black students (Hochschild, 1984). In the context of sex desegregation, many programs have found it especially hard to encourage male students to enroll in vocational programs preparing for occupations seen as female (for example, cosmetology), while females have shown great reluctance to enroll in some male-dominated fields, such as automotive repair. Programs encouraging atypical sex enrollments may heighten students' awareness of the sex link to occupations and make such enrollments less likely.[6]

Special programs that segregate and label some students as exceptional, as bilingual and special education programs necessarily do, may exacerbate the conditions such remedies are intended to redress. Using the interaction perspective described in Chapter 2 and closely inspecting the labeling of students in ways that are obvious to other students, we can see that such programs may occasion serious problems. They may negatively stigmatize those students and lead schools and teachers to reduce their expectations for student achievement.[7] At the same time, there is no question that each of these groups of students, and perhaps others, have had and continue to have legitimate complaints about the education they receive. Legal and legislative pressures have forced schools to attend to needs of students who were not otherwise being well served and have been the only way many of these students have received any education at all. Perry Zirkel, a professor of law and education, in reviewing recent litigation concerning special education, asks a telling question: "The educational and legal maelstroms of desegregation and bilingual education have not ended, and now the push-pull forces of special education are starting the same sort of swirl. With all the solutions to choose from for these sink-or-swim problems, why do there continue to be so many drownings in the mainstream?" (1989, 411)

THE ARTICLES

The articles included in this section all address different facets of the issues raised in this introduction. Together, they provide a good introduction to the benefits and the perils of becoming the object of "special" attention.

Basing his remarks on an extensive research project, Hawley reviews the recent history of school desegregation efforts, including problems encoun-

---

[6]For good examples of the research and policy literature on this topic, see Herzog (1982) and Friedman and Huling (1982).

[7]See Gartner and Lipsky (1987) for a detailed critical review of the implementation of PL 94-142, the Education of All Handicapped Act. The article by Christensen, Gerber, and Everhart in this chapter is also illustrative of these concerns. The discussion on tracking in the introduction to Chapter 6 offers further insight into how teacher expectations are shaped by labels.

tered in the implementation phase of integration plans. While there have been disappointments and unintended consequences, such as white flight from desegregated schools, he argues that much of the current cynicism surrounding desegregation is unfounded. When desegregation plans are designed to take into account the knowledge gained from the analysis of prior plans, many of the difficulties that have plagued desegregation can be reduced.

Stockard provides a thorough review of the research evidence on discrimination against females in schools. She examines sex differences in depiction in the curriculum, treatment by teachers, and rates of educational success. Overall, she contends that schools seem to favor females as often as they do not. Hence, Stockard strongly argues that our attention should be more closely focused on the labor market than on education. She concludes that "the inequalities women face in the occupational world cannot be traced, except in a most limited and tenuous manner, to educational achievements or experiences." An implication of her analysis is that attention devoted to schooling draws attention away from the importance of discrimination in the labor market. Several aspects of her analysis of the occupational world anticipate the readings in Chapter 9, where the relations between education and the labor market are more fully explored.

The article by Ovando discusses recent research and controversy surrounding bilingual education. While acknowledging the lack of solid research supporting the contention that limited-English-speaking (LEP) students do better in bilingual classrooms and English-as-a-second-language (ESL) classes, he nevertheless makes a strong case for the special instructional needs of these students. Definitive research is not available to support most instructional programs, yet the evidence is clear that language problems are at the core of many students' difficulties in school. But bilingual education involves more than instruction. It also includes an acknowledgment of students' culture and their different experiences. Ovando provides a good introduction to those issues as well.[8]

The category of special education has not received extensive attention from social scientists outside of the field of educational psychology. Yet, with about 10 to 12 percent of *all* students now being classified as in need of special educational services (Gartner and Lipsky, 1987: 371), analysis of this group is essential and the subject of a growing literature.[9] Key problems in special education concern how students in need of special education are identified, how their needs are assessed, and how special educational services are delivered to them.

The article by Christensen and her colleagues is especially concerned with a fairly new subcategory of special education, learning disability.[10] They raise

---

[8]The recent book by Hakuta (1986) provides an excellent review of all of the relevant literature.

[9]To get an idea of the magnitudes involved here, New York City has well over 100,000 special education students.

[10]Refer back to our earlier comments in this introduction about the consequences of special education categories. Also see Carrier (1983, 1986), Gartner and Lipsky (1987), and Milofsky

serious questions about its validity and explore reasons for its recent wide use. They point to the ironic possibility that by emphasizing the psychological and neurological basis of students' problems—which may or may not be responsible for the difficulties these students have in school—educators divert attention from the more important social and educational issues that may be responsible for students' problems. Viewing these problems as having a psychological or medical origin helps to explain—accurately or not—students' failure, but does not lead to educational success. Moreover, the emphasis on the problems of students takes attention away from the problems of schools themselves.

CONCLUSIONS

As these selections demonstrate, we have accomplished much in acknowledging the special needs of students. Education today is far more accessible and less overtly discriminatory than in the days before *Brown*. Nevertheless, we have a long way to go in providing all students with an education that is truly equal and avoids unintended negative consequences that may be worse than the problems we have set out to eliminate.

REFERENCES

Arias, M. Beatriz (ed.). 1986. "The Education of Hispanic Americans: A Challenge for the Future." *American Journal of Education* 95 (November): whole issue.

Burstein, Paul. 1985. *Discrimination, Jobs and Politics: The Struggle for Equal Employment Opportunity in the United States Since the New Deal.* Chicago: University of Chicago Press.

Carrier, James G. 1983. "Masking the Social in Educational Knowledge: The Case of Learning Disability Theory." *American Journal of Sociology* 88 (March): 948–974.

_____. 1986. "Sociology and Special Education: Differentiation and Allocation in Mass Education." *American Journal of Education* 94 (May): 281–312.

Coles, Gerald. 1987. *The Learning Mystique: A Critical Look at "Learning Disabilities".* New York: Pantheon Books.

Dreeben, Robert. 1968. *On What Is Learned in School.* Boston: Addison-Wesley. (See the excerpt in Chapter 7.)

Elliott, R. 1987. *Litigating Intelligence: IQ Tests, Special Education and Social Science in the Courtroom.* Dover, MA: Auburn.

Friedman, Ruth, and Tracy Huling. 1982. *Their Proper Place: A Report on Sex Discrimination in New York City's Vocational High Schools.* New York: Center for Public Advocacy Research, Inc.

Gamson, William A. 1975. *The Strategy of Social Protest.* Homewood, IL: Dorsey.

(1974) for discussions of the evolution of this category, along with more general discussions of special education.

Gartner, Alan, and Dorothy Kerzner Lipsky. 1987. "Beyond Special Education: Toward a Quality System for All Students." *Harvard Educational Review* 57 (November): 367–395.

Hakuta, Kenji. 1986. *Mirror of Language: The Debate on Bilingualism.* New York: Basic Books.

Herzog, A. Regula. 1982. "High School Seniors' Occupational Plans and Values: Trends in Sex Differences, 1976 Through 1980." *Sociology of Education* 55 (January): 1–13.

Hochschild, Jennifer L. 1984. *The New American Dilemma: Liberal Democracy and School Desegregation.* New Haven, CT: Yale University Press.

Jarvis, Melvin E. 1984. "Current Trends in Federal Court Intervention in Public Education." Paper presented at the annual meeting of the American Educational Research Association, New Orleans.

Kirp, David L. 1977. "Law, Politics, and Equal Educational Opportunity: The Limits of Judicial Involvement." *Harvard Educational Review* 47 (May): 117–137.

Milofsky, Carl. 1974. "Why Special Education Isn't Special." *Harvard Educational Review* 44 (November): 437–458.

_____. 1986. "Is the Growth of Special Education Evolutionary or Cyclic? A Response to Carrier." *American Journal of Education* 94 (May): 313–321.

O'Neil, John. 1988. "How 'Special' Should the Special Education Curriculum Be?" *Curriculum Update* (September): Alexandria, VA: Association for Supervision and Curriculum Development.

Rist, Ray C., and Ronald J. Anson (eds.). 1977. *Education, Social Science, and the Judicial Process.* New York: Teachers College Press.

Sexton, John. 1979. "Minority-Admissions Programs After Bakke." *Harvard Educational Review* 49 (August): 313–339.

Stevens, Edward, and George H. Wood. 1987. *Justice, Ideology, and Education.* New York: Random House.

Teitelbaum, Herbert, and Richard J. Hiller. 1977. "Bilingual Education: The Legal Mandate." *Harvard Educational Review* 47 (May): 138–170.

Tilly, Charles. 1978. *From Mobilization to Revolution.* Reading, MA: Addison-Wesley.

Zald, Meyer N., and John D. McCarthy. 1987. *Social Movements in an Organizational Society.* New Brunswick, NJ: Transaction Books.

Zirkel, Perry A. 1989. "Sink or Swim in the Mainstream." *Phi Delta Kappan* 70 (January): 411–412.

Achieving Quality Integrated Education—With or Without Federal Help

WILLIS D. HAWLEY

Vanderbilt University

Is school desegration a policy whose time has come and gone? Probably not. Hundreds of school systems, including some of the largest in the U.S., are involved in the desegregation of racial and ethnic groups. This does not seem likely to change dramatically. Although the flow of new cases into the courts has slowed substantially, courts continue to find that districts must desegregate, and most efforts to achieve relief from the jurisdiction of the courts are unsuccessful.

But two important developments in the last two years suggest that desegregation will not be the same issue in the years to come. First, many education policy makers seem to have decided that high-quality education rather than equal educational opportunity should be the primary goal of public education. (I will resist the temptation to argue that other concerns have *always* been more important than equal educational opportunity.) Clearly, the future acceptance of desegregation by both whites and minorities will depend, much more than it has in the past, on the belief that excellence and equity are mutually reinforcing, rather than competing, goals. Second, the Reagan Administration has reduced both the federal pressure to desegregate and the federal support for desegregation efforts. The Administration opposes mandatory desegregation (i.e., busing) and has essentially repealed the Emergency School Aid Act (ESAA), the primary mechanism through which the federal government encouraged voluntary desegregation. ESAA funds also increased the probabilities that academic achievement would be enhanced when schools desegregated.[1]

Given these changes in attitudes and in federal policies, how can desegregation result in quality integrated education and what can the federal government do to promote this outcome? In trying to answer these questions, I will identify several strategies that school systems can use to increase the benefits of desegregation for students. These strategies do not depend on federal support for their efficacy. Then I will explore some low-cost, nonintrusive actions that the federal government can take to improve the quality of education in districts in the process of desegregation.

OVERVIEW

Students in desegregated school systems usually exhibit the full range of learning capabilities. Thus effective educational strategies for students in desegregated schools should be a combination of the strategies that are most effective for children who are handicapped, have limited or no English-speaking ability, require compensatory education, are academically gifted, and have no special needs. In other words, most strategies work for different types of children whether their schools are desegregated or not.

In some ways, of course, desegregation makes it more difficult to provide effective education. But before I discuss these problems and their possible solutions, let me call attention to the opportunities that desegregation can create to enhance the education of students. Desegregation can create possibilities for (and sometimes enforce) changes in curricula, classroom structures, instructional practices, and the behavior of teachers and administrators. Moreover, racially integrated schools have one certain advantage over racially isolated schools: They offer opportunities to learn from and about people of different races. In most cases, students in desegregated schools will also have more interaction with persons of different social backgrounds than will students in school systems that have not been desegregated.

The evidence on the overall effects of desegregation shows that in desegregated schools the educational achievement of minorities improves and the achievement of whites is not undermined.[2] Moreover, race relations usually improve where schools take appropriate action to achieve this end.[3] There is also evidence that desegregation in schools improves students' prospects for future employment and increases their chances of attending a desegregated college.[4] These contributions of desegregation to the education of young people are surprising, not only because they fly in the face of popular notions but also because they have been achieved amid considerable opposition, half-hearted implementation, and a lack of shared knowledge about the process. What follows is *not* a full prescription for effective education. I intend to suggest some practices that appear to be important in desegregated schools *in addition* to those that should provide all children with a high-quality education.

People differ on their definition of "quality education." For purposes here, I define quality or effectiveness in terms of 1) academic achievement in mathematics and language arts and 2) tolerance and understanding of people of different races and social backgrounds.

My conclusions are based primarily on the findings of a recent study that reviewed and synthesized 1) the conclusions of about 1,200 books, articles, papers, reports, and commentaries on the effects of desegregation;[5] 2) surveys of educators;[6] and 3) the results of interviews with 135 local and national desegregation experts.[7] Evidence from more recent research is also discussed.

CHANGES AFTER DESEGREGATION

When school systems desegregate, the relationship of the community to its schools changes. Changes also occur in the context and circumstances in which instruction takes place and educational programs are presented. These alterations in the "conditions of schooling" require special attention if schools are to reap the benefits of otherwise productive educational practices and if the advantages of desegregation are to outweigh its costs. Most of the specific changes in the conditions of schooling that result from desegregation can be grouped into four general categories.

- *Diversity.* Because race is associated with socioeconomic status, interracial schools and classrooms tend to be more heterogeneous academically than their racially segregated counterparts. Traditional instructional strategies are poorly suited to settings in which students have so broad a range of educational needs.[8]

- *Potential conflict.* The possibility of interracial conflict in desegregated schools worries many parents.[9] Moreover, the key challenge of desegregation is to increase student interaction across racial lines so as to enhance race relations in schools and in the larger society.[10]

- *Discontinuity.* Both students and parents feel this change. Parents may feel that desegregated schools are not accessible, because they are far away and unfamiliar. Students may find themselves in environments in which the expectations they experience at home and in their neighborhoods are very different from those they experience in school.[11]

- *Change.* In desegregated schools, teachers, administrators, and students experience substantial change that simultaneously affects the social environment, the nature of instruction and curricula, and personal beliefs. For example, desegregation often requires teachers to take part in a broader range of educational programs, some of which may involve externally imposed requirements and paperwork. Such multidimensional change can greatly increase the workload and sometimes lead to a loss of self-confidence.

Diversity, conflict, discontinuity, and change characterize many schools. But schools that are desegregated by explicit social policy are more likely than others to face these problems and to be forced to resolve them all at once.

These challenges are also opportunities through which more effective education can be achieved. Some school systems have seized these opportunities; others have not. Those that have not seized these opportunities have had their effectiveness reduced and their progress impeded; those that have seized them have often become more effective than they were before desegregation.

STRATEGIES OF RESPONSE

The challenges posed by the diversity, conflict, discontinuity, and change that often characterize a desegregated school can be met by one or more of a dozen practices.

1. *Desegregate children as early as possible.* Differences in the achievement of students of different races are narrower in early grades, and racial prejudices are not yet ingrained. Thus possibilities for positive, equal interaction among races are greatest at early ages. Such interaction is critical to the mitigation of racial prejudice.[12] In addition, it appears that the positive effects of desegregation on the academic achievement of minorities are greatest in the early grades.[13]

2. *Employ instructional strategies that retain heterogeneous classes and work groups.* Such practices avoid resegregation and encourage teachers to retain high expectations for students of all groups. They also deemphasize competition and encourage student interaction. Examples of such practices are cooperative team learning,[14] the multi-ability classroom,[15] and peer tutoring.[16] Evidence of the effectiveness of such strategies on enhancing achievement and improving race relations is strong.[17] Similarly, there is growing evidence that pull-out strategies are ineffective.[18]

3. *Avoid tracking and other rigid forms of ability grouping.* Tracking usually leads to resegregation within schools and the denial of educational opportunity to low achievers. The increased diversity of students and programs in desegregated schools often leads to a proliferation of pull-out programs and special education assignments. Such assignments may have the effect of tracking and resegregation.[19] Without expertise in classroom management and knowledge of instructional strategies most appropriate for heteogeneous classes, most teachers will be frustrated by extreme student diversity, and the learning needs of students will not be met.[20] Clearly, some students will require special classes if their needs are to be met. But the possible misuse of special programs should be monitored closely.

4. *Retain a critical mass of the minority students in each school and classroom.* When students are in too small a minority, they may be excluded by the majority or withdraw of their own accord. A critical mass of 15% to 20% of students of a given race may help to avoid this problem in

desegregated schools.[21] However, in multiracial or multiethnic situations, intergroup conflict tends to be highest when the two groups are about equal in size. Some evidence also suggests that this potential for conflict may be greatest when the students involved are of low socioeconomic status.[22]

5. *Employ minority teachers and counselors.* Minority teachers may act as models for minority children. Some weak but positive evidence exists that minority students do better when they have minority teachers.[23] There is also evidence that minority teachers are less likely to misassign and stereotype students and that they are more likely to relate effectively to minority parents.[24]

6. *Develop a comprehensive approach to human relations that involves substantial interracial contact.* Human relations should be an integral part of the curriculum both in its substance and in the way material is taught. Human relations programs that involve parents are more effective than those that do not,[25] and the most effective human relations programs are those that embody substantial interracial contact.[26] A multiethnic curriculum provides substantive material that may be more meaningful to minority students, and it can provide opportunities for discussing issues that are important to the students' relations with one another. But curricular change alone is not likely to be enough to improve human relations; what teachers do with that curriculum makes all the difference.[27]

7. *Develop interracial extracurricular activities.* Extracurricular activities can offer a chance for success to students whose academic achievement affords them little status within the school. Moreover, extracurricular activities can provide opportunities for interracial contact in cooperative, nonthreatening situations that often require teamwork.[28]

8. *Develop a rigorous but fair disciplinary program.* Developing a well-defined and widely understood code of student conduct and enforcing that code in consistent, firm, and equitable ways are essential elements of an effectively desegregated school. Such a program can help dispel parental anxiety,[29] minimize conflict,[30] and maximize learning.[31]

9. *Create smaller and more supportive learning environments.* Fostering continuity of instruction that avoids anonymity among students and creating a feeling of community that derives from shared values are effective ways to increase order and improve teachers' responses to student needs. Smaller schools and classrooms are not essential to this strategy, but they make it easier to employ flexible instructional strategies and to create manageable environments.[32]

10. *Involve parents directly in the education of their children.* In order to reduce the discontinuity between home and school environments, schools should engage parents directly in the education of their children. Studies on the importance of parental involvement in desegregated schools generally support this conclusion.[33]

11. *Once the desegregation plan is in effect, make an effort to maintain some stability in the educational experiences of the child.* Such stability helps teachers focus on the educational needs of students, reduces parental anxiety, and gives students a greater sense of security.[34]

12. *Develop a comprehensive program for inservice training.* Staff training is always important, but it becomes even more important when large changes have taken place.[35]

Each of these several strategies responds to at least one of the four conditions of desegregated schooling. Some are positive responses to one or more of the conditions, but they tend to exacerbate one of the others. For example, avoiding tracking and rigid approaches to ability grouping is an appropriate way to respond to student diversity, but it makes it harder for teachers to manage their classrooms.

IMPLICATIONS FOR FEDERAL POLICY

With the demise of the Emergency School Aid Act, the federal government cannot exert the influence it once could on the educational effectiveness of desegregated schools. Through its enforcement powers, the Office for Civil Rights can insist that racial isolation in school systems that have engaged in *intentional* segregation be reduced. Thus it can affect the conditions under which desegregated schools operate. Moreover, housing and employment polices and actions of the Justice Department can affect desegregated schools, but these federal actions do not usually affect the learning process. Assuming that the federal role will no longer involve substantial expenditures or assertive action to require desegregation, let me suggest some general ways that the federal government could enhance the potential educational and social benefits of desegregation for elementary and secondary school students.

Collection and Dissemination of Information

A fair amount is known about how desegregated schools can become more effective, and many school systems have already implemented successful practices. This information needs to be collected, synthesized, and disseminated. Some steps in systematically collecting information have been taken, but much more needs to be done. The dissemination of research findings has not even reached the federally funded Desegregation Assistance Centers.[36] Among the more than 240 "Ideas That Work" that are publicized by the National Diffusion Network, only *one* deals directly with school desegregation. The National Institute of Education and various federal programs that provide technical assistance and that support professional development could become major vehicles for disseminating information about school desegregation.

Technical Assistance and Professional Development

The largest single federal resource that could influence the instruction students receive in desegregated schools is the set of technical assistance and professional development programs authorized by Title IV of the Civil Rights Act. We now know a good deal more about what works in desegregated schools than we did just a few years ago. But the current "system" that provides assistance is decentralized and uneven in quality. Refocusing these programs—the Desegregation Assistance Centers, the training institutes, state education agencies, and direct discretionary grants to school systems—on improving the education children receive in desegregated schools could make a substantial difference.

Research and Development

The federal effort in research and development (especially in the area of desegregation) has been less effective than it might be. Two of the most significant reasons for this failure are the shotgun approach to research funding and the absence of a research and development *system.* . . .

Parental Involvement

Direct involvement of parents in the education of their children seems to be of significant educational benefit. Moreover, parents may increase the sensitivity of educators to discriminatory practices.[37] Most school systems, however, have been ambivalent or even hostile to meaningful parental involvement, though some of the reluctance of educators may be due to a lack of knowledge about ways that parents can be constructively involved.

Federal policies should encourage or require, depending on the program, that districts receiving federal funds actively involve parents. There is no one best way to involve parents, but parent advisory councils at the district level are *not* one of the effective alternatives. Districts should be allowed to construct their own plans to involve parents, and they should be required to make their plans public before they implement them. But parents need to be involved more directly than district-level councils permit. Various technical assistance agencies should know the full range of alternative strategies for involving parents, and the National Institute of Education could publish a handbook on the subject.

Gertrude Stein might have said that a good school is a good school is a good school. But desegregated schools face special challenges in their quest for excellence. With or without federal assistance, desegregated schools can do a great deal to meet those challenges. However, the ability of local school systems to provide high-quality integrated education would surely be enhanced by the relatively inexpensive and non-intrusive federal actions suggested above.

There is no necessary trade-off between equity and high quality. Desegregation creates conditions that require changes in schools, in instruction, and in professional behavior. But the major problems posed by desegregation are not educational; they are political. Most objections that focus on the negative effects of desegregation on students do not hold water. Evidence from research and experience indicates that the difficulties can be overcome and that education in many desegregated districts has improved—especially for minority students.

But the public does not believe the best evidence we have. The reasons for this disbelief raise serious doubt about the possibility of providing high-quality education for all children. Desegregation is more than a challenge to the capacity of schools to provide high-quality education. It is a test of our national commitment to social mobility and to racial equality. So far, we have been doing less well on this test than our schoolchildren have a right to expect. The federal government could help us pass the test by accurately representing the story of the nation's progress to its people.

NOTES

1. John E. Coulson and Anne H. MacQueen, *Emergency School Aid Act (ESAA) Evaluation: Overview of Findings from Supplemental Analyses* (Santa Monica, Calif.: System Development Corp., 1978).

2. Robert L. Crain and Rita E. Mahard, "Some Policy Implications of the Desegration/Minority Achievement Literature," in Willis D. Hawley, ed., *Assessment of Current Knowledge About the Effectiveness of School Desegregation Strategies, Vol. V* (Nashville, Tenn.: Vanderbilt University, Institute for Public Policy Studies, Center for Education and Human Development Policy, April 1981).

3. Janet W. Schofield, "Desegregation School Practices and Student Race Relations Outcomes," in Hawley, ed., *Assessment of Current Knowledge . . . Vol. V;* and John B. McConahay, "Reducing Racial Prejudice in Desegregated Schools," in Willis D. Hawley, ed., *Effective School Desegregation: Equity, Quality, and Feasibility* (Beverly Hills, Calif.: Sage, 1981).

4. James M. McPartland and Jomills H. Braddock, "Going to College and Getting a Good Job," in Hawley, ed., *Effective School Desegregation. . . .*

5. Willis D. Hawley et al., *Strategies for Effective Desegregation: Lessons from Research* (Lexington, Mass.: Lexington Books, D.C. Health, 1982).

6. William T. Trent, "Expert Opinion on School Desegregation: Findings from the Interviews," in Hawley, ed., *Assessment of Current Knowledge . . . Vol. V.*

7. Ibid.

8. Valerie Cook, Janet Eyler, and Leslie Ward, *Effective Strategies for Avoiding Within-School Resegregation* (Nashville, Tenn.: Vanderbilt University, Institute for Public Policy Studies, Education Policy Development Center for Desegregation, December 1981).

9. John B. McConahay and Willis D. Hawley, *Reactions to Busing in Louisville: Summary of Adult Opinions in 1976 and 1977* (Durham, N.C.: Duke University, Institute of Policy Sciences and Public Affairs, 1978).

10. McConahay, "Reducing Racial Prejudice. . . ."

11. William J. Tikunoff and José A. Vasquez-Faria, *Effective Instruction for Bilingual Schooling* (San Francisco: Far West Regional Laboratory for Educational Research and Development, 1982), pp. 22–24.

12. Schofield, "Desegregation School Practices. . . ."

13. Crain and Mahard, "Some Policy Implications. . . ."

14. Robert E. Slavin, "Cooperative Learning and Desegregation," in Hawley, ed., *Effective School Desegregation. . . .*

15. Elizabeth G. Cohen, "A Multi-Ability Approach to the Integrated Classroom," paper presented at the annual meeting of the American Psychological Association, Montreal, 1980.

16. Hawley, et al., *Strategies for Effective Desegregation. . . .*

17. Robert Slavin, "Cooperative Learning in Teams: State of the Art," *Educational Psychologist,* vol. 15, 1980, pp. 93–111; and Shlomo Sharan, "Cooperative Learning in Small Groups; Research Methods and Effects on Achievement, Attitudes, and Ethnic Relations," *Review of Educational Research,* vol. 50, 1980, pp. 241–72.

18. H. Carl Haywood, "Compensatory Education," paper prepared for the National Institute of Education, Vanderbilt University, Peabody College for Teachers, January 1982; and Cook, Eyler, and Ward, *Effective Strategies for Avoiding. . . .*

19. Cook, Eyler, and Ward, *Effective Strategies for Avoiding. . .* ; *Roger Mills and Miriam M. Bryan, Testing . . . Grouping: The New Segregation in Southern Schools* (Atlanta: Southern Regional Council, 1976); and Joyce Epstein, "After the Bus Arrives: Resegregation in Desegregated Schools," paper presented at the annual meeting of the American Educational Research Association, Boston, 1980.

20. Carolyn M. Everston, Julie P. Sanford, and Edmund T. Emmer, "Effects of Class Heterogeneity in Junior High School," *American Educational Research Journal*, vol. 18, 1981, pp. 219–32.

21. Hawley et al., *Strategies for Effective Desegregation. . . .*

22. Willis D. Hawley, "Effective Educational Strategies for Desegregated Schools," *Peabody Journal of Education*, July 1982, pp. 209–33.

23. Gary Bridge, Charles Judd, and Peter Moock, *The Determinants of Educational Outcomes: The Effects of Families, Peers, Teachers, and Schools* (New York: Teachers College Press, 1979).

24. Epstein, "After the Bus Arrives. . . ."

25. System Development Corporation, *Human Relations Study: Investigations of Effective Human Relations Strategies, Vol. 2* (Santa Monica, Calif.: System Development Corp., June 1980).

26. Schofield, "Desegregation School Practices. . . ."

27. Robert E. Slavin and Nancy Madden, "School Practices That Improve Race Relations," *American Educational Research Journal*, vol. 16, 1979, pp. 169–80.

28. Cook, Eyler, and Ward, *Effective Strategies for Avoiding. . . .*

29. Peter O. Peretti, "Effects of Teachers' Attitudes on Discipline Problems in Schools Recently Desegregated," *Education*, vol. 97, 1976, pp. 136–40.

30. Gary D. Gottfredson and Denise C. Daiger, *Disruption in 600 Schools* (Baltimore: Johns Hopkins University, Center for the Social Organization of Schools, Technical Report No. 289, 1979).

31. Stewart C. Purkey and Marshall S. Smith, "Effective Schools—A Review," *Elementary School Journal*, in press.

32. Hawley, "Effective Educational Strategies. . . ."

33. Coulson and MacQueen, *Emergency School Aid Act (ESAA) Evaluation. . .* ; and Jean B. Wellisch et al., *An In-Depth Study of Emergency School Aid Act (ESAA) Schools: 1974–1975* (Santa Monica, Calif.: System Development Corp., July 1976).

34. Purkey and Smith, "Effective Schools—A Review. . . ."

35. Willaim J. Genova and Herbert J. Walberg, *A Practitioner's Guide for Achieving Student Integration in City High Schools* (Washington, D.C.: National Institute of Education, November 1980); and Mark A. Smylie and Willis D. Hawley, *Increasing the Effectiveness of Inservice Training for Desegregation: A Synthesis of Current Research* (Washington, D.C.: National Education Association, 1982).

36. Willis D. Hawley and Barry Schapira, *The Title IV Race Desegregation Technical Assistance Centers: Some Directions for Change* (Nashville, Tenn.: Vanderbilt University, Institute for Public Policy Studies. Center for Education and Human Development Policy, December 1981).

37. Jennifer Hochschild and Valerie Hadrick, *The Character and Effectiveness of Citizen Monitoring Groups in Implementing Civil Rights in Public Schools* (Washington, D.C.: National Institute of Education and the Office for Civil Rights, 1980).

Bilingual/Bicultural Education: Its Legacy And Its Future

CARLOS J. OVANDO

Oregon State University

Like the intricate baobab tree of Africa, which is a natural haven for myriad fauna, bilingual/bicultural education has become an educational phenomenon that serves many different groups. Beyond this point, however, the simile takes a different turn. For, unlike the baobab tree, with its largely self-regulating web of life, bilingual/bicultural education has many wardens who monitor its status with a great deal of interest. At one extreme are parents who (understandably) want to know what is going on inside the bilingual or English-as-a-second-language (ESL) classroom in terms of curricular content, first- and second-language development, and cultural emphasis. At the other extreme are politicians and journalists who are eager to extract a great deal of mileage from a topic that has consistently, during the past 15 years, touched some of the most sensitive sociopolitical and pedagogical nerves in U.S. society.

Both participants and observers view bilingual/bicultural education in a variety of ways. Some embrace with zeal the revitalization of languages and cultures through the public schools. They see bilingual education as a natural consequence of the sociocultural realities of a pluralistic society. For them, dual language instruction is a logical vehicle for cognitive and language development for those students with limited proficiency in English—and for those students whose first language is English, as well. They believe that bilingual/bicultural education will be personally satisfying to all students and that it will help them to develop the interpersonal skills and attitudes that are essential to a healthy society. Students with limited proficiency in English, these advocates would argue, are entitled to a fair share of the goods and services of the society, and this includes equal access to high-quality educational opportunities through the use of the language spoken in each student's home.

Those individuals at the other extreme argue that the positive effects of bilingual education on academic achievement, dual language development, cultural affirmation, national integration, and psychological well-being have been exaggerated. Such critics often suggest that support for bilingual education springs from faith, not from empirical evidence. They fear that the institutionalization of bilingual education in the public schools will further fracture social cohesion by encouraging youngsters to depend on languages other than English and to adhere to cultural patterns that may be in conflict with the mainstream U.S. culture. Such results, these critics argue, will only hamper upward mobility for students with limited proficiency in English.

Somewhere between these two extremes are those individuals who concede, on ideological and pedagogical grounds, that students with limited proficiency in English are entitled to schooling in their primary language until such time as they can assume the demands of an all-English curriculum—but the sooner, the better. Where this view of bilingual education is dominant, students with limited proficiency in English are generally removed from the bilingual program—somewhat arbitrarily—after one or two years of instruction. Bilingual education is only a means of pushing and pulling the speaker of limited English as quickly as possible into the mainstream American culture (whatever that is).

Finally, some individuals believe in the importance of nurturing ancestral languages and cultures, but they also believe that such endeavors should take place somewhere other than in the public schools. Consider, for example, the Korean community of about 2,000 in Anchorage, Alaska. Sensitive to the fact that its children were forgetting their mother tongue, becoming alienated from their culture, and having trouble communicating with their parents (who speak limited English), the Korean community, with help from the Korean consulate, started a Saturday school to teach these youngsters the Korean culture and language. The Japanese community in Anchorage also operates such a school, as do many other ethnic groups throughout the U.S.

Although it is useful to isolate and examine the myriad voices competing for attention on the topic of bilingual/bicultural education, the debate is much less clear in reality. The formulation of a national policy on language would compel the articulation and examination of language-related issues. Such a policy could function as a sounding board for debates on the homogenization or the pluralization of U.S. society. To what extent, why, how, and by what means should we move in one direction or the other? A national policy on language would resolve the often conflicting language policies that the U.S. has randomly and almost unconsciously followed to date. The National Defense Education Act (NDEA) of 1957 and the Title VII bilingual education legislation of 1968 epitomize this conflict. The NDEA affirmed the significance of foreign languages as integral components of national security; the bilingual education legislation, by contrast, was designed to allow the rich linguistic experiences of the immigrant and indigenous minority communities in the U.S. to atrophy.

To establish the need for a national policy on language, we must look back at the pedagogical and the sociopolitical development of bilingual/bicultural education since the late 1960s. By isolating these two closely interrelated strands of development, we can see that both the pedagogy and the sociopolitics of bilingual education have suffered from a general lack of direction. The usual approach has been one of ad hoc experimentation. This is natural in the early stages of developing a new program, but it also demonstrates more clearly the need for a national policy on language.

BILINGUAL PEDAGOGY

Pedagogically, bilingual education was based on the assumption that building instruction on what students with limited proficiency in English already knew would result in more learning than would total instruction in a second language. Those who held this view also assumed that cognitive skills acquired in one language can be transferred to other languages and cultures. The general objective of bilingual education was to open up two-way communication between the world of the limited-English-speaking student and the school in subject-area content, in first- and second-language development, and in cultural awareness. The long-term goal was to improve the academic achievement of students with limited proficiency in English.

The partial institutionalization of bilingual education in U.S. public schools was an admission that defects in the regular curriculum accounted, at least in part, for the poor academic showing of limited-English-speaking students. Through bilingual/bicultural education, educators, parents, and policy makers expected to improve the marginal academic achievement and the equally marginal sociocultural status of these students.

But those educators charged with carrying out this dual mission had no reliable research to guide them. In fact, not until federally sponsored bilingual education was 10 years old, in 1978, did the now-defunct Department of Health, Education, and Welfare direct a Title VII committee to monitor a research agenda in the following areas: 1) assessment of national needs for bilingual education, 2) improvement in the effectiveness of services for students, and 3) improvement in Title VII program management and operations.[1] The data from these research efforts were to be ready for the congressional hearings for reauthorization of Title VII in 1983.

Approaches to language delivery illustrate the experimental nature of bilingual education during the Seventies. Teachers who were bilingual themselves often used the concurrent method—switching back and forth between two languages during lessons—for delivery of content and development of students' language. The concurrent method was a commonly prescribed mode of delivery in early Title VII programs. More recently, this approach has come into disrepute, however. Teachers have found it time-consuming, tedious, and—more important—not conducive to the development of a second language. Rather than actively listening to the second language, students learn to wait passively until the teacher returns to their first language. Similarly, teachers tried and then often discarded many varieties of the alternate and preview/review models for delivering language.

As with modes of language delivery, approaches for developing literacy skills in the bilingual classroom have varied tremendously. Some programs have introduced reading skills exclusively through the first language, while English as a second language is developed separately. Other programs have chosen to immerse children in English exclusively. Still others have experimented with introducing reading and writing simultaneously in students' first and second languages.[2]

Two of the most debated issues in bilingual education have concerned *who* should participate and *for how long*. Educators have used a wide variety of instruments to assess the language skills of learners slated for entry into or exit from bilingual or English-as-a-second-language programs. Some educators have been interested in instruments that would identify only those students most in need of bilingual instruction—and that would deem these youngsters ready for exit from such programs as quickly as possible. Others have looked for instruments that would identify many students with diverse language needs and that would demand higher levels of achievement in the areas of language and literacy before returning these youngsters to regular instructional programs. It was not until 1978 that Title VII made provisions to assess all four language skills—listening, speaking, reading, and writing. Even then, a gap existed between this policy and the availability of instruments to carry out these tasks with sufficient validity and reliability.

The policy regarding which youngsters to include in bilingual/bicultural programs has also been subject to change. The major intent of early bilingual legislation, for example, was to address the needs of limited-English speakers, who were frequently children of poverty. But a 1978 amendment to Title VII encouraged the inclusion of other students, provided that they did not exceed 40% of the total classroom population. Thus it was possible to have in one classroom indigenous minority students whose parents wanted them to reclaim their ancestral languages, English-dominant majority students whose parents saw the benefits of acquiring a second language, highly bilingual children whose parents wanted them to develop in both languages, and students with limited proficiency in English. The instructional implications for each of these groups are quite different. For instance, indigenous minority students whose dominant—or only—language is English may have endured negative experiences associated with their linguistic or cultural identities. To focus in the classroom on a language or culture that a student has rejected may be a delicate endeavor. Furthermore, such children—even though their dominant language is English—may in fact speak a nonstandard version of English. Often, their needs are overshadowed by the glaring language deficits of limited-English-speaking students—and thus not given the attention they deserve.

Such instructional problems stem in part from the shortage of classroom-tested research findings to shape and buttress program designs. Bilingual teachers, many of them novices, have been given a complex charge. They must 1) provide literacy instruction in two languages for a variety of students; 2) understand and apply theories of language acquisition; 3) organize their classrooms for the triple goals of language development, cognitive growth, and intercultural awareness; 4) stay abreast of the latest research findings; and 5) keep up to date on the constantly changing federal, state, and school district regulations. Simultaneously, bilingual teachers must manage their classes, which are characterized by linguistic, cultural, and academic diversity.

What have we learned during the past 15 years that can help us realize more fully the promise of bilingual education? To begin with, linguists have made important progress in understanding first- and second-language acquisition. Their research suggests that the developmental process is similar and predictable for both children and adults. Thus the acquisition of a second language requires time and experiences that are tailored to a learner's developmental stage.

One stage is manifested in the informal language that we all use as we deal with our immediate environments. Because the context is clear, this level of language is characterized by incomplete responses, a limited vocabulary, and many nonverbal cues. An average non-English-speaking student learns to communicate at this level after about two years of instruction.

A second developmental level consists of the language used in school and in many facets of adult life. Here the context is less clear; instead, communication depends on a speaker's (or writer's) ability to manipulate the vocabulary and syntax with precision. Students with limited proficiency in English need at least five to seven years of instruction to master this formal language.[3]

The implications for timing the exit of students from bilingual programs into the regular curriculum are clear. In assessing the language proficiency of such students, we must be certain that they can handle this formal (i.e., context-reduced) language. However, assessments during the Seventies of children with limited proficiency in English often measured only context-embedded communication, not the formal language that students need for sustained academic growth.

During the past 15 years we have also learned that certain methods promote natural acquisition of language, while other methods promote only a mechanical ability to manipulate rules of grammar. Moreover, because learners follow a neurologically programmed sequence of stages in acquiring a second language, we now recognize that our expectations for second-language production should follow that sequence. Likewise, the language to which teachers expose learners during language lessons should reflect those stages. To be comprehensible, teachers should begin with concrete objects, firsthand experiences, and visual contexts. In other words, students with limited proficiency in English are likely to make more progress in one hour of carefully designed, *comprehensible* input than in many hours of simply sitting in a regular classroom listening to what, to them, is "noise." In addition, Stephen Krashen has found that students' attitudes toward the second language are as important as their talents for learning languages; the students' ages, their previous exposures to the second language, and their levels of acculturation are also factors that teachers must take into account.[4]

We have also learned that bilingualism and biculturalism are not detrimental to cognitive development, and that cognitive skills are transferable across cultures and languages. In fact, some evidence suggests that bilingualism may encourage the development of divergent thinking and creativity.[5] This new view of bilingualism challenges the view that researchers held from the Thirties through the Fifties: that bilingualism hindered cognitive and linguistic development because the brain could not deal with multiple linguistic tracks.

The evolution of bilingual education has caused us to recognize the fact that social context affects learning outcomes in bilingual settings. For example, programs that immerse youngsters in a second language are successful only when they do not stigmatize the students' primary languages and home cultures. Thus the attitudes of the host society toward groups that speak another language have an enormous impact on minority students' perceptions of themselves and of the school.

Much pedagogical experimentation and learning took place during the Seventies in the areas of language and cognitive development, but not all the findings were pleasant. The most publicized negative findings were those of the report by the American Institutes of Research (AIR),[6] which suggested that students enrolled in Title VII bilingual programs did not achieve at a higher level than counterparts who were not enrolled in such programs. However, Doris Gunderson points out that:

> Although there is insufficient research documenting the effects of bilingual education, there is no research to substantiate the claim that bilingual education and bilingualism are harmful. Moreover, the available research indicates that bilingual education is either beneficial or neutral in terms of scholastic achievement, giving the student the added advantage of exposure to two languages.[7]

A variety of longitudinal studies have also revealed positive academic gains for students who have been enrolled in bilingual programs for at least four years.[8]

To date, many students who would qualify for bilingual or English-as-a-second-language programs have not received such instruction—and, in general, such students are still not achieving on a par with students whose native language is English. There is still much work to be done. As bilingual educators become better acquainted with theories of language acquisition and the methods they imply, with the relationships that research is disclosing between cognition and language, and with the findings related to the optimal organization of classroom programs and resources, bilingual education will become increasingly effective. But better bilingual education also depends on a supportive sociopolitical environment.

The war of words regarding bilingual/bicultural education has centered on three disputed issues: 1) the use of public funds for special educational programs for students with limited proficiency in English, 2) the function of language as a bonding or polarizing force in society, and 3) the extent to which language—and not other socioeconomic and cultural factors—is responsible for academic failure. Historically, bilingual programs emerged in the U.S. wherever ethnic communities believed that it was in their interest to create such programs. But 1968 marked the beginning of an uneasy relationship between the federal government and such ethnic communities, brought about by the enactment of Title VII of the Elementary and Secondary Education Act. The primary purpose of Title VII was to improve the academic performance of economically deprived children who also had difficulty with English. Congress appropriated the initial funds to teach such students in their home languages, but these students were to transfer into the all-English curriculum as soon as they were able to handle such instruction. Congress did not intend the legislation either to promote minority languages or to pluralize society. Rather, the intention was to use the home languages and firsthand experiences of these students to assimilate them as rapidly as possible into the regular (i.e., English-dominant) school program. Congress supported Title VII on the premise that these low-income youngsters needed all the help they could get to overcome their linguistic, cultural, and environmental handicaps and thus to equalize their opportunities for success in U.S. society.

Title VII recognized the importance of building on what the students already knew. However, this legislation was not intended to maintain the rich linguistic resources that these children represented. Much of the debate about bilingual education during the Seventies focused on this issue. One side favored prolonged attempts by the schools to maintain children's home languages; the other side believed that the period of bilingual instruction should be as short as possible. As the debate on the length of programs grew more heated, participants focused less attention on the quality of bilingual instruction.

From the debate about language maintenance versus rapid transition to English, a second question arose that the public found more worrisome: would bilingual education cause students to develop divided linguistic and cultural loyalties? The federal guidelines for Title VII implied that the schools would encourage a common culture, since they would eventually return bilingual students to regular classes. At the community level, however, ethnic minorities were beginning to see that they could join the societal mainstream politically, educationally, and econominically without forgetting their first languages and their cultural traditions.

Should linguistic minority groups have the right to participate fully in American life without being completely assimilated into the mainstream culture? This issue is still not resolved. Court decisions have consistently affirmed the civil rights of all residents without regard to race, language, or national origin.[9] However, many defenders of monolingualism and monoculturalism have argued that, with respect to bilingual education, the courts have limited the rights of local communities to run their schools as they see fit. Therefore, even thought the intent of the courts has been to protect the civil rights of all students, many individuals have interpreted these decisions as invidious vehicles for social engineering.

Moreover, bilingual education is intertwined with such sensitive issues as governmental attitudes toward immigrants and indigenous minorities. The U.S. has received in the recent past large numbers of political refugees, economic refugees, and undocumented workers. But consistent policies regarding who can enter the U.S. and on what criteria are nonexistent. Nor do clear policies exist with regard to trade relations with the developing nations or political relations with oppressive regimes. It is hard to examine the pedagogical value of bilingual instruction without becoming entangled in such sensitive political issues as the rights and status of undocumented workers.

Given these tensions and the current trend toward less federal involvement in education, some observers feel that bilingual programs are doomed to extinction. However, the 1982 cutbacks in bilingual education were no more severe than those in other federal programs, and it looks as though Congress will reauthorize funding in 1983. Furthermore, extensive state legislation is now in place to continue the funding of bilingual education. It would be pedagogically unsound and sociopolitically imprudent to return to the sink-or-swim methods of the past. Bilingual education is a reality that even Nathan Glazer, one of its most ardent critics, admits is here to stay.[10]

This does not mean that bilingual education will have smooth sailing. As we reflect on the experiences of the past 15 years and consider the political, demographic, and economic realities of the future, we must recognize the need to define more clearly the mission of bilingual education. This mission is to meet—rationally and realistically—the linguistic and cognitive needs of students with limited proficiency in English. This mission assumes greater importance when we consider that the non-English-speaking population in the U.S. is expected to increase from 30 million in 1980 to about 39.5 million in the year 2000.[11] There will never be a more appropriate time for the U.S. to develop a clear language policy.

An official language policy toward ethnolinguistic minorities would create a better balance between the learning needs of students with limited proficiency in English and the national interest. Such a policy would stress the universal language needs of all learners; it would also consider both the importance of breaking down the social barriers between ethnic groups and the potential for cognitive development of intracultural and cross-cultural affirmation. Likewise, such a policy would recognize the role of language in the promotion of academic excellence, and it would encourage the development of multilingualism in the larger society. In this era of global interdependence, such multilingualism would help to advance U.S. trade and political interests. Although it is difficult to quantify, the humanistic rationale for encouraging individuals to maintain or acquire a second language is also important. Through language, human beings discover one another's worlds.

The public is still somewhat uncertain today about the content and the process of bilingual education, about its posture regarding goals for national unity, and about the balance that bilingual education strikes between benefits and costs. But despite these uncertainties, most Americans seem to agree that language development and cross-cultural studies advance national interests. The final report of the President's Commission on Foreign Language and International Studies, *Strength Through Wisdom: A Critique of U.S. Capability*,[12] confirms this positive attitude. Largely as a result of the commission's recommendations, a consortium of 10 organizations involved in language instruction—called the Joint National Committee for Language—has begun to assess governmental support for a more coherent national policy on language.

Such a language policy must be responsive to the desires and needs of local communities. As it relates to the education of children with limited proficiency in English, however, this policy could aim to accomplish three general goals: 1) the affirmation of children's right to maintain their home languages, 2) the collection and dissemination of research findings on the role of the home language in cognitive development, and 3) the collection and dissemination of research findings that compare the outcomes of carefully designed bilingual education programs with those of undifferentiated instruction in an all-English environment.

The U.S. should nurture the rich linguistic resources that ethnic minorities provide. A national language policy will increase the likelihood of a flexible support system for children whose home language is other than English. Such a policy will also foster the acquisition of second languages among English-speaking students and can be adjusted to meet the needs of local communities.

NOTES

1. Betty J. Mace-Matluck, *Literacy Instruction in Bilingual Settings: A Synthesis of Current Research* (Los Alamitos, Calif.: National Center for Bilingual Reserach, 1982), pp. 19–20.

2. Eleanor W. Thonis, "Reading Instruction for Language Minority Students," in *Schooling and Language Minority Students: A Theoretical Framework* (Los Angeles: Evaluation, Dissemination, and Assessment Center, California State University, 1981), pp. 162–67.

3. Jim Cummins, "Four Misconceptions About Language Proficiency in Bilingual Education," *NABE Journal*, Spring, 1981, pp. 31–44.

4. Stephen D. Krashen, "Bilingual Education and Second Language Acquisition Theory," in *Schooling and Language Minority Students. . .* , pp. 76–77.

5. Elizabeth Peal and Wallace E. Lambert, "The Relation of Bilingualism to Intelligence," *Psychological Monographs: General and Applied*, no. 76, 1962, pp. 1–23.

6. Malcolm Danoff, *Evaluation of the Impact of ESEA Title VII Spanish/English Bilingual Education Program* (Palo Alto, Calif.: American Institutes for Research, 1978), pp. 1–19.

7. Doris V. Gunderson, "Bilingual Education," in Harold E. Mitzel, ed., *Encyclopedia of Educational Research*, Vol. I, 5th ed. (New York: Free Press, 1982), p. 210.

8. See, for example, Wallace E. Lambert and Richard Tucker, *Bilingual Education of Children: The St. Lambert Experiment* (Rowley, Mass.: Newbury House, 1972); William Mackey and Von Nieda Beebe, *Bilingual Schools for a Bicultural Community: Miami's Adaptation to the Cuban Refugees* (Rowley, Mass.: Newbury House, 1977); and Bernard Spolsky, "Bilingual Education

in the United States," in James E. Alatis, ed., *Georgetown University Round Table on Languages and Linguistics: International Dimensions of Bilingual Education* (Washington, D.C.: Georgetown University Press, 1978).

9. See, for example, *Aspiria of New York* v. *Board of Education of the City of New York,* 423 F. Supp. 647 (S.D.N.Y. 1967); *Lau* v. *Nichols,* 414 U.S. 563, 566 (1974); and *Castañeda* v. *Pickard,* 648 F. 2d 989 (5th Cir., 1981).

10. Nathan Glazer, "Pluralism and Ethnicity," in Martin Ridge, ed., *The New Bilingualism: An American Dilemma* (Los Angeles: University of Southern California Press, 1982), p. 58.

11. *The Prospects for Bilingual Education in the Nation: Fifth Annual Report of the National Advisory Council for Bilingual Education, 1980–81,* p. xii.

12. President's Commission on Foreign Language and International Studies, *Strength Through Wisdom: A Critique of U.S. Capability* (Washington, D.C.: U.S. Government Printing Office, 1979).

Education and Gender Equality: A Critical View

JEAN STOCKARD
University of Oregon

A number of authors have discussed how educational experiences influence gender inequality. To combat these influences the popular media and educators encourage women and girls to pursue advanced training if they want to "get ahead," often stressing the importance of training in mathematics. Educators design courses to help women overcome "math anxiety" and to encourage promising young girls to pursue mathematics training. Likewise, girls are encouraged to enter nontraditional vocations; and counselors and teachers, as well as parents, are reminded to encourage young women to enter fields typically seen as appropriate for men. Researchers urge teachers and counselors to monitor their interactions with male and female students so that males are not favored over females. Writers of textbooks and tests are encouraged to use equal numbers of examples about males and females, to picture members of both groups in equal numbers, and to avoid sex-typed descriptions of activities.

Much of this advice appears to be based on the assumption that if women gain more education, train in typically male areas, increase their mathematical skills, are properly encouraged by adult role models, and/or are exposed to nongender-biased curricula, then gender inequality in the adult occupational world should lessen. The evidence to support this assumption, however, appears to be minimal. Each of these modifications may be laudable in and of itself, and each may produce some level of change. Nevertheless, I will show in what follows that the evidence suggests that it would be unreasonable to expect alterations in these areas of education to change segregation of males and females in the occupational world or to lessen the gender gap in income

From *Research in Sociology of Education and Socialization* 5 (1985): 299–326. Copyright © 1985 by JAI Press, Inc. Reprinted with permission of the publisher.

in any marked way. In other words, the linkage between gender differences in educational experiences and gender inequalities in the adult occupational world is probably much more tenuous than commonly believed. . . .

GENDER DIFFERENCES IN ACADEMIC ACHIEVEMENT

Studies of gender differences in academic achievement have involved learning disabilities, grades, scores on achievement tests—especially in mathematics—and underachievement. Interestingly enough, many of the gender differences which occur in academic achievement involve advantages which accrue to females rather than to males.

Grades, Behavior and Learning Problems, and Achievement

Females receive higher grades than males throughout school, from the elementary years through college (Lavin, 1965; Davis, 1964). This advantage appears in total grade averages and in specific subject areas such as English and mathematics (deWolf, 1981) and despite the fact that males and females usually score equally well on composite tests of achievement (McCandless, et al., 1974; Stockard, et al., 1985).

In addition, girls appear more likely to be well adjusted to school. Males suffer various learning disabilities, exhibit more behavior problems, are referred more often for remedial work, and in general, are rated lower than females on many dimensions of behavior by teachers and other adults. Only a small part of this discrepancy can be explained by a tendency to underreport girls' problems (Barfield, 1976; Cruickshank, 1977; Blom, 1971). Both official records and self-reports show that males commit various kinds of illegal activities more often than females (Feyerherm, 1981; Schur, 1984:213–200). High school girls also report spending much more time doing homework, report greater participation in extracurricular activities of all types (except sports) more often than boys (Grant and Eiden, 1982:71–72), value academic achievement more highly than boys (Lueptow, 1975, 1980), and report "liking" school more than boys (Sexton, 1969).

Nevertheless, some gender differences exist in the areas in which students achieve. . . . Results obtained from the National Assessment of Educational Progress (NAEP), a set of achievement tests given to a nationally representative sample of students from 1975 to 1980, . . . support many studies which show that from the first years of school and continuing through adulthood, girls score higher than boys on various tests of verbal reasoning and achievement (e.g., Maccoby and Jacklin, 1974; Herman, 1975). Beginning around adolescence, boys score higher on tests of mathematics achievement, especially those involving spatial-visual skills, a special kind of perceptual ability (Aiken, 1976; Fennema, 1974; Maccoby and Jacklin, 1974).

Mathematics Achievement

As noted, much of the commentary on gender differences in achievement has focused on mathematics. Researchers suggest that mathematics is a crucial filtering device, serving to sort out students who are eligible for studying lucrative, male-dominated fields such as engineering, architecture, or computer science (Ernest, 1976; Sells, 1978). Some authors focus on math anxiety, "feelings of tension and anxiety that interfere with . . . the solving of mathematical problems" (Richardson and Suinn, 1972:551). It is suggested that women experience math anxiety more often than men and that this helps prevent women from achieving their full potential (Tobias, 1978; Betz, 1978). Special coursework, counseling, and other training procedures are advocated to cure this anxiety. Yet, not all analyses of the actual prevalence of math anxiety indicate that gender differences exist (Resnick, et al., 1982), and the severity of this problem has not been fully documented.

Just as gender differences in math anxiety may be small, gender differences in mathematics achievement are also small. For instance, the gender differences in 17-year-old students' mathematics NAEP test scores are smaller than the differences in reading, music, or science. In addition, the variation in NAEP scores (in all subject areas) by region of the country, race, parental education, or size and type of community is larger, often by many times, than the variations by sex (Grant and Eiden, 1982:20–27).

Gender differences in mathematics achievement are also small when compared to gender differences in adult income. For instance, the average mathematics SAT score of females is approximately 90% of the average score of males (computed from 1980–81 data, CEEB, 1981), and the median mathematics NAEP score for 17-year-old females is 96% that of 17-year-old males. In contrast, the median income of all women full-time, year-round workers in 1982 was about three-fifths of that of all full-time, year-round men workers. These figures suggest that equalizing men's and women's mathematics achievement is insufficient to end gender inequality in overall income.

Moreover, simply increasing women's mathematical achievement would not necessarily alter the sex segregation of occupations. Forty-two percent of all bachelor's degree recipients in mathematics in 1979-1980 were women, a figure close to the proportion of women bachelor degree recipients in the biological and the social sciences. Women receive a much smaller share of the degrees in fields where one is expected to apply mathematics, such as economics, chemistry, physics, and computer science. This discrepancy may reflect differential abilities of males and females to apply mathematical knowledge, rather than to learn mathematical concepts. Yet, it might also reflect women's avoidance of occupational areas which are perceived as inappropriate for females. For example, mathematics may be seen as an appropriate major for women in undergraduate school, for it can lead to a career in teaching, a traditionally female-typed field of work and the traditional career choice of the majority of women who major in mathematics in college (Handley and Hickson, 1978). Fewer options may be perceived as available for women majoring in areas such as chemistry, physics, economics, or computer science. If this suggestion is true, gender differences in mathematics achievement may not be as much of a bar to equality in the occupational world as women's perceptions of opportunities for employment.

Underachievement

Even though gender differences in academic achievement may be relatively small, it is still possible, as some authors have suggested, that women downplay their abilities and underachieve more often than men, especially beginning in the high school years. This appears to involve two separate areas: academic underachievement, receiving grades which are lower than would be expected given one's scores on ability tests (Coleman, 1961; Shaw and McCuen, 1960; Fitzpatrick, 1978) and a more general, social avoidance of achievement which might offend males whom females wish to attract as potential partners (e.g., Komarovsky, 1953; Weitzman, 1984). The latter is said to involve behavior patterns such as "hiding one's intelligence" and not appearing superior to a male partner.

Recent analyses have suggested that the conclusions about academic underachievement could have been erroneous and that at least Coleman's (1961) conclusions were based on a potentially incomplete analysis of the data. Academic underachievement (in total grade averages, as well as in English and mathematics) appears to be more common among males than females. Boys consistently have grades lower than would be predicted by their ability (Stockard and Wood, 1984). The often-cited work on women's "motive-to-avoid success" (Horner, 1970) has also been discounted. Numerous replications have led to the suggestion that this phenomenon may appear among men as well as women and that it probably involves a reflection of social reality, including reactions of others to achievement patterns, more than a deep-seated fear of achievement (Tresemer, 1977; Condry and Dyer, 1976).

Even though females may not receive grades lower than would be predicted by their ability and females may not have a generalized "motive-to-avoid success," they may still downplay their achievements when interacting with males whom they see as potential dating or marital partners. Komarovsky (1953) first documented this pattern and others have noted its continuing presence (e.g., Frazier and Sadker, 1973:127), although some suggest the pattern may have altered in recent years (Weitzman, 1984). Whatever the current prevalence of this behavior, it probably reflects anticipated sex-roles within the family and the desire of young women to attract a spouse (see Stockard and Johnson, 1980:256–259). Its relation to policies or programs of schools is unclear.

ATTENTION GIVEN TO MALES AND FEMALES

While the formal obligation of schools is to instruct students in academic areas such as mathematics and English, much of the learning which takes place involves informal interactions or what social scientists have called the "hidden curriculum" (Jackson, 1968). When examining gender differences in this hidden curriculum researchers have looked at subtle messages about gender roles given in texts and examination questions, and at interactions between teachers and students, suggesting that gender inequalities in these areas help promote gender inequalities in the adult occupational world.

Curricular Materials

Many studies have noted an overrepresentation of males as characters in stories, in pictures, and even as the focus for examination questions in curricular materials. Such bias has been documented in a wide range of subjects (Weitzman and Rizzo, 1974; Saario, et al., 1973). As noted above, it is suggested that these stereotypes in the curricular material help influence girls' choices of occupations and generally reinforce students' views of sex-stereotyped roles and thus their career aspirations.

Males' overrepresentation in curricular materials probably reflects to some extent the greater valuation of males within our society as a whole. Extensive analyses of language usage, religious practices, and the mass media document the greater attention and value given to males and their activities, not unlike the emphasis found on male activities in school textbooks and tests (see Stockard and Johnson, 1980:4–10; Schur, 1984:34–37). While altering curricular materials may have a short-term effect on older students' views of occupations which are potential choices (Vincenzi, 1977) and on preschool children's sex-role stereotypes (Koblinsky and Sugawara, 1984), consistent results with such attempts to alter curriculum have not yet been demonstrated (e.g., Weeks and Porter, 1983). Given the negative portrayal of women in all media, it would be very difficult to isolate the impact of curricular material on students' adult lives from influences of other areas of society (Moulton, et al., 1978).

In addition, if employers are not willing to hire women in non-traditional occupations, encouraging women to aspire to such fields through curricular materials is an indirect way to promote change in these occupations. Some in the counseling profession note that it may also involve a potential misrepresentation of the nature of the job world to young people (Overs, 1975: Birk, et al., 1979). Finally, if women perceive that they will continue to face the predominant responsibilities of caring for their home and family during their adult lives, a situation which currently appears to be true (e.g., Pleck, 1977; also Stockard and Johnson, 1980:51–59), urging them to also add the burden of a career to this load may not be a productive means of change.

Interactions with Students

A number of studies have also noted differences in the amount and type of attention which teachers give to boys and girls. Interestingly enough, this appears to involve both more positive and more negative sanctions to boys. Among very young students boys appear to receive more loud reprimands than girls and more responses when they exhibit aggressive behaviors. They also receive more nurturant and instructional attention while behaving appropriately (Serbin, et al., 1973). Studies of elementary school children suggest that boys are criticized and reprimanded more often than girls (Jackson and Lahaderne, 1967; Dweck, et al., 1978), especially if they are underachievers or have behavior problems (Martin, 1972), but that boys also receive more academic attention and praise (Meyer and Thompson, 1963). A study of interactions in high school geometry classes provides similar evidence (Becker, 1981).

Some authors speculate that these differences in interaction patterns help reinforce girls' conformity to traditional feminine roles (Weitzman, 1984:186) and boys' greater independence and autonomy (Sears and Feldman, 1966) as well as their greater mathematics achievement (Becker, 1981). In addition, Dweck and associates (1978) suggest that boys' extensive experience with negative feedback contributes to their tendency to discount negative evaluations and to a more resilient sense of self-confidence. There is, however, little empirical evidence that males are actually more independent or autonomous than females, or that they have more positive self-concepts or higher self-esteem (See Maccoby and Jacklin, 1974), or that they have substantially greater mathematics achievement (see prior discussion). In addition, girls' reluctance to pursue careers and their conformity to traditional roles may result more from the difficulty of actually pursuing active careers while carrying the double burden of home and work responsibilities, than from the influence of interactional patterns in school.

While the greater attention teachers give to boys probably reflects, to at least some extent, the greater cultural valuation placed on males and their activities, it could also be an attempt, perhaps unconscious, to motivate students perceived as unwilling to learn. Teachers' interactions with boys in the classroom also reflect a need to control them. While it is obvious that most of the negative interactions involve reprimands and attempts at control, many of the positive interactions could also have this theme, given the current emphasis on positive reinforcement as a means of behavior management. Because the girls misbehave less often and value academic achievement more (see prior discussion), they require fewer such interactions (Jackson and Lahaderne, 1967; Serbin, et al., 1973; Kedar-Voivadas, 1983).

In general, there may be logical problems in linking the hidden curriculum to gender inequality in adult life. While there may be an as yet undocumented more direct negative effect, at this time it appears that any effect that negative portrayals and interactions may have on adult gender inequality is undoubtedly subtle and not immediate.

EDUCATIONAL ATTAINMENT

When people apply for jobs employers usually do not assess their knowledge of particular subject areas. Instead, they are often interested in how much schooling an applicant has received. In general, although there are historical variations, females and males within the same social class group have quite similar patterns of educational attainment. . . .

Since the late 1970s over half of all college students have been women. Much of the increased enrollment of women reflects a growing representation of older women (those over 35) in undergraduate work, perhaps as these women return to school to gain the education given to their brothers or husbands in earlier years. The increased enrollment of women also involves an increased representation of women, including those under 35 years of age, in graduate programs (see Figure 1, Grant and Eiden, 1982:93).

THE EDUCATION-INCOME ASSOCIATION

. . . One could ask whether income disparities between men and women correspond to disparities in educational attainment of various age cohorts in the population. To investigate this question, information on educational attainment and income of men and women in various age cohorts in the labor force in 1962, 1972, and 1982 is summarized in Table 1. The first columns of data give the median years of education of female workers and male workers. Clearly, the gender variations in educational attainment over time are minimal. In the older cohorts women tended to have more education than men, reflecting the greater high school drop-out rate of men and the relatively low proportion of the population which attended college. In the younger cohorts the women have slightly lower median educational levels than the men, reflecting the increasing high school completion rate of men and the growing prevalence of college attendance. The median educational level of women workers varies from 97% to 103% of that of men workers. (It is, of course, possible that the women in the younger cohorts have not yet completed their education, and the eventual disparity may be somewhat smaller.)[1]

When compared to the gender disparities in income, the variations in average educational attainment are virtually nonexistent, for the yearly incomes of full-time, year-round women workers range from only 52% to 72% of that of comparable men (see Table 1). Examination of the complete table indicates that the income ratio of female to male workers does not appear to vary with their relative education. When educational levels are very similar, income ratios are not high, by cohort or period. The income ratio varies somewhat from one historical period to the next, being most favorable to women in 1982 and least favorable in 1962. To some extent, the experiences of each cohort follow these overall patterns, with women in each age group and cohort earning more relative to men in 1962 or 1982 than in 1972. The exceptions involve age variations. Younger women (the 1928–37 cohort in 1962, the 1938–47 cohort in 1972, and the 1948–57 cohort in 1982) tend to earn more relative to men than do their older sisters in a given year. This probably reflects the relatively flat lifetime earnings curve of women (Johnson and Stafford, 1975; King, 1977). Men's earnings tend to increase over the life cycle much more than women's, even when work experience is taken into account, and this contributes to a greater sex disparity in incomes among older workers. The 1948–57 cohort in 1982 has the highest income relative to men reported in the table. This cohort is most likely to have benefited from various affirmative action and equal opportunity laws when they entered the work force. It is possible then that they may not experience this "flat lifetime earnings curve" to the same extent as older cohorts (see also Blau, 1984b). In general, however, the results in this table suggest that gender differences in income, at least to this time, are largely unrelated to gender differences in educational attainment for specific age cohorts.

The analysis in Table 1 combined individuals with a wide range of educational levels. Similar results, however, appear when comparisons are

TABLE 1. Relative Years of Education and Income of Female and Male Workers, Age 25–64, By Age Cohort in 1962, 1972, and 1982

Cohort		Median Years of Education 1982 (1972)[1]		Ratio of Median Incomes of Female/Male Full-Time, Year-Round Earnings		
Age in 1982	Year of Birth	Females	Males	1962	1972	1982
75–84	(1898–1907)	— (9.0²)	— (8.7²)	.64	—	—
65–74	(1908–1917)	11.4² (12.1)	11.1² (11.7)	.59	.56	.58
55–64	(1918–1927)	12.4 (12.3)	12.4 (12.3)	.54	.52	.56
45–54	(1928–1937)	12.5 (12.4)	12.7 (12.5)	.63	.52	.59
34–44	(1938–1947)	12.7 (12.6)	13.1 (12.7)	—	.65	.72
25–34	(1948–1957)	12.9 (—)	13.0 (—)	—	p	.63
Total²		12.6 (12.2)	12.7 (12.3)	.59	.57	

Source: U.S. Bureau of the Census, *Current Population Reports*, Series P–60, "Income of Families and Persons in the United States: 1962," No. 41, October 21, 1963; "Money Income in 1972 of Families and Persons in the United States," No. 90, 1973; and "Money Income of Households, Families, and Persons in the United States: 1982," No. 142, 1984. U.S. Government Printing Office, Washington, D.C.

[1] Figures in parentheses are for 1972. Data were not available on education for 1962. Data on education is for all workers, full or part-time.

[2] This includes data for workers 65 years of age and older.

made between males and females with similar levels of education. Table 2 gives the median income of year-round, full-time workers in each gender and major race category and with various levels of education. Within each gender group people who have less education and are nonwhite earn less than those with more education and who are white. Yet, in each of the education and race categories females earn far less than males. The advantage of white males is especially striking, for the gender difference is somewhat smaller among nonwhites than among whites. White males with a high school education have higher average yearly incomes than college graduates in any of the other groups. They also earn more than women, of either race, who have done college graduate work.

Even when various human capital variables such as work experience, training, and occupational status are taken into account a large wage gap between men and women remains. Many studies demonstrate that women appear to benefit less than men from advanced education, working in male dominated areas, and having continuous work histories (Treiman and Terrell, 1975; Suter and Miller, 1973; Featherman and Hauser, 1976; Blau, 1984a). Some studies have tried to categorize occupations by the level of skill or training which they require and then compare the salaries of male and female workers within each of these occupational levels. The results consistently confirm the conclusion that women receive less pay than do men with similar levels of skill and training (Stevenson, 1975). . . .

EDUCATION AND CHANGING GENDER INEQUALITY

The picture of gender differences in education drawn above is not one of blatant inequality and women's low academic achievement, but primarily one of general equality and female academic success and achievement. Most women attend as many years of school as men of similar social class backgrounds. Females value academic achievement more highly than males, they get better grades, they behave better in school, and they are less likely to underachieve. Even though females are underrepresented in textbooks and testing materials, this does not appear to affect their scholastic achievement, and any independent effect on long-range achievement appears tenuous. In general, it appears that females in this country do remarkably well in education and have substantially fewer problems than males.

How then do we account for the fact that women are accorded second rank positions in the adult occupational world and generally have less access to prestige and power once they have left school? How can we explain the fact that males, who often do less well than females within schools, manage to do so much better in the adult occupational world?

A Theoretical Perspective

The answer may not be found by focusing on education as a social institution, but by examining the economy and the family, social institutions

TABLE 2. Median Yearly Incomes of Full-Time Year-Round Workers, Age 25 and Over, 1982, By Race, Gender, and Educational Level

	Elementary	High School		College			
	(1–8)	(1–3 years)	4 years	1–3 yrs.	4 yrs.	5+ yrs.	Total
Whites							
Males	$14,875	$18,203	$21,856	$24,179	$28,745	$32,542	$23,549
Females	$ 9,255	$10,803	$13,458	$15,721	$17,596	$21,474	$14,734
Blacks							
Males	$11,734	$15,104	$16,469	$18,839	$18,829	$25,204	$16,534
Females	$ 9,197	$10,353	$12,105	$15,177	$16,183	$21,112	$12,674

Source: U.S. Bureau of the Census, Current Population Reports, Series P-60, No. 142, *Money Income of Households, Families and Persons in the United States: 1982*, U.S. Government Printing Office, Washington, D.C., 1984, pp. 156–163.

which may be more closely linked to the sources and perpetuation of male dominance. In a book published in 1980 my colleague, Miriam Johnson, and I (Stockard and Johnson, 1980) examine the nature of male dominance and its persistence. We review evidence that male dominance (defined as beliefs, values, and cultural meanings that give higher value and prestige to masculinity than to feminity) exists in our cultural symbol system, in informal everyday interactions, and in social institutions and roles. We suggest that gender stratification, or hierarchical ranking of the gender groups and the separation of their activities, is reproduced in each generation, in social institutions, and in the personalities of individuals as men's motive to deprecate women develops along with their early notions of gender identity. We suggest that this system of gender stratification underlies the differential rewards men and women receive in the occupational world.

While we accept the possibility that some sex differences may have a biological basis, we review psychological studies which show few gender differences in basic capacities. Those that do appear as people grow older can generally be better explained by the different social roles that males and females are expected to play. Children first develop their understandings of these different social roles and boys first develop the motive underlying male dominance in their interactions in the family. As children grow older and interact more with their peers, their notions of appropriate sex roles are elaborated. We suggest that the male peer group may be especially important in reinforcing the deprecation of women and the expectation that men and women should have different roles.

We end the book by discussing changes that might be necessary to produce a society without male dominance. We suggest that the most fruitful way to approach change is not to focus directly on individual motivation but on how the structure of social institutions and the patterns of interactions within them reinforce gender inequalities on the institutional, individual, and cultural levels. While legal guarantees to equality and increased education are probably necessary steps for gaining greater gender equality, we believe that changes in the polity and in education are probably not sufficient to guarantee the end of male dominance. Instead, we suggest that changes in both the economy and the family will be necessary to lessen inequality in social institutions and to decrease men's motive to devalue women and to separate their activities from those of women. These changes should be accompanied by, and reflected in, alterations in cultural beliefs and values.

In suggesting ways to deal with sex stratification in the economy we note the need to maintain affirmative action programs, equal employment opportunity laws, and other means to promote the equitable hiring and pay of women and men. The comparable worth movement advocates paying occupants of predominantly female jobs wages which are similar to those received by occupants of predominantly male jobs requiring similar levels of training and education (Treiman and Hartman, 1981). This may be another important means of promoting greater economic equality, for it directly deals with the problem of occupational sex segregation and the lower pay of female-typed jobs. Yet, given the persistence of occupational sex segregation and sex disparities in income, we suggest that economic changes are necessary, but not sufficient, to produce lasting changes in gender inequality. Simply focusing on women's work role does not appear to directly change the attention men give to the family role, nor does it assure that the various laws regarding economic equality will be followed. To deal with these problems and specifically with psychological motives underlying male dominance we turn to additional changes that focus on the family.

We suggest that one step that might minimize the psychological motives underlying male dominance is for men to become more involved in the nurturing of young children. We hypothesize that as men become more involved in nurturing young children, gender identity will not disappear but will become less problematic and less salient. This in turn could lead to lessened motivations to deprecate the activities of women and promote strong gender role differentiation (see also Stockard and Johnson, 1979). Because sex objectification and male dominance are strongly reinforced in the male peer group, we suggest that it will also be important to devise ways to strengthen ties between males and females that are not necessarily sexually oriented and that can compete with the bonds of the male peer group.

Implications of this Analysis

It is undoubtedly true that educational equality is a necessary condition for gender equality in the occupational world. Cross-cultural evidence indicates that education is an important tool in advancing greater rights of women. For instance, the increasing education of women in both Italy and Japan has been linked to women's greater economic and social participation (Stockard and Johnson, 1980:85–6; Koyama, et al., 1967), educational changes in Muslim countries have been linked to growing political rights for women (Youssef, 1976), and the growth of the feminist movement in the late 1960s in the United States has been linked to women's greater involvement in higher education in that period (Stockard and Johnson, 1980:84). In general, the major role of education in minimizing gender inequalities may well involve the encouragement of pressure for change.

Certainly some of the reforms discussed above may have some impact on occupational sex segregation and gender differences in adult income, although the influence is probably more indirect than many authors seem to assume. For instance, young women probably learn in school about the gender-typed nature of occupations. Perhaps as more women are encouraged to enter fields that are currently typed as appropriate for males, they will exert pressures that could eventually lead to a lessening of gender segregation in those fields. The proportion of law school graduates who are women has grown substantially in recent years, from 2.3% in 1960 to 30.2% in 1980 (Grant and Eiden, 1982:126). The majority of women lawyers have traditionally specialized in areas where they do not have direct contacts with clients (Patterson and Engelberg, 1978) and it will be important to trace any changes in segregation within this field and others experiencing such change in the coming years.

Another area of educational reform that may help minimize gender inequalities, although again in an indirect manner, is the greater integration of males and females mandated by the Title IX legislation. To the extent that this greater contact tends to counteract the influence of the male peer group by promoting ties between males and females that are not sexually oriented, it can serve to mitigate the influence of the male peer group on boys' motives to deprecate women (cf. Stockard and Johnson, 1980:281). In general, this analysis does not necessarily imply that curricular materials, classroom interactions, or other reforms are totally ineffective means of changing gender inequality.

Because most classrooms in this country are integrated by gender, the male peer group now probably finds its greatest expression in extracurricular sports activities that are still segregated (the "contact sports") and in informal interactions both within and outside the classroom. Analyses of peer group interactions suggest that the devaluation of women and the expectation that to be a "real man" one must avoid female-typed behavior are often expressed within these settings (see Stockard and Johnson, 1980:241–247). Educators interested in finding other ways to minimize gender inequalities in the adult occupational world might want to focus on mitigating the devaluation of women which is supported by these interactions. While many of these interactions occur outside the influence of school authorities, some, including those on the football field or in the locker room or on the playground in elementary schools, are well within the authority of school officials. Just as school officials outlaw racist interactions and protect other people who are potentially subject to abuse by peers, those who are concerned with eliminating gender inequalities could try to minimize sexist interactions (cf. Best, 1983).

While all of these educational reforms may be necessary conditions for gender equality in other institutional areas, they are probably far from sufficient. Change efforts, at least in this country, need to focus on institutions such as the economy and family in addition to education.

Social scientists conversant with literature in the sociology of education are no doubt familiar with arguments which discount the effectiveness of educational reforms in promoting alterations in other areas (e.g., Coleman, et al., 1966; Jencks, et al., 1972). Yet, as noted above, social scientists specializing in the study of gender roles, including those with extensive knowledge of the education literature, seem to persist in suggesting that changes in education may be an important means toward more equitable gender roles in the adult occupational world. The analysis presented here suggests that the inequalities women face in the occupational world cannot be traced, except in a most limited and tenuous manner, to educational achievement or experiences. Analyses of gender inequality and education, as well as prescriptions for change, might be enhanced by considering this conclusion.

ACKNOWLEDGMENTS

I would like to thank Patricia Gwartney-Gibbs, Miriam Johnson, and Alan Kerckhoff for helpful comments on earlier drafts of this paper. Support of the

Center for the Study of Women in Society is gratefully acknowledged. All opinions expressed in the paper are those of the author and do not necessarily represent those of the Center.

NOTES

1. It should be noted that the ratio of years of education of males and females in Table 1 was computed from data for all workers (full- or part-time) because data on the educational level of male and female full-time, year-round workers were not available. The income ratios were computed from data for only full-time, year-round workers because more women than men tend to work part-time and computations using data for all workers would tend to greatly overstate the wage gap. It is unclear how much bias results from this discrepancy, but it is doubtful that it is large.

   One possible way to assess the discrepancy is to assume that those without incomes are similar to those with part-time employment. Data to answer this question are available for 1982. Within each age group both men and women without incomes have lower levels of education than those with incomes. Yet, when the educational levels of men and women without incomes are compared to each other, the women have levels which are quite close to those of the men in the youngest cohort, but somewhat higher than those of the men in the three older cohorts. (The latter probably reflects the presence of the unemployed, but well-educated, housewife among the women with no incomes. For the older men, not having an income more likely reflects hard-core poverty.) If the group of part-time workers is like those with no incomes, the male-female educational ratio for part-time workers in the youngest cohort would be very similar to that for all workers, while that for the older cohorts would be substantially higher. This would then imply that for full-time workers the female/male ratios of educational attainment for the older cohort would be slightly lower than those reported in the text. However, the magnitude of the differences would probably not be large and the ratios would still be much larger than those computed for income and shown in Table 1.

REFERENCES

Aiken, L. R., Jr. 1976. "Update on attitudes and other affective variables in learning mathematics." Review of Educational Research 46:293–311.

Almquist, Elizabeth McTaggart. 1984. "Race and ethnicity in the lives of minority women." In Jo Freeman (ed.), Women: A Feminist Perspective. Palo Alto, Calif.: Mayfield.

Astin, Helen S. and Alan Bayer. 1973. "Sex discrimination in academe." In Alice Rosse and Ann Calderwood (eds.), Academic Women on the Move. New York: Russell Sage Foundation.

Barfield, Ashton. 1976. "Biological influences on sex differences in behavior." In Sex Differences: Social and Biological Perspectives (M. Teitelbaum, ed.). Garden City, NY: Anchor Books.

Becker, Joanne Rosse. 1981. "Differential treatment of females and males in mathematics classes." Journal for Research in Mathematics Education 12:40–53.

Best, Raphaela. 1983. We've All Got Scars: What Boys and Girls Learn in Elementary School. Bloomington: Indiana University Press.

Betz, Nancy E. 1978. "Prevalence, distribution, and correlates of math anxiety in college students." Journal of Counseling Psychology 25:441–448.

Birk, Janice M., Mary Faith Tanney, and Jacqueline F. Cooper. 1979. "A case of blurred vision: stereotyping in career information illustrations." Journal of Vocational Behavior 15:247–257.

Blau, Francine D. 1984a. "Discrimination against Women: theory and evidence," In William Darity, Jr.(ed.) Labor Economics: Modern Views, Boston: Martinus Nijhoff.

_____ . 1984b. "Women in the labor force: an overview." In Jo Freeman (ed.) Women: A Feminist Perspective (3rd edition). Palo Alto, Calif.: Mayfield.

Blom, G. E. 1971. "Sex differences in reading disability." In Reading Forum (E. Calkins, ed.). National Institute of Neurological Disease and Strokes, Bethesda, Maryland.

Braverman, Harry. 1974. Labor and Monopoly Capital: The Degradation of Work in the Twentieth Century. New York: Monthly Review Press.

Campbell, J. W. 1973. "Women drop back in: educational innovation in the sixties." In A. S. Rossi and A. Calderwood (eds.) Academic Women on the Move. New York: Russell Sage Foundation.

Coleman, James S. 1961. The Adolescent Society. New York: Free Press.

Coleman, James S. et al. 1966. Equality of Educational Opportunity. Washington, D.C.: U.S. Government Printing Office.

_____ . College Entrance Examination Board. 1981. National Report on College-Bound Seniors.

College Placement Council, Inc. n.d. A Study of Beginning Offers. Bethlehem, Pennsylvania: College Placement Council, Inc.

Condry, John and Sharon Dyer. 1976. "Fear of success: attribution of cause to the victim." Journal of Social Issues 32:63–83.

Coser, Rose Laub. 1981. "Where have all the women gone?" In Cynthia Fuchs Epstein and Rose Laub Coser (eds.) Access to Power: Cross-National Studies of Women and Elites. London: George Allen and Unwin.

Cruickshank, W. 1977. Learning Disabilities in Home, School and Community. Syracuse University Press.

Davis, James A. 1964. Great Aspirations: the Graduate School Plans of America's College Seniors. Aldine, Chicago.

de Wolf, Virginia A. 1981. "High school mathematics preparation and sex differences in quantitative abilities." Psychology of Women Quarterly 5:555–567.

Donahue, T. J. and J. W. Costar. 1977. "Counselor discrimination against women in career selection." Journal of Counseling Psychology 24:481–486.

Dweck, Carol S., William Davidson, Sharon Nelson, and Bradley Enna. 1978. "Sex differences in learned helplessness:II. The contingencies of evaluation feedback in the classroom and III. An Experimental Analysis." Developmental Psychology 14:268–276.

England, Paula. 1981. "Assessing Trends in occupational sex segregation, 1900–1976." In Ivar Berg (ed.) Sociological Perspectives on Labor Markets. New York: Academic Press.

England, Paula and Steven D. McLaughlin. 1979. "Sex segregation of jobs and male-female income differentials." In Rodolfo Alvarez, Kenneth Lutterman, and associates (eds.) Discrimination in Organizations. San Francisco: Jossey-Bass.

Ernest, John. 1976. "Mathematics and Sex." American Mathematical Monthly 83:595–614.

Featherman, David L. and Robert M. Hauser. 1976. "Sexual inequalities and socioeconomic achievement in the United States, 1962–1973." American Sociological Review 41:462–483.

Fennema, Elizabeth. 1974. "Mathematics learning and the sexes: a review." Journal for Research in Mathematics Education 5:126–139.

Feyerherm, William. 1981. "Gender differences in delinquency." In Lee H. Bowlen, ed., Women and Crime in America. New York. MacMillan.

Fitzpatrick, J. L. 1978. "Academic underachievement, other direction, and attitudes toward women's roles in bright adolescent females." Journal of Educational Psychology 70:645–650.

Fox, Lynn H. 1970. "Sex differences in mathematical precocity: bridging the gap." In Daniel P. Keating, ed., Intellectual Talent: Research and Development. Baltimore: Johns Hopkins University Press.

Fox, Mary Frank. 1981. "Sex segregation and salary structures in academia." Sociology of Work and Occupations 8:39–60.

_____ . 1984. "Women and higher education: sex differentials in the status of student and scholars." In Jo Freeman (ed.), Women: A Feminist Perspective. Palo Alto, Calif.: Mayfield.

Frazier, Nancy and Myra Sadker. 1973. Sexism in School and Society. New York: Harper and Row.

Grant, W. Vance and Leo G. Eiden. 1982. Digest of Education Statistics. Washington, D.C.: National Center for Education Statistics.

Grant, W. V. and T. Snyder. 1983. Digest of Education Statistics, 1983–84. Washington, D.C.: National Center for Education Statistics.

Grout, H. Theodore, David W. Chilson, and Arthur G. Neal. 1982. "Sex stratification among three cohorts of recent university graduates." Sociology and Social Research 66: 269–288.

Handley, Herbert M. and Joyce F. Hickson. 1978. "Background and career orientations of women with mathematical aptitude." Journal of Vocational Behavior 13:255:262.

Herman, M. 1975. Male-Female Achievement in Eight Learning Areas. Denver: Education Commission of the States.

Horner, Matina. 1970. "Femininity and successful achievement: a basic inconsistency." In Judith Bardwick, et al., (eds.), Feminine Personality and Conflict. Belmont, Calif.: Brooks-Cole.

Jackson, Philip. 1968. Life in Classrooms. New York: Holt, Rinehart and Winston.

Jackson, P. and H. M. Lahaderne. 1967. "Inequalities of teacher-pupil contacts." Psychology in the Schools 4:204–211.

Jencks, Christopher, Marshall Smith, Henry Arland, Mary Jo Bane, David Cohen, Herbert Gintis, Barbara Heyns, and Stephen Mickelson. 1972. Inequality: A Reassessment of the Effect of Family and Schooling in America. New York: Harper and Row.

Johnson, George E. and Frank P. Stafford. 1975. "Women and the academic labor market." In Cynthia B. Lloyd (ed.), Sex, Discrimination, and the Division of Labor. New York: Columbia University Press.

Kedar-Voivodas, Gita. 1983. "The impact of elementary children's school roles and sex roles on teacher attitudes: an interactional analysis." Review of Educational Research 53:415–437.

King, Allan G. 1977. "Is occupational segregation the cause of flatter experience earnings profiles of women?" Journal of Human Resources 12:541–549.

Koblinsky, Sally A. and Alan I. Sugawara. 1984. "Nonsexist curricula, sex of teacher, and children's sex-role learning." Sex Roles 10:357–367.

Komarovsky, Mirra. 1953. Women in the Modern World. Boston: Little Brown.

Koyama, Takashi, H. Nakamura, and M. Hiramatsu. 1967. "Japan." In Raphael Patai (ed.) Women in the Modern World. New York: Free Press.

Lavin, D. E. 1965. The Prediction of Academic Performance. New York: Russell Sage Foundation.

Lipman-Blumen, Jean. 1984. Gender Roles and Power. Englewood Cliffs, N.J.: Prentice Hall.

Lueptow, Lloyd B. 1975. "Parental status and influence and the achievement orientations of high school seniors." Sociology of Education 48:91–110.

–––––– . 1980. "Social change and sex-role change in adolescent orientations toward life, work and achievement: 1964–1975." Social Psychology Quarterly 43:48–59.

Maccoby, E. and C. Jacklin. 1974. The Psychology of Sex Differences. Stanford University Press.

Madden, Janice F. 1978. "Economic rationale for sex differences in education." Southern Economic Journal 44:778–797.

Malkiel, B. G. and J. A. Malkiel. 1973. "Male-female pay differentials in professional employment." American Economic Review 63:693–705.

Martin, R. 1972, "Student sex and behavior as determinants of the type of frequency of teacher-student contact." Journal of School Psychology 10:339–344.

McCandless, B. R., A. Roberts, and T. Starnes. 1974. "Teachers' marks, achievement test scores, and aptitude relations with respect to social class, race and sex." Journal of Educational Psychology 63:153–159.

Meyer, W. J. and G. Thompson. 1963. "Teachers' interactions with boys as contrasted with girls." In Psychological Studies of Human Development (Kuhlena, R. G., and Thompson, G. G., eds.). Englewood Cliffs, NJ: Prentice-Hall.

Moulton, J. M., G. M. Robinson, and C. Elias. 1978. "Sex bias in language use: neutral pronouns that aren't." American Psychologist 33:1032–1036.

Oppenheimer, Valerie Kincade. 1968. "The sex-labeling of jobs." Industrial Relations 7:219–234.

–––––– . 1970. "The female labor force in the United States: demographic and economic factors governing its growth and changing composition." Population Monograph, Series No. 5, University of California, Berkeley: Institute of International Studies.

Overs, R. P. 1975. "Comment on bias in OOH illustrations." The Vocational Guidance Quarterly 23:340–341.

Patterson, Michelle and Laurie Engleberg. 1978. "Women in male dominated professions." In Ann H. Stromberg and Shirley Harkess (eds)., Women Working, Palo Alto, Calif.: Mayfield.

Pleck, Joseph H. 1977. "The work-family role system." Social Problems 24:417–27.

Polachek, Solomon W. 1978. "Sex differences in education: an analysis of the determinants of college major." Industrial and Labor Relations Review 31:498–508.

Quadragno, Jill. 1976. "Occupational sex-typing and internal labor market distributions: an assessment of medical specialties." Social Problems 23:442–453.

Resnick, Harvey, John Vieke, and Sanford Segal. 1982. "Is math anxiety a local phenomenon? a study of prevalence and dimensionality." Journal of Counseling Psychology 29:39–47.

Richardson, F. C. and R. M. Suinn. 1972. "The mathematics anxiety rating scale: psychometric date." Journal of Counseling Psychology 19:551–554.

Richardson, Laurel Walum. 1981. The Dynamics of Sex and Gender: A Sociological Perspective. Boston: Houghton-Mifflin.

Roby, Pamela A. 1973. "Toward full equality: more job education for women." School Review 84:181–211.

Rossi, Alice S. 1984. "The presidential address: gender and parenthood." American Sociological Review 49:1–19.

Saario, T. N., C. N. Jacklin and C. K. Tittle. 1973. "Sex role stereotyping in the public schools." Harvard Educational Review 43:386–416.

Schmuck, Patricia. 1980. "Differentiation by sex in educational professions." In J. Stockard, et al., Sex Equity in Education. New York: Academic Press.

Schur, Edwin M. 1984. Labeling Women Deviant: Gender, Stigma, and Social Control. New York: Random House.

Sears, Pauline and David Feldman. 1966. "Teacher interactions with boys and girls." National Elementary Principal 46 (November):30–35.

Sells, Lucy. 1978. "Mathematics—a critical filter." Science Teacher (February):28–9.

Serbin, L. A., K. K. O'Leary, R. N. Kent and I. J. Tonick. 1973. "A comparison of teacher response to the preacademic and problem behavior of boys and girls." Child Development 44:796–804.

Sexton, Patricia C. 1969. The Feminized Male: Classrooms, White Collars and the Decline of Manliness. New York: Vintage.

Shaw, M. and J. McCuen. 1960. "The onset of academic underachievement in bright children." Journal of Educational Psychology 51:103–108.

Smith, M. L. 1980. "Sex bias in counseling and psychotherapy." Psychological Bulletin 87:392–407.

Stevenson, Mary H. 1975. "Relative wages and sex segregation by occupation." In Cynthia B. Lloyd (ed.), Sex, Discrimination, and the Division of Labor. New York: Columbia University Press.

Stockard, Jean and Miriam M. Johnson. 1979. "The social origins of male dominance." Sex Roles 5:199–218.

_____ . 1980. Sex Roles: Sex Inequality and Sex Role Development. Englewood Cliffs, N.J.: Prentice-Hall.

Stockard, Jean. 1980. "Sex inequities in the experience of students." In J. Stockard, et al., Sex Equity in Education. New York Academic Press.

Stockard, Jean, Dwight Lang, and J. Walter Wood. 1985. "Academic merit, status variables, and students' grades." Journal of Research and Development in Education 18:12–20.

Stockard, Jean and J. Walter Wood. 1984. "The myth of female underachievement: a re-examination of sex differences in academic underachievement." American Educational Research Journal 21:825–838.

Suter, L. E. and H. P. Miller. 1973. "Income differences between men and career women." American Journal of Sociology 78:962–974.

Tobias, Shelia. 1978. Overcoming Math Anxiety. New York. W. W. Norton.

Treiman, D. J. and Heidi Hartman (eds.) 1981. Women, Work and Wages: Equal Pay for Jobs of Equal Value. Washington, D.C.: National Academy Press.

Treiman, D. J. and K. Terrell. 1975. "Sex and the process of status attainment: a comparison of working women and men." American Sociological Review 40:174–200.

Tresemer, David W. 1977. Fear of Success. New York: Plenum.

United States Bureau of the Census. 1983. Statistical Abstract of the United States: 1984. (104th edition). Washington, D.C.: U.S. Government Printing Office.

Vincenzi, Harry. 1977. "Minimizing occupational stereotypes." The Vocational Guidance Quarterly 25: 265–8.

Weeks, M. O'Neal and Emily Prior Porter. 1983. "A second look at the impact of non-traditional vocational role models and curriculum on the vocational role preferences of kindergarten children." Journal of Vocational Behavior 23:64–71.

Weitzman, Lenore J. 1984. "Sex-role socialization: a focus on women." In Jo Freeman (ed.) Women: A Feminist Perspective. Palo Alto, Calif.: Mayfield.

Weitzman, L. and D. Rizzo. 1974. "Images of males and females in elementary school books." In Biased Textbooks, The National Foundation for the Improvement of Education, Washington, D.C.

Youssef, Nadia H. 1976. "Women in the Muslin world." In L. B. Iglitzin and R. Ross (eds.) Women in the World: A Comparative Study. Santa Barbara, Calif.: Clio Books.

Toward a Sociological Perspective on Learning Disabilities

CAROL A. CHRISTENSEN
San Jose State University

MICHAEL M. GERBER
University of California, Santa Barbara

ROBERT B. EVERHART
Portland State University

In 1975, the Education for All Handicapped Children Act (PL 94-142) was enacted by Congress. It mandates that only those students who are identified as handicapped and whose handicap prevents them from benefiting from regular classroom instruction may be placed in special education. The legislation identifies handicaps which may result from physical or sensory impairments, cognitive disabilities, or emotional disturbance.

Prior to PL 94-142, there had been a long history of providing special education services to students with physical or sensory handicaps such as blindness or deafness, and students who were mentally retarded.[1] More recently (and in part fueled by the implementation of PL 94–142), a new category of handicap, "learning disability," has been introduced to education. The term "learning disability" (LD) was coined by Samuel Kirk in 1962 to describe students who displayed inadequate achievement in speech, language, spelling, writing, or arithmetic that resulted from cerebral dysfunction. The disorder was not considered to be the primary result of mental

From *Educational Theory* 36, 4 (Fall 1986): 317–331. Copyright © 1986 by Educational Theory. Reprinted with the permission of the publisher retardation, sensory deprivation or cultural or institutional factors and manifested itself as a discrepancy between the child's achievement and apparent capacity to learn.

Parallel with the existence of the category of learning disability as a relatively new phenomenon in the field of special education has been an explosive growth in the number of children identified as learning disabled.[2] The National Center for Education Statistics reported that in 1963, none of the 1,431,520 handicapped children was labeled learning disabled.[3] By 1970, the Center reported that 1,160,000, or 24 percent of the handicapped population, were identified as learning disabled,[4] and by 1980, the number of students identified as learning disabled had risen to 1,262,535, or 39 percent of handicapped students.[5] By 1982, over 1.7 million students were classified as learning disabled, almost 4.6 percent of all students enrolled in school.[6]

Since the introduction of the category, thousands of children who have been labeled learning disabled have been placed in special education programs. Yet, from its outset, the field of learning disability has been plagued by conflict and controversy based on the demonstration of chronic inconsistencies and contradictions between learning disability theory and practice.[7] This, of course, poses the question as to the appropriateness of those student placements.

Learning disability theory posits a model of psychological deviance to explain school failure by students whose failure is otherwise inexplicable. However, researchers have increasingly observed that many children who are actually identified by schools as learning disabled do not fit the theoretical model.[8] Thus, learning disability theory is inadequate for explaining the identification and treatment of children in schools. There is irony in the fact that this theory, developed originally from a psychological perspective, has been most severely challenged by findings from research using conventional psychological assumptions, methods, and tools. While researchers using the psychological model initially did not seek to question the reality of learning disabilities, they were forced to acknowledge that their psychological theories of learning disability lack explanatory power when applied to the social and institutional reality of schools.[9]

Unfortunately, the issues raised by this research show little movement toward resolution. For example, Ysseldyke and Algozzine have indicated present practices in identification and education of learning disabled children as indefensible and called for a new approach to learning disability.[10] Scriven has concluded that while we cannot say what "a pessimist would say about research and practice in special education . . . an optimist could say that we have a wonderful opportunity to start over."[11] However, neither the research that resulted in comments such as these nor the comments themselves seem to suggest the direction which such a new start would take.

A new and fruitful direction might begin with the recognition that psychological analyses have masked sociological forces underlying the development and implementation of learning disability theory.[12] Therefore, to explicate these fundamental yet covert influences it is necessary to move beyond psychological approaches and employ a different paradigm. Through application of constructs developed in the field of sociology of education, new insights into the learning disability dilemma can emerge. . . .

TRADITIONAL APPROACHES TO THE FIELD

Traditional learning disability theory is based upon a medical model. The pioneering work in the field was conducted by Strauss and Lehtinen who noted that many children exhibiting academic and behavioral difficulties performed similarly to children who were known to have sustained brain damage.[13] Therefore, they argued that if brain injury produced certain types of behavior, then it could be inferred that children who exhibited similar behavior may also have suffered brain injury.

Subsequent researchers and practitioners were less tentative in applying this logic. Consequently, in the early 1960s, prevailing professional opinion about children with normal intelligence test scores from reasonably advantaged families who failed to achieve as expected rested strongly on the assumption that their learning problems resulted from some neurological, cognitive, or perceptual abnormality.[14] A variety of psychophysiological variables were developed to account for the poor performance of learning-disabled students. These have included, for example, inadequacies in motor development,[15] visual and auditory perception,[16] psycholinguistic ability,[17] and memory and information processing skills.[18] Over the ensuing years, a variety of labels have been applied to these children, including brain injured, hyperkinetic, neurologically impaired, dyslexic, and aphasic.[19]

In 1977, federal regulations subsumed the variety of medico-educational terms applied to low-achieving children under the one category, specific learning disability, using as a definition one not substantially different from Kirk's original suggestion. According to federal regulations, learning disability

> means a disorder in one or more of the basic psychological processes involved in understanding or in using language, spoken or written, which may manifest itself in an imperfect ability to listen, think, read, spell, or do mathematical calculations. . . . The term does not include children who have learning problems which are primarily the result of visual, hearing, or motor handicaps, of mental retardation, or emotional disturbance, or of environmental, cultural, or economic disadvantage.[20]

The focus of this and most other definitions of learning disability has been on the identification of dysfunction or pathology in the child that is responsible for the child's failure to learn. The exclusionary criteria attempt to ensure that students identified as learning disabled are apparently normal (do not demonstrate any physical, intellectual, or emotional handicap) and generally come from the middle or upper classes (are not culturally disadvantaged).

While parent advocates lobbied successfully for federal recognition of learning disability as a category of handicap, there has never been complete consensus among professionals about how to define or operationalize the concept. A survey by Tucker, Stevens and Ysseldyke has shown that there is overwhelming agreement among "experts" and leaders in the field that learning disability is, in fact, a viable category and that it is clinically identifiable.[21] Yet a small band of persistent critics, buttressed by steadily accumulating data, have begun to cast serious doubts on the viability of the concept of learning disability as a within-child, neurogenic "condition."[22] In fact, as soon as the current definition of learning disability was formulated, critics identified substantial inadequacies in it.

Kirk's inclusion of a number of exclusionary criteria in the definition (the disorder is not due to mental retardation, sensory impairment, or cultural or instructional factors) was indicative of the problems which would emerge as policymakers attempted to translate the clinical concept of learning disability into mandated school practices.

Learning disability, as a category for legitimizing allocations of educational resources and services, lacks the specificity and universality criteria necessary for a viable classificatory tool. As a number of writers have observed,[23] when a phenomenon is defined in terms of what it is not rather than what it is, questions about the viability of the concept naturally follow. The behaviors manifested by the school-identified learning-disabled population are neither specific to that population nor universal within it. Behaviors attributed to learning-disabled children are shared by children labelled mentally retarded and emotionally disturbed, as well as by many nonhandicapped children.[24]

Yet, for at least fifteen years, the chronic disparity between formal definition of learning disability, recommended diagnostic instruments or clinical procedures, and characteristics of those actually identified by schools has been blithely regarded as correctable by policymakers, practitioners, and researchers alike. Learning disability identification based on the diagnosis of a neurological impairment has proven so elusive that present legislation has returned to Kirk's suggestion that, operationally, learning-disabled children are those who demonstrate a discrepancy between achievement and capacity to learn. In consequence, then, the psychometric or clinical determination that there is a "severe" discrepancy between the child's achievement and ability[25] leads unavoidably to the inference that an organic disorder lies at the heart of the measured discrepancy.

This inference, however, has not been supported by data collected on identification procedures and characteristics of the learning disabled. Diagnostic procedures indicate that children identified as learning disabled rarely show demonstrable signs of neurological problems or psychological-process disturbance. In fact, research has repeatedly demonstrated that children identified by schools as learning disabled are virtually indistinguishable from other, poorly achieving students. For example, in a recent study of one state's population of students identified by schools as learning disabled, less than one percent demonstrated any "hard" neurological signs of brain abnormality.[26] A small minority of students showed less interpretable "soft" signs (i.e., sometimes regarded as indicative of neurodevelopmental differences rather than defect), 4.7 percent demonstrated clinical signs that were considered "high-quality evidence" of processing deficits, and 11.1 percent presented what was termed "medium-quality" clinical evidence of processing deficits. The vast majority (97 percent) of students identified by schools as learning disabled in this study showed no signs of physiological impairment. Even when rather weak clinical criteria were applied, fewer than 43 percent of the assessments reviewed yielded evidence consistent with any conventional criteria for classifying children as learning disabled.

Other research has similarly reported that school-identified learning-disabled and low-achieving children are indistinguishable on tests of neurological functioning.[27] In fact, standard psychological assessment only differentiates school-identified learning-disabled children from their "nondisabled" peers at about a chance level.[28]

Extensive examinations of the population served by the Child Service Demonstration Centers between 1971 and 1980 found that children were identified as learning disabled for a variety of reasons, including emotional disturbance, mental retardation, and cultural deprivation.[29] These investigations have generally revealed enormous heterogeneity of characteristics among children identified for service. This had led Mann et al. to suggest that "underachievement and learning disability are often the same thing in the eyes of the diagnoser."[30] It was further argued that Child Service Demonstration Centers appeared to serve all underachieving children, provided that they were not blind, deaf, or severely mentally retarded, and therefore tended to identify a racially and ethnically biased population.

What explanation can be offered for the apparent discrepancy between clinical models of learning disabilities and the extreme variability of student characteristics in those identified as learning disabled by schools? Are assessment personnel sufficiently trained to identify "learning disabilities"? There is evidence indicating questionable technical adequacy of tests used by school psychologists and other assessment personnel to classify children as learning disabled. Cole, for example, has shown that there are gross technical inadequacies in the ten most frequently recommended procedures for the identification of learning-disabled students.[31]

Other researchers have questioned the way tests are used in schools. On simulated decision tasks, assessment personnel used more adequate instruments in the early stages of information gathering, but as these professionals increased the number of tests, they tended to select less adequate instruments.[32] During actual assessment, a similar trend is seen. From three to thirty-nine different instruments reportedly have been used by Child Service Demonstration Centers in assessing children for "learning disabilities."[33] In schools, relatively adequate tests are used more often than not, but evidence shows that a disconcerting number of assessment personnel tend to misinterpret[34] or simply to discount[35] the considerable amount of information accumulated from testing. While it is true that assessment personnel are sometimes confused about what psychometric or clinical results constitute evidence of a "severe" discrepancy between academic achievement and potential, neither technical adequacy of instruments nor competence of assessment personnel appears to resolve variability in school practices. Instead, the social processes of referral and assessment, much more so than the quality of data collected from diagnostic procedures, emerge as more powerfully explanatory of persistent differences between abstract descriptions of learning disabilities and characteristics of those students actually identified by schools.[36] Thus, even if valid statistical and clinical procedures were reliably applied to the problem of discriminating learning-disabled students from other underachievers, the critical decision on when a "discrepancy" is so "severe" that students require differential treatment is largely based on a social judgment, one that cannot be made on a psychometric basis alone.[37]

Moreover, the very notion that learning-disabled children fail to learn commensurate with their "potential" is an intriguing one. Since the learning-disabled population is assumed to be a subgroup of low-achieving children, the discrepancy position relies on a further assumption that some children (i.e., non-learning-disabled low achievers) should fail to learn in school while others (learning-disabled students) have greater "potential" and should not fail. According to advocates for learning disability, some children, due to a disorder of "basic psychological processes," have potential beyond that which otherwise would be indicated by their low levels of achievement. Yet, logic suggests that potential for achievement by neurologically impaired students would be limited by virtue of their neurological limitations. Nevertheless, learning disability "specialists" give scant attention to the reasonable position that if neurological impairment produces poor learning, then neurologically impaired students who demonstrate poor learning are achieving according to their "potential." Instead, the field has clung steadfastly to the assumptions underlying the medical model, holding out its promise of curative or remedial treatment. It has erected the edifice of learning disability as an innately handicapping condition. Thus, correct "diagnosis" is assumed to lead to "prescriptive" educational, psychological, and sometimes pharmacological "treatment."

In sum, an increasing number of investigators have shown that a variety of traditional assumptions about learning disability are untenable when applied to school practice. It has become more common to hear unusually strident expressions of dissatisfaction with the continued search for psychological methods for discovering neurological and other within-student causes of learning failure. Ysseldyke, for example, has called practices in the identification and treatment of learning disabled students "indefensible,"[38] and Algozzine has called the category "ludicrous."[39] However, while these and other criticisms of practice have succeeded in arousing concern, they have generally failed to explain either the forces that created this current policy dilemma or the phenomenal growth and variability in classifying children as learning disabled. Psychology-oriented empiricists who have catalogued discrepancies and inconsistencies between learning disability theory and practice have not questioned the fundamental premises upon which learning disability theory rests. Following the logic of the field, they have established that the system does not work the way it should, but they are unable to explain why this is so or suggest how it can be changed. A different set of assumptions needs to be made, and a different set of questions needs to be asked. . . .

THE SOCIOLOGY OF LEARNING DISABILITIES

Learning Disability and Student Stratification

Many of the behaviors attributed to neurological impairment in learning-disabled students can be interpreted equally well as indications of student resistance to school culture. Traditionally, learning disability theory has cited disruptive behavior associated with student failure as evidence of neuropathology. Impulsivity, hyperactivity, hyperkinesis, and attentional disorders are but a few of the medico-educational terms applied to children who engage in a variety of teacher-irritating behaviors from nail-biting and thumb-sucking to physical aggression.[40] When accompanied by low achievement, these behaviors are frequently cited as evidence of learning disability. For example, Bryan and Bryan have reported that the most frequently mentioned characteristics of learning-disabled students are hyperactivity, short attention span, and distractibility.[41] Hyperactivity was defined by Bryan and Bryan as "behavior which is disruptive to the group,"[42] while a short attention span or distractibility "reflects the child's interests in things other than those on which he should be concentrating."[43]

Few investigators have questioned the assumption that these disrupting behaviors are indicative of an underlying neurological problem. Although little research has been conducted into alternatives to neurological explanations for learning-disabled students' behavior, the behaviors frequently labelled as hyperactivity, distractibility, or impulsivity are indistinguishable from the unruliness that Apple refers to as a manifestation of student resistance. Thus, it can be argued that many learning-disabled students frequently behave in ways that may be interpreted as resistance to the school culture.

Support for the notion that learning-disabled students demonstrate resistant behavior can be found in the literature on the characteristics of identified students. The increasing trend to identify disproportionate numbers of minority students as learning disabled[44] suggests that behavior typical of low-socioeconomic-status students may facilitate their identification as learning disabled. As Willis and Everhart have pointed out,[45] the low achievement of many students in school is a manifestation of their resistance to instruction rather than of innate or biological deficiency within the student.

The resistant nature of students' behavior has largely gone unrecognized in special education research based on psychology-oriented paradigms. Recently, however, a few researchers working within a sociological paradigm have demonstrated that learning-disabled students' behavior is marked by both active and passive resistance to instructional practices that are inappropriate to meet their educational needs. For example, Malmstad, Ginsburg, and Croft conducted an ethnographic study of a summer remedial program for learning-disabled students.[46] They found that the students engaged in both overt and covert forms of resistance in response to pedagogical techniques that were inadequate in remediating their learning problems. Overt resistance took the form of behavior which was intended to disrupt and irritate teachers and peers, while covert or passive resistance did not disturb others but sabotaged any learning that was intended to occur. Passive resistance was manifested by sitting quietly, daydreaming, or, as Malmstad et al. note, "tuning out and turning inwards rather than seeking guidance."[47]

Certain instructional episodes appeared to provoke student resistance. In particular, students engaged in resistant activity when tasks were too difficult or when given instructions which they did not understand.

As workers control the employment of their skills, so students can refuse to participate in the learning process. This behavior has been interpreted by traditional psychological approaches through constructs such as "learned helplessness," which regards the child's behavior as inadequate to meet the situation requirements. However, a sociological analysis views the child's behavior as a meaningful response to the situation. While both approaches recognize the deleterious effects of resistant behavior on the student's learning, the sociological analysis views the student as an active participant in the instructional process, not merely as a passive recipient of school messages. Resistant behavior, which is often misconstrued as deviance or learned helplessness, may in fact be a manifestation of the child's moral and political indignation when confronted with alien cultural expectations.

The only consistent defining feature of the learning-disabled population is poor achievement.[48] Learning-disabled students appear to be a subgroup of students with particularly poor achievement; unruly student behavior traditionally associated with the social stratification of low-socioeconomic-status groups is also highly characteristic of learning-disabled children. It then appears reasonable to suggest that learning disability programs function similarly to other special education programs in providing differential treatment to students who will occupy the lower-socioeconomic-status positions in society. If this is so, the unrivaled popularity which the learning disability label enjoys compared with other handicapping labels and the phenomenal growth of learning disability programs in the last two decades appear inexplicable.

Unlike Ysseldyke, who has called current practices "indefensible," most educators, researchers, administrators, and parents appear pleased with and supportive of the growth of the field.[49] Given the limited utility of traditional approaches to learning disability in terms of the remediation of learning problems, the lack of clear evidence that special education is effective for these children, and the potential role of learning disability classification in social stratification, this attitude is somewhat perplexing.

Clearly, the attraction of the learning disability label does not result from its role in the social stratification of low-achieving children. Rather, its acceptability rests on its power to explain and justify poor school performance in terms of child attributes instead of institutional attributes. The label of the learning-disabled child then not only helps stratify students along hierarchical dimensions but also serves to legitimize that stratification. . . .

Institutional Factors Contributing to Learning Disability

While evidence has been mounting on the futility of pursuing a neurological approach to many learning problems, there has been a steady accumulation of evidence that suggests that specified instructional practices can aggravate or alleviate the effect of individual differences in learning. Schools tend to treat groups of students as homogeneous and are thus relatively inflexible in response to diversity in student characteristics. For example, the lock-step grade level system serves such a homogenizing function through the process of grouping students whose ages vary by approximately a year into a single grade. Once students are identified with a grade, each individual is expected to perform according to the established grade standard.

There is some evidence to suggest that institutional rigidity in response to student diversity contributes to student "problems" which later become labeled as "disabilities." For example, Ames found that a number of students labeled as "disabled" were significantly younger than their same-grade peers and consequently were less cognitively capable of benefiting from instruction designed for older students.[50] Age at entry to first grade, where students are often given their first experience of formal reading and mathematics instruction, appears particularly crucial in predisposing a child for identification as being disabled in later grades.[51]

In addition to finding that students experiencing problems are often younger than normally achieving students, there are data to suggest that learning-disabled students tend to be less mature than their same-age nondisabled peers. Poor readers show more signs of neuromaturational delay when compared with good readers,[52] and in the area of mathematics many learning-disabled students demonstrate a developmental delay in the use of age-appropriate cognitive strategies in problem solving, thereby performing like younger, less mature students.[53] This suggests that the provision of instruction that is congruent with the child's grade level rather than his/her developmental level may contribute to poor academic performance. Students then might be better served if schools demonstrated greater flexibility in response to the age and maturational diversity of students rather than relying on the learning disability label to explain and justify inadequate student performance.

In addition to basing instruction on grade standard expectation, schools tend to use uniform curricula and to demand student homogeneity in terms of interest in curriculum and materials in the classroom. In this regard, Elkind suggests that many children may be curriculum disabled rather than learning disabled.[54] He argues that many children fail to benefit from instruction because the curriculum and materials are perceptually or cognitively inappropriate, confusing, boring, or in conflict with the learning styles and strategies of students. For these children failure is attributable to a mismatch between the curriculum and the individual rather than to a malfunction in the child's brain.

In addition, texts tend to portray the values, attitudes, and life styles of the predominant middle class.[55] This middle-class bias in school materials frequently conflicts with the values and attitudes of students who come from poor or ethnic/racial-minority backgrounds, thus contributing to the alienation which many of these students feel toward school and learning. The relationship between culturally appropriate materials and the acquisition of reading skills has been established.[56] Consequently, the poor performance of many minority children can be explained, at least in part, by the inappropriate messages encoded into many introductory reading texts. By calling many of these children "learning disabled" and seeking to identify within the child deficits that explain the student's problems, schools exempt from examination the institutional factors which could account for the child's poor achievement.

There is also evidence that inadequate instruction can play a fundamental role in the achievement problems of learning-disabled children. For example, Janksy and de Hirsch demonstrated a relationship between what was judged to be competent classroom instruction and learning disability.[57] The number of students found to be eligible for learning disability classification in classrooms taught by teachers classified by school-site principals as competent at the beginning of the school year was reduced by 50 percent by the end of the school year. Yet it is almost unknown for schools to examine failure in terms of curricular or instructional inadequacy. In a National Education Association poll only 5 percent of teachers from a national survey felt that poor teaching or schools could be responsible for student failure.[58] Smith, in an investigation of team meetings making special education placement decisions, found that attempts to explain the child's behavior as being a result of teaching methods or curriculum were severely sanctioned by school personnel.[59]

This is not to suggest that there is no variability in students' ability to benefit from instruction or that educators in some way conspire with the elite social groups to limit the educational outcomes of some children. Rather, the meritocratic assumptions of the dominant hegemony often serve to mask the stratification and legitimizing functions of the school from all participants, including teachers, parents, and students. This masking process is crucial because, as Ysseldyke and his colleagues suggested,[60] meaningful intervention programs for learning-disabled students must be implemented at the point of referral, in the regular classroom. However, the medical mystique that has been generated by learning disability theory inhibits this process from occurring. Belief that learning disability has a biological etiology rather than an instructional one effectively precludes appropriate remedial measures from being taken and reinforces belief in an overriding biological determinism to social structure.

SUMMARY AND CONCLUSIONS

This paper has focused on the concept of learning disability and the manner in which the premises underlying this concept affect research and practice. We have reviewed some of the many inconsistencies which are inherent in the medical and psychological models used to define such disabilities and offered that adherence to these models masks some of the underlying structural conditions accompanying the behavior of learning-disabled students. We concluded that by legitimizing student impairment as a rationale for student failure, special education facilitates the very social stratification in schools which it professes to minimize.

At the level of practice, at least two areas demand the attention of special educators. Concerning first the area of instruction, educators need to realize that while there are a number of students in school who are difficult to teach, the instructional technology required to instruct these students is available. In the case of learning-disabled students this technology is not mystical, based on psychomedical rhetoric, but utilizes the same procedures that have proven successful with all types of students.[61] These techniques involve direct instruction in the content area in which the student is experiencing difficulty. Rosenshine, for example, has synthesized the literature on direct instruction and identified six teaching functions which characterize effective instruction.[62] More systematic use of these procedures could enhance the skill development of learning-disabled students.

A second area of practice demanding careful scrutiny is that of the referral process. Although special education legislation appears to dictate specific procedures for the identification and treatment of handicapped children, research indicates that these mandates are not adequate to explain the referral and placement of learning-disabled students. For example, Mehan found that the individual Education Plan (IEP) meetings did not typically make the determination of handicap and placement decisions as prescribed by law.[63] Rather, such decisions were made through a complex and relatively covert process which preceded the meeting. The IEP meeting became a somewhat ritualistic event where professionals gathered the necessary parent consent for decisions which had already been made.

Mehan also reported that a number of students placed in special education classes did not meet the criteria for identification as handicapped as mandated by law.[64] However, a search of student records revealed that several children who did meet the criteria attended regular classes in the school. These children had never been referred to assessment for special education placement. These findings are in keeping with the work of other researchers who have found that many children labeled learning disabled do not meet the traditionally accepted criteria for identification.[65]

Research is needed to explicate the mechanisms which discriminate who is identified as learning disabled from who is not. Research has established that the identification process cannot be explained by legal mandates or theoretical definitions of learning disabilities. However, few insights have emerged into the characteristics and behaviors which students demonstrate that lead to referral and identification as learning disabled. If, as the present sociological analysis suggests, student resistance to classroom instruction plays a fundamental role in learning failure, then a research agenda needs to be developed which is concerned with the investigation of student perceptions, goals, attitudes to classroom processes, and the social context in which they exist.

The assumptions supporting concepts such as learning disability need to be unmasked at the same time local changes are implemented. By seeing as problematic the assumptions that the school is a neutral allocator of cultural capital and that individuals occupy positions in the social hierarchy according to individual merit based on biologically determined traits, new solutions can emerge. Rejection of the position that failure is the result of individual deficit allows institutional forces to be employed to intervene in the process of the systematic differentiation of students.

Reform in special education then can proceed only as a critique of education itself. Until special educators perceive children labelled learning disabled not as neurologically impaired but as children with teaching or instructional disabilities, special education will continue to provide the justification for practices which are detrimental to those students unfortunate enough to become its clients.

NOTES

1. J. E. Wallin, *The Education of Handicapped Children* (Boston: Houghton Mifflin, 1924).
2. B. Algozzine and L. Korinek, "Where is Special Education for Students with High Prevalence Handicaps Going?" *Exceptional Children* 51, no. 5 (1985): 388–94; M. M. Gerber, "The Department of Education's Sixth Annual Report to Congress on P.L. 94–142: Is Congress Getting the Full Story?" *Exceptional Children* 51, no. 3 (1984): 209–24.
3. National Center for Education Statistics, *Digest of Education Statistics 1966* (Washington, D.C.: Government Printing Office).
4. National Center for Education Statistics, *Digest of Education Statistics 1981* Washington, D.C.: Government Printing Office).
5. National Center for Education Statistics, *Digest of Education Statistics 1983–84* (Washington, D.C.: Government Printing Office).
6. Gerber, "The Department of Education's Sixth Annual Report."
7. B. Algozzine and J. E. Ysseldyke, "Learning Disabilities as a Subset of School Failure: The Over-Sophistication of a Concept," *Exceptional Children* 50, no. 3 (1983): 242–46; G. S. Cole, "The Learning-Disabilities Test Battery: Empirical and Social Issues," *Harvard Educational Review* 48, no. 3 (1978): 313–40.
8. L. Mann, C. H. Davis, C. W. Boyer, C. M. Metz, and B. Wolford, "LD or Not LD, That Was the Question: A Retrospective Analysis of Child Service Demonstration Centers' Compliance with the Federal Definition of Learning Disabilities," *Journal of Learning Disabilities* 16, no. 1 (1983): 14–17; Cole, "Learning-Disabilities Test Battery."
9. Algozzine and Ysseldyke, "Learning Disabilities as a Subset of School Failure"; Cole, "Learning-Disability Test Battery"; M. M. Gerber and M. I. Semmel, "Teachers as Imperfect Test: Reconceptualizing the Referral Process," *Educational Psychologist* 19, no. 3 (1984): 137–48.
10. Algozzine and Ysseldyke, "Learning Disabilities as a Subset of School Failure."
11. M. Scriven, "Comments on Gene Glass's Paper Presented at the Wingspread Conference on Public Policy and the Special Education Task of the 1980s" (Racine, Wisconsin, September 1981), 10.
12. J. G. Carrier, "Masking the Social in Educational Knowledge: The Case of Learning Disability Theory," *American Journal of Sociology* 39, no. 1 (1983): 949–73, and "Sociology and Special Education: Differentiation and Allocation in Mass Education," *American Journal of Education* 94, no. (1986): 281–312.
13. A. Strauss and L. Lehtinen, *Psychopathology and Education of the Brain Injured Child* (New York: Grune & Stratton, 1947).
14. Carrier, "Masking the Social in Educational Knowledge."
15. N. C. Kepart, *The Slow Learner in the Classroom* (Columbus, Ohio: Merrill, 1960).
16. M. Frostig, "Visual Perception, Integrative Functions and Academic Learning," *Journal of Learning Disabilities* 5, no. 1 (1972): 1–15; J. Wepman, *Auditory Discrimination Test* (Chicago: Language Research Associates, 1958).

17. S. A. Kirk and W. P. Kirk, *Psycholinguistic Learning Disabilities: Diagnosis and Remediation* (Champaign, Ill.: University of Illinois Press, 1972).

18. F. P. Connor, "Improving School Instruction for Learning Disabled Children: The Teachers' College Institute," *Exceptional Education Quarterly* 4, no. 1 (1983): 23–44.

19. P. Schrag and D. Divoky, *The Myth of the Hyperactive Child* (New York: Pantheon Books, 1975).

20. U.S. Office of Education, "Education of Handicapped Children: Implementation of Part B of Education of the Handicapped Act," *Federal Register* 1977, 42.

21. J. Tucker, L. J. Stevens, and J. E. Ysseldyke, "Learning Disabilities: The Experts Speak Out," *Journal of Learning Disabilities* 16, no. 1 (1983): 6–14.

22. J. Ysseldyke, B. Algozzine, and M. Thurlow, "On Interpreting Institute Research: A Response to McKinney," *Exceptional Education Quarterly* 4, no. 1 (1983): 1945–47.

23. D. P. Hallahan and J. M. Kauffman, "Labels, Categories, Behaviors: ED, LD and EMR Reconsidered," *Journal of Special Education* 11, no. 2 (1977): 139–49.

24. Algozzine and Ysseldyke, "Learning Disabilities as a Subset of School Failure": S. A. Kirk and J. Elkins, "Learning Disabilities: Characteristics of Children Enrolled in the Child Service Demonstration Centers," *Journal of Learning Disabilities* 8, no. 10 (1975): 630–37; Mann et al., "LD or Not LD, That Was the Question."

25. U.S. Office of Education, "Education of Handicapped Children."

26. L. A. Shepard, M. L. Smith, and C. P. Vojir, "Characteristics of Pupils Identified as Learning Disabled," *American Educational Research Journal* 20, no. 3 (1983): 309–11.

27. J. Ysseldyke, B. Algozzine, and S. Epps, "A Logical and Empirical Analysis of Current Practice in Classifying Students as Handicapped," *Exceptional Children* 50, no. 2 (1983): 160–66.

28. J. Ysseldyke, B. Algozzine, M. R. Shinn, and M. McGue, "Similarities and Differences between Low Achievers and Students Classified as Learning Disabled," *Journal of Special Education* 16, no. 1 (1979): 73–83.

29. Mann et al., "LD or Not LD, That Was the Question"; see also Kirk and Elkins, "Learning Disabilities"; C. A. Norman and N. Zigmond, "Characteristics of Children Labelled and Served as Learning Disabled in School Systems with Child Service Demonstration Centers," *Journal of Learning Disabilities* 13, no. 10 (1980): 546–47.

30. Mann et al., "LD or Not LD, That Was the Question," 16.

31. Cole, "The Learning-Disabilities Test Battery."

32. J. Ysseldyke, B. Algozzine, R. Regan, and M. Potter, "Technical Adequacy of Tests Used by Professionals in Similated Decision Making," *Psychology in the Schools* 17 (1980): 202–9.

33. J. Ysseldyke and M. Thurlow, "Psychoeducational Assessment and Decision Making: A Review," in their *Synthesis of the Knowledge Base: Identification and Assessment of Learning Disabled Children*, Monograph No. 2 (Minneapolis: University of Minnesota Institute for Research on Learning Disabilities, 1979).

34. See, for instance, W. A. Davis and L. A. Shepard, "Specialists' Use of Tests and Clinical Judgement in the Diagnosis of Learning Disabilities," *Learning Disability Quarterly* 6, no. 2 (1983): 128–38.

35. See, for instance, J. Ysseldyke, B. Algozzine, L. Richey, and J. Graden, "Declaring Students Eligible for Learning Disability Services: Why Bother with the Data?" *Learning Disability Quarterly* 5, no. 1 (1982): 37–44.

36. Gerber and Semmel, "Teachers as Imperfect Test"; M. L. Smith, *How Educators Decide Who Is Learning Disabled* (Springfield, Ill.: Charles C. Thomas, 1982); J. Ysseldyke, "Current Practices in Making Psychoeducational Decisions about Learning Disabled Students," *Journal of Learning Disabilities* 16, no. 4 (1983): 226–33.

37. Gerber and Semmel, "Teachers as Imperfect Test."

38. Ysseldyke, Algozzine, and Thurlow, "On Interpreting Institute Research."

39. Cited in Tucker, Stevens, and Ysseldyke, "Learning Disabilities."

40. Schrag and Divoky, *The Myth of the Hyperactive Child.*

41. T. H. Bryan and J. H. Bryan, *Understanding Learning Disabilities* (Sherman Oaks, Calif.: Alfred Publishing, 1975).

42. Ibid., 34.

43. Ibid., 35.

44. J. A. Tucker, "Ethnic Proportions in Classes for the Learning Disabled: Issues in Nonbiased Assessment," *Journal of Special Education* 14, no. 2 (1980): 93–105; Mann et al., "LD or Not LD, That Was the Question."

45. Willis, *Learning to Labor; Everhart, Reading, Writing and Resistance.*

46. B. J. Malmstad, M. B. Ginsburg, and J. C. Croft, "The Social Construction of Reading Lessons: Resistance and Social Reproduction," *Journal of Education* 165 (1983): 359–73.

47. Ibid.

48. Algozzine and Ysseldyke, "Learning Disabilities as a Subset of School Failure."

49. Tucker, Stevens, and Ysseldyke, "Learning Disabilities."

50. L. B. Ames, "Learning Disability: Truth or Trap?" *Journal of Learning Disabilities* 16, no. 1 (1983): 19–20.

51. C. D. Maddux, "First-grade Entry Age in a Sample of Children Labeled Learning Disabled," *Learning Disability Quarterly* 3, no. 5 (1980): 79–83.

52. R. L. Gottesman, L. Croen, and L. Rotken, "Urban Second Grade Children: A Profile of Good and Poor Readers," *Journal of Learning Disabilities* 15, no. 1 (1982): 268–72.

53. Connor, "Improving School Instruction for Learning Disabled Children."

54. D. Elkind, "Viewpoint: The Curriculum-Disabled Child," *Topics in Learning and Learning Disabilities* 3, no. 3 (1983): 71–78.

55. G. E. Blom, "The Role of Content in the Teaching of Reading," in *What Research Has to Say about Reading Instruction,* ed. S. J. Samuels (Newark, Del.: International Reading Association, 1978).

56. G. Whipple, "Multicultural Primers for Today's Children," *Education Digest* 29 (1964): 26–29.

57. J. Janksy and K. de Hirsch, *Preventing Reading Failure* (New York: Harper and Row, 1972).

58. National Education Association, "Teacher Opinion Poll," *Today's Education* 68, no. 10 (1979).

59. Smith, *How Educators Decide.*

60. Ysseldyke, Algozzine, and Thurlow, "On Interpreting Institute Research."

61. Ibid.

62. B. Rosenshine, "Teaching Functions in Instructional Programs," *The Elementary School Journal* 83 (1983): 335–51.

63. H. Mehan, personal communication, 1984.

64. Ibid.

65. Mann et al., "LD or not LD, That Was the Question."

9

Education, Occupation, and Income

We have come to the end of students' educational lifecourse. Having followed them through school in the preceding three chapters, we now pick them up as they emerge from school and enter the labor force. This transition used to be much less structured in times past, when education had little connection to work. But over the course of this century, schooling has become tightly entwined with the occupational and class structures of advanced industrial societies. High levels of education have become a prerequisite for entrance into the professions and, often, the ranks of management. A high school diploma, meanwhile, has become necessary simply for securing a respectable job.

Social scientists agree on education's importance in job placement. But they disagree sharply over the reasons for this. Is it because education provides important technical skills that employers value, as functionalists claim? Is it because it provides docile workers who have accepted the work hierarchy, as many Marxists argue? Or is it because higher educational credentials provide a convenient device to raise an occupation's status and restrict job access to people of a certain background, as Weberians claim? The readings in this chapter examine the main explanations that have been given for education's role in job placement and explore what educational requirements are likely to be in the next 20 years.

Table 1 depicts the strong relationship between educational attainment and economic success in the United States. The first part of Table 1 gives the incomes attained by recipients of different educational credentials. As can be seen, college graduates on the average earn considerably higher salaries than do less educated people.[1] The second part gives the occupations attained by

---

[1]Various studies put the correlation between years of education attained and income between 0.2 and 0.5 (on a scale from 0 to 1, which is a perfect correlation), with the best estimate being around 0.4 (Jencks and others, 1979: 168–169, 178–179; Sewell and Hauser, 1975: 72).

TABLE 1 The Relationship Between Education and Economic Success
in the United States

	Median Personal Income by Level of Education (1986)*			
	Four or More Years of College ($)	One to Three Years of College ($)	High School Only ($)	One to Three Years of High School ($)
Men	33,304	23,738	19,772	13,401
Women	18,065	11,574	8,366	5,831

	Occupations Attained by Level of Education (1987)†				
	Professional and Managerial (%)	Technical, Sales, and Administrative (%)	Service (%)	Blue Collar (Precision Production, Operators) (%)	Total (%)
Four Years of College or More	68	23	3	5	100
One to Three Years of College	26	41	10	20	100
Four Years of High School Only	12	36	14	35	100
Less than Four Years of High School	5	13	22	53	100

*U.S. Bureau of the Census (1987: Table 7). Data refer to persons 15 years of age and older working either full-time or part-time. The lower incomes of women reflect not only such factors as fewer hours worked and less labor force experience, but also restriction to female-dominated jobs and unequal pay for equal work.

†U.S. Bureau of the Census (1988: Table 629). Data are for the civilian noninstitutionalized population age 25 and over. The percentages add up horizontally. The list of occupations is not exhaustive, so the figures will not total 100 percent. The category of precision production includes skilled workers such as carpenters and tool and die makers.

people with a given educational credential. It demonstrates that on the average college graduates enter considerably more prestigious occupations than less educated people.[2] Two-thirds of college graduates have entered professional and managerial occupations, with the remainder largely entering

[2]The correlation between educational attainment and occupational status is variously estimated to fall around 0.60 (Blau and Duncan, 1967: 169; Featherman and Hauser, 1978: 259; Jencks and others, 1979: 168–169).

technical, sales, and administrative (largely clerical) occupations.[3] Meanwhile, high school graduates rarely enter professional and managerial jobs and end up about equally split among technical, sales, and administrative occupations, and blue collar jobs.

People's economic success is affected not just by the *amount* of schooling they receive but also by the *type*. A variety of studies indicate, for example, that whether one begins at a four-year versus a two-year college or a highly selective versus an unselective college has a significant impact, over and above other factors, on economic attainment (Dougherty, 1987; Jencks and others, 1979: 186–187; Karabel and McClelland, 1987; Solmon and Taubman, 1973; Useem and Karabel, 1986). For example, Useem and Karabel (1986) find that graduates of elite colleges and professional schools such as Harvard or Stanford are significantly better able to attain the topmost corporate positions than are graduates of nonelite institutions. Among top corporate managers, the very top officers—those who are chief executive officers, members of several boards of directors, and members of the major business associations— are more likely to have received a bachelor's degree or business or law degree from an elite institution than are less highly placed executives.[4]

The strong association between the educational credentials people receive and the incomes and occupations they attain is striking, but it should not be taken simply at face value. There is no inherent and unchangeable relationship between a given level of education and a given job. This can be seen in three ways.

First, the relationship between education and occupation and income is historically variable. The strong relationship we see now is relatively recent and largely restricted to industrial societies.[5] In preindustrial societies, such as the United States prior to the Civil War and Mali and Ecuador today, schools tend to have little connection to the economy. For the most part, schools are largely places to acquire rudimentary reading, writing, and arithmetic skills. Few go on to high school and college to acquire more advanced learning. Except for the clergy, preindustrial societies have little need for college graduates' skills or credentials. However, as societies begin to industrialize and national governments become more powerful, as the United States began to do in the 1840s and as many societies are doing today, education begins to develop a closer tie to the economy. Employers (ranging from business firms to the government) increasingly demand certain educational credentials in hiring in order to secure workers who are more skilled and better motivated. Many occupations try to professionalize, raising their

[3]This figure pertains to all college graduates above the age of 25. The percentage for recent college graduates will be somewhat lower because of the "underemployment" of college graduates that began to appear in the early 1970s. See below for more discussion.

[4]This educational effect holds even when one controls for class background, which also affects chance of success. Useem and Karabel (1986) find that upper-class origins provide a powerful stimulus to corporate success over and above the fact that upper-class people tend to receive better educational credentials.

[5]See Paci (1977) for a discussion of different stages in the relationship between education and the economy.

educational requirements as a means to increase their pay and prestige (Collins, 1979: chap. 6; Larson, 1977). Governments develop civil service systems that rely on educational credentials. Moreover, they encourage mass education as means to unify their nations (Boli, Ramirez, and Meyer, 1985; Collins, 1977), thus increasing the demand for teachers.[6] Meanwhile, alternative ways of acquiring job skills, such as apprenticeship, began to wither.[7]

Even though the relationship between education and economic success is now very strong in the United States, it is still subject to change. During the 1970s, the labor market demand for college graduates weakened sharply, although they continued to enjoy a strong advantage over high school graduates. Between 1970 and 1978 only 46 percent of college graduates entered professional or technical jobs, while 73 percent of those graduating between 1962 and 1969 entered these jobs (Smith, 1986).[8]

A second reason for maintaining a certain skepticism about the strong association between educational and economic success is that a good part of this association is not due to any unique effect of education. It represents instead the effect of family background and other extraeducational variables. Better educated people get better jobs in part because they come from economically and culturally more advantaged families and score better on exams than less educated people. These characteristics would help better educated people get desirable jobs even if they did not happen to be highly educated. In fact, several studies find that controlling for family background and test scores reduces the association between educational attainment and occupational status and income by as much as half (Featherman and Hauser, 1978: 258–259; Jencks and others, 1979: 167–172, 180–183).[9]

Finally, the general economic payoff to education is deceptive in that it does not hold uniformly across different kinds of students. Studies repeatedly find that, among blacks and whites with similar family background and test scores, blacks receive a smaller payoff to their education than do whites (Featherman and Hauser, 1978: 340, 344–345, 357–359, 367–375; Jencks and others, 1979: 174, 197).[10] Similarly, women get a smaller economic payoff on

---

[6]Educators have not been passive in this process, but have pioneered new connections between education and the economy (Dougherty, 1988).

[7]A major exception to this withering away of the apprenticeship system is West Germany (Hamilton, 1987).

[8]The extent, causes, and implications of this drop are subject to considerable debate (Featherman and Hauser, 1978: 276–283; Freeman, 1976; Smith, 1986). For example, even if true, the declining economic returns to a college degree do not mean that the *relative* advantage of a college degree disappeared. College graduates continue to enjoy a decided advantage over high school graduates. Still, the absolute benefits of a college degree have suffered and this is reflected in student attitudes (Hammack, 1987–1988).

[9]These studies find that controlling for family background and test scores reduces the apparent economic payoff of elementary and secondary schooling much more than that of higher education. The reduction is as much as 40 to 60 percent in the first case and about 12 to 40 percent in the second.

[10]This racial disparity holds especially for elementary and secondary schooling. The occupational and income gap is smallest between black and white college graduates (Featherman and Hauser, 1978: 342; and Jencks and others, 1979: 200).

their education than do men with similar marital status and labor force characteristics (England, Farkas, Kilbourne, and Dou, 1988; Tienda, Smith, and Ortiz, 1987).[11] Finally, students with blue collar fathers tend to get a lower occupational payoff to their education than those with white collar fathers (but there seems to be no difference in the income payoff) (Jencks and others, 1979: 175, 186, 355).

EXPLAINING THE ASSOCIATION BETWEEN EDUCATIONAL AND ECONOMIC SUCCESS

Granted that schooling has a strong independent association with economic success, how do we explain this association? Sociologists and economists have provided three main answers to this question, ones corresponding to the functionalist, Marxist, and Weberian theories described in Chapter 2.

Functionalism

The functionalist position has two slightly different variants: functionalist theory in sociology and human capital theory in economics. But both advance basically the same explanation of the connection between education and economic success. The fundamental argument is that people with higher educational credentials typically receive better jobs because those jobs require greater skills and these skills are acquired through advanced education. And advanced industrial societies have highly educated populations because they need complex skills that can only be acquired through extended education.

Within this general framework, sociological and economic functionalists strike somewhat different positions. Sociological functionalists focus on why better educated people receive more prestigious jobs, while economic functionalists focus on why they receive better paying jobs. Moreover, sociologists simply argue that better educated people get better jobs because their skills allow them to perform better, while economists argue that better educated people get those jobs because their skills make them more productive and thus more profitable to employers.

The selection by Johns, Morphet, and Alexander, "Human Capital and the Economic Benefits of Education," presents the dominant version of the economic functionalist explanation of the education-economy connection.[12] This argument typically goes by the name of "human capital" theory. It argues that employers are willing to pay more for better educated employees because those employees have more "human capital" (skills and other traits) than less educated employees and because this human capital makes them

---

[11]These studies examine the impact of years of education on income, for women and men separately, controlling for differences in marital status, amount of hours worked, labor force experience, proportion female of occupation, and many other variables.

[12]For statements of the sociological version of the functionalist argument, see Clark (1962) and Trow (1961).

more productive and therefore more profitable to employers.[13] Johns and his colleagues describe this human capital as taking such forms as good health, work skills, work habits, and capacity to learn quickly and adapt to changes. These skills and traits are described as a form of capital because they are instruments of production and because workers can invest in them (for example, by paying tuition to go to college). Besides describing the forms of human capital, Johns and his colleagues explain how economists calculate the rate of return to education: that is, the net economic payoff to education, once one takes into account the cost of education and the earnings one gave up in order to secure an education.

The functionalist argument at first seems very compelling. It agrees with schools' self-description as institutions that transmit job-relevant skills. And it has provided much of the rationale for government programs to eliminate poverty and unemployment through vocational education and manpower training. As a result, human capital theory and functionalist theory generally have received powerful support from the highly educated, higher education leaders, and government officials.[14]

But very powerful objections have been raised against functionalist theory. The selection by Gregory Squires, "Education, Jobs, and Inequality: Functional and Conflict Models of Social Stratification in the United States," reviews the main objections to functionalist theory and sketches an alternative explanation of the education-economy relationship.[15] Squires finds evidence for four claims that go directly against the "techno-democratic" (functionalist) argument that education's association with occupation is due to the fact that it supplies job-relevant skills. He argues that the supply of advanced education has outrun any evident increase in the skills demanded by our economy; that younger workers are usually better educated but may be doing no more difficult work than older workers in the same job; that greater education often makes a worker no more (and perhaps even less) productive than a less educated worker; and that workers (even professionals) usually learn their skills outside of school, often on the job.[16]

Marxism

In place of the functionalist argument, Squires proposes an essentially Marxist explanation. He argues that employers give preference to more educated workers in hiring and pay because they believe that such workers are more willing to accept corporations' hierarchical structure. Squires does

---

[13]Credit for the development of human capital theory usually goes to Theodore W. Schultz (1961) and Gary Becker (1964). But human capital theory arguably goes back to the 19th-century economist Alfred Marshall (Karabel and Halsey, 1977: 12).

[14]For more on the appeals of human capital theory, see Karabel and Halsey (1977: 13, 307–308).

[15]Squires's argument is much indebted to the work of Randall Collins (1979: chaps. 1–2) and Ivar Berg (1971).

[16]This criticism of the job relevance of school-learned skills is applicable even to specifically vocational education. See Grasso and Shea (1979), Grubb (1977), and Reubens (1974).

not explain why more educated workers are more docile. But since his argument resembles Bowles and Gintis's (1976) argument about why employers value better educated workers, we can bring them in to fill out the Marxist argument. They argue that different levels of education inculcate different kinds of work orientation: elementary and secondary schooling stresses unquestioning obedience of rules; community colleges a small degree of initiative; and advanced higher education the initiative necessary to command an industrial apparatus. This difference in training is due to a "correspondence" between the way education is organized at different levels of the school system and the manner in which work is organized at different levels of the corporate hierarchy.[17]

Weberianism

A third major explanation for the education-occupation association is advanced by Weberians. They join Marxists in holding that employers often prefer the better educated because education makes workers more docile. But in contrast to Marxists, Weberians go on to argue that educational and economic success are connected also because advanced education provides a handy way for those in desirable occupations to enhance the prestige of their occupations and to pass them on to people of their choice. For example, Collins (1979: chap. 6) argues that the elite of the legal profession pushed to increase the educational requirements for entrance into law—requiring attendance of law school and passage of a bar exam rather than the apprenticeship system under which Abraham Lincoln, among others, qualified. Their motive was to reduce the number of non-upper-class, often radical lawyers around the turn of the century.

Weberians have also noted that occupational elites have increased educational requirements as a way of enhancing the prestige of their occupation. The more educated the members of an occupation, the more willing employers and the public are to accede to their demands for greater prestige, higher pay, and more control over their conditions of work (Collins, 1979: chap. 6; Larson, 1977).

The selection by Hammack, "The Changing Relationship Between Education and Occupation: The Case of Nursing," takes up this second Weberian argument. He examines the current efforts of the leaders of the nursing profession to improve the prestige and power of their occupation by, among other things, increasing the educational requirement for entrance into nursing. They are calling for requiring all registered nurses to hold at least a bachelor's degree from a regular college, thus eliminating the long-standing path of entry through three-year hospital "diploma" programs. As he notes, this move is dictated much less by the technical skill requirements of nursing than the need to counter the greater prestige and power of the doctors they work under.

[17]See the selection by Anyon in Chapter 7 for an elaboration of Bowles and Gintis's "correspondence principle."

THE ECONOMY'S FUTURE DEMANDS ON EDUCATION AND THE PROBLEM OF OVEREDUCATION

The Marxian and Weberian explanations both deny that the education-economy nexus is largely due to the schools' providing job-relevant skills.[18] Hence, they suggest the possibility that the supply of educational credentials could well outrun the demands of the economy. And indeed this seems to be the case. In the early 1970s, observers began to note a significant number of "underemployed" college graduates: that is, graduates who were taking jobs that were not typical "college jobs" and that could well be filled by high school graduates (V. Burris, 1983; B. Burris, 1983; Freeman, 1976; Rumberger, 1981; Smith, 1986).[19] This raises the question of what the likely future of the education-economy nexus is.

The selection by the economist Henry Levin—"Jobs: A Changing Work-force, a Changing Education?"—argues against the current belief that our nation's economic salvation lies in the growth of jobs in high technology and that our economy will be demanding larger numbers of college graduates. Levin notes that very few of the jobs created in 1982–1995 will be in high technology. Moreover, only a quarter of the jobs will require college skills. The bulk of newly created jobs will be in such low-skilled occupations as custodian, sales clerk, and secretary. This prediction is important, for it contradicts a very popular argument, that the main reason American industry has been slipping in competition with Japan and Germany has been a dearth of highly trained workers.[20] Levin's argument is sobering, so he ends with several economic and educational policy recommendations for ensuring the production of good jobs rather than passively accepting the low-skill jobs likely to be produced.

CONCLUSION

The debates over how much impact education has on its graduates' occupations and incomes and the causes of this impact are not simply academic

---

[18]Weberians, such as Collins (1979), are particularly emphatic in denying the importance of job skills. More Marxist-influenced scholars are more willing to argue that, while schools exert their main influence by shaping attitudes, they do also inculcate job-relevant skills. See, for example, Walters and Rubinson (1983).

[19]However, this change in the *absolute* economic payoff to a college education has not greatly diminished its *relative* payoff. College graduates still do better than high school graduates, whose prospects have fallen as well. This stability in the *relative* payoff of different levels of education is reflected in the stability of the correlation between educational and occupational attainment (Featherman and Hauser, 1978: 276–280).

[20]This argument is given great prominence in several recent educational reports, most notably that of the National Commission on Excellence in Education (1983). For further discussion, see Chapter 10.

issues. As we will see in the concluding chapter of this book, American schools are under criticism as ineffective, above all in preparing students for occupational life. In fact, the National Commission on Excellence in Education (1983) argued that American schools are largely to blame for why the United States has been slipping in its economic competition with Japan. Consequently, a fundamental feature of recent proposals for reform in American schools has been to improve their capacity for vocational training. These proposals are usually based, however, on a functionalist perspective of the relationship between education and occupation. Hence, in evaluating the current reform recommendations, it is important to keep in mind the debate in this chapter between the functionalist and antifunctionalist explanations of the education-economy relationship.

REFERENCES

Becker, Gary. 1964. *Human Capital*. New York: National Bureau of Economic Research.

Berg, Ivar. 1971. *Education and Jobs*. Boston: Beacon Press.

Blau, Peter, and Otis D. Duncan. 1967. *The American Occupational Structure*. New York: Wiley.

Boli, John, Francisco O. Ramirez, and John W. Meyer. 1985. "Exploring the Origins and Expansion of Mass Education." *Comparative Education Review* 29: 145–170.

Bowles, Samuel, and Herbert Gintis. 1976. *Schooling in Capitalist America*. New York: Basic Books.

Burris, Beverly. 1983. *No Room at the Top*. New York: Praeger.

Burris, Val. 1983. "The Social and Political Consequences of Overeducation." *American Sociological Review* 48 (August): 454–67.

Clark, Burton. 1962. *Educating the Expert Society*. San Francisco: Chandler.

Collins, Randall. 1977. "Some Comparative Principles of Educational Stratification." *Harvard Educational Review* 47:1–27. (Excerpted in Chapter 2 of this book.)

———. 1979. *The Credential Society*. New York: Academic Press.

Dougherty, Kevin. 1987. "The Effects of Community Colleges: Aid or Hindrance to Socioeconomic Attainment?" *Sociology of Education* 60 (April): 86–103. (Excerpted in Chapter 5 of this book.)

———. 1988. "Educational Policymaking and the Relative Autonomy of the State: The Case of Occupational Education in the Community College." *Sociological Forum* 3 (summer): 400–432.

England, Paula, George Farkas, Barbara Stanek Kilbourne, and Thomas Dou. 1988. "Explaining Occupational Sex Segregation and Wages: Findings from a Model with Fixed Effects." *American Sociological Review* 53 (August): 544–558.

Featherman, David L., and Robert M. Hauser. 1978. *Opportunity and Change*. New York: Academic Press.

Freeman, Richard. 1976. *The Overeducated American*. New York: Academic Press.

Grasso, John, and John Shea. 1979. *Vocational Education and Training*. Berkeley, CA: Carnegie Council for Policy Studies in Higher Education.

Grubb, W. Norton. 1977. "The Phoenix of Vocational Education." In U.S. National Institute of Education, *Planning Papers for the Vocational Education Study.* Washington, DC: National Institute of Education.

Hamilton, Stephen F. 1987. "Apprenticeship as a Transition to Adulthood in West Germany." *American Journal of Education* 95 (February): 314–345.

Hammack, Floyd M. 1987–1988. "The Decline in Critical and Historical Sensibility Among College Students: What Has Changed?" *The Gallatin Review* 7 (winter): 27–33.

Jencks, Christopher, Marshall Smith, Henry Acland, Mary Jo Bane, David Cohen, Herbert Gintis, Barbara Heyns, and Stephan Michelson. 1972. *Inequality.* New York: Basic Books.

_____, Susan Bartlett, Mary Corcoran, James Crouse, David Eaglesfield, Gregory Jackson, Kent McClelland, Peter Mueser, Michael Olneck, Joseph Schwartz, Sherry Ward, and Jill Williams. 1979. *Who Gets Ahead?* New York: Basic Books.

Karabel, Jerome, and A. H. Halsey (eds.). 1977. *Power and Ideology in Education.* New York: Oxford University Press.

_____, and Katherine McClelland. 1987. "Occupational Advancement and the Impact of College Rank on Labor Market Outcomes." *Sociological Inquiry* 57 (fall): 323–347.

Larson, Magali Sarfatti. 1977. *The Rise of Professionalism.* Berkeley: University of California Press.

National Commission on Excellence in Education. 1983. *A Nation at Risk.* Washington, DC: Government Printing Office. (Excerpted in Chapter 10.)

Paci, Massimo. 1977. "Education and the Capitalist Labor Market." In Jerome Karabel and A. H. Halsey (eds.), *Power and Ideology in Education*, pp. 340–355. New York: Oxford University Press.

Reubens, Beatrice. 1974. "Education for *All* in High School?" In James O'Toole (ed.), *Work and the Quality of Life*, pp. 299–337. Cambridge, MA: MIT Press.

Rumberger, Russell. 1981. *Overeducation in the U.S. Labor Market.* New York: Praeger.

Schultz, Theodore W. 1961. "Investment in Human Capital." *American Economic Review* 51 (March): 1–17. Reprinted in Jerome Karabel and A. H. Halsey (eds.), *Power and Ideology in Education*, pp. 313–324. New York: Oxford University Press, 1977.

Sewell, William H., and Robert M. Hauser. 1975. *Education, Occupation, and Earnings.* New York: Academic Press.

Smith, Herbert. 1986. "Overeducation and Underemployment: An Agnostic Review." *Sociology of Education* 59 (April): 85–99.

Solmon, Lewis, and Paul Taubman (eds.) 1973. *Does College Matter?* New York: Academic Press.

Tienda, Marta, Shelley A. Smith, and Vilma Ortiz. 1987. "Industrial Restructuring, Gender Segregation, and Sex Differences in Earnings." *American Sociological Review* 52 (April): 195–210.

Trow, Martin. 1961. "The Second Transformation of American Secondary Schooling." *International Journal of Comparative Sociology* 2: 144–166. Reprinted in Jerome Karabel and A. H. Halsey (eds.), *Power and Ideology in Education*, pp. 105–118. New York: Oxford University Press, 1977.

U.S. Bureau of the Census. 1987. "Money Income and Poverty Status of Families and Persons in the United States: 1986." Current Population Reports, Series P-60, No. 157. Washington, DC: Government Printing Office.

U.S. Bureau of the Census. 1988. *Statistical Abstract of the United States, 1988*. Washington, DC: Government Printing Office.

U.S. Department of Education. Center for Education Statistics. 1987. *Digest of Education Statistics, 1987*. Washington, DC: Government Printing Office.

Useem, Michael, and Jerome Karabel. 1986. "Pathways to Top Corporate Management." *American Sociological Review* 51: 184–200.

Walters, Pamela B., and Richard Rubinson. 1983. "Educational Expansion and Economic Output in the United States, 1890–1969." *American Sociological Review* 48: 480–493.

Human Capital and the
Economic Benefits of Education

ROE L. JOHNS
University of Florida

EDGAR L. MORPHET
University of California, Berkeley

KERN ALEXANDER
University of Florida

The value of the human being to a nation is evidenced historically by the physical strength of conquering armies, both ancient and modern. In its crudest form, human value was recognized by the treatment of human beings as property in slave trade throughout the centuries. Value of the human being was largely determined by physical rather than mental capability. Human valuation and the labor of individuals have shaped markets, whether provided by freemen, serfs, or slaves.[1] The market value of the human changes dramatically with fluctuations in the supply of workers; as Tuchman observes, a decline in population caused by the bubonic plague of the fourteenth century placed such a premium on the laborer that the value of the individual was reflected in wage reforms which swept western Europe and affected commerce for centuries.[2]

Throughout these earlier eras, valuation was based on people's physical productivity as "hewers of wood and drawers of water," not as philosophers, scientists, teachers, or physicians. According to this method of valuing the individual, the nation with the greatest population had the greatest human capital value. The fallacy in this approach became apparent in the nineteenth and twentieth centuries, as the world's work force became less "labor intensive" and more "brain intensive." The country with the greatest population was not necessarily the most productive or influential. If sheer numbers had been the measure of human value then England would have been a dependency of India rather than vice versa.

It was not until the 1960s that an awakening to the real value of human capital actually occurred. Guided by Theodore W. Schultz, later to win the Nobel Prize for Economic Science, economists and educators began to recognize the economic importance of the human being in the production process and to begin to seek ways to measure the magnitude of human capital.[3] This is not to say that human knowledge and skill were never observed before, but it is certainly true that no attempts were made in an economic sense to quantify the value of human capital. The economist Petty had earlier observed "that the value of mankind is worth twenty times the present annual earning of labor,"[4] but Petty's estimates were without empirical base. Though he recognized the value of human capital his imprecision of measurement tended to create problems of academic credibility. . . .

MEASURING THE BENEFITS OF EDUCATION

. . .

Cash Value Approach

Educational benefits can also be measured by relating earnings to the educational level of individuals. On the average, individuals with a high-school education will have higher earnings than those with only a tenth-grade education, and college graduates will earn more than high-school graduates. This pattern has held for many years. In 1939, the average annual earnings of a high-school graduate was 64 percent of the college graduate; in 1949 the figure was 61 percent; in 1957, 60 percent; and in 1968, 69 percent. Today, the earnings of high-school graduates remain about two-thirds those of college graduates. Table 1 shows how the differential broadens when a graduate-school education of five or more years is compared with a high-school education.

Figure 1 shows age-income profiles by levels of education without costs taken into account. In other words, this figure shows the cash value of education over the working life of an individual, by elementary, high-school, and college level. The line ABC shows the average pattern of income for the elementary-school graduate. DEF gives the pattern for the high-school graduate, and GHI shows that of the college graduate.

The continuity of the relationship between more education and higher earnings rebuts earlier warnings by such economists as Seymour Harris of Harvard, who in 1949 warned that a persistent increase in college graduates would flood the employment market and make relative earning power fall. He had erroneously concluded that "college students within the next twenty

TABLE 1 1978 Mean Income by Educational Level

Educational Level	Mean Annual Income		
	25-34	25 years and over	18+
Elementary School			
dropout (less than 8 years)	$ 8,174	$ 7,149	$11,297
graduate	9,553	9,367	13,561
High School			
dropout (1–3 years)	10,699	11,784	14,194
graduate	13,505	15,152	16,385
College			
dropout (1–3 years)	14,328	16,708	18,273
graduate (4 years or more)	17,471	23,724	25,974
graduate (5 years or more)	18,424	25,687	28,509

Source: U.S. Bureau of the Census, Current Population Reports, *Consumer Income: Money Income of Families and Persons in the United States: 1978,* Series P–60, No. 123, (June 1980), Table 50, pp. 212–15. Data refer to males of all races by age groups.

years are doomed to disappointment after graduation, as the number of coveted openings will be substantially less than the numbers seeking them."[5]

Such conclusions overlook the expansive influence of education on the economy; a better-educated work force will create economic demand for products which can only be produced by a better-educated employee. "The demand for highly trained workers has kept pace with the supply, so that

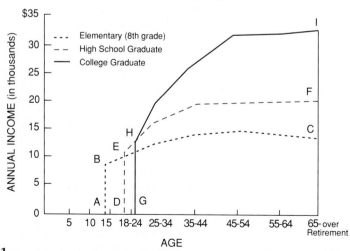

MEAN YEAR-ROUND FULL-TIME WORKERS' INCOME
BY AGE AND EDUCATION, 1978

FIGURE 1

they are, by and large, fully employed."[6] Thus, the monetary benefits to education are well documented and a person progressing ever upward through the educational system can be comforted by the knowledge that he or she, on the average, stands a better chance of having a higher income throughout a lifetime. This does not, of course, assure that every individual will earn more than if he or she had only completed, say, the tenth grade. Our history is replete with examples of "self-made" persons, who without formal education became economically independent. Actuarially, though, the odds are much better for one to become economically successful if he or she has more education than less.

Costs.   At different school levels, the direct-monetary-returns approach to measuring the economic desirability of obtaining an education does not give the entire picture, for although it is accurate as far as it goes, it does not take into account the important element of costs. It only looks at the benefits. To take costs into account requires a more complex analysis of the value of education.

The benefit-cost approach is schematically represented in Figure 2. Notice how this differs from Figure 1 in that costs are a negative feature, which must be overcome by income in order for there to be a positive return at retirement age. This schematic is, of course, not to scale. If it were, the costs would possibly show an even more dramatic difference because of foregone income. If we assume that the profile represents individual or private returns on educational investment, and we further assume that the education is taking place in a public school, then the costs to the individual at the elementary level ABC are quite small. Foregone income is very little, since the value of annual earnings of an illiterate or semiliterate person amounts to very little. Additionally, the individual does not incur direct costs in attending a public school, since the state pays for the education in its entirety. Thus, benefit-costs of elementary education to the individual can be expected to be quite impressive, since the costs are so low. On the other hand, if one is considering social benefits, then the direct costs of schooling must be taken into account, thereby reducing the benefit-cost ratio (see Figure 2).

With a public high-school education, the costs, FGH, are expected to be greater for the individual because of foregone income. The benefit-cost ratio will therefore be reduced somewhat even though income, HIJ, of the high-school graduate is greater.

The individual costs to a college graduate are relatively greater than to either the elementary- or high-school graduate, since the state does not pay the full cost of a higher education and the student must pay out of pocket for tuition, books, room and board, in addition to greater foregone earnings. In the schematic, then, KLM is of greater magnitude and the income, MNO, must be correspondingly higher to offset costs and potential interest thereon over the working life of the individual.

Cost-Benefit Approach
An alternative method of showing the value of education is to relate costs of education to the benefit to be derived, and from this calculate rates-

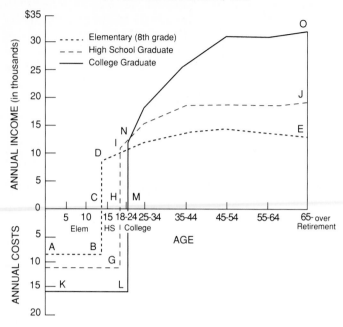

FIGURE 2

of-return or cost-benefit ratios. This is a method of net valuing education wherein the costs of obtaining an education are deducted from monetary gains over the working life of the individual.

Costs.   Education has both private and social costs, which may be both direct and indirect. If the student is attending a private school, direct private costs are incurred for tuition, fees, books, room and board. In a public school, the majority of these costs are subsumed by the public treasury, and, thus become social costs. Indirect costs of education are embodied in the earnings which are foregone by all persons of working age, but foregone earnings are also a cost to society, a reduction in the total productivity of the nation. This may be viewed in macroeconomic terms, but can also be measured in the amount of tax funds which a state foregoes when an individual is not employed. Of course, the state here assumes, as does the individual, that earnings foregone for the sake of education at some early point in the person's career will yield greater returns later. This is the essence of the idea of investment in education. Table 2 shows the major types and categories of costs.

It is within the realm of costs that much of the disenchantment with rate-of-return studies has been generated. Schultz maintained that only about half of the total social cost for education should be considered as an investment. It must be acknowledged that all education is not undertaken as an investment. Much of the educational experience of most persons is simply

TABLE 2   Types and Categories of Social and Private
Educational Costs

	Categories of Costs	
Types of Costs	Social	Private
Direct Costs	1. Salaries of teachers, administrators, and nonprofessional personnel	Tuition and fees
	2. Books, supplies and equipment (total)	Books, supplies, and equipment (out-of-pocket expenditures)
	3. Transportation (total)	Extra travel
	4. Room and board (total)	Room and board
	5. Scholarship and other subsidies to students	
	6. Capital expenditures	
Indirect Costs	7. Earnings foregone	Earnings foregone

consumed and enjoyed with no thought to what the expenses for the education will earn them in the future. Does the student make an economically rational choice to invest in education, as he or she would in stocks and bonds?

Shaffer has maintained that the entire notion of rate-of-return analysis of education has no place in economic theory because there is no way to appropriately apportion costs between consumption and benefit. He says that:

> Any attempt to show that rational individuals tend to undertake expenditure on education up to the point where the marginal productivity of the human capital produced by the process of education equals the rate of interest—a point at which the marginal expenditure on education yields a return equal to the return on marginal expenditure for any other factor of production—would be a mockery of economic theory.[7]

Shaffer admittedly represents a rather extreme viewpoint, which rejects the idea of education being treated as a pecuniary benefit, but even an advocate of investment must admit that there is much imprecision of measurement introduced by the intractable problems of delineating consumption from investment. If, for example, only one-half the costs of education were attributable to consumption, then the benefits derived, compared to actual investment, would be doubled. As Bowen observes, for those who say that the college years were the "best years of his life," the consumption portion may even be more than one-half.[8] Too, the study of humanities, art, and music may well have a much higher consumption purpose than the study of business, education, or law. Certainly, there would appear to be less consumption in vocational training, which is designed specifically for a particular job.

This issue has not been satisfactorily resolved and is not likely to be. Yet, education advocates may be secure in knowing that in most studies few or none of the costs are attributable to consumption and most or all costs are assumed to be investment; thus rates of return to education are generally understated.

Benefits. Benefits from education may be either monetary or non-monetary and either private (individual) or social. Monetary returns are measurable and are therefore most commonly used in cost-benefit studies. The social externalities of education are difficult to quantify and are, therefore, seldom relied on in estimating returns to education. A discussion of social nonmonetary benefits is presented later in this chapter. Table 3 presents a categorization of both private and social benefits of education.

Direct benefits to the individual are typically measured by increases in earning power after completion of the educational program. Natural ability of the individual, ambition, family connections, family social and economic status, inherited wealth, race, sex, and education of parents may all have a bearing on future earning potential, but cannot be accurately quantified. For example, it has been estimated that anywhere from 5 to 35 percent of income differentials are attributable to differences in ability,[9] while Griliches and Mason have calculated the bias attributable to ability at only about 10 percent.[10] While estimates of the influence of native ability on economic returns vary widely, the overstatement does not appear to be a serious source of bias to determination of returns to investment in education.[11]

The most widely used method of calculating the cost-benefit of education is through rate-of-return analysis. This approach takes into account the costs of education to both the individual and society and relates them to the benefits of each. Benefits are measured only in terms of higher earnings throughout the working life of those who acquire the education. Rate-of-return analysis represents a major alternative to manpower studies for educational planning. The manpower method seeks to estimate the supply and demand of the work force by various educational levels and types, while the rate-of-return approach determines the economic benefits of acquiring higher levels and different types of education. For example, one may calculate the rates-of-return to various vocational training programs or to investment in teacher or legal education in universities.[12] Rate-of-return analysis measures the demand for a certain type of training among various types of occupational groups.

Rates-of-return are the interaction between several supply-and-demand effects. These groups will probably operate differently over time in various age groups. An oversupply of lawyers will likely drive down legal fees,

TABLE 3   Private and Social Benefits of Education

Private (Individual) Benefits	Social Benefits
Direct Benefits	

Monetary
    Net increase in earnings after taxes
 	
    Additional fringe benefits
	Increase in taxes paid by the educated as a result of education

Nonmonetary Increased satisfaction derived from exposure to new knowledge and cultural opportunities for both students and parents	
Indirect Benefits	

Monetary
    Work options available at each educational level
 	
    Increased consumption of goods and services due to extra income
	Increases in other income
	a) due to increasing productivity of future generations as children become better educated (intergeneration effect)

Nonmonetary
    Intergenerational effect between parent and child
 	
    Job satisfaction
	b) due to previously unemployed workers taking jobs vacated by program participants (vacuum effect)—indirect income effect

	c) due to reduced tax burden (tax effects)
	d) due to incremental productivity and earnings of workers (indirect income effect)
	Availability to employer of well-trained and skilled labor force
	Improved living conditions of neighbors

Source: Adapted from table by Asefa Gabregiorgis, "Rate of Return on Secondary Education in the Bahamas." (Ph.D. dissertation, University of Alberta), p. 75.

reducing the return to investment in legal education. Although the freedom of the marketplace does not operate as fully for public school teachers as for lawyers because of the state's control of salaries, nevertheless, a scarcity of teachers in a certain geographical area or in a particular field of study would likely be reflected in higher wages to attract competent teachers and a resultingly higher rate of return.

Two methods are used for the measurement of costs and benefits, the net-present-value approach and the internal rate-of-return. The net present value is the sum of the benefits minus the sum of costs, both discounted at an appropriate rate. The result is the net value today of payments in the future.[13] The net present value requires that benefits minus costs be larger than zero. To explain more fully, the value of both benefits and costs may be determined at any point in time. If one is looking into the future, it must be assumed that money invested today in education could have also been invested in alternative sources of income. It is, therefore, necessary to take into account the interest (or discount rate) that could have been earned by this alternative investment. Studies of this type will usually include two or three alternative discount rates of possibly 5, 8, and 12 percent. The net-present-value approach includes the discount rate in the formula and it is modified until the present value of benefits equates to the present value of costs.

Another model is the internal rate-of-return (IROR), which does not use the discount rate internal to the formula. Instead, the IROR is concerned only with the relationship of costs to benefits, not the total value of each. In this calculation the rate-of-return is derived and then compared to a chosen discount rate. For example, if it is found that a high-school education produces a rate-of-return of 16 percent and if a realistic alternative investment would produce a 10 percent rate, then the investment in education is more favorable by 6 percent. Those who want to delve more deeply into rate-of-return analysis may wish to refer to formulas given by Psacharopoulos, Cohn, and Alexander and Melcher.[14]

The IROR may be graphically represented as the interest rate which equates the present value of benefits with the present value of costs. The discount rate (or interest rate), r, at which the curve for benefits intersects the curve for costs, is the internal rate-of-return (see Figure 3).

A third model is the benefit-cost ratio, which compares benefits where a ratio is produced, which, if exceeding unity, denotes a positive payoff. Where the present value of benefits divided by the present value of costs exceeds one, then the project is worthwhile. For example, if the present value of benefits is $3,000 and the present value of costs is $1,000, then the benefit-cost ratio would be $3000/1000 = 3$. Since 3 is greater than unity, the investment would be a good investment. . . .

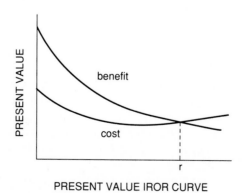

PRESENT VALUE IROR CURVE

FIGURE 3

EXTERNAL BENEFITS TO INVESTMENT IN EDUCATION

To this point we have considered only a portion of the benefits to investment in education. The entire value of education must also be viewed in light of its social possibilities and consequences. The monetary benefits considered in rates-of-return include only the value of increased earnings of the individual and the value of additional taxes collected by the state. Actually, the direct monetary returns are not inclusive of all the economic returns accruable from investment in education. In the broader economic context, benefits include:

(1) anything which increases production; (2) anything which reduces the need to incur costs such as for law enforcement, thereby releasing resources for alternative uses; and (3) anything which increases welfare possibilities directly, such as development of public-spiritedness or social consciousness of one's neighbor.[15]

Increased Labor Productivity.   The first of these refers to the overall strengthening of the economic system through increased worker productivity. This is not a direct monetary return to education, but a broader economic externality of education. Of course, as Denison documents, human capital does not alone determine the optimum productivity of a country, but it is a major contributor. In recent years, the United States has experienced a relative decline in worker productivity which cannot be attributed to a decrease in educational level but rather to inadequacy of capital formation and obsolescence of physical assets of many of the major industrial firms in the United States. Further, in some cases, the relative decline may also be attributed to poor planning and questionable management practices.

By and large, though, education can improve the general environment in which production takes place, having a positive effect beyond that to those who are actually receiving the education. The educated may be better prepared to pass on or receive training than the uneducated or may more adequately enhance productive psychological and motivational factors.

Even though the value of education as it relates to work has been drawn into the question and an all-out attack on credentialism has been launched in recent years,[16] the value of education for employment is readily apparent. The more educated person in the job market receives preferential treatment from the employer. Whether this is justified is largely irrelevant if the marketplace responds in this manner. Employers appear to recognize that the educated worker has favorable external effects on other workers and on the firm in general. An interdependence exists whereby both the worker and the firm have a financial interest in the education of fellow workers.[17]

Employers believe that education of the employee improves the financial potential of the firm. There is a definite positive relationship between the amount of formal education and on-the-job training received.[18] Firms apparently have found that greater productivity can be achieved with less cost of investing in the more educated employees. Greater benefits can be obtained by grafting job training on to the knowledge already acquired from formal schooling.[19] It may also be that the employer responds in part to the worker's own willingness to invest in himself, since employer investment in the worker appears to increase in about the same proportion as the worker's self-investment in schooling.

The less-educated experience a greater amount of unemployment. On the average, "job losers" have almost a year and a half less education than "job keepers."[20] Labor turnover and unemployment are related to consumer demand for goods and services. Even though the correlation is rather weak, the more educated, being more generally employed in service jobs, have greater employment stability.[21] Some evidence also shows that in certain areas of the economy, physical capital is more likely to be substituted for unskilled than for skilled labor. Consequently, the less-educated labor force is more susceptible to layoffs due to advances in technology and fluctuations in types of goods produced and methods of production.[22] Thus, education may be viewed as a type of private (and social) hedge against technological displacement. Weisbrod called this the "hedging option," the value of which is difficult to quantify.[23] Further, inexperienced and uneducated workers who earn less than minimum wage have higher unemployment. Better-educated workers may well have the edge in communication, discipline of the mind, flexibility, and adaptability. Also, the more educated the worker, the more likely he or she is to be receptive to new ideas and knowledge.[24]

The production process may be regarded as the transformation of resources into goods and services. Transformation is generally more efficient if the process utilizes educated workers, even though the precise nature of the interaction between education and economic productivity is not known. Bowen lists six ways that worker productivity is increased by education:

(1) *Quantity of product*—workers with higher levels of education produce more goods and services in a given time period because of their greater skill, dexterity, and knowledge.

(2) *Quality of product*—the more educated produce better goods and render services with greater skill and/or sensitivity to human conditions.

(3) *Product mix*—educated workers may be able to produce goods and services which are more highly prized by society than those produced by workers with less education.

(4) *Participation in the labor force*—educated workers are less susceptible to lost time from unemployment and illness, and are usually characterized by higher aspirations.

(5) *Allocative ability*—workers, through education, may be better able to assess their own talents; to achieve greater skills; and to be more receptive to new technologies, new products, and new ideas.

(6) *Job satisfaction*—the educated may have greater job satisfaction because they tend to acquire jobs with greater psychic rewards.[25]

Machlup has summarized the effects of education on increased productivity as follows:

> It is with regard to . . . improvements in the quality of labor, that education can play a really significant role. Positive effects may be expected on five scores: (a) better working habits and discipline, increased labor efforts, and greater reliability; (b) better health through more wholesome and sanitary ways of living; (c) improved skills, better comprehension of working requirements, and increased efficiency; (d) prompter adaptability to momentary changes, especially in jobs which require quick evaluation of new information, and, in general, fast reactions; and (e) increased capability to move into more productive occupations when opportunities arise. All levels of education may contribute to improving the quality of labor.[26]

Education differs in a basic way from most other major social or public services in that it constitutes an investment in knowledge and skills which can yield economic and social benefits in the future. It differs materially from governmental welfare or health expenditures, which may be characterized as maintenance of human capital rather than development. While it is true that payment of health bills for the needy may help heal and return them to the work force or that welfare payments for food or shelter preserve human capital, it is nevertheless important to note that neither of these public programs actually increases the worth of human capital. The same human raw material is maintained but not necessarily enhanced. More nonproductive yet is public expenditure for police protection and prison systems. While every society expends large sums on these public functions, the benefits cannot be classified as investments in the development of human capital except in a limited sense where rehabilitation of prisoners actually works and the individual is returned to the labor force as a positive factor in the production process. Largely, though, penal expenditures must be viewed as nonproductive in the economic sense. While it is true that benefits from these public services cannot be completely self-contained, it is obvious that provision of public education is quite different from those services characterized as social services, and education should not be treated in the same light by legislators. There is a fundamental difference between the mere maintenance of human capital and the development of human capital.

Reduced Need for Other Services.   This is not to say, of course, that public expenditures for health and welfare are not desirable and necessary on humanitarian grounds, nor is it to say public expenditures for law enforcement should or can be reduced; but it is important to note that education must be considered in a different context—as a remedy to the problems and not as a problem itself. Increased investment in education will tend to reduce the necessity of placing more public revenue into health, welfare, and the penal system. An increment of education reduces government expenditures on crime prevention, fire protection, public health, and medical care.[27] It may be argued that education reduces crime primarily because education reduces unemployment, and the employed commit fewer crimes.[28] Some portion of criminal behavior can be attributed to a lack of education.[29] With a rise in family income, a corresponding decrease in delinquency may be found; since more education and greater income are related, a similar relationship exists between education and crime.[30] . . .

NOTES

1. For an excellent discussion of the history of human capital see Elchanan Cohn, *The Economics of Education*, rev. ed. (Cambridge, Mass.: Ballinger Publishing Company, 1979), pp. 13–26.

2. Barbara W. Tuchman, *A Distant Mirror: The Calamitous 14th Century* (New York: Alfred A. Knopf, 1978), pp. 119–20.

3. Theodore W. Schultz, "Investment in Human Capital," *American Economic Review,* 51 (March 1961), 1–17.

4. Sir William Petty, *Political Arithmetick, or A Discourse Concerning the Extent and Value of Lands, Buildings, etc.* (London: 1666).

5. Seymour E. Harris, *The Market for College Graduates and Related Aspects of Education and Income* (Cambridge, Mass.: Harvard University Press, 1949), p. 64.

6. Herman P. Miller, *Rich Man, Poor Man* (New York: Thomas Y. Crowell Company, Inc., 1971), p. 168.

7. H. G. Shaffer, "Investment in Human Capital: Comment," *American Economic Review* 52, No. 4 (1961), 1026–35.

8. W. G. Bowen, "Assessing the Economic Contribution of Education: An Appraisal of Alternative Approaches," *Higher Education. Report of the Committee under the Chairmanship of Lord Robbins, Report: 961–63* (London: H.M.S.O., 1963), 73–96.

9. Paul Taubman and Terence Wales, "Education as an Investment and a Screening Device," in *Education, Income and Human Behavior,* ed. F. Thomas Juster (New York: McGraw-Hill Book Company 1975), pp. 95–121; and Paul Taubman "Personal Characteristics and the Distribution of Earnings," in *The Personal Distribution of Incomes,* ed. A. B. Atkinson (London: George Allen and Unwin, 1976), pp. 193–226.

10. Zvi Griliches and William M. Mason, "Education, Income and Ability," in *Investment in Education,* ed. T. W. Schultz (Chicago: University of Chicago Press, 1971), p. 87.

11. John C. Hause, "Earnings Profile: Ability and Schooling," in ed., T. W. Schultz, *op. cit.* in note 10, p. 131.

12. Richard S. Eckaus, *Estimating the Returns to Education: A Disaggregated Approach* (Berkeley, Calif.: Carnegie Commission on Higher Education, 1973).

13. Asefa Gabregiorgis, *Rate of Return on Secondary Education in the Bahamas,* (Ph.D. dissertation, University of Alberta), p. 117.

14. George Psacharopoulos, *Returns to Education* (San Francisco: Jossey-Bass, Inc., Publishers, 1973). Cohn, *op. cit.;* Kern Alexander and Thomas Melcher, *A Computerized System for Benefit-Cost Analysis in Vocational Education* (Gainesville, Fla.: Institute for Educational Finance, University of Florida, 1980).

15. Burton A. Weisbrod, *External Benefits of Public Education* (Princeton, N.J.: Princeton University, Industrial Relations Section, Department of Economics, 1964), p. 17.

16. *Work in America,* Report of a Special Task Force to the Secretary of Health, Education and Welfare (Cambridge, Mass.: MIT Press, 1973), pp. 134–52.

17. Burton A. Weisbrod, "Investing in Human Capital," in *Education and the Economics of Human Capital,* ed. Ronald A. Wykstra (New York: Free Press, 1971), pp. 79–81.

18. Jacob Mincer, "On-the-Job Training: Costs, Returns, and Some Implications," *Journal of Political Economy* 70 (October 1962 Supp.).

19. Richard Perlman, *The Economics of Education* (New York: McGraw-Hill Book Company, 1973), p. 32.

20. John D. Owen, *School Inequality and the Welfare State* (Baltimore: Johns Hopkins University Press, 1974), p. 91.

21. *Ibid.*
22. *Ibid.*
23. Weisbrod, *op. cit.* in note 15.
24. J. Ronnie Davis, "The Social and Economic Externalities of Education," in *Economic Factors Affecting the Financing of Education*, Vol. 2, eds. R. L. Johns and others (Gainesville, Fla.: National Educational Finance Project, 1970), p. 66.
25. H. R. Bowen, *Investment in Learning* (San Francisco: Jossey-Bass, Inc., Publishers, 1977), pp. 159–60.
26. Fritz Machlup, *Education and Economic Growth* (Lincoln, Nebr.: University of Nebraska Press, 1970), pp. 7–8.
27. Carl S. Shoup, *Public Finance* (Chicago: Aldine Publishing Co., 1969), p. 97.
28. Weisbrod, *op. cit.*, p. 31.
29. Werner Hirsch, Elbert W. Segalhorst, and Morton J. Marcus, *Spillover of Public Education Costs and Benefits* (Berkeley: University of California Press, 1964), p. 342.
30. Belton Fleisher, "The Effect of Income on Delinquency," *American Economic Review* 56, No. 1 (March 1966), 118–37.

SELECTED REFERENCES

Blaug, Mark. *An Introduction to the Economics of Education*. New York: Penguin Books, 1970.

Bowen, Howard R. *Investment in Learning*. San Francisco: Jossey-Bass, Inc., Publishers, 1977.

Cohn, Elchanan. *The Economics of Education*. Cambridge, Mass.: Ballinger Publishing Company, 1979.

Eckaus, Richard S. *Estimating the Returns to Education: A Disaggregated Approach*. Berkeley, Calif.: Carnegie Commission on Higher Education, 1973.

Ginsberg, Eli. *The Human Economy*. New York: McGraw-Hill Book Company, 1976.

Harbison, Frederick H. *Human Resources as the Wealth of Nations*. New York: Oxford University Press, 1973.

Johns, Roe L., and others, eds. *Economic Factors Affecting the Financing of Education*. Gainsville, Fla.: National Educational Finance Project. Vol. 2, 1970.

Machlup, Fritz. *Education and Economic Growth*. Lincoln, Nebr.: University of Nebraska Press, 1970.

Miller, Herman P. *Rich Man, Poor Man*. New York: Thomas Y. Crowell Company, Inc., 1971.

Psacharopoulos, George. *Returns to Education*. San Francisco: Jossey-Bass, Inc. Publishers, 1973.

Rogers, Daniel C., and Hirsch S. Ruchlin. *Economics and Education: Principles and Applications*. New York: Free Press, 1971.

Schultz, Theodore W. *Investment in Human Capital*. New York: Free Press, 1971.

Schultz, Theodore W., ed. *Investment in Education: The Equity-Efficiendy Quandary*. Chicago: University of Chicago Press, 1972.

Schultz, Theodore W. *Investing in People: The Economics of Population Quality*. Berkeley: University of California Press, 1981.

Vaizey, John. *The Economics of Education*. London: Faber & Faber, 1962.

Education, Jobs, and Inequality: Functional and Conflict Models of Social Stratification in the United States*

GREGORY D. SQUIRES

University of Wisconsin, Milwaukee

. . . industry places a high value on the college degree, not because it is convinced that the four years of schooling insure that individuals acquire maturity and technical competence, but rather because it provides an initial starting point of division between those more trained and those less trained; those better motivated and those less motivated; those with more social experience and those with less (Gordon and Howell, 1959: 121).

Formal education has expanded throughout the history of the United States, particularly since World War II. With each passing generation more people are attending school, staying in school longer, and spending more on formal education. The school year is longer and students attend a higher percentage of their classes (U.S. National Center for Education Statistics, 1975: 34–35). One of the major attractions of formal education is the higher level of economic reward available to the better educated. Yet there is debate

University of California Press Journals. From *Social Problems*, Vol. 24 No. 4 (April 1977): 436–450. Copyright © 1977 by the Society for the Study of Social Problems: Used with permission of the publisher and the author.

*Some of this material appeared in a book by the author, *Education and Jobs: The Imbalancing of the Social Machinery*, Transaction Books, 1979.

over what constitutes the link between education and jobs, and the dynamics of social stratification.

Several explanations exist for the expansion of education, the relation between educational attainment and occupational status, and the nature of social inequality in the United States, but most follow two basic models. One, the techno-democratic model, maintains that education has expanded in response to the rising technical skill requirements of jobs (Cubberley, 1909: 18–19; Kerr, et. al., 1974: 70–77; Killingsworth, 1966: 106–116) and to create greater equality, or at least equality of opportunity (President's Commission on Higher Education, 1947: Vol. I & II; Commager, 1950; Lipset and Bendix, 1959: 101; Cremin, 1961: vii–ix, 3–22; Schultz, 1961: 16; U.S. Commission on Civil Rights, 1974: 87), and social mobility for all segments of the population (Blau and Duncan, 1967: Hechinger, 1976). Rooted primarily in functional sociological theory and human capital economic theory, this model emphasizes the differences in the cognitive abilities (marginal productivity) of individuals in accounting for inequality, and points to the nation's schools as the key for providing people with the skills required to compete in American society.

This perspective has been challenged in recent years, mainly from the perspective of a class conflict model. In this view, formal education expanded to meet the rising social control problems generated by industrialization and urbanization in the United States by imparting noncognitive traits of obedience, disciplining, and respect for authority in students rather than by responding to the changing technical skill requirements of jobs, or desires to reduce inequality or increase mobility (Katz, 1971; Greer, 1972; Spring, 1972). The primary function of education is to socialize workers into the socioeconomic status of their parents and perpetuate the class structure (Bowles and Gintis, 1976; Karier, 1972; Friedenberg, 1965; Goodman, 1964; Illich, 1971). Educational credentials are used to rank workers rather than measure a level of skills (Thurow, 1975); to allocate workers to existing, unequal slots within the occupational structure (Jencks, et. al., 1972); and to restrict access to more desirable jobs (Collins, 1971; Stiglitz, 1975; Griliches and Mason, 1972; Taubman and Wales, 1974). Inequality is rooted in the dynamics of the class structure and inherent in a capitalist mode of production, rather than in the characteristics of individuals. Education has served to legitimize class relationships in a capitalist economy. Until those relationships are dealt with directly, educational expansion or reform is unlikely to alter the distribution of rewards.

This study examines a variety of empirical data to determine which model more adequately reflects the education-jobs nexus and the dynamics of social stratification. Evidence will be examined for answers to the following questions:

1. Can the expansion of formal education in the United States be explained in terms of technological advances or changes in the technical skill requirements of jobs? . . .

2. While education has long been associated with income and occupational status, is it the noncognitive characteristics or the technical skills inculcated by formal schooling which are rewarded in the occupational structure?

TECHNOLOGY AND EDUCATION

Whether advancing technology has been a primary determinant of educational expansion will be assessed by looking at the following: (1) the relation between changes in the technical skill requirements of jobs and changes in educational attainment and job performance; (2) the kinds of training workers use in learning the skill requirements of their jobs; and (3) a simulated longitudinal analysis of the educational attainment of workers within selected occupations.

Technical Skill Requirements of Jobs and Educational Attainment of Workers

U.S. Department of Labor estimates of changes in the amount of formal education dictated by changes in the technical skill requirements of jobs,[1] and U.S. Census Bureau reports on the increasing educational attainment of workers, show that attainment has far surpassed the level which functional requirements could explain. Berg found that as of 1950, 1.1 million jobs required a college degree while 4.1 million workers were college graduates. In 1960, 1.4 million jobs required a degree while 6.0 million workers were graduates. This methodology was used in other studies, yielding similar results (Rawlins and Ulman, 1974; Miller, 1971).

That educational attainment has risen faster than technical skill requirements, and that functional requirements cannot explain the expansion of formal education, is further indicated by an increase in the educational attainment of workers in all occupational groups, not just in the highly skilled professions. For example, between 1948 and 1973, the median number of school years attained by farmers and farm laborers increased from 8.0 to 10.7, for service workers the increase was from 8.7 to 12.0, for all blue-collar workers the comparable figures are 9.0 and 12.1, while for professional and managerial workers the increase was from 12.8 to 15.6 (U.S. Department of Labor, 1974a: 303).

The Impact of Technological Change on the Skill Requirements of Jobs

A review of over five hundred bibliographic titles, published between the early 1950's and mid 1960's on the effects of technological change on job skill requirements yielded the following conclusion:

From the current literature one cannot generalize about the effects of automation and technological change upon job content and skill requirements, except to say that they differ (Horowitz and Herrnstadt, 1966: 230).

In perhaps the most exhaustive case studies of the effects of mechanization and automation on job skills, Bright concluded:

> the net effect of automation in almost every plant I studied was still to reduce—or at least not to increase—the demand for skills and abilities of the direct labor force (1966: 214).

One finds that when the technical skill requirements of jobs are affected by technological change, workers learn whatever additional skills are required informally on the job, and rarely participate in a formal training program (Bright, 1958; Collins, 1969; Fine, 1964; Jaffe and Froomkin, 1968; Mueller, 1969).

Recent historical analyses of the labor process and the bureaucratization of work have illustrated how, in part as a result of the advent of Taylor's principles of scientific management, skilled occupations have been fragmented into several unskilled jobs, thus reducing the skill requirements for many clerical, service, craft, sales, and some professional and technical occupations (Aronowitz, 1973: 291–322; Braverman, 1974: 155–245, 292–409; Marglin, 1974; Stone, 1974). Shifts in the occupational structure from farm laborer to operative or from blue-collar to white-collar occupations are often misinterpreted as representing an upgrading of skill requirements. This interpretation rests on conventional assumptions about the nature of U.S. Census Bureau occupational classifications, when the skills required on jobs actually have been reduced (Braverman, 1974: 424–449). An assembly line worker may use more sophisticated machinery than the small family farmer, but operatives are not therefore more highly skilled workers. While the proportion of white collar jobs has been expanding, the largest growth has been in clerical occupations (U.S. Census Bureau, 1960: 74; U.S. Census Bureau, 1974a: 350), not clearly distinguishable from many blue-collar occupations, which often pay more (U.S. Census Bureau, 1973c: Tables 227 & 228).

No doubt jobs have been created as a result of technological changes requiring newer and higher levels of skill. But the available evidence indicates that skill requirements of jobs throughout the occupational structure have not undergone massive upgrading. When changes have occurred, they have not resulted in a demand for extensive formal retraining or educational programs.

The Effects of Formal Education on Job Performance

While employers have been steadily increasing educational requirements of jobs, few attempt to validate this selection criterion (Berg, 1971: 15) and even fewer are willing to make public the results of studies which are conducted in an attempt to determine whether or not better educated workers are more productive. I wrote to sixty companies asking for such information.[2] Of the twenty-nine which responded, nine said it was company policy not to provide such information for the public, three said they had done some analysis along these lines in the past, and seventeen said they never conducted this kind of research. Available information suggests why employers are not anxious to cooperate.

Berg (1971: 85–176) found that in terms of productivity, turnover, absenteeism, supervisors' ratings, and rates of promotion, education was frequently inversely related to job performance for jobs throughout the occupational structure. In a study of entry level jobs Diamond and Bedrosian (1970: 6) concluded, "little or no difference in job performance could be attributed to differences in education." A study of tool and die makers (Horowitz and Herrnstadt, 1969) concluded that the relation between type of training (ranging from formal schooling to "just picked it up on the job") and competence was not statistically significant.

Employers are aware of such findings, but they do not appear to affect hiring practices. A Bank of America Vice-President argued, "The banking business isn't so mysterious that an employee need hold more than one degree" (*Business Week*, 1972: 51). However, the proportion of male bank officers and financial managers with five or more years of college ranges from 9.6% of those between the ages of 55 and 64 to 15.4% of those between 25 and 34 (U.S. Census Bureau, 1973b: 54). There apparently is a trend towards hiring workers with more than one degree.

In a study of the promotion rates of the 1600 employees in one division of one of the major automobile manufacturers, workers with bachelor's degrees progressed at a faster rate than those with master's and Ph.D.'s and, based on current trends, would surpass the income levels of those with advanced degrees after fifteen years (Forum on Graduate Student Employment, 1974). A company representative informed me, however, that the firm had no intention of dropping the master's degree requirement.

Standard Oil of California is one company which acknowledged an attempt to validate its educational requirements. In a letter from a professional employment coordinator I was told:

> . . . some years ago we did a study to determine if there was any correlation between achievement in college and performance on the job (GPA vs. highest rank achieved). Unfortunately after several months of study and much data gathering for 6,000 unclassified (professional) employees we found there was *no* correlation at all!

Although evidence is fragmentary, the relationship between educational attainment and occupational status cannot be explained by superior levels of performance by better educated workers. When educational requirements are established they serve to disqualify people from those positions, but such requirements do not determine workers in terms of their abilities to perform on the job.

How Are Job Skills Learned?

If modern technology is an important determinant of the expansion of formal education, one would expect that formal education is an important means for workers to learn their jobs. This is not the case. In 1963 the Labor Department conducted the only nationwide survey of how workers learned their jobs (U.S. Department of Labor, 1964). Only 30.2% of those with less than three years of college (over 85% of the civilian labor force) said they used formal training, compared to 56% who cited on-the-job training and 45% who cited other informal methods. Those with three or more years of college were asked a different set of questions, so no comparable findings could be reported for this group of worrkers. Even if one assumes that all of the better educated workers relied on formal training, this leaves almost 60% of the civilian labor force not using formal training to learn skills required on their jobs.

No doubt professional workers depend more on their formal training than do others, but available evidence on how much even highly skilled workers rely on formal and informal training suggests they, too, use skills learned informally as often as those learned in the classroom (Pierson, 1959: 127–140; Rawlins and Ulman, 1974: 208–211; Bird, 1975: 96–105).

Age and Education of Similarly Employed Workers: A Simulated Longitudinal Analysis

One way to test the relative merits of the techno-democratic and class conflict models is to examine the age and educational attainment of workers within specific occupations. If technical skill requirements dictate educational requirements and attainment, there should be little variation by age in the education of workers within a given job. If education is used to allocate workers to unequal slots within the occupational structure and to restrict access to jobs, one would expect younger workers to have higher levels of educational attainment than older workers in the same job, for employers will raise requirements when better educated workers are available.

When the age and educational attainment of workers in specific occupations is examined, it is clear that educational attainment has increased. Of the seventy-three professional, managerial, sales, and clerical occupations for which age and education are reported in *Earnings by Occupation and Education: 1970 Census of Population* those between the ages of twenty-five and thirty-four were better educated than those between fifty-five and sixty-four in sixty-five (89%) of them (U.S. Census Bureau, 1973b: Table 1). The average difference in the percentage of each group with four or more years of college in these sixty-five occupations was fourteen percentage points.

The difference between specific jobs could be suppressed in an analysis of census occupations. Younger workers may simply hold the more highly skilled jobs within these occupations. In order to examine this relationship among workers holding the same job, performing the same duties within the same organization, data were obtained for 1701 workers in thirty-nine entry level positions currently requiring a college degree, in five private firms.[3] In thirty-three (84.6%) of the thirty-nine jobs the percentage of those under thirty-five with a bachelor's degree was higher than the percentage of those thirty-five or older who held a degree. The average difference in the percentage of each group with a degree was 33.8 percentage points. . . .

Assuming that the younger, more recent entrants into the job market are those most recently receiving their degree, it is again clear that educational requirements have increased, above the level of some veteran workers, for reasons other than technical skill requirements. Recruiters from two of the six firms told me that educational requirements have been raised simply as a response to the available supply of better educated workers.

That changes in the technical skill requirements of jobs cannot explain the educational expansion that has taken place is further demonstrated by the growing phenomenon of underemployment, particularly among college graduates. Several labor market experts have noted that the problem of underemployment for graduates is increasing every year (Shingleton, 1972: 1; Johnston, 1973: O'Toole, 1975: Rosenthal, 1973). In 1973 the Carnegie Commission on Higher Education estimated that at least 10% of those graduating from college in the 1970's would be underemployed (Carnegie Commission on Higher Education, 1973: 4). And the gap between the supply and demand for college graduates in jobs traditionally held by graduates is expected to increase in the 1980's (Rosenthal, 1973).

As college graduates dip further down in the job market, those with less education will have even fewer opportunities (Rosenthal, 1973: 24–25; Johnston, 1973: 28). For example, the percentage of high school graduates entering professional and managerial jobs declined from 8.6% of 1966 graduates to 2.3% of 1972 graduates (U.S. Department of Labor, 1973: A-12; U.S. Department of Labor, 1969: A-8). Better educated workers do earn more and do obtain more attractive jobs, but it is evident that it is the amount of schooling rather than the content of a particular amount of education or the skill requirements of jobs which accounts for the relationship between educational attainment and occupational status. . . .

WHAT ARE EMPLOYERS LOOKING FOR?

Another way to test the validity of these two models is to ask employers what attributes they seek in their employees and what attributes they associate with educational credentials. According to the techno-democratic model employers should cite specific technical or cognitive abilities. The class conflict model would predict that employers express greater concern for behavioral, noncognitive traits. Schooling does cultivate such noncognitive characteristics as discipline, obedience, and acceptance of traditional norms and values in general, while frequently discouraging such traits as creativity, initiative, and unorthodox beliefs (Gintis, 1971; Rist, 1970; Howe and Lauter, 1972; Cottle, 1974). The issue is whether employers value education more for its technical training component or its socialization function.

The Emphasis on Personality

Over the last thiry years many surveys have been conducted to elicit information about what employers want. Invariably such noncognitive traits as personalilty, motivation, ability to get along and work with others are rated higher than indicators of cognitive ability like previous work experience, knowledge of a specific subject, or grades (Thomas, 1956: 326–337; Drake,

Kaplan, and Stone, 1972; Keyser, 1974; Ma, 1969; Michigan State University Placement Services, 1974: 41–43; Berg, 1971). I asked Frank Endicott, Placement Director at Northwestern University, if his office had conducted any studies to determine whether employers were more concerned with personality and other noncognitive traits or technical abilities and other cognitive abilities. He replied in the winter of 1975:

> It seems to me that we have nailed this one to the wall. PERSONAL QUALITIES are most important in getting a job, in keeping a job, and in succeeding in it over a long period of time, with special reference to college graduates (emphasis in original).

Employers don't mind admitting it is the noncognitive rather than the cognitive traits learned in school which makes college graduates good employees. In a series of twenty-five discussions I had with recruiters at Michigan State University in the spring of 1975, the following were typical of the comments they volunteered:

- college graduates are more productive retail sales representatives not because of the information learned in school but because of the social interaction skills developed in school . . . the content of most courses is irrelevant to the outside world . . . a bachelor's degree is an important indicator of the kind of employee we are seeking because the degree indicates a tendency on the part of an individual to complete a program;
- college graduates are sought [for sales, managerial, and junior executive positions] because a person develops a sense of maturity in college;
- we like our engineers to have a college degree not because of the specific knowledge learned in school, but for the social skills developed in school.

Perhaps the best statement of employers' attitudes toward a college degree is the following line in a Mobil Oil advertisement aimed at future marketing representatives:

> You need a bachelor's degree to apply. We really don't care what it's in. Because the most important requirements are sales ability and motivation. And those are things you can't major in (Michigan State University Placement Services: Fall, 1973: inside front cover).

The Issue of Control

These testimonials raise the question why employers value these noncognitive characteristics. According to the class conflict model these preferences reflect an underlying concern for the maintenance of social control within the firm and throughout the class structure in general.

Evidence for this perspective appears in many sources. In a study of one hundred Lockheed employees in California, recently graduated from a Los Angeles high school, Brenner (1968) found that teachers' ratings of student work habits and cooperation, grade point averages, and school absences were correlated with supervisors' ratings (Brenner, 1968). Analysis showed that when teachers' ratings of student work habits, cooperation, and school absences were controlled, grades had no additional predictive value of job performance. In other words grades predicted job performance only through their noncognitive component (Bowles, Gintis, and Meyer, 1975). Educational requirements for jobs are highest for those positions and within those organizations where employers express the greatest concern for the behavioral characteristics of workers and for social control in general. Concern for job related technical skills or the extent of technological innovation are not as closely related to educational requirements as is the concern for stability and control (Noland and Bakke, 1949: 176–177, 183–185; Collins, 1969: 202–209; Collins, 1974; Edwards, 1975).

Employers are more concerned with the noncognitive, behavioral characteristics of their employees than with the cognitive abilities they possess, and the value of formal education is viewed in terms of the noncognitive traits it imparts. This does not mean that employers are uninterested in the technical capabilities of their workers. But when they choose among several prospective employees using educational credentials in that process, they seek primarily noncognitive attributes of workers. This emphasis reflects employers' underlying concern with the maintenance of social control within the organization.

TECHNOLOGY, IDEOLOGY, AND EDUCATION

This study evaluated two competing perspectives of the relationship between education and the occupational structure, and the dynamics of social stratification in the United States. The evidence presented shows that the expansion of formal education and the upgrading of educational requirements of jobs cannot be explained in terms of the changing technical skill requirements of jobs. . . .

Educational requirements of jobs are frequently raised in response to the increasing supply of better educated workers and educational attainment of workers is used to allocate workers to unequal slots within the occupational structure. One consequence, no doubt, is that individuals have responded by seeking higher levels of educational attainment to improve or maintain their competitive position with the labor force, thus completing the vicious circle of spiralling attainment and requirements. The ranking of employees according to their level of educational attainment has not been a completely arbitrary practice on the part of employers. Better educated workers, particularly college graduates, are valued for the noncognitive attributes imparted by the schooling process because such workers provide employers with a more stable work force. Therefore the class conflict model provides a more adequate explanatory framework.

The basic problem with the techno-democratic model, as well as the functional and human capital theories it rests on, is its focus on the assumed differences among individuals in terms of their cognitive abilities. The structural constraints under which individuals compete are either ignored or treated as unalterable givens. The private ownership of productive resources, the operation of those resources for the personal enrichment of the owners, and the exploitive set of relationships in that system permitting selected individuals to accumulate wealth, are not recognized as central determinants of who gets what and why in American society.

By recognizing that inequality and exploitation are rooted in the class structure of American capitalism rather than in the marginal productivities of individuals who interact within that system, it becomes clear that some ideological mechanism must be created to maintain the system's stability. The inability of technological change to account for the expansion of formal education, the resilience of economic inequality in the face of substantial reduction of educational inequality, and employers' expressed concern for the behavioral characteristics of workers and the socialization function of education make it clear that formal education has long constituted a key element of that ideological mechanism. . . .

NOTES

1. Labor Department estimates for 4000 jobs in 1949 were reported in *Estimates of Worker Trait Requirements for 4000 Jobs as Defined in the 1949 Dictionary of Occupational Titles*, 1957. A revision entitled *Selected Characteristics of Occupations (Physical Demands, Working Conditions, Training Time) 1966—A Supplement to the Dictionary of Occupational Titles* provided similar information for 14,000 jobs in 1965. These estimates were based on job descriptions provided in the second and third editions of the *Dictionary of Occupational Titles*. In order to compare functional requirements with educational attainment, GED scores in the *Dictionary* must be translated into years of schooling, a problem compounded by the fact that the seven point GED scale used in the second edition was collapsed into a six point scale in the third edition. For a description of how these estimates were made see *Estimates*, pp. iv–ix and 110–158 and Berg, 1971, pp. 43–45.

2. These companies were selected from a list of those recruiting at Michigan State University. Those companies most likely to maintain this kind of information, according to Jack Shingleton, Director of Placement Services at Michigan State University, were chosen.

3. The organizations include: (1) a retail clothing chain; (2) a beer manufacturer; (3) a meat processor; (4) a pharmaceutical drug manufacturer; and (5) a communications equipment manufacturer. For a more complete description of the data see Squires (1976: Appendices B and C).

REFERENCES

Aronowitz, Stanley. 1973. False Promises. New York: McGraw-Hill Book Company.

Berg, Ivar. 1971. Education and Jobs: The Great Training Robbery. Boston: Beacon Press.

Bird, Caroline. 1975. The Case Against College. New York: David McKay Company.

Blau, Peter M. and Otis Dudley Duncan. 1967. The American Occupational Structure. New York: John Wiley and Sons.

Bowles, Samuel and Herbert Gintis. 1976. Schooling in Capitalist America. New York: Basic Books, Inc.

Bowles, Samuel, Herbert Gintis, and Peter Meyer. 1975. "The long shadow of work: education, the family, and the reproduction of the social division of labor." The Insurgent Sociologist (summer).

Braverman, Harry. 1974. Labor and Monopoly Capital. New York: Monthly Review Press.

Brenner, Marshall H. 1968. "Use of high school data to predict work performance." Journal of Applied Psychology 52 (February): 29–30.

Bright, James R. 1958. Automation and Management. Boston: Harvard Business School.

———.1966. "The relationship of increasing automation to skill requirements." In The Employment Impact of Technological Change.Washington, D.C.: Government Printing Office.

Business Week 1972 "The job gap for college graduates." 2247 (September 23): 48–58.

Carnegie Commission on Higher Education. 1973. College Graduates and Jobs. New York: McGraw-Hill Book Company.

Collins, Randall. 1969. "Education and employment: a study in the dynamics of stratification." Unpublished Ph.D. Dissertation, University of California at Berkeley.

———.1971. "Functional and conflict theories of educational stratification." American Sociological Review 36(December): 1002–1019.

———.1974. "Where are educational requirements for employment highest?" Sociology of Education 47(fall): 419–442.

Commager, Henry Steele. 1950. The American Mind. New Haven: Yale University Press. Cited in Colin Greer. The Great School Legend [1972]. New York: Basic Books, Inc.

Cottle, Thomas J. 1974. "What tracking did to Ollie Taylor." Social Policy 5(July-August): 21–24.

Cremin, Lawrence. 1961. The Transformation of the School. New York: Knopf. Cited in Colin Greer. The Great School Legend. [1972]. New York: Basic Books, Inc.

Cubberley, Ellwood P. 1909. Changing Conceptions of Education. Boston: Houghton Mifflin: Cited in Richard C. Edwards, Michael Reich, and Thomas Weisskopf (Eds.) The Capitalist System. [1972]. Englewood Cliffs: Prentice-Hall.

Diamond, Daniel E. and Hrach Bedrosian. 1970. Hiring Standards and Job Peformance. Washington, D.C.: Government Printing Office.

Drake, Larry R., H. Roy Kaplan, and Russell A. Stone. 1972. "How do employers value the interview?" Journal of College Placement 32(Febraury-March): 47–51.

Edwards, Richard C. 1975. "The social relations of production in the firm and labor market structure." Politics and Society 5:83–108.

Fine, Sidney A. 1964. The Nature of Automated Jobs and Their Educational and Training Requirements. McLean: Human Sciences Research, Inc.

Forum on Graduate Student Employment. 1974. Michigan State University. (October 24).

Friedenberg, Edgar. 1965. Coming of Age in America. New York: Vintage Books.

Gintis, Herbert. 1971. "Education technology, and the characteristics of worker productivity." American Economic Review 61(May): 266–279.

Goodman, Paul. 1964. Compulsory Mis-Education. New York: Vintage Books.

Goodman, S. M. 1959. The Assessment of School Quality. Albany: New York State Education Department.

Gordon, Robert A. and James E. Howell. 1959. Higher Education for Business. New York: Columbia University Press.

Greer, Colin. 1972. The Great School Legend. New York: Basic Books, Inc.

Griliches, Zvi and William M. Mason. 1972. "Education, income, and ability." Journal of Political Economy 80(May-June): 74–103.

Harrison, Bennett. 1972. "Education and underemployment in the urban ghetto." American Econmic Review 62(December): 796–812.

Hechinger, Fred. 1976. "Murder in academe: the demise of education." Saturday Review (March 20).

Horowitz, Morris A. and Irwin L. Herrnstadt. 1966. "Changes in the skill requirements of occupations in selected industries." The Employment Impact of Technological Change. Washington D.C.: Goverment Printing Office.
1969. The Training of Tool and Die Makers. Boston: Department of Economics. Northeastern University.

Howe, Florence and Paul Lauter. 1972. "How the school system is rigged for failure." Richard C. Edwards, Michael Reich, and Thomas E. Weisskopf (Eds.) the Capitalist System. Englewood Cliffs: Prentice-Hall.

Illich, Ivan. 1971. Deschooling Society. New York: Harper and Row.

Jaffe, A. J. and Joseph Froomkin. 1968. Technology and Jobs. New York: Praeger Publishers.

Jencks, Christopher et al. 1973. Inequality. New York: Harper and Row.

Johnston, Denis F. 1973. "Education of workers: projections to 1990." Monthly Labor Review 96(November): 22–31.

Karier, Clarence J. 1972. "Testing for order and control in the corporate liberal state." Educational Theory 22(Spring): 154–180.

Katz, Michael. 1972. Class, Bureaucracy, and Schools. New York: Praeger Publishers.

Kerr, Clark et al. 1974. "The logic of industrialism." Bertram Silverman and Murray Yanowitch (Eds.) The Worker in "Post-Industrial" Capitalism. New York: The Free Press.

Keyser, Marshall. 1974. "How to apply for a job." Journal of College Placement 35(Fall): 63–65.

Killingsworth, Charles C. 1966. "Automation, jobs, and manpower: the case for structural unemployment." The Manpower Revolution. Garden City: Anchor Books.

Lampman, Robert J. 1962. The Share of Top Wealth Holders in National Wealth. Princeton University Press.

Lipset, Seymour Martin, and Reinhard Bendix. 1959. Social Mobility. . . .

Ma, James C. 1969. "Current trends in recruiting practices." Journal of College Placement 29(April-May): 113–114.

Marglin, Stephen A. 1974. "What do bosses do?" The Review of Radical Political Economics 6(Summer): 60–112.

McDill, Edward and Leo Rigsby. 1973. The Academic Impact of Educational Climates. Baltimore: John Hopkins University Press.

Michigan State University Placement Services. 1973. Placement Manual. Rahway: Placement Publications, Inc. (Fall)
1974. Recruiting Trends Survey. East Lansing: Michigan State University Placement Services.

Miller, Ann. 1971. Occupations of the Labor Force According to the Dictionary of Occupational Titles. Washington, D.C.: Office of Management and Budget.

Mollenkopf, W. G. and S. D. Melville. 1956. A Study of Secondary School Characteristics as Related to Test Scores. Princeton: Educational Testing Service.

Mueller, Eva. 1969. Technological Advance in an Expanding Economy. Ann Arbor: Institute for Social Research.

National Urban League Research Department. 1975. Quarterly Economic Report on the Black Worker. Washington, D.C.: National Urban League.

Noland, E. William and E. Wright Bakke. 1949. Workers Wanted. New York: Harper and Brothers.

O'Toole, James. 1975. "The reserve army of the underemployed." Change Magazine 7(May): 26–33, 63.

Pierson, Frank C. 1959. The Education of American Businessmen. New York: McGraw-Hill Book Company.

President's Commission on Higher Education. 1947. Higher Education for American Democracy. Washington, D.C.: Government Printing Office.

Rawlins, V. Lane and Lloyd Ulman. 1974. "The utilization of college trained manpower in the United States." In Margaret S. Gordon (Ed.) Higher Education and the Labor Market. A Report of the Carnegie Commission on Higher Education. New York: McGraw-Hill Book Company.

Risk, Ray C. 1970. "Student social class and teacher expectations: the self-fulfilling prophecy in ghetto education." Harvard Educational Review 40 (August): 411–451.

Rosenthal, Neal H. 1973. "The United States economy in 1985: projected changes in occupations." Monthly Labor Review 96(December): 18–26.

Schultz, Theodore W. 1961. "Investment in Human Capital." American Economic Review 51(March): 1–17 Reprinted in Jerome Karabel and A. H. Halsey (eds.), Power and Ideology in Education, pp 313–324. New York: Oxford University Press.

Shingleton, Jack. 1972. "Prognosis of employment of future graduates." Presentation to Administrative Group at Michigan State University (January 4).

Spring, Joel. 1972. Education and the Rise of the Corporate State. Boston: Beacon Press.

Squires, Gregory D. 1976. "Education, jobs, and the U.S. class structure." Unpublished Ph.D. Dissertation, Michigan State University.

Stiglitz, Joseph E. 1975. "The theory of 'screening,' education, and the distribution of income." American Economic Review 65(June): 283–300.

Stone, Katherine. 1974. "The origins of job structures in the steel industry." Review of Radical Political Economics 6(Summer): 113–173.

Taubman, Paul and Terence Wales. 1974. Higher Education and Earnings. A Report of the Carnegie Commission on Higher Education. New York: McGraw-Hill Book Company.

Thomas, Lawrence. 1956. The Occupational Structure and Education. Englewood Cliffs: Prentice-Hall, Inc.

Thurow, Lester C. 1975. Generating Inequality. New York: Basic Books, Inc.

U.S.Bureau of the Census. 1960. Historical Statistics of the United States: Colonial Times to 1957.

———— .1973b Earnings by Occupation and Education: 1970 Census of Population.

———— .1973c Age and Earnings by Occupation for the United States: 1970 Census of Population.

———— .1974a Statistical Abstract of the United States 1974.

U.S. Commission on Civil Rights. 1974. Twenty Years After Brown: The Shadows of the Past.

U.S. Department of Labor. 1957. Estimate of Worker Trait Requirements for 4,000 Jobs as Defined in the. 1949. Dictionary of Occupational Titles.

———— .1964. Formal Occupational Training of Adult Workers.

———— .1965. Selected Characteristics of Occupations, (Physical Demands, Working Conditions, Training Time). 1966—A Supplement to the Dictionary of Occupational Titles.

———— .1969. Employment of High School Graduates and Dropouts, October. 1968. Special Labor Force Report 108.

———— .1973. Employment of High School Graduates and Dropouts, October. 1972. Special Labor Force Report

U.S. National Center for Education Statistics. 1975. Digest of Educational Statistics, 1974.

The Changing Relationship Between Education and Occupation: The Case of Nursing

FLOYD M. HAMMACK
New York University

Education in the United States has expanded by almost any measure: More students are in schools and colleges, staying longer, and studying an increasing variety of subjects. The causes of this expansion are complex and not fully understood.[1] Some of its consequences, however, are becoming clear. According to many observers, one important consequence has been a changed relationship between education and work.

Until recently, educational achievement was only one of several routes by which individuals reached the same positions. Indeed, many states allowed candidates for the state bar examination to qualify by "reading for the law" under the supervision of a practicing attorney (who did not necessarily hold a baccalaureate degree) in place of attending a law school.

With the expansion of schooling, however, the requirement of some kind of formal higher education, or "credentialing" as this requirement has come to be called, is on the rise. The effect is to close off other, informal routes into many occupations (Rodriguez, 1978). Formal education at the postsecondary level is now widespread, allowing a growing number of employers and occupational groups to use education as an entry requirement. In 1960, 7.7 percent of the population 25 years old or older had completed four or more years of college. By 1970, this figure was 11.0 percent; by 1980, it was 17.0 percent; and by 1985, it had risen to 19.4 percent. For those in the younger age

Revision of "Education for Nursing: Problems and Prospects" by Floyd M. Hammack from *New York University Education Quarterly* (winter 1982): 8–14. Copyright © N.Y.U. Education Quarterly. Reprinted with permission of the publisher.

group of 25 to 29, the same figures are 11.1 percent, 16.4 percent, and 22.6 percent, and by 1985 had dropped back slightly to 22.2 percent (U.S. Department of Education, 1986: 13).

Thus, an examination of the generally "tightening bond" (Tyler, 1977) between education and work is timely and important. This paper presents a discussion of the nature of this changing relationship for one occupational group: nursing.

Some leaders in nursing had called for collegiate education for nurses before the turn of the century (the first college-based nursing school was founded before 1910). But it is only recently that college-educated nurses, holding an associate or baccalaureate degree, have outnumbered graduates of hospital-based diploma programs among those entering nursing. The majority of working nurses, however, remain graduates of the hospital diploma programs.

COLLECTIVE MOBILITY

Several professional associations of nursing have recently proposed that all preparatory education for nursing be located in higher education settings rather than in hospitals. In 1965 the American Nurses' Association issued its *Educational Preparation for Nurse Practitioners and Assistants to Nurses: A Position Paper,* which asserted that all beginning "professional" (registered) nurses should have a baccalaureate degree in nursing, and that all practical nursing programs should be replaced with technical nursing programs in community colleges. This plan meant the closing of hospital-based nursing education programs and implied the eventual restriction of professional practice to persons who hold at least a baccalaureate degree in nursing. The proposal has been supported by several state nurses' associations, which are attempting to have state laws rewritten to reflect the recommendations (McClure, 1978). Not all professional nursing groups, however, favor the proposal, and it remains controversial among other health-related groups as well (American Nurses' Association, 1978).

Although the functions of nursing are not always described in the proposals for new educational standards, many nursing leaders are calling for new roles for registered nurses, new relationships with other health-care workers, and new places and forms of practice. The development of private nurse practitioners who collect fees directly for care provided, the reorganization of and expansion of nursing duties emphasizing primary or initial care and assessment of outpatients in hospitals and clinics, and nurse clinicians who have extensive expertise in a specialized care area are examples of efforts to change traditional patterns of nursing practice located primarily in hospitals and nursing homes.

Thus, not only have there been calls for changing the education of nurses, but efforts are also being directed at expanding the work in which they engage. In sum, nursing may be characterized as attempting to enhance its occupational status—to professionalize. In Glaser and Strauss's (1971) terms, nursing is engaged in a collective mobility project. Individual nurses are aspiring to higher salaries, higher status, and greater recognition among those with whom they work and in the larger society. Their individual efforts, however, are also finding support in the work of their professional associations, work groups, and unions. The destiny of an individual nurse, as with members of other work groups, is inextricably linked with the prospects of the occupation as a whole. Because nursing is licensed by state governments, which control the profession's rights and prerogatives, the activities of individual nurses take place within a legal context as well as one that includes their employing organizations, other health-related occupations, and the public at large.

THE CURRENT STATUS OF THE NURSING PROFESSION

As an occupation, nursing has long been associated with organized health-care delivery. Since the end of World War I, it has been practiced mostly inside hospitals, nursing homes, or other organizations that employ nurses directly. Prior to the War, nursing students provided care in hospitals, and registered nurses were employed primarily by patients themselves in private duty. Hospitals were largely places for the indigent; more affluent patients avoided hospitals and were cared for at home (Brown, 1966).

The upgrading of hospitals and their clientele, which began after World War I, had the effect of providing more job opportunities and security for nurses. At the same time, however, nurses' ability to support themselves independently was reduced. Where previously they worked on a one-to-one basis with physicians, both of them separately employed by patients, the market for nursing's services became restricted to large health-care organizations—hospitals, primarily. The practice of medicine was less affected by this shift than was nursing, as many physicians were able to maintain a private practice. For contemporary nurses, however, while private duty remains an option, relatively few nurses can support themselves outside of large health-care facilities.

In its new context, nursing was defined as the provision of practical service under the supervision and at the direction of physicians. It is important to note that until this time (the end of World War I), physicians had few real tools with which to change the course of illnesses or health problems. While some forms of surgery and setting broken bones, for example, were well developed, there were few really effective drugs until World War II (Riser, 1978). Much of the practice of medicine was placebo medicine. Excellent nursing care by private duty nurses was undoubtedly as beneficial, and probably more beneficial than, the care provided by the doctor. With the medical advances provided by science, the reform of medical education, and the improvement of hospitals during the first two decades of this century, however, the ability of medical practice to affect the course of disease and treat other problems increased substantially. Physicians became the occupational group controlling the right to apply scientific knowledge to health care.[2] Consequently, nursing was subsumed under the larger mandate of medicine. Nursing service became institutionalized while physicians maintained the pattern of independent practice.[3] In 1980, a majority (65.7 percent) of employed registered nurses worked in hospitals and 8 percent worked in nursing homes, 6.6 percent were employed in public and community health settings, and 5.7 percent were employed in doctors' offices (American Nurses' Association, 1985). Even smaller percentages worked in education and occupational health fields and as exclusively private-duty nurses or otherwise self-employed.

As noted above, the majority of nurses employed—69.6 percent—have a diploma from a hospital-based nursing school or an associate's degree. Most of the rest (24.7 percent) hold a B.A. degree in nursing, and 5.7 percent have a master's or doctorate (American Nurses' Association, 1985). Since 1970, the proportion of nurses holding only a diploma or associate's degree has decreased from 86 percent, and baccalaureate degree holders have increased as a proportion of the work force from 12 percent. Only 3 percent of nurses in 1970 held a master's degree or doctorate (American Nurses' Association, 1977).

While each of the three basic nursing education programs (diploma, associate, and baccalaureate) will be briefly described below, it is important to note that graduates of all three are qualified to take the state licensing examination for the registererd nurse license. Graduates of all three programs compete with each other for employment; distinctions based on the type of education leading to licensure are *not* built into many employers' personnel policies. Moreover, many employers do not use level of education to determine salary or suitability for assignment or promotion. Job advancement strongly depends on experience or in-service education. Some employers do reward degrees (the U.S. Public Health Service is one example) and many help their nurses to pay for tuition costs in seeking baccalaureate- and master's-level education. Nevertheless, the current shortage of nurses has not allowed employers the relative luxury of closing off opportunities to nurses without academic degrees nor have the professional associations consistently endorsed increasing the educational requirements for entry.[4]

The hospital-based diploma programs are generally three years in length and have remained the most practice-oriented of the programs. Students spend much of their time working in the hospital, becoming familiar with most of the duties normally included in general hospital nursing and with the specialty-care areas such as coronary-care units, the emergency room, and so on. Students take courses taught by faculty drawn from the hospital's nursing and medical staff, by the school's own faculty, and sometimes at local colleges. Diploma schools are increasingly linking themselves with local two- and four-year colleges to offer combined diploma and degree programs. Of those entering nursing for the first time in 1982–83, 15.8 percent were graduates of these schools (American Nurses' Association, 1985).

Associate degree programs, begun in 1952, are usually two years in length and require liberal arts as well as science and nursing coursework together with some clinical experience. These programs have been the fastest growing of all nurse education programs. Although this growth has slowed recently, associate degree programs currently constitute the largest single source of basic education for entering nurses. In 1982–83, 52.9 percent of those entering nursing were prepared in associate degree programs (American Nurses' Association, 1985).

Baccalaureate programs, usually four years long, also require liberal arts and sciences courses, courses specific to nursing, and laboratory and clinical experiences. These programs began early in the century and have grown steadily. In 1982–83, 31.3 percent of entering nurses possessed baccalaureate degrees in nursing (American Nurses' Association, 1985).

Until recently, the nursing curriculum followed the medical curriculum in that its courses concerned body systems, different kinds of pathophysiology, age-related health problems, locus of problem (for example, mental or physical), and appropriate nursing treatments. The curriculum is now likely to be an integrated one which takes a holistic view of nursing and stresses the relationship of physical, social, and emotional factors in illness and health (Notter and Robey, 1979). What this means for the curriculum, for example, is the addition of material from psychology and sociology and attention to the effects of stress on patients and family relations.

In the care setting, nurses seek to provide technical services, and perhaps more important for the nurses, counseling and attention to patients' and their families' reactions to the illness or health problem. This newer, integrated curriculum is found in varying degrees in all three educational settings, but is most strongly associated with the baccalaureate programs, which appear to be more self-consciously professional in orientation. Baccalaureate programs also stress the application of nursing knowledge to many settings in addition to the hospital: public health, health education, school nursing, and work in industry.

THE PROFESSIONAL SEARCH: NEW ROLES

The development of a unique knowledge base for nursing has been a major concern of nurse educators, researchers, and theorists.[5] This enterprise is closely associated by nursing's leaders with attempts to separate nursing from the medical perspective on illness and health and from the control of the medical profession. These attempts, moreover, are tied to efforts to provide new services in non–medically controlled settings. The specific content and orientation of this new knowledge base is not, however, a matter about which nurses have attained a consensus.

For example, some advocate that nursing move more deeply into the diagnosis and treatment of patients, utilizing knowledge concerning cure as well as care (Brodt, 1978; Gordon, 1978). Many of these nurses argue for a greater involvement in the primary care of patients and advocate that, for example, independent nurse practitioners become the first health workers to whom patients are exposed. Others cite health education, preventive care, and public health as areas into which nursing could move more fully. Efforts to rewrite legislation governing the practice of nursing and to obtain rights to third-party payment (such as from insurance companies) are among the objectives of these nursing leaders.

While this expanded conception of nursing service is the objective of some nurses, others agree with the thesis that "the primary task in the movement toward professional autonomy by nurses is to clearly and definitely differentiate the arena of nursing from the arena of medicine" (Tomich, 1978: 299). In contrast to physicians' concern with the pathological conditions of patients, "nursing approaches the work of healing from the perspective of patient needs with the emphasis of care rather than cure, on health or wellness rather than illness. What nursing has not yet effected is a basic generic focus differentiating the nursing arena from medicine" (Tomich, 1978: 201). This account continues to emphasize the need for nursing to devote its attention to the social aspects of the nurse-patient relationship.

Goode addresses the core problem with respect to the nursing curriculum. He asserts that dominant occupations are granted a monopoly on the most highly developed knowledge in the relevant field: "The society, in effect, gives the authority of knowledge to the professions as centers of knowledge from which the knowledge used by subordinate occupations will flow" (1969: 287).

Friedson (1970) agrees, noting that in the health-care field, medicine's comprehensiveness and strategic importance gives it superiority over others. The other health-care occupations, including nursing, remain under the supervision and often at the order of physicians (Freidson, 1970: 69). Freidson goes on to observe that professional autonomy in medically related occupations must be built on control of a discrete function or area of work that can be practiced independently of medicine. Health-related occupations in this country have not, he asserts, had much success in accomplishing this, although dentistry is one exception.

There is, however, one additional element that also must be reckoned with. While Freidson (1970) emphasizes autonomy, Larson (1977) specifies the need for an occupation to develop and control a market for its services. She sees professionalization as "the process by which producers of special services sought to constitute and control a market for their expertise" (1977: xvi). This argument stresses both the expertise and the provisions created to dispense the services derived from the expertise. This point will be more fully developed below.

The Usefulness of Higher Education

Nurses have yet to create large markets that they could dominate outside of hospitals and nursing homes. This may relate partly to the lack of a single educational route and a single, standardized curriculum. Larson argues that the best education to create a market, and especially a market for which an occupational group is granted a monopoly, is one that clearly defines the problems to be addressed by the members of the group and specifies the techniques or processes that will be used to treat or solve those problems. The education "must be specific enough to impart distinctiveness to the professional 'commodity'; it must be formalized or codified enough to allow for standardization of the 'product' " (1977: 31). This will help create a single, clear public understanding of the occupation and its role. Having three distinctly different types of programs preparing nurses for practice does not evidence much standardization. Nor does the lack of agreement among nursing leaders on the nature of the "product" of nurse education aid in the identification and control over a market outside of those in which nurses currently find employment.

Yet efforts are being made to create greater standardization. As nurse education has moved more prominently into higher educational settings, curriculum development has become an important consideration for nursing's further professional development. The learning-through-work model of apprenticeship education lost much of its attractiveness for an occupational group seeking higher status. Colleges and universities are not, of course, dependent on the labor of students, which is the case in diploma school–affiliated hospitals. Moreover, collegiate nursing students are required to meet many of the same general education requirements as other students for degrees, and the nursing faculties have to defend their courses against the measures applied to other fields of study. These measures, which stress the theoretical basis of course content, contribute to collegiate nursing's more theoretical, integrated curriculum. And at least in four-year colleges and universities, the faculty are expected to undertake research that contributes to their field. Such research is meant, among other things, to be fed back into the content of courses. Thus, the traditional applied and practical curriculum of diploma schools needed to be made more theoretical and research based once nurse education entered colleges.

This upgrading was sought by many nursing leaders as they anticipated that the development of more nursing theory and research would help nursing provide better service and would aid in their attempts to improve the standing of the occupation. Developing faculty for degree programs meant the expansion of master's and doctoral degree programs. This expansion has begun, though there are still reports of a shortage of faculty.

Giving attention to graduate study, the American Nurses' Association has said, "The major purpose of graduate study in nursing should be the preparation of nurse clinicians capable of improving nursing care through the advancement of nursing theory and science" (1969: 2). The National League for Nursing asserts: "The significant general characteristics of graduate education in nursing derive from its essential purpose: the preparation of leaders in nursing—that is, those who will influence the practice and the study of nursing by generating higher levels of competence and by teaching, administering, and investigating professional practice" (1974: 34).

In building graduate education, nursing has had to create a field about which it can theorize and in which it can undertake research, identify problems, establish methods, and found journals. It has had to accomplish these tasks without overlapping previously established fields of study, like the physical and social sciences, or, at least, by combining them in new ways.

One recent paper recommends that graduate nurse education maintain its attention to the patient while combining a greater emphasis on developing a stronger research orientation for nursing activities. The author of this paper quotes the work of Leininger, who states:

> Today health providers are being reawakened to consider the significant and critical role that humanism plays in helping people get well and maintain a high level of wellness. As medical science has rapidly developed new drugs, treatments and instruments, there is genuine concern that the humanistic dimensions of health care have not paralleled these scientific achievements. . . . The challenge to the nursing profession is to discover and interrelate the two dimensions in graduate curriculums; how to frame graduate curriculums within a humanistic posture so that that posture is maintained in the preparation for and delivery of scientifically sound health care (Hamilton, 1975: 25).

It is such a basis, however vague in current development, that many nurse leaders hope will allow for the growth of graduate education and for the development of new services and sites for the provision of those services. They also believe that the improvement of instruction and curriculum in undergraduate education will follow. In additon, graduate degree nurses who find employment in traditional settings will be more likely to establish and maintain egalitarian relationships with physicians who, it is hoped, will come to recognize the beneficial nature of the new knowledge these nurses bring to patient care.

ASSESSMENT OF THE PROFESSION'S STANDING

Perhaps the matter of increased status for nursing comes to whether nursing has attained enough momentum and power to overcome the barriers to further professionalization, such as the three separate routes to entry, a not yet fully developed and unique knowledge base, a lack of explicit public understanding of nurses' roles in health care, and employment in settings dominated by physicians.

It is in the hospital setting, the largest employer of nurses, that they find the greatest dissatisfaction. For example, Kramer (1974) reports that many beginning nurses, and especially baccalaureate graduates, experience "reality shock" entering hospital work. This shock derives, she asserts, from new nurses' inability to practice nursing as it was taught to them. All the nurses she studied experienced conflict between professional perspectives learned in school and the bureaucratic norms of the employing hospitals. Earlier, Davis, Olesen, and Whittaker (1966) had found among their baccalaureate nurses a progressive disenchantment with hospital nursing. They argued that the explanation of this stemmed from the disjunction between the educational philosophy of the school from which the nurses were graduated—which stressed the interpersonal aspects of nurse-patient relationships and comprehensive approaches to nursing care and health teaching—and the hospital's bureau-cracy, depersonalization, and obsessive concern with technical nursing.

More recently, Lurie's (1981) study of graduates of a nurse practitioner certificate program (which only admitted registered nurses), who worked in a variety of traditional and some of the newer work settings, found that "the existing structure of the work setting and the expectations of more powerful actors in the work setting exerted an influence on nurse practitioners counter to the program's model" (1981: 46). These nurse practitioners usually had greater autonomy in their positions than traditional nurses had, yet they still had difficulty in establishing and maintaining positive work relationships with doctors, hospitals, and other health institutions and personnel. Among the difficulties they experienced was gaining access to hospitals as an independent nurse practitioner; it was often difficult or impossible.

A recent American Nurses' Association report confirms the problem. It argues that the Association's concern with controlling routes into nursing (as exemplified by the 1965 position paper) "gave little consideration to work-world realities. . . . Now as then, the rhetoric about professional nursing practice in nursing literature is not easy to reconcile with existing work-world conceptions of jobs or practice" (1978: 8). The report notes the growth of primary-care nursing, nurse practitioners, and other expanded roles. Yet, it asserts that "these professional roles have developed and spread without reference to the [1965 paper's] conceptualization of technical and profes-sional, and, more telling, without discriminating educational requirements for entry" into these positions. "We must conclude," it continues, "that the position paper's premise that there is a direct relationship between level of education and level or type of nursing practice is not yet generally sanctioned or supported in the work world" (1978: 9). The real work to be done is "in realizing the professional practice role and the contribution education makes to nursing practice in the practice setting" (1978: 11–12).

Nurses have expended great effort in developing their own higher education programs, though they have not been successful in moving all nurse education into such settings or in implementing the baccalaureate degree as the basic entry requirement. In fact, the associate's degree has become the most common education for entering nurses. Though nurses have attempted to develop a field of learning that is their own, they are less far along in translating their newer conceptions of nursing into general practice in hospitals and nursing homes, where most nurses work.

Moreover, their attempt to create their own market in the larger health and illness markets is not yet solidified, and leads directly to conflict with the legal and social authority of physicians. For example, it is still generally illegal for nursing to expand into primary care of patients for payment by third parties (insurance companies and state medical benefit plans) and to order diagnostic tests, such as X-rays or blood tests, without a physician's signature. Nurse practice laws, however, are being rewritten in some states to allow more freedom for nurses, often as a result of nursing's efforts combined with the work of state and joint nurse-physician practice committees (Bullough, 1978).

Finally, nurses' efforts to increase the prestige of the occupation face another kind of challenge. The national shortage of nurses, acute in both urban and rural areas, has altered the dynamics of nursing's efforts at professionalization. First, the shortage is making work on hospital floors even less attractive than it was before the shortage became acute. Overwork, in part due to the heavy demands imposed by increasingly elderly and sicker patients, has exacerbated dissatisfactions already present in hospital work. The application of Diagnostic Related Groups (DRGs), a cost-containment measure, has meant patients' hospital stays are usually shorter than in the past and thus patients are generally in need of greater nursing attention.[6] But the kind of care these patients need is traditional; there is little time for newer, more personalized attention from more highly educated graduates of baccalaureate degree programs.

The implications of the nursing shortage for the professionalization project of nursing are twofold. On the one hand, the shortage has put a premium on nurses, and has raised salaries and encouraged altered working conditions in line with the aspirations of nurse professionals. On the other hand, as noted earlier, there are fewer nurses on the hospital floors today and the nature of the care they provide patients has not changed significantly. Moreover, the two-year programs have become the primary route into nursing.

An opportunity for independent practice of nursing has been opened by the advent of DRGs. As patients are staying fewer days in hospitals with each illness, they are returning home less well. With more two-worker families today, there are not many homes into which such patients can go without outside help. Thus, the private-duty nursing market is on the rise.

Many nurses, moreover, are convinced that their personal opportunities, such as moving into administrative positions, will be limited without at least a baccalaureate, or increasingly, a master's degree in nursing. Even without a formal shift to limit the educational routes into nursing, the market seems to be encouraging higher levels of education in nursing, even if not for entry.

CONCLUSIONS

This examination of nursing has provided an excellent context within which to explore the developing relations between education and occupations and professions. Without reiterating the importance of formal education for professional development, it is worth noting several aspects of nursing's experience. Educational upgrading is not an easy or simple process. Once alternative educational routes have been formed and used, resistance to eliminating them is likely to be strong (Fondiller, 1983).

Moreover, the professional payoff of increased educational requirements, especially for entry, seems to depend on a variety of factors, including the nature of the advanced education offered and the availability of settings in which to utilize the new knowledge. Clearly, different things will be learned as the site of professional preparation is changed, in this case from the workplace to the schools, and hence removed from the practice of the work. These new skills and perspectives on work learned in the new educational settings will produce a conflict for the practitioners and for the profession if the settings into which graduates move do not reward them. New forms of education imply new kinds of work and often new work settings. For nursing, the new work settings have not emerged in the quantity envisioned by the early proponents of advanced education nor have the existing settings changed significantly. The importance of the relationship between education and the nature of the work and its setting is highlighted by nursing's experiences.

NOTES

1. For a review of this issue see Meyer and Hannan (1979) and Craig (1981).
2. Some other groups, such as dentists, exercise this right, but only in regard to specific parts of our bodies. In the case of eyes, there can be several levels of care available: opticians in some states can provide limited independent service, though mostly they are like pharmacists, filling prescriptions written by doctors; optometrists can examine and prescribe lenses but not drugs and cannot perform surgery on the eye; and finally ophthalmologists are MDs specializing in the eye, and can do all that is restricted to others. This control by physicians is well documented by Freidson (1970) and Starr (1982).
3. There is a large literature on medicine, hospitals, and the organization of health care in the United States. See Starr (1982), Mechanic (1968), Freidson (1970), and Larson (1977). More relevant to the general topic of professionals and professionalization are Johnson (1972) and Halmos (1973).
4. See Fondiller (1983) for an excellent discussion of the problems professional associations in nursing have faced as they considered educational requirements for entry.
5. Examples of this literature include Stevens (1978), Roy and Roberts (1981), and Newman (1979).
6. Diagnostic related groups refers to a schedule of cost reimbursement that is based on a diagnosis, not on the costs of the hospital stay and doctors' fees. Thus, a patient having a kidney stone removed, for example, will be reimbursed a fixed amount, within certain parameters (such as age), no matter what the costs are. Of course, doctors and hospitals have begun to treat patients within the confines of the reimbursement.

REFERENCES

Aiken, Linda. 1983. "Nurses." Pp. 407–431 in David Mechanic (ed.), *Handbook of Health, Health Care, and the Health Professions.* New York: Free Press.

American Nurses' Association. 1965. *Educational Preparation for Nurse Practitioners and Assistants to Nurses: A Position Paper.* Kansas City: Author.

_____. 1969. *Statement on Graduate Education in Nursing.* Kansas City: Author.

_____.n.d. *1977 National Sample Survey of Registered Nurses: A Report on the Nurse Population and Factors Affecting Their Supply.* Springfield, VA.: National Technical Information Service.

_____. 1978. *Entry into Professional Practice: The New York Proposal.* Kansas City: Author.

_____. 1985. *Facts About Nursing, 1984–1985.* Kansas City: Author.

Brodt, Dagmar. 1978. "The Nursing Process." Pp. 256–263 in Norma L. Chaska, (ed.), *The Nursing Profession: Views Through the Mist.* New York: McGraw-Hill.

Brown, Esther L. 1966. "Nursing and Patient Care." Pp. 176–201 in Fred Davis (ed.), *The Nursing Profession: Five Sociological Essays*. New York: Wiley.

Bullough, Bonnie. 1978. "The Law and the Expanding Nursing Role." Pp. 309–319 in Norma L. Chaska (ed.), *The Nursing Profession: Views Through the Mist*. New York: McGraw-Hill.

Craig, John. 1981. "The Expansion of Education." Pp. 151–213 in David C. Berliner (ed.), *Review of Research in Education*. Washington, DC: American Educational Research Association.

Davis, Fred, Virginia L. Oleson, and Elvi W. Whittaker. 1966. "Problems and Issues in Collegiate Nursing Education." Pp. 138–175 in Fred Davis (ed.), *The Nursing Profession: Five Sociological Essays*. New York: Wiley.

Fondiller, Shirley H. 1983. *The Entry Dilemma: The National League for Nursing and the Higher Education Movement*. New York: National League for Nursing.

Freidson, Eliot. 1970. *Profession of Medicine: A Study of the Sociology of Applied Knowledge*. New York: Dodd, Mead.

Glaser, Barney, and Anselm Strauss. 1971. *Status Passage: A Formal Theory*. Chicago: Aldine.

Goode, William J. 1969. "The Theoretical Limits of Professionalization." Pp. 266–313, in Amitai Etzioni (ed.), *The Semi-Professions and Their Organization: Teachers, Nurses and Social Workers*. New York: Free Press.

Gordon, Marjory. 1978. "Nursing Diagnosis and the Diagnostic Process." Pp. 264–268 in Norma Chaska (ed.), *The Nursing Profession: Views Through the Mist*. New York: McGraw-Hill.

Halmos, Paul (ed). 1973. *Professionalization and Social Change*. Keele, England: University of Keele.

Hamilton, Mae J. 1975. "Identification of Needs Affecting Curriculum in Graduate Education in Nursing." Pp. 21–27, in National League of Nursing, *Curriculum in Graduate Education In Nursing*, Part 1. New York: Author.

Johnson, Terence J. 1972. *Professions and Power*. London: Macmillan.

Kramer, Marlene. 1974. *Reality Shock: Why Nurses Leave Nursing*. St. Louis: Mosby.

Larson, Magali S. 1977. *The Rise of Professionalism: A Sociological Analysis*. Berkeley: University of California Press.

Light, Donald. 1983. "Medical and Nursing Education: Surface Behavior and Deep Structure." Pp. 455–478 in David Mechanic (ed.), *Handbook of Health, Health Care, and the Health Professions*. New York: Free Press.

Lurie, Elinore E. 1981. "Nurse Practitioners: Issues in Professionalization Socialization." *Health and Social Behavior* 22 (March): 31–48.

McClure, Margaret L. 1978. "Entry into Professional Practice: The New York Proposal." Pp. 93–99 in Norma Chaska (Ed.), *The Nursing Profession: Views Through the Mist*. New York: McGraw-Hill.

Mechanic, David. 1968. *Medical Sociology*. New York: Free Press.

Meyer, John, and Michael Hannan (eds). 1979. *National Development and the World System: Educational, Economic, and Political Change, 1950–1970*. Chicago: University of Chicago Press.

National League for Nursing. 1974. *Characteristics of Graduate Education in Nursing*. New York: Author.

Newman, Margaret A. 1979. *Theory Development in Nursing*. Philadelphia: Davis.

Notter, Lucile E., and Marguerite Robey. 1979. *The Open Curriculum in Nursing Education*. New York: National League for Nursing.

Riser, Stanley J. 1978. *Medicine and the Reign of Technology*. Cambridge, England: Cambridge University Press.

Rodriguez, Orlando. 1978. "Occupational Shifts and Educational Upgrading in the American Labor Force Between 1950 and 1970." *Sociology of Education* 51 (January): 55–67.

Roy, Sister Callista, and Sharon L. Roberts. 1981. *Theory Construction in Nursing: An Adaptation Model*. Englewood Cliffs, NJ: Prentice-Hall.

Starr, Paul. 1982. *The Social Transformation of American Medicine*. New York: Basic Books.

Stevens, Barbara J. 1978. *Nursing Theory: Analysis, Application, Evaluation*. Boston: Little Brown.

Tomich, Jean H. 1978. "The Expanded Role of the Nurse: Current Status and Future Prospects." Pp. 299–308 in Norma Chaska (ed.), *The Nursing Profession: Views Through the Mist*. New York: McGraw-Hill.

Tyler, William. 1977. *The Sociology of Educational Inequality*. London: Methuen.

U.S. Department of Education. 1986. *Digest of Educational Statistics*. Washington, DC: Author.

Vaughn, John C. 1981. "Educational Preparation for Nursing—1980." *Nursing and Health Care* (September): 386–395.

Jobs: A Changing Workforce, a Changing Education?

HENRY M. LEVIN
Stanford University

The United States is preparing to enter a new age, an unprecedented period in which high technology products and processes will play an increasingly significant role in the life of the individual, and affect the structure of society as a whole, to a degree at this point unknown. Certainly such a revolution will have profound effects on our entire educational system but especially in the area of higher education.

High technology generally refers to the development and application of computers, lasers, communications technologies, robotics, and bioengineering. These technologies are closely associated with research and development activities and are heavily dependent upon workers with advanced education and training. Indeed, the media are already predicting substantial erosion of the labor force if the education of the population is not upgraded substantially. This contention is based upon the view that traditional industries are being replaced by ones that use the new technologies, with new job requirements demanding higher levels of worker sophistication than those of the old jobs. Some pundits even predict the demise of entry-level jobs requiring little education.

Before the effect of the new technologies on education can be fully understood, it is necessary to explore exactly what changes will be required of workers, and what new jobs will be created by the information age and its technologies.

WHERE WILL THE JOBS BE?

In considering where the jobs will be and their educational requirements, it is necessary to avoid two fallacies that are reflected in popular discussions of the subject. First is the fallacy that equates high technology industries with jobs that require high skill levels and advanced education. Second is the fallacy that assumes that the fastest growing job categories in terms of relative growth or percentage growth are also the ones that will provide the most new jobs in the future.

The question of what is a high technology industry is very much open to debate. The U.S. Department of Labor uses three definitions: (1) industries in which technology-oriented workers (engineers, scientists, etc.) accounted for a proportion of total employment that was at least one and one-half times the average for all industries; (2) industries in which the ratio of R & D expenditures to net sales was at least twice the average for all industries; and (3) combination of the first two criteria.

Even when such industries were singled out, only a relatively small portion of jobs in these areas required high tech workers in terms of skills and educational requirements. For example, in electronic components firms, only about 15 percent of the jobs were technologically oriented, while 61 percent were blue collar jobs. What is often forgotten is that firms selling products must hire large numbers of assemblers, clerks, warehouse workers, secretaries, and so on. Even the computer and data processing industry had only one-quarter of its labor force in technically-oriented positions. For the automobile industry, the percentage of such positions was less than 6 percent. The growth of high technology industries does not mean that all or even most of the new jobs created will require high levels of technical skills. Most new jobs in these industries will require high school diplomas rather than advanced education and training.

Thus, the concern over education should focus on the expansion of jobs in high technology occupations and in other higher level occupations, rather than in so-called high technology industries. The most sophisticated job projections to date have been carried out by the U.S. Department of Labor, Bureau of Labor Statistics (BLS). The BLS method takes account of alternative economic growth rates, technological change as it affects occupational requirements and production techniques, and a wide variety of other criteria. Table 1 shows the forty occupations with the largest expected job growth from 1982-95. The top five occupations by numbers of jobs projected are building custodians, cashiers, secretaries, general office clerks, and sales clerks.

No high technology occupations are included among the top eighteen expected to contribute the most jobs to the American economy. Although fast food workers, guards and doorkeepers, kitchen helpers, and janitors are found among the top occupations, high tech occupations are far down the list. While it is expected that some 200,000 additional computer programmers will be needed by 1995, the increase in jobs for building custodians, fast food workers, and kitchen helpers is expected to be more than 1.3 million. It is

TABLE 1 Forty occupations with largest job growth, 1982–95

Occupation	Change in total employment (in thousands)	Percentage of total job growth	Percent change
Building custodians	779	3.0	27.5
Cashiers	744	2.9	47.4
Secretaries	719	2.8	29.5
General clerks, office	696	2.7	29.6
Sales clerks	685	2.7	23.5
Nurses, registered	642	2.5	48.9
Waiters and waitresses	562	2.2	33.8
Teachers, kindergarten and elementary	511	2.0	37.4
Truck drivers	425	1.7	26.5
Nursing aides and orderlies	423	1.7	34.8
Sales representatives, technical	386	1.5	29.3
Accountants and auditors	344	1.3	40.2
Automotive mechanics	324	1.3	38.3
Supervisors of blue-collar workers	319	1.2	26.6
Kitchen helpers	305	1.2	35.9
Guards and doorkeepers	300	1.2	47.3
Food preparation and service workers, fast food restaurants	297	1.2	36.7
Managers, store	292	1.1	30.1
Carpenters	247	1.0	28.6
Electrical and electronic technicians	222	.9	60.7
Licensed practical nurses	220	.9	37.1
Computer systems analysts	217	.8	85.3
Electrical engineers	209	.8	65.3
Computer programmers	205	.8	76.9
Maintenance repairers, general utility	193	.8	27.8
Helpers, trades	190	.7	31.2
Receptionists	189	.7	48.8
Electricians	173	.7	31.8
Physicians	163	.7	34.0
Clerical supervisors	162	.6	34.6
Computer operators	160	.6	75.8

TABLE 1   *(continued)*

Occupation	Change in total employment (in thousands)	Percentage of total job growth	Percent change
Sales representatives, nontechnical	160	.6	27.4
Lawyers	159	.6	34.3
Stock clerks, stockroom and warehouse	156	.6	18.8
Typists	155	.6	15.7
Delivery and route workers	153	.6	19.2
Bookkeepers, hand	152	.6	15.9
Cooks, restaurants	149	.6	42.3
Bank tellers	142	.6	30.0
Cooks, short order, specialty and fast food	141	.6	32.2

Note: Includes only detailed occupations with 1982 employment of 25,000 or more. Data for 1995 are based on moderate-trend projections.
Source—Silvestri, George T., John M. Lukasiewicz, and Marcus E. Einstein. "Occupational Employment Projections through 1995." *Monthly Labor Review*, (November 1983), pp. 37–49.

obvious that most job growth will be in areas requiring at most a high school diploma or some community college training. Relatively few jobs will require the skills of a college graduate or any post-graduate training. The BLS estimates that only about one-quarter of the forty jobs with the largest expected contribution to job growth will require a college degree.

How can these results be reconciled with the persistent signals that high technology jobs are the ones growing most rapidly and that educational requirements for these jobs will be high? Part of the answer is that, in percentage or relative terms, many of the occupations with the most rapid growth rates are in high technology occupations as shown in Table 2. But, although these job categories are growing at a rapid rate in relative terms, this growth occurs in occupations with numerically small numbers, so that rapid growth rates produce relatively few new jobs. For example, although employment of computer systems analysts is expected to rise by about 85 percent during the 1982–95 period, only about 200,000 new jobs are expected to emerge from this growth.

A second explanation for the puzzle is the assumption that high tech jobs all require advanced education. Although it is projected that the number of jobs for computer operators will rise by 76 percent during this period, it should be recognized that those jobs typically require no education beyond high school. This is also true of the increasing number of computer and micro-processor repair positions which use highly sophisticated diagnostic equip-

TABLE 2   Twenty fastest growing occupations, 1982–95

Occupation	Percent growth in employment
Computer service technicians	96.8
Legal assistants	94.3
Computer systems analysts	85.3
Computer programmers	76.9
Computer operators	75.8
Office machine repairers	71.7
Physical therapy assistants	67.8
Electrical engineers	65.3
Civil engineering technicians	63.9
Peripheral EDP equipment operators	63.5
Insurance clerks, medical	62.2
Electrical and electronic technicians	60.7
Occupational therapists	59.8
Surveyor helpers	58.6
Credit clerks, banking and insurance	54.1
Physical therapists	53.6
Employment interviewers	52.5
Mechanical engineers	52.1
Mechanical engineering technicians	51.6
Compression and injection mold machine operators, plastics	50.3

NOTE: Includes only detailed occupations with 1982 employment of 25,000 or more. Data for 1995 are based on moderate-trend projections.
Source—Silvestri, George T., John M. Lukasiewicz, and Marcus E. Einstein. "Occupational Employment Projections through 1995." *Monthly Labor Review*, (November 1983), pp. 37–49

ment that automatically identifies problems, and simple component and circuit-board construction that allows component replacement requiring little sophisticated knowledge.

The BLS has defined high technology occupations as including engineers, life and physical scientists, mathematical specialists, engineering and science technicians, and computer specialists. Workers in these occupations typically need advanced training at least to an associate degree level, and up to the Ph.D. level in some cases. Although the growth of these occupations will be at a rate about twice that of all wage and salary workers, the actual number of new jobs expected to emerge in these areas will be about 1.5 million out of an expected 23–28 million new jobs. It is expected that only about 6 percent of the new jobs in the economy will be in high technology occupations, about the same proportion as in the 1970s.

What of the effects of high technology on other occupations? Will high technology require increased skills in those occupations? The available evidence suggests that the principal impact of micro-processors and robotics on traditional occupations will be to displace some workers and to reduce the skills of other workers. This conclusion is consistent with studies of the impact of machine automation done in earlier periods, where it was found that new production technologies tend to reduce skill requirements. This is also logical, since an investment in new capital can only be profitable if it reduces overall costs for any given output. Reduced labor costs can be derived from using fewer people in the production process, using persons with lower skill levels and wages, or some combination of these. It is the latter that seems most applicable.

One example of such effects in the workplace can be found as secretaries are being replaced by word processors at a very rapid rate. Traditionally, secretaries were required to know the appropriate formats for reports and correspondence, and have almost perfect typing skills. In addition, they needed strong spelling skills and a basic understanding of grammar. However, word processors can correct typing errors automatically, so letter-perfect typing and strong spelling are no longer required of operators. Formats for different types of documents can be programmed into the word processor, and even grammatical revisions can be done through syntactical programs. The result is that many of the traditional functions of the secretary have been replaced by the machine. Additionally, the increased productivity of word-processing reduces the need for office workers, and the shift from a typewriter to a word-processor requires relatively little training. One of the major suppliers of temporary manpower has found that it can prepare typists who lack background on word processing equipment with only one day of intensive instruction.

A second example is found in the field of computer programming. Not only were earlier computers larger and more expensive than today's computers, but they were far more cumbersome to program. The power of the technology itself has rendered unnecessary many of the earlier skills required of the programmer, with the transition from circuit logic and plug boards to machine language, macro-assembly languages, science- and business-oriented user languages and the relatively simple languages that are in use today. Increasingly, powerful software packages allow highly sophisticated applications to broad classes of problems, with the programmer only required to provide data and select from among a menu of options. Now, even present simple programming languages will be replaced with "natural" languages (the language of the user), simple mechanical devices such as the computer "mouse," and voice recognition. Although a small number of programmers using highly advanced systems will require very sophisticated skills, the average programmer will not, and software will replace programmers.

Similar stories can be told for computer and computerized machine repair, data processing, auto repair, design, drafting, and many other occupations. Just as a modern automobile with six or seven micro-processors requires far less skill to drive than a primitive Model T, the vast majority of high technology applications create a reduction in the skill requirements of the operator. Many workers will be displaced by the new technologies, and far more will see their jobs reduced to ones requiring minimal training and skills. As a portent of this, it should be noted that many American multi-national firms are producing sophisticated silicon chips in such third world countries as Malaysia, where young women from rural areas with a few years of primary education have displaced American assembly workers.

WHAT SHOULD BE DONE?

The advent of high technology will expand the capabilities of the economy, reduce prices, offer a large array of new products, and contribute in other ways to society. Yet, contrary to popular reports, it is not likely to add large numbers of jobs for highly educated and trained persons; many workers will likely be replaced by new technology, and it appears the skill requirements of broad classes of traditional occupations will be reduced. What should be done?

It is clear that high technology cannot solve the employment problem. Such expectation has actually undermined traditional jobs by ignoring the large number of jobs—even in smokestack industries—that are necessary to our economy, and that can be saved through judicious policy making. First, decisions must be made concerning which jobs in declining industries, beset by foreign competition, are worth saving, and what the cost will be. In many cases, high technology will be part of the solution, since major investments in high technology can increase productivity enormously. It is absurd to think that the U.S. will produce only information services, computer software, and work in research development, and that all other goods and services will be imported from third world countries. The U.S. will continue to be a major manufacturer of steel and metal products, automobiles, machine tools, and many other basic products. The question is how America can improve its performance and compete more effectively in both domestic and world markets, not how to pursue the purposive abandonment of such industries.

Most new jobs are created in small and medium-size firms rather than in large corporations or in government. To the degree that Fortune 500 firms have increased employment, it has been done largely through acquisitions and foreign subsidiaries. Many of the largest corporations have been reducing employment over the long run while expanding output through labor-saving approaches. Accordingly, entrepreneurship must be promoted, and the establishment and survival of substantial numbers of smaller businesses must be encouraged. Such businesses not only have greater employment potential, but they also are the major incubators for product innovation in America, according to U.S. Small Business Administration figures. Government assistance should be provided in the form of technical help, information on markets, and reduced interest rates. Present national deficits and other aspects of national economic policy have kept interest rates high, and this is the single worst enemy of small businesses.

The family farm is still the most efficient segment of American agriculture; this has been one of the most consistent findings in the literature on agricultural economics. Such farms are more productive in terms of total factor inputs, and they provide considerably more employment per unit of investment than the large corporate entities. Yet, agricultural policy—and particularly high interest rates—are undermining the family farm while providing the largest benefits from tax policies, agricultural subsidies, and water subsidies (particularly in the West) to the wealthiest corporations in America. Clearly, a more even-handed policy is in order, or one that promotes the family farm. Such farmers need assistance in terms of access to credit as well as through the application of high technologies that will keep them competitive. This is another area in which overall employment can be maintained or increased.

In order to compete more effectively in world markets, a much more aggressive policy to promote trade is necessary. Businesses need more information about foreign markets and the requirements for entering and competing in them. At the state level, businesses need guidance as to where opportunities will be and how to take advantage of them. None of this will easily overcome a strong dollar making American goods expensive to foreigners. However, as interest rates come down over the longer run, America must be in a position to exploit the resulting improvement in the attractiveness of U.S. prices to foreign purchasers. Even under existing exchange rates much higher employment levels can be generated in the foreign trade sector.

Finally, educationally intensive activities should be emphasized. Much of Japan's success has been achieved by continually upgrading the workforce and creating technological change in materials and capital-savings forms. For example, some 61 percent of process innovations initially introduced between 1945 and 1974 in the U.S. were labor-saving as compared with only 16 percent of those introduced in Japan and 18 percent of those introduced in Europe. In contrast, only about 19 percent of such innovations introduced in the U.S. were material savings in comparison with about 50 percent in Japan and Europe. Yet, both Japan and Western Europe increased their labor productivity considerably more than the U.S. did during this period, despite a failure to adopt labor saving devices at the rate of the Americans. Another example of an industrially competitive organization with high labor input is the producer cooperative movement of Mondragon in Spain that has produced over a billion dollars a year of industrial and high technology products, with far greater labor inputs and higher productivity than comparable firms organized in traditional ways.

IMPLICATIONS FOR EDUCATION

It is clear that the structure of American industry is changing dramatically, resulting in massive repercussions for the workforce. Many workers will be displaced and will need new training to acquire new jobs, while others will need to be retrained to accommodate new technologies. Retraining does not mean that higher level skills will be needed as much as different ones. In some cases the training will take hours or days, while in other cases the need will be for weeks, months, or even years. A policy of recurrent education must be established to make it possible for individuals to move from the workplace to retraining programs and back into the workplace, a system in which education and work follow a recurring pattern. At the present, there is no centralized source of information or coordination of the large numbers of federal, state, local, and privately sponsored programs with employers, school districts, community colleges, unions, proprietary schools, universities, and local training entities providing educational and training services. Sources and modes of finance are also highly fragmented. The challenge is to construct an overall system of education and finance that will be efficient, responsive, and that will draw upon all elements of the postsecondary educational system.

The number and kind of jobs that will be available to any individual over a lifetime cannot be predicted. While job projections give some idea of the array of employment opportunities that will be available at a future time, they cannot forecast precisely what will be available and what skills will be required for any particular individual situation. Accordingly, it is important to stress a broad array of fundamental skills in higher education for the vast majority of students, rather than narrow vocational preparation. These skills include written and oral expression, mathematics, sciences, fine and performing arts, analytical skills, social sciences, and foreign languages. These will provide a firm basis for obtaining the applied training that will be needed at each stage of the career.

Much more emphasis should be placed on the training of entrepreneurs and on the fostering of creativity in virtually all of higher education. This can be done by restructuring courses and curricula to provide greater analytic work in creative problem solving as well as providing greater incentives for imaginative solutions in contrast to rote learning. Higher education should also provide incentives and encouragement for greater risk-taking among students in their choice of classes, the nature of their assignments, and in the careers that they pursue. These measures could result in great improvement in the entrepreneurial capabilities of the population, through our colleges and universities.

Finally, the current dearth of common knowledge concerning foreign languages and cultures among our citizens does not augur well for successful competition in world markets. Virtually all students in higher education should be required to obtain proficiency in at least one foreign language and the study of another culture, and much of the curriculum should reflect cross-cultural rather than narrow egocentric thinking. If the U.S. cannot communicate with and understand other cultures, it is unlikely to respond to their needs and successfully compete for their business.

These analyses of the implications of the high technology for jobs and higher education in the United States are not optimistic if it is blindly assumed that the high technology revolution will provide plenty of jobs for highly trained individuals. Accepting the realities of high tech societies and making conscious choices with both economics and education in mind can improve the future considerably. Ignoring the problem will lead to serious consequences for both the labor force and the educational sector.

10

Educational Policy
and Reform

Since 1983 there have been uncounted numbers of national, state, and local reports by blue ribbon commissions recommending reforms in education.[1] The report of the President's National Commission on Excellence in Education, *A Nation at Risk* (April 1983), is usually credited with beginning the national rexamination of education. Highly critical of the quality of schooling being provided in our schools and colleges, this report links the decline in our international economic competitiveness with a decline in the quality of our school system: "A rising tide of mediocrity . . . threatens our very future as a Nation and a people. . . . We have, in effect, been committing an act of unthinking, unilateral education disarmament" (1983: 1).

What is most startling about this report is the enormous amount of attention it received and the additional studies and reports it generated (several of the most important of which are excerpted in this chapter). As important as the publicity the report received, the movement it spawned has resulted in state legislatures and governors spearheading change in the laws and policy under which schooling is conducted in the various states. The National Governors' Association (1986) proposed an elaborate set of objectives for all states to improve their educational systems.

Three important issues are raised by these reports and their extended impact. The first issue deals with the specifics of the reformers' proposals. What reforms are being proposed? Second, what evidence is there that the reports are right about what is wrong with our educational system and that their proposed reforms will produce the desired effects? Third, why has

---

[1]The most frequently cited reform reports are Adler (1982), Boyer (1983), Business–Higher Education Forum (1983), Education Commission of the States (1983), National Commission on Excellence in Education (1983), National Science Board (1983), and Twentieth Century Fund (1983).

educational reform risen to such prominence on the national political agenda in the 1980s? Why have so many reports appeared?

This introduction will describe the general outlines of the educational reforms that are being proposed and implemented, review the main criticisms of the reports, and analyze the developing explanation of why the reform movement appeared when it did and why it has been so robust. The selections that follow provide more detail on the specifics of the proposals, analyze their arguments, and raise questions about their assumptions, objectives, and consequences.

DESCRIPTIONS OF THE REFORMS

Although the reports' recommendations and policymakers' actions vary somewhat, a working consensus has arisen about the problems of education and, less firmly, about what should be done about them. First and most important, the reports generally agree that students are not learning the basic intellectual skills well enough and are not spending enough time mastering the traditional academic curriculum (English, history, mathematics, sciences, and foreign languages). The reason, according to the reports, is that too often students are enrolled in schools without strong leadership or a clear focus on what will enhance cognitive achievement. Many administrators and teachers, it is argued, do not expect students to do well and in fact may sometimes conspire with students to keep the school orderly instead of effective.[2] This lack of a central academic focus is often attributed to a confused mission. Schools are expected to perform so many different academic and nonacademic functions that none can be performed well or even adequately.

The solutions most frequently suggested include a greater focus on fundamental skills, more frequent assessment of student progress, stricter standards for student promotion and graduation, and tying school funding formulas to students' test scores.[3] In addition, many districts are developing secondary schools that are smaller and more focused: for example, using a vocational interest to orient the curriculum. Often designated as magnet schools, these schools use aviation or health or business careers as a common thread for their curricula. Finally, an effort has recently begun to provide a measure of school autonomy (from the central school district) that would allow for school-based planning and management, with administrators, teachers, and parents all sharing in the decision-making process (Clune and White, 1988).

It is useful to trace the history of the recent reform movement in order to see how it has evolved and to be able to place the various reports and their

[2]The tie is clear between the recommendations of the reports and the "effective schools movement" discussed in Chapter 6, including its emphasis on the effective use of academic learning time. The reports draw rather heavily on these earlier findings.

[3]On this last point, some states such as New Jersey are experimenting with the threat of "educational bankruptcy" and state-mandated closure or takeover of schools and even districts if student performance does not improve.

recommendations in perspective. The focus of the movement was originally on secondary education, but it has expanded to elementary and postsecondary education. Most recently, the reform movement has focused on the preparation of teachers and the enhancement of teaching's professionalization. As the movement has gained strength, the initially strident rhetoric of national crisis has become muted, though it has by no means disappeared. Rather the language of reform today combines the economic and political arguments of businesspeople and government officials with the concerns of educators such as Theodore Sizer and John Goodlad.

The excerpt from the report *A Nation at Risk* by the President's National Commission on Excellence in Education (1983) illustrates the early economic concerns most starkly. While this report addresses the consequences for individuals, its primary concern is with the economic, political, and military health of the nation. Our national neglect of education, it asserts, has resulted in "unilateral disarmament." The consequences of this neglect directly affect our ability to compete economically and, perhaps, militarily. The report recommends increasing the number of years of basic academic studies high school students should have for graduation and higher levels of local and state support for schooling, while being silent on more federal assistance. More time should be spent on a limited number of subjects, and the school year should be longer. Higher standards for performance are to be encouraged by standardized testing, especially at major transition points such as from elementary to secondary schooling. No national standards exist about such things, and the report asserts they should be implemented. Teachers should be of higher quality, paid better, and have the opportunities career-ladder and merit-pay plans afford. A career-ladder plan provides steps between beginning and advanced teachers and administrators. In most schools today, there are no or very few steps between these positions. A merit-pay system awards salary increases on the basis of a review of the individual teacher's annual performance.[4]

The next selection, "A New Agenda for Education"—by Eileen Gardner of the Heritage Foundation (a conservative thinktank)—also heavily influenced the Reagan Administration's educational policies. This report is as concerned with the breakdown of what it defines as moral standards as *A Nation At Risk* is with economic, political, and military concerns. For example, regarding one legislative funding program administered by the U.S. Department of Education, it argues that the Women's Educational Equity Act has put forth a radical feminist agenda and needs to be repealed. The Heritage report identifies the federal government as sapping state and local control, and turning schools over to "vested interests" such as teachers' unions whose pursuits of self-interest has led to a breakdown of the schools' authority.

---

[4]The majority of schools, lacking a merit system, grant the same increases to all teachers, depending only on years of service and degrees or credits attained. Although administrators in these schools review the performance of beginning teachers before they are granted tenure, the review of tenured teachers is often less thorough and without the consequences for salary a merit plan dictates.

The differences between these two reports clearly show that conservatives are not uniform in their view of the federal role in education. The Heritage Foundation's report directly expresses the ideological commitments of the "New Right," among whose goals are an end to the federal role in education and promotion of tuition tax credits and vouchers to expand parental choice of schooling for their children. The Excellence Commission's report avoided these controversial ideological topics in order to generate a wider consensus for improving education.

The concern for a reemphasis on basic academic subjects has evolved in another way as well. The work of E. D. Hirsch, represented here by his article, "Restoring Cultural Literacy in the Early Grades," has recently received wide attention. Hirsch advocates a curriculum that imparts "traditional literate culture," including knowledge of history and geography, to children. His thesis is that schools have let various "slogans" deflect them from providing students with what they need to know in order to function as literate citizens of this country. This literacy "is more effectively taught when [students] are successfully taught durable, traditional subjects like Ulysses and the Cyclops than when they are taught ephemera like Dick and Jane at the Supermarket."

Liberals and others have responded to the *A Nation at Risk* report and to the Heritage Foundation's proposals. Theodore Sizer, a well-known educational writer and researcher, is most troubled by the impossibility of the task teachers confront in a typical school. In "High School Reform: The Need for Engineering," he is not as concerned with national defense as he is with schools' lack of a clear sense of what they are about. Sizer favors an academic curriculum with teachers heavily involved in creating and designing it. He wants smaller, more focused schools that are more autonomous from state regulation than is currently allowed. In some ways, particularly in his concern with improving school quality, Sizer shares common ground with conservatives. But Sizer also rejects tracking in schools and strongly supports greater teacher autonomy, a theme we will pick up in greater detail later. In these last two respects, his position is quite distinct from those of conservatives.

Ann Bastian and her colleagues are much more explicit in their rejection of the conservative agenda and restate the case for emphasizing equality in schooling in their selection entitled "Choosing Equality." They see the crisis in schooling as a crisis of inequality and citizenship. Strenuously arguing for greater local control and parental involvement, these authors view the national reform reports not as universal solutions but as elitist prescriptions. Our primary concern should lie with the acute failure to provide low-income and minority students with decent schools and skills. Instead, according to Bastian and her colleagues, the reform reports have been primarily concerned with improving the test performance of middle- and upper-class students. Minority and urban issues were ignored in the initial round of reports.[5]

---

[5]More recent commissions have not been as narrow in their conception of our educational problems. See the report sponsored by the William T. Grant Foundation (1988) under the title *The*

More recently, several national commissions have projected a future teacher shortage and decried the poor qualifications and training of new teachers. All new reforms for education are seen to depend on qualified and enthusiastic teachers who are in short supply. These "second" or "third" generation reform proposals are particularly focused on where instruction takes place, that is, in classrooms. Enhancing the quality of teachers, the sharing of power through school-based decision making, and new instructional techniques (like the cooperative learning models developed by Slavin, 1988) are now seen as better ways to improve the quality of education provided students. The focus of earlier "generations" of reform reports—advancing standards or improving the leadership of principals and the climate of schools—are now seen as more difficult or less promising than increasing teacher quality and their decision-making power.

For example, the Holmes Group of deans of schools of education (1986) proposes enhancing the salary and working conditions of teachers so as to improve the attractiveness of teaching as a profession and, in turn, the quality of students entering teaching. The selection by Frank Murray, "Goals for the Reform of Teacher Education: An Executive Summary of the Holmes Group Report," outlines their recommended changes in the education of prospective teachers, including eliminating the bachelor's degree in education and requiring a master's degree. It emphasizes the need for all teachers to have a strong liberal arts background specializing in a field taught in schools. Moreover, less time should be devoted to traditional education courses and prospective students should have extensive preservice or student teaching experience.[6]

Teachers with improved qualifications are likely to find the current organization and working conditions of education stifling. The Holmes Group speaks of the need to empower teachers in their classrooms, in schools, and in the larger educational system. Such a reform implies providing teachers with new levels of classroom autonomy and new relationships among themselves and with administrators.[7]

The educational reform agenda has not been restricted to elementary and secondary schooling and the preparation of teachers but has expanded to include higher education generally (Association of American Colleges, 1985; Bennett, 1984; National Institute of Education, 1984). Again, although there are differences among these reports, their similarities are strong. They argue that colleges need to focus on the core arts and sciences curriculum, to

---

Forgotten Half. Other examples include the Hispanic Policy Development Project's report (1984) and the Committee for Economic Development's report *Children in Need* (1985).

[6]The 1986 report of the Carnegie Forum on Education and the Economy echoes the Holmes Group's report, but goes one step further. It called for the formation of a national teacher board that would certify the competence of master teachers. A board has been appointed and has begun its work. Whether it can create criteria acceptable to teachers and to school boards and come to be as powerful as the medical specialty boards remains to be seen.

[7]The reforms intended to enhance teachers' autonomy can be related with the workplace democracy efforts found in industry. Zwerdling (1980) provides a good introduction to this literature. Also see Maeroff (1988).

emphasize teaching and student needs as opposed to the current emphasis place on research, and to assess the cognitive and affective changes brought about in students (Hammack, 1985). The "assessment movement," as this nationwide movement is now known, has grown very fast and is forcing many higher education institutions to refine their objectives for students and how they plan to achieve those goals (Adelman, 1986; Ewell, 1987).

For example, the state of Florida has recently decided to specify higher statewide standards of student achievement and academic progress. All students at public colleges and universities and those who receive state financial aid at private schools must take a standard test (the CLAST—College Level Academic Skills Test) to be able to go on to the junior year and to complete their degree programs. The test is meant to influence the curricular requirements of colleges so that their sophomores will pass the test.

Because the federal government, under President Reagan, has attempted to reduce its educational role, the activities of states and their governors are particularly interesting. The National Governors' Association report *A Time For Results: The Governors' 1991 Report on Education* (1986) outlines policy initiatives selected by the Governors' Association for the next five years. They have chosen to seek local and state action in seven broad areas. They want states to move to link teacher pay to assessments of teaching performance; to improve school leadership; to increase parental choice among public schools; to improve the schooling of poor children and to keep them in school longer; to more fully and effectively use our educational facilities; to adopt and use new instructional technologies; and, finally, to assess what college students are learning. In each case, the report outlines recommendations and discusses how the Governors' Association intends to follow up on its work during the next five years. In short, the governors have included just about all of the reform initiatives, and even some of the aims of critics of the initial reform reports.[8]

Governors are clearly an important group for setting the educational agenda, as education is a state function under our constitution. That their national association has set so ambitious and public an agenda for education is a good indicator of the current importance being attributed to education. Moreover, it is important to note that while the reform movement originated at the national level, its recommendations have been enacted at the state and local levels. There has been a significant decline in federal expenditures for education and virtually no new federal legislative initiatives. Meanwhile, many states now have minimum competency tests for students and for teachers. Some have mandated curricular changes. And others are in the process of enacting new funding formulas.

---

[8]In his first speech to Congress, President Bush reiterated several of these goals: "The most important competitiveness program of all is one which improves education in America" ("Text of President Bush's Address," 1989). The President stressed the following objectives: to increase parental choice among schools, to increase the accountability of teachers and administrators, and to foster programs that reduce the dropout rate.

CRITICISM OF THE REPORTS

The reports and studies that have emerged in the last few years have generated skepticism and controversy as well as praise. The selection by Lawrence Stedman and Marshall Smith, "Recent Reform Proposals for American Education," provides an analysis of several reports that asks how good their data are. They find that the reports often make claims about poor levels of academic achievement that are unsupported by the evidence. Furthermore, they fault the reports for making recommendations without specifying how they could be implemented and for ignoring the needs of the poor and minorities.

Their criticisms are primarily technical, but others have questioned the underlying assumptions of the reports. For example, the assumption of a close link between our educational system and economic productivity and competitiveness, as Chapter 9 has shown, is not universally accepted. Few doubt the importance of literacy and numeracy for our economy, but many question how important other school-related skills are. The economy needs many able workers, but relatively few engineers or other highly trained workers. Perhaps more important, as our economy becomes primarily oriented toward services as opposed to manufacturing, the relation of education to economic growth becomes increasingly tenuous. Many more jobs are being created for janitors and restaurant workers than are being created for computer programmers and physicians. Thus, while test scores and our nation's economy have declined together, there is considerable doubt as to whether the first drop caused the second (Levin, 1984; Rumberger, 1984).

Some critics of recent educational reforms are concerned that the reforms will themselves produce negative consequences. The selection by Natriello, McDill, and Pallas, "School Reform and Potential Dropouts," argues that tighter requirements for graduation may well lead students already having difficulties to drop out even earlier. The imposition of stronger academic demands, when the existing ones are not being met, is likely to alienate and discourage failing students who might have stuck it out. Whatever the true nature of the relation of education to the economy, we know that those who do not have a high school diploma are much less likely to be employed. While we all want higher levels of performance in schools, this should not be achieved by forcing out those who do not perform well. Rather, such students need better programs and encouragement to stay in school as long as they can benefit from it.

ACCOUNTING FOR THE REFORMS

Organizations develop policy to state objectives and the means of attaining them. Educational policies are statements about what should be the objectives of teachers and students and how they should conduct themselves to achieve those aims.

How policy objectives are determined by government is the heart of politics. Changes in aims or the means for achieving those aims are the result of efforts by interested groups promoting them, frequently in the face of opposition from other groups either wanting to keep things as they are or proposing yet other aims or means.

Thus, in order to explain the education reform movement, we need to determine who has been pushing for reforms, what their interests are (what they gain from the reforms), and how they have articulated their desires for change. At the same time, it is important to keep in mind that interests are not always formally articulated; they may reside in the taken-for-granted way things are done and can also be hidden behind the actions of others (Lukes, 1974).

The reports each provide an explanation for their existence and for their recommendations. For example, the National Commission on Excellence in Education asserts: "To keep and improve on the slim competitive edge we still retain in world markets, we must dedicate ourselves to the reform of our educational system" (1983: 5). And the National Governors' report states that governors have become interested in education because of jobs. "More than anything else, it is the threat to the jobs of the people who elected us" (1986: 5).

The argument that our economic and military strength is dependent on educational reform is reminiscent of functional explanations of the interdependence of society's parts and the commonality of values and interests. Chapter 2 of this book has outlined this theoretical position and the positions of its critics. But there are other explanations for the reform movement that, as one might expect, reflect other theoretical positions.

Other analysts argue that attention needs to be focused on economic elites who shape social and educational policy in their interests. Historian Joel Spring argues that the origin of the reform movement "lies in the demographic changes of the last two decades and the responses of U.S. business to those changes. The connection between changes in educational policy and industrial needs is direct" (1984: 534). A labor shortage is on the horizon, according to Spring, and more highly educated workers are needed; thus, employers are demanding improved education.

Other Marxist and critical theorists stress the economic roots of the reform movement, but see it as the consequence of a more conflictual process. H. Svi Shapiro argues: "Contrary to some assertions, educational reform is in no sense to be understood as a simple 'knee-jerk' response to the demands of a monolithic ruling class or to what is needed to accelerate the accumulation of capital" (1985: 57–58). Rather, he argues, the reports need to be seen as representing a reaction by more liberal parts of the dominant class against the Reagan administration's attempts to reduce the federal role in education. The reform movement arises, then, out of internal conflicts within the dominant class over the role of the state and of private interests (but see Stedman, 1987).

Kingston (1986: 648) argues a Weberian position. He asserts that the liberal reforms of the early 1960s and 1970s to increase equality in schooling (social promotion, bilingual education, programs for the handicapped and the poor) constituted a threat to the middle classes. These reforms made their academic achievements more commonplace and hence less economically valuable. Kingston argues that in response middle class parents have wanted to reestablish the market value of schooling. Because education is critical for middle-class occupations and professions, middle-class parents want to distinguish their children from the disadvantaged and enable them to compete with elite groups (1986: 649–649).

While Kingston's analysis focuses on middle-class parents, he makes brief reference to another actor: professional educators. In fact, the role of professional educators deserves a great deal of attention. Many of the reform proponents are themselves educators. For example, of the 18 members of the National Commission on Excellence in Education, 11 were school and college faculty or administrators and 3 were members of state or local boards of education. Only one member was clearly a business executive.

Other reform advocates such as John Goodlad, Theodore Sizer, Mortimer Adler, and Ernest Boyer are present or former educators. Moreover, there is reason to believe that these educators-reformers had concerns of their own that were not reducible to the interests of business or even of the middle class. Many educators have been distressed with education's sharp loss of prestige and political and financial support over the last 15 years. They have needed a way to make a case for education in terms that would attract the support of the business-conservative political coalition that became dominant in the late 1970s and early 1980s. Hence, it would be natural for them to relate educational reform to national economic challenges. This use of a rhetoric of national crisis was made easy by the successful use of such rhetoric in the past. In the late 1950s the launching of the Soviet satellite Sputnik was used as symbol to mobilize support for major educational reform.

Just as educators did not simply respond to popular pressure but also used it as a base for realizing their own interests, so have governors. Governors have supported reform for reasons in addition to popular demand. One reason is ideology. Many of the governors are deeply committed to the individual and social benefits of education. They also see it as a way of making a distinctive contribution during their term in office. Finally, governors have believed that a strong program of educational reform could bring electoral benefits. Even if voters are not demanding a particular educational program, they may vote for an elected official who champions that program simply because of voters' interest in and support of education. Moreover, governors have also hoped that educational reform would generate voter support by spurring economic growth. They are aware that, in times of large shifts in our industrial base and consequent unemployment, the incumbent party is usually punished at the polls.[9]

That educators and governors have had their own reasons for calling for reform in education does not disallow a role for the middle-class and business interests. The current educational reform movement is not a cohesive whole, but made up of a variety of groups with diverse concerns.

[9]For more on the role of educators and governors, see Dougherty (1989).

Because of its diversity, the reform movement's future is likely to be like its past: conflictual and with a rapidly changing focus. One primary conflict today is between those who, like the Holmes Group, want greater teacher empowerment and local school-based management and, on the other hand, those who have less trust in teachers and local school initiatives to improve student achievement. Another pair of conflicting impulses is between those who want tighter links between education and the economy and those, like Bastian and her colleagues, who want education's larger citizenship role to be dominant.

CODA

Education in the United States is larger and more complex than in any other country. A major reason for this is that our society uses education differently. We allow great adult inequality, but want to limit the degree to which such inequalities are passed on to our children. Education is the primary means we have come to use to limit the inheritance of inequality, taking the place of the welfare policies chosen by other countries (Heidenheimer, 1981). But education cannot overcome the inequalities our economic and political system creates or the wide cultural differences that exist in our society (Jencks and others, 1972; Bowles and Gintis, 1976). What we ask of education, then, cannot be given. Education can mitigate, but cannot eliminate, inequality. Because of this inherent contradiction in our expectations, repeated controversy over the purposes and quality of education is inevitable.

REFERENCES

Adelman, Clifford (ed.). 1986. *Assessment in American Higher Education: Issues and Contexts*. Washington DC: Government Printing Office.

Adler, Mortimer J. 1982. *The Paideia Proposal*. New York: Macmillian.

Association of American Colleges, Project on Redefining the Meaning and Purpose of Baccalaureate Degrees. 1985. *Integrity in the College Curriculum: A Report to the Academic Community*. Washington, DC: Author.

Bachrach, Peter, and Morton Baratz. 1962. "The Two Faces of Power." *American Political Science Review* 57 (December): 947–952.

Bennett, William J. 1984. *To Reclaim a Legacy*. Washington, DC: National Endowment for the Humanities.

Bowles, Samuel, and Herbert Gintis. 1976. *Schooling in Capitalist America*. New York: Basic Books.

Boyer, Ernest. 1983. *High School*. New York: Harper & Row.

Business–Higher Education Forum. 1983. *America's Competitive Challenge: The Need for a National Response*. Washington, DC: American Council on Education.

Carnegie Forum on Education and the Economy, Task Force on Teaching as a Profession. 1986. *A Nation Prepared: Teachers for the 21st Century*. New York: Author.

Clune, William H., and Paula A. White. 1988. *School-Based Management: Institutional Variation, Implementation and Issues for Further Research.* New Brunswick, NJ: Center for Policy Research in Education.

Collins, Randall. 1979. *The Credential Society.* New York: Academic Press.

Committee for Economic Development, Research and Policy Committee. 1985. *Children in Need: Investment Strategies for the Educationally Disadvantaged.* New York: Committee for Economic Development.

Dougherty, Kevin J. 1989. "The Politics of Educational Excellence." Unpublished paper, Department of Sociology, Manhattan College.

Education Commission of the States. 1983. *Action for Excellence: A Comprehensive Plan to Improve Our Nation's Schools.* Denver, CO: Author. (ERIC ED 235 588)

Ewell, Peter T. 1987. "Assessment: Where are We?" *Change* (January/February). pp. 23–28.

Gardner, Eileen (ed.). 1985. *A New Agenda for Education.* Washington, DC: Heritage Foundation.

Goodlad, John I. 1983. *A Place Called School: Prospects for the Future.* St. Louis, MO: McGraw-Hill.

Hammack, Floyd M. 1985. Review of *Liberating Education* by Zelda Gamson. *American Journal of Education* 94: 128–134.

Heidenheimer, Arnold J. 1981. "Education and Social Security Entitlements in Europe and America." In Peter Flora and Arnold J. Heidenheimer (eds.), *The Development of Welfare States in Europe and America,* pp. 269–304. New Brunswick, N.J.: Transaction Books.

Hispanic Policy Development Project. 1984. *Make Something Happen: Hispanics and Urban High School Reform.* Washington DC: Author.

Holmes Group. 1986. *Tomorrow's Teachers: A Report of the Holmes Group.* East Lansing, MI: Author.

James, Thomas, and David Tyack. 1983. "Learning from Past Efforts to Reform the High School." *Phi Delta Kappan* 64 (February): 400–406.

Jencks, Christopher, Marshall Smith, Henry Acland, Mary Jo Bane, David Cohen, Herbert Gintis, Barbara Heyns, and Stephen Michelson. 1972. *Inequality: A Reassessment of the Effects of Family and Schooling in America.* New York: Harper & Row.

Kingston, Paul William. 1986. "Theory at Risk: Accounting for the Excellence Movement." *Sociological Forum* 1:632–656.

Levin, Henry M. 1984. "Jobs: A Changing Workforce, A Changing Education?" *Change* 16 (October): 32–37. (Reprinted in Chapter 9 of this book.)

Lukes, Steven. 1974. *Power: A Radical Analysis.* London: Macmillan.

Maeroff, Gene I. 1988. *The Empowerment of Teacher: Overcoming the Crisis of Confidence.* New York: Teachers College Press.

National Commission on Excellence in Education. 1983. *A Nation at Risk.* Washington, DC: Government Printing Office. (ERIC ED 226 006)

National Governors' Association. 1986. *A Time For Results: The Governors' 1991 Report on Education.* Washington, DC: Author. (ERIC ED 279 603)

National Institute of Education, Study Group on the Conditions of Excellence in American Higher Education. 1984. *Involvement in Learning: Realizing the Potential of American Higher Education.* Washington DC: Government Printing Office.

National Science Board Commission on Precollege Education in Mathematics, Science, and Technology. 1983. *Educating Americans for the 21st Century.* Washington, DC: National Science Foundation.

Peterson, Paul. 1983. "Did the Education Commissions Say Anything?" *Brookings Review* 2: 3–11.

Rubinson, Richard. 1986. "Class Formation, Politics, and Institutions: Schooling in the United States." *American Journal of Sociology* 92: 519–548.

Rumberger, Russell. 1984. "The Job Market For College Graduates, 1960–1990." *Journal of Higher Education* 55 (July/August): 433–454.

Shapiro, H. Svi. 1985. "Capitalism at Risk: The Political Economy of the Educational Reports of 1983." *Educational Theory* 35: 57–72.

Slavin, Robert E. 1988. "Synthesis of Research on Grouping in Elementary and Secondary Schools." *Educational Leadership* 46 (September): 67–77.

Spring, Joel. 1984. "Education and the Sony War." *Phi Delta Kappan* 65 (April): 534–537.

Stedman, Lawrence. 1987. "It's Time We Changed the Effective Schools Formula." *Phi Delta Kappan* 69 (November): 215–224.

"Text of President Bush's Address to a Joint Session of Congress." 1989. *New York Times.*(February 10): A17.

Twentieth Century Fund Task Force on Federal Elementary and Secondary Education Policy. 1983. *Making the Grade.* New York: Author. (ERIC ED 233 112)

William T. Grant Foundation Commission on Work, Family, and Citizenship. 1988. *The Forgotten Half: Pathways to Success for America's Youth and Young Families.* Washington DC: William T. Grant Foundation.

Zwerdling, Daniel. 1980. *Workplace Democracy.* New York: Harper & Row.

A Nation at Risk

NATIONAL COMMISSION ON EXCELLENCE IN EDUCATION

Our Nation is at risk. Our once unchallenged preeminence in commerce, industry, science, and technological innovation is being overtaken by competitors throughout the world. This report is concerned with only one of the many causes and dimensions of the problem, but it is the one that undergirds American prosperity, security, and civility. We report to the American people that while we can take justifiable pride in what our schools and colleges have historically accomplished and contributed to the United States and the well-being of its people, the educational foundations of our society are presently being eroded by a rising tide of mediocrity that threatens our very future as a Nation and a people. What was unimaginable a generation ago has begun to occur—others are matching and surpassing our educational attainments.

If an unfriendly foreign power had attempted to impose on America the mediocre educational performance that exits today, we might well have viewed it as an act of war. As it stands, we have allowed this to happen to ourselves. We have even squandered the gains in student achievement made in the wake of the Sputnik challenge. Moreover, we have dismantled essential support systems which helped make those gains possible. We have, in effect, been committing an act of unthinking, unilateral educational disarmament.

Our society and its educational institutions seem to have lost sight of the basic purposes of schooling, and of the high expectations and disciplined effort needed to attain them. This report, the result of 18 months of study, seeks to generate reform of our educational system in fundamental ways and to renew the Nation's commitment to schools and colleges of high quality throughout the length and breadth of our land.

That we have compromised this commitment is, upon reflection, hardly surprising, given the multitude of often conflicting demands we have placed

Excerpt from *A Nation at Risk*. 1983. Washington, D.C. Government Printing Office.

on our Nation's schools and colleges. They are routinely called on to provide solutions to personal, social, and political problems that the home and other institutions either will not or cannot resolve. We must understand that these demands on our schools and colleges often exact an educational cost as well as a financial one.

On the occasion of the Commission's first meeting, President Reagan noted the central importance of education in American life when he said: "Certainly there are few areas of American life as important to cur society, to our people, and to our families as our schools and colleges." This report, therefore, is as much an open letter to the American people as it is a report to the Secretary of Education. We are confident that the American people, properly informed, will do what is right for their children and for the generations to come.

THE RISK

History is not kind to idlers. The time is long past when America's destiny was assured simply by an abundance of natural resources and inexhaustible human enthusiasm, and by our relative isolation from the malignant problems of older civilizations. The world is indeed one global village. We live among determined, well-educated, and strongly motivated competitors. We compete with them for international standing and markets, not only with products but also with the ideas of our laboratories and neighborhood workshops. America's position in the world may once have been reasonably secure with only a few exceptionally well-trained men and women. It is no longer.

The risk is not only that the Japanese make automobiles more efficiently than Americans and have government subsidies for development and export. It is not just that the South Koreans recently built the world's most efficient steel mill, or that American machine tools, once the pride of the world, are being displaced by German products. It is also that these developments signify a redistribution of trained capability throughout the globe. Knowledge, learning, information, and skilled intelligence are the new raw materials of international commerce and are today spreading throughout the world as vigorously as miracle drugs, synthetic fertilizers, and blue jeans did earlier. If only to keep and improve on the slim competitive edge we still retain in world markets, we must dedicate ourselves to the reform of our educational system for the benefit of all—old and young alike, affluent and poor, majority and minority. Learning is the indispensible investment required for success in the "information age" we are entering.

Our concern, however, goes well beyond matters such as industry and commerce. It also includes the intellectual, moral, and spiritual strengths of our people which knit together the very fabric of our society. The people of the United States need to know that individuals in our society who do not possess the levels of skill, literacy, and training essential to this new era will be effectively disenfranchised, not simply from the material rewards that accompany competent performance, but also from the chance to participate fully in our national life. A high level of shared education is essential to a free, democratic society and to the fostering of a common culture, especially in a country that prides itself on pluralism and individual freedom.

For our country to function, citizens must be able to reach some common understandings on complex issues, often on short notice and on the basis of conflicting or incomplete evidence. Education helps form these common understandings, a point Thomas Jefferson made long ago in his justly famous dictum:

> I know no safe depository of the ultimate powers of the society but the people themselves; and if we think them not enlightened enough to exercise their control with a wholesome discretion, the remedy is not to take it from them but to inform their discretion.

Part of what is at risk is the promise first made on this continent: All, regardless of race or class or economic status, are entitled to a fair chance and to the tools for developing their individual powers of mind and spirit to the utmost. This promise means that all children by virtue of their own efforts, competently guided, can hope to attain the mature and informed judgment needed to secure gainful employment and to manage their own lives, thereby serving not only their own interests but also the progress of society itself.

INDICATORS OF THE RISK

The educational dimensions of the risk before us have been amply documented in testimony received by the Commission. For example:

- International comparisons of student achievement, completed a decade ago, reveal that on 19 academic tests American students were never first or second and, in comparison with other industrialized nations, were last seven times.

- Some 23 million American adults are functionally illiterate by the simplest tests of everyday reading, writing, and comprehension.

- About 13 percent of all 17-year-olds in the United States can be considered functionally illiterate. Functional illiteracy among minority youth may run as high as 40 percent.

- Average achievement of high school students on most standardized tests is now lower than 26 years ago when Sputnik was launched.

- Over half the population of gifted students do not match their tested ability with comparable achievement in school.

- The College Board's Scholastic Aptitude Tests (SAT) demonstrate a virtually unbroken decline from 1963 to 1980. Average verbal scores fell over 50 points and average mathematics scores dropped nearly 40 points.

- College Board achievement tests also reveal consistent declines in recent years in such subjects as physics and English.
- Both the number and proportion of students demonstrating superior achievement on the SATs (i.e., those with scores of 650 or higher) have also dramatically declined.
- Many 17-year-olds do not possess the "higher order" intellectual skills we should expect of them. Nearly 40 percent cannot draw inferences from written material; only one-fifth can write a persuasive essay; and only one-third can solve a mathematics problem requiring several steps.
- There was a steady decline in science achievement scores of U.S. 17-year-olds as measured by national assessments of science in 1969, 1973, and 1977.
- Between 1975 and 1980, remedial mathematics courses in public 4-year colleges increased by 72 percent and now constitute one-quarter of all mathematics courses taught in those institutions.
- Average tested achievement of students graduating from college is also lower.
- Business and military leaders complain that they are required to spend millions of dollars on costly remedial education and training programs in such basic skills as reading, writing, spelling, and computation. The Department of the Navy, for example, reported to the Commission that one-quarter of its recent recruits cannot read at the ninth grade level, the minimum needed simply to understand written safety instructions. Without remedial work they cannot even begin, much less complete, the sophisticated training essential in much of the modern military.

These deficiencies come at a time when the demand for highly skilled workers in new fields is accelerating rapidly. For example:

- Computers and computer-controlled equipment are penetrating every aspect of our lives—homes, factories, and offices.
- One estimate indicates that by the turn of the century millions of jobs will involve laser technology and robotics.
- Technology is radically transforming a host of other occupations. They include health care, medical science, energy production, food processing, construction, and the building, repair, and maintenance of sophisticated scientific, educational, military, and industrial equipment. . . .

EXCELLENCE IN EDUCATION

We define "excellence" to mean several related things. At the level of the *individual learner*, it means performing on the boundary of individual ability in ways that test and push back personal limits, in school and in the workplace. Excellence characterizes a *school or college* that sets high expectations and goals for all learners, then tries in every way possible to help students reach them.

Excellence characterizes a *society* that has adopted these policies, for it will then be prepared through the education and skill of its people to respond to the challenges of a rapidly changing world. Our Nation's people and its schools and colleges must be committed to achieving excellence in all these senses.

We do not believe that a public commitment to excellence and educational reform must be made at the expense of a strong public commitment to the equitable treatment of our diverse population. The twin goals of equity and high-quality schooling have profound and practical meaning for our economy and society, and we cannot permit one to yield to the other either in principle or in practice. To do so would deny young people their chance to learn and live according to their aspirations and abilities. It also would lead to a generalized accommodation to mediocrity in our society on the one hand or the creation of an undemocratic elitism on the other.

Our goal must be to develop the talents of all to their fullest. Attaining that goal requires that we expect and assist all students to work to the limits of their capabilities. We should expect schools to have genuinely high standards rather than minimum ones, and parents to support and encourage their children to make the most of their talents and abilities.

The search for solutions to our educational problems must also include a commitment to life-long learning. The task of rebuilding our system of learning is enormous and must be properly understood and taken seriously: Although a million and a half new workers enter the economy each year from our schools and colleges, the adults working today will still make up about 75 percent of the workforce in the year 2000. These workers, and new entrants into the workforce, will need further education and retraining if they—and we as a Nation—are to thrive and prosper. . . .

FINDINGS

We conclude that declines in educational performance are in large part the result of disturbing inadequacies in the way the educational process itself is often conducted. The findings that follow, culled from a much more extensive list, reflect four important aspects of the educational process: content, expectations, time, and teaching.

Findings Regarding Content

By content we mean the very "stuff" of education, the curriculum. Because of our concern about the curriculum, the Commission examined patterns of courses high school students took in 1964–1969 compared with course patterns in 1976–81. On the basis of these analyses we conclude:

- Secondary school curricula have been homogenized, diluted, and diffused to the point that they no longer have a central purpose. In effect, we have a cafeteria-style curriculum in which the appetizers and desserts can easily be mistaken for the main courses. Students have migrated from vocational and college prepatory programs to "general track" courses in large numbers. The proportion of students taking a general program of study has increased from 12 percent in 1964 to 42 percent in 1979.

- This curricular smorgasbord, combined with extensive student choice, explains a great deal about where we find ourselves today. We offer intermediate algebra, but only 31 percent of our recent high school graduates complete it; we offer French I, but only 13 percent complete it, and we offer geography, but only 16 percent complete it. Calculus is available in schools enrolling about 60 percent of all students, but only 6 percent of all students complete it.

- Twenty-five percent of the credits earned by general track high school students are in physical and health education, work experience outside the school, remedial English and mathematics, and personal service and development courses, such as training for adulthood and marriage.

Findings Regarding Expectations

We define expectations in terms of the level of knowledge, abilities, and skills school and college graduates should possess. They also refer to the time, hard work, behavior, self-discipline, and motivation that are essential for high student achievement. . . .

Our analyses in each of these areas indicate notable deficiencies:

- The amount of homework for high school seniors has decreased (two-thirds report less than 1 hour a night) and grades have risen as average student achievement has been declining.

- In many other industrialized nations, courses in mathematics (other than arithmetic or general mathematics), biology, chemistry, physics, and geography start in grade 6 and are required of *all* students. The time spent on these subjects, based on class hours, is about three times that spent by even the most science-oriented U.S. students, i.e., those who select 4 years of science and mathematics in secondary school.

- A 1980 State-by-State survey of high school diploma requirements reveals that only eight States require high schools to offer foreign language instruction, but none requires students to take the courses. Thirty-five States require only 1 year of mathematics, and 36 require only 1 year of science for a diploma.

- In 13 States, 50 percent or more of the units required for high school graduation may be electives chosen by the student. Given this freedom to choose the substance of half or more of the education, many students opt for less demanding personal service courses, such as bachelor living.

- "Minimum competency" examinations (now required in 37 States) fall short of what is needed, as the "minimum" tends to become the "maximum," thus lowering educational standards for all.

- One-fifth of all 4-year public colleges in the United States must accept every high school graduate within the State regardless of program followed or grades, thereby serving notice to high school students that they can expect to attend college even if they do not follow a demanding course of study in high school or perform well.

- About 23 percent of our more selective colleges and universities reported that their general level of selectivity declined during the 1970s, and 29 percent reported reducing the number of specific high school courses required for admission (usually by dropping foreign language requirements, which are now specified as a condition for admission by only one-fifth of our institutions of higher education).

- Too few experienced teachers and scholars are involved in writing textbooks. During the past decade or so a large number of texts have been "written down" by their publishers to ever-lower reading levels in response to perceived market demands.

- A recent study by Education Products Information Exchange revealed that a majority of students were able to master 80 percent of the material in some of their subject-matter texts before they had even opened the books. Many books do not challenge the students to whom they are assigned.

- Expenditures for textbooks and other instructional materials have declined by 50 percent over the past 17 years. While some recommend a level of spending on texts of between 5 and 10 percent of the operating costs of schools, the budgets for basal texts and related materials have been dropping during the past decade and a half to only 0.7 percent today.

Findings Regarding Time

Evidence presented to the Commission demonstrates three disturbing facts about the use that American schools and students make of time: (1) compared to other nations, American students spend much less time on school work; (2) time spent in the classroom and on homework is often used ineffectively; and (3) schools are not doing enough to help students develop either the study skills required to use time well or the willingness to spend more time on school work.

- In England and other industrialized countries, it is not unusual for academic high school students to spend 8 hours a day at school, 220 days per year. In the United States, by contrast, the typical school day lasts 6 hours and the school year is 180 days.

- In many schools, the time spent learning how to cook and drive counts as much toward a high school diploma as the time spent studying mathematics, English, chemistry, U.S. history, or biology.

- A study of the school week in the United States found that some schools provided students only 17 hours of academic instruction during the week, and the average school provided about 22.

- A California study of individual classrooms found that because of poor management of classroom time, some elementary students received only one-fifth of the instruction others received in reading comprehension.

- In most schools, the teaching of study skills is haphazard and unplanned. Consequently, many students complete high school and enter college without disciplined and systematic study habits.

Findings Regarding Teaching

The Commission found that not enough of the academically able students are being attracted to teaching; that teacher preparation programs need substantial improvement; that the professional working life of teachers is on the whole unacceptable; and that a serious shortage of teachers exists in key fields.

- Too many teachers are being drawn from the bottom quarter of graduating high school and college students.

- The teacher preparation curriculum is weighted heavily with courses in "educational methods" at the expense of courses in subjects to be taught. A survey of 1,350 institutions training teachers indicated that 41 percent of the time of elementary school teacher candidates is spent in education courses, which reduces the amount of time available for subject matter courses.

- The average salary after 12 years of teaching is only $17,000 per year, and many teachers are required to supplement their income with part-time and summer employment. In addition, individual teachers have little influence in such critical professional decisions as, for example, textbook selection.

- Despite widespread publicity about an overpopulation of teachers, severe shortages of certain kinds of teachers exist: in the fields of mathematics, science, and foreign languages; and among specialists in education for gifted and talented, language minority, and handicapped students.

- The shortage of teachers in mathematics and science is particularly severe. A 1981 survey of 45 States revealed shortages of mathematics teachers in 43 States, critical shortages of earth sciences teachers in 33 States, and of physics teachers everywhere.

- Half of the newly employed mathematics, science, and English teachers are not qualified to teach these subjects; fewer than one-third of U.S. high schools offer physics taught by qualified teachers.

RECOMMENDATIONS

In light of the urgent need for improvement, both immediate and long term, this Commission has agreed on a set of recommendations that the American people can begin to act on now, that can be implemented over the next several years, and that promise lasting reform. The topics are familiar; there is little mystery about what we believe must be done. Many schools, districts, and States are already giving serious and constructive attention to these matters, even though their plans may differ from our recommendations in some details.

We wish to note that we refer to public, private, and parochial schools and colleges alike. All are valuable national resources. Examples of actions similar to those recommended below can be found in each of them.

We must emphasize that the variety of student aspirations, abilities, and preparation requires that appropriate content be available to satisfy diverse needs. Attention must be directed to both the nature of the content available and to the needs of particular learners. The most gifted students, for example, may need a curriculum enriched and accelerated beyond even the needs of other students of high ability. Similarly, educationally disadvantaged students may require special curriculum materials, smaller classes, or individual tutoring to help them master the material presented. Nevertheless, there remains a common expectation: We must demand the best effort and performance from all students, whether they are gifted or less able, affluent or disadvantaged, whether destined for college, the farm, or industry.

Our recommendations are based on the beliefs that everyone can learn, that everyone is born with an *urge* to learn which can be nurtured, that a solid high school education is within the reach of virtually all, and that life-long learning will equip people with the skills required for new careers and for citizenship.

Recommendation A: Content

We recommend that State and local high school graduation requirements be strengthened and that, *at a minimum,* *all* students seeking a diploma be required to lay the foundations in the Five New Basics by taking the following curriculum during their 4 years of high school: (a) 4 years of English; (b) 3 years of mathematics; (c) 3 years of science; (d) 3 years of social studies; and (e) one-half year of computer science. For the college-bound, 2 years of foreign language in high school are strongly recommended in addition to those taken earlier.

. . .

Recommendation B: Standards and Expectations

We recommend that schools, colleges, and universities adopt more rigorous and measurable standards, and higher expectations, for academic performance and student conduct, and that 4-year colleges and universities raise their requirements for admission. This will help students do their best educationally with challenging materials in an environment that supports learning and authentic accomplishment.

. . .

Recommendation C: Time

We recommend that significantly more time be devoted to learning the New Basics. This will require more effective use of the existing school day, a longer school day, or a lengthened school year.

. . .

Recommendation D: Teaching

This recommendation consists of seven parts. Each is intended to improve the preparation of teachers or to make teaching a more rewarding and respected profession. Each of the seven stands on its own and should not be considered solely as an implementing recommendation.

1. Persons preparing to teach should be required to meet high educational standards, to demonstrate an aptitude for teaching, and to demonstrate competence in an academic discipline. Colleges and universities offering teacher preparation programs should be judged by how well their graduates meet these criteria.

2. Salaries for the teaching profession should be increased and should be professionally competitive, market-sensitive, and performance-based. Salary, promotion, tenure, and retention decisions should be tied to an effective evaluation system that includes peer review so that superior teachers can be rewarded, averages ones encouraged, and poor ones either improved or terminated.

3. School boards should adopt an 11-month contract for teachers. This would ensure time for curriculum and professional development, programs for students with special needs, and a more adequate level of teacher compensation.

4. School boards, administrators, and teachers should cooperate to develop career ladders for teachers that distinguish among the beginning instructor, the experienced teacher, and the master teacher.

5. Substantial nonschool personnel resources should be employed to help solve the immediate problem of the shortage of mathematics and science teachers. Qualified individuals including recent graduates with mathematics and science degrees, graduate students, and industrial and retired scientists could, with appropriate preparation, immediately begin teaching in these fields. A number of our leading science centers have the capacity to begin educating and retraining teachers immediately. Other areas of critical teacher need, such as English, must also be addressed.

6. Incentives, such as grants and loans, should be made available to attract outstanding students to the teaching profession, particularly in those areas of critical shortage.

7. Master teachers should be involved in designing teacher preparation programs and in supervising teachers during their probationary years.

Recommendation E: Leadership and Fiscal Support

We recommend that citizens across the Nation hold educators responsible for providing the leadership necessary to achieve these reforms, and that citizens provide the fiscal support and stability required to bring about the reforms we propose.

. . .

A New Agenda for Education

EILEEN GARDNER

The recurring theme of this volume is that centralized control of education has failed.

Teacher training has fallen under the control of university departments of education and education accreditation agencies that perpetuate questionable social ideologies and shun high standards. Teachers' unions (most notably, the NEA) have stripped administrators of power, opposed plans to share responsibility for education with parents, sought to control the curriculum without collaboration with those whose children they are educating, and demanded more money while rejecting accountability. What is worse, these unions support political candidates who agree to advance their interests.

Centralized control of elementary and secondary education has redirected local and state education priorities into subsidiary agendas. It has skewed balanced education programs and crowded out the core of competencies. Control has been taken from the people and placed in the hands of small but powerful lobbies motivated by flawed premises. Special interest programs based on these flawed premises are then advanced. The inevitable result has been the sacrifice of educational excellence and integrity.

American universities have allowed traditional academic ideals to be undermined by accepting the federal agendas (such as affirmative action) that accompany federal money. As a result, political goals have usurped those of higher education, and the very purpose of the university has been altered dramatically—to the detriment of quality teaching and academic standards.

To make matters worse, the Supreme Court has applied the Constitution to education without prior precedent. So doing, it has established a comprehensive national policy in several critical areas, including public aid to nonpublic schools, prayer and spiritual values, racial segregation, and student rights. Courts decisions have reinterpreted the Establishment Clause, triggering endless conflicts over church/state affairs; usurped states' rights to prescribe moral and spiritual instruction in their public schools, opening the classroom doors to "values-free" education; established judicial supervision of desegregation, creating white flight and the resegregation of the schools; and arrogated to the judiciary the right to set local school disciplinary standards, thereby crippling the power of school authorities to effect discipline in their own schools. Caught in its owned tangled web, the Court is only now seeking ways to free itself and the nation from these counterproductive decisions.

Major changes are needed to reverse the damage from the hammerlock of centralized control on education. The following specific actions should help place U.S. schooling once again on sound, independent footing, where it works best.

THE TEACHING PROFESSION

1. Separate departments of education in the nation's schools and colleges should be eliminated or reformed. Pedagogical instruction should be transferred to departments of academic instruction.
2. Aspiring teachers should pass an examination testing their mastery of academic disciplines and aptitude for teaching.
3. Every novice teacher should serve a year's apprenticeship under competent supervision.
4. Outstanding teachers should be recognized formally and rewarded as Master Teachers, which would make them exemplars for others and supervisors of apprentice teachers.
5. Advancement of teachers via "career ladders" and merit pay should be determined by teaching success, not by accumulation of seniority and education credits.
6. To retain certification, teachers should be retested after fixed periods on the job, with successive examinations progressively more exacting.

PUBLIC AND PRIVATE SCHOOLS

1. Passage of tuition tax credit and voucher legislation at the federal and/or state levels should be a top legislative priority.
2. Legislation specifically should state that those institutions benefitting from tuition tax credits or vouchers are not to be deemed recipients of federal aid or subsidies.
3. As long as a religion is not being established by the state, public aid to religious schools should not be considered unconstitutional.

THE GROWTH OF THE FEDERAL ROLE IN EDUCATION

1. The President should encourage a national debate on the merits of centralized vis-à-vis decentralized education. He should appoint a

national commission to hold hearings across the country, review the ample evidence, and publish a report.

2. The Commission should study and make recommendations on what constitutes a proper education for handicapped children and who has the primary responsibility for this education.

3. Chapter 1 of the 1981 Omnibus Budget Reconciliation Act should be reconstituted as a voucher program, as the Reagan Administration has proposed, or folded into a block grant and turned over to the states. Chapter 1 has failed to accomplish its aim of significantly and permanently raising the academic achievement of low-income, slow students. The costs are excessively disproportionate to its benefits, and it has created a new deprived group—the high achievers. The way to help educationally deprived, low-income students is to give parents real discretion (through vouchers) in choosing the schools their children attend or (through block grants) to spend the money locally to meet the unique needs of each school district.

4. The U.S. must confirm English unequivocally as the nation's one and only official language. To support bilingual education is to encourage fragmentation. All students who attend U.S. schools should be taught—from the beginning—in English.

5. The Women's Educational Equity Act has advanced a radical feminist agenda in our public schools. It should be repealed.

HIGHER EDUCATION

1. Through legislation, Congress should narrow the federal government's authority to intervene in academic affairs. Federal guidelines and the accompanying paperwork should apply only to those schools that accept direct federal support. The federal government should retain its authority to prosecute an institution violating federal antidiscrimination statues. A school that does not accept direct federal support, however, should not be subject to federal regulations merely because its student body includes some recipients of government loans. Congress should end the uncertainty and make this point clear.

2. Affirmative action programs must be revamped, so that government efforts to prevent illegal discrimination do not burden nonliable institutions with onerous paperwork. Unless there is evidence of illegal discrimination, Washington should not interfere in the academic affairs of an institution. Federal agencies should not set quotas for the admission of students or the appointment of faculty members.

3. When Washington's research needs can be met by university resources (though nonacademic research institutions may be equally capable of filling those needs), the appropriate federal agency should enter a contractual relationship with the school involved. Federal research grants do not justify Washington's involvement in the school's general academic affairs. Nor should the U.S. Department of Education be

involved in what should be a simple contractual relationship between a university and another arm of the federal government.

THE COURTS AND EDUCATION

1. The Supreme Court's 1983 decision in *Mueller v. Allen* established the legality of the Minnesota law allowing parents of public and nonpublic school children to deduct tuition and additional education expenses from their income taxes. Other states should take advantage of this ruling and adopt a similar or identical program.

2. The *Everson* Supreme Court decision of 1947, which reinterpreted the Establishment Clause to mandate an "absolute wall of separation between church and state" has little basis in constitutional law or tradition. On this, most constitution scholars agree.[1] The ruling has produced more conflict than it has resolutions of church/state interactions. The Constitution clearly contemplates local resolution of this issue. Therefore, the Court should take the first opportunity to overturn the *Everson* decision, as it has overturned others.

3. There needs to be a national desegregation remedy other than forced busing, which would place the power of decision in the hands of the minorities involved. Such national voluntary school integration recently has been proposed by Dennis Cuddy, a senior associate with the National Institute of Education. Dr. Cuddy argues that forced busing to achieve racial balance discriminates against the minority race, because it is bused in greater proportion to the majority race. Forced busing, therefore, should be prohibited, and no one should be denied the right to attend his or her neighborhood school. To avoid coercive resegregation, Dr. Cuddy proposes that any student receive free transportation to attend any school within the district if the court rules that racial discrimination in educational opportunities exists in his or her home school.[2]

4. There needs to be a national discussion about the impact of the Supreme Court decisions—most notably *Tinker v. Des Moines* which extended First Amendment rights to students—that have replaced the traditional student/teacher relationship with an adversarial, legal model and have usurped the right of state and local education officials to set their own disciplinary standards. This appears to have damaged the teacher/student relationship. The Supreme Court is not always aware of the long-run social effects of its rulings. A Commission should be established, therefore, as a focal point for discussion and a source of recommendations to the Court.

* * *

The reversal of most of these flawed policies could be effected over the next four years of the Reagan Administration. Such measures are compatible with many other goals of the Reagan mandate, in which the people have indicated their desire to return social policy to the local and state levels. Given such impetus, it seems clear that the time for a new agenda is now.

NOTES

1. Peter J. Ferrara, *Religion and the Constitution: A Reinterpretation* (Washington, DC: Free Congress Research & Education Foundation, 1983).
2. Dennis L. Cuddy, "The Problems of Forced Busing and a Possible Solution," *Phi Delta Kappan*, September 1984, pp. 55–56.

Restoring Cultural Literacy in the Early Grades

E. D. HIRSCH, JR.
University of Virginia

In recent decades we have assumed that the early curriculum should be "child-centered" and "skill-centered." Yet there is a growing consensus among reading researchers that adequate literacy depends upon the specific information called "cultural literacy," and we should therefore begin to impart traditional literate culture to children at the earliest possible age.[1]

The need to begin such instruction early is based on technical as well as social considerations. From a purely technical standpoint, our children need traditional background information early to make sense of significant reading materials, and thus gain further information that enables them to make further progress in reading and learning. From a social standpoint, the need to start as early as possible is even more urgent. Young children from the middle class sometimes receive necessary literate information outside the school, but disadvantaged children rarely have access to literate background information outside the school.[2] Therefore, to change the cycle of illiteracy that debars disadvantaged children from high literacy, we need to impart enough literate information from preschool through third grade to ensure continued progress in literacy on the part of all our children.

EXAMINING THE EDUCATIONAL SLOGANS

Now that these basic truths are becoming widely known, it is time to question and qualify some educational slogans inconsistent with those truths that have actively hindered the teaching of literate information to young children. I do

From *Educational Leadership* 45 (December 1987/January 1988): 63–70. Copyright © E. D. Hirsch, Jr. Reprinted with the permission of the author.

not suggest that the three slogans I shall examine constitute all the intellectual barriers to curriculum reform in the early grades (sheer inertia must never be underestimated). But the harmful slogans are powerful and widely spread. Calling them into doubt might help foster the urgently needed reform of giving young children early instruction in our traditional literate culture.

1. *The home is more decisive for literacy than the school.* No one with common sense would doubt that a child whose parents actively encourage conscientious performance in school will do better, all things equal, than a child whose parents discourage academic performance. We know that many children are all too heavily influenced by the anti-academic values (usually defensive reactions) of their parents and peers. Every conscientious teacher, principal, and supervisor tries to counteract the anti-school ethic that is especially powerful and self-defeating among just those disadvantaged children who are most in need of a pro-school ethic. Although few of us in education have the time or opportunity to abolish the anti-school ethic in all its defensive manifestations, one good sign of the times is that we are getting help. Parents and the public at large have identified the problem, and are trying to help the schools combat it.

But quite apart from lamenting the negative influences of anti-academic attitudes, some educators have held a rather defeatist view about the possibility of breaking the illiteracy cycle. They accept as axiomatic the slogan that the educational and economic level of the home is more decisive for high literacy than the school can ever be, no matter how supportive the attitudes of the home. This defeatist attitude dates, of course, from the first Coleman report of 1966. Since that time, the slogan that the socioeconomic status of the home is inherently decisive for academic achievement has been part of the received wisdom of many specialists in education.[3]

The slogan is, of course, truth as a description of educational outcomes under our current educational arrangements. Children from middle-class homes perform better on the whole than children from poor homes, no matter what schools they attend or what moral support they receive in the home. Viewed in broad, statistical terms, a child's socioeconomic status is at present the decisive factor in academic performance. But two inferences from the first Coleman report are open to serious criticism: first, the inference that the state of affairs described by the report is inherent and inevitable, and, second (a corollary of the first), that any attempt to reverse the sociological finding by specific school policies would be futile. These doleful inferences are used to support the claim that we can at best try to change the attitudes and actions of parents, but that nothing of consequence regarding the cycle of illiteracy will be accomplished by changing the policies of our already-beleaguered schools.

We must, of course, acknowledge that all attempts to reinforce children's education within the home are welcome. Parental help is useful not only for motivating students, but also for increasing their time-on-task and attitude to learning. My aim in criticizing the slogan of the decisiveness of the home is not to discourage vigorous appeals to parents to help, supervise, and encourage their children's learning. My purpose, rather, is to insist that, despite the importance of the home, our schools can do a much better job of teaching literacy to all students, even without effective reinforcement from the home.

There is positive evidence, not considered by the first Coleman report, that under a different curriculum our schools can make children acceptably literate even when they come from illiterate homes. The positive evidence is just as compelling as the negative evidence cited in the report. In fact, the positive evidence is more compelling, because it takes into account a larger number of instances and a greater amount of experimental data. I mean by this the historical record.

In the later nineteenth and early twentieth century, American schools succeeded in creating a literate middle class by teaching children of illiterate parents. One factor in their success, lacking in our schools today, was the use of a traditional literate curriculum. Ruth Elson has demonstrated the uniformity of American textbooks in the 19th century, and to her study may now be added Kathryn Neeley's examination of school readers between the 1840s and 1940s.[4] Both studies find a consistent tendency in earlier schoolbooks to teach common, traditional materials. The commonalty of our elementary curriculum in the early twentieth century gave students from literate and illiterate families alike a common foundation in the literate culture, which, as I show in *Cultural Literacy*, is a prerequisite to mature literacy.

Looking outside the United States and taking a still broader historical view of home influence produces evidence that is even more decisive. In the eighteenth century, the establishment of wide-scale national literacy in Britain, France, and Germany (and every other literate country) was first accomplished through the school, not through the home.[5] In Perpignan, for example, literacy in the French language was achieved by schools that taught children who heard and spoke no French in their homes. Indeed, their Catalan-speaking parents were not literate in any language, and were in fact *opposed* to their children's learning French in school.

The only way national literacy could have been achieved in such large multilinguistic nations as France and Great Britain was through the deliberate agency of a national school system that conveyed a common core of literate culture. Parents in Wales, for example, did not always approve of or cooperate with schools that taught English to their children. Nonetheless, Welsh schools graduated pupils who were literate in English language and culture. The cooperation of parents was certainly not available in the schools of Brittany, where Breton-speaking parents opposed the teaching of French. But that did not prevent the schools of Brittany from producing pupils who were literate in French language and culture. In short, the schools can impart high literacy even under severe handicaps, if they do so by teaching not only the mechanical skills of decoding but also the literate national culture. Ernest Gellner has pointed out that all literate national cultures in the modern world have been school-transmitted cultures rather than home-transmitted cultures, and has explained in detail why the pattern has necessarily been followed in every modern nation.[6]

Why, then, did we accept the slogan that the socioeconomic status of the home is more decisive than the policies of the school in achieving mature literacy? What lies behind the well-documented findings of the first Coleman report?

The best explanation I can devise is this: Up to about 1945 in many schools (give or take a decade to allow for the slowness of curricular change), literacy *had* been effectively taught to disadvantaged students under a largely traditional curriculum. It was not until the 1940s that older generations of teachers and administrators had retired in large numbers and were replaced by disciples of Dewey and Kilpatrick who imposed the latest child- and skill-centered textbooks. Up to the 1940s or so, many of our schools were still able to graduate highly literate students who had come from illiterate homes. They effected this transformation through a traditional curriculum both for native black children as well as for children from immigrant European families.

But by the 1940s, with the newer theories ever more dominant in teachers, administrators, and textbooks, our public schools were turning slowly and overwhelmingly to less traditional, more up-to-date, child-centered materials that gradually ceased to transmit our traditional literate culture. This curricular change constituted a particularly catastrophic turn for the early grades. The effects of the change were not immediately noticed, because the earlier curriculum had already created a large number of literate homes that continued to supply their children with the traditional literate information that had disappeared from the schools.

Thus the new curriculum was not at first disabling for those children who were lucky enough to come from highly literate homes, where they received traditional (originally school-transmitted) literate culture. But the new curriculum did cease to supply literate background information to children from illiterate homes, and consequently those unfortunates did not receive the needed information from any source. This hypothesis probably explains why the Coleman report of 1966 turned out to be inconsistent with the larger historical record. Unhappily, this hypothesis about the effects of the new curriculum may also explain why our schools in the past four decades have done little to improve the educational and economic status of children from illiterate homes.

The practical implication of these historical observations, when coupled with the data from reading research, is to suggest that we should once again teach all our children the elements of our traditional literate culture, starting at an early age. That means, for instance, teaching Mother Goose at school, instead of assuming the Mother Goose rhymes might bore children who have already heard them. The argument about boredom has an easy answer; if parents don't want their children to be bored, and if they know that our schools are going to teach Mother Goose, they can read their kids *Pat the Bunny* or *The Cat in the Hat* or whatever else they choose, with full confidence that "Jack and Jill" are on the way.

In sum, we cannot validly generalize the findings of the Coleman report of 1966. We cannot justifiably continue to repeat the easy slogan that the home is the fundamental determinant of literacy. Our children are not trapped in a cycle of sociological determinism. As late as the 1930s and 1940s our schools were our chief, and at times our only conveyors of our literate traditions. History and common sense suggest that our schools can successfully resume that primary responsibility with better results than ever before. The home should, of course, foster a pro-school ethic, and should, where possible, enhance, enlarge, and encourage the teaching of our literate traditions. But it is our schools which must make sure that our literate traditions are successfully conveyed to every child from every sort of home.

2. *Schools should stress general skills and broad understanding, not mere facts.* Along with the new child- and skill-centered curriculum went an antipathy to "mere facts." The phrases "rote-learning" and "piling up of facts" are still used today as scapegoat terms against a traditional education that has not in fact existed in our public schools for several decades. In the 1920s such terms of abuse radiated from lectures at Teachers College, Columbia, and slowly spread to schools of education throughout the nation.[7] You will immediately recognize that these scapegoat terms still function as banner slogans, even though the education they attack has long since vanished from the scene. On the other hand, the typical terms of approval in educational writing since the '20s continue to be such phrases as "relevant materials" that are "meaningful to the child," and that inculate "higher-order skills."

Since we now know that, in order to become literate, young children must gain a store of traditional information at an early age, it is time to reconsider the pejorative use of phrases like "memorization," (better to say "learning by heart") and "piling up facts" as though they were insult terms. Many "higher-order skills" of literacy are gained *only* by piling up information. No study of language acquisition, for instance, has challenged the common-sense observation that children learn the names of objects by repeatedly being told those names until they remember them.[8] Thus, at the very roots of language acquisition we find memorization and the piling up of facts. Later on, in earliest training, children must learn the alphabet by heart. I cannot conceive how a child could acquire the alphabet other than by memorization and the piling up of facts. The same applies to the multiplication table, the days of the week, and the months of the year. There's no other way of acquiring those skills.

Of course everybody knows these things. I do not wish to make the shibboleths of modern educational theory seem totally without merit. My point is subtler and gentler. Only recently have we come to understand that "Jack and Jill" and "George Washington" belong to an alphabet that must be learned by heart, and which is no less essential to higher-order literacy skills than the alphabet itself. Certain linguistically based concepts (researchers call them "schemata") belong to the very ABCs of literacy.[9] The methods by which children learn these higher-order ABCs can be exciting and fun, or they can be deadening and painful. Good teachers always try to choose the pleasant over the painful, if only because the pleasant is more effective. But learning the higher-order ABCs, like learning the alphabet itself, does require learning by heart and piling up information.

The negative connotations of terms like "mere facts" and "memorization" arise from the theory that acquiring facts is inferior to "meaningful" learning experiences that cause children to take interest in and understand the significance of what they are being taught. It is assumed that the piling up of information cannot be meaningful, or interesting, or motivational to children. Given such alternatives, who would choose to be meaningless and dull? To reinforce this anti-fact, anti-memorization view, psychology since the time of Herbart has instructed us that the only materials that are meaningful to children are those that resonate with their own imaginations and experiences. Hence, the human principle of meaningful, nonrote instruction has been reinforced by the scientific principle that curricular materials should connect directly with the experiences of young children.

But expert teaching and well-conceived texts, not modernity of content, are the bridges of relevance that connect reading materials with a child's experience. The life experiences of children who enter American classrooms are much too varied to form a definite content basis for child-centered materials. Moreover, most of the literate culture that children will need for later life consists of traditional, intergenerational materials. Consequently, their literacy is more effectively enhanced when they are successfully taught durable, traditional subjects like Ulysses and the Cyclops than when they are taught ephemera like Dick and Jane at the Supermarket.

It's quite doubtful that "mere facts" are really meaningless to young children, any more than they are to adults. We should unblinkingly face the truth that many of the facts we adults know are not perfectly interconnected in our minds. Meaningfulness does not require complete clarity and coherence, or even powerful emotion. E. B. White once said that he learned how to drive, without understanding what went on under the hood. How many adults can explain coherently what happens when they switch on a TV set? Most of us just know the less-than-coherent facts about TV: the picture comes on when we punch the power switch, it changes when we change the channel switch, and it goes off when we punch the power switch again. In the technological era, many of us still live in the "magic years"; things happen for us as they happen for children in ways that we do not fully understand and cannot accurately explain.

Take another example. The names that we give to objects and concepts rarely have any coherent logic to them. It is the nature of language to be arbitrary. *Dog* has no more inherent rightness or logical aptness than *chien* or *Hund*. We have just gotten used to the words. This is as true for adults as for children. In short, the world of adults, like that of children, is at least partly incoherent and arbitrary. The child's world is less coherent and certainly less accurate than our own, but the differences are of degree, not kind. Perhaps many differences between children and adults have been, as Mark Twain said of reports of his death, greatly exaggerated.

Much of the essential information that we adults need can be gained only by being "piled up" as schemata in our memories. If parents and teachers waited until children could adequately understand the alphabet, they would wait until the first year of a doctoral program in linguistics. If they waited until children could adequately understand the first line of "My country, 'tis of thee," they would wait until tenth grade before divulging the words of the song. (Does anyone know an elementary school child who can explain the linguistic meaning of the words "My country, 'tis of thee?") For that matter, does anyone believe that a first-grader can understand "The Star-Spangled Banner," whose readability score probably ranks at the eleventh- or twelfth-grade level? Shall we therefore defer teaching "The Star-Spangled Banner" until twelfth grade?

Even the most ardent proponents of "meaningful" instruction and "higher-order skills acquisition" must accept such inconsistencies when slogans about developmental learning readiness are applied to the early grades. I don't know anyone who is so opposed to learning by heart as to deplore the teaching of the alphabet, or "The Star-Spangled Banner," or "America." But if we acquiesce in accepting *those* incompletely understood elements into the curriculum, why should we exclude other "mere facts" that are equally useful to literacy? Answer: We should *not* exclude those traditional facts, but recognize that young children need many, many items of traditional information that are no less necessary to literacy than the alphabet and "The Star-Spangled Banner."

Another grave weakness in the theory that children are interested only in immediately meaningful, child-centered materials is that young children take great joy in learning vaguely understood information that will only later be fully meaningful to them. Although many of the facts that children need to learn are meaningless to them in a linguistic sense, they are nonetheless highly meaningful to them in a social sense. Children give their own context to such items, and correctly believe them to belong to the fabric of the adult community they wish to join. Children thrive only as members of a community. From the cradle, they take to language and culture like ducks to water. They come into the world with an appetite for acculturation. It is impractical, indeed absurd, to thwart that *natural* appetite for culture on the basis of an abstract theory about learning readiness. Nothing better expresses the absurdity than Dewey's deploring of the "facility" with which young children absorb the cultural facts we pile upon them, or his approval of Rousseau's fatuous remark that "the apparent ease with which children learn is their ruin."

3. *The optimal contents of a language arts curriculum can be determined on scientific principles.* This doctrine about the early curriculum is less a slogan than an unexamined assumption. Science is a neutral servant of our educational purposes. Science represents the reality principle in education. It does not set our goals; it serves them. It helps define their inherent limits, and indicates the best avenues for us to follow in order to achieve them. Any more substantial claim for the role of science in education is a misleading claim.

Suppose, for example, that our primary goal is to achieve high literacy for all children. How can science guide us in choosing the *specific* materials to reach that goal? One currently used, so-called "scientific" approach is to use a quantitatively determined first-grade vocabulary for first grade, a second-grade vocabulary for second grade, and so on. And how does science yield up these graded vocabularies? By word frequency studies. The most frequent words should be taught first, the next frequent next, and so on.

There are serious difficulties hidden under this apparently neutral, apparently scientific approach. Assuming that makers of children's texts use common sense, as McGuffey did long before there were any word frequency studies, they wouldn't have to take special measures to supply young children with the most frequent words of English. They could assume that children would encounter those primary words with approximately the standard frequency in *any* reasonably chosen reading materials. They could rely on the fact that any diverse sampling of texts in a language will produce a similar list of its most frequent words. For instance, the Francis-Kucera frequency list, taken from the huge Brown University corpus consisting of several million words, puts the word *from* in position 26.[10] The Carroll-Davies-Richman (CDR) frequency list, taken from a corpus of elementary and secondary school materials, puts the word *from* in position 23.[11] It is safe to assume that *any* intelligently chosen materials for the early grades will provide automatic reinforcement of the most frequent words of the English language.

An even stronger reason for not depending on word frequencies to determine suitable elementary reading materials is that after a certain point—somewhere after the top few thousand words—word frequencies depend entirely on the particular corpus of texts chosen to determine them. But what is the right corpus for the early grades? No one can answer that question on neutral scientific grounds. There is no purely objective, scientific way of choosing the right corpus for determining the correct grade-level of words. Consider, for example, some complications for choosing proper names in texts for early grades by means of the Carroll-Davies-Richman frequency list. On the basis of the most frequent words from 1 to 10,000, the corpus tells us that early texts should contain:

- The Alamo *but not* The Iliad
- Jack and Jill *but not* Cinderella
- Blake *but not* Milton
- Helen Keller *but not* Joan of Arc
- Moses *but not* Jesus
- Galileo *but not* Copernicus
- John Glenn *but not* Charles Lindbergh
- Louis Pasteur *but not* Marie Curie
- Scrooge *but not* Dickens
- Edison *but not* Locke
- Einstein *but not* Socrates
- Hitler *but not* Churchill

This list on its face suggests the inappropriateness of using word frequency as a "scientific" basis for the content of the language arts curriculum.

In fact, such a use of word frequency is quite *unscientific* when we simply take the existing word frequencies that are found in current school materials as "objective" guides for determining the proper frequencies for new school materials.

Understanding this, suppose we did agree upon an appropriate corpus for determining grade-by-grade vocabulary according to word frequency. One characteristic of such a corpus would be that it must be constantly revised to reflect changes in the literate culture. Otherwise, the frequency analysis might become quite misleading. Consider this example. The biggest analyzed corpus of English that we have is the one at Brown University, compiled by Francis and Kucera. This corpus not only takes materials from a deliberately indiscriminate sampling of genres, it also remains stuck in the year 1961. Thus, according to the frequencies of the Brown corpus, the first surname that our children should learn after Washington is Khruschev.

What inference should we draw from this interesting fact? Not, of course, that first-graders should be taught about Nikita Khrushchev before they are taught about Abraham Lincoln. Rather, we should draw the inference that it is all too easy to misapply scientific data. Consider, by contrast, the *scientific* virtues of simply asking a group of literate adults to choose the words and concepts that are most important for children to know to become literate adults. These people will do a much better job than either the Brown or the CDR frequency lists, in part because the corpus of texts they have read will be many, many times bigger than even the huge Brown corpus, and in part because their sense of the most appropriate words will be constantly adjusting itself to significant cultural change. Consequently, their judgments will be far less likely to exhibit the Khrushchev effect. This advantage alone will make their judgments more, not less, scientific than the current word frequency approach. Of course, these observations imply no criticism of the valuable work of Carroll, Davies, and Richman, Francis, and Kucera, but are directed toward the unsound, uncritical use of quantitative research.

Other examples of pseudoscience in education could teach us the same moral: there can be no substitute for informed judgments by educated adults regarding the most important contents to be taught to children. If we as a nation decide that we want our children to possess mature literacy, there is no substitute for asking literate persons collectively to decide upon the contents required for mature literacy. After we make that determination, we need to develop an effective sequence of those core contents and effectively present them during the 13 years of schooling. Science can surely help us accomplish those jobs, but science alone is not in a position to tell us which words, concepts, and facts we need to teach.

CHANGING A LOSING GAME

In criticizing certain slogans and assumptions that are current among some educators, my purpose has, of course, been a constructive one. I take no pleasure in showing prized educational doctrines to be half-truths. Rather, I have tried to focus on just those doctrines, slogans, and assumptions that have actively impeded the teaching of traditional literate information to young children. Only by imparting that information early can we achieve higher literacy and greater social justice. Any half-truth or slogan, no matter how dearly held, that stands in the way of that aim should be ruthlessly cast aside. Our children are more important than our theories.

We have given our theories a reasonable chance during the past four decades, and in light of the current ignorance explosion among young people, our results do not tend to confirm our theories. Even those educators who do not agree with my specific proposals for higher national literacy may nonetheless readily agree with the great tennis player Bill Tilden, whose immortal strategic advice holds for educational policy just as well as for tennis matches: "Always change a losing game."

NOTES

1. R. C. Anderson, *Becoming a Nation of Readers* (Washington, D.C.: U.S. Department of Education, 1985).
2. E. D. Hirsch, Jr., *Cultural Literacy: What Every American Needs to Know* (Boston: Houghton Mifflin, 1987).
3. James S. Coleman et al., *Equality in Educational Opportunity* (Washington, D.C.: Government Printing Office, 1966).
4. Ruth Miller Elsen, *Guardians of Tradition: American Schoolbooks of the Nineteenth Century* (Lincoln: University of Nebraska Press, 1964). Kathryn Neeley, "From Tradition to Fragmentation: American College Readers from 1840 to 1980" (unpublished paper).
5. Francois Furet and Jacques Ozouf, *Reading and Writing: Literacy in France from Calvin to Jules Ferry* (Cambridge: Cambridge University Press, 1982).
6. Ernest Gellner, *Nations and Nationalism* (Ithaca, N.Y.: Cornell University Press, 1983).
7. L. A. Cremin, *The Transformation of the School: Progressivism in American Education, 1876–1957* (New York: Knopf, 1964).
8. Roger Brown, *A First Language: The Early States* Cambridge: Harvard University Press, 1973).
9. See, for example, Rand J. Spiro, "Constructive Processes in Prose Comprehension and Recall," in Rand J. Spiro et al., *Theoretical Issues in Reading Comprehension* (Hillsdale, N.J.: Erlbaum Associates, 1980).
10. W. N. Francis and Henry Kucera, *Frequency Analysis of English Usage: Lexicon and Grammar* (Boston: Houghton Mifflin. 1982).
11. John B. Carroll, Peter Davies, and Barry Richman, *Word Frequency Book* (Boston: Houghton Mifflin, 1971).

High School Reform: The Need for Engineering

THEODORE R. SIZER
Brown University

The first question following my talk to an audience of professionals in an eastern city came from the veteran principal of a large senior high school. I knew what was coming as soon as he stood up. I had heard it before.

"I certainly agree with you, Mr. Sizer, that we need to coach students more on their writing skills and that age-grading hurts as many kids as it helps. I know that trying to teach 175 different students each day is difficult. Most of what you said is very good, very nice. But let me tell you about my school. They sent me two kids this morning who read at the fourth-grade level. I've got to help them. We have 50 Cambodians who can't speak a word of English. My people have to help them. However, my staff is shrinking faster than the student body. I have almost no math or science teachers left who really know their subjects. The mayor makes promises to us but always reneges. No one seems to give a damn any more—parents, politicians, even teachers. Now, Mr. Sizer, your ideas are very nice, but they don't help me very much. I wish they did."

Technically, his remarks were not a question. They were a painful confession, and an accusing one. My response was limp: "I know, I know well, what you're facing. Unless we get more public support behind schools such as yours, no progress can be made. I share your anger and frustration." He sat down with a sarcastic smile, masking his anger. The next question was easier: "How do your ideas compare to those of Mortimer Adler's *Paideia Proposal*?" Kicking philosophies around allows for precision that the real world of adolescents never accommodates—and it carries few costs. The principal's concern could be swept under the rug.

Two days later I had lunch with an able, energetic assistant professor of social studies education at a university in the same city. We talked about her student teachers, now a small number compared with the late Sixties but still "placed" in public and private schools throughout the community. We reflected on the age-old student teacher's problem of tempering idealism with newly faced realism. The talk switched easily to the assistant professor's future, the realism with which she was living. Three years remained on her contract; then she would probably be out of a job. Not even John Dewey could get tenure these days. Not a single social studies education position was advertised in the *Chronicle of Higher Education* during the last 12 months, she reported. Today some front-rank state universities have only one faculty member for all teacher preparation in social studies—this in institutions that had bustling departments of 10 or more people as little as 15 years ago.

"How about a high school department chair's position?"

"They don't hire from the outside, and they don't like ex-professors."

"State department work?"

"There are cutbacks there."

"City schools' central offices?"

"More cutbacks."

"What are you going to do?"

"Go into business. That's where the interesting work is."

She told me of a large, high-tech company that required up to six weeks' intensive inservice training each year for all of its professional staff. The programs at their training center were, apparently, well planned and imaginative. An individual could select morning, afternoon, or evening presentations (in effect, a class schedule for every cognitive metabolism), and he or she "graduated" whenever a final test was passed. If an individual passed in four weeks, for example, the remaining two weeks of the prescribed program were given to him or her as a vacation, with a bonus thrown in. "The incentives," she observed wryly, "are right."

THE GRIP OF STRUCTURE

These kinds of experiences are particularly familiar to those of us who are trying to understand the contemporary American high school system and who are obliged to suggest practical ways of strengthening it. At professional meetings, we present our observations and analyses, many of which are critical, and few professionals or school board members seriously disagree with the main themes of our presentations. However, when we suggest remedies, the reactions usually start with disbelief, move through skepticism, and end up with the kind of exasperated frustration that my city high school principal exhibited.

None of this should be surprising. Most of the central problems crippling U.S. high schools are obvious, well understood, and of long standing. Educators and their critics have been rhetorically hammering away at them for several decades. It is the remedies that seem problematic. None seems to stick.

The reason lies in the basic structure of the high school. Its organizing framework dates from the late 19th century and persists today with remarkable consistency across all regions of the country and across public and private sectors. Most adolescents attend high schools with a thousand or more age-mates. They find there a structure that is highly fractionated—horizontally by age group and vertically by program track. The program revolves around subjects taught by specialists—another element of fragmentation—and the students "cover" a succession of topics each day, seemingly at random. The social rituals of schools are numerous and widely uniform, even down to the names students give to their informal cliques.

It is not that there are no exceptions. There are, usually among rural public schools, small private schools, and a variety of "alternative" schools. Nonetheless, the uniformity of the structure of the majority of schools is astonishing, given the geographical diversity and scale of the U.S. and its apparently decentralized school governance.

It is not that school structure has remained totally unchanged over the last 40 years. It has changed, but the changes have been remarkably small relative to those in American living patterns, careers, values, needs, and technologies.

It is not that some schools do not seem more effective than others. They do appear to be so, but whatever special effectiveness is apparent emerges from the same framework. And that framework seriously limits our expectations.

High schools are complicated organisms. To be orderly, the pieces must work together smoothly. In a typical school of 1,500 pupils, almost 10,000 individual place changes occur in a five-hour period—students and teachers moving from classroom to classroom to cafeteria and so forth. The successful orchestration of so much traffic is just the beginning of the problem. Everything impinges on everything else. For example, if 15 special education students drawn from three grades must meet for tutoring with a specialist teacher (who is also on a rigid schedule) from 11:15 a.m. to 12:04 p.m. every other Tuesday, this must be accommodated, but without sacrificing important work that those students would ordinarily do at that time. Adjustments must be made. Or for reasons having to do with bus schedules, students must leave the school building at different times. Or for reasons stemming from a court order, each curriculum track must have certain racial quotas. Or the cafeteria can seat only 500 people at once, and the three "seatings" must be coordinated with everything else. And the list goes on.

Not surprisingly, any significant change in structure and procedure that is proposed must usually be vetoed on practical grounds; it disturbs too many things. Or it is spun off as an "alternative" program, in effect a school-within-a-school with its own structure. In these purposeful, pessimistic 1980s, when orderliness is a cardinal virtue, these alternatives are all too rare.

Thus things remain the same because it is impossible to change very much without changing most of everything. The result is paralysis.

HIGH SCHOOLS' PROBLEMS

There are, of course, many things that are *right* about American high schools. They are, on the whole, happy places, settings that most adolescents find inviting, staffed by adults who genuinely care for youngsters. (The far-too-well-publicized exceptions merely prove the rule.) Virtually no young American lacks access to some high school, and some segments of the population—the physically handicapped, for example—have never had greater access to schooling. These kinds of achievement of attitude and accommodation are remarkable and deserve high visibility. However, there are problems, too. And it is on these problems that the attention of those of us now studying high schools has properly focused.

A list of some of these problems makes familiar reading.

- The goals for high schools are numerous and seem to continue multiplying, with little regard for the severe limits imposed by a lack of school staff, equipment, and time.

- Many adolescents complete high school unprepared for what follows in their lives; they are marginally literate, uninspired, possessed of only rudimentary skills, and imbued with a narrow view of the world.

- Productivity is low. Young people, who may spend well over 12,000 hours in school and who are maintained there at substantial expense, are nonetheless unprepared to take their places in society. In a narrower economic sense, schooling has become progressively less productive over the last decades. Greater investments seem not to have produced correspondingly greater yields, however defined.

- Many students find little incentive in hard academic work. Although they want their diplomas, they earn them primarily by doggedly dutiful attendance rather than by an exhibition of mastery of the substance of study. Thus there is little need to suffer the pain of stretching one's mind.

- Students are rarely expected to educate themselves. They are "delivered a service" and are expected to carry few burdens in their schools—even for simple custodial obligations. For all too many, school is an entitlement and thus, curiously, is not respected as much as those activities that require adolescents to make a significant personal investment.

- The labels of subjects are ambiguous and often misleading. In the same breath with which policy makers piously assert the need for "four years of English for all students," they admit that "English" in practice is currently a ragbag of ends and means. High school "improvement" thus ends up as a juggling of slogans.

- A premium is put on coverage at the expense of thoroughness. We need to get to the Civil War by Christmas, even though we don't understand what the colonialism of the 1760s meant. We value three papers written more than one paper written well. In biology we value covering numerous phyla rather than understanding one phylum well. More is better, or so it seems. The torrent of facts poured over students is overwhelming, and the only way teachers can keep up the flow is to lecture—to feed students knowledge rather than expect them to forage on their own.

- The daily activities, academic and otherwise, in which a typical high school student engages are numerous: five or six classes on widely differing topics taken in a random sequence are mixed with some nonacademic activity and lots of usually frenetic socializing. The high school scene is as colorful and feverish as it is inimical to the reflection that inescapably accompanies learning to use one's mind.

- The academic reward system revolves around time, with quick being better. "Ahead of grade level" is absolutely preferred to solid, ultimate mastery. This grade-level tracking system and the remarkably uniform pedagogies that accompany it exist despite the overwhelming evidence of both behavioral science and common observation that all of us learn at different rates, at different times, and in different ways and that, if these learning rates and learning styles are accommodated, most students can master the material that the typical high school places before them.

- In spite of strenuous efforts on many sides to eliminate it, segregation of the schools by social class is profound and no less visible at the school level today than it was more than 50 years ago when observed by the Lynds in *Middletown*. The poor are tracked to be poor, the rich to be rich. Related racial and ethnic stereotyping is pervasive.

- Schools connect poorly with the outside world. Traditional vocational and technical education has been devastatingly challenged, but still it goes on largely unaffected by the evidence of its malfunctions. The connection between nonschool technologies, such as television and computers, and the schools is at best rudimentary. The fact that most high school students hold jobs during the school year is ignored or cursed but rarely used constructively.

- Inevitably, schools are places where values are learned. But, sadly, few schools have well-articulated and thoroughly argued approaches in this area. Thus zealots dominate discussions of questions of value.

- Teachers know that time on task (up to a point) is important for all students and that personal attention to each student pays great dividends. However, most high school teachers deal with well over a hundred young people daily, in groups that gather for less than an hour. In such circumstances, only an exceptional instructor can come anywhere near individualizing instruction.

- The teaching profession has a very limited career line. A teacher has roughly the same responsibility at the end of a professional lifetime as on the first day of work. As much as anything else, this state of affairs drives many able and ambitious people from the classroom.

- Teachers' salaries and benefits are not competitive with those in fields that require comparable preparation—particularly at the top levels. Moreover, teachers' salaries have fallen in real dollars over the last decade. The psychic rewards of teaching provide some compensation— but they don't pay dental bills.

- Even though policy makers universally agree on the need to strengthen the teaching profession, many of them support policies that both patronize teachers and undermine their autonomy—that essential element of self-esteem. The teacher's role is codified today, all the way down to minutes-per-year-per-subject. (One wonders how the American Bar Association would react to minutes-per-year-per-case.) Teachers are told that their own competence is to be measured by credit hours of college courses taken, even though there is little evidence that quality derives from credits earned. Thus the system insults the intelligence of teachers. Policies seem to be drafted to squeeze the incompetents out of the profession rather than to attract the able into it.

- Their rhetoric notwithstanding, public leaders are uninterested in the schools. Regulation and coercion, which don't cost much, get great play today. The politics of education is sufficiently unexplored that a President is applauded for announcing an "initiative" for science and mathematics instruction to affect America's almost 50 million schoolchildren, even though in the first year of the program he proposes to spend a sum that would barely buy two F-18 jets.

Even when spiced with such pinches of angry sarcasm as I have added here, these assertions elicit nods of agreement from most of my fellow educators, such as my urban principal. Along with such agreement, however, comes fiery resentment, as few of us want things to be this way. We protest, giving examples of exceptions. In our frustration we lash back at critics, blaming the message on the messenger. We confuse criticism of long-established school structures with criticism of us as people and professionals. We call the woes of the schools a public relations problem. They aren't. They are a problem of the structure of the institution we are working hard to improve. Cursing the critics may be therapeutic, but it isn't productive. Re-engineering the structure could be.

ENGINEERING

In 1971 Seymour Sarason wrote, "It is inordinately difficult to adopt approaches that require us to recognize and suspend our values in the quest of achieving distance from our habitual ways of thinking and working." In 1983 we still seem stuck with our habits, incapable of considering substantially new ways to achieve old and worthy ends. We live with a curriculum of labels (English-mathematics-social studies-science-physical education . . .), with students grouped according to their birthdays, and with school routines suited nicely to 180 six-hour days. These features of schooling seem beyond challenge.

The first step in our search for better schools will be to clear our minds of what Sarason calls the "regularities" of school-keeping. Some of these well-intentioned traditions simply don't work very well. Part of the frustration experienced by the urban principal who responded to my talk stemmed from his inability to visualize a constructive, if radical, alternative—and to have faith that anything of the kind was conceivable in practice and politics.

Institutional structures are hard to change. Many aspects of schooling have become more important for their form than for their substance. What is the real significance of graduating with one's class? Does it matter who would run the junior prom if there were no age-grading? Parents not only count on daily babysitting for their adolescent children 180 days a year but defend it as their unchallengeable entitlement. Because high school is so complex, with everything impinging on everything else, any significant change in one part changes everything else. Certainly it is difficult to conceive of a different way of working. But it is even more difficult to build a consensus to try a new form of school and to allow its staff the time to work out its bugs. Change costs money, too. Working up alternatives takes teacher and administrator time, and time is money. Leaving routines in place is cheaper.

Nonetheless, the hard fact remains that there is no serious way to improve high schools without revamping their structure. Politically painful though such a renovation may be, it is inescapable. What might it involve? Let me return to the list of problems I mentioned above and examine the logic that might be pressed—and the pain it might create.

1. In most high schools, a shorter, simpler, better-defined list of goals is necessary; this will involve shelving the long-standing claims of certain subject areas. For example, driver education may have to give way to English. Athletic and chorus trips may no longer be allowed to preempt teaching time, which might mean curtailing interscholastic athletic and arts programs. Chemistry may have to be dropped as a separate subject in order that biology and physics can be taught well. The list must be long, and the necessary constrictions will be as painful as they are inescapable.

2. Students entering high school unable to read, write, and cipher adequately will have to concentrate exclusively on these subjects. These are the foundations of secondary school work, and, until they are mastered, studying much else is wasteful. Teachers will need substantial time to work with these youngsters, as the students almost certainly will be demoralized and ready to fail.

3. Higher-order thinking skills—reasoning, imagining, analyzing, synthesizing—are the core of senior high school work, and they are learned through confrontation, through dialog. One isn't *told* how to think; one reasons and has that reasoning critiqued. Inescapably, this process requires different kinds of teaching formats and lower teaching loads than are now the rule.

4. Until mastery of subject matter determines whether or not a diploma is granted, students will see minimal incentives for achieving such mastery. There must be some kind of culminating examination or other exhibition of mastery to place the emphasis of schooling squarely on learning. (Today the emphasis is primarily on dutiful attendance.)

5. A central goal of schooling is for students to be able to teach themselves and to wish to do so. (We forget most of the facts we learn in schools; what stays with us, if we're lucky, is the knowledge of how to gain knowledge.) The way one learns to teach oneself is to practice doing it and to have that practice critiqued. This absolutely requires serious independent work (homework) and time available both for teachers to challenge students' efforts and for students to struggle with this process of learning to learn. Certainly, any course with such a focus will be able to "cover" fewer facts than is now the case. The world history course will cover fewer centuries; the mathematics sequence will not get to calculus; the biology course will no longer include some phyla. We will be required to let go of many cherished sectors of the curriculum in our pursuit of the aphorism, "Less is more."

6. Sorting out what students require inescapably uncovers the inadequacy of traditional interpretations of the subjects of study. Absolutely fundamental skills of thinking and expression cut across the domains of existing departments. Thus they are often given short shrift. The fractionated curriculum that the high schools have inherited from the 1890s serves us poorly. To reconstruct it will infuriate many academic scholars, scare many teachers who have been narrowly trained by those scholars, and send shivers of apprehension down the spines of parents. The core academic structure of high school, legitimized by the Committee of Ten in 1893, maintains a ferocious hold on our thinking.

7. The frenetic quality of many high schools needs to be eased, the pace slowed, and larger blocks of time made available for the kind of dialectical teaching that is a necessary part of helping adolescents learn to think clearly and constructively. This will mean that some things will have to go. The snippets of this and that (e.g., 10 minutes a day in every 10th-grade social studies class to consider the state driver manual) will have to give way.

8. Age-grading must cease, and students must be allowed to progress at their own rates. Adult attitudes about "where a student should be" will also have to change; the assumption must always be that mastery is not only possible but expected. We will need to adapt instruction to students' differing learning styles. Such policies follow necessarily from what we know about human learning. To ignore these complicating realities is to hurt students and engage in prodigious waste. Age-grading and standardized instruction are as efficient to administer as they are inefficient pedagogically. To adapt our school structures to a more complicated view of learning will be a bureaucrats' nightmare, but adapt they must.

9. Lessening segregation and stereotyping by class, race, gender, and ethnicity requires not only unprejudiced attitudes on the parts of

those of us who work in schools but also changes in the structure of schooling. Mastery of the basic core of high school work should be the goal for everybody—a common purpose even if addressed through widely differing means. Diversions from this through early tracking (e.g., decisions on vocational education made at the end of ninth grade) or through magnet programs (sometimes thinly disguised devices to perpetuate segregation) must be resisted. People, especially the more affluent people, *like* tracking. Any challenge to their enclaves (normally suburban schools in neighborhoods insulated by high property costs) will be fiercely fought.

10. The way to connect the world of school and the world outside of school is to make thoughtful use of the latter bear usefully on the former. If a high school diploma is awarded as a validation of a student's mastery, then *how* that learning is mastered is not very important. It could be learned at home or on the job as well as in class. Adolescents can and will learn much from the tumble of information and experience that pervades modern life. Schools should seize upon the best of that learning and give incentives to students to use their out-of-school opportunities in ways that help them learn still more.

11. Teachers cannot provide the kind of teaching required to help students learn higher-order thinking skills in groups of 30 or more and with overall teaching loads of 130 to 175 students. A practical way to reduce these loads somewhat is for a greater percentage of the school staff to teach and for each teacher to become less specialized. Students will learn more if they are taught English and social studies by the same teacher than if they are taught by separate specialists. A single teacher has to work with about 80 students; two specialists must try to know 160 each. However, launching a challenge against specialization in high schools will be difficult, especially in states where job descriptions are frozen into certificates and legislation.

12. Proper accommodation of individual student differences demands that teachers have control over their own and their students' schedules and programs. Standardized procedures (30 minutes per week of physical education; no fewer than 215 minutes per week of English) fly in the face of common sense—save that of administrators who do not trust their teachers or who run schools so understaffed that such rigid policies are necessary simply to maintain order. Giving teachers autonomy also flies in the face of the belief in the value of scientific management in education—a conviction spawned by the turn-of-the-century Progressives and accepted today as virtual dogma, alas.

13. Good teachers value their autonomy. They know they need it to do a first-class job. If they are denied autonomy, they do mediocre work—or leave teaching. If we want to attract and hold top professionals in teaching, we will have to give them appropriate autonomy. Despite rhetoric to the contrary, the trends today are working to weaken the teaching profession. Ever more regulation comes from the top. There

is a sort of vicious circle at work: teachers are weak, and therefore they must be regulated; if teaching is heavily regulated, good people will avoid the profession; therefore, teachers are weak. . . .

14. Top professionals want a career that gradually develops, with more responsibility and compensation following experience and demonstrated excellence. This requires differentiated staffing within teaching and salaries that follow this differentiation. Such schemes require us to redefine the ways of deploying teachers in schools. The record of schools being able to carry out such redefinitions is disappointing. The notion that every teacher is just like every other teacher has substantial momentum.

One can continue. The list of conditions that reasonable educators agree need changing but that they believe cannot be changed is depressingly long. It is easier for "reformers" to look for less controversial initiatives: say, a small summer program for students identified as talented in mathematics and science, not controversial, kept well off to the side; or more money for teacher education or for loans to prospective teachers; or fresh curriculum development efforts—all of which *assume* the traditional five-times-a-week, 50-minute classes for groups of 18 to 35 students; or hyping up principals as "instructional leaders." All of these are worthwhile projects. They simply miss the center of the target, which is the dysfunctional structure of the American high school.

Taking this line of argument still persuades neither my urban principal critic nor my assistant professor friend. Be realistic, they say. And I protest that I *am* being realistic in admitting candidly what clearly is not functioning well. It is unrealistic to accept the existing structure of the high school. Trying to reform it within that structure is like trying to push a large square of Jello across a plate with the sharpened point of a pencil. You can do it, but you certainly don't get much traction.

I find I do better with my colleague-critics over a few beers than in an auditorium where I deliver a speech. The fury, as well as the personal defensiveness that lies behind it, fades a bit in less formal surroundings. We start talking of the future, wondering what might the answers be. They all point in the same direction: high school reform will start as an effort in exploratory *engineering*, designing and testing new structures appropriate to the adolescents, the teachers, and the culture of the 1980s. We need new models of schooling that attempt several new approaches at once—a necessity, given how most of the important aspects of high school structure affect every other aspect.

Such a strategy of "model" schools will bring us back to the "alternative school" approach of the 1960s, but this time the "alternatives" will not be spinoffs to accommodate a special, atypical group of students. Rather, they will be experiments that ultimately should affect the central system—indeed, that should replace it. The best analogy is to the Progressive experiments of the early 20th century—the Dalton Public Schools, the Little Red Schoolhouse, and the schools in Eight-Year Study.

That should have been my initial response to my urban principal critic. "Your school system must do two things at once: help you cope well with that semi-literate 10th-grader and your needy Cambodian refugees *and* set up a truly unfettered alternative experiment that ultimately may make it easier for you to do your job far better." Both short-range and long-range needs must now be addressed. We must not let our desperation about meeting the former prevent us from tackling the latter.

My response to my assistant professor friend is shakier. "Use your skills as an educational engineer to design a better structure, and try to find a school system that needs you and your design and that wants you to try it out." Her sensible rebuttal would be that there is neither money nor political will for this sort of thing. And she'd be right.

That's why the burden is on those of us who have been given the privilege of studying and writing about high schools. It is our duty to join with colleagues to persuade the American political system—its public authorities *and* its great private philanthropies—that investment in imaginative educational engineering is absolutely essential if we are to have a secondary school system worthy of the talent and promise of American adolescents.

Choosing Equality: The Case for Democratic Schooling

ANN BASTIAN
New World Foundation

NORMAN FRUCHTER
Educational Consultant

MARILYN GITTELL
Queens College, City University of New York

COLIN GREER
New World Foundation

KENNETH HASKINS
Harvard University

. . . We have come to a number of conclusions that we feel represent the case for democratic schooling:

1. The crisis of achievement in American education is twofold: there is a crisis of inequality and a crisis of citizenship. Our primary concern should lie with the acute failure to provide a vast number of low-income and minority students with decent schools and skills. We also need to recognize a chronic failure to enhance all children's capacities to think critically and to acquire social knowledge.

2. Massive school failure is primarily the long-term consequence of meritocratic school practices, which have created distinctly different conditions in elite and mass education. Moreover, meritocracy rationalizes school failure by attributing it to individual deficiences, rather than to schools that do not serve children well. Today, as in the past, school resources, expectations, and services are highly unequal, both absolutely and relative to student needs. Competitive standards and methods of achievement compound social and educational advantages and disadvantages, and force unfair trade-offs between different kinds of needs. Our school system has thus reproduced the prevailing pattern of social stratification, not transcended it.

3. Today's schools are not suffering an erosion of quality due to excessive egalitarian reform: the problem is not that schools have shortchanged those on the top, but that schools have so completely underserved those on the bottom. Overall, the equity reforms of the 1960s and 1970s accomplished a shift from exclusive meritocracy, which shut many students out, to inclusive meritocracy, which granted students access but not the resources to achieve. In the 1980s, even inclusion is being undermined, as elitist get-tough prescriptions erect new barriers and push more students out of school.

4. Economic realities do not justify the claim that a more competitive school regime will raise productivity and widely enhance job opportunities. The growing polarization of the workforce into a small professional strata and a large pool of low-wage, de-skilled service and production workers indicates that education will mean more for a few and less for many, in terms of economic reward. The logic of today's marketplace is to lower expectations and limit chances for the majority of children, and elitist schooling reinforces this logic.

5. Schools do not have to mirror economic imperatives; they can also respond to social imperatives. If education were constructed around the social needs of children, families, communities, and a democratic society, the priority would be to endow all children with the basic and higher-order skills needed to fulfill personal and citizenship roles. The mission of schooling would be individual and social empowerment, which itself would promote more equitable chances of survival in the labor market. We believe schools can make a difference in our quality of life, but realizing this potential will require different schools.

6. School improvement and effective instruction cannot be legislated by quantitatively raising requirements, by imposing reward-and-punish systems of performance, or by singling out aspects of school practice that can be technically manipulated. More of the same is not better, when traditional practice has contributed to both school failure and alienation. Successful approaches to improving performance recognize the need to qualitatively change the environmental context—the school culture—that conditions the learning process. Effective reform

must be multi-dimensional, must address structural, organizational, and managerial issues, and must account for the quality of relationships among staff and students.

7. In the debate over instructional reform, the differences between democratic and elitist approaches to improving instruction cannot be reduced to false choices between permissiveness and authority, or low and high standards. The differences represent conflicts over what constitutes achievement and who should achieve. These conflicts are expressed in general terms as the opposition between universal or selective access; between inclusive or exclusive advancement; between supportive or punitive motivation; between cooperative or competitive achievement; between collaborative or hierarchic management; between bottom-up and top-down change processes.

8. The approaches that constitute democratic education are known to promote school improvement in deprived and deficient schools; they can also work to make all schools more engaging, more attuned to individual potential, more collectively rewarding. Likewise, the conditions of educational achievement found in advantaged schools—such as better staffing ratios, greater community accountability, more resources for enrichment and supportive services—are conditions that can be provided in all schools. Equality does not dictate mediocrity any more than quality depends on privilege. Since we know a great deal about what makes all kinds of schools more effective, the issue is why we use that knowledge for some and not all children.

9. Addressing the crises in public education thus necessitates a challenge to the priorities we have set and to the way we set priorities. Progressive change must include reforming the political processes that determine our choices, both within the institution and in government. Today, the grassroots constituents of education—parents, teachers, community members—are increasingly distanced from the centers of power. As in other social institutions, control over school policy and practice is concentrated in the hands of administrative and professional bureaucrats, special interests, and political elites.

10. Progressive reform therefore requires empowering the constituents of schooling as both essential elements of school culture and indispensable agents for change. Progressive reform also requires renewing our conception of the school as a community institution, both drawing on and adding to community resources. The conception that schools should be socially responsive does not detract from their primary function of instruction; on the contrary, schools must respond to the societal conditions that influence them in order to perform well for all students.

11. Promoting constituent activism around school needs both generates and requires new power relationships. In advocating the construction of progressive federalism in education, we are calling for all levels of

government to play a redistributive role in regard to governance as well as funding. The local governance of local schools is a core issue of school improvement and constituent empowerment, but will occur only with major policy shifts at the state level, an arena of education politics where progressives must direct new energy. Locating basic decision-making power at the school site also means that power-sharing mechanisms and equity standards must be more, not less, rigorously promoted at the state and federal levels. Alongside the policy goals of progressive federalism, it is necessary to renew our national sense of public ownership in education, defending schools as public institutions through which citizens rightfully assert social needs and priorities for their children and communities.

There is one more argument to add to these conclusions and to our debate with the new elitists. The emphasis they place on standardization and technique has been used on occasion to imply that financial resources are not at the heart of the school crisis, except perhaps in regard to teacher pay and shortages. Yet nearly every progressive measure that we have identified requires a higher level of fiscal support, as well as redistribution of funding to those who are currently underserved. If the majority of American school children cannot rely on either meritocracy or the marketplace to secure their right to productive knowledge, if education can advance only through its democratic mission, then we have far to go in fulfilling our commitments. Democratic education can be pursued, but it cannot be achieved without substantially increasing funding to education—funding for equity, for inno-vation, for participatory institutions linked to community and social needs. Money is never a solution, but it is an essential means to an end. To those who argue that equality of results simply costs too much, Tom Bethell offers the best reply: "Compared to what?"[1] . . .

NOTE

1. Thomas N. Bethell, "Now Let's Talk About Jobs Again," *Rural Coalition Report*, no. 10, December 1984, p. 11.

Goals for the Reform of Teacher Education: An Executive Summary of the Holmes Group Report

FRANK B. MURRAY

University of Delaware

A small group of education deans conducted a series of meetings and deliberations on the enduring problems associated with the generally low quality of teacher preparation in the United States. Out of these meetings grew the Holmes Group. The deans' initial discussions focused on the lax standards that continue to be tolerated. Weak accreditation policies and practices and the historic disinterest in teacher preparation on the part of the major research universities were topics that also received special attention. Clearly, weak accreditation and the low priority assigned to teacher education at major universities were not independent phenomena, and in the end this connection became the focus of the group's work.

Over a three-year period, the deans, in consultation with many of their peers, saw that the problems they faced were so great and so complicated that solving them would require a long-term commitment of like-minded institutions to a reform agenda. They proposed a plan for a consortium and outlined a set of goals for it.

The institutions whose deans are members of the Holmes Group, though they span a fairly wide range of quality themselves, are the leading research institutions in their respective states and regions. By any commonly accepted standard, they are at the top 10% of U.S. institutions engaged in teacher education—even though in some cases their teacher education programs are not currently among the nation's best. The deficiencies of the teacher education programs in some of the member institutions are all the more reason for the existence of the consortium, which is simply a means by which members can improve and reform their own programs. However, the consortium must become more than a self-help group because its vision of the kind of teacher who should be permitted to teach in U.S. schools requires the consortium to work equally hard to change the teaching profession itself. The consortium wishes to see nothing less than the transformation of teaching from an occupation into a genuine profession, and to this end it has aligned itself with other organizations, agencies, and institutions that support its goals and general directions.

The consortium seeks to provide the nation with teachers who have all the attributes of genuine professionals—including the prestige, high earnings, and autonomy that accrue to competent people who are engaged in important matters in ways that are beyond the talent or training of the ordinary person. Those educated at Holmes Group universities will be entrusted *fully* with the education of their pupils. They will be people who, by a combination of natural talent and training, can be *fully* responsive to the immediate demands of the classroom. They will be people who will make significant decisions in pedagogy and in educational policy because they are competent to make them and because *no other person* will be more qualified or in a better position to do so.

Thus the consortium is organized around twin goals: the reform of teacher education and the reform of the teaching profession. It assumes that these reforms will prosper if the nation's best universities are committed to teacher education. It assumes also that teacher education programs will be different in these institutions for all the reasons that make these institutions so academically powerful in every other respect. They are institutions that attract more than their share of the best and the brightest students; their faculty members are, on the whole, the nation's best and most authoritative sources of information in their fields; they command substantial resources; and, in the case of education, they are the institutions that have educated and will continue to educate the professoriate in education. A consortium of institutions that educate teacher educators is needed, if only to insure that the teachers of teachers do their graduate work in institutions that have exemplary teacher education programs. This consortium is the Holmes Group.

With these points in mind, the members of the Holmes Group recognize that powerful forces work against major reform in education. One of these forces is the dramatic increase in the demand for teachers that will occur in the next 10 years. If states and localities respond to this demand as they have in the past—by giving certification to unqualified persons and by allowing certified teachers to teach outside their fields of competence—then efforts to reform teacher education will be substantially undermined once again.

Another force working against a major reform of teacher education is, ironically, the education reform movement itself. Recent reform proposals have suggested that attracting higher-quality people to teaching is a key component of the effort to reform education—a recommendation we endorse as well. The reformers have also recommended that attention be given to such ideas as increased subject-matter competence, more standardized testing, the addition of a fifth year to teacher preparation programs, differentiated career opportunities, increased clinical experience, higher salaries for teachers, and the like. But few of the reformers have seen that these issues are interrelated and more complex than each by itself would suggest, because each by itself could become a superficial and symbolic reform that could actually worsen the problems it was meant to solve. The current reform proposals will fail, as they have in the past, because they attempt to reform education simply by telling teachers (and everyone else) what to do, rather than by empowering them to do what must be done.

The quality of teachers is tied, of course, to the quality of their education. And we cannot improve teacher education very much by changing colleges of education without also changing the universities, the credentialing systems, and the schools themselves. The rewards and career opportunities for teachers; the standards, nature, and substance of professional education; the quality and coherence of the liberal arts and subject-matter fields; and the professional certification and licensing apparatus must all be changed—but not changed merely for the sake of change. They must be changed *only* in mutually supportive ways that will yield the kind of teachers we envision.

The policy changes recommended by reformers are only the first stage of lasting reform. Regrettably, most reform efforts end with the publication of a report. Past attempts at large-scale reform demonstrate that changes imposed from above, without the concurrence and collaboration of those who must implement them, have limited effects. Changes in the structure and content of teacher education depend on long-term and genuine reform efforts by policy makers, scholars, and practitioners. For this reason, the Holmes Group has proposed for itself long-term goals as both a regional and a national organization. We recognize that in implementing our proposed agenda, there will be many mistakes, false starts, and unanticipated problems. We also recognize that solutions that work in one setting must inevitably be adapted to work in another setting. For this reason, the plans of member institutions for achieving the group's goals will differ. We foresee that in the years ahead we will learn much from one another about the strengths and limits of our proposed agenda. Hence the Holmes Group is committed to exploring a range of alternative solutions organized around five themes and to sharing the outcomes of our experiments among ourselves and with others. As we become more confident of solutions to the problems of building a teaching profession, we commit ourselves as teacher education institutions to establish accreditation standards for ourselves that reflect the following five major goals.

1. To make the education of teachers intellectually sound. Competent teaching is a compound of four kinds of knowledge: 1) a broad general and liberal education, 2) the subject matter of the teaching field, 3) the literature of education, and 4) reflective practical experience. Over time, the established professions have developed their own bodies of knowledge, which are transmitted through professional education and clinical practice. Their legitimate claims to professional status rest *solely* on the utility of this body of knowledge. For the occupation of teaching, a defensible claim for such special knowledge has emerged only within the last 20 years. Efforts to reform the preparation of teachers and the profession of teaching must begin, therefore, with improvements both in scholarship in education and in the articulation of education with the more mature academic disciplines. With this in mind, the Holmes Group commits itself to the development of programs in teacher education that *guarantee* the student's mastery of the four kinds of knowledge cited above.

The Holmes Group sees mastery of the liberal arts as essential in the preparation of teachers, because teaching, more than any other profession, is about knowledge. However, the Holmes Group finds that most undergraduate programs lack coherence and a focus on enduring questions and ideas. The disciplinary and departmental structure of universities—the source of so much strength in the modern university—is also responsible for the lack of attention to educational issues that extend beyond the boundaries of the academic major. This inattention weakens all students' understanding of the fundamental ideas that distinguish the truly educated person. Moreover, little in the contemporary university encourages university faculty members to go beyond the firmly held—but naive—view of teaching as merely presenting or telling correctly.

The reform of teacher education must be coupled with changes in the education that undergraduates receive in the arts and sciences. Courses in the core subjects that elaborate both the structure of a discipline and its powerful and generative ideas must be developed. Currently, most prospective high school teachers major in their teaching field and engage in general liberal studies, leaving little room for the study of pedagogy and the reformulation of their college major into a teachable secondary school subject. Prospective elementary teachers, on the other hand, spend substantially more time on pedagogy, but they do so at the expense of essential knowledge of subject matter. Members of the Holmes Group commit themselves to the development of both a university-level pedagogical curriculum and a coherent program of professional education.

Despite the fact that clinical experience is almost universally praised by teachers, it presents some of the most serious problems in teacher education as it is currently practiced. We are committed to developing clinical experiences in a number of different settings, and, rather than merely exposing prospective teachers to experienced teachers, we are also committed to focusing clinical experience on the systematic development of practice and experimentation. It is clear that acquiring a general liberal education, mastering the content of the teaching field(s), and undertaking the study of and disciplined practice in pedagogy will take more time than is currently available in the traditional four-year undergraduate program. Thus the traditional program must be reorganized and inevitably extended—by about 25%, in our estimation. This reorganization and extension would mean, in most cases, that the deans of education would recommend for certification *only* persons who had completed a reformed academic major in their teaching subject, a true program of liberal studies, and a modern graduate program of pedagogical studies.

2. To recognize differences in knowledge, skill, and commitment among teachers. Improved teacher education must also be accompanied by changes in the structure of the profession of teaching; making university programs more demanding and costly will attract competent applicants *only if* the rewards of teaching and the opportunities for professional advancement are also increased substantially. In our view, a differentiated structure consisting of at least three levels is a prerequisite for the construction of a profession of teaching that will be responsive to the demands of the next decade.

Career professional teachers would be people capable of assuming not only full responsibility for the classroom but also for certain aspects of the administration of the school and even of the university. The *professional teacher* would be an autonomous teacher in the classroom. And the *instructor,* a person whose ultimate career aspirations lie elsewhere, would teach for a few years under the supervision of a career professional teacher.

The Holmes Group commits itself to make the changes in teacher education necessary to prepare teachers for a differentiated structure along these general lines and to use its influence to change state and local policy in these directions.

3. To create honest standards of entry into the profession of teaching. The hallmark of a profession is the responsibility it assumes for the competence of its members. This responsibility is twofold: responsibility to the public at large that its members possess the knowledge and skill needed to be effective and responsibility to the prospective members of the profession that they will receive just value for their investment in preparation. The Holmes Group commits itself to develop and administer a series of professional teacher examinations that will provide a credible basis for issuing teaching credentials and licenses. Because of the current limitations of even the best standardized tests in predicting the performance of teachers, the Holmes Group commits itself to require students to demonstrate mastery of important knowledge and skill through multiple evaluations in realistic and honest formats and settings. These examinations will provide a basis for evaluation not only of prospective teachers but also of the institutions themselves.

The Holmes Group also recognizes its responsibility to help create a profession that is representative of the larger pluralistic society. The most difficult problem in this regard is minority representation. Minority under-graduate enrollments and minority entry into teaching have been declining rapidly at the very time when the proportion of minority children in schools has been increasing. As a result, the teacher force may soon be composed overwhelmingly of people from majority backgrounds teaching students who are primarily from minority backgrounds. The Holmes Group institutions commit themselves to significantly increasing the number of minorities in their teacher education programs. Moreover, the Holmes Group does not see this goal as incompatible with its other goals.

4. To connect schools of education with schools. The professionalization of teaching depends on the contributions that teachers and professors make to the creation of knowledge about their profession and to teachers' ability to form collegial relationships beyond their immediate working environment and to grow intellectually throughout their careers. The improvement of teacher education depends on teachers' contributions to pedagogical knowledge and to reflective practice. These two facts lead Holmes Group institutions to commit themselves to establishing professional development schools and other working partnerships among university faculty members, practicing teachers, and administrators.

These professional development schools, analogous to teaching hospitals in the medical profession, will bring practicing teachers and administrators together with university faculty members in partnerships based on the principles of *reciprocity* (the mutual exchange and benefit between research and practice), *experimentation* (a willingness to try and carefully evaluate new forms of practice and structure), and *diversity* (commitment to the development of teaching strategies for a broad range of children with different backgrounds, abilities, and learning styles).

5. To make schools better places in which teachers can work and learn. Constructing a profession through the improvement of professional education, the development of a differentiated structure for professional opportunity, the creation of honest standards for entry, and the creation of settings for mutual exchange between research and practice will have profound effects on the competence and aspirations of new teachers. The current working conditions of teachers—especially the division of authority between administrators and teachers—are seriously out of step with the notion of a truly professional teacher who would not need the levels of guidance, supervision, and external support that many districts now attempt to provide.

The Holmes Group will develop models for more appropriate divisions of authority between teachers and administrators in professional development schools and will make the professional education of administrators compatible with the requirements of a genuine profession of teaching.

The Holmes Group report, *Tomorrow's Teachers*, assesses the obstacles to lasting reform of education and sets forth a vision of teaching as a genuine profession. The report is not to be taken as dogma or as a schematic diagram for removing these obstacles. Nor is it a prescription for the one best way to educate teachers. Instead, it sets forth five themes or goals and challenges its members to adopt these goals and to propose individual plans to address them. The reason this consortium exists is, of course, that a single institution needs help to accomplish these five goals. Obviously, the reform of the schools and the teaching profession is far beyond the capacity of even the strongest universities acting individually. Given the research orientation of each member institution, there is every expectation that these institutional plans, apart from being shaped by their local contexts, will be experimental and will reflect the same kind of inquiring attitude that characterizes sound research in any field.

The plans are to be submitted jointly by the chief academic officer of each university and by the dean of the college of education. They will show how the institution, over a period of years, will go about making its teacher education program more intellectually solid and accomplishing the other goals of the Holmes Group. Each successful plan will call for extensive collaboration between the college of education and the faculties of arts and sciences, the local schools, state departments of education, state legislatures, and so on. In the end, the value of the consortium will be the rich diversity of solutions to the common problem of transforming teaching into a true profession.

In recognition of the nation's regional diversity, the Holmes Group plans to pursue these larger goals at both the regional and national levels. For this reason, it has organized itself into five regions with at least one member institution for each 25,000 teachers within a region. Through a national office, the Holmes Group will address reform measures common to the entire profession, and, in each region, the schools of education and their partners will address the unique educational features of their states and regions. In addition, the consortium has standing committees on four topics: curriculum development, state planning and policy, testing and evaluation, and membership.

Currently, the Holmes Group is establishing its charter membership and furthering its plans for implementation of its agenda. In keeping with the view that a focused effort among a reasonable number of research universities will increase the chance of successful reform, invitations for charter membership in the Holmes Group have been issued jointly to the chief academic officer and the dean of education at 123 institutions. At least one leading public university in each state has been invited, and at least one institution for each 25,000 teachers in each of the five regions has been asked to join.

Institutions that belong to the American Association of Universities have been invited to become charter members of the Holmes Group, as have other institutions identified in studies of institutional reputation for the excellence of their research and development in education. Other factors taken into account include whether or not an institution offers a doctoral program in education, the past record of investment in research and development activity on the part of the institution as a whole, and the percentage of minority enrollment at the institution.

To become a charter member of the Holmes Group, the chief academic officer and the education dean at the institution must support the goals of the Holmes Group. And they must describe their general plans for encouraging development and implementation of reform efforts at their institution.

Once charter membership has been established and pilot programs for implementation of the Holmes Group reform effort are under way, the group's membership committee will accept applications for participation from the deans and academic officers of other institutions that wish to affiliate with the group. We anticipate that application for membership in the Holmes Group will be open to other research-intensive institutions within three to five years.

Recent Reform Proposals for American Education

LAWRENCE C. STEDMAN

University of Wisconsin, Madison

MARSHALL S. SMITH

Stanford University

During the past few months, several commissions have published reports proposing major reforms for our educational system. Four of these reports . . . have received widespread attention. Their publication (with special credit to the National Commission) has spurred the greatest national debate on education since the launching of Sputnik in 1957. In this review, we describe each commission and its report, and examine their case for reform and their recommendations. Our focus is on the quality of their analysis and their recommendations rather than on the rhetorical or political importance of the documents. Our analysis is intended to be provocative rather than conclusive.

THE COMMISSIONS AND THEIR REPORTS

A Nation At Risk

The National Commission on Excellence was an 18-member panel appointed by Education Secretary Terrel H. Bell in 1981. Its chair was David P.

From *Contemporary Education Review* 2 (Fall 1983). Copyright © 1983, American Educational Research Association, Washington, D.C. Reprinted by permission of the publisher.

Preparation of this paper was supported in part by the Wisconsin Center for Education Research which is supported in part by a grant from the National Institute of Education (Grant No. NIE-G-81–0009). The opinions expressed in this paper do not necessarily reflect the position, policy, or endorsement of the National Institute of Education.

Gardner, president of the University of Utah, and president-designate of the University of California. The panel included Yale University president A. Bartlett Giamatti, former Minnesota governor Albert H. Quie, a retired chairman of the board of Bell Labs, the immediate past president of the San Diego School Board, a Harvard physicist, and the 1981–1982 National Teacher of the Year. The panel was charged with making practical recommendations to foster academic excellence in our nation's schools. To prepare its report, the panel commissioned research papers, met with administrators, teachers and representatives of professional and public organizations, and studied existing analyses of educational problems. Its recommendations focus on upgrading content, raising academic standards, increasing time on academic subjects, and providing greater financial rewards and status for teachers. Specific recommendations include an emphasis on the "new basics," including social studies and computer competency, 7-hour school days and 200- to 220-day school years, and a 3-tiered system for ranking and paying teachers: beginner, experienced, and master.

Action for Excellence

The national Task Force on Education for Economic Growth was established by the Education Commission of the States. The task force, chaired by James Hunt, governor of North Carolina, and co-chaired by Pierre duPont, governor of Delaware, and Frank Cary, chairman of the executive committee of IBM, was composed of governors, legislators, corporate chief executives, educators, and labor leaders. It was primarily concerned with the role education could play in solving the crisis in American economic productivity and growth. Although many of its recommendations are similar to those of the National Commission on Excellence—focusing on the new basics, increased academic time, and teacher quality—two major proposals are quite different. The report calls for governors to take leadership in the reform effort and to appoint state task forces on education for economic growth to promote improvement. It also calls for the creation of partnerships between businesses and schools, including courses taught in factories and offices and team teaching using specialists from industry.

Academic Preparation for College

The College Entrance Examination Board's study was an outgrowth of an earlier report by the Education Equality Project on improving high school students' intellectual skills. The new report represents, therefore, the efforts of 1,400 college and high school teachers and administrators, parents and students, and representatives of professional organizations who have worked together since 1980 on the problem of college preparation (Watkins, 1983, p. 14). The report presents guidelines for each academic subject—English, the arts, mathematics, science, social studies, and foreign language—outlining the skills necessary for college.

The report differs from the *Nation at Risk* and *Action for Excellence* reports in that it stresses academic content over academic time. It is also the only one of the four reports to recommend improving student competence in the arts, giving equal weight to the humanistic aspects of education and to math and science.

Making the Grade

The Twentieth Century Fund, founded in 1919 and endowed by Edward A. Filene, is an "independent research foundation which undertakes policy studies of economic, political, and social institutions and issues" (1983, p. iv). Its Board of Trustees includes Hodding Carter, III, Patricia Roberts Harris, Arthur Schlesinger, Jr., William Ruckelshaus, and Shirley Williams, former British Member of Parliament. Its task force on education was chaired by Robert Wood, the director of Urban Studies at the University of Massachusetts and former superintendent of schools in Boston. Other members of the task force included Carlos Hortas, chairman of romance languages at Hunter College; Diane Ravitch, Columbia University professor, educational historian, and author of *The Revisionists Revised;* Wilson Riles, former superintendent of public instruction for California; and Patricia Graham, dean of the Harvard Graduate School of Education. The report focuses on the role the federal government should play in the current economic and educational crisis. This federal policy focus is unique among the four reports. Nevertheless, many recommendations display the same concern with academic content and teacher quality that is present in the other reports. One major proposal, for example, calls for the creation of a National Master Teacher Program with rewards and grants going to state-level selected master teachers. Other proposals reveal the task force's interest in uniform national approaches, such as the recommendation that federal requirements and funds for children with limited proficiency in English be focused on language immersion and English-as-a-second-language programs rather than bilingual programs. Finally, there is a proposal, not universally endorsed by members of the task force, for the creation of a federally financed public school voucher scheme for educationally disadvantaged students.

THE CASE FOR REFORM

The four commissions were responding to the current American economic crisis, particularly the decay in our industrial base and the decline in our economic power relative to that of foreign countries. They were also responding to what is considered to be two decades of American educational failure, to what one report describes as a "rising tide of mediocrity that threatens our very future as a Nation and a people" (National Commission on Excellence in Education, 1983, p. 5). Their recommendations are designed to cure our educational failures and to prepare students for a new society—for a future economy based on high technology, emphasizing information processing and computers. By adopting these recommendations, the commissions believe, the United States can recapture its economic vigor and regain its competitive edge in the world economy.

At the outset, it should be recognized that these reports are political documents; the case they make takes the form of a polemic, not a reasoned treatise. Rather than carefully marshalling facts to prove their case, they present a litany of charges without examining the veracity of their evidence or its sources. By presenting their material starkly, and often eloquently, the commissions hoped to jar the public into action, and to a great extent they have been successful. Caveats and detailed analysis of evidence might have lessened the reports' impact.

The argument for reform was spelled out in detail in *A Nation at Risk*, and the case it makes forms the basis of our critique. We focus on three aspects: the quality of the evidence for the poor state of American education, the claim that the U.S. education system is inferior to those of foreign countries, and the assumption that a high-technology (hi-tech) revolution is sweeping the American economic system. After considering these aspects of the argument, we review the four reports' recommendations and discuss their viability.

The Nature of the Evidence on Academic Performance and Standards

The rhetoric of the reports concerning the decline in student performance and the relaxation of educational standards is reminiscent of the 1950s attacks on progressive education (see, e.g., Lynd, 1953; there were also calls for excellence, see, e.g., Gardner, 1961). The argument primarily rests on the ability of the report to evoke a sympathetic reaction of the reader: to nod and say "Yes, we've heard that before, we've retreated from academics and excellence," and to accept the "Back to the basics" shibboleth. The widespread perception of an undisciplined 1960s has guaranteed a national acceptance of the commissions' argument despite the reports' poor documentation.

Academic performance. The National Commission presents 13 representative indicators of "the educational dimensions of the risk." One indicator contrasts achievement in the United States with other nations and will be discussed later; 5 describe contemporary U.S. achievement; and 7 contrast past achievement with present. Viewed critically they provide more convincing evidence of the lack of quality of our indicators than of our educational system.

Two of the five contemporary snapshots cite data about the prevalence of illiteracy in America and are neither current nor without controversy. The first stated that "23 million American adults are functionally illiterate by the simplest tests of everyday reading" (p. 8). This measure comes from a study carried out a decade ago that has been extensively criticized by the National Institute of Education (NIE) (Fisher, 1978). The other found that 13 percent of 17-year-olds were functionally illiterate in 1974 and again in 1975. These data were collected by the National Assessment of Educational Progress (NAEP); many of the same items were also given in 1971. The data indicate that the 1974 and 1975 cohorts of 17-year-olds scored higher than the 1971 cohort. (Fisher, 1978; Gadway & Wilson, 1975). Apart from the problem of defining "literacy" at any given moment in history, and that the definition has changed over time to become more rigorous as society has changed its demands, it is clear from almost every recent report that the problem of illiteracy for young adults is very heavily concentrated in the poor and minority (particularly male) population, a fact that goes unmentioned in the report.

The third snapshot is insufficiently explained. It finds that "over half the population of gifted students do not match their tested ability with comparable achievement in school" (p. 8). This may suggest as much about our skill in assessing "ability" and "achievement" as it does about the quality of the educational system. Given the imperfect reliability of our tests over time, the Commission's statement sounds suspiciously like "over half of the sample scores below the median."

The last two of the contemporary indicators are more persuasive. The first pointed out that 25 percent of Navy recruits required remedial reading in order to understand written safety instructions. The other was recent National Assessment data that showed many of the nation's 17-year-olds cannot carry out reasonably complex intellectual tasks. This latter case has been forcefully made by other commentators (Holmes, 1982).

The case for a serious "decline," though rhetorically compelling, also does not stand up very well. Three of the Commission's seven indicators of decline are drawn from the College Entrance Examination Board (the College Board) data. One cited the drop in SAT scores over the past 20 years, with no mention that the population taking the tests has changed fairly dramatically during the same period (College Entrance Examination Board, 1977). A second found "consistent achievement test declines in recent years in such subjects as physics and English" (p. 9), without also pointing out that "mean grades increased between 1969 and 1979 on all College Board advanced placement tests in science and mathematics as did the number of students who took each test" (Jones, 1981, p. 415). A third College Board indicator found the number and percentage of very high test scores dropping substantially over the past two decades. This seems to us to be a valid indicator and a matter for legitimate concern.

Of the other four indicators of decline, only one deserves serious attention. The Commission cited a "steady decline in science achievement scores of U.S. 17-year-olds as measured by the NAEP in 1969, 1973, and 1977" (p. 9). This decline, however, is small, amounting to a drop of only 4.7 percentage points correct over an 8-year period (NAEP, 1978). Over the past decade, declines in other tested areas of the NAEP, such as math and writing, were also small (NAEP, 1979, 1980, 1981), whereas in reading the performance of "American youth improved for young students, while teenagers tended to hold their ground" (Holmes, 1982, p. xi).

Our purpose in being critical of the Commission's indicators is not to deny that test scores of American youth have declined or that they shouldn't be higher. Rather, we wish to point out the poor quality of their treatment of the data and, with the exception of National Assessment, the abominable nature of national data on school performance. Even so, it is conceivable that careful treatment of the existing evidence on academic performance in areas such as the incidence of literacy (which suggests a focus on the poor, the minorities, and urban school children) and the acquisition of higher order skills (which suggests changes in strategies of instruction and sequencing of content) might have led to more carefully honed recommendations than those reached by the Commission.

Academic Standards. Here, too, the evidence is weak. The National Commission, for example, argued that a widespread growth of electives had diminished the academic focus and claimed that the secondary school curriculum has been "homogenized, diluted, and diffused" (p. 18) and that the resulting "curricular smorgasbord . . . explains a great deal about where we find ourselves today" (p. 18). This generalization rests primarily on a supplementary study conducted by Adelman (1983), which analyzed changes in high school transcripts of two samples, one covering 1964–1969 and the second, 1975–1981. The problem with the study is that these two samples are not comparable. The early one was of only 27 high schools, with little Southern representation and no schools from cities of population over 1 million. The second was a national sampling of households. There is no longitudinal study of a given set of high schools on which the Commission's claims rest.

Even if the two samples were comparable, the evidence presented in the Adelman report barely justified the claim made. Although the later sample showed a threefold increase in the percentage of students in the general track and substantial increases in such courses as driver's education and marriage training, the total time spent on academics was much less different for the two samples. Taking all high school graduates together, the percentages of all credits received that were generated by academic subjects were 69 percent in the first sample and 62 percent in the second (Adelman, 1983, Appendix F). Although the second sample had lower credits in a number of academic subjects, in many others the differences were small. Chemistry and intermediate algebra credits, for example, differed by 6 percent, Spanish 1 by 7 percent, and biology by only 3 percent. In the general track, the percentage of students in the second sample taking such academic subjects was higher, not lower. (Geometry rose from 22 percent to 32 percent, intermediate algebra from 18 percent to 19 percent, and chemistry from 10 percent to 19 percent.) These data, therefore, lend only weak support to the claim that academics have been seriously weakened.

Other data drawn from representative samples indicate only a modest overall decline in academic emphasis. Table I presents our preliminary analyses comparing the senior classes of 1972 and 1980 for nationally representative samples. These data do show some reduction in the percentages of "all" students in academic classes over the 8-year period from 46 percent in 1972 to 39 percent in 1980. They also show concomitant increases in the percentages of "all" students in the general and vocational tracks. But overall data may be obscuring important interactions, for example, the changes between whites and blacks. In 1972 roughly 28 percent of blacks were enrolled in academic tracks, while almost 50 percent of whites were in the academic tracks. By 1980 the gap had been reduced by over 70 percent. The

TABLE I   Percentages of High School Seniors (self-reported)
Enrolled in Different Tracks in 1972 and 1980

Track	Black		White		All[a]	
	1972	1980	1972	1980	1972	1980
General	37.6	36.4	31.4	36.8	32.6	36.8
Academic	27.8	34.0	49.6	40.0	46.2	38.7
Vocational	34.6	29.6	19.0	23.1	21.2	24.5

[a]Includes other minorities.

Note. 1980–20 percent random sample of "High School and Beyond" seniors (from National Center for Education Statistics, U.S. Dept. of Education).

1972–20 percent random sample of the Class of '72, "National Longitudinal Survey," seniors (from National Center for Education Statistics, U.S. Dept. of Education).

The analyses above were performed by Ki-Seok Kim of the Wisconsin Center for Education Research, University of Wisconsin, Madison.

black percentage enrollment in the academic track had increased to 34 percent, while the white percentage had dropped to 40 percent. Such dramatic differences indicate the need for further study.

Academic content, of course, was not the only example presented of weaker school practices. The various commissions also cited declining amounts of homework required, the relaxing of discipline, and the giving of higher grades for the same work. Though much of their evidence was anecdotal, data do exist on changes in homework requirements *and* on "grade inflation" (Takai, 1983). However, with the exception of homework, there are no hard data on the effects of these changes on achievement, and in the case of homework the results are often contradictory (see, e.g., Ginsburg, Milne, Myers, & Ellman, 1983; Wolf, 1977).

Even if there were changes in some school practices, it is not clear that these were responsible for the decline in performance. A major study of the SAT decline, for example, suggested that the decline had little to do with changing school practices. The College Board, in *On Further Examination* (1977), found that between two-thirds and three-fourths of the decline from 1964–1973 could be attributed to the changing social composition of the test takers. A smaller percentage of the decline from 1973 could be attributed to population changes. The remaining portion of the decline was not soley attributable to the schools but also to changing social conditions such as student unrest, increase in television watching, and so on. A supplementary study by Echternacht (1977) compared high schools whose SAT scores had remained stable or risen slightly between 1965 and 1976 to a group whose scores had declined more than the national average. He found that differences in the number of academic courses taken in the "effective" and "ineffective" schools were tiny. English curriculums were similar; pass-fail grading and nontraditional offerings had expanded to the same extent.

Rather than abandoning academics, many high schools with decreasing scores had increased homework and expanded basic skill instruction. Echternacht (1977) concluded, "Changes in the curriculum explain little of the SAT decline for this study's sample of schools" (p. 5).

Similarly, Peterson (1983), in an excellent review of the status of American education published as part of the Twentieth Century Fund report, concluded, "Nothing in these data permits the conclusion that educational institutions have deteriorated badly" (p. 59). The Fund's Task Force, however, argued as if they had. This is one of a number of examples where the commissions ignored the findings of their supplementary reports.[1]

International Comparisons

The commissions argue that, because U.S. schools fail to teach as well as those in other countries, we need to copy them to improve our test scores and technical preparation. The main features they recommended copying are time spent on academics, in particular longer school days and school years, with academic content, specifically curricula with a strong emphasis on math and science. There are major difficulties with this line of reasoning. First is the claim that U.S. students uniformly perform worse than those in other countries. The National Commission relies on the International Assessment of Educational Achievement (IEA), which has been the only major systematic international study. The data available to the Commission were gathered over a decade ago during the years 1964 to 1971. The Commission used country averages reported by the IEA to make their comparison. This approach has been strongly criticized (Husén, 1983). The averages were generated from noncomparable student bodies—in most other countries a small select group of students attending academic schools was tested, while in the United States both college- and noncollege-bound students attending comprehensive high schools were tested. The selectivity of the foreign systems is reflected, in part, by the percentages of students remaining in school. In West Germany, for example, only 9 percent of the age cohort reached their terminal year of high school in the early 1970s, whereas in the United States approximately 75 percent did (Comber & Keeves, 1973, p. 159). It should not be surprising that a more academically select group would perform better than the average U.S. student. As one observer remarked on the science scores, "The scores at age 18 diverged widely by country and are associated with the percentages of students still in school at that age" (Walberg, 1983, p. 7). There has, therefore, been no proper international comparison of the academic performance of the average high schooler.[2]

To make international comparisons using the IEA data, researchers often study the performance of the top students in each country. This still does not tell us how well the various countries prepare the average student but does indicate how well each country prepares a secondary school elite. After making such a comparison, Husén (1983) concluded,

> the international survey of both mathematics and science demonstrated that the top 5 percent to 10 percent at the end of secondary

education (i.e., the elite) tended to perform at nearly the same level in both comprehensive and selective systems of secondary education. Thus the elite among U.S. high school seniors did not differ considerably in their performance from their age-mates in France, England, or Germany. (p. 456)[3]

Indeed, if we again look at the most recent IEA results (1970–1971) we see that the "top" 9 percent of U.S. students in their terminal year of high school do better than those in foreign countries at the same level. The data in Table II indicate that, although the U.S. mean for reading comprehension exceeded only 3 of the 14 assessed countries, the top 9 percent of U.S. students exceeded the top 9 percent of *each* of the other countries. These data are strikingly different from those highlighted by the various commissions— though, as with the commissions' data, they are over 10 years old.

These elite comparisons still may be misleading, however, because IEA researchers did not disaggregate data by the type or number of courses taken. In science, for example, we do not know how U.S. students who took 4 years of science did compared to, say, German students who completed a similar sequence.

Perhaps more devastating to such comparisons is that they involve only secondary school students. This ignores the fact that the U.S. educational system is organized differently from those in foreign countries. We have striven for universal postsecondary education, relying on our technical schools, colleges, and universities rather than our high schools to provide technical training and professional specialization. With a marked edge over

TABLE II   Number of Countries Above and Below the U.S. Mean for the Entire Population of Sampled Terminal Year High School Students and for an Estimated Top 9 Percent of Age Group in the Terminal Year

Population	Science		Reading comprehension		Literature		Civic education	
	Above	Below	Above	Below	Above	Below	Above	Below
All tested terminal year students	13	4	11	3	4	5	5	2
Estimated top 9% of terminal year group students	6	11	0	14	0	9	1	6

Note. Numbers differ for each subject. Taken from Wolf (1977, p. 54).

foreign countries in college and university enrollment, having proportionately, for example, twice as many postsecondary students as Japan (*A Nation at Risk,* p. 34), the effectiveness of our educational system should be evaluated in terms of college performance as well as high school performance. This is particularly true in light of recent reports describing the poor quality of Japanese higher education, with its high absenteeism rates for both professors and students, with rampant grade inflation, and with lax standards (Fiske, 1983a, 1983b, 1983c, 1983d; Zeugner, 1983). No evidence, however, was presented in the Commissions' reports about the performance of our college students relative to those in foreign countries, nor, given the concern with high technology, that our university math and science graduates are less well prepared.

We do not know, therefore, how U.S. students in the late 1960s and early 1970s actually compared to students in other countries. Nor do we know their comparative performance since then. (This may soon be corrected in math as the results of a second recently implemented IEA study become known.)

The commissions also presumed that academic emphasis, particularly increased time, was the crucial factor in the supposedly better performance of students in these foreign countries. A number of findings from IEA studies bear on this supposition. Teachers in different countries, for example, were asked whether their students had been exposed to course material that covered the topics assessed by the various tests. Of course, the coverage of the information in courses affected the country's average test scores. To the extent that increasing course requirements increases the coverage of information that is measured by the test, we can expect test scores to rise.

TABLE A   Number of Countries Above and Below the United States Mean in Each Subject at Two Population Levels

Subject	Population I[a] (full-time students ages 10.0–10.11)		Population II (full-time students ages 14.0–14.11)	
	Above U.S. mean	Below U.S. mean	Above U.S. mean	Below U.S. mean
Science	4	11	7	10
Reading comprehension	8	5	2	12
Literature			2	7
Civics			2	6
French Reading comprehension			5	0

Note. From Wolf (1977, p. 54).
[a]Testing in Population I was limited to science and reading comprehension.

This approach to increasing time, however, must be distinguished from increasing the time during a school year that is given to a subject. The IEA study of mathematics, for example, found that variations in the amount of instructional time in mathematics and the amount of time on mathematics homework had only small effects on the achievement levels of different countries (Husén, 1967, pp. 182–189).

Length of the school day and year also do not explain variations in countries' achievement. Many of the Western European nations and Japan have longer school days and school years than the United States, but nevertheless had markedly divergent performance levels. Factors other than time must be considered salient. Cultural differences, in particular, can influence school performance and make copying school practices difficult. Japan is a prime example. By focusing on time, the commissions overlooked the more dramatic differences between the Japanese and the U.S. educational systems. The Japanese have extensive school solidarity, built upon student responsibility for cleaning buildings and serving meals, and upon weekly school assemblies punctuated by inspirational messages and songs. The cultural context for education is different. Students work for the honor of their class, school, and family and seek to do well on the rigorous high school and university entrance examinations. Authority relations are different, reflecting cultural factors such as the respect accorded elders. Teachers' desks are on raised platforms, desks are fixed in rows, students rise to greet the teacher, and students give a thank-you bow at the end of lessons. The pedagogy is quite different. There is extensive tutoring of younger by older children, heavy dictation and memorization, and a widespread network of academic centers providing in-service training (see Fiske, 1983a, 1983b, 1983c, 1983d; Hurn & Burn, 1982).

Finally, the commissions' call for copying other systems rests on a mismatch of school practices and achievement data. Given that the student assessments were carried out over a decade ago, a cross-national comparison of *contemporary* school practices is inappropriate. The commissions should have studied what the Japanese and West European school systems were doing then compared to what we had been doing then. What they were doing, more than now, was the early sorting of students by examinations into separate academic and vocational high schools (Hurn & Burn, 1982, pp. 12–13). Such practices would be anathema to most American educators and local school officials. What we had been doing, given that a high school senior in 1964 (the year of the mathematics test) would have begun public schooling in 1952, was traditional schooling, presumably with all the homework, grades, and discipline the commissions are now calling for.

A Hi-Tech Future?

Their third contention is that educational reforms, particularly those centered on math, science, and computers, are essential to restoring the American economic position. Developing computer competency and increasing mathematical and scientific literacy for the general population is a good idea, but we are skeptical that it will lead to our economic recovery. There is little evidence that the American economy is undergoing a *wholesale* transformation to a high-technology society. Although the use of high technology will certainly increase, we expect that most of the economy will look the same in 1995 as it does now. Bureau of Labor Statistics projections, for example, show that most new jobs created during the next decades will *not* be in engineering or the computer fields, but will be concentrated in clerical and retail positions (Bureau of Labor Statistics; 1982; Levin & Rumberger, 1983).[4] Nor does the increase in the use of computers in the work place necessarily demand a more highly trained work force (Carnevale & Goldstein, 1983, p. 13; Levin & Rumberger, 1983). The introduction of computers often results in a simplification of job skills and an increase in job routinization. Many of the jobs generated around computers, for example, often require little skill other than typing. Data entry positions are a prime example.

On the other side of this argument are those who challenge the conclusion reached by the Bureau of Labor Statistics (see, e.g., Tucker, 1983). These analysts see the changes in office technology requiring personnel with greater, not less, intellectual ability. The point, simply put, is that we are as uncertain about future occupational demands as we have always been. This is a good reason for training people to think and to be adaptable. But it does not necessarily justify increased training in math and science.

Finally, we are certain that educational reform is not critical for our *short-term* economic recovery because there is no evidence that our current economic malaise is due to an educational failure. There is, for example, no clear evidence of a shortage of qualified engineers or computer scientists (Walberg, 1983, p. 2). We believe the United States is experiencing high unemployment and low productivity not because of a lack of a technically skilled work force, but because of a worldwide recession, a failure to modernize our industrial plants, and a mismanaged federal budget.

These criticisms do not mean that there is not an educational crisis or that school reforms are unnecessary, or that an improved educational system will not improve our nation's human capital. Certainly we cannot afford to be complacent at a time when half of our high school graduates take no math or science after 10th grade, nearly 40 percent of 17-year-olds cannot draw inferences from written material, and only one-third can solve a mathematics problem requiring several steps (National Commission, 1983, p. 9; Task Force on Education, 1983, p. 23). But our criticisms suggest that in seeking solutions we need to be less concerned with the test score decline and trying to reestablish school practices that existed before the decline, that we should spend less time looking for foreign countries as models, and that we may not need to be as concerned about shaping our reforms to a particular vision of a hi-tech future. Our schools, historically, have failed to educate well a majority of our youth, whether this is measured by college graduation, the capacity to write a cogent essay, mastery of advanced mathematical and scientific concepts, training in literature and foreign languages, or the acquisition of higher-order reasoning and problem-solving skills. This in itself should be sufficient motivation for change. It also suggests that marginal correction may not be sufficient—at the least we should *consider* fundamental institutional changes.

THE RECOMMENDATIONS

An important contribution of the commissions is that they have not resorted to elitist solutions. They have not, as they very well might have, proposed extensive adoption of gifted and talented programs, the resurrection of systematic tracking by early test scores, or the introduction of specialized math and science programs for the academic high achievers. Instead they have proposed a redefinition of the basic skills, consisting of an expansion and upgrading of the fundamental abilities schools should impart, and at least three of the four commissions argued that the goal of the reforms is not to train an academic elite but to raise the performance of the average student. The National Commission on Excellence, for example, called for a "high level of shared education" (p. 7), and commented, "We do not believe that a public commitment to excellence and educational reform must be made at the expense of a strong public commitment to the equitable treatment of our diverse population" (p. 13). The Task Force on Education for Economic Growth stated, "We must improve the quality of instruction for all students— not just for an elite, but for all" (p. 18); and the Twentieth Century Fund task force proposed, "the skills that were once possessed by only a few must now be held by the many" (p. 4). The College Board's focus was confined to the preparation of students who plan to attend college, but their project has emphasized expanding opportunities for minorities. We strongly agree with the commissions that this twin focus on higher order skills and general improvement is necessary if we hope to remedy the historical failure of schools to teach the majority.

Yet, even though the rhetoric is egalitarian, the analysis and the recommendations failed to address the needs of the poor, the minorities, and inner city youth. Strategies to encourage dropouts to remain in school, for example, were not considered by three of the commissions, and were treated superficially by the fourth. The commissions also failed to deal with the problem of enticing good teachers to work in the inner cities and overlooked the desperate lack of employment for many inner city youth. The Twentieth Century Fund task force did propose extending compensatory education programs for poor, low-scoring, and handicapped students, but their attention was slight. The agenda of the nation is shifting away from equal opportunity. We are concerned that there will be trade-offs made between the efforts proposed by the commissions and traditional efforts made on behalf of the poor and educationally disadvantaged. As we review the commission's recommendations, it will be useful to keep this in mind.

The recommendations can be grouped into four categories: leadership, time, content, and teachers (see Table III). In subsequent sections, we briefly describe the recommendations of each commission.

TABLE III   Commissions' Recommendations

A Nation at Risk National Commission on Excellence	Action for Excellence Task Force on Education for Economic Growth	Academic Preparation The College Board	Making The Grade Twentieth Century Fund
Leadership			
State and local government should take primary responsibility for reforms Role of federal government: —identify national interest in education —provide research, resources, support for special groups	Governors should develop —state plans —state task forces Business-school partnerships should be formed —team teaching —instruction in offices and factories Principals as instructional leaders	Colleges and secondary schools should take lead in improvements	Federal government should —emphasize the need for better schools —promote literacy in English as the number one goal Continue federal role for poor and handicapped Impact aid shifted from military to immigrants Federal vouchers for educationally disadvantaged
Time			
more time			
7-hour school days 200- 220-day years Tighten attendance policies	Longer school days Improved attendance policies (revitalize curriculum, flexible scheduling)		
More homework	More homework		

more efficient use of time			
Order and discipline	Order and discipline		
Tougher grading	Tougher grading		
Periodic testing	Periodic testing		
Train students in work and study skills	Study skills		
Placement and grouping by performance, not age			

Content

(Curriculum)

Increase high school graduation requirements to (at a minimum):	*New Basics* (competencies)	*Academic Subject Competencies* in English, math, science, social studies, computers, foreign language, the arts	*Stress on* English literacy (end bilingual programs), math-science (loans for teachers, grants for students), foreign language (government should help train language teachers)
"New Basics" (suggested required years)	Reading, writing, speaking, listening, reasoning, economics		
English (4), math (3), science (3), social studies (3), computer (1/2), foreign language (4–6) (2 in high school). The report also limited key competencies in the subjects.	Basic employment	*General Academic Competencies* Reading, writing, speaking, listening, reasoning, mathematics, study skills	
	College entrance requirements increased		
	Gifted students' programs		
Implement a national system of standardized tests of achievement for certification and identification of needs		College preparation should be strengthened	
Work and study skills			
College entrance requirements increased			

Teachers		
Three-tiered system: beginner, experienced, master	Enrich career path, increase responsibility	National master teacher program
Salaries tied to effectiveness	Salaries tied to effectiveness (principals, also)	
Grants and loans for outstanding students in subject matter shortage areas	Financial incentives for shortage areas	
Higher requirements for teacher preparation	Renew teacher preparation curriculum; adopt rigorous standards	
Textbook improvements: national effort by schools and teachers to improve books and materials; publishers should prove educational effectiveness; states and local agencies should evaluate books and require data	Flexible certification	
	In-service training	

There are two major omissions in the recommendations. The first is that while the commissions were extensively concerned with content and time, that is, the questions "What is taught?" and "For how long?," they ignored the problem of pedagogy, namely the question "How is it taught?" The second is that the commissions failed to consider the implications of the recommendations, particularly the difficulties attending their implementation and the ramifications of adopting them. We can understand why these aspects were omitted; the commissions felt the reports needed to be short and simple to reach a wide public. Details on implementation might have distracted attention from the major message—that the educational system had reached a crisis point—and could have drowned out the reform suggestions. Such omissions also provide local school systems and states with the flexibility to make their own decisions in light of their particular circumstances.

Nevertheless, the failure to include even the briefest analysis of what the policy recommendations would entail weakens their argument. Practitioners, in particular, will consider many suggestions unrealistic. For example, the National Commission on Excellence recommends a 200- to 220-day school year. At first glance lengthening the school year seems a reasonable suggestion—many foreign nations have schools years of this length— and the increased time on academics should raise our students' academic achievement. But lengthening the school year, particularly by almost a quarter, has such practical difficulties that the recommendation seems unworkable. First, substantial new curriculum material would have to be developed. Second, it is certainly possible that not all school systems would lengthen their school years to the same extent. What would then happen in our highly mobile society as students moved from one district to another? Third, are teachers to be paid more? Where will the funds come from? What will the position of teachers' unions be on extending the school year 40 days? Fourth, what will the impact on students be? A longer school year could increase alienation and decrease motivation and, consequently, actually hamper performance. Many such implementation problems can be raised about each recommendation. The commissions also failed to take into account the decentralized nature of the American governmental system. The "top-down" flavor of their recommendations appears more in line with Western European systems, in which the federal government controls education. In such centralized systems the problems of articulation, cost, and side effects are part of a national planning process for major changes in the system. Here, those making recommendations, and in the case of state and federal governments, those making policy, are neither responsible for implementation nor can they easily be held responsible for failure.

Leadership

The commissions differ in what they consider the proper source of leadership for the reforms. The National Commission on Excellence believes that the federal government has the primary responsibility for identifying the national interest in education (as does the Twentieth Century Fund Task Force), including providing some resources, research, and support for special groups (handicapped, minorities, etc.), but that it is the states and local school systems that have the primary responsibility for implementation. In this, they are not as specific as the Task Force on Education for Economic Growth, which also emphasizes state and local leadership, but which directs governors to take the leadership role, creating state plans and statewide task forces that include business leaders to promote reforms. Local efforts would be guided by business-school partnerships and principals acting as instructional leaders within the schools. The College Board recommends that colleges and secondary schools carry out their proposals for strengthening high school curriculums and college entrance requirements.

How these various sources of leadership are supposed to coordinate efforts is unspecified; there could be a marriage of purpose or a clash of responsibility. What is ignored is the growing conviction among effective schools researchers that leadership must come from school-site management (Finn, 1983; Levin, 1983; Purkey & Smith, 1983). The staff of schools must be given the responsibility to construct their own reform efforts, to develop their own plans, to change their own programs, albeit within a framework established by local, state, and federal government. In these reports, however, the leadership comes only from the top. Even the important involvement of parents and community groups goes unmentioned, though the National Commission does have appendices directed at students and parents urging greater attention to academic endeavors.

Finally, there is little recognition of the political ramifications of the leadership sources. This is particularly true of the Task Force on Education for Economic Growth. How closely should business work with the schools? The issue is not only one of vocational education, of keeping dropouts in school longer, or of making the curriculum relevant to the work place, but also one of the influence that private interests should have over a public institution. Through team teaching by industry specialists and public school teachers, and classes taught in the offices and factories (and a host of other cooperative efforts), business will receive major benefits from the *public* training of future employees and can influence the nature and direction of the curriculum. *Action for Excellence*, for example, calls for the transmission of two economic competencies: "the ability to understand personal economics and its relationship to skills required for employment and promotability, the ability to understand our basic economic system (e.g., profits, revenues, basic law of supply and demand, etc.)" (p. 50). Can one doubt that with the involvement of the business community in school, understanding "promotability" and "our basic economic system" will mean an emphasis on corporate values rather than social responsibility? The danger of such an arrangement is suggested in the historic battles against vocational tracking and industrial education (Bowles & Gintis, 1976; Cremin, 1961). All of us recognize that education is more than the production of human capital, but this recognition is obscured when the commissions focus on training students for a hi-tech future or call for reform to be guided by task forces promoting economic growth.

Time

The recommendations for time come in two forms: those that call for increases in the amount of academic time and those that call for more efficient use of time. As can be seen from Table III, time was *not* a focus of the College Board or the Twentieth Century Fund reports. The other two reports contained similar recommendations. Both called for longer school days, improved attendance policies to reduce absenteeism, tougher grading, increased homework, more order and strict, fair discipline, and frequent testing of students. There were some differences. The Task Force on Economic Growth called for introducing critical academic subjects, such as science, earlier in students' schooling. The National Commission on Excellence called for 200- to 220-day school years, whereas the Task Force did not call for lengthening the school year. The National Commission also called for placement and grouping by academic performance, not by age.

In one recommendation, one of the commissions did move beyond simply stating the need for an effective policy and described what might be entailed. On the issue of attendance policies, the Task Force on Economic Growth recognized that the problems of absenteeism and dropouts are linked to the curriculum and the students' alienation. They called for revitalizing the curriculum to retain such students and for helping them set standards for themselves. Yet even here their call raises more questions. What is meant by revitalizing the curriculum? Does this differ from their main recommendation to make the general program more academically demanding and the environment more disciplined, changes which could increase dropout rates?

Finally, there are the recommendations for longer school days and longer school years. We are impressed, as many are, that the average Japanese high school graduate will have spent the equivalent of 4 more years in school than his American counterpart. Although we would agree that increasing academic time should somewhat raise achievement, we would argue that time is not *the* crucial element in higher achievement. More important seems to be the coverage of content. (See, e.g., the discussion of the "opportunity to learn" variable in the IEA studies, Wolf, 1977.) This factor and the various cultural and pedagogical elements discussed previously are more likely the major determinants of high Japanese achievement.

In addition, the most recent analyses of the "time" prescription recognize that quantity is a relatively minor variable in the production of achievement compared to quality, that is, how that time is used. Karweit (1982), for example, in a background paper prepared for the National Commission, concluded that

> present studies of time and learning, contrary to widely publicized statements, have not produced overwhelming evidence connecting time-on-task to learning . . . it is what is done in time and how appropriate it is that affects the learning that takes place. (pp. 51–52)

Thus, rather than simply calling for increased time, researchers are now focused on coverage of content, classroom organization, and teaching techniques that maximize the use of the given time and produce higher achievement.

Content

All four reports propose strengthening the curriculum and increasing the requirements. As can be seen in Table III, they all propose improvements in math and science and stress English literacy. Three emphasize work skills, two mention study skills (the commissions apparently believe as we do that the need to teach study skills has been overlooked by schools or has been poorly done), three call for increasing graduation requirements (two include increasing college entrance requirements), three stress computer competency, and three stress foreign language. The unique recommendations include the National Commission's proposal that textbook publishers demonstrate their books' effectiveness, the Task Force on Economic Growth's proposal to expand gifted programs, and the College Board's emphasis on the arts. The last is one of the most unusual recommendations in the four reports. At a time when the technological emphasis is paramount, only the Board has issued a strong statement of the need for strengthening the humanistic aspects of the curriculum.

Our major concern with how much the recommendations will strengthen the curriculum centers on the "new" basic skills. With the exception of the emphasis on computers (and the Board's arts proposal), the descriptions of the "strengthened" curriculum read like current curriculum goals. The National Commission on Excellence, for example, proposed the following for three important subjects:

> math: understand geometric and algebraic concepts, understand elementary probability and statistics, apply mathematics in everyday situations, and estimate, approximate, measure, and test the accuracy of calculations. . . .
>
> science: the concepts, laws, and process of the physical and biological sciences; the methods of scientific inquiry and reasoning; the application of scientific knowledge to everyday life; and the social and environmental implications of scientific and technological development. . . .
>
> social studies: enable students to fix their places and possibilities within the larger social and cultural structure, understand the broad sweep of both ancient and contemporary ideas that have shaped our world; understand the fundamentals of how our economic systems work and how our political system functions; grasp the difference between free and repressive societies. (pp. 25–26)

Not to mention the obvious problems with agreeing on what some of these mean (consider the last—"grasping the difference between free and repressive societies" in relationship to the debate about U.N. ambassador Jeane Kirkpatrick's distinction between totalitarian and authoritarian regimes), few high school math, science, or social studies teachers would find anything novel in these descriptions. The Task Force on Economic Growth and the College Board did not propose specific numbers of years for each subject, but rather listed competencies that should be acquired in a variety of areas, including speaking and listening, writing, reading, math, and science. Many of these are also the current goals of contemporary secondary schooling. Many high school English curricula, for example, already have as their goals the following writing competencies proposed by the Task Force:

> the ability to organize, select and relate ideas and to outline and develop them into coherent paragraphs.
>
> the ability to write Standard English sentences . . .
>
> the ability to improve one's own writing by restructuring, correcting errors and rewriting
>
> the ability to gather information from primary and secondary sources, and to write a report using this research; . . . and to cite sources properly (p. 48)

One way of thinking about this issue is not to question whether these are appropriate goals, but to ask how we can ensure that classes are organized so students acquire these skills. Beyond suggesting more homework and more frequent testing, the reports are silent on this issue. Given, however, our historical failure to transmit these skills to many of our students, restating the goals and calling for increased academic time without changing the teaching method and instructional climate contributes little. In this way, these reports have much in common with simplistic calls for a "return to basics." Certainly, we might all agree, as the College Board stated, that foreign language competency should involve the "ability to ask and answer questions and maintain a simple conversation" and "to pronounce the language well enough to be intelligible to native speakers," and, as the National Commission recommends, that 4 to 6 years of language study are needed, including at least 2 in high school. But given the atrocious performance of our schools in producing language fluency, these recommendations are hardly enough. We are not sure, in fact, that increasing the years spent would be beneficial without a major reorganization of the way foreign languages are taught. It could well be detrimental. It might be better to spend the money on sending students to the respective foreign country for the summer or for a semester.

Teachers

Silent on pedagogy, the reports suggest only one way to improve the quality of teaching, and that is to improve the quality of teachers. The critique of teacher quality centers on five factors: their low test scores relative to majors in other professional areas; teacher preparation programs that concentrate on methods at the expense of subject matter; their low salaries relative to other occupations; shortages in critical areas such as math and science; and the hiring of unqualified teachers, particularly in these critical areas. Each of these factors, however, has another side which wasn't mentioned in the reports.

1. Teachers historically have had low test scores relative to other majors, which suggests that the test score decline (e.g., student SATs, etc.) cannot be attributed to the teachers' low test scores (Twentieth Century Fund, 1983, p. 27). In addition, studies have shown only a tiny relationship between teachers' standardized test scores and student achievement (Jencks et al., 1973, p. 96, and footnote 111, p. 127).

2. In most teacher education institutions, students preparing to teach at the secondary level must major in their academic subject in *addition* to taking the required methods courses (Clark & Marker, 1983, pp. 55–56); sometimes they are required to take even more courses in their subject areas. For example, in mathematics a history of mathematics course or courses in additional divisions within mathematics might be required. At the University of Wisconsin-Madison, for instance, future secondary school teachers must meet a state requirement of 34 credits in their major subject, whereas liberal arts majors typically need only 30 credits.

3. Studies have *not* found that higher teacher salaries are associated with higher student achievement (see, e.g., Jencks et al., 1973, p. 149). The implication that teachers are not working hard now or are ineffective because of low pay, or that they would behave differently if they were paid more, has not been substantiated. Moreover, the argument that higher salaries are required to attract or retain teachers in critical areas, such as math, must be considered in light of recent data that show only 5 percent of experienced math teachers leave the profession yearly, and some for retirement (Pelavin, Reisner, & Hendrickson, 1983, p. 9).

   In our view, teacher effectiveness should be related to a larger vision of working conditions—competitive salary is a part of this, but social status and work place responsibility are others.

4. In spite of the publicity attending the math and science teacher shortage, some school systems are laying off math teachers, not hiring them (National Center for Education Statistics, 1982, p. 101). This presumably is due, in large part, to declining enrollments and severe budget crunches. In addition, the supply and demand forces of the marketplace should, in the long term, greatly increase the supply of qualified personnel. For example, students at the University of Wisconsin-Madison, presumably spurred by knowledge of math teacher shortages, are already enrolling in math education at increasing rates.

5. The hiring of uncredentialed or partially credentialed teachers must be distinguished from the hiring of unqualified teachers. The reports did not document that the students of undercredentialed teachers performed worse than those of credentialed teachers. Indeed, there could be more incentive for an untenured, undercredentialed teacher to perform well than for a tenured, fully credentialed teacher. In addition, school systems require undercredentialed teachers to take courses to become credentialed. Taking an evening class in the subject or its methodology while teaching the subject can sometimes provide a direct avenue for applying what is being learned and for understanding the role of the student struggling to comprehend new concepts. Both can improve the teaching.

In spite of these weaknesses in their critique of teacher quality, the commissions have proposed one major change that we feel could lead to improved student performance. The commissions have called for relating status and salary to teacher effectiveness. Over the past few months this has led to considerable discussion of the strengths and weaknesses of various merit pay and master teacher approaches. To a considerable degree this debate has been fruitful, leading to a sense that the "merit pay" approach may not be a particularly effective way of improving instruction or retaining good teachers. The "master teacher" strategy, however, has withstood some initial scrutiny and plans are being proposed throughout the nation. The National Commission on Excellence called for a three-tiered system of beginning, experienced, and master teachers, whereas the Task Force on

Economic Growth was less specific, calling for enriched career paths with increasing responsibility. The Twentieth Century Fund group proposed a National Master Teacher program. The difficulty, once again, is that the recommendation raises many questions. Who will judge the effectiveness of a teacher? On what criteria? What role will teacher unions have in these decisions? The reports do not discuss these issues.

As can be seen from Table III, the National Commission on Excellence and the Task Force on Economic Growth made virtually identical recommendations in the area of teacher quality. The Task Force did recommend flexible certification procedures to allow specialists and industry workers to teach, even if they might not have all the required courses, and called for extensive in-service training for current teachers and principals. The College Board was silent on the issue of teacher quality.

CONCLUSION

The commissions used weak arguments and poor data to make their case. Neither the decline in test scores, the international comparisons, nor the growth of hi-tech employment provided a clear rationale for reform. By ignoring their background reports and carelessly handling data, their reports further lost credibility. In particular, the commissions made simplistic recommendations and failed to consider their ramifications. They proposed increasing time without altering pedagogy, instituting merit schemes without describing procedures, and adopting the "new basics" without changing old definitions. They ignored numerous problems—teenage unemployment, teacher burnout, and high dropout rates—that must be solved before American education can be considered sound. They did not address the special needs of the poor and minorities. A blind acceptance of these recommendations could lead to little improvement. Worse, a rapid adoption in the hopes of a speedy improvement could lead to a disenchantment with reform. There is today a crucial dilemma facing education policy. On the one hand, there appears to be a legitimate desire to impose new and more rigorous standards on our nation's schools. On the other hand, recent studies of school effectiveness indicate the need to rest considerable responsibility for a school's instructional program on the shoulders of the staff of the school. Over and over we find that without the commitment of the school staff, topdown mandates will fail. Local school systems and state governments, therefore, should examine these reports carefully before adopting any of their recommendations.

In spite of these criticisms, the commissions have made a number of important recommendations. Their calls for increased academic requirements, curriculum reform, computer competency, and career ladders for teachers could improve the quality of education. The commissions also have been successful in making the educational crisis a public concern. The current focus on education increases the likelihood that successful reforms can be made. The ongoing debate over master teacher plans in many states and local districts is an example. Educators should follow these efforts closely. Their success or failure will be the ultimate test of the worth of the four commissions' reports.

A final note: Part of the fault with the poor handling of data lies with the poor quality of data that are currently available. We recommend two major improvements that could, at a relatively small expense, remedy the present deficiencies: (a) upgrade the quality of national educational data, and (b) expand federal involvement in and funding of U.S. participation in IEA studies. In particular, we suggest that the NAEP become more regular, more frequent, and include extensive information on time and content variables such as the number of homework hours and the number and type of courses students are enrolled in. This would produce a longitudinal data base that could be used to check assertions about changing educational practices and to test hypotheses about the causes of achievement. Participation in IEA studies should be done as part of a greater research effort in comparative education. It would shed light on American educational practice and suggest possible improvements originating elsewhere.

NOTES

1. The examples include overstating the decline, asserting across the board foreign educational superiority, ignoring cultural factors in the Japanese educational performance, and placing an improper emphasis on time as an explanatory factor in higher achievement.
2. The 1970–1971 IEA testing also compared 10- and 14-year-olds across a variety of countries, age groups at which nearly 100 percent are in school. The U.S. students fared reasonably well on the science, reading comprehension, literature, and civic education tests. For tests of proficiency in French, U.S. students did poorly compared to students in other nations. See Table A for selected comparisons. On the mathematics test given in 1964, U.S. 13-year-olds did quite poorly.
3. These data, however, were not completely clear-cut. (See chart on achievement presented in Husén, 1983). The top 4 percent of U.S. math students ranked 9th among 12 advanced nations, and achieved well below the top two nations, Japan and Sweden. In science, the differences between the elite performers in each country were smaller, and the U.S., ranking 9th of 14, was closer to the highest ranking countries.
4. BLS projections typically have a high degree of uncertainty. See, for example, Berlin (1983, pp. 25–30). In raising the concern about the limited number of jobs that will require hi-tech skills, we are not denying that the supply of well-trained personnel can affect the location of capital and investment.

REFERENCES

Adelman, C. *Devaluation, diffusion, and the college connection: A study of high school transcripts, 1964–1981*. Paper prepared for the National Commission on Excellence in Education, 1983. (Available from the U.S. Department of Education, 1200 19th Street, N.W., Washington, D.C. 20208)

Berlin, G. *Not working: Unskilled youth and displaced adults*. New York: Ford Foundation, 1983. (Available from the Ford Foundation, Office of Reports, 320 East 43rd Street, New York, N.Y. 10017)

Bowles, S., & Gintis, H. *Schooling in capitalist America*. New York: Basic Books, 1976.

Bureau of Labor Statistics. *Economic projection to 1990* (Bulletin 2121). Washington, D.C.: Department of Labor, 1982.

Carnevale, A., & Goldstein, H. *Employee Training: Its changing role and an analysis of new data.* Washington, D.C.: American Society for Training and Development, 1983.

Clark, D. L. & Marker, G. The institutionalization of teacher education. In *Teacher education, the seventy-fourth yearbook of the national society for the study of education.* Chicago: University of Chicago Press, 1983.

College Entrance Examination Board. *On further examination.* New York: College Entrance Examination Board, 1977.

Comber, L. C., & Keeves, J. P. *Science education in nineteen countries:* New York: John Wiley, 1973.

Cremin, L. A. *The transformation of the school.* New York: Vintage Books, 1961.

Echternacht, G. J. *A comparative study of secondary schools with different score patterns.* (Appendix to College Entrance Examination Board, *On further examination*). New York: College Entrance Examination Board, 1977.

Finn, C. E., Jr. *Toward strategic independence: Policy considerations for enhancing school effectiveness* (Contract No. 400–79–0035). Washington, D.C.: National Institute of Education, 1983.

Fisher, D. L. *Functional literacy and the schools.* (No. 623–545/173). Washington, D.C.: U.S. Government Printing Office, 1978.

Fiske, E. B. Japan's schools: Intent about the basics. *New York Times,* July 10, 1983, p. 1. (a)

Fiske, E. B. Japan's schools stress group and discourage individuality. *New York Times,* July 11, 1983, p. 1. (b)

Fiske, E. B. Japan's schools: Exam ordeal rules each student's destiny. *New York Times,* July 12, 1983, p. 1. (c)

Fiske, E. B. Balance sheet on schools: Experts doubt the ailing American system can learn much from Japan. *New York Times,* July 13, 1983, p. 1. (d)

Gadway, C., & Wilson, A. J. *Functional literacy: Basic reading performance.* Denver: National Assessment of Educational Progress, Education Commission of the States, 1975.

Gardner, J. W. *Excellence.* New York: Harper & Row, 1961.

Ginsburg, A., Milne, A. M., Myers, D. E., & Ellman, F. M. *Single parents, working mothers and the educational achievement of elementary school age children.* Washington, D.C.: U.S. Department of Education, 1983.

Holmes, B. J. *Reading, science, and mathematics trends: A closer look* (No. SY-RSM-50). Denver: National Assessment of Educational Progress, Education Commission of the States, 1982.

Hurn, C. J. & Burn, B. B. *An analytical comparison of educational systems: Overview of purposes, policies, structures and outcomes.* Background paper presented to the National Commission on Excellence in Education, February 1982. (Available from the U.S. Department of Education, 1200 19th Street, N.W., Washington, D.C. 20208)

Husen, T. (Ed.). *International study of achievement in mathematics: A comparison between twelve countries* (Vol. 2). New York: Wiley, 1967.

Husen, T. Are standards in U.S. schools really lagging behind those in other countries? *Phi Delta Kappan,* 1983, *64,* 455–461.

Jencks, C., Smith, M., Acland, H., Bane, M. J., Cohen, D., Gintis, H., Heyns, B., & Michelson, S. *Inequality.* New York: Harper & Row, 1973.

Jones, L. V. Achievement test scores in mathematics and science. *Science,* 1981, *213,* 412–416.

Karweit, N. *Time on task: A research review.* Background paper presented to the National Commission on Excellence in Education, 1982. (Available from the U.S. Department of Education, 1200 19th Street, N.W., Washington, D.C. 20208)

Levin, H. M. Reawakening the vigor of urban schools. *Education Week,* May 18, 1983, p. 24.

Levin, H., & Rumberger, R. Hi-tech requires few brains. *Washington Post,* January 30, 1983, p. C5.

Lynd, A. *Quackery in the public schools.* Boston: Little, Brown, 1953.

National Assessment of Educational Progress. *Three national assessments of science: Changes in achievement, 1969–1977* (Report No. 08–S–300). Denver: Education Commission of the States, 1978 (ERIC Document Reproduction Service No. ED 159 026)

National Assessment of Educational Progress. *Changes in mathematical achievement, 1973–78* (Report No. 09-MA-01). Denver: Education Commission of the States, 1979. (ERIC Document Reproduction Service No. ED 177 011)

National Assessment of Educational Progress. *Writing achievement, 1969–1979* (Report No. 10-W-35). Denver: Education Commission of the States, 1980. (ERIC Document Reproduction Service No. ED 196 044)

National Assessment of Educational Progress. *Three national assessments of reading: Changes in performance, 1970–1980* (Report No. 11-R-301). Denver: Education Commission of the States, 1981. (ERIC Document Reproduction Service No. ED 200 898)

National Center for Education Statistics. *The condition of education.* Washington, D.C.: U.S. Government Printing Office, 1982.

Pelavin, S. H., Reisner, E. R., & Hendrickson, G. *Analysis of the national availability of mathematics and science teachers* (Draft). Washington, D.C.: Pelavin Associates, 1983.

Peterson, P. E. Background paper. In *Making the grade.* New York: Twentieth Century Fund Task Force on Federal Elementary and Secondary Education Policy, 1983.

Purkey, S. C., & Smith, M. S. Effective schools: A review. *Elementary School Journal,* 1983, *83,* 427–452.

Takai, R. *Grade inflation and time spent on homework.* Washington, D.C.: National Center for Education Statistics, U.S. Department of Education, 1983.

Tucker, M. S. *Computers in the schools: The federal role.* Paper presented at the meeting of the Special Interest Group on Computer Uses in Education of the Association for Computing Machinery, Spring Hill Center, Wayzata, Minnesota, September 1983.

Walberg, H. J. Scientific literacy and economic productivity in international perspective. *Daedalus,* 1983, *112* 1–28

Watkins, B. Mastery of 6 basic subjects and 6 intellectual skills urged for college bound students. *Chronicle of Higher Education,* May 18, 1983, pp. 1; 14.

Wolf, R. M. *Achievement in America.* New York: Teachers College Press, 1977.

Zeugner, J. Japan's non-education. *New York Times,* June 24, 1983, op ed page.

School Reform and Potential Dropouts

GARY NATRIELLO

Teachers College, Columbia University

EDWARD L. MCDILL

Johns Hopkins University

AARON M. PALLAS

Teachers College, Columbia University

School leaders have cause for both celebration and caution. Education has finally returned to the forefront of policy discussions at the state and national levels, and educators have both an opportunity and a responsibility to secure increased support for American schools. However, as with all widespread movements, the current reform effort has its own direction and momentum; while it directs attention to certain problems in schools, it may divert much-needed attention from problems that are equally pressing, such as the growing number of high school dropouts.

THE SEVERITY AND NATURE OF THE DROPOUT PROBLEM

Nearly one-third of respondents in a 1979 national survey of school administrators cited early dropouts as a problem in their districts; over half of the administrators in districts with more than 25,000 students reported that early dropouts are a problem.

From *Educational Leadership* (1985): 161–166. Copyright © 1985 by ASCD. Reprinted with permission of the Association for Supervision and Curriculum Development and the author.

While reliable statistics on school attendance are difficult to obtain, it is estimated that approximately 25 percent of all 18-year-olds have not graduated from high school. Although different sources present different figures, this rate has remained fairly stable over the last decade. Most youngsters who drop out do so after they have entered the 9th grade (Dearman and Plisko, 1979).

The economic costs of dropping out are also difficult to estimate, but Levin (1972) projected $71 billion of lost tax revenue from high school dropouts aged 25–34, welfare and unemployment costs of $3 billion, and crime and crime prevention costs of $3 billion.

Students drop out of high school for a variety of often interrelated reasons, which generally fall into three major categories:

1. *Poor academic performance*, primarily low grades, is the most common reason students leave high school. Students who perform at one or more years below grade level or have failed one or more grades are most likely to drop out. In addition to poor grades and academic performance, expulsion and suspension also indicate school problems that lead to dropping out. It is not surprising that students who do not perform well in school seek to leave the environment that provides negative feedback.

2. *Conditions in the student's family* can lead to an increased likelihood of dropping out. Students from single-parent homes are twice as likely to drop out of school as are students living with both parents, and eight of ten teenage mothers under the age of 17 never finish high school.

3. *Economic issues*, such as a disadvantaged family background, also increase the probability of dropping out; and many students report leaving school to go to work. Twenty-five percent of all 14-year-olds and over 50 percent of all 17-year-olds were employed at least part-time in 1979 (Michael and Tuma, 1983). High school seniors who worked averaged 15 to 18 hours of work per week, and very intensive work involvement is associated with higher rates of dropping out for at least some groups of youths (D'Amico, 1984). Serious economic pressures lead many students to drop out of school.

THE CURRENT SCHOOL REFORM MOVEMENT: THE COMMISSIONS AND THEIR OMISSIONS

In examining the current movement for school reform and its implications for potential dropouts, we must consider the national commission reports that generated the latest wave of school reform and the responses of policymakers to the recommendations made in these reports. Both almost totally ignore the dropout problem in considering ways to improve education. Recommendations to raise standards fall into three broad areas:

1. *Course content.* The National Commission on Excellence (1983) advocates five new basics: four years of English; three years each of

mathematics, science, and social studies; and one-half year of computer science. Other reports have advocated more science and mathematics courses (National Science Board Commission, 1983) or the elimination of the soft, nonessential courses (Task Force on Education for Economic Growth, 1983), but the general message is the same: students should pursue more demanding sequences of basic courses. If these recommendations are implemented, students will have fewer choices in selecting courses, and curriculums will offer a more restricted range of courses. While seldom fully adopting the commissions' recommendations, at least 40 states have increased the number of academic courses required for high school graduation (Fiske, 1984).

2. *The use of time for instruction and learning.* The National Commission on Excellence and the Task Force on Education for Economic Growth recommend longer school days and years. The National Science Board Commission also suggests a longer school week to provide the time necessary for increased science and mathematics instruction. Both the National Commission on Excellence and the Task Force on Education for Economic Growth argue for increases in homework requirements and attention to attendance requirements. They are joined by Goodlad (1983) in stressing that better use should be made of in-school time.

   The state-level response has typically concerned increasing in-school time. Twenty-three states have taken steps in increase the time students spend in school (Fiske, 1984). Local districts have moved to establish or increase homework requirements; for example, Oklahoma City's new homework policy requires 30 minutes of homework each night for elementary students and two hours each night for high school students (U.S. Department of Education, 1984).

3. *Student achievement.* Both the National Commission on Excellence and the Task Force on Education for Economic Growth have called for the use of grades solely to indicate achievement, not as motivational devices reflective of student effort. A second form of achievement standard calls for the end of social promotion and the use of rigorous grade promotion policies by which students will be promoted only when it is academically justified (National Commission on Excellence, 1983; National Science Board Commission, 1983; Task Force on Education for Economic Growth, 1983). Finally, several reports have recommended the use of standardized tests to monitor student achievement at specified intervals. Boyer (1983) argues for the use of a language proficiency test prior to high school admission with remediation of any deficiencies during the summer. The National Commission on Excellence recommends the use of achievement tests at major transition points, particularly in the move from high school to college. The Task Force on Education for Economic Growth advocates periodic testing of achievement and skills.

State-level activity in this area actually pre-dated the recent commission reports. In the late 1970s, states started requiring testing of students to ensure certain levels of achievement. By 1984, 29 states had established some type of testing program, and 13 additional states were considering adopting one (U.S. Department of Education, 1984). While the standards set by many states may appear low, these tests represent yet another hurdle for students hoping to graduate from high school.

Taken together, the call for higher standards in curriculum content, learning time, and achievement levels seems to be based on five assumptions: (1) current standards are too low, (2) more demanding content and more time allocated to school will lead to greater individual student effort, (3) greater student effort will lead to improved achievement, (4) the relationships between standards and effort and between effort and achievement will hold for all students, and (5) no negative consequences will be associated with the more demanding standards. These assumptions, like the specific commission recommendations based on them, fail to consider our population at risk— potential dropouts.

HIGHER STANDARDS AND POTENTIAL DROPOUTS

In an analysis of data from the Educational Testing Service's Study of Academic Prediction and Growth, Alexander and Pallas (1984) showed that although the overall advantages of increasing core requirements in the "new basics" are clear, these core requirements seem to have little effect on the performance of students with relatively low grade point averages. In fact, they conclude that the lowest performing youngsters are apparently a little bit better off outside the core.

Not only the substance, but the resulting form of the curriculum—a single pattern of courses taken by most students—may also have negative effects. The core curriculum is mainly composed of academic courses, all of which tap ability along a narrow range. Implementing the new curriculum requirements will restrict the variation in school experiences for students, limit the number of dimensions of ability deemed legitimate within the school, and curtail student choice in constructing a program of study. Potential dropouts, typically students with limited ability along this one dimension, may have to face repeated failure with little opportunity to engage in other school activities that might afford them some sense of success.

Increasing the time students spend on school tasks does seem to have positive effects on learning, even for students likely to be potential dropouts. For example, Keith (1982), in an analysis of data from the High School and Beyond Study, found that low-ability students who do one to three hours of homework weekly achieve grades commensurate with those of average students who do no homework. The problem is not that increased time on school tasks is ineffective; rather, the problem is motivating students to spend additional time on school tasks.

Longer school days and years may not result in greater time on school tasks, as these increases may require additional breaks, and teachers and students may encounter problems with fatigue. An additional 30 minutes at the end of the school day or an additional week at the end of the school year may add little to real learning time. Moreover, such demands may be problematic for potential dropouts, who are more likely than other students to have assumed adult responsibilities related to families and jobs. Furthermore, increasing time spent on school work and homework may prevent participation in extracurricular activities, thus denying students who do not perform well in the classroom access to activities that build a normative attachment to the school and provide avenues of success (Otto and Alwin, 1981). Increasing the time demands on potential dropouts may present them with a severe conflict that may be most easily resolved by leaving school.

The impact of higher achievement standards on potential dropouts is apparently mixed. A series of studies reported by Natriello and Dornbusch (1984) found that students in classrooms with very low standards were more likely to cut class than students in classrooms with more demanding standards. Moreover, a higher demand level in the classroom was found to be associated with greater student effort even when the students' ability level was controlled. In the low-demand classrooms, the highest proportion of students reported that they felt the teacher should make them work harder. However, these studies also showed that high-demand classrooms often lose low-ability students, who try less hard when the pace is too fast.

These dual effects of raising achievement standards, (sometimes challenging students, sometimes frustrating them) appear in the limited information we have on the impact of minimal competency testing. While systematic, evaluative studies on the impact of minimal competency testing are currently unavailable, the failure rates on such tests are clearly much higher for economically disadvantaged and minority students, two sociodemographic groups with high dropout rates (Jaeger, 1982). If academic standards are raised and students are not provided substantial remediation within the limited time they can devote to school tasks, socially and academically disadvantaged students will be more likely to experience frustration and failure, which can result in notable increases in dropping out.

IMPLICATIONS FOR SCHOOL ADMINISTRATORS

If we are to avoid some of the serious negative effects of the current reforms on potential dropouts, discussions of the problem that have been uncommon at the national and state levels must become common at the district and building levels. It is there that the dropout problem cannot be ignored. Accordingly, we suggest that school administrators:

1. *Redouble efforts to monitor dropouts at the district and building level.* It is difficult and time consuming to collect valid information on students who leave high school prior to graduation; they often disappear without formal warning, becoming invisible problems. To fully under-

stand the dimensions and patterns of their particular dropout problems, local administrators must collect systematic information on students who drop out, and use it in at least three ways. First, internal variations in the patterns of dropouts within schools and districts can alert administrators to potential policies that might encourage students to complete their high school education. Second, information collected on dropout rates can, over time, help in understanding the impact of changes such as those currently being implemented as part of the current wave of reforms. Third, hard evidence on the magnitude of the dropout problem can be used to bring the dropout problem to the attention of state and national policymakers.

2. *Insist on adequate evaluation of the new reform policies.* Careful program evaluation is expensive and time consuming; yet it is essential to judging the efficacy of changing standards for performance. While individual districts and schools can monitor the impact of new policies on their students, only state-level evaluation efforts can examine their impact across districts within a state, and only national evaluation efforts can examine the impact of diverse state policies on schools and districts in various states. If school administrators are to be held accountable for the performance of their schools, they should hold governors, legislators, and national commissions accountable for the effectiveness of their reform policies. Despite the tone of the recent commission reports and the quick action by various states, it is not clear how to raise standards for uniformly good effect.

3. *Insist that effects on potential dropouts be considered in any assessments of the reforms.* To assess the true impact of the reforms in terms of aggregate outcome measures requires the use of what we refer to as a "full-enrollment" approach in calculating such measures, as opposed to a "survivor" approach, as is typically done at present. The survivor approach includes final outcome scores only for those students who remain enrolled through the 12th grade, or whenever outcome measures are collected. Under a full-enrollment approach, aggregate performance measures would include scores of students who dropped out of school before graduation. Scores for dropouts might be estimated on the basis of their earlier test scores and background characteristics. In any case, such an approach would reduce aggregate scores by making them reflective of outcomes for both students who graduate and those who drop out. This would prevent policymakers from claiming as successful those reforms that simply rid the schools of students with performance problems.

4. *Continue to serve potential dropouts with special programs that have proven successful in the past.* While there has been relatively little systematic evaluation of many of these programs, certain features appear to work well with potential dropouts, including (1) relatively small programs or schools that offer more responsive environments for students;

(2) individualized curriculums and instructional approaches that tailor course content and mode and pace of instruction to the aptitudes and interests of students; and (3) learning climates characterized by clear and fair rules, reward systems reflective of individual student effort and progress, and a normative emphasis on academic excellence (U.S. Department of Justice, 1980).

5. *Provide educational services with flexible time options.* Our analysis suggests that potential dropouts are subject to severe time constraints. Since the economic and family demands placed on such students typically cannot be alleviated, school administrators should modify the time demands the educational system places on them by experimenting with programs that are less concentrated and of longer duration. It may be reasonable for many potential dropouts to achieve higher standards by planning to participate in high school for an additional year, thereby reducing their course load. It would be important to remove the stigma of failure from such an option; planning to remain in high school part-time for an additional year should have a different meaning than being retained in a grade and repeating a full course load. College administrators have grown accustomed to students who stretch out their undergraduate careers without any sense of failure, and high school administrators should be encouraged to do the same. Only in this way will many potential dropouts escape the severe time conflicts that prevent them from doing well initially and benefiting from remedial services when necessary.

CONCLUSION

We have listed a full and heavy agenda of responsibilities for district- and building-level administrators. Parents, the local community, and state and national policymakers may be enlisted to help, but recent experience suggests that it is *local educational leaders* who will have to keep the dropout problem in the public eye.

REFERENCES

Alexander, K. L., and Pallas, A. M. "Curriculum Reform and School Performance: An Evaluation of the 'New Basics.' " *American Journal of Education* 92 (1984): 391–420.

Boyer, E. L. *High School: A Report on Secondary Education in America.* Washington, D.C.: Carnegie Foundation, 1983.

D'Amico, R. "Does Employment During High School Impair Economic Progress?" *Sociology of Education* 57 (1984): 152–164.

Dearman, N. B., and Plisko, V. W. *The Condition of Education: 1979 Edition.* Washington, D.C.: U.S. Government Printing Office, 1979.

Edson, C. H. "Risking the Nation: Historical Dimensions on Survival and Educational Reform." *Issues in Education* 1 (1983): 171–184.

Fiske, E. B. "Concern Over Schools Spurs Extensive Efforts at Reform." *The New York Times*, September 9, 1984, pp. 1, 68.

Goodlad, J. I. *A Place Called School: Prospects for the Future.* New York: McGraw-Hill, 1983.

Jaeger, R. M. "The Final Hurdle: Minimum Competency Achievement Testing." In *The Rise and Fall of National Test Scores*, pp. 223–246. Edited by G. R. Austin and H. Garber. New York: Academic Press, 1982.

Keith, T. Z. "Time Spent on Homework and High School Grades: A Large-Sample Path Analysis." *Journal of Educational Psychology* 74 (1982): 248–253.

Levin, H. "The Costs to the Nation of Inadequate Education." Report to the Select Committee on Equal Educational Opportunity, United States Senate. Washington, D.C.: U.S. Government Printing Office, 1972.

Michael, R., and Tuma, N. B. "Youth Employment: Does Life Begin at 16?" Paper presented at the annual meeting of the Population Association of America, Pittsburgh, Penn., 1983.

National Commission on Excellence. *A Nation at Risk: The Imperative for Educational Reform.* Washington, D.C.: U.S. Government Printing Office, 1983.

National Science Board Commission on Precollege Education in Mathematics, Science and Technology. *Educating Americans for the 21st Century.* Washington, D.C.: National Science Foundation, 1983.

Natriello, G., and Dornbusch, S. M. *Teacher Evaluative Standards and Student Effort.* New York: Longman, 1984.

Neill, S. B. "Keeping Students in School: Problems and Solutions." AASA Critical Issues Report. Arlington, Va.: American Association of School Administrators, 1979.

Otto, L. B., and Alwin, D. F. "Athletics, Aspirations, and Attainments." *Sociology of Education* 54 (1981): 132–140.

Task Force on Education for Economic Growth. *Action for Excellence: A Comprehensive Plan to Improve Our Nation's Schools.* Denver, Colo.: Education Commission of the States, 1983.

U.S. Department of Education. *The Nation Responds: Recent Efforts to Improve Education.* Washington, D.C.: U.S. Government Printing Office, 1984.

U.S. Department of Justice, Office of Juvenile Delinquency Prevention. *Program Announcement: Prevention of Delinquency Through Alternative Education.* Washington, D.C.: U.S. Government Printing Office, 1980.

Index